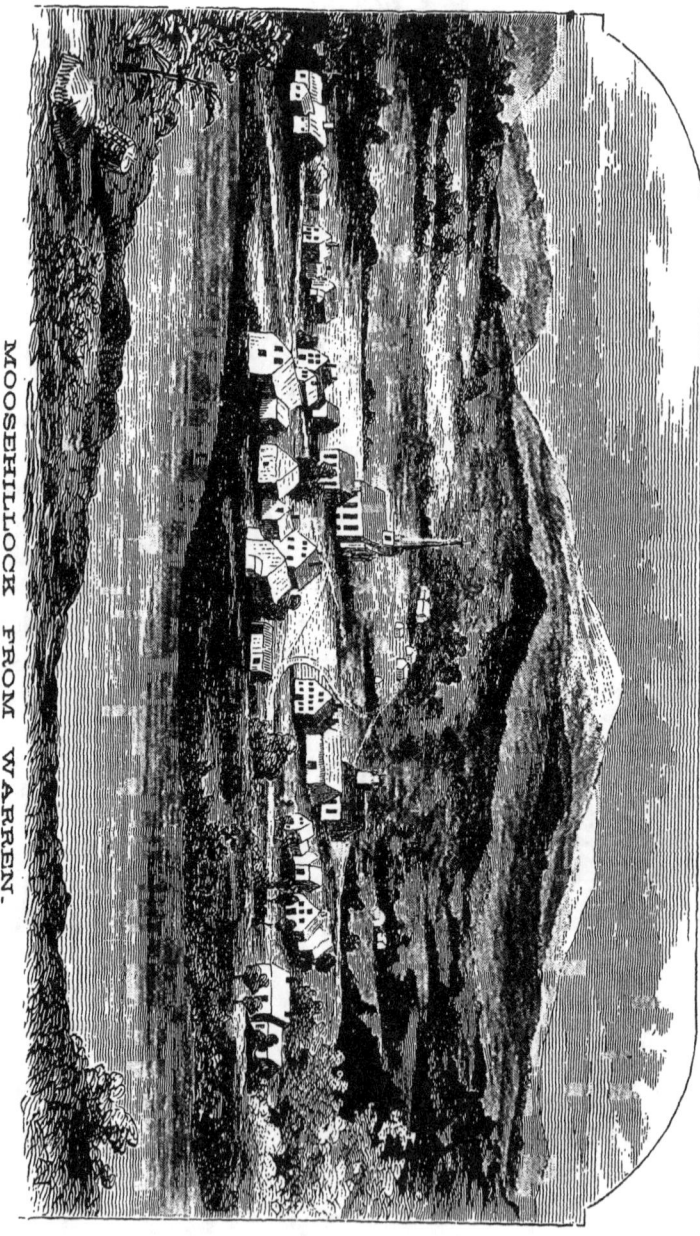
MOOSEHILLOCK FROM WARREN.

THE HISTORY OF WARREN

A Mountain Hamlet
Located Among
the
White Hills
of
New Hampshire

William Little

HERITAGE BOOKS
2015

HERITAGE BOOKS
AN IMPRINT OF HERITAGE BOOKS, INC.

Books, CDs, and more—Worldwide

For our listing of thousands of titles see our website
at
www.HeritageBooks.com

A Facsimile Reprint
Published 2015 by
HERITAGE BOOKS, INC.
Publishing Division
5810 Ruatan Street
Berwyn Heights, Md. 20740

with the cooperation of
The Warren Historical Society
and
Robert W. Averill, M.D.

Entered according to Act of Congress, in the year 1870, by William Little,
in the office of the Librarian of Congress, at Washington

The illustrations in this volume were mostly made by
Amos F. Clough, Artist, Warren, New Hampshire

— Publisher's Notice —
In reprints such as this, it is often not possible to remove blemishes from the original. We feel the contents of this book warrant its reissue despite these blemishes and hope you will agree and read it with pleasure.

International Standard Book Numbers
Paperbound: 978-1-55613-774-7
Clothbound: 978-0-7884-6127-9

PREFACE
to the 1993 Edition

William Little died a century ago, and after his death his History of Warren (1870) became a scarce treasure known and available to a few local families, book collectors, and historians. This rarity was partly due to the limited number of original copies, perhaps 600 or so, and the use of an acidic wood-pulp based paper, similar to that seen in old newspapers. This last feature produced an increasingly fragile book, with pages that crumbled easily and rapidly if folded in any way. Not surprisingly those who had a copy of the History were apt to treat it as one of the family jewels, loaning it rarely if at all.

A review written in 1871 seems oddly prophetic: "... we predict that it will be sought for in coming years by collectors as one of the rare, quaint books of New England origin." And yet, its stories are still fresh and its interest to those familiar with this town at the base of Mt. Moosilauke still great. Many have considered it a "unique" town history, but of course all town histories are unique. At least it is a uniquely readable, "brimful of humor," as its reviewer comments.*

It seems fitting to make Little's fine narrative available once more in this the centenary year of his death. His own introduction to this second printing might have read as follows, taken from his Address at the Warren Centennial, July 14, 1863:

> All the events which make up the great drama of the world have a certain interest, but each man, as he has been educated, looks at some particular scene with more intent than at others; so each man, regarding his whole country, has a greater interest in some spot or locality — the place of his birth, the scenes of his early years. Men, in contemplating a particular period of time, often lose sight of eternity, that incomprehensible something which is lost in the past and unfathomable in the future. In a like manner, what one of us does not recollect when the blue horizon, resting upon its rim of green hills which girt us round, seemed the boundary of space, and the outer world was unknown or forgotten.
>
> — *The Warren Historical Society*

---

* The New-England Historical & Genealogical Register and Antiquarian Journal, 1871, Vol. 25, p.304.

PREFACE.

To preserve the Indian traditions, tales of border wars, the memories of the old proprietors and first white settlers, the legends, anecdotes, and events of our mountain hamlet, and to afford some slight assistance to the great historian of New Hampshire who shall come hereafter, was why this book was written.

The author was sailing chip boats on Aiken brook one day when a very small boy. A companion, several years older, now Rev. William Merrill, was planting potatoes near by. For amusement he told the story of James Aiken, how his house was burned up, who did it, and why, and showed the old cellar. An interest was excited; it grew as the years went by, and the result is this history.

The writing of it has not been a labor. It has been a pleasant pastime, a source of amusement — " good fun." If any are disposed to smile at the writer's efforts, let them remember that every one must have a little recreation of some kind, and that while the writer's friends have enjoyed themselves some by hunting and fishing, some by music and dancing, some by cards and gaming, some by squinting through glass tumblers and worshipping the god Bacchus, some by paying their devotions at the shrine of Venus, some by buying pictures and costly libraries, some by sporting fine horses and carriages and building magnificent houses, some by preaching and praying and singing psalms and songs, and some in divers other ways too numerous to mention, the author of these pages has passed many pleasant and happy hours preserving the incidents of his native town.

But we wish all our readers to know that this pleasant pastime, writing a town history, is a costly one; that we have not, cannot, and shall not make a cent out of it; that, to use an expression of the vulgar world, "We are a good deal out of pocket by the operation;" and that the whole thing is well illustrated by the wise maxim that "those who dance shall pay the fiddler."

We claim that this history has one merit over ordinary town histories, and that is unity. That instead of being heterogeneous matter thrown together without any regard to connection of thought, and with no unity except perhaps that of time, and with no interest to any one except persons particularly acquainted with the town, we have grouped our facts together, giving unity of thought, unity of time, and we hope some interest to the general reader.

We know that the first two books of this history are no more applicable to the town of Warren than to any other of the neighboring towns. But it seemed necessary to write them in order that it might be known how this wild northern country came to be cultivated and settled.

The citizens of Warren should be very happy that they have this history. Their acts and those of their ancestors and their friends will be preserved as long as the State exists. They have a bright and shining page, while Wentworth, Romney, Ellsworth, Woodstock, Benton, and Piermont, and all the other neighboring lands round about, have lost the pleasant memories of their early settlers; and all their historical data, so rich, so entertaining, has passed away forever. To-day the inhabitants of those regions are no better off than the Negroes, Hottentots, or the dwellers on the Cannibal Islands. They have no place in history, and perhaps never will have.

To those who have assisted us in producing this work, we tender our most grateful acknowledgements. We would mention Col. Stevens M. Dow, Anson Merrill, Amos F. Clough, Geo. Libbey, Nathaniel Richardson, James Clement, Mrs. Susan C. Little, Miss Hannah B. Knight, all the town clerks, and particularly Russell K. Clement, as persons who have materially aided us. We would also return our most sincere thanks to those pleasant writers who gave "Knickerbocker's History of New York," "Margaret," and "Rural Life." We have helped ourselves freely to such portions of those works as pleased us, and while the authors of them will not suffer, we believe the good folks of Warren will be much happier by reason of our literary larceny. We have also derived great assistance from Vol. vii. of the N. H. Hist. Coll., a book dry as a chip to the general reader, but one of the most valuable historical works ever published in New Hampshire. But most especially do we feel thankful to those persons who have encouraged us in writing this book, by placing their names in our list of subscribers. We shall hold them in happy recollection to the latest day of our life.

In closing, we hope that those who look over these pages may be in some degree amused, pleased, edified, and entertained; and that some one, a native of Warren, may, many years hence, revise, add to, and continue this history, making a book ten times better than ours.

CONTENTS.

INTRODUCTION. - - - - - - - - - - - - - 17

BOOK I.

CONTAINING A HISTORY OF A TRIBE OF INDIANS NEVER BEFORE WRITTEN BY ANY OTHER HISTORIAN.

CHAP. I. Of the name of this tribe, or how they called themselves one name while foreigners called them another, together with where they resided in the most permanent manner, and what great tribes lived around them. 23

CHAP. II. Containing the origin of the Pemigewassetts with a few profound theories very interesting to know. - - - - - - - - - 29

CHAP. III. About Acteon,—politely called old Acteon,—and what he as well as others said of the manners and customs of the Pemigewassetts. 33

CHAP. IV. The first account of the Nipmucks, or the earliest history of the Pemigewassetts, and of their union with other tribes; also how a Bashaba was killed, with a description of a very polite way of treating captives, and a foreshadowing of something dreadful to happen. - - 41

CHAP. V. Of a terrible war, pestilence, and famine, the heroes of which are all dead and their names forgotten. - - - - - - - - 47

CHAP. VI. How the Pemigewassetts and the rest of the Nipmucks were compelled to enter a new league to protect themselves from the Mohogs, Marquas or Mohawks, with a slight sketch of another great man who came to be Bashaba. - - - - - - - - - - 51

CHAP. VII. In which is set forth the manner the Pemigewassetts sometimes enjoyed themselves, while the new Bashaba lived, and then of a slight war that arose which was exceedingly entertaining to them, together with its pious close at Quocheco. - - - - - - 58

CHAP. VIII. How according to tradition the Pemigewassetts were present at a great court at Quocheco, where the laws were very legally executed and justice done—according to the idea of certain exasperated red men.   64

CHAP. IX. Containing a slight attempt at biography, or the early life of Waternomee, otherwise Wattanumon, sometimes vulgarly called Walternumus, last chief of the Pemigewassetts. - - - - -   69

CHAP. X. How the Pemigewassetts engaged in Queen Anne's war—of sundry expeditions—and how several Pemigewassetts were surprised and slain by five terrible Marquas led by the brave Caleb Lyman.   73

CHAP. XI. Of several things that happened during the progress of the war, and how, as one of the results, the Pemigewassett tribe was destroyed and their hunting grounds, of which Warren was a part, became a solitude. - - - - - - - - - - - - -   80

BOOK II.

TREATING OF INDIAN FIGHTS AND MASSACRES, EXPEDITIONS AND EXPLORATIONS, RESULTING IN OPENING TO THE WHITE MAN THE LAND OF THE PEMIGEWASSETTS, AND MAKING THE VALLEY NOW CALLED WARREN, AND ALL THE ADJACENT COUNTRY, A SAFE PLACE TO LIVE IN.

CHAP. I. Of two wars and more than a dozen battles. - - - - -   87

CHAP. II. A beautiful solitude, and how there was an attempt to build two forts above the Pemigewassett country, and what came of it. -   99

CHAP. III. Giving an account of a hunting party on the Asquamchumauke; how two young men were captivated in the most captivating manner—concluding with how one got his back tickled with the oil of birch, while the other did not, much to the delight of all concerned. - - - 103

CHAP. IV. How the salvages, Sabatis and Christo, stole two negroes from the settlement at Canterbury and the excitement it caused, together with a grand result before hinted at. - - - - - - - 107

CHAP. V. How the road was cut through the woods, and how the great and mighty nation of Arosagunticooks, composed of all the Nipmuck tribes, including our Pemigewassetts and some others, sent a flag of truce to Number Four. Concluding with a general back out. - - - - - 110

CHAP. VI. How Sabatis and Plausawa fared in the hands of Peter Bowen, together with the miraculous opening of the jail. Concluding with a captivating account of a whole family who were politely invited to go to Canada, by "the gentle salvages." - - - - - - - 114

CHAP. VII. How Capt. Peter Powers marched gallantly through the Pemigewassett country to the land of the Coosucks; of a brave exploit and a heroic retreat. - - - - - - - - - - - 120

CHAP. VIII. Of a gallant exploit on the New Hampshire frontier,—of an excited camp on the shore of Wachipauka pond, with other entertaining and curious matter, very interesting to know. - - - - - 126

CHAP. IX. Account of the manner the brave Arosagunticooks of St. Francis passed Captain Goffe; the capture of the Johnson family, with other incidents no doubt very interesting to the participants, together with the first campaign of the old French war. - - - - - - 132

CHAP. X. Treating of the assembling of the regiment, and the building of the log fortress at Coos, with other interesting adventures, in the country about Lake Champlain. - - - - - - - - - - 136

CHAP. XI. A long march through the woods; a terrible attack on an Indian village; a bloody butchery—awful to the participants—but withal very pleasant to read about. - - - - - - - - - - 141

CHAP. XII. The retreat and its horrors. The camp on the Coos interval under the shadow of the mighty Moosilauke; concluding with a beautiful and golden tradition that has been repeated around the farmer's fireside for a hundred years. - - - - - - - - - 147

CHAP. XIII. How the surviving rangers all got safely home and how thenceforward the Pemigewassett land containing the pleasant little territory of Warren, became a very safe country in which to sojourn. - 154

BOOK III.

OF THE BIRTH OF A MOUNTAIN HAMLET, OR THE PRECISE AND ACCURATE HISTORY OF THE ACTS OF SIXTY-SIX DISTINGUISHED MEN, OTHERWISE KNOWN AS THE PROPRIETORS OF WARREN.

CHAP. I. Concerning a great shaggy wood, and numerous hunters therein; and then of a sweet little feud between three royal governors, and how one of them politely "euchered" the others, much to their delight. - 157

CHAP. II. Of a fine old Governor of 'ye ancient days, and of his royal Secretary; how these two worthies built golden castles in the air, and finally grew quite rich. - - - - - - - - - - 162

CHAP. III. What John Page, Esq., did, or how he procured a royal charter of our mountain hamlet, Warren, conferring many glorious privileges and only a few conditions very easy to be complied with. - - - - 166

CHAP. IV. Of eager men,—how they held several meetings—also of a gay and festive corporation dinner; concluding with a powerful effort to obtain a surveyor of the King's Woods. - - - - - - 176

CHAP. V. How the lines were run round about Warren; a camp in the forest; a roaring, raging equinoctial storm worth seeing, and a report of the whole affair by surveyor Leavitt. - - - - - - - - 182

CHAP. VI. Conditions hard and terrible,—road made of an Indian trail,—rich lots of land drawn by lot, and how men felt rich but anxious. - 187

CHAP. VII. How the proprietors' prospects got desperate—so much so that they were willing to give away some of their lands; how Phillips White, Esq., came to the rescue—got them out of a terrible difficulty, and finally procured a new charter, which ends this book and introduces us to an altogether new life in Warren. - - - - - - 194

BOOK IV.

WHICH RELATES HOW OUR WILD MOUNTAIN HAMLET WAS CULTIVATED AND SETTLED.

CHAP. I. Of divers and sundry sounds, heard on the head-waters of the Asquamchumauke, and of two hotels in which not a drop of "grog" could be got either for love or money. - - - - - - - - 201

CHAP. II. About Joseph Patch, the first white settler of Warren, and how he had a few hungry visitors which ate up all his provisions. - - - 207

CHAP. III. How eighteen families and two single gentlemen came to Warren to reside, and amused themselves building cabins, clearing land, hunting moose and deer on the hills, and fishing in the clear, rapid trout streams. - - - - - - - - - - - - 214

CHAP. IV. Of how the early settlers of our mountain hamlet took great thought about the manner they should be sheltered, and what they should eat, and of the building of mills; concluding with the mighty leaps of the salmon, and a delectable swim by the boys. - - - - 236

CHAP. V. Narrating how two men, Stevens Merrill and James Aiken loved each other,—how the laws were executed, and a house burned up,—concluding with a "pious inquiry" worthy of all good christians. - 243

CHAP. VI. Mount Carr; its ancient inhabitants, and then of the grand old huntings that were had about it, with a beautiful Moosehillock description thrown in for variety. - - - - - - - - - 247

CHAP. VII. Of a provision for religious meetings; grandiloquent description of one, and how it closed with a cup of sweet comfort and peace, as was the custom in ancient times. - - - - - - - - 257

CHAP. VIII. War! How it reared its horrid front and its din resounded even across the boundaries of Warren, together with what part our early settlers took in it. - - - - - - - - - - - 263

BOOK V.

CONCERNING THE MIGHTY MARCH OF EVENTS IN THE GREAT CIVIL HISTORY OF WARREN.

CHAP. I. Of the organization of the hamlet, and how certain men achieved immortal glory by getting elected to town office. - - - - - - 275

CHAP. II. How the revenue was raised to carry on the war, much to the delight of several patriotic gentlemen called tories; and what soldiers were furnished to fill Warren's quota, with other very interesting and entertaining matter. - - - - - - - - - - - 282

CHAP. III. The first funeral of a white man in Warren; or how John Mills died and was buried. - - - - - - - - - - - 294

CHAP. IV. About a great army in Warren, how it marched and counter-marched; of the pretty names it was called, and how it was subsisted. 297

CHAP. V. Thanksgiving day, or how there was feasting, dancing and merry-making in our hamlet among the hills. - - - - - - - - 304

CHAP. VI. The first schools of Warren, or how the young idea was taught to shoot; and of a certain oil much used in ye ancient days. - - - 313

CHAP. VII. How Sarah Whitcher was lost in the woods, what happened and how they hunted for her, together with a remarkable dream, and how a bushel of beans suddenly disappeared. - - - - - - - - 322

CHAP. VIII. Of a mighty battle fought between two ambitious office seekers, and how each gained the victory, much to his great delight. - - 329

CHAP. IX. Concerning a great boundary feud and what came of it. - - 335

CHAP. X. Of the mighty requisites necessary to make a perfect democracy, all graphically portrayed in the most attractive manner. - - - - 340

BOOK VI.

IN WHICH THE MIGHTY MARCH MENTIONED AT THE BEGINNING OF BOOK V. IS CONTINUED.

CHAP. I. How several religions came to Warren; of tythingmen who fined men for traveling Sunday, thereby making them exceedingly happy; concluding with an account of a camp-meeting, where several pious youth sounded a horn in the night and disturbed the slumbers of the godly. - - - - - - - - - - - - - - - 361

CHAP. II. Of grand huntings, fowlings, and fishings; concluding with how a 'squire, a doctor, and a minister were perfectly delighted trying to catch every fish in Wachipauka pond. - - - - - - - - 370

CHAP. III. How the turnpike was built, and of divers things that happened thereby. - - - - - - - - - - - - 384

CHAP. IV. About the 1812 war; of drafting and volunteering; closing with a grand muster, when Warren's hills heard louder music than ever before. - - - - - - - - - - - - 390

CHAP. V. How the first covered stage, accompanied by sweet music, ran through Warren, with an account of the first post-office, and who delivered the letters. - - - - - - - - - - 398

CHAP. VI. The Black Plague, otherwise called the Spotted Fever, or the greatest horror Warren people ever had. - - - - - - 404

CHAP. VII. How almost a famine, then a hurricane came, and then a history of one of the most pleasant years Warren ever experienced. - - 408

CHAP. VIII. What a woman can do and how she did it; or the accomplishment of one of the greatest "requisites" of the last century, viz: the building of a meeting-house. - - - - - - - - - 422

CHAP. IX. A gay little chapter about witches. - - - - - - 431

CHAP. X. The first store in Warren, and its successors, and of a roaring, raging canal that never was built. - - - - - - - - 441

BOOK VII.

WHICH BOOK IS BUT A CONTINUATION OF BOOKS V. AND VI., AND CONTAINS THE HISTORY OF THE THIRD GENERATION OF WARREN'S WHITE INHABITANTS.

CHAP. I. How gold, silver, and diamonds were discovered in Warren; and of several individuals who got immensely rich mining, especially in their imaginations. - - - - - - - - - - 449

CHAP. II. How the Berry brook road was built, and a path on to Moosehillock was cut, with a pleasant account of several individuals who nicknamed each other in the happiest manner. - - - - - - 454

CHAP. III. Of a great lawsuit about Mrs. Sarah Weeks, whom foolish people called a witch, concluding with pleasant recollections of a paring bee and a "shin-dig," if anybody knows what that is. - - - - - 461

CHAP. IV. A chapter on fires. - - - - - - - - - 467

xiii.

CHAP. V. How and when the railroad was built, which will be a wonder to future generations, but is quite a common thing now. - - - - 472

CHAP. VI. A brief account of two murders. - - - - - - 478

CHAP. VII. Concerning a great rivalry between charitable religious societies, which resulted in moving and remodelling the old meeting-house, in a town-house, a new school-house, a beautiful common, and in improving the graveyard, all which is an honor to the town and the pride of the inhabitants. - - - - - - - - - - - 483

CHAP. VIII.. Of a delectable visit to Moosehillock, and what can be seen there—the weather permitting. - - - - - - - - 490

CHAP. IX. How several individuals got rich manufacturing, or ought to, with the glorious results of it. - - - - - - - - - 499

CHAP. X. Of several things that happened; concluding this History with sincere thanks and many kind wishes. - - - - - - - . 508

APPENDIX.

Explanatory Notes.
Natural History of Warren.
Selectmen, Representatives, and other Town Officers.
Town Statistics.
Lawyers, Doctors, and Ministers.
Military Officers.
Town Lots.
First Inventory and Tax List.
Longevity.
Genealogies.
Miscellaneous.
The Poets of Warren.
Amos F. Clough's Diary, kept on Moosehillock.
Chronology.

INDEX.

ILLUSTRATIONS.

1. Moosehillock, from Warren, opposite title page.
2. Map of Warren 17
3. Webster Slide and Wachipauka Pond 23
4. Oak Falls 23
5. Rocky Falls 87
6. Portrait of Amos F. Clough, Artist 157
7. Map of Warren 171
8. Mount Carr 201
9. Waternomee Falls 201
10. Old Barn built by Joseph Patch 240
11. Breaking and Swingling Flax 274
12. Old Boundary Lines 336
13. Our Grandmothers' Pastime 360
14. Portrait of Rev. Joseph Merrill 399
15. Portrait of Rev. Moses H. Bixby 426
16. Map of Modern Warren 448
17. Portrait of Samuel B. Page, Esq. 462
18. Church and Village School-House 486
19. Town House 486
20. Sugaring off 486
21. McCarter, the Hermit 486
22. Moosilauke Falls 486
23. The Forks School-House 486
24. Moosehillock from Indian Rock 493
25. Prospect House, Summit of Moosehillock . . · 493
26. Portrait of Dr. Worcester E. Boynton . . . 502
27. Portrait of Gen. Natt Head 510

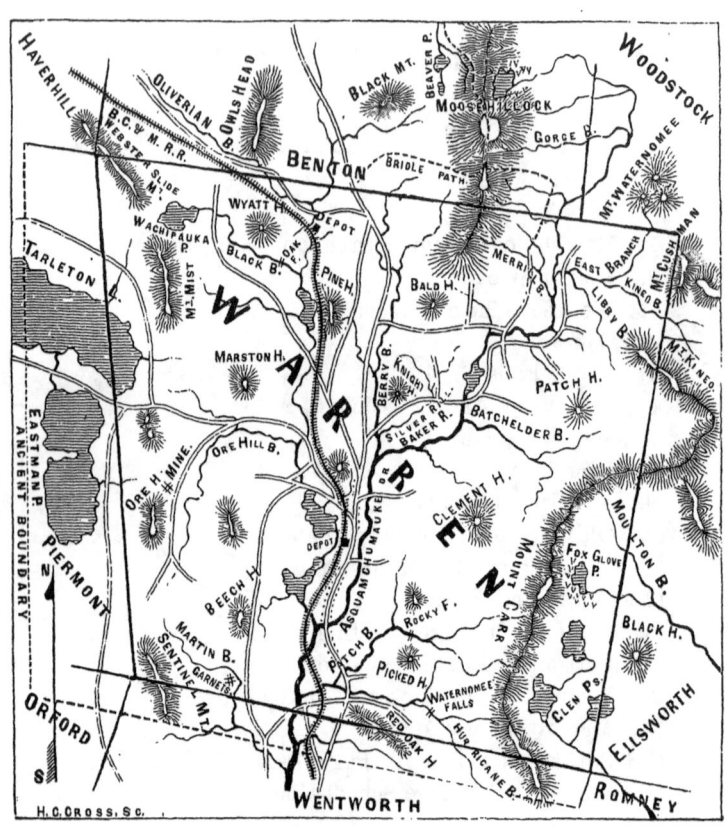

MAP OF MODERN WARREN

INTRODUCTION.

WHICH GIVES A CONCISE ACCOUNT OF THE DISCOVERY OF AMERICA; ITS SETTLEMENT BY THE ENGLISH; THE LOCALITY OF WARREN, ITS BOUNDARIES, MOUNTAINS, HILLS, STREAMS, PRODUCTIONS, AND INHABITANTS.

AMERICA was discovered by Christopher Columbus in 1492. The first permanent English settlement was made at Jamestown, Virginia, in 1607. New Hampshire, another British province, was settled in 1623. These are facts that every one is presumed to know.

Warren, the history of which we now undertake to write, is a town in New Hampshire. It is situated in latitude forty-four degrees north, longitude six degrees east from Washington, and became a geographical fact July 14th, 1763. Admiral Warren, a gallant commander of an English man-of-war, was its godfather. These are facts which every one is not presumed to know.

For further information we would say that Warren is a mountainous hamlet, situated in one of the western valleys of the great White Mountain range. The latter is a cluster of lofty peaks, located a little north of the centre of the State, which vary from three thousand to six thousand three hundred feet in height. Four great roads pass through these mountains, connecting the northern and southern portions of the State. One leads through the Pinkham notch, another through the White Mountain

---

The White Hills were called by the Indians, Waumbekketmethna; Waumbekket signifies White, and Methna, mountains.

notch, a third through the Franconia notch, and the fourth and most western one through the Oliverian notch. Warren is situated on the last mentioned thoroughfare.

That there may be no mistake about the locality of the town, gazetteers say that it is in the very centre of Grafton County, is fourteen miles from Haverhill, one of the shire towns of the county, seventy miles from Concord, the State Capital, and ninety-three from Portsmouth, New Hampshire's only seaport.

The boundaries of Warren are the gifts of nature. Its eastern line runs over the crests of three lofty mountains. Mt. Cushman on the north rises like a dark wave of the ocean 3,306 feet high. Mt. Kineo, a hundred feet higher, sweeps away in wavy crested summits to the southeast, and Mount Carr, blue, forest-clad, and the last of the trio, is 3,500 feet in height. The south line bends down the slopes of Red-Oak hill, crosses the pebbly-bottomed Asquamchumauke, and creeps up to the elevation of 2,059 feet over Mt. Sentinel. The western line is over a spur of the latter mountain, crosses Tarleton lake and Mt. Mist—so called from the vapor that sails up to its summit from the blue waves—and finds its northern termination on Webster Slide mountain. The latter is 2,170 feet above sea-level, and its precipitous face slopes down 800 feet to the deep shadows of Wachipauka or Meader pond. The northern line rests upon the flanks of Owl's Head mountain, 3,206 feet high, Mt. Black 3,550 feet, *Moosilauke about 5,000 feet,† and Mt. Waternomee, a woody elevation of about 3,000 feet. The first is a most curiously shaped mountain. Like a whale—its head a sharp angular peak, piercing the blue ether, its dorsal fin white jagged rocks, rising from the dark forest of firs, its tail a dizzy precipice, sinking perpendicularly a hundred fathoms down,—it turns up its huge back to be fanned by the rude winds. The second, Mt. Black without a white spot upon it, is a dark, sombre monument, rising in the city of mountains; the third, Moosilauke, head and shoulders above the others, is monarch of all, and the

---

The height of these mountains was ascertained by Prof. Guyot, of Princeton College, in 1857.

*Moosilauke was so called by the Indians from Moosi, bald, and Auke, a place—Bald-place. On the first maps it was written Mooshelauke, then Mooshelock, then Moosehillock. Many persons suppose it was so called from the large number of moose once found about the mountain.

† Some say 5,051 feet; others say 4,802 feet high.

fourth, Mt. Waternomee, is a green wooded mountain with three round crests, and is sometimes known as the southern spur of the Pemigewassett range.

The exact centre of Warren is the summit of Knight hill. Standing on the top, one is surrounded on all sides by lofty crests, and the forest hamlet appears like a huge bowl, with another bowl transparent, formed of blue sky inverted and placed over it, and resting upon the rim of mountains.

Warren is well watered. The principal stream is the Asquamchumauke, now called Baker river. It rises in a little meadow pond on the north side of Moosilauke mountain. At first a wild torrent, then a bright pebbly-bottomed stream, and lastly a deep blue river, it empties into the Pemigewassett. Its Warren tributaries from the west are Merrill, Berry, and Black brooks; on the east, East Branch, Batchelder, and Patch brooks. Through the north part of the town, running into the Connecticut, is Oliverian brook. These are the principal streams; but small yet never-failing rivulets gush from the mountain springs situated in every ravine, while there is scarcely a meadow which does not contain a fountain whose waters, cool and crystalline, bubble up from the white sands. More than a hundred of these musical streamlets make Warren one of the best watered towns in New Hampshire.

Five sparkling ponds lie sleeping high up among Warren's mountains. Over on the east side of Mount Carr two bright gems gleam in the greenwood, which from their locality are called the Glen ponds. Near Mt. Mist is Kelley pond, furnishing a stream for an old mill, and under the face of precipitous Webster Slide mountain is the before-mentioned Wachipauka or Meader pond. West of Mt. Mist, and kissing its sloping base, a crystal sheen in an emerald setting, is Tarleton lake.

Within the town are numerous hills, some of which deserve mention. Red Oak, Picked, Clement, and Patch, each rise about a thousand feet high on the east side of the Asquamchumauke. Bald, and Knight, wood-crowned heights of about the same elevation, are situated between the Asquamchumauke and Berry brook.

The Indians 'called Black brook Mikaseota, or with full spelling it was *Mikkasseotque.*— Acteon.

Pine hill is a long rolling ridge, terminating abruptly in Keyes ledge, or Mt. Helen, and stands between Black and Berry brooks. Wyatt, Marston, and Beech hills are on the western border.

Warren is rich in minerals. On Sentinel mountain is a large and productive vein of ore. Gold, silver, iron, copper, lead, zinc, plumbago, molybdenum, calc-spar, rutil, epidote, beryl, garnets, quartz crystals, tourmalines, and many others are found. Near the Summit are large quantities of limestone. Gneiss and mica slate abound, and the underlying granite which crops out on Webster Slide mountain and Mount Carr affords excellent building material.

The first road through Warren was the old Indian trail entering the town where the Asquamchumauke leaves it, and following the Mikaseota to its source in Wachipauka pond, it descended the slope of Webster Slide to the valley of the Oliverian. The second was built by the first white proprietors, and wound over the Height o' land and round the east shore of Tarleton lake. The third was the turnpike. Then the road over Pine hill and through the Oliverian notch was constructed, and last of all the railroad, which follows the old Indian trail with little variation and leaves the town by the above-mentioned notch. Numerous other roads have been made, for the accommodation of the later inhabitants, among which is the bridle-path over Moosilauke mountain.

The climate is very healthy. Residents of the town have seen the snows of a hundred winters. Owing to the elevation of the valley, and to the mountains which surround it, good sleighing often lasts from December to April. The snow then suddenly disappears, frequently causing destructive freshets. Summer treads quickly in the footsteps of winter, the crops spring forth as if by magic, and autumn never fails of returning an abundant harvest to cheer the heart of the husbandman.

The physical formation of a country has much to do with moulding the character of its people. The Indians of New Hampshire, to whom we shall devote the first book of this history, especially those who inhabited the central part of the State, must have been a race of mountaineers. As such, a love of freedom, the spirit of adventure, and a granite hardihood must have characterized them. Their wars with the early English pioneers will form the material of book the second of this very sedate and truthful history.

The acts of the sixty-five distinguished men, otherwise known as the provincial proprietors of Warren, will be accurately narrated in book the third.

The present inhabitants of Warren are mostly farmers. They are tenacious of their rights and political privileges, and are just such a hardy race as one might expect to find dwelling among granite boulders, leaping torrents, and high hills. In the Revolution about one-fourth of those capable of bearing arms served in the army. In the 1812 war they furnished their quota of troops cheerfully, all who went going as volunteers. The adventures of the early settlers of Warren and those of their descendants will form the subject of the remaining books of this, we trust, most entertaining history.

HISTORY OF WARREN.

BOOK I.

CONTAINING A HISTORY OF A TRIBE OF INDIANS NEVER BEFORE WRITTEN BY ANY OTHER HISTORIAN.

CHAPTER I.

OF THE NAME OF THIS TRIBE, OR HOW THEY CALLED THEMSELVES BY ONE NAME WHILE FOREIGNERS CALLED THEM BY ANOTHER, TOGETHER WITH WHERE THEY RESIDED IN THE MOST PERMANENT MANNER, AND WHAT GREAT TRIBES LIVED AROUND THEM.

THE first sunlight of history begins to dawn upon that little territory now called Warren, of which we have just given such a full description, about the last years of the seventeenth century. It reveals a pleasant valley surrounded by lofty mountains, watered by a rapid river and a hundred tumbling trout brooks sparkling down from the hills, and inhabited by a portion of a small tribe of Indians known in after years as the Pemigewassetts.

This people belonged to the Algonquin race, which occupied the whole Atlantic coast from the gulf of the St. Lawrence to Cape Fear.*

---
*Bancroft's Hist. of U. S. Vol. iii, Chap. 22. Whiton's Hist. of N. H. 9.

They called themselves NIPMUCKS,* a word derived from "nipe," meaning fresh water, and "auke," a place, an "m" being thrown in by skillful manufacturers of Indian words for the sake of euphony,—the whole meaning fresh-water Indians, a name used to distinguish them from those who resided on the immediate sea coast. †

These Nipmuck Indians were divided into numerous tribes or families, each having a head or chief, and we are told that as neighbors of the Pemigewassetts "a great and powerful tribe" lived on the Nashua stream and were called NASHUAS. ‡ That another lived on the Souhegan river, and of course were called SOUHEGANS. A third lived at Amoskeag falls, and were called AMOSKEAGS. A fourth inhabited the beautiful interval at Concord, called by the Indians Pennacook, and they were PENNACOOKS. A fifth dwelt on Squamscott river, now Exeter, and for the same reason were called SQUAMSCOTTS. A sixth stopped at Newichannock, and they were NEWICHANNOCKS. A seventh stayed at Piscataqua river, and they were PASCATAQUAUKES. An eighth built a wigwam city at Ossipee lake, and they were the cultivated OSSIPEES, with mounds and forts like more civilized nations. A ninth built flourishing villages in the fertile valley of the Pequawket river, and were known as the pious PEQUAWKEES, who worshipped the great Manitou of the cloud-capped Agiochook. A tenth had their home by the clear Lake Winnepisseogee, and were esteemed "the beautiful WINNEPISSAUKIES." An eleventh set up their lodges of spruce bark by the banks of the wild and turbulent Androscoggin river, and were known as "the death-dealing AMARISCOGGINS." A twelfth cultivated the Coos intervals on the

---

* Drake's Biog. of Indians, 13, 281. Hist. of New England, 636.
† The Indians from the interior were known and called among the tribes upon the seashore by the general name of Nipmucks, or Fresh-water Indians, and, true to their name, the Nipmucks usually had their residences upon places of still water, the ponds, lakes, and rivers of the interior. But the Indians in the Merrimack valley, although properly Nipmucks and living in distinct bands or tribes, were usually called by the English, Pennacooks, etc.
‡ *Nashua* means the river with a pebbly bottom. *Souhegan* is a contraction of Souheganash, meaning worn-out lands. *Amoskeag* is derived from Namaos (a fish) and Auke (a place). *Pennacook* is derived from Pennaqui (crooked) and Auke. *Squamscott*, from Asquam (water) and Auke. *Newichannock*, from Nee (my), Week (a contraction for Wigwam), and Owannock (come). *Pascataquauke*, from Pos (great), Attuck (a deer), and Auke. *Ossipee*, from Cooash (pines) and Sipe (a river). *Pequawkees*, from Pequakis (crooked) and Auke. *Winnepissaukies*, from Winne (beautiful), Nipe (water), Kees (high), and Auke. *Amariscoggins*, from Namaos (fish), Kees (high), and Auke. *Coosucks*, from Cooash, pines.—Potter's Hist. of Manchester.

Connecticut, and were called "the swift deer-hunting COOSUCKS." Besides these twelve tribes, just equal in number to the tribes of the children of Israel, the Pemigewassetts also had as neighbors in New Hampshire, and along its present borders, the WINNECOWETTS,* inhabiting a beautiful pine-tree-place in the southeast corner of the State, the Wachusetts living about the mountain of that name in Massachusetts, the Agawams residing at the mouth of the Merrimack, the Pawtuckets, who fished at Pawtucket falls, and several small tribes upon the banks of the Connecticut river whose names are unknown.

All these various tribes derived their pretty names from some prominent object in the territory which they inhabited. Thus the Pemigewassetts are so called from the principal river that flowed through their hunting grounds. That the places inhabited by the Indians, neighboring to the Pemigewassetts, did not derive their names from the name of the tribe, can be seen by examining the derivation of the names themselves. For instance, we are told that Pascataqua means "great deer place." Now we have too much respect for the memory of the noble Pascataquaukes to believe they would like to be called great deer. or rather great cowards. Again, Nashua means the river with a pebbly bottom; and we cannot think those red men intended to call themselves the *pebbly-bottomed Indians.* The literal significance of the word Pemigewassett is "the crooked mountain pine place"—a name that will answer well enough for a river, but would not at all describe the hardy race of Indian mountaineers that hunted in the pleasant territory of Warren. They were not crooked children but straight as arrows; they were not mountains, except in firmness and strength; nor were they pines, for that is a soft, brittle wood, and they were tough as oaks. We conclude that the Pemigewassetts, and all those numerous tribes who called themselves Nipmucks, received their name from foreigners in pretty much the same manner that Boston men are called Bostonians and the highly moral men of Gotham, Gothamites.

The different families of these several tribes, neighbors of our Pemigewassetts, were not very careful to confine their residences

---

* *Winnecowetts*, from Winne (beautiful), Cooash, and Auke.—Potter's Hist. of Manchester, 28.

to any particular locality,* but generally changed them several times in a year, and changed their names as often as they changed their residences. Consequently when a few families went to Amoskeag falls to fish they were Amoskeags; if they went to the rich intervals of Pennacook to plant they were Pennacooks; if they went later in the season to Winnepissiogee lake, where they could fish through the ice and hunt on the hills, to spend the winter, they were Winnepissaukies,—and, furthermore, any tribe had but to say *presto* and travel, and they immediately changed into some other great tribe.

Where in Warren, "the beautiful bowl of the mountains," did the Pemigewassetts live? They had numerous camping-grounds, but several places are particularly shown, where it is said they built their wigwams.

On the right bank of the Asquamchumauke, and a few rods below the large railroad bridge that spans its waters, was a fertile meadow. Here was a planting place. Arrow-heads have been found there, and the ridges where the corn grew were seen by the first settlers. But the Indians who sometimes lived here left a monument more enduring than the little mounds where they hilled their corn. Twenty rods back from the river, and fifty feet higher than the running water, a trap dyke cuts across a high ledge, known as

INDIAN ROCK.

On its top are formed four smoothly cut bowls. Lines connecting them would point east and west, north and south. Such regularity shows that they cannot be "pot-holes," and they were without doubt formed by the Indians. This settlement was on the Indian trail.

---

*From thick warm valleys where they winter they remove a little nearer to their summer fields. When it is warm spring they remove to their fields, where they plant corn. In middle summer, because of the abundance of fleas which the dust of the house breeds, they will fly and remove on a sudden to a fresh place. And sometimes having fields a mile or two or many miles assunder, when the work of one field is over they remove hence to the other. If death call in amongst them, they presently remove to a fresh place. If an enemy approach they remove to a thicket or swamp, unless they have some fort to remove into. Sometimes they remove to a hunting house in the end of the year and forsake it not until the snow lies thick; and then will travel home, men women and children, through the snow thirty, yea fifty or sixty miles. But their great remove is from their summer fields to warm and thick woody bottoms, where they winter. They are quick in half a day, yea sometimes in a few hours warning to be gone, and the house is up elsewhere, especially if they have a few stakes ready pitched for their mats. I once in my travels lodged at a house at which in my return I hoped to have lodged again the next night, but the house was gone in that interim and I was glad to lodge under a tree.—Roger Williams' Key, 3 Mass. Hist. Coll. 213.

Then there were indications of another settlement near Beach-hill bridge over Black brook, or, as they called it, the Mikaseota. This was a favorite place, and old Indians came back and camped there even after white settlers had moved into the valley.

A high embankment known as the Blue ridge connects the base of Keyes ledge with the foot of Sentinel mountain. This is the southern shore to what is now called Runaway pond. Where the water burst through is plain to be seen, and on the rocks of the former beach are yet the marks scored by the tumbling waves and dashing ice. The broad acres, once the bed of the pond, are now fertile meadows. They were never fully overgrown by forest trees. Mounds, where the Indians stored their corn; ashes, where burned the wigwam fires; pieces of rude pottery, axes of stone, arrow-heads turned up by the ploughshare, and graves under the shadow of Marston hill, tell that here once was an Indian village. By it ran the trail* leading to the land of the Coosucks. In front wound their Mikaseota, silent and dark, and near by the bright water of Ore hill brook flashed in the rocky glen. Here the steep hills, that once sloped down to the curling waves, protected from the chill winds the Indian's maize, his pumpkins, squashes, and beans, which grew in these most fertile meadows.

Then by the mouth of Berry brook,— the stream that comes down through the dark ravine from Moosilauke,— was a planting place. Debris from the wigwams, rude implements of husbandry, of hunting and fishing, have been found here.

High up on a plateau of Moosilauke mountain lies one of the most fertile farms of Warren. On its eastern side is a dark ravine a hundred fathoms deep. Through this rushes a foaming torrent, the head-waters of the Asquamchumauke. On the north the lofty Moosilauke shoots up five thousand feet; Mts. Waternomee, Cushman, and Kineo are on the left, a woody mountain ridge runs to the valley on the right, in front are Mount Carr and Mt. Sentinel, and through the passes and over hills may be seen the distant mountains of the southwest. Near the eastern edge of the plateau bubbles up a clear, cold spring. A little stream flowing therefrom winds for a considerable distance nearly parallel to the

---

*It is admirable to see what paths their naked hardened feet have made in the wilderness, in most stoney and rocky places.— Roger Williams' Key.

brink of the ravine and then, flashing among the boulders, leaps down through a deep gully to the torrent. Between the spring and the brink, in a grove of tall hemlocks, Indian implements* discovered show that here also was once an Indian village.

But the Pemigewassetts, as we have gently intimated before, were not confined to the woody territory of Warren. They had ample hunting grounds, larger than any of the other great tribes we have mentioned. The Height o' land was their northern boundary and the Connecticut river was on the west. The great White mountains were on the east, while on the south was the land of the Pennacooks and the Winnepissaukies.

Their's was a beautiful country. No clearer and more sparkling rivers could be found in the world than the Asquamchumauke and Pemigewassett; no brighter and more smiling lakes than the Newfound and the Squam, and no more glorious mountains than Moosilauke and the Haystacks. By Sawheganet and Livermore falls were the best of fishing places, and at the confluence of the Asquamchumauke and Pemigewassett were the broad and beautiful intervals of the tribe. No place more fertile can be found in New England. Luxuriant grasses and wild flowers growing with tropical exuberance, clusters of noble elms with waving branches, a dense forest, hills and wood-crowned summits on the border, and lofty mountains in the distance, often snow-capped at midsummer, made this spot a wild paradise. Ridges where the corn was planted, ashes where the wigwam was built, mattocks made from the bone of a moose's thigh, rude pestles and knives of stone, gouges, and arrow and spear-heads here found, show that this was the chief planting place of the tribe.† Here also was frequently the royal residence, and without doubt the Indians had encamped here for centuries.

There was really but one tribe of Indians in New Hampshire, the Nipmucks, as they called themselves. The division of this tribe into ten or fifteen small but distinguished tribes is but a pleasant fancy of great Indian Historians, and we have been pleased to humor that fancy. The Nipmucks belonged as much to one section of the State as to another, and inhabited all sections, setting up their wigwams wherever they could find good hunting grounds, fishing waters, and planting places. Potter says the New Hampshire Indians were all Nipmucks, and Drake says the same thing — and they have given the matter more research than all others who have written upon the subject. *Every town in New Hampshire has had a portion of a tribe of Indians at some time residing within its borders, and that was the Nipmuck.*
*Nathaniel Merrill, 2d, found a beautiful Indian freestone bowl at this place.
† At the mouth of Baker river, in the town of Plymouth, N. H., the Indians had a settlement, where have been found Indian graves, bones, gun-barrels, stone mortars, pestles, and other utensils in use among them.—I. Farmer & Moore's Col. 128.

CHAPTER II.

CONTAINING THE ORIGIN OF THE PEMIGEWASSETTS, WITH A FEW PROFOUND THEORIES VERY INTERESTING TO KNOW.

WHENCE came the Pemigewassetts? Whence all the red men? These are not easily answered.

Naturally one would turn to the Indians and seek the information from them. The medicine man, priest, or panisee, when asked the question would reply, as he often has, as follows:

"The first pair of mortals crept from a hole in the earth, climbing up by a grape-vine," to inhabit a world that, as some say, had "grown out of a tortoise's back," or as others, "the globe reconstructed from the earth clutched in a muskrat's paw."

Or the great legend man of another tribe would say that man was brought to earth on the back of the white-winged bird of heaven.

The traditions of another would have it that the land was peopled by "a few wanderers from the seven caves (if any one can tell where they are), veiling their god-like powers of terror with hissing rattlesnakes fearful only to others."

Then it was often told round the wigwam fire how a mammoth bull jumped over the great lakes with the first Indians on his back, and how a grape-vine carried a whole tribe across the Mississippi.

Now these, and very many more like them, were all satisfactory answers to the Indians themselves, but did not at all clear up the mystery of the origin of the Indians to the minds of the pious missionaries who first came among them, or the host of Indian historians who have sprung up in later years. Consequently theories without number have been started, a few of which the most important we will mention briefly, as they will aid the enquiring reader greatly in solving the momentous question.

Christopher Colon—otherwise the great Columbus—immediately upon his discovering the red men in the West Indies began to theorise upon their origin, and concluded they were the people of the ancient Ophir, from whence Solomon procured the gold to embellish the temple at Jerusalem, and "imagined that he saw the remains of furnaces of veritable Hebraic construction employed in refining the precious ore."

Numerous writers, following the great discoverer, asserted without the least hesitation that the Jews were the early settlers of America, and many pious authors rejoiced that they had found at last the abode of the ten lost tribes of the children of Israel.

Then learned authors arose who said North America was peopled by a colony of Norwegians, and a generation of later writers were sure that the newly discovered land was peopled in remote ages by the Chinese.

As time passed on, one distinguished historian ascribed the settlement of America to the Egyptians; another to the Scandinavians; a third to the Gauls; a fourth to the Celts; a fifth to the Phœnicians, and a sixth to the Carthagenians, and numerous others to as many different peoples and nations,—each author bringing a cloud of witnesses and numerous tomes of written evidence to support his theory.

In later times distinguished antiquarians, bringing to bear the light of natural science and modern geographical discoveries, have come to the conclusion that America was not peopled by the Norwegians, Celts, or Gauls,—marching from Europe by a pleasant route across frozen rivers and arms of the sea through Iceland, Greenland, and Labrador; neither that they sailed direct from Egypt, Phœnicia, or Carthage, westward across the Atlantic, or from China eastward across the Pacific; but that they came in veritable birch canoes from the northeast corner of Asia, coasting with a pleasant breeze along the Aleutian isles, or sailing in the most daring manner directly across Behring's straits—forty-four miles wide—with three small islands intervening at equal distances for convenient resting places.

Others are so kind that they have constructed in remote ages an exceedingly strong bridge of ice across the above-named strait, over which the red men could pass dry shod.

It is said, with how much truth we know not, that the Esquimaux of Asia and those of America are of the same origin, as is proved by the affinity of their language, and the latter probably emigrated from the former country—coming over in canoes or on the convenient bridge of ice. Also that the Tungusians of Asia* are identical with the red men of America; only this cannot be proved by their language, but by similarity of features, hair, and complexion.

Certain it is there are many who do not believe the last mentioned theories any more than the former, and assert that the Indians had an Adam and Eve of their own, who lived more than a hundred and fifty thousand years ago upon that strip of land seen to the northward from the top of our Pemigewassett's loved Moosilauke, and which was once the only land in the whole world, an island washed on every side by a boundless and unknown ocean.

From this we are to infer that Asia was peopled from America, and not vice versa, as was gravely asserted in former times.

Others there are who, discarding all the former theories, assert that the human race had diverse origins, by the development process, as unfolded by the great Darwin, in which he makes man to have descended by natural selections and gradual development from the—oyster, or some other equally distinguished creation of animal life. Our noble tribe on the banks of the Pemigewassett must have felt honored had they but known from what noble ancestors they descended.

Dissenters, who do not believe in the unity of the human race, affirm that the five species of men each had a different origin—five different pairs of first parents.† But these are only an aristocratical sort of people, who do not like to acknowledge themselves

---

* Captain Ray, of the whaleship Superior, testifies that while he was fishing at Behring's straits he saw canoes going from one continent to the other. The origin of the native Americans is thus evidently explained. It has also been observed that North Americans have habits and manners similar to the Tchuktchians, Kamtschatkans, Yakoutsks, and Koriaks of Asia. A similarity in the language has also been discovered.—History of the Abnakis, 13.

† They say it would have been just as easy for the Creator to have made five or twenty-five different races of men as it was to have made one.

to be cousins to the Hindus, Hottentots, and Negroes, perhaps to the gorillas and orang-otangs.

We do not propose to go further in this antiquarian or anthropological expedition, but think that our readers, from what has been thus briefly presented, will come to the sage conclusion that the Pemigewassetts came from somewhere, the Lord only knows where, and inhabited the fair valley of the Asquamchumauke for long centuries before the advent of the white man.

CHAPTER III.

ABOUT ACTEON—POLITELY CALLED OLD ACTEON—AND WHAT HE AS WELL AS OTHERS SAID OF THE MANNERS AND CUSTOMS OF THE PEMIGEWASSETTS.

IN a little old legendary manuscript history, where the handwriting was decidedly poor and the spelling none of the best, said to have been written by Colonel Obadiah Clement in his younger and palmiest days, are related many and wonderful things, reported to have been told the Colonel by an Indian * who had seen more than a hundred and twenty winters, and who was wont to stop at his inn, about the red men that once resided on the head waters of the Asquamchumauke. We have made the most diligent search for this exceedingly entertaining work, and although we found his few poems and a lengthy religious experience written out, and numerous other interesting papers, yet we were never able to lay our hands upon it. But we have no doubt that a work written by Colonel Clement, containing divers and sundry facts, did once exist, which like many another great production is now lost to the world forever. In fact, we have met with one person who claims to have read the identical history, and from him we learned many a fond tale which he said his grandfather's manuscript recounted. These we have scrupulously written down, preferring to give them as heard rather than to trick them out in all the beautiful adornings and gay images of rhetoric.

The old Indian, whose name was Acteon, as tradition has it,

---

* Joseph Clement and James Clement both vouch for the Indian.
In 1726 this same Acteon, at the head of ten Indians, surprised the family of Phillip Durrell, at Kennebunk, Me., burned the house and carried away ten persons into captivity. Acteon was a Nipmuck, although there was much dispute as to where he was born.— Drake's Ind. Biog, 336.

narrated how that the Pemigewassett tribe were a jovial set of wandering hunters, going from one end of their hunting grounds to the other in a single season, and building for themselves every time they stopped to plant, fish, or hunt fairy wigwams* to protect them from the weather. These mountain Indians had a taste for the beautiful, and their forest halls were elaborately constructed, splendidly ornamented, and furnished with the most artistic skill. A smooth plat of ground was chosen among the embowering trees, near which a bright cold spring gushed up from the white sand, or by which a sparkling brook danced in circling eddies among the rocks. Sometimes they chose the bank of the river, and again the margin of the shining lake.

In building their palaces they were the sole architects and artificers, and, being able to do so many things, they would have been termed in Yankee land jacks-at-all-trades.

Yet they reared no marble or granite halls. They planted numerous sapling poles in the ground, at equal distances from a given point called the centre; these were all bent toward each other till they met and formed a sharp cone, when they were there fastened. Spruce or birch bark was neatly shingled all over this light framework, save a small opening on the top and another about two feet wide and three feet high, on the southeast side. The first was never closed, no doubt being left open that the smoke of the fire, which was always built in the centre of the palace, might easily escape,—perhaps also for ventilation—while the second, which answered for a royal entrance, and was really larger than that through which the dirty philosopher Diogenes entered his tub, was stopped by the shaggy skin of a bear. Mats were placed upon the ground, and these were covered with rich furs. Dishes of birch bark, shells, and gourds; bows and arrow-filled quivers, tomahawks and scalping-knives; spears, paddles, pipes, and tobacco—in fine, all the treasures of mighty warriors, together with the scalps of enemies, were hung, like trophies in old baronial halls, upon the pillars, architraves, cornices, fluted shafts, friezes, and capitals of the stately pole and bark edifice.†

---

* The men make the poles or stakes, but the women make and set up, take down, order, and carry the household stuff.—Roger Williams' Key.
† Deer skins, or those of some other animal, were hung at these apertures to take the place of doors, and were pushed aside when they wished to enter or pass

ACTEON. 35

The palace of Versailles, the Kremlin of Moscow, or the halls of St. James have not half the beauties these woodland lodges and their surroundings possessed. Fountains and baths in silvery sands, with flowers smiling on the mossy rim; long aisles amid the mighty colonnade of trees; terraces on the green slopes, planted with flowering shrubs; leafy canopies echoing with the fairy notes of the light-winged winds, or thrilling with the sweetest madrigals of a thousand birds, with plumage dyed in the brightest rainbow hues; arches of sky of the sweetest blue, or ebon vaults glowing with diamond stars—all these emparadised the forest lodges of the Pemigewassetts.

But, said old Acteon, although we don't use his exact language, let no one who has common sense suppose for a moment that these almost ephemeral wigwams were free from the numerous cares that harass and perplex humanity. The Pemigewassetts, like other men, must eat. Their bodies were sensible to the scorching rays of the summer sun and also felt the chilly blast and biting frost. Toil might procure them food, but from heat and cold their palaces afforded only a weak protection.

Still they had one advantage over ordinary civilized mortals: No frowns, scowls, or cross looks on the lovely faces of their squaw-queens ever troubled them on washing or cleaning days. In fact, it required no great outlay of elbow-grease to keep their castles clean, nor coats of whitewash to make them look comely. If a dirty mud-puddle stank before the entrance, or if all the chinks and cranies of the low-arched hall swarmed with fleas and lice, as was frequently the case, all that was necessary to be done was to move out the treasures, apply the torch, let the devouring element do its work—and then no forest flower could grow half so quick as a second royal wigwam.*

How did the Pemigewassetts subsist? Old Acteon, in a story-

---

out. They had *gourds* of various kinds. The common gourd they cultivated for dippers and musical instruments, use and pleasure. The *bow* of the Pemigewasset was usually made of white ash or hemlock. The *arrow* was pointed with stone; sometimes of fine granite, but oftener of quartz and slate. The *spear-head* and *knife* were of the same materials. When bending the bow the string was drawn with three fingers, while the forefinger and thumb held the arrow. In this manner a strong man could bend a very stiff bow, which would throw an arrow with very great velocity. *Paddles* were made of light bass wood or ash. *Pipes* were made of freestone.

*The wigwam for the summer was a frail and temporary affair, as it was removed from the winter encampment to the fishing place, and from thence to the

telling mood, often related to Colonel Obadiah how it was,—and as they were just like all the rest of the New England Indians their manners and customs can also be learned from the early English Indian historians among them, and perhaps the most entertaining is John Josselyn, Gent., as he was accustomed to sign himself.

Cultivating the land, fishing, fowling, and hunting occupied for the most part their attention.

The braves did not like to work, and the women were compelled to strengthen their feeble constitutions by cultivating the wild fields with mattocks of wood, bone, or shell. They planted the maize, scared away the crows, hoed the beans, and trained the flowering vines.

While their women were thus employed and kept out of mischief the men would gamble, tell their brave exploits in war, sing their rude songs, engage in wild sports, or eat, smoke, and sleep. When they were tired of this lazy way of existence they would dig out their boats, construct their birchen canoes, * repair the wigwams, and make bows, arrows, spears, and tomahawks.

When they wanted moderate excitement, and did not care to fight, they would engage in fishing, fowling, and hunting. It is said that in the first they used a spear, a net, and rude hooks of bone.† But Old Acteon said the Pemigewassetts and their Nipmuck cousins down the river had no need of such artificial contrivances. So plenty were the fish in the Merrimack and its tributaries that all they had to do was to jump into the water and with their hands throw out a hundred dozen or so, just as their delicate appetites happened to crave.

In the ponds and rivers, at certain seasons, wild-fowl congregated in immense flocks. Then fleets of birchen canoes would

---

planting grounds; then from one field to another, and then again oftentimes from one spot in the field to another, to get rid of the fleas, which were numerous in hot weather, and which insect they call *Poppek* from its celerity of movement.—Potter's History of Manchester, 47.

* The *canoe* was made of birch bark: A suitable tree was cut down and the bark peeled off in one piece. Then a framework of spruce was made and the bark fitted or sewed to it with spruce or other roots. The holes were stopped with pitch. They were really beautiful and graceful structures, and one that weighed less than forty pounds would carry five persons. A man could easily carry one on his shoulders around falls or from place to place.

† Up higher from the sea, at the falls of great rivers, they used to take salmon, shad, and alewives that used in great quantities, more than cartloads, in the spring to pass up into the fresh water ponds and lakes to spawn.—Ms. H. C. iii. s. vol. v. 30.

surround them, and gradually narrowing their circle they would rapidly huddle them into some narrow creek or cove, and then in wantonness destroy them by thousands.

In hunting they set spring traps* for deer, snares for partridges and rabbits, and kulheags for bears, coons, fisher-cats, minks, muskrats, and sable. In early autumn, when moose and deer fed at night on the grassy shores of the lakes and rivers, the Indian hunter, with rude lantern brightly flashing in front, placed in the prow of the canoe, would paddle noiselessly in the dark shadow behind, and when sufficiently near his spell-bound victim would send his feathered shaft on its silent but fatal mission. Every dark night of autumn these spectral fires might be seen gliding like will-o'-the-wisps over the rivers, ponds, and lakes in the Pemigewassett country.

But the most exciting and the most attractive of all were their grand hunting-parties. As they had no hawks, hounds, nor horses, and as it was difficult for a single hunter to capture the larger game, these huntings were necessary. They would select some woody glen or pass of the hills, such as can be found anywhere in the East-parte regions, or like the notch of the Oliverian, which they would nearly hedge across by an abattis of trees placed in the form of the letter V — the apex being left slightly open, so that the game could pass through. The skillful spear and bow men stationed themselves near the open apex. Some of the more inexperienced hunters, together with the women and children, would go out on the hillsides, while others stood in a semi-circle across the valley. Then with shouts, and yells, and wild whoops, the moose and deer, bears and wolves, were roused with the smaller game. Narrowing their semicircle, they drove the wild

---

* In November, 1620, soon after the arrival of the Mayflower, as Stephen Hopkins, William Bradford and others were walking in the woods they came to a tree where a young sprit was bowed down over a bow and some acorns strewed underneath. As Bradford went about it it gave a sudden jerk up and he was immediately caught up by his legs and hung dangling in the air.—Potter's Hist. of Manchester, 42.

They hunt by traps of several sorts. To which purpose after they have observed in spring-time and summer the haunt of the deer then about harvest they go ten or twenty together, and sometimes more, and withal if it be not too far, wives and children also, where they build up little hunting houses of barks and rushes, not comparable to their dwelling-houses; and so each man takes his bounds of two, three, or four miles, where he sets thirty, forty, or fifty traps, and baits them with that food the deer loves, and once in two days he walks his round to view his traps where they lie at what comes at them, for the deer, whom they conceive have a divine power in them, will soon smell all and be gone.—Roger Williams' Key, 233.

herd toward the restricted opening of the abattis. The moose and deer were shot, as bounding forward they endeavored to escape. Bears generally took to the trees, but the bowmen brought them down, while the lesser game, confused and crowded, was easily captured by the shouting drivers.*

Such scenes were yearly witnessed in all the Nipmuck country, and especially in the Asquamchumauke valley, where game was so plenty. In this manner they procured a large supply of meat which, smoked, lasted through the winter, as well as an abundance of furs and skins for clothing and blankets.

When the strawberry crimsoned the banks of the Asquamchumauke, the wild cherry and sugar plum tempted the songster by Berry brook and the Mikaseota; when the raspberry and blackberry grew by the wild maize fields, and the blueberry and huckleberry ripened on the rocky heights of Owl's Head and Webster Slide and along the shores of the sedgy ponds, rosy-cheeked girls and bright-eyed boys of the Pemigewassett tribe had a joyous time gathering the luscious store.

But when the green corn was ripe enough to roast, and the fishings, or fowlings, or huntings were over; when the squaws had gathered the silken ears, or had cooked the geese, the ducks, and the partridges, or the golden-fleshed salmon or rich fat trout; or had roasted the moose meat and the venison and bear steaks,— then began the feast and jubilant festivals; then the archways of their forest temples echoed with wild harmonious choruses and deep-resounding music; then on the fire-lit lawn symmetrical forms circled in the mazy green corn dance, the salmon dance, and the hunters' dance; then vows were plighted, nuptials celebrated, and the old men recounted the legends of the tribe.

Acteon said that the Pemigewassetts never considered Warren —the land upon the head-waters of the Asquamchumauke—as a very good planting ground. Plymouth, and the rich meadows of Coos, were much better. But as a good hunting region, about the lofty Moosilauke, or as containing excellent fishing waters, no better place could be found.

---

*When they pursue their game, especially deer—which is the general and wonderful plenteous hunting in the country—they pursue in 20, 40, 50, yea 200 or 300 in a company, as I have seen when they drive the woods before them.—Roger Williams' Key, 236.

The Pemigewassetts like all the rest of the Nipmucks hunted, or fished, or planted, every day in the year. There was no Sunday for them. Still they were somewhat piously disposed and observed religious rites whenever the spirit moved. They had no God, as we understand Him. Their deities were infinite; but some were superior to others. Every thing that showed life or motion had a divinity, and they saw a god in every blade of springing grass, in the waving of the forest trees; they saw him smiling in the blue river and heard him in the dashing of the great lakes, in the music of the leaping waterfalls, in the sighing of the trickling drops of the grotto, and in the winds shrieking on the cliffs. To them there was a bright Shade dancing in the stars, gliding on the moonbeams, smiling in the rosy dawn of morning, and the last tinges of the setting sun.

Then there was a divinity—a guardian angel—for the trout, the salmon, and the shad; for every kind of fish, for the songster that sang by the wigwam, and the eagle that screamed above the mountains; for the beaver, the bear, the deer, the moose, and for every creeping thing. This divinity, this "shade," would never die. When its mission on earth was ended it flew to the "happy hunting grounds" of the far southwest, along with the noble shades of the dusky departed Indians, and there it would live forever.

But the great god, Gitchie Manito, of the Pemigewassetts had his home on the mountains, and they heard him in the voices of the storm and the mighty torrent, and in the thunder that muttered in the dark gorges and rumbled low over the crests. They saw him in the rosy hue that kindled on the peaks in early morning, or in the sharp flash of the lightning that leaped from the murky clouds.

His home they seldom visited, and the Indian had a bold spirit who dared to climb the bald crest of the mountain.

To him they sacrificed. The first fruits of the chase, the early green maize, the golden salmon, the wild duck, the goose, and the partridge were their offerings. But, like more modern Christians, they believed in evil spirits as well as good ones, and the former came in for their share and received their portion,—the same as the ancient Greeks were accustomed to sacrifice five white sheep to the good gods and ten black ones to the bad.

Many other things, as Acteon said, the Pemigewassetts were wont to do, such as to marry and be given in marriage, and now and then obtain a divorce, as is the custom in later days; to die and be buried, to weep and mourn, and then to engage in the pleasant pastime of war, as we shall be most happy to narrate.

---

* When they come to the grave they lay the dead by the grave's mouth and then all sit down and lament; that I have seen tears run down the cheeks of stoutest captains, as well as little children, in abundance. And after the dead are laid in the grave and sometimes in some parts some goods cast in with them, they have the second great lamentation. And upon the grave is spread the mat the party died on, the dish he eat in, and sometimes a fair coat of skin hung upon the next tree to the grave, which none will touch, but suffer it there to rot with the dead.—Roger Williams' Key, 238.

CHAPTER IV.

THE FIRST ACCOUNT OF THE NIPMUCKS, OR THE EARLIEST HISTORY OF THE PEMIGEWASSETTS, AND OF THEIR UNION WITH OTHER TRIBES; ALSO HOW A BASHABA WAS KILLED, WITH A DESCRIPTION OF A VERY POLITE WAY OF TREATING CAPTIVES, AND A FORESHADOWING OF SOMETHING DREADFUL TO HAPPEN.

CAPTAIN JOHN SMITH deserves honorable mention in this and every other great history. He was the bravest man of that company of adventurers who founded Jamestown, Virginia. He would have been leader whether chosen by the London Company or not, for as a general thing the bravest man in trying times takes the lead. Smith was courageous. There was a sort of a bull-dog crossed with a rat-terrier look in his countenance. He had stamina, gumption — pluck in abundance. With his cocked hat, blue coat and bright buttons, sword, buff-breeches, leggins, shoes and buckles, he presented an imposing appearance, which showed that he was the man for the times and the occasion. He arranged the affairs of the colony, explored the country, met with his Pocahontas adventure, went twice to England and returned, made a map of all the American coast claimed by his sovereign, King James, and then all for glory went to fight in the wars of some eastern prince.

This same Capt. John Smith, many thanks to him, claimed to be something of an author. He explored the coast of New England, kept a journal, and afterwards published an account of his travels. From him we learn all about this beautiful land — called by some a rock-bound coast — how it was full of bays and inlets, and how bright rivers came down from the mountains seen rising from the far interior forests.

We also learn from him how many and what Indians resided here. He tells us of the cruel Micmacs of Nova Scotia, who, with the New Brunswick Indians, were called Tarentines. They were jolly fighters, and delighted in blood and carnage. He also tells us of the Scotucks, a tribe with a beautiful name, admired by all, and of the Penobscots, who inhabited the Kennebec country, and were celebrated in the songs of the red men as a tall race of noble warriors. He says the Sokokis dwelt on the Saco river and fished at its falls; that the Pascataquas were at the Isles of Shoals, and built handsome wigwams on the shores of the beautiful bay, at Strawberry Bank. The Massachusetts lived at Trimountain, the Paconikicks at Cape Cod, and west were the warlike Pequots and the bloody Narragansetts. In the interior of Massachusetts and New Hampshire were the Nipemucks, and the Noridgewolks were seated on the upper Kennebec and Moosehead lake.

All these tribes were divided into numerous clans, and the famous Capt. Smith tells all their musical, easily pronounced names, such as the Aumughcawgens, Pauhuntanucks, Pocopassums, Taughtanakagnets, Mauherosquick, Pasanack, and many others equally pretty, with as much particularity as he would mention the hundred names of all the great and powerful German states.

This voyage of exploration, when Smith made such wonderful discoveries, which resulted in his giving us the earliest account of the Nipmucks extant, happened in 1614. At this time the Marquas,* or Mohawks, on the Hudson, were a powerful race of warriors. Their wild maurauding parties frequently crossed the Green mountains and fell on the dwellers of the coast. Then the bloody Tarentines of the east were continually panting for glory and triumphs — not unlike the Romans — and the consequence was that all the above-mentioned tribes were compelled to join in a league for mutual protection.

The Penobscot Indians were at the head of this league. They were a valiant race, and their chief was superior to all of his

---
*To sum up all concerning the Marquas you may see in the foregoing discourse that they are a stout though cruel people, much addicted to bloodshed and cruelty, very prone to vex and spoil the peaceable Indians.— Gookin, Ms. Hist. Col. 167.

The Mohawks were a powerful tribe and made frequent incursions among the New England Indians.— 3 Ms. Hist. Soc. Col. iii. 21, 22.

time. Of powerful frame, no Indian could hurl the tomahawk with more precision, could shoot an arrow higher, paddle the canoe faster, or run swifter than himself. In the council he was eloquent, and commanded the closest attention; in the fight his whoop was the loudest and his blow the most deadly; as a medicine man he was unequalled, and as a sorcerer all the subtle spirits stood ready to do his bidding. Of commanding appearance, with eagle plumes in his straight black hair, with an eye flashing like lightning, high cheek bones, broad nose and firmly set jaws; with necklace of panthers' claws, and a rattlesnake skin on his tawny red arm; naked to the waist, a robe of fox-skins with tails pendant extending to the knee; bear-skin breeches, with flowing hair, and moccasins of moose-hide,—the chief of the Penobscots —the Bashaba of New England—was the idol of his braves.

This great Bashaba had numerous chiefs of his own tribe under him, and so in all the other tribes. Even our Pemigewassetts had several chiefs, according to Acteon's narrative: a war chief, who led the army of braves to battle; chiefs in the council, who sat as head men of the deliberations,—and every one of these great chiefs acknowledged fealty to the Bashaba.

But this great man did not long survive the visit of Capt. Smith, and then the league went to pieces. How it happened is very interesting to know:

The young warriors of the Tarentines* were thirsting for glory. They feasted in the groves where the wigwams were planted; by their fire they sang the war-song and danced the war-dance in the shadowy night, and all who danced enlisted. As the full moon waned, a score of parties, each numbering from three to forty, were ready for the march. Their outfit was simple. A bow and quiver of arrows, tomahawk, scalping-knife, pipe and tobacco, with pouch of parched corn provided, and they were ready for a month's campaign. They make themselves hideous with black and red paint, they sing the farewell song to their women and children, and they are gone.

Round the Bay of Fundy, where the foam-crested tide was rushing, across the rivers St. John and St. Croix, for weeks they thread the pathless wilderness towards the southwest. They

---

* They were sometimes called the Abnaki Indians of the east.

place no watch at night. They pray to their fetiches and, like the panther, lie down feeling secure. Arrived in the land of the Penobscots, for days together they hide in deep ravines and among the spruces of the mountains. When the moon is sleeping in the western waves, when the first blush of morning tinges the eastern sky, when sleep is soundest and sweetest, they rush upon the Penobscot villages. Like the tornado they sweep them away. The warriors of the Bashaba are slain. The Tarentine brave twists the scalp lock in his left hand, places his foot on the neck, cuts a circular gash around the head with the scalping knife, gives an accompanying dexterous jerk, and the scalp is his. Even the Bashaba himself, fighting bravely, finds a death-couch upon the bodies of half-a-dozen Tarentines. The score of war parties have a hundred scalps. The richest wampum, the choicest skins, strong bows, ornamented quivers full of arrows tipped with rose quartz, spears and nets, are among the spoils. Yet they return home with few captives.

As they approached their own villages they announced their return in triumph with loud yells of exultation. To celebrate their victory they renew the feast and dance the scalp dance. The latter was a unique performance. The scalps taken in former battles are attached to their girdles. With heads bent forward they hold by the hair the fresh scalps in their teeth. Then they howl and stamp around the fire in the centre of their cluster of wigwams, cutting all the uncouth antics imaginable, performing gyrations innumerable, and screaming and yelling in their intense jollification, "as though," in the language of a pious writer, " bedlam had broken loose and all hell was in an uproar."

But this very interesting ceremony was only a gentle prelude to the good time that followed. Let no one be shocked at the recital. Men are the creatures of education. The effeminate and refined queen of Spain enjoys a bull-baiting on the Sabbath as much as northern Christians enjoy psalm singing and hosannas. Some of our near neighbors take a peculiar delight in cock-fighting, and the Roman matrons of old reached the acme of their bliss when they saw fierce gladiators butchering each other or contending with ferocious wild beasts. After the scalp dance had ceased the few Penobscot captives were brought forward. The young Micmacs were enjoined by the old men to do well. A young brave from the west was to undergo the ordeal. With scornful eye and air of defiance he presents his hands to be crushed between the rough stones. His fingers are torn off one by one, yet not a cry escapes him. His nose is cut off—his tongue torn out—and still he does not flinch. His joints are separated; he is flayed like a deer—and then the cold shivering spirits are driven away by pushing him up to the fire that he may enjoy the hot ones. Yet he survives this exquisite torture; and pitch faggots are thrust into his involuntary, quivering flesh, and lighted—at which all the assembled braves, the tawny squaws, and their sunburnt daughters laugh and shout, in fiendish glee at the sickening misery. At dawn, if still alive, he is dragged beyond the wigwams and there hacked in pieces. Such was the practice, not only of the Tarentines, but of all gentle Indians.*

Some cunning writers, to show off the fine points of their heroes, draw a parallel between them and other notable characters. One might be set forth in this manner: Did the most Holy Pope of the Christian Catholic Church apply thumbscrews in the Inquisition—the Micmacs had as pleasing a torture in putting hands between the mashing rocks. Did his holiness unjoint limbs on the rack—the more primitive savage could unjoint them as well with his hands. Did God's vicegerent break limbs—Indians could do the same with a stone beetle. Did the good John Calvin burn Michael Servetus at the stake—Micmacs could roast the flayed victim and laugh at the sound of the quivering flesh cooked by the faggots. Did the Puritans scourge the backs, crop the ears, cut out the tongues of unoffending Quakers, and hang witches—the "brave" with as keen an avidity could cut off the nose, tear out the tongue, and hack in pieces.

But we will not carry this refined comparison further. There is a dark side to everything. If we looked only to the failings of men we might run mad with melancholy. The Indians have been strangely venerated. We are sometimes disposed to admire them.

---

*For an account of their method of torturing see V. Bancroft, Chap. 28.

One William Moody unhappily resigned himself into the hands of some French Mohawks, who most inhumanly tortured him by fastening him unto a stake and roasting him alive, whose flesh they afterwards devoured.—Penhallow's Indian Wars, N. H. Hist. Soc. Col. 61.

There is a disposition from some cause to hide their faults, but, for the sake of truth, their character should be correctly presented. Yet after all we do not see as they are much worse than many others who have pretended to vastly better things.

For a long time the Penobscot tribe was ruined. The Bashaba dead — all the New England Indians, including our Pemigewassetts, who were no doubt exceedingly interested in passing events, were at sea without compass or rudder. The bond of union was broken. Each tribe now struggled for the supremacy. Like the earlier times, when Milton's Satan and his good angels showed a belligerent spirit in Paradise, primeval war raged.* It extended from the Hudson river to the St. John. How this very amiable contest, in which our proud Pemigewassetts engaged with delight, was conducted and ended, we shall endeavor most faithfully to narrate.

---

*After the death of the Bashaba the public business running to confusion for want of a head, the rest of his great sagamores fell at variance amongst themselves, spoiled and destroyed each other's people and provision, and famine took hold of many; which was seconded by a great and general plague, which so violently reigned for three years together that in a manner a greater part of the land was left desert, without any to disturb or oppose a free and peaceable possession thereof.— Sir Ferdinando Gorges' Des. of N. E., vii. Ms. Hist. Soc. Col. 3 Ser. vol. vi. 90.

CHAPTER V.

OF A TERRIBLE WAR, PESTILENCE, AND FAMINE, THE HEROES OF WHICH ARE ALL DEAD AND THEIR NAMES FORGOTTEN.

IT is much to be lamented that there were no historians among the Indians to record the names of their heroes and their victories. But the wild hordes of Asia, the highly enlightened darkies of Africa, who have had their *bright* civilization crushed out by powerful European armies, which so frequently have ravished their beautiful lands at the sources of the Nile, have no place in history and never had. The Indians may thank their lucky stars that their European exterminators have taken so much pains to preserve the remembrance of the benevolent acts that thrust them out of existence and on to the page of history, where they still live. In this they have the advantage of the Esquimaux, the Negroes, some of the Asiatics, and their numerous cousins in the Pacific isles. The author of this excellent history has had occasion to be thankful to the renowned and the redoubtable Capt. John Smith for his notes on the Indians, and he here renews his thanks.

To take up the thread of this to us very interesting subject, we would say we are sure there was a most fierce fight among the Indians on the death of the Bashaba. Capt. Smith says so. In what tribe it commenced we never could learn, but when begun it proved universal. The strong fought for supremacy, the weak for existence. There was no necessity for the war-song or the war-dance. Every brave was compelled to enlist whether he would or not. The signal fire gleamed on the hill-top. The war-whoop was heard in the valley. New England, before nor since, never saw such carnage within her borders. The French war and the

Revolution were nothing compared to it. The battles of the Scottish clans, or those of the old Norsemen, might have been somewhat similar, yet there were many points of difference. In fact, the red Indians had decidedly a style of their own—original, and one that could not well be imitated. The children of the forest were early to bed and early to rise, and they generally fought in the morning. The shrill war-whoop, the whistling arrow, the whirr of the tomahawk, the yells in the savage onslaught, or of the wounded who refused to groan though hurt to death, were a wild matin hymn to their fierce war-god, who smiled upon them in the blood-red streaks of dawn. All the tribes on the seacoast with euphonious names fought with wild frenzy. Numerous were the warriors slain, the captives taken, the scalp locks hanging on the poles of the wigwam.*

But the fiercest fighters of all were the mountaineers of New Hampshire. From their secret lurking places in the dark ravines they would steal out and drop silent and still as the falling dew into the pleasant villages of the coast. Then leaping up fiery and fierce, and shouting and yelling like fiends incarnate, they would massacre every inhabitant. They would traverse the passes of the mountains, and flying down swift as the scudding mist, in a few hours they would secure scalps enough to astonish their village. Then retreating up the beds of the torrents they would elude all pursuit. Invincible as their own mountains, and secret as the panther that crouched in the pathless forest gloom, their enemies fell beneath their blows like frost work under the morning sun.

Thus the war went on, and every tribe seemed about to be exterminated, when a foe more terrible than the mountain Indian entered the villages, and cut down alike men, women, and children.

The plague † first appeared on the coast. But it soon journeyed inland and preyed on every tribe. Its ravages were terrible. One individual of a village smitten down, and despair seated

---

*Divisions arose as to the succession to the Bashaba, of which the Tarentines taking the advantage soon overpowered the other tribes of Maine, and extended a war of extermination along the coast of Massachusetts.— Potter's Hist. of Manchester, 23.
Drake's Indian Biography, 81.
† Drake's Indian Biography, 3.
Not long before the English came into the country, happened a great mortality amongst them, especially where the English afterwards planted. The east and

itself on the countenances of all. Flight was hopeless. One by one they would lie down and die. The dead were unburied. A terrible stench tainted the air. Strong warriors, who had coped with death in a thousand forms, lay rotting in the wigwams. Infants lay on the breasts of their dead mothers, striving in vain to draw life from the bosoms that would never throb again. The strong and vigorous youth, the beautiful maiden, were alike a prey to it. In a few weeks whole villages were depopulated, and whole tribes ceased to exist.

Inland the crops were neglected, and when winter came the famine was as terrible as the plague. As the snow grew deeper, and the cold more intense, and the wind howled back the shrieks of the spectre famine, attenuated forms with haggard faces and sunken eyes and cheeks would sit for days in the smoke of their wigwam fires. Then with tottering steps they would reel into the woods for food, and there, chilled, would lie down and die.

Three summers the plague came, until on the seacoast not an Indian village remained; and for many leagues along the shore not five Indians in a hundred were alive. When the Pilgrim bark anchored in Plymouth Bay, " the hardy few found the country a solitude."

One thing has troubled exceedingly in writing the above very minute and accurate account of this war, pestilence, and famine. A particular description cannot be given. The names of the warriors who fell, the men, women, and children who sickened

---

northern parts were sore smitten with the contagion, first by the plague, afterward when the English came by the small pox.—John Josselyn, Gent., 2 Voyages to N. E. 123.

For that war had commenced, the Bashaba and most of the great sagamores, with such men of action as followed them, were killed, and those that remained were sore afflicted by the plague. [1616–1617.] So that the country in a manner was left void of inhabitants. Notwithstanding Vines and the rest with him that lay in the cabins with those people that died, some more some less nightly, (blessed be God for it!) not one of them ever felt their heads to ache while they staid there.— Sir F. Gorges' Description of New England, Chap. 10 Ms. H. C. 3 s. v. 6, 57.

"It seems God has provided this country for our nation, destroying them by the plague, it not touching our Englishmen, though many traded and conversant amongst them, for they had three plagues in three years successively, neare two hundred miles along the sea-coast, that in some places there scarce remained five in a hundred. * * * * But most certain there was an exceedingly great plague amongst them; for where I had seen two or three hundred, within three years after there remained scarcely thirty.— Ms. H. C. vol. iii. 3 s. 40.

Thomas Morton, in his "New England Canaan," p. 23, says: "But contrarywise [the Indians having said they were so many that God could not kill them, when one of the Frenchmen rebuked them for their wickedness, telling them God would destroy them] in a short time after the hand of God fell heavily upon them with such a mortal stroke that they died in heaps as they lay in their houses, and

and died, or of those who starved, cannot be told. Thucydides narrates how in the plague of Athens, during the Thirty Years War, such and such a distinguished man was stricken down. Our sympathies are particularly excited at the death of the noble and renowned Pericles and his doubtful wife, Aspasia, with their sweet children. Hume, in his narrative of the great plague in London, makes his history decidedly entertaining in giving the minute particulars, and Moses of old, likewise, in telling of the plagues of Egypt. These great historians have all the advantage there, and one can but mourn that time has buried the names of all the old Indian heroes in oblivion.

---

the living that were able to shift for themselves would run away and let them dy, and let their karkases ly above ground without buriall. For in a place where many inhabited there hath been but one left alive to tell what became of the rest. The living being (as it seems) not able to bury the dead. They were left for crows, kites, and vermin to prey upon. And the bones and skulls upon the several places of their habitations made such a spectacle, after my coming into these parts, that as I travelled in that forest nere Mass. it seemed to me a new-found Golgotha."

CHAPTER VI.

HOW THE PEMIGEWASSETTS AND THE REST OF THE NIPMUCKS WERE COMPELLED TO ENTER A NEW LEAGUE TO PROTECT THEMSELVES FROM THE MOHOGS, MARQUAS, OR MOHAWKS, WITH A SLIGHT SKETCH OF ANOTHER GREAT MAN WHO CAME TO BE BASHABA.

THE war is over. The famine and the pestilence, mighty woes in the land of the Nipmucks, have passed. Peace comes again—and once more there is plenty in the wigwams.

But the terrible Mohawks still dwell in the west and the bloody Tarentine war-whoop still resounds from beyond the hunting grounds of the Sokokis and the Penobscots.

There is no safety but in union; and our Nipmucks, whom we are pleased to style Pemigewassetts, are compelled to enter into another mighty league, which is formed among all the Nipmuck tribes, with a new Bashaba* at its head.

This great ruler, the second Bashaba, standing as he does on the confines of civilization, with the mellow twilight of history casting a halo of romance about him, seems to us one of the most prominent characters in our annals. He makes his first appearance in 1623. Acteon well remembered him, and as he was much beloved by our Pemigewassetts and all the rest of the Nipmucks, and was their great protector, we cannot pass him by without a brief notice.

Born, as tradition has it, about 1540, by his bravery and genius he won at length his proud position. Indian legends tell of his great prowess, and of his sanguinary battles fought and

---

* Potter's History of Manchester, 54.
Mass. Hist. Col. 3 series, vol. viii. 173.

won in the deep forests on the streams and mountains. These Indian tales, collated and adorned, might prove to Indian lovers as interesting as the account of the twelve labors of Hercules, or the voyage of the Argonautic Jason. But we cannot loiter in these pleasant fields. The demands of our most important history of a most important tribe compel us to hurry rapidly through these interesting chapters.

When the little province of Mariana, alias Laconia, otherwise New Hampshire, was first settled he was about eighty years old, and at this early period of life, having been schooled in all the cunning wiles of the forest, had won for himself the title of PASSACONAWAY*—"The Child of the Bear."

Of powerful frame, he was more than six feet tall. He could leap like a catamount across the streams, and bound like a wild deer through the pathless woods. No warrior could bend his bow, and his feathered arrows were lost in the deep blue of the sky. A cap of red plumes on his head, his quiver at his back, his bow in his hand, clothed only in a robe of the richest furs, shod with moccasins of the toughest moose hide, with flashing eye and haughty mien, the Nipmuck Bashaba was the most noble Indian that ever trod the Granite hills.†

But we must assure our readers that we draw the above picture by reasoning *a posteriori*. He was Bashaba—only such an Indian could be a Bashaba—therefore such was Passaconaway.

Yet his appearance is much changed from this when he makes his first mythical bow in 1623. Modern painters (who have seen him) put a royal crown on his head in the shape of a dowdy skull

---

*His name is indicative of his warlike character: Papisseconewa, as written by himself, meaning the child of the bear. Being derived from *papoeis*, a child, and *Kunnaway*, a bear.—Potter's Hist of Man. 48, 54.

† Laws made by the Apostle Elliot for Passaconaway and his people:
  1st. That if any man be idle a week, at most a fortnight, hee shall pay five shillings.
  2d. If any unmarried man shall lie with a young woman unmarried hee shall pay twenty shillings.
  3d. If any man shall beat his wife his hands shall be tied behind him and he be carried to the place of justice to be severely punished.
  4th. Every young man, if not another's servant, and if unmarried, he shall be compelled to set up a wigwam and plant for himself, and not live shifting up and down to other wigwams.
  5th. If any woman shall not have her hair tied up, but hang loose or be cut as men's hair, she shall pay five shillings.
  6th. If any woman goe with naked breasts she shall pay two shillings sixpence.
  7th. All those men that weare long locks shall pay five shillings.
  8th. If any shall kill their lice between their teeth they shall pay five shillings.
—Mass. H. C. vol. iv. series 3.

cap, with a crooked horn about four inches in length rising from its apex. Sashes of furs are worn on his shoulders, a pipe, a pouch, a bear's face — the Nipmuck totem — are attached to his girdle; his teeth are gone, his face is shrunk up, and his sunken eyes, shaded by the high cheek bones and the massive forehead, only gleam with their wonted fire when fierce excitement fills his breast.

His disposition is also changed. From what the English saw of him we should say that he had more the spirit of John Howard the philanthropist, coupled with that of old Potter the juggler, than of Julius Cæsar or Napoleon Bonaparte. He had lost the war spirit of former years, and loved the retirement of his wigwams. About them he assembled his council and his statesmen. To them the children of the forest brought his tribute. This did not always consist of soft furs, shad or salmon, venison or bear steaks, maize, squashes, or pumpkins, stone axes, arrow-heads, or gouges, canoes, paddles, spears or fish-nets — none of these. But when they saw the water in the freestone bowl burning with a blue flame; when they saw him sailing on a cake of ice over the shining lake on the hottest summer day, or at night changed into a will-o'-wisp and dancing a wild cotillon with the mighty forest trees; or weaving for himself garlands from snow-born flowers, and wreaths of honor from oak leaves growing on fields of glaring ice, and holding in his hand a writhing snake, sprung to life from the dead skin, the badge of honor on his left arm — they paid him a mighty tribute and great honor by opening their mouths in right good earnest to the fullest extent, while their eyes involuntarily started from their sockets. By such astounding juggling feats Passaconaway in his old age extorted his tribute and retained his mighty power.

Another gift also aided Passaconaway to maintain his influence. He was a great medicine man. He could beat all the renowned homeopaths, clairvoyants, and healing mediums of to-day clear out of sight. If one of his subjects was sick, he placed him in a tight wigwam or lodge. Vessels of water were set by his side, and in them were put fiery hot stones. A warm steam naturally arose like a great cloud and filled the lodge. Passaconaway then dressed in the most agreeable manner possible, painting himself all over like a striped pig. With his head covered with a porcupine skin, a drum in his hands, and tinkling bells attached to his legs, he went howling and stamping round and round the lodge full a hundred times, all the while keeping step to the soul-stirring peals of his drum and the soft voluptuous notes of his tinklers. This was done to drive away the evil spirits. Then he oped his mouth and set his teeth firmly together; then gentle twitches spasmodically jerked all the muscles of his fair countenance; then he rolled up the whites of his eyes, and then slowly rolled them down, where they remained set like those of a dying calf; then his jaws relaxed, his tongue began to wag, and he pronounced incantations thirty-one, all different, to invoke the healing spirits. For a full hour and a half he thus performed, like a medium, the steaming and sweating being only a preliminary of little use, while the aforesaid howls, music, and incantations effected the cure, pretty much in the same manner as the homeopaths' very little doses from the smallest possible bottles, with just nothing at all in them, effect extraordinary cures at the present day.*

Passaconaway was an orator.† His eloquence was great, and with it he could mould the council at his will. Several splendid speeches which it is said he made are still extant. These have been handed down to us by the politeness of the historians. The first, as given by Hubbard, is said to have been delivered at a great public fish-feast, when all the Indians were assembled at Pawtucket falls, and is as follows:

"I am now ready to die," said Passaconaway, "and not likely to see you ever meet together any more. I will now leave this word of counsel with you, that you may take heed how you quarrel with the English; for though you may do them much mischief, yet assuredly you will all be destroyed and rooted off the earth if you do; for I was as much an enemy to the English on their first coming into these parts as any one whatsoever; and I did try all ways and means possible to have destroyed them, at least to have prevented their sitting down here; but I could in no way effect

---

*Force's Historical Tracts, vol. ii. New England Canaan, 25, 26. John Josselyn, Gent., 2 Voyages to New England, 131.
†Drake's Indian Biography, 277. Hubbard, Indian Wars. 67, 68.

it. [Meaning by his incantations and sorceries.] Therefore I advise you never to contend with the English nor make war with them."

Dr. Bouton, a celebrated modern historian, gives the following much prettier version, as he had probably a reporter on the spot: "Hearken to the last words of your dying father. I shall meet you no more. The white men are the sons of the morning, and the sun shines bright above them. In vain I opposed their coming; vain were my arts to destroy them; never make war with them; sure as you light the fires, the breath of heaven will turn the flames to consume you. Listen to my advice. It is the last I shall ever give you. Remember it and live!"*

Now there is much beauty in all this, as well as in many other speeches that have been attributed to him, and what is better a great probability that the old chief delivered the speech quoted. Hubbard says it was done at Pawtucket in 1660, and was his dying speech to his tribe. Bouton in his book says the speech he gives is the identical one delivered by Passaconaway in 1660, and we may well believe it, for he affirms that it was delivered at the same place, to the same audience, and at the same time as Hubbard's. We come to the probably correct conclusion that Passaconaway said something very pretty and exceedingly eloquent sometime.†

When he had seen the snows of a hundred winters or so pass away he concluded, like many another sinner, to join the church. To the apostle Elliot, who had left friends, home, and happy coun-

---

*Bouton's History of Concord, N. H., 30.

†Barstow gives the following: "Hearken," said Passaconaway, "to the last words of your father and friend. The white men are the sons of the morning. The Great Spirit is their father. His sun shines bright about them. Never make war with them. Sure as you light the fires the breath of heaven will turn the flames upon you and destroy you. Listen to my advice. It is the last I shall be allowed to give you. Remember it and live!"— Hist. of N. H., 68.

Hon. Chandler E. Potter gives this fanciful version: "Hearken to the words of your father. I am an old oak that has withstood the storms of more than an hundred winters. Leaves and branches have been stripped from me by the winds and frosts; my eyes are dim — my limbs totter — I must soon fall. But when young and sturdy — when my bow no young man of the Pennacooks could bend — when my arrows would pierce a deer at a hundred yards, and I could bury my hatchet in a sapling to the eye, — no wigwam had so many furs, no pole so many scalp-locks as Passaconaway's. Then I was delighted in war. The whoop of the Pennacook was heard on the Mohawk, and no voice so loud as Passaconaway's. The scalps upon the pole of my wigwam told the story of Mohawk suffering.

"The English came. They seized our lands. *I sat me down at Pennacook.* They followed upon my footsteps. I made war upon them, but they fought with fire and thunder; my young men were swept down before me when no one was

try to cross the ocean on an errand of mercy, is due his conversion. He left off juggling and became a very good man. He was benevolent, peaceful, and forgiving. We think it fortunate for the very kind-hearted and well-disposed colonists who came to Massachusetts and New Hampshire that, like Massasoit, he was not fightingly disposed. It is a notorious fact that the English trespassed on his hunting-grounds and stole his lands.* Yet he never stole anything from them. They killed his warriors—yet he never killed a white man, woman, or child. They captured and imprisoned his sons† and daughters—yet he never led a captive into the wilderness. Once the proudest and most noble Bashaba of New England, he passed his extreme old age poor, forsaken, and robbed of all that was dear to him, by those to whom he had been a firm friend for nearly half a century.

Passaconaway had six children—four sons and two daughters whom we read of—and perhaps he had more. The exceedingly pretty names of the boy pappooses were as follows: Nanamocomuck, who first was sachem or sagamore of the Wachusetts in Massachusetts, and secondly with his whole tribe was changed into the great Amariscoggin nation, of which he continued chief; Wonalancet, a peaceable man, who trod in the footsteps of his father; Unanunquosset, of whom we know but little, and Nonatomenut. We are much grieved that the name of the eldest daughter has not come down to us. It only transpires that she was the squaw-queen of the royal Nobhow. The youngest was

---

near them. I tried sorcery against them, but they still increased and prevailed over me and mine, and I gave place and retired to my beautiful island of Naticook. I can make the dry leaf turn green and live again; I can take the rattlesnake in my palm as a worm without harm. I, who have had communion with the Great Spirit—dreaming and awake—I am powerless before the pale faces.

"The oak will soon break before the whirlwind—it shivers and shakes even now. Soon its trunk will be prostrate, the ant and the worm will sport upon it. Then think, my children, of what I say. I commune with the Great Spirit. He whispers me now: 'Tell your people, peace! Peace is the only hope of your race. I have given fire and thunder to the pale faces for weapons. I have made them plentier than the leaves of the forest, and still shall they increase. These meadows shall they turn with the plow—these forests shall fall by their axe; the pale faces shall live upon your hunting grounds, and make their villages upon your fishing places.' The Great Spirit says this, and it must be so. We are few and powerless before them. We must bend before the storm. The wind blows hard. The old oak trembles! The branches are gone. Its sap is frozen. It bends! It falls! Peace, peace with the white man, is the command of the Great Spirit, and the wish—the last wish—of Passaconaway.—Hist. of Manchester, 60.

IV. Mass. H. C. series 3, 82.
* Potter's Hist. of Manchester, 61.
† When the gov't of Ms. sent forty men to arrest Passaconaway they did not succeed, but captured his sonne Wonalancet.—Winthrop's Journal.
  Drake's Indian Biog. 279.

INDIAN ROMANCE.

Wetamoo, the beautiful squaw of Monatawampatee, the haughty sagamore of Saugus. From the poet Whittier we learn that the marriage of this beautiful Indian girl was celebrated in great state, and that the bride was escorted to her lord's wigwam or palace by a noble train of warriors; that homesick the Saugus chief returned her to visit Passaconaway with like pomp, and that in due time he demanded her back with the same formality. But old Passaconaway had got sick of this foolery and vain show, and would not take the trouble to restore her. Whereupon, the poem states, she left her father's wigwam at Pennacook—by the way, Passaconaway never had a wigwam there—to sail down the Merrimack home, but unfortunately perished on the foaming falls of Amoskeag; a very poetical idea, but an exceedingly improbable tale. Wetamoo was known as a grass widow for many years.*

We give this somewhat extended account of Passaconaway, for his life illustrates some of the finest traits of Indian character. As Bashaba he was obeyed by all the Indians of New Hampshire, and by many other of the New England tribes. He died about 1663. In the deep wood, at a place now unknown, the noblest of the Nipmuck Indians, their last and greatest Bashaba, was laid to rest in the burial place of his ancestors.

*Morton's New England Canaan.

CHAPTER VII.

IN WHICH IS SET FORTH THE MANNER THE PEMIGEWASSETTS SOMETIMES ENJOYED THEMSELVES WHILE THE NEW BASHABA LIVED, AND THEN OF A SLIGHT WAR THAT AROSE, WHICH WAS EXCEEDINGLY ENTERTAINING TO THEM, TOGETHER WITH ITS PIOUS CLOSE AT QUOCHECO.

THE Pemigewassetts, a tribe of the great Nipmuck nation, belonging to the widely extended Algonquin race, were at peace with the English for fifty years after the first settlements were made at Dover Neck and Strawberry Bank. The same is true as far as the thirteen other great tribes of New Hampshire were concerned. But with the Marquas or Mohawks — sometimes called Mohogs — their relations were not always the most friendly. How many fierce battles, cunning ambuscades, or gray-of-the-morning surprises our Pemigewassetts encountered or inflicted upon them, cannot now be told. We lament this ignorance, but there is no remedy, for their birch-bark histories, if they ever had any, are all burnt up; their story-telling legend-men are all dead, while the just and worthy English settlers had such a holy horror and pious hatred of red-skins that they would have disdained to record their great wars, even if they had known anything about them. In fact, the reasons why the learned historians of those days say so little and frequently nothing about our beloved Pemigewassetts are just these: First, because they lived far in the interior, and did not travel down to the coast very often to report themselves, and when they did they had somehow changed into some other great tribe, being known as the Amoskeags, Nashuas, or Winnecowetts, just as it happened, the name depending upon the place of their temporary sojourn and changing with their removal. Secondly, the English scarcely ever visited them; for it must be remembered that ten other great tribes of New Hampshire always intervened. Thirdly, the Puritans believed the Indians to be the children of the devil, and their Quaker-loving, witch-hanging religion forbade them to associate with such low offspring; and fourthly, being religiously inclined to blot out the devil and his works, they would take especial pains to destroy rather than preserve the history of our happy Pemigewassetts. Still we know enough of that history to be assured that in battle they did sometimes distinguish and immortalize themselves among all good fighting Indians.

Old Acteon used to tell how often a large number of brave war-parties, each consisting of three or more fierce, glory-seeking soldiers, all painted and plumed, went majestically forth to fight the Mohawks. They have danced the war-dance, taken leave of the women and children, and having gathered around their chosen chief, depart from the shadows of Moosilauke and the Haystacks. The Indian story-teller of two hundred years ago, listening, might have heard them singing as they crossed the long river of pines — the Connecticut —

> "The eagles scream on high,
> They whet their forked beaks;
> Raise, raise the battle-cry,
> 'Tis fame our leader seeks."

Or he might have heard the whistling of their arrows, the whirr of their tomahawks, and their savage shouts in the valleys of the Hudson and Mohawk rivers, or in the dark glens of the Green mountains. We can well believe that such brave mountaineers were often victorious, and returned triumphant with rich trophies of dangling scalps. But as all great military commanders know that the fortunes of battle are fickle, it is nothing more than fair to presume that the war chief sometimes came back with a huge flea in his ear, more scalps having been left among the festive Mohawk fighters than he would well care to acknowledge.

Thus the Pemigewassetts found the wildest kind of enjoyment, and we suppose pretty much all the rest of the New England Indians lived in the same way, even to the time of the death of the great Bashaba, Passaconaway.

But in 1675 a great war with the English arose, in which many of the Nipmucks engaged, and which was exceedingly interesting to the Pemigewassetts who lived among our hills.

Philip of Mount Hope, sachem of the Wampanoags, known in Indian tongue as the renowned Pometacom, waged the first war with the peaceable Puritans. The English had arrested and executed his warriors without his consent. He himself with his child they had captured and sold into slavery. The chieftain was stung to the quick; madness seized upon him; hatred tormented him, and soon his heart burned for revenge. Besides, the encroachments of his white-faced enemy were driving him from his hunting-grounds. War was inaugurated. What Alexander or Hannibal was to the ancients, or Bonaparte to the last generation, was Philip to the Indians. The bravest in the fight, the most skilled in diplomacy, and eloquent above all others in the council, the great sachem enlisted nearly every New England tribe in his cause.

Wonalancet, in part successor to Passaconaway, true to the teachings of his father and the apostle Elliot, refused to join him. This Nipmuck sachem could not break his faith pledged to the English, neither could he be a traitor to his own race and fight against Philip. Beset on one hand to fight for the English, on the other Philip endeavored to gain him as an ally; refusing to join the first he was suspected of treachery, and holding himself aloof from the second, he was hated by all the hostile Indians.

There was no safety for him at home on the beautiful island of Wickasauke, where he had long resided, and he fled to the land of the Pennacooks. And here let us notice a very novel idea, once before slightly alluded to. Wonalancet, by almost every writer on the subject, has been styled the sachem of the Pennacooks. Yet all his life, up to the period referred to, he had lived amongst the Pawtucket Indians, and we have no record of his ever residing in the Pennacook country until he was compelled to seek refuge in it at this time. Yet he only copies the historical style of his father, Passaconaway, who, likewise called the Pennacook sachem, never lived in that country at all.

The withdrawal of Wonalancet with his few followers alarmed the courageous colonists very much. Runners were sent "to

Natacooke, Penagooge, *or other people of those northern Indians*," inviting Wonalancet or any other of the principal men to return. But Wonalancet did not choose to accept the polite invitation, which was very much in the form of a peremptory summons, and Captain Mosely, the noted Indian fighter, was sent to disperse the Indian enemy "at Penagooge said to be gathered there for the purpose of mischief." But the valiant captain could not find him, and he had to content himself with burning wigwams, and destroying dried fish which had been cured for winter use.

Wonalancet was off to the fastnesses of the mountains, "where," as Major Gookin says, "*was a place of good hunting for moose, deer, bear, aud other such wild beasts.*"

Late in the autumn all the Wamesits, alias the Wauchusetts, alias the Pawtuckets, joined him. They had been basely treated, had been driven from their homes, and only found Wonalancet in his safe hiding-place after much toil, privation, and suffering. Numphow, their sagamore, Mystic George, a teacher, "besides divers other men, women, and children perished by the way." An old legend, told first perhaps by Acteon, then repeated by our grandfathers, seated at evening around their great cabin fireplaces, says that the above-mentioned two lie buried on the banks of the Asquamchumauke.

Many other Indians joined Wonalancet in his retreat. Among them was * Monocco, or one-eyed John, and † Shoshamin, or Sagamore Sam, a valiant chief who had fought under Philip. Some of these refugees even went to the head-waters of the Connecticut, and during the long and cold winter suffered severely.

Philip's war closed in the summer of 1676. Wonalancet with his people then returned to the south part of the State. On the sixth of July he with several others made a treaty with the Eng-

---

* Monocco, so called by his countrymen, but by the English, One-eyed-John, was termed by an early writer a notable fellow. When Philip's war began he lived near Lancaster, Mass. He had frequently served in the wars against the Mohawks. With 600 Indians he burned Lancaster and carried all the inhabitants into captivity. He afterwards burned Groton, and boasted much what he was going to do. He was one of those who were captured at Cocheco, was taken to Boston, marched through the streets with a halter about his neck, "and hanged at the town's end, Sept. 26, 1676."— Drake's Ind. Biog. 267.

Niles' History of the Indian and French Wars, Ms. H. C. 3d series, vol. vi. 202.

† Shoshamin, alias Uskatugun, and called by the English, Sagamore Sam. He was a high-minded, "magnanimous sachem." At the burning of Lancaster he took an active part. He was hanged with Monocco.—Drake's Indian Biog. 268.

lish. By it they agreed to live in peace; that they would deliver up, for a reward, all hostile Indians who should come among them, or give notice where they were; and that the English on their part should attend to their own business, and if they meddled with the Indians or their estates the offenders should be tried by English laws—and these by the way generally found the whites innocent as turtle doves. It was signed on the one part by Mr. Richard Waldron, to be mentioned hereafter, Nic. Shapleigh, and Thos. Daniel; on the other by Wonalancet, Squando,* Doney,† Serogumba,‡ and others.

This same Richard Waldron, or the "Major," as he was commonly termed, had been engaged in the above-board business of persuading Indians to desert Philip. Three hundred of these, together with Wonalancet and a hundred handsome Nipmucks, came to Quocheco on the first of September, at the invitation of "the good Major." A few days later Captains Syell and Hathorn, brave trooping men, with their companies also arrived in town. They were marching to the eastern country. Their orders were to seize all Indians, and they wanted to fall upon Major Waldron's four hundred guests at once. But he dissented. He was afraid both friends and foes would be killed. By his advice a little friendly strategy was put in practice. A grand sham-fight was arranged. The English were on one side—the Indians on the other. The latter were furnished with a piece of cannon, on wheels, loaded by English gunners. As the unsuspecting Indians manned the drag-ropes, the gun by the merest accident ranging along their lines, strange to say it went off, no one knew how — perhaps by spontaneous combustion—and several were killed. The rest, including wounded, were taken prisoners. A hundred

---

* Squando was also a sagamore of Saco or Sokokis. He was one of the chief beginners and chief actors in the war, 1675-8. He was roused to a hatred of the English by the rude and indiscreet act of some English seamen, who either for mischief overset a canoe in which was Squando's wife and child, or to see if young Indians could swim naturally, like animals of the brute creation, as some had reported. [John Josselyn, Gent., said they could swim like dogs.] The child went to the bottom, but was saved from drowning by the mother's diving down and bringing it up. Yet within a while after the said child died. The whites did not believe the death of the child was owing to the immersion; still, we must allow, the Indians knew as well as they. He was engaged in several battles, one of which was the attack upon Saco in 1675. He was a brave Indian.—Drake's Ind. Biog. 286.

† Doney was a Saco sachem. He signed an Indian treaty in 1698. He once had a captive by the name of *Thomas Baker*. What Doney's fate was is uncertain.—Drake's Ind. Biog. 308.

‡ Serogumba was a sagamore.

or so of them were hanged. Two hundred were sold into slavery, while the hundred up-country Indians, including some of our Pemigewassetts, were dismissed to their homes. Thither they went, exceedingly well-pleased with their kind treatment, and firmly convinced that their pale-faced entertainers were the most honest, reliable, and pious set of cut-throats with whom they ever had the happiness to become acquainted.

CHAPTER VIII.

HOW ACCORDING TO TRADITION THE PEMIGEWASSETTS WERE PRESENT AT A GREAT COURT AT QUOCHECO, WHERE THE LAWS WERE VERY LEGALLY EXECUTED AND JUSTICE DONE — ACCORDING TO THE IDEAS OF CERTAIN EXASPERATED RED MEN.

THE valiant deeds of Major Waldron and the brave captains at Quocheco were well remembered by the northern Indians, among whom were numbered the Pemigewassetts. They believed that the pious Quocheco settlers and their allies had committed a great sin. After thinking the subject over for ten years or more, and after having had their thoughts quickened from time to time by the Indian slaves, many of whom had returned, they came to the solemn conclusion that it was their duty to take the law into their own hands and see it properly executed. Accordingly they planned an expedition to teach Major Waldron and his friends a lesson, if nothing more.

The leader was Kancamagus; and as he often sat down in the Pemigewassett country, being a Pemigewassett chief when there, we must give him a passing notice. He was "grant-son" of Passaconaway. For many years he was chief of the Amariscoggins, sometimes of the Pequawkees, and finally a Pennacook sachem. At one time he was the firm ally of the renowned Worombo,* and with him maintained a strong fort far in the wilderness, on the

---

* Worombo was a sachem of the Amariscoggins. He had a fort on the river bank. It was captured by Col. Church in 1690, Sept. 14. Two of Worombo's children were taken prisoners and carried to Plymouth. Seven days after, Kancamagus and Worombo fell upon Church by surprise at Casco, Maine, killed seven of his men and wounded twenty-four more, two of whom died. The Indians were beaten off only after a long and desperate fight. He was a brave Indian. What became of him is uncertain.

banks of the Androscoggin. He was a brave and politic chief, and had a little of the forgiving spirit of his grandfather Passaconaway and uncle Wonalancet, but his mercy did not endure forever. In person he was tall and well-proportioned; he possessed great strength, was fleet of foot, and had an eye like an eagle.

When the gentle sachem Wonalancet fled away as he did to the land of the Arosagunticooks, otherwise known as the St. Francis Indians, with a portion of his tribe, Kancamagus took up his residence in the fertile meadows of the Pennacooks. Cranfield* the English governor at the time, did not like the idea of his residing in the hunting grounds of his ancestors, and being a scrupulous man he went to New York and entered into an engagement with the gentle fighting Mohawks † to come and drive him and his people away. Kancamagus heard of the design, and addressed several letters to the "Honur Governor my friend," and sent him presents of beaver-skins, but without much effect. In fact, the governor was firm in his purpose; the Mohawks sent word that they were coming, and Kancamagus and his braves, giving up the idea of taking their revenge just then, fled far into the northern wilderness.

But he did not remain long away. When King William's war broke out he was back again upon the banks of the Merrimack. Around the council fire they recounted the treachery at Quocheco; how their brothers had some been butchered, others sold into slavery; some hung upon trees in Boston or shot down in the streets at noon-day; and how they had been burnt in the wigwams by the dozen in time of peace; and now, as the wartimes offered an excellent opportunity, the old plans for revenge were fully determined upon. Under the trees on the banks of the river they danced the war-dance—the war-paint was prepared —and Amariscoggins, Coosucks, Pequawkees, Winnepissaukies, Amoskeags, Pennacooks, Pemigewassetts, in fine all the Nipmucks remaining, were ready to put their plans of revenge in execution.

But Major Waldron and his friends might have been saved. When the plan was maturing, friendly Indians communicated it

---

* He was authorized as early as March 22, 1683, by the Council of Massachusetts to do this.—Potter's Hist. of Man. 83.

† The Mohawks were sometimes called Mauquawogs, i. e., man-eaters.

E

to Captain Thomas Hinchman, of Chelmsford, Mass., and he immediately dispatched a messenger to the governor. But the latter was careless, heeded it not, thought nor cared but little about it.

June 27th, 1689, the woods about Quocheco were full of Indians. Our valiant tribes had come down. Yet the inhabitants mistrusted nothing; they felt secure, for as yet the governor's messenger had not arrived with the warning.

Night came on, and two squaws, as the plan intended, went to each of the garrison houses and asked leave to lodge by the fire. In the night, when the people were asleep, they were to open the doors and gates and give the signal by a whistle, when the Indians should rush in and take their long-meditated revenge. These squaws, in pairs, were admitted into every garrison but one, and the people at their request showed them how to open the doors in case they should have occasion to go out in the night. Mesandowit, a chieftain under Kancamagus, was a guest of Major Waldron. At supper, with his usual familiarity, he said: "Brother Waldron, what would you do if the strange Indians should come?" The Major carelessly answered that he could assemble a hundred men by lifting his finger. In this unsuspecting confidence the garrison retired to rest.

When the gates were opened the signal was given. The Indians rushed in, and the butchery commenced. The Major, awakened by the noise, jumped out of bed, and though advanced in life to the age of eighty years, he retained so much vigor as to be able to drive them through two or three doors; but as he was returning for his other arms, they came behind and stunned him with a hatchet, drew him into his hall, and seating him in an elbow chair mounted on a long table, insultingly asked him, "Who shall judge Indians now?" They then obliged the people in the house to get them some supper, and when they had done eating they cut the Major across the breast and belly with knives, each one with his stroke saying, "I cross out my account!" They then cut off his nose and ears, forcing them into his mouth; and when, spent with the loss of blood, he was fast falling down from the table, one of them held his sword under him, which quick put an end to his misery. Five or six houses, and all the mills, were burned; twenty-three people were killed, and twenty-nine were carried away captive. Before the morning the Indians were off to their fastnesses among the mountains.

Gov. Cranfield's messenger arrived at Quocheco that very afternoon, but too late to prevent the slaughter.

An instance of generous forbearance on the part of a warrior is related: Mrs. Heard was by chance fastened outside of her husband's garrison house. She hid herself in the bushes near by, so near that she witnessed the wild massacre and the burning of the buildings. A young Indian came towards her with a hatchet as if to kill her, but when he looked in her face he turned away with a yell and fled. When the four hundred were seized in 1676, an Indian boy took refuge in her house, where she concealed him until he was able to effect his escape in safety. The young warrior was that boy. He had not forgotten her, and her kindness to him saved her life.

The Nipmucks had taken their revenge—their wrongs were in part cancelled.

The colonies were amazed—awe-struck. Kancamagus was outlawed, and a price set upon his head. Captain Noyes, with soldiers, marched to Pennacook, but the Indians had fled. Nothing was found but some corn, which was destroyed. Other soldiers went as far north as the White mountains, and so much were the Indians pressed, as Acteon relates, that even the Pemigewassetts were compelled to leave their hunting grounds, and hurry away to the head-waters of the Connecticut and across the border into Canada.

About this time the first Indian captives were carried into our northern wilderness. In 1695, Isaac Bradley, aged 15, and William Whittaker, aged 11, were taken prisoners and carried to Winnepissiogee lake.—Ms. H. C. 2d series, vol. 4, 128.

In 1697 the celebrated *Hannah Duston* was captured at Haverhill, Mass., and went up the Merrimack river towards our Pemigewassett country, as far as the mouth of the Contoocook river. Here they lodged upon an island for some time and Mrs. Duston formed the plan of killing the whole party. Two other prisoners, Mrs. Neff and an English boy, readily agreed to assist her. To the art of killing and scalping she was a stranger, and that there should be no failure in the business, Mrs. Duston instructed the boy, who, from his long residence with them had become as one of the Indians, to inquire of one of the men how it was done. He did so, and the Indian showed him without mistrusting the origin of the inquiry. It was now March 31st, and in the dead of night following, this bloody tragedy was enacted. When the Indians were in the most sound sleep these three captives arose, and softly arming themselves with the tomahawks of their masters, allotted the number each should kill: and so truly did they direct their blows that but one escaped whom they designed to kill. This was a woman whom they badly wounded. There was also a boy, who for some reason they did not wish to harm, and accordingly he was allowed to escape unhurt. Mrs. Duston killed her master, and the boy, Leonardson, killed the man who but one day before had so freely told him where to deal the deadly blow and how to take off a scalp.

Kancamagus did not long remain idle. Captain Church, a noted Indian fighter, had attacked Worombo's fort, captured it, and with it the wife and child of Kancamagus. This stung the chieftain to the quick. With Worombo he fought Church at Casco, killed seven white men, and wounded twenty-four more, two mortally, as we have before narrated. His wife and child were then restored to him.

This famous Indian died about 1691, and tradition has it that he was buried in the land of the Pemigewassetts.

All was over before the dawn of day, and all things were got ready for leaving this place of blood. All the boats but one were scuttled, to prevent being pursued, and with what arms and provisions the Indian camp afforded, they embarked upon the boat remaining, and slowly and silently took the course of the Merrimack river to their homes, where they all soon after arrived without accident.

Several other white captives were carried into the New Hampshire woods about this time, and in this manner, probably, the first white persons entered the Asquamchumauke valley.

CHAPTER IX.

CONTAINING A SLIGHT ATTEMPT AT BIOGRAPHY, OR THE EARLY LIFE OF WATERNOMEE, OTHERWISE WATTANUMON,* SOMETIMES VULGARLY CALLED WALTERNUMUS, LAST CHIEF OF THE PEMIGEWASSETTS.

IN a wigwam beside the Asquamchumauke, long years ago, as old Acteon said, was born a young pappoose, whose history is better known than that of any other member of the Pemigewassett tribe. At first, lashed to its cradle, it was borne about from place to place by its mother, or hung upon a branch of a tree while she was at work. Then the boy ran by the bright stream in springtime, plucked wild flowers, and chased the butterflies. As the young Waternomee grew in years, he journeyed with his family throughout the whole length and breadth of the Nipmuck territory. When he arrived at manhood he became the chief of his individual tribe, and often went back to the old hunting grounds, the land of his birth.

It was there Acteon first saw him. He said he was well built, tall, "straight as a pickerel," a fine smooth face, and with "an eye like a hawk." He was a good hunter, and was much given to farming (hence his name), and could use a spear better than any other man of his tribe. On the river he could make his canoe fairly fly, and he had marched through the forest a hundred miles in a day.† He was the admiration of his tribe, and

---

*The word Wattanumon means a farmer, or planter.—Potter, 258.
There were other Indians by the same name: One lived at Concord, long after the death of the Pemigewassett chief.

†They are generally quick on foot, brought up from the breasts to running; their legs being also from the womb stretched and bound up in a strange way on their cradle backward, as also annointed. Yet they have some that excel: So that

he soon had great influence in every other clan among the whole Nipmuck people.*

In 1689 he is first mentioned in English history, as a brave but kind-hearted Indian. March 5th of that year "Waternumon, an Indian who lived at Newbury," as he is described and his name spelt, in a company of thirty or forty Indians made an attack upon Andover and killed five persons. Colonel Dudley Bradstreet and family were his friends, and when there was danger of their being killed, he rushed forward and preserved them.

The same year, in May, he went northward to his old haunts, and he is reported by those who went to treat with the northern Indians as one of the chief captains of Wonalancet.

At the attack on Quocheco, as ancient tradition has it, he was present under Kancamagus, and witnessed one of the wildest slaughters that ever happened on the New Hampshire frontier. The part he took in it, however, is now unknown.

Then came ten years of peace, and the chief Waternomee went back among the mountains and made his home in the pleasant hunting-grounds of his boyhood.

There was a beautiful planting place at the confluence of the Pemigewassett and Asquamchumauke rivers; good fishing waters were at Sawheganet and Livermore falls, and round about was the best of hunting in all the northern woods. Moose and deer were in the valleys and upon the hills, and he got large supplies of beaver skins from the solitary beaver meadows and ponds, high up on the streams, even to their very sources among the mountains. Waternomee was a most successful hunter, and he well

---

I have known many of them run between fourscore or an hundred miles in a day, and back within two days. They do also practice running races, and commonly in the summer they delight to go without shoes, although they have them hanging at their backs. They are so exquisitely skilled in all the body and bowels of the country by reasons of their huntings, that I have often been guided twenty, thirty, yea sometimes forty miles through the woods a straight course, out of any path.— Roger Williams' Key, 3 Mass. H. C. 234.

*Waternomee, it is said, had as friends, who lived up and down the river, Tohanto, Sagurmoy, Weranumpee Sagurmoy, Pacohunte, Quangecun, Nascum, Monamusque, and Pehaungun. The latter was a well known warrior, and his name was indicative of his character, *Pehaungun* meaning, "Beware of Me!" He was killed in a drunken frolic in 1732, at the age of 124 years, and was buried very carefully — the Indians treading the dirt in his grave, crying all the time like maniacs, "He no get up," "He no come back now." They feared his ghost would return from the land of shades to haunt them.

Drake more particularly locates the Nipmucks upon the Nashua river, a branch of the Merrimack. He gives the following spellings of the name: Nopnats, Nipnets, or Nipmuks.—Ind. Biog. 82.

knew every pond and stream, and flashing waterfall in all his pleasant country.

Acteon saw his wigwam fire blazing once by the mouth of the Mikaseota or Black brook, and heard the crack of his rifle, as he shot some of the smaller game up by "Indian Rock." Then, as he once travelled northward to the land of the Coosucks, he encamped, as the Indians were wont to do, by Wachipauka pond, the leaping waters of Oak falls making pleasant music in his ears.

Tradition avers that Acteon told the story how Waternomee, with a few other Indians, once followed the Asquamchumauke up to its very source in the mountains. There they camped beside a beaver pond, where the beaver, Tummunk, had built houses. These they did not molest, but set out, just as the sun rose, to go over Moosilauke to the "Quonnecticut" valley.

Not often did the Indians climb the mountain, and they only did it now to save time and distance. It was a hard ascent for their moccasined feet, over the stones and through the hackmatacks, as they called the dwarf firs and spruces; but upon the bald mountain crest the way was easier, and the little birds, Psukses, were whistling and singing among the lichens and rocks. When they reached the summit, the heaven, Kesuk, was cloudless, and the view unobscured.

It was a sight, the like of which they had never seen before. Great mountains, Wadchu, were piled and scattered in the wildest confusion in all the land; and silver lakes, Sipes, were sparkling; and bright rivers, Sepoes, were gleaming from the forest.

As they sat upon that topmost peak, the wind was still, and they could hear the moose bellowing in the gorges below; could hear the wolf, Muquoshim, howling; and now and then the great war-eagle, Keneu, screamed and hurtled through the air.

A feeling of superstitious reverence took possession of those Indians as they drank in the strange sights and wild sounds, for they believed that the peak was the home of Gitche Manito, their Great Spirit. Does the unlettered Catholic have reverence at the altar?—much more was the untutored savage filled with awe as he stood in the very dwelling place of his God, afraid that the deity would be angry at the almost sacrilegious invasion.

As the sun, Nepauz, was going down the western sky, a light

mist collected around the eastern peaks, and above all the river valleys in the west, clouds, at first no larger than a man's hand, began to gather. Soon hanging over every valley was a shower—the heavens above them clear—the sun shining brightly upon the vapor. Quickly the wind freshened, and the great clouds, purple and gold and crimson above, black as ink below, hurried from every quarter towards the crest of Moosilauke. Then thunder, Pahtuquohan, began to bellow, and the lightning, Ukkutshaumun, leaped from cloud to cloud, and streamed blinding down to the hills beneath, while the great rain-drops and hailstones, crashing upon the infinite thick woods, sent up a roar loud as a hundred mountain torrents.

"It is Gitche Manito coming to his home angry," muttered Waternomee, as with his companions he hurried down the mountain to the thick spruce forest, Soshsumonk, for shelter. Such scenes, the wildest exhibitions of nature, made the mountain summits to be dreaded, and he was a brave Indian who dared ascend them.*

Through all his hunting grounds, never tarrying long in any place, he travelled—building his wigwam now beside the fishing-place, then by the maize-field, and then where game was plentiest. Thus the years went by, and the Pemigewassett chief with all his people lived happily and greatly increased in numbers. Their range was far away in the wilderness, and their English friends had as yet never invaded their homes. But this state of things could not long continue, for causes were at work whereby war would be brought about in the old world, and the Indians would be again compelled to dig up the tomahawk in the new.

---

*For a vocabulary of Nipmuck words see Schoolcraft, vol. i. 291.

CHAPTER X

HOW THE PEMIGEWASSETTS ENGAGED IN QUEEN ANNE'S WAR,—OF SUNDRY EXPEDITIONS—AND HOW SEVERAL PEMIGEWASSETTS WERE SURPRISED AND SLAIN BY FIVE TERRIBLE MARQUAS, LED BY THE BRAVE CALEB LYMAN.

WHILE the eastern continent shook to the bloody tread of the great Marlborough, and Eugene of Savoy, the primitive "salvage" of the western world was playing his part on a narrower though equally as bloody stage. Did those loving nations, England and France, but set the sanguinary ball in motion, and the peaceable forest children, instigated by pious emissaries, immediately dug up the tomahawk.

The New England colonists had heard of the war commenced in Europe, and well knowing its reciprocal influence and effect in the new world, they immediately began to bestir themselves, to avert as much as possible the storm that was sure to burst. They conceived that it would be an excellent idea to make a solemn treaty with their red-skinned foes, and keep peace if possible in the great northern forest, where with numerous other tribes the Pemigewassetts resided. Accordingly the good Gov. Dudley, who at that time was ruler over the Colony of Massachusetts Bay, sent messengers to all the northern and eastern tribes and invited their chiefs to meet him and his council on the peninsula of Falmouth, Maine, to make a treaty of friendship. This accomplished the red warriors at least would not fight on the side of the French.

On June 20th, 1702, they came together in great numbers. Mauxis and Hopehood,* from Norridgewolk; Wanungunt and

---

* Wahowa, alias Hopehood, was son of Robinhood. His career was a series of warlike and bloody exploits. His attacks upon Berwick, Salmon Falls, and at Fox Point, are among his most celebrated acts. At the latter place 14 whites were

Wanadugunbuent, from Penobscot; Adiwando and Hegan, from Pennacook and Pigwacket; Messambomett and Wexar, from Amascouty, with two hundred and fifty men in sixty-five canoes, all came to Falmouth peninsula. The several chieftains with their adherents were well armed and mostly painted with a variety of colors. It was a rude gathering there in the wilderness—the Governor and his white friends, painted savages, rough wigwams, camp fires burning, and on the shore a fleet of birchen canoes. All were seemingly affable and kind, although in some instances causes of jealousy and distrust were not wanting.

But they did not proceed immediately to business. Wattanumon,* otherwise Waternomee, whom we so politely introduced in our last entertaining chapter, as a chieftain from the northwest, had not arrived, and the other chiefs were unwilling to proceed until he came.†

After waiting several days, in a tent which had been fixed for their lodgment, the Governor made them a short brotherly speech, saying he desired to settle every difficulty which had happened between them.

Captain Simmo, a warrior, replied as follows: "*We thank you, good brother, for coming so far to talk with us. It is a great favor. The clouds fly and darken—but we still sing with love the songs of peace. Believe my words. So far as the sun is above the earth are our thoughts from war or the least rupture between us.*"

A belt of wampum was then presented to the Governor, and they invited him and his white friends to the two pillars of stone which were erected at a former treaty and called by the significant name of the "Two Brothers," unto which also both parties went and added a great number of stones.

Everything now seemed lovely. Many presents were given. There was singing and dancing. Loud acclamations of joy were heard, and the English began to feel that Queen Anne's War in

---

killed, six captivated, (sic) and several houses burned. The pious Cotton Mather says this was as easily done "as to have spoiled an ordinary hen-roost." The same author says that shortly after he went to the westward with a design to bewitch another crew at Aquadocta into his assistance. Some time after he was met by some Canada Indians, who, taking him to be of the Iroquois nation, slew him, with many of his companions.— Drake's Ind. Biog. 302.

*He is mentioned in Penhallow's Indian Wars as from Pigwacket.
† Hubbard's History of Maine.

Europe would not trouble them much in America. But they were destined to be terribly mistaken, and quickly got an inkling of what might happen. A parting salute must be fired. The very polite—not a bit jealous—English wished to honor the Indians by having them fire first, and when they did so the English were greatly alarmed at discovering that the guns of the Indians were loaded with balls, which rattled terribly among the leaves and dry branches of the trees overhead. Very greatly alarmed—and this notwithstanding the curious fact that their own muskets were likewise fully charged for service.

Some of the Indians furthermore had gently intimated that certain French Jesuits had recently come among them and endeavored to seduce them from their allegiance to the crown of England, but without success, for, as they said, they were "as firm as mountains, and should continue so as long as the sun and moon endured."

But all this was a pleasant kind of cheat. The gentle salvages did not mean a word they said. They did not expect the warrior Wattanumon—our Waternomee of the mountains—at the treaty of peace at all. He was to come at the head of a war party, and Governor Dudley with his English friends were to be swept from existence. Three days after they were gone back to Boston, two hundred more French and Indians were sounding their war whoop in the forest where the Two Brothers were erected. Six weeks later, and Queen Anne's war had broken out in fury, and the whole frontier was in a blaze. Not a house was standing nor a garrison unassaulted. Woe to him then whose musket bore no lead.

War raged universally in New England, and our beloved Pemigewassett tribe of course took a hand in it. So fierce were the incursions of the Northern Indians that Massachusetts was exceedingly alarmed. Her general assembly was convened, and a law passed offering a bounty of forty pounds for every Indian scalp that could be procured.

So tempting an offer could not long be withstood, and Capt. Tyng, a brave Indian fighter, was the first to embrace the tender. In the deep mid-winter of 1703, he with his party went on snow-shoes to the head-quarters of the Indians among the mountains, and got five scalps. Massachusetts was prompt, and paid him two hundred pounds for them.*

But the Indians took a sweet revenge for all this, and Haverhill, Deerfield, and other settlements in Massachusetts were attacked, and more than two hundred whites were killed and captured. Ample reparation for five Indian scalps.

This would not do. More than ever the colonies were alive to the fact that the Indians must be punished and subdued. So Major Hilton,† with five companies, and Captain Stevens with one, ranged all the northern woods, went up the Pemigewasset and the Asquamchumauke and eastward along the base of the White mountains, but not an Indian did they discover.

Waternomee with his people were too careful for these marching parties. The old men, women, and children were off to the fastnesses of the mountains and the deep, impenetrable swamps, where pursuit was useless.

But one man, at the head of five Marquas, Mohog, or Mohawk Indians, accomplished more than the six great marching companies together. By chance some of the Pemigewassetts had crossed the highlands, as old Acteon reported, and had set down to plant on the banks of the Connecticut. The Coosucks, with a strong fort, were on the great meadows above them, and on the banks of the stream below were numerous other families of friendly Indians. Thus surrounded they thought themselves secure.

Some time in May, 1704, word came from Albany that the Mohawks had discovered the fort upon the Connecticut river and knew that the Coosucks were planting corn there.

June 6th, Mr. Caleb Lyman, a brave man, placed himself at the head of five Mohawk warriors, and leaving Northampton,

---

* Another party marched directly up the Merrimack river to the Pemigewassett land. The fourth day from home they discovered an Indian settlement a short distance from the river; and after carefully reconoitering and finding that the number of the Indians was less than their own, they advanced to the attack. The Indians did not discover the English until they were close upon them, when they were accidentally observed by a young warrior who cried, "Owanux, Owanux!"—"Englishmen, Englishmen!" This frightened the other Indians, who, rising up quickly, were fired upon by the Englishmen, who killed eight upon the spot. The rest immediately fled, and the company, with considerable booty and the scalps of the slain Indians, returned home without the loss of a man.

† In the spring of 1704 Col. Winthrop Hilton commanded a party to scour the woods to the heads of the Winnepisseogee and Pemigewassett, and was not only this summer but most of the time, when not engaged in more important and distant expeditions, employed in ranging the frontier from Massachusetts to Maine.—1 Farmer & Moore's Col. 246.

Massachusetts, struck into the wilderness. They were soon in the enemy's country. They found his tracks and heard the noise of his guns in the woods. For nine days they pursued their course northward. Then, discovering fresh tracks, they followed them till they came to the river. Supposing that hostile Indians were in the immediate neighborhood they halted, consulted what method was best to pursue, and soon concluded to send out a spy — with green leaves for a cap and vest, to prevent his own discovery, and to find out the enemy.

But before he was out of sight they saw two Indians at a considerable distance in a canoe, and immediately called him back. Soon after they also heard the firing of a gun up the river, upon which they concluded to keep close until sunset, and then, if they could make any further discovery of the enemy, to attack if possible in the night.

Sitting down concealed upon the south shore they looked out upon the scene. The noble river swept round a little wood-crowned height in the east, and then ran straight into the west, till, meeting the low bluff on that side of the meadow, it turned short and flowed away to the south. Before them was the long reach of sparkling water, reflecting the green woods upon its bank; in the light fairy canoe, near where the river came out of the forest in the east, were the two Indians spearing fish; and looking in over the green hills beyond them was the round, bald top of Moosilauke, gemmed with snow fields not yet melted in the summer sun. Even the wood-thrush — sweetest songster of the forest — was here; and with the frogs in the swamp, and the partridges' drumming, and the warbling of the white-throated finch, made melody in the solitude.

When the evening came on they moved up the river, and at the distance of half a mile saw a smoke and found where the wigwams were built. At two o'clock in the morning everything was quiet, and the deadly Marquas with Caleb Lyman were within twelve rods of the slumbering Pemigewassetts.

Here they met a difficulty which, as Mr. Lyman in his narrative relates, nearly ruined their plan. For the space of five rods the ground was thickly covered with dry sticks and brush, over which they could not pass without danger of alarming their enemy and giving him a chance to escape. But while they were contriving how they might compass their design, God—as the pious Caleb* would have it—in his good Providence assisted them with a miracle. A very small cloud arose. It gave a smart clap of thunder and a sudden shower of rain descended. The Mohawks with their leader rush forward, they clear the thicket, come unperceived in full sight of the wigwams, and discover by the noise that the enemy within are awake. Creeping still nearer on their hands and knees, in a moment they are at the side of the rude dwellings. Rising, they pour into them a murderous fire; then, flinging down their guns, with their clubs and hatchets they knock on the head every Indian they meet. Two only of the whole number of Pemigewassetts escape, one mortally wounded, the other, as was afterwards learned, unhurt.

On looking over the ground, seven Indians were found killed on the spot, six of whom they scalped, leaving the other untouched, the Mohawks patriotically saying they would give one scalp to the country. Each would then have one, which would make him rich enough.

Then they took their scalps and plunder, such as guns, skins, etc., loaded them into the canoes of the enemy, and started down the river. The stars shone in the sky above, and the gibbous moon, sinking behind the trees in the west, looked red. Owls hooted in the forest, the frogs sang a lullaby in the grass and lilypads, and the muskrats splashed by the shore. When the sun came up they were twelve miles down the river, and knowing that more "strange Indians" were between them and home, they broke up and abandoned their canoes, and took to the woods.

They were now a hundred miles from the white settlements; they had but one meal of victuals left, and as they soon came upon the trail of thirty Indians they dared not hunt for a subsistence. Caleb Lyman says that for five long days they marched, eating nothing "but the buds of trees, grass, and strawberry leaves, when, through the goodness of God, we safely arrived at Northampton, on the 19th or 20th of the aforesaid June."

The Great and General Court of Massachusetts, being humbly petitioned, granted thirty-one pounds for these services. Why

---

*He was an elder of a church in Boston that sometimes hung witches.

they did not get £240, as they deserved, is more than we can tell. At any rate they merited it more than Captain Tyng, for it was a braver exploit.

The captain of the Marquas, Caleb Lyman, sagely concludes "That in consequence of this action the enemy were generally alarmed, and immediately forsook their fort and corn at Cowassuck and never returned to this day as we could hear off to renew their settlement in that place."

That they were greatly alarmed there is no doubt, but that the Indians did not leave this upper country just then is a fact very well known to all great historians. For several more years they sojourned here; and during the war fought a number of great battles, as we shall be highly pleased to narrate.

CHAPTER XI.

OF SEVERAL THINGS THAT HAPPENED DURING THE PROGRESS OF THE WAR, AND HOW AS ONE OF THE RESULTS THE PEMIGEWASSETT TRIBE WAS DESTROYED AND THEIR HUNTING GROUND —OF WHICH WARREN WAS A PART—MADE A SOLITUDE.

AND now there was marching and hurrying through all the wildwood. The Indians came down like wolves on the fold. Hadley and Quabaug,* Nashua, and Groton were attacked. Then, dividing into small parties, the red foe fell upon Amesbury, Haverhill, and Exeter, and did much mischief.

Captain Tyng and Captain How entertained a warm and slightly cordial dispute with them, but came off second-best, that is, got whipped; and then company after company of Englishmen went northward, and tramped the forest through and through, but had the poorest kind of luck in finding the head-quarters of the Indians. The latter were off to the swamps, the morasses, and the strongholds of the mountains.

Among those who ranged the woods was the brave Colonel Hilton. He came upon a trail and killed four Indians. At the same time he took a squaw alive, with a pappoose at her breast, both of whom he preserved. She was of great service in conducting him to a body of eighteen Indians. These he succeeded in surprising, about break of day, as they lay asleep, and slew all but one, whom he made a prisoner. This was accounted a great feat of arms.

One Captain Wright also ventured far into the enemy's country and fought the Indians with varying success.†

---

*Now Brookfield, Mass.
†Penhallow's Indian Wars, 1 N. H. Hist. Col. 60.

Then the Indians, in the most terrible manner, would retaliate. One party killed Colonel Hilton and another slew Major Tyng.* They scalped the Colonel, struck their hatchets into his brain, and left a lance in his heart. Major Tyng was rescued and carried to Chelmsford, where he soon expired.

Colonel Walton, with two companies of men, hastened away for revenge. He went to the ponds north of "Winnepisseocay" lake, where there were places of general resort for fishing, fowling, and hunting. But he found no Indians—only a few deserted wigwams; for, as Mr. Penhallow politely says, being so closely pursued from one place to another, they removed to other nations, leaving only a few cut-throats behind, which kept the country in a constant state of alarm.

Thus, mutually killing and burning, the war went on with varying fortune, the English, afterwards called Yankees, having the poor luck to get the worst of it as a general thing, until near its close, when an expedition was planned and a blow struck by which our Pemigewassetts were annihilated.

In the year 1709, February 27th, Thomas Baker was taken captive from Deerfield, Massachusetts. They took him straight up the Connecticut river, over the carrying-place to Memphremagog lake, and from thence to the happy land of Canada. He was ransomed a year afterwards, and came home well knowing one of the routes to the haunts of the Indians. He also learned something during his captivity about the great tribes we have mentioned, their homes and hunting grounds, and in the spring of 1712—the border war raging fiercer than ever—he raised a company of thirty-four men to fight some of the enemy, who lived in a beautiful place he had heard of while in Canada. Thirty-three of his company were white soldiers, and there was one friendly Indian to guide them across the highlands.

Lieutenant Baker left Northampton,† Mass., in April, as soon as the snow was gone, and pursued his old route up Connecticut

---

* Formerly Capt. Tyng. He had been promoted.
† In the county of Hampshire.

Lieut. Thomas Baker was born at Northampton, Mass., May 14, 1682. He married Christine Otis, otherwise Margaret Otis, and lived once at Brookfield, and afterwards at Dover, N. H. He died about 1753, of lethargy. Margaret Otis was once taken prisoner by the Indians, carried to Canada, and was there called Christine Otis by the French.

F

river. In four days he was upon the Cowassuck intervals. Snow banks were still scattered about, and the eastern mountains were white as winter. The friendly Indian had told him of the old Indian trail up the Oliverian, and by nightfall they had looked at the mighty precipice of Owl's Head mountain and were camped on the shore of Wachipauka pond.

The next morning, passing Oak falls, they proceeded down the Mikaseota, as Acteon called it, now plain Black brook, and discovering signs of Indians, who appeared to have been in the neighborhood hunting, they marched all day on the right bank of the Asquamchumauke with great caution.

At night Lieutenant Baker and his men camped without fire, and ate a cold supper, for they knew they were in the immediate neighborhood of the Indians.

In the morning early he sent out scouts to reconnoitre. These cautiously advanced, and at about eight o'clock discovered numerous Indian wigwams grouped in a circle upon the east bank of the river.* Some squaws were at work near by, seeming to be getting ready to plant corn. A few men were fashioning a canoe and several children were playing among the trees upon the shore. A large portion of the warriors, as was afterwards learned, were away hunting. The scouts, after gazing upon this scene a few moments, returned and reported their discovery.

The Lieutenant, after a short consultation with his men, now moved forward with all possible circumspection. No sound — not even the breaking of a twig or the snap of a gun-lock — warned the Pemigewassetts of their impending fate. He chose his position, and at a given signal his company opened a tremendous fire upon the Indians, which carried death through their village, and was as sudden to them as a clap of thunder. Some shouted that the English were upon them, and that dreaded name echoed from mouth to mouth, filling all with dismay. Many of the children of the forest bit the dust in death, but those who survived ran to call in the hunters.

The company immediately crossed the river in pursuit, but all who were able to flee were beyond their reach. They fired the

---

*1 Farmer & Moore's N. H. Hist. Col. 128.
Whiton's Hist. of N. H., 70.

wigwams, and as the flames streamed upward and the smoke rolled aloft on the air, a shout from the Indians came sounding down the valley, informing Lieutenant Baker that the warriors were collecting to give him battle.

While the wigwams were being kindled, part of the company were searching for booty. They found a rich store of furs deposited in holes in the banks, in the manner bank-swallows dig to make their nests. Having obtained these, Lieutenant Baker ordered a retreat, knowing that the Indians would soon return, and he feared in too great numbers to be resisted by his single company. As they moved swiftly down the river, the sounds of the war-whoop greeted their ears. This served to accelerate their speed. Often it was repeated and each time grew nearer. When they had reached a poplar plain,* in what is now the town of Bridgewater, a shrill, maddened yell, and a volley of musketry in their rear, told Baker that the Indians were upon him, and that he must immediately prepare for action. This they did by retreating to a more dense wood.

The Indians, commanded by their chief, Waternomee—called vulgarly by some historian, Walternumus—immediately pursued, and, swarming on all sides, poured volleys of musketry into the woods which concealed their enemies. On the other hand, the little party, concealing themselves behind rocks and trees, plied their muskets vigorously and with good effect. Balls rattled in showers around, scattering twigs and branches of the trees in every direction.

While the battle was going on, Waternomee, who was leading the Indians, accidentally encountered Lieutenant Baker. They knew each other well, having met on the frontier and in Canada. They saw each other at the same moment, and fired almost simultaneously. The ball from the sachem's gun grazed Baker's left eye-brow, but did him no injury. Baker's bullet went through the breast of the chief. Immediately upon being struck, with a loud whoop, he leaped four or five feet high and fell dead.

Waternomee was richly attired, and Baker snatched his blan-

---
* Mr. Dearborn has visited that plain and seen and examined a number of skulls which he supposed fell in that engagement. One or two of them were perforated by a bullet.—Power's Hist. of Coos, 171.

ket, which was covered with silver brooches, his powder-horn and other ornaments, and hastened to join the main body of his men.*

The Indians having now lost their chief, and a considerable number of their warriors being wounded, and a few killed, retired.

Lieutenant Baker also immediately collected his men and again ordered a retreat, for he believed that the Indians, though repulsed, would soon rally to the attack, and their numbers constantly swell by those who would join them. On he went, allowing his men no refreshment after the battle, For many miles they travelled without food, until, hunger oppressing them, they declared that they might as well die by the red men's bullets as by famine. At length, upon crossing a stream in New Chester, Lieutenant Baker, finding it useless to try to proceed further, ordered a halt, and the men prepared to refresh themselves. While building the fires to cook their food, the friendly Indian who had acted as guide proposed a stratagem by which the warriors when they came up would be deceived, in regard to the number of men in Lieutenant Baker's marching party. He told each one to build as many fires as he possibly could in a given time, and in roasting the meat to use several forks about the same piece; then, when they were done, to leave an equal number around each fire. This advice was followed, and after enjoying a hasty meal they again moved swiftly on.

The Indian warriors, coming up shortly after, found the fires still burning; they counted the array of forks, and being alarmed at the supposed number of the English they whooped a retreat, and Baker and his men were no more annoyed by them on their return.

Without the loss of a man, Lieutenant Baker and his marching party hurried down the Merrimack river to Dunstable, and on the 8th of May, 1712, made application in Boston for the bounty. They brought but one scalp, yet claimed pay for many more, as they believed they had killed several Indians, but were unable to

---

*These trophies were kept among Captain Baker's descendants for many years. Long afterwards he used to show them to the Indians; they would shed tears and make gestures as though they would sometime kill him when war once more arose. — Genealogical Register.

get their scalps. The governor and council heard this statement and allowed them twenty pounds, or pay for two scalps, and wages for the Lieutenant and company from the 24th of March, to the 16th of May, 1712.*

But this did not satisfy Lieutenant Thomas Baker and his men. They drew up a petition and presented the evidence of the Indians themselves, and on Wednesday, June 11th, were allowed twenty pounds additional for two more Indians proved to have been killed. Captain Baker, in addition to a promotion in rank, also received another honor. The stream on which the battle commenced, and called by the Indians the "Asquamchumauke,"† has ever since been known as *Baker river*.

On the retreat of the Indians they visited the battle-field and looked with sorrow on the once proud forms of their brothers. After burying their dead, they went to the place of their formerly beautiful village. Through fear the survivors had not collected, and, as the warriors approached, their hearts were filled with emotions far different from those which but a few hours before possessed them. All was ruin.

> "No wigwam smoke is curling there,
> The very earth is scorched and bare;
> And they pause and listen to catch a sound
> Of breathing life, but there comes not one —
> Save the fox's bark and the rabbit's bound —
> And here and there on the blackening ground
> White bones are glistening in the sun."

Here, too, the last sad offices were performed to departed shades. This done, they erected a few temporary wigwams, and gradually the fugitives who had fled from the assault of the Eng-

---

Allowed to Thos. Baker's Company.
* "Resolved that the sum of Ten pounds be allowed and paid out of the Public Treasury to Thomas Baker, commander of a company of marching forces in the late expedition against the enemy to Coos and from thence to the west branch of the Merrimack river and so to Dunstable, in behalf of himself and company, for one enemy Indian, besides that which they scalped, which seems so very probable to be slain.
Consented to, J. Dudley."

Additional allowance to Lieut.Thos.Baker & Company for scalps.
"Wednesday, June 11th, 1712.
Upon reading a petition from Lieut. Thomas Baker, commander of a party in a late expedition to Coos and over to Merrimack river, praying for a further allowance for more of the Indian enemy killed by them than they could recover or their scalps, *as reported by the enemy themselves*.
Concurred with a resolve passed thereon, viz: That the sum of twenty pounds be allowed and paid out of the Public Treasury to the petitioner and Company.
Consented to, J. Dudley."
—Journal of the Mass. Legislature for 1712.

† Asquamchumauke is from *Asquam*, water, *Wadchu*, mountain, and *Auke*,—mountain-water-place.

lish were gathered together. A few days later the remainder of their tribe joined them, and after a long council it was decided to unite with the Arosagunticooks, or St. Francis Indians, as many other eastern tribes were doing. It was hard to leave their pleasant hunting grounds, but stern necessity compelled them, and in a few days those dear and sacred places were solitary and deserted. A few of the tribe remained about the shores and islands of Squam lake, occasionally visiting Lake Winnepisseogee, and there dwelt, a passive people, until the settling of the towns around them. Thus the Pemigewassett country, including the beautiful valley of Warren, once possessed by a brave people, became a solitude, and for many years after was seldom visited, save by a few white hunters, or straggling bands of hostile St. Francis, on their way to or from the English frontiers.

BOOK II.

TREATING OF INDIAN FIGHTS AND MASSACRES, EXPEDITIONS AND EXPLORATIONS, RESULTING IN OPENING TO THE WHITE MAN THE LAND OF THE PEMIGEWASSETTS, AND MAKING THE VALLEY NOW CALLED WARREN—AND ALL THE ADJACENT COUNTRY—A SAFE PLACE TO LIVE IN.

CHAPTER I.

OF TWO WARS AND MORE THAN A DOZEN BATTLES.

IN the previous book we have shown how the Indians were dispossessed of our beautiful Asquamchumauke valley. But the driving out of the red men did not render the land a safe place for white people. Hunters and frontiermen equally were liable to have their scalps taken off, or daylight made to shine through them by a bullet, and in order that this history may be complete, it will be necessary to relate the whole series of remarkable events that opened to the hardy settlers our woodland paradise. Consequently this second book must be one of general history, applying alike to a large section of country of which the little territory of Warren is the centre.

Now, in the first place, we have seen how all the Nipmucks of New Hampshire had gone to Canada, except a few called Pequawkees, and the Amariscoggins, and that these Nipmuck braves in Canada formed a considerable part of the great Arosagunticook tribe, sometimes known as the St. Francis Indians.

But under another name the Nipmucks had not forgotten the wrongs which they fancied the English had done them, and their priests, the French Jesuits, helped to keep their recollection fresh upon these subjects; for the Jesuits hated the Protestant English. So when, in 1723, King Williams' war was about to break out, our Indians began to annoy their English neighbors, "killing their cattle, burning their stacks of hay, and robbing and insulting them."

In 1724 two men, Nathan Cross and Thomas Blanchard, were taken captive at Old Dunstable, now Nashua, and started towards Canada. Ten brave men went out in pursuit, under the direction of Lieut. French, and were all killed beside the Merrimack river, at Thornton Ferry, except Josiah Farwell, who took to his heels and escaped.

Everybody was terribly excited at this, and the famous Captain Lovewell raised a scout of thirty men and started north into the woods for revenge. He also wanted a slight bounty of a hundred pounds per scalp for every Indian he could kill. With his company he marched beyond Lake Winnepisseogee to the Pemigewassett country, up towards the land to be called Warren, and discovered an Indian wigwam in which was a man and a boy.

December 19th, 1724, they killed and scalped the man, and brought the boy alive to Boston, where they received the promised reward of two hundred pounds, and the Massachusetts Legislature kindly gave them a gratuity of two shillings and sixpence per man by way of encouragement.

By reason of this success Captain John Lovewell's party was augmented to seventy. They marched again in midwinter, visited the Pemigewassett land, found the dead body of the Indian they had before scalped still lying in the wigwam, and then turned off eastwardly towards the country of the Pequawkees. About the middle of February the Captain discovered the trail of a party of Indians, fresh upon the war-path.

February 20th, the tracks becoming fresher, the scout marched with more wariness some five miles on, and came upon a wigwam but lately deserted, and pursuing "two miles further discovered their smokes." This was near sunset, and the Indians were encamped for the night. Lovewell's party laid in concealment till after midnight, when they advanced and discovered ten Indians asleep round a large fire by the side of a frozen pond.

Lovewell now determined to make sure work, and placing his men conveniently, ordered a part of them to fire—five at a time, as quick after each other as possible—and another part to reserve their fire. He gave the signal by firing his own gun which killed two of them; the men, firing according to order, killed five more upon the spot; the other three starting up from their sleep, two of them were immediately shot dead by the reserve. The other, though wounded, attempted to escape by crossing the pond, but was seized by a dog and held fast till they killed him.*

Then the brave company, with the ten scalps stretched on hoops and elevated on poles, entered Dover in triumph and proceeded thence to Boston, where they received the bounty of one hundred pounds for each out of the public treasury.

This success was hailed with joy and triumph throughout the Provinces. Other expeditions were immediately set on foot. Captain Samuel Willard, with forty-seven able-bodied men, went up the Pemigewassett river and looked up the Asquamchumauke. He was gone thirty-five days, but did not find an Indian. Captain Jabez Fairbanks also traversed the whole country south of the White mountains, and went up the Asquamchumauke valley even to Coos, but with no better luck. Colonel Tyng, of Dunstable, also headed an expedition, and marched into the country betwixt Pemigewassett and Winnepisseogee, but after a month's absence returned without taking a scalp.

Lovewell was greatly elated with his success. He raised another company and boldly marched through the southerly portion of the Pemigewassett country towards Pequawket to obtain a few Pequawkee scalps. Paugus was chief of the tribe, and his name was a terror to the frontier.

 " 'Twas Paugus led the Pequ'k't tribe;
 As runs the fox, would Paugus run;
 As howls the wild wolf would he howl;
 A huge bear-skin had Paugus on."

On Friday, May 7th, 1725, they had reached the Saco river,

---

*These Indians were marching from Canada, well furnished with new guns and plenty of ammunition, they had also a large number of spare blankets, mockaseens, and snow shoes for the prisoners whom they expected to take, and were within two days' march of the frontiers. The pond by which this exploit was performed has ever since borne the name of Lovewell's pond.—Belknap, 200. 209.

Penhallow adds: "Their arms were so good and new that most of them were

and on the morning of the 8th (May 19th new style) Ensign Wyman discovered an Indian on a stony point of land running into a pond from the east. He had in one hand some black ducks he had just killed, and in the other two guns. The Indian, seeing death was his fate, as quick as thought levelled his gun, fired, and Lovewell fell badly wounded. Ensign Wyman, taking deliberate aim, shot the poor hunter, and he was scalped by the chaplain. The latter had been very anxious for the conflict, and in the morning thus patriotically prayed: "We came out to meet the enemy; we have all along prayed God we might find them; we had rather trust Providence with our lives, yea, die for our country, than try to return without seeing them, if we might, and be called cowards for our pains."

In the meantime Paugus with eighty Indians was watching the English, and when the latter marched again by the way they came, to recover their packs, he prepared an ambush to cut them off or take them prisoners, as fortune should will.

When these Indians rose from their coverts they nearly encircled the English, and at first offered to give the latter quarter. This only encouraged Lovewell and his men, who answered: "Quarter only at the muzzles of our guns!" and then, rushing towards the Indians, fired and killed several of them. But they soon rallied, forced the English to retreat, and killed nine of them, Captain Lovewell with the rest.

The party then retreated to the shore of the pond, where they had a brook on the right, a pile of large boulders on the left, and to the north and front of them a swamp partly filled with water, forming a long, narrow peninsula, only accessible from the plain at the westerly extremity, over the pile of rocks. Here they fought all day long. At one time the Indians ceased firing and drew off among the pines at a little distance to *pow-wow* over their success. They had got earnestly engaged in the ceremony, dancing, jumping, howling, and beating the ground — in a word, *pow-wowing*, — when the intrepid Wyman crept up behind the

---

sold for seven pounds apiece, and each of them had two blankets, with a great many moccasons, which were supposed to be for the supply of captives that they expected to have taken. The plunder was but a few skins: but during the march our men were well entertained with moose, bear, and deer, together with salmon trout, some of which were three feet long, and weighed twelve pounds apiece."— N. H. Hist. Col. vol. i. 113.

rocks and trees and fired upon the principal actor, killing him on the spot. This man was supposed to be the celebrated chief, Wahowa.

The fight was then renewed and continued with greater earnestness. Towards night John Chamberlin and Paugus both went down to the pond at the same moment to wash out their guns. They knew each other, agreed to finish washing, and to commence to load at the same time. In loading, Paugus got the advantage; his ball was so small as to roll down the barrel, while Chamberlin had to force his down with his rod. Paugus, seeing his advantage, quickly said, "Me kill you!" and took up his gun to prime. Chamberlin threw down his rod, and bringing the breech of his gun a smart blow upon the hard sand, brought it to his face and fired. Paugus fell pierced through the heart. Chamberlin's gun, being worn from long use, *primed itself*, and the knowledge of this saved the bold hunter's life.

Then the battle gradually ceased, and at midnight all who were able began to retreat. Lovewell went into the fight with thirty-four men, but only fourteen ever lived to reach home. More Indians than English were killed, and a party of fifty, who went to this most terrible battle-field of Indian wars, found and buried Captain Lovewell and many of his brave soldiers who had died beside him. They also found and opened the grave of Paugus. After this the Indians resided no more at Pequawket.

King William's war closed soon after the opening of these interesting adventures, and then the wilderness—hereafter to be called Warren—was solitary enough for a score of years, being visited only by hunters and trappers, Englishmen and Indians, hostile and friendly by turns.

But in 1745 King George's war broke out, and then began another series of interesting adventures and great Indian campaigns, the history of which every son of our town of Warren ought to know, because it relates some of the great events which produced such happy results.

The first of these grand campaigns in our wild solitudes took place in "King George's War" shortly after the fall of Louisburg, the Dunkirk of America, in 1745, and when Benning Wentworth was the royal governor of New Hampshire. The French were highly exasperated to think that their strong fortress had been captured by a few rough woodsmen under Colonel Pepperell, or as they felt, "Colonel Pepper-them-well," and they immediately resorted to their old method of warfare, to wit: to send a few of their very gentle "salvages," to "scrape" a slight acquaintance with the English borderers, and to form a lasting friendship by sealing it in a gentle effusion of blood.

Governor Wentworth and his wise counsellors had a sort of a presentiment, founded, like most other presentiments, on very logical premises, that such might be the case, and so sent a garrison to Captain Jeremiah Clough's fort, in Canterbury. But the Indians, like deer, scented the fort a long distance, slyly hied down the Connecticut, and at the great meadow, now Walpole, kindly removed one William Phipps from all trouble in this world, taking only his scalp as a reward for their services, and then proceeding to upper Ashuelot, now Keene, there feloniously and wilfully and of malice aforethought committed the same outrage upon one James Fisher.

As no one pursued them to wreak revenge, the courage of the Frenchman's humane allies, our Nipmucks, greatly increased. That very season they went down the Merrimack on campaign number two. They did not trouble themselves to visit the fort at Canterbury, thinking it too bad to disturb the garrison there of its quiet and repose. Near Suncook they thought to relieve the monotony of their life by a little miscellaneous practice at target shooting. Accordingly they found a couple of suitable marks in the persons of James McQuade and John Burns, of Bedford, who had been to Pennacook, now Concord, to procure corn, and were returning home. McQuade was shot dead; but Burns, running zigzag, and the Indians not being able to shoot round a corner, escaped. The Indians were off to Canada before this great battle was reported.

When the news of this brilliant campaign reached Portsmouth it is said Governor Wentworth gnashed his teeth and stamped his foot. "How dared the haughty foe to pass the impregnable fortress at Canterbury?" But he would meet them on their own ground, that is, in the woods. The order was given, a company of men was enlisted, and Captain John Goffe, of Harrytown, was detached by Colonel Blanchard to command the hazardous expedition. His company of thirty-four men was selected from the large number who presented themselves. None were enrolled but such as were noted for courage and sagacity. The first of January they started up the Merrimack on a scout. How far they went we were never able to learn. Whether they proceeded as far as Coos is very doubtful. We cannot tell, though we wish we could, whether they even went as far as the forks of the Merrimack, where the golden salmon in the springs of olden time are said to have parted company with the shad; all we know is that they scouted valiantly all the long winter, with excellent success at— scouting; but not discovering even so much as one of the moccasin footprints of the enemy, April 6th, 1746, they disbanded. But the chiefs who led the renowned war parties in the campaigns of the previous season were heroes in the eyes of their own little Arosagunticook nation at home, and many a brave fellow who had rested on soft furs in his smoky wigwam all winter, now stimulated by an abundant supply of " French pap," was burning for deeds of glory.

Down through the wild Coos, about which the snowy mountains were gleaming, they came on the run. Over the highlands and down the Asquamchumauke they hurried, and on April 26th, 1746, like the crafty crusader, Bohemond, at the siege of Antioch, contrived to enter an open door of the garrison house in New Hopkinton, now minus the "New," and plain Hopkinton. They found all the people fast asleep, and easily took as prisoners Samuel Burbank, his sons Caleb and Jonathan, Daniel Wordwell, his wife, and three children, Benjamin, Thomas, and Mary.

This splendid victory was the crowning achievment of campaign number four. But a more blood-thirsty army, numbering three braves, took Timothy Brown and one Mr. Moffatt prisoners, at Lower Ashuelot, killed Seth Putnam at Number Four, and made campaign number five full as brilliant as any other.

New Hampshire was now in a terrible state of alarm. There was running and riding through all the wild border. The stoutest heart beat faster at the slightest noise after dark. Women turned pale at the shriek of the night hawk, or at the bark of the watch dog, and the naughtiest child in all the province, affrighted, would cower still at its mother's side at the bare name of Indian. Captain Goffe, who was really a brave officer, of good ability, was ordered to the frontier with a company of fifty men. In a sorrowful yet firm letter, written from Pennacook to Governor Wentworth, he complained of the lurking ambuscade tactics of the Indian enemy. But although he could not see the wisdom of their movements, we of a later day can admire the skill and bravery of the Arosagunticooks as much as the oblique movements of Epaminondas, the new Greek fire, or the harrow-shaped columns which Napoleon hurled with such terrible effect on his foes.

Captain Goffe marched up the Merrimack, scouted along the Pemigewassett, looked up the Asquamchumauke, visited all the great "camping places" in the adjacent country, and returned by Lake Winnepisseogee. Not an Indian could he find. But Governor Wentworth was not to be thus thwarted by his very open enemy that skulked through the woods. A very brilliant idea took possession of his head. "To train in the troop has always been considered about as good as to join the church," and the worthy Governor thought it very proper to patronize the horse companies. So he ordered detachments of Captain Odlin's and Captain Hanson's cavalry to proceed immediately to relieve the forts at New Hopkinton and Canterbury. Prompt to respond, the brave mounted men went up the east bank of the Merrimack. Like a sweeping avalanche they rush on. No common obstacle could check their swift, wild march. Without a particle of doubt the bright sun of the second morn would see them debouch from the forest and with their glittering trappings rein up their prancing steeds, champing upon the impatient bit, before the massive gate of the strong fortress of Canterbury. But how uncertain are the things of this world. This brilliant expedition was destined to be a sad failure. The gallant troopers slackened their headlong course on the banks of the broad, deep Suncook river, the breadth of which to-day is about fifty long feet, and the dark depth about eighteen inches. No bridge spanned the surging flood, and to ford it was impossible. For hours they attempted to overcome this great barrier of nature, but in vain, and they were forced to return on their trail. At a meeting of the Legislature the Honorable Governor recommended that a bridge be constructed across the mighty river. But though the cavalry companies made a glorious return, yet that the Indians might be thoroughly conquered, Captain Samuel Barr, of Londonderry, was also sent north with nineteen men. He was out nineteen days, and met with the same brilliant success as the other bold captains. As New Hampshire would in no manner be behind her sister colonies, a large number of soldiers were raised, to join a great expedition to Canada. In after years it was known as the Honorable Gov. Shirley's Quixotic success. As the expedition was a heavy body, and slow to start, the soldiers were sent into quarters on the shore of Lake Winnepisseogee, where they were to fight the Indians. But, instead of long marches through the pleasant solitudes they enjoyed themselves immensely, hunting and fishing on the shore of the beautiful lake—but not an Indian was seen.

Notwithstanding all this marshalling in battle array, the St. Francis braves, now including the entire Nipmuck nation and some other savages, gallantly accomplished campaign number six. June 27th they fought a successful battle at Rochester, with five Englishmen, who were at work in a field. The Indians sent out one of their number as a decoy, who drew the fire of the enemy. They then charged upon their white foe and drove them with the blunt points of their muskets into a deserted house. Here the white men long held them in check; but with true Indian cunning they unroofed the house and then coolly shot and killed Joseph Hurd, Joseph Richards, John Wentworth, and Gersham Downs. John Richards, the only survivor, was taken prisoner. Reclining for a short time upon a sloping bank, beneath a shady tree, in which forest songsters warbled war-pæans in honor of their glorious triumph, they recover their exhausted energies. Then, as the sun bids good-bye to the flashing zenith, the brave war-party rush upon another company of laborers in a field near by. Again glorious victory perches on their banners, but the spoils were less. All the English escaped except one poor lad named Jonathan Door. Long before night the Indians, with scalps and prisoners, returned to the fastnesses of the deep wood.

Madam Rumor, with her thousand tongues, circulated an account of this campaign in double-quick time.

New Hampshire men again flew to arms, Capt. Nathaniel Drake, of Hampton, was ordered out, "with fifteen of his troopers to scout at and about Nottingham, fitted with their horses for fourteen days." Capt. Andrew Todd, of Londonderry, with twenty-three men, flew to Canterbury. Capt. Daniel Ladd, of Exeter, with a company of foot, ranged the woods by Massabesic lake to Pennacook, and returning scouted across the country to Nottingham; as usual, though scouting valiantly, not an enemy was discovered.

By the first of August, Capt. Drake's brave troopers were at home again, having sweat themselves and horses terribly doing nothing. Capt. Todd had returned even before this, and Capt. Ladd had dismissed his men until August fifth.

August tenth the Indians came to Pennacook, but Capt. Ladd at the same time came also.

The Indians were keen enough to discover the fact, but Capt. Ladd did not, consequently the former grew very religious, and resolved not to fight, as it was the Sabbath. In this they did differently from many other great military peoples, who have improved this day for battle. The Indians retired into a deep black wood for solemn meditation.

The following day, Monday, they were fresh for the contest. They made a snug little ambush on the path leading from Pennacook to Hopkinton. It was about half a mile from the church which they did not attack the previous day. When a portion of Capt. Ladd's company came along, rather irregularly, the Indians gave them a warm welcome. Daniel Goodman had gone forward to fire at a hawk, which sat on a dry stub by the path. Obadiah Peters was resting under the rustling leaves of a poplar tree, while the rest of the party behind walked leisurely up. With the warwhoop ringing, and the echo of the musketry reverberating from the distant hills, the smoke curled slowly away through the trees, and showed five men, drenching the mossy hillside with their blood. Lieut. Jonathan Bradley, Samuel Bradley, John Luffkin, John Bean, and Obadiah Peters were dead; but the quick eye of the Lieutenant had caught sight of the Indians, and he killed, before he received his death wound, the only Indian that fell during this great war.

MORE INDIAN CAMPAIGNS.

With their dead comrade buried, howling and yelling, with the scalps, and two prisoners, this brave wild war party of forty Arosagunticooks returned to Canada.

In the language of one of the first historians of the times, this campaign produced "dire consternation throughout all the province. New Hampshire armed herself in her might." She was determined to defend herself. In the way she did it, she won an imperishable glory. Forts and block houses sprung up all along the frontier, a garrison was placed in each, and at the head of Little Bay, in the present town of Sanbornton, Fort Atkinson was built of rough stone, and strongly manned. If the Indians had only attacked one of these, there is no doubt but that a most gallant defence would have been made. But that was not the Indians' style; they did not care a rush for forts, blockhouses, or garrisons.

In the spring of 1747, they opened another brilliant campaign, the eighth. On the morning of May 10th, they fell upon two men at Suncook; one they killed and scalped, the other escaped. At night they fired upon four others, but, much to their chagrin, missed them. By this time the settlers had all got snugly inside the garrison house, and the Indians not believing anything was to be made by attacking it, very quietly decamped. A few days afterwards scouts pursued them, as usual, and with the usual success.

Campaign the ninth was disastrous to the Indians. They approached Pennacook, and this time a scout did actually discover them. But they were off like a smoke in a high wind, leaving all their vast military train, to wit: things stolen, provision bags, ropes for the prisoners, and blankets, in the possession of the English.

Campaign the tenth was more successful. August 21st, they took the house of Charles McCoy, in Epsom, captured Mrs. McCoy, stole all the apples off a single tree that composed their orchard, burned the house, and then cleared for Canada by Coos interval and Lake Champlain. Away went the English scouts after them, with the same glorious success as ever.

Campaign eleventh was an attack on Hinsdale. They killed several, took a number of prisoners, and achieved a splendid victory, without any scout to pursue them.

Campaign twelfth they grew so heroic, on account of previous success, that they even besieged Number Four, and somehow managed to take several prisoners.

These were the great campaigns of 1745-6-7. In 1748 there was a little skirmishing with the enemy's pickets. Several men were frightened, and possibly a few might have been hurt. But the treaty of Aix-la-Chapelle put an end to the war, and the brave Arosagunticooks buried the tomahawk.

This border war was a source of great suffering to the English, as well as mortification. Many of their number had fallen, and many were pining in captivity. The Indians had the advantage in the whole contest. But one of their number had been killed, and they never had returned to Canada but once without a scalp or a captive. The Arosagunticooks knew well where to find the English. The latter, brave as their painted enemy, looked in vain for Indians. Like the Persians advancing on the Hellespont, the Indians were well acquainted with the country they had to pass. The English scouting parties, like the Greeks, dare not venture across the great wild solitudes of our beloved Pemigewassett land, which stretched between themselves and the home of their enemy. Captain Baker and Captain John Lovewell had fought the Indians valiantly on their own ground, and could Captain Goffe have been as successful in finding them he would have fought equally as well. But he and the other brave captains had wholly failed of meeting them, and consequently could not fight them, and they now retired to their farms with about as much glory, and feeling about as well, as the noble lion in his lair stung half to death, while all his despicable enemies, the wasps, were uninjured.

CHAPTER II.

A BEAUTIFUL SOLITUDE; AND HOW THERE WAS AN ATTEMPT TO BUILD TWO FORTS ABOVE THE PEMIGEWASSETT COUNTRY, AND WHAT CAME OF IT.

A few years now passed, and a deeper shade filled the solitudes—the wilds of the Asquamchumauke—or, as modern civilians delight to term it, Baker river, once the land of the Pemigewassett Indians. True it is that down by the grass-grown intervals of Coos, where the Connecticut sweeps around the great oxbow, then up the Indian trail by the wild, roistering Oliverian brook, marauding parties of the French and Indians from St. Francis, Canada, occasionally travelled; but when they had gone back the solitudes grew grimmer, and every thing would have been still as chaos and old night, but for the lowing of the antlered moose and the howling of the wolf and panther.

This land of the Pemigewassetts, which included the little territory of Warren, together with the whole upper country once inhabited by the Coosucks, our solitudes, was now debateable ground, claimed both by the English and St. Francis Indians. Scouts and captives who had been there said it was a delightful region, and the old soldiers of Captain Baker descanted wonderfully upon its being a perfect paradise; and now that King George's war was over, New Hampshire men began to have extraordinary desires for obtaining it. Besides, it was a great strategic point, worth having if another war should arise; for the meadows of lower Coos had been a sort of a rendezvous for the Arosagunticook Indians, from which, in the wars just mentioned, they had sallied forth down either the Connecticut or Merrimack rivers. Consequently the public mind was greatly roused, the attention of all was turned towards possessing this upper country, in the exact centre of which was our little mountain valley, Warren, and a pleasant series of most entertaining adventures was carried on for the accomplishment of that purpose, as we shall endeavor most faithfully to show.

The first thing that happened, as we have just intimated, was an immense amount of talking. Then a petition, numerously signed, was presented to the General Assembly of New Hampshire. It prayed that a road might be surveyed and cut from Bakerstown, a settlement that had been pushed far up on the frontier, to the Coos intervals, and that two forts might be built, one on each side of the Connecticut, for the benefit of settlers and the protection of the lower country. The General Assembly was deeply interested, and the Governor and Council most favorably disposed. They had fretted and fumed through King George's war, and now they were ready and willing to do almost anything to keep back the dire and savage Arosagunticooks, and increase the number of settlements and subjects.

Numerous plans for settling this upper country, building and garrisoning forts, were presented. Finally in the winter of 1752, the following very nice one was agreed upon:

A tract of land on Connecticut river was to be laid out into five hundred suitable portions. It was then to be granted to five hundred brave men. The conditions of the grant were that they should pay a small quit-rent and should occupy the lands immediately.

Furthermore, two townships should be laid out, one on each side of the river. A regular garrison should be built in each of them. The latter should encompass fifteen or more acres of land, in a square or parallelogram form. A line should be drawn around their area, just as the ancients marked out their cities, and on it were to be built log houses, at considerable distances apart — and a log house was certainly to be erected at each corner. The spaces between the houses were to be filled up with a palisade of square timbers, making a wall so strong and high that the nimble Arosagunticooks should not be nimble enough to leap over it, even if they should be foolish enough to make the attempt.

In the centre of this great square, and upon a rising plat of ground, if such could be found, was to be built a strong and impregnable citadel, such as the Greeks and Persians were in the habit of building within their cities. Here should be the granary of the colony, and here should be the last refuge of the inhabitants, if they should be driven from the outer enclosure. Within hailing distance on each bank of the noble river, either fortification was to assist the other, in case of an emergency.

As an addenda to the above brilliant plan, a form of government was prescribed. Courts were to be established, and justice and equity were to be administered in all civil causes. That every thing might go smoothly, and that there might not be the least possible chance for jar or discord, the governor-general of these already renowned fortresses was to have the power to proclaim martial law at any time, and to put every inhabitant under strict military discipline. The above plan having been matured and decided upon, a committee was immediately chosen to carry it into effect. This committee was composed of resolute and energetic men. They quickly made all necessary arrangments. Partings were hastily taken with kind friends and families, for it was a hazardous enterprise upon which they were entering, and each hurried to the rendezvous at Bakerstown, from which place they were to make the desperate attempt to penetrate the dark solitudes of the to them hitherto unexplored north.

It was a bright day when they set out. Old Winter had just taken up his march to the double-quick-time tune of "The hot sun's a coming," and all nature was bursting into life. On the trees the young leaves were expanding, and the little wild-flowers springing up among the gnarled roots lent a delicious fragrance to the air. The birds carolled in the branches, making merry music to cheer the woodsmen, or rather the committee-men, as they pushed their canoes up the Merrimack, toted them round the falls of the Pemigewassett, and with setting poles drove them up the "rips" of the Asquamchumauke.

Suffice it to say, that they must have left them in the shoal head waters of the stream and then toiled slowly through the woods by the old Indian trail across our valley to the Connecticut.

Here they rested themselves, as men naturally would, looked

over the land on the eastern bank of the broad stream, and then, crossing to the western shore, ascended the rocky bluff to obtain a better view of the country. Although rough woodsmen, they could not have been insensible to the magnificence of the scene. At their feet the Connecticut wound like a band of silver through a seeming garden. Noble elms grew upon the river banks. Beneath their shade the wild deer sported and with their mottled fawns beside them cropped the luxuriant herbage. A mighty forest just clothing itself in young verdure covered the lesser hills of New Hampshire, while far in the distance the great peaks of the Haystacks shot up into the transparent ether. To the south, the long, swelling summit of Moosilauke, still flecked with snow-fields, lay mirroring itself in the blue heaven. They also noted where the streams came down from the highlands and entered the river; where lay the broadest and richest intervals, and where the rising plats of ground afforded the best sites for their forts.

Descending from the eminence that commanded such an enchanting scene, and was also so serviceable in showing the natural facilities of the country, they selected the places for the forts and located the townships. This done, and their provisions being nearly spent, they hurried back to their canoes and floated rapidly down stream through the woods to the settlements.

They gave so flattering an account of the beauty, richness, and fertility of the intervals that four hundred men were immediately enlisted to settle this paradise of New England. Active preparations for the journey to this upper country were commenced, and another autumn bid fair to have seen two forts gleaming with bayonets on the banks of the Connecticut.

But how illusory are the plans of men. The Indians had watched the acts of the committee with a jealous eye. Like men of common sense, they judged the loss of their planting grounds would be a serious evil. To counteract it and to preserve their lands they commenced what was to themselves an entertaining series of hostilities—but which meant death or captivity for the poor whites. We shall now endeavor to show how the migratory would-be English colonists were for a time thwarted, and that part of our pleasant land of the Pemigewassetts now called Warren hindered from being settled.

CHAPTER III.

GIVING AN ACCOUNT OF A HUNTING PARTY ON THE ASQUAMCHUM-
AUKE, HOW TWO YOUNG MEN WERE CAPTIVATED IN THE MOST
CAPTIVATING MANNER, CONCLUDING WITH HOW ONE GOT HIS
BACK TICKLED WITH THE OIL OF BIRCH, WHILE THE OTHER
DID NOT — MUCH TO THE DELIGHT OF ALL CONCERNED.

THE Indian runner must have been fleet-footed who bore the news of the committee's acts at the Coos intervals to the village of the St. Francis. Like a shower of toads, an old-fashioned, time-out-of-mind war party, under the generalship of Acteon,* some say Francis Titagaw, others the young chief, Peer, was hopping over the logs and stealing through the thickets which lined the banks of the Asquamchumauke almost as soon as the committee had gone in their canoes down the Merrimack.

Now it so happened that some of those daring spirits who always delight to live upon the frontier, and are never contented unless, like their red-skin cousins, they were strolling through the woods whether it paid or not, were trapping upon the Asquamchumauke, and along a little black mountain stream in the present town of Romney. They were brave fellows every one of them, and their names, as is known to all who have read the oft-told story, were William and John Stark, David Stinson, and Amos Eastman.

They had come up from their homes at Amoskeag falls, and had worked most industriously at trapping. They had sable,

---
*Acteon was a Nipmuck Indian, and married an Arosagunticook woman. He was sometimes called Capt. Moses. He was at one time an associate with Wahowa, and was the same Indian that in his old age sometimes made his home with Colonel Obadiah Clement.
Peer was a young chief.

marten, mink, and beaver traps, set on three long ranges or "lines," one up Stinson brook to the head waters of the Pemigewassett, another up the "South Branch" to the water shed of the Mascoma, and a third far up the Asquamchumauke to Moosilauke mountain. They had been very successful in their avocation, and had gathered furs amounting to more than five hundred and sixty pounds in value.* But the long days had come; corn-fields and potato-patches must be improved, and so they made ready to return. Another circumstance that quickened their departure was the discovery of fresh, moccasined footprints on the Indian trail.

All day long they had worked diligently in gathering their traps, and on the morrow they were to break up their camp. It was nearly evening. The long shadows began to steal across the water, and the last rays of the setting sun were streaming full upon the face of craggy Rattlesnake mountain, when John Stark, who was stooping to take a steel trap from the water, was startled by a sharp hiss. Jumping up he saw the Indians, and the muzzles of half a dozen muskets, staring at him within three feet of his head, told him that escape was hopeless.

That night he lay bound among his captors, and in the morning was early roused to proceed down the river, where they were to lay in ambush for the rest of the hunters. The latter had guessed the cause of Stark's absence, and at the earliest dawn packed their furs, traps, and camp equipage into their canoe and started. Eastman was upon the shore, while William Stark and Stinson guided the frail craft as it floated down in the rapid current. The Indians easily captured the former, and then bid Stark hail those in the canoe, and invite them to come on shore. Stark complied so far as to tell them to pull to the opposite bank and then run for their lives, as the Indians had got him and would have them too unless they were quick in getting away.

Curses and blows fell thick upon the head of the dutiful but unfrightened hunter, and then the Indians leveled their muskets to fire upon the retreating men. "Not yet, my friends," said the belabored Stark, as he struck up their guns at the moment of discharge. For this he got another shower of kicks and cuffs, and when a second time they attempted to fire he again endeavored to

---
* Potter's Hist. of Manchester, 277.

stop them, but not so successfully as before. Stinson was killed in the act of leaping upon the shore, and fell backward, his blood staining the clear water. The paddle in the hand of William Stark was shivered with bullets, but leaping from the canoe like a deer he took to the woods and escaped.*

The Indians in their usually polite and gentlemanly manner now wished for a slight memorial of young Stinson to take to St. Francis. They crossed the stream, dragged his body ashore, dexterously took off his scalp, and after giving John Stark a sound beating for his daring interference, told the two captives to take up what was to them a not very agreeable march to the happy land of Canada.

The first night they camped on the Coos intervals, close by the Connecticut. As he lay bound between two of his captors John Stark could hear the murmuring of the river and see its dark waters gleaming in the moonlight, as the full orb rose slowly up over the bow-backed summit of Moosilauke mountain.

It was a long march up the Connecticut, across the highlands, and down the sluggish St. Francis river to the St. Lawrence. Meanwhile the Indians determined that the captives should run the gauntlet when they reached the village, and so to beguile the way they taught Eastman and Stark a sentence in Indian, which they should recite during that interesting ceremony, the tenor of which was: *"I'll beat all your young men!"*

On their arrival two long lines of warriors were formed, and between them the captives were to run. Each warrior had a club, with the right to beat the prisoner as much as he chose as he passed along. To each of the runners the Indians gave a pole about six feet in length upon the end of which was stretched the skin of some animal. Upon Stark's was a loon skin. Eastman's turn came first. When the young Indians heard him cry out, "I'll beat all your young men!" they cudgelled him most unmercifully, and he came out of the lines more dead than alive. But young Stark was made of different mettle. He marched up to the start-

---
*When the news of the capture of Eastman and Stark reached Rumford, a party was raised, who proceeded to Baker river, found and buried the body of Stinson in the woods, and brought home one of the paddles of the canoe, which was pierced with several shot holes. It was possessed a long time by the Virgin family.

Jacob Hoyt, Esq., says that in this party were Phineas Virgin, Joseph Eastman (called deacon), and Moses Eastman.—Hist. of Concord, 193.

ing point with firm step, astonished the braves with the cry, "*I'll kiss all your young women!*" and then bounded into the lines. He knocked down the first Indian he met, and continued to lay about him with so much vigor that the astonished natives suffered him to pass through with scarcely a blow.

The old men were pleased at the consternation of their young warriors, and so greatly admired the bravery of Stark that they wished to adopt him as their chief. But the hero of Bennington had no notion of passing his life in the wilds of Canada, and plainly told them so. Afterwards they bid him hoe corn. He complied so far as to cut it up by the roots and then throw his hoe into the river, declaring that such work was fit only for squaws. This only heightened their admiration for him, and they did not ask him to do any more work.

Late in the autumn Captain Stevens, of Number Four, and Mr. Wheelwright, of Boston, went to St. Francis to redeem the prisoners. For Eastman they paid a ransom of sixty dollars, for Stark one hundred and three dollars, showing how much higher they prized the courage of the latter above the timidity of the former.

They returned home by Lake Champlain and Number Four— Eastman to lead the life of an industrious farmer, Stark to plan and execute new hunting or trapping excursions, to procure means to pay his ransom, or to serve as guide through the wilderness he had explored, all of which disciplined him for achieving those immortal deeds in the old French war and the Revolution. We hear of him the next summer down in the wilds of Maine, trapping on the Androscoggin; but previous to this he was pilot for a large party which made one more attempt to explore the north country, that historical land containing our mountain hamlet— Warren.

CHAPTER IV.

HOW THE SALVAGES, SABATIS AND CHRISTO, STOLE TWO NEGROES FROM THE SETTLEMENT AT CANTERBURY, AND THE EXCITEMENT IT CAUSED; TOGETHER WITH A GRAND RESULT BEFORE HINTED AT.

THE capture of the hunters and the murder of Stinson in the Pemigewassett country caused the New Hampshire people considerable alarm, and communicated in fact a little palpitation of the heart to the Governor himself. But, like any other nine days' wonder, it soon died away. Yet quiet only reigned for a moment, and then the excitement commenced again.

There were two big, burly savages, who sometimes resided at St. Francis, but more often on the head waters of the Merrimack. Their names were Sabatis and Christo. Like most of the Indians of that degenerate Indian time they would get drunk, and then would boast of their wicked deeds done in the wars. They were a source of terror to the women and children, and many a time it was whispered at night when the family was gathered around the huge old-fashioned fire-place, where the burning logs were glowing, how these men, stealing from the northern solitudes, had buried their tomahawks in the settlers' heads; and how Sabatis, sleeping on the hearth as he was wont, would start and groan and scream, as he said his victims did. Yet the settlers treated them kindly, and for some time they shared the hospitality of two men, Miles and Lindsey.

Now it chanced that two negroes were living in Canterbury, the property of said Miles and Lindsey, and our red-skins, not having the fear of the law before their eyes, and never having heard the teachings of certain abolitionists who lived at a later day — how wicked it was to hold black chattels in bondage — at once experienced a strong desire to appropriate said chattels to their own use. Accordingly, like other men-stealers, they immediately began to form plans to "captivate" the negroes.

It was a bright summer morning. Men were repairing to the fields, and the two would-be kidnappers started for a stroll in the woods. They met the negroes, asked them to show a path that led to a certain locality, and the darkies, good honest souls, complied. When they were a considerable distance in the forest, the Indians seized the negroes, bound their hands, fettered their little heels, and then, instead of taking them down south, like kidnappers of a later day, they engineered the first underground railroad, and started their chattels towards Canada.

But one night, when they were far on the road, one of the negroes managed to unfetter himself, and in terse Indian nomenclature, "him run fast," and escaped to his "ole massa" again.

But the other negro was not so fortunate. His Indian captors waded him across the "river of pines," the dark flowing Connecticut, feasted his keen ideality on the wild beauties of the rolling Green mountains, and delighted his vision with the sight of the sparkling Lake Champlain. Suffice it to say, the kidnapped darkey saw the frowning battlements of Crown Point, where his humane captors sold him to a French officer. Whether he was redeemed or not is too insignificant a matter for this history to investigate.

But one great result grew out of these Indian depredations. Petitions were again circulated, signatures procured, and when the great and dignified Assembly of New Hampshire — characterized then as now more by its size and numbers than by its ability — met, it was memorialized. The petitioners humbly prayed that a road might be marked, cut, and made, from the settlements on the Merrimack, through the Pemigewassett land to the Coos meadows. Then the forts would surely be built. Then bristling bayonets, gleaming over the bright waters of the Indian gardenland, would keep those self-same Indians who pretended to own the aforesaid garden — yearly planted with pumpkins, corn, and beans — from committing their depredations upon innocent, brave hunters, sable trappers, and white squatters, who of right roamed upon the frontier. In other words there should be a guard at the Coos meadows, who, ever vigilant, should make the settlers feel more secure in their new homes.

They never dreamed that the Indians could leave the Connecticut higher up, and come down through the notch by the Haystacks, where they could learn one lesson of stern grandeur from the Old Man of the Mountain; or that they could go round by the green hills of the west and, crossing the Connecticut below, reach the Asquamchumauke by Baker ponds. There were no such contingencies about it in their minds; the forts once built, they were safe.

But New Hampshire then, as now, was poor. It would be great expense to cut the road and maintain the forts. But after considering the matter for a long time, it was determined that so weighty a petition could not be disregarded; that the interests of the State demanded immediate action; and so they voted to assume the expense of cutting and making the road, and appointed a committee to survey and mark the same. That committee consisted of Zacheus Lovewell, of Dunstable, a relative of that Captain Lovewell who fought Paugus; John Tolford, of Chester, and Caleb Page, of Starkstown; and they hired John Stark to assist them. The Assembly sat in the winter of 1752-3, and in the spring following the committee commenced the work—looking toward the beloved land of this history.

CHAPTER V.

HOW THE ROAD WAS CUT THROUGH THE WOODS, AND HOW THE GREAT AND MIGHTY NATION OF AROSAGUNTICOOKS — COMPOSED OF ALL THE NIPMUCK TRIBES, INCLUDING OUR PEMIGEWASSETTS AND SOME OTHERS — SENT A FLAG OF TRUCE TO NUMBER FOUR. CONCLUDING WITH A GENERAL BACKOUT.

THE committee were no laggards. The General Assembly of New Hampshire made a wise choice. They immediately rendezvoused at Amoskeag falls, the place where John Stark lived, and where daring spirits like Waternomee, Kancamagus, and Passaconaway congregated in times long ago. Philosophers say that associations form human character. Tell, amid his native mountains, was brave and daring; the inhabitant of India is cowardly and effeminate. Consequently, the great rocky barrier at Amoskeag, the white, foaming water, ever roaring, the northern granite mountains — all conspired to make such men as John Stark and his friends.

The committee hired sixteen men, and Stark was to pilot them through the Pemigewassett country to the Coos intervals. Robert Rogers, the most daring ranger of the old French war, was one of the number.

It was March 10th, 1753, when the surveying party left Amoskeag. The river was yet frozen over. Each man had a pair of snow-shoes on his feet. His blanket, twenty-five days' provision, and his cooking utensils, were strapped to his back. Half the party had guns. Almost all had axes or hatchets, and Caleb Page carried a compass and other materials suitable for making a plan of the survey.

THE ROAD BLAZED TO COOS.

Thus equipped they proceeded up the river on the ice as far as Bakerstown, now Franklin, N. H. They stopped one night at the most northern settler's hut, and rested their weary limbs on the floor by the blazing hearth. On the bright ensuing morn, when the sun gleamed on the myriad diamond points of the frozen snow, and the red-crested woodpecker drummed a merry tune on the hollow beech-tree, they struck into the woods. Their route was now up the west bank of the Merrimack. A part of the company would perform the day's march in the forenoon, construct the camp, cut the wood for the night fire, prepare and cook the provisions, and make everything as comfortable as possible for the tired road choppers and surveyors. At different points on the route they left a portion of their supplies, to be used on their return. The snow was four feet deep; yet they pushed on without faltering. Not a man lagged behind. One day, in what is now our good town of Wentworth, they started a moose. The whistling balls of half a dozen rifles, in sailors' phrase, "brought him to," and at evening, when night's shadows were creeping through the forest, the gleaming knives of nineteen hardy borderers flashed before the campfire, as they carved out the choicest morsels and over them cracked their merry jokes. In fifteen days they had blazed a pathway through the wilderness, and were encamped on the intervals at Coos.

They occupied six days in returning, and when they disbanded at Amoskeag on the 31st day of March, the great province of New Hampshire, with Benning Wentworth for Governor, was indebted to this indomitable surveying party in the sum of 684*l*. 5*s*. old tenor. Caleb Page got 22*l*. extra for surveying, and John Stark more pay than his fellows, for additional work and services as guide.

But our mighty Arosagunticook, or St. Francis tribe of redskins, heard of the act of the General Assembly of New Hampshire almost as soon as it was passed. Although they had no governor, they had a chief; if they had no legislature, they could sit smoking around the council-fire, and debate matters concerning their rude nation of eighteen hundred souls, in a manner more dignified and grave than even the Roman Senate; if they had no money to pay the expense of an expedition to the English settlements, still, their resolve once determined upon, they could find daring, painted, tufted-headed desperadoes enough, to whom the pleasureable prospect — the excitement of burning buildings, groaning victims, sighing captives, and dangling scalp-locks — would be a sufficient inducement to undertake such enterprise.

With a little prompting from the French the war-council decided upon war. But, be it said to their credit, they had learned one principle of christian civilized warfare mentioned in the books that treat of the laws of nations. That was, before open hostilities were commenced in the usual ambuscade fashion, they determined to notify the enemy. Accordingly in the winter of the passage of the act, even before our noted committee with its hardy surveying party had performed its labors, six Indians, (for Indians in those days were as hardy as white men) braved the chill winds of 'Magog lake, rustled the snow from the evergreen firs of the swamps, and with a flag of truce suddenly appeared at the fort in Number Four, now Charleston, N. H.

Captain Stevens, the commander received them in true military style, even as did Cyrus the younger the Queen of Silesia, only not quite so affectionately perhaps; or the great Hannibal, Scipio; or Bonaparte, Lord Wellington. They fared sumptuously upon the good viands within the log fort, dined upon hearty moose-beef and supped upon corn-cakes, washed down with sundry mugs of flip, made hissing-hot with the old-fashioned loggerhead, which was always kept at a white heat.

On the day following their arrival they stated their message. Their orator, drawing himself up full height, asserted their title to the corn patches and pumpkin fields at the long river of pines, which runs through the meadows, under the shadow of the snowy mountain, Moosilauke. "*Our fathers*," said he, "*gave it to us. We have never sold it, never bargained it for the deadly firewater. Why do you trespass upon it? Why wrongfully seek to drive us from our inheritance? Already have your armed men visited it. Already have forts been staked out upon it. We say now, desist! Let not the English come to Cowass. If they do — sure as the heavens above the mountain peaks shall blush in the rosy morning, you shall have war, and it shall be a strong war! Like a wolf on your flocks we will rush on your wives and child-*

ren; like a hurricane uprooting the forest, we will pluck you from the soil!"

This message delivered, the Indians, jolly roisterers, managed to dispose of sundry other mugs of flip, heated in the before-mentioned manner, cut numberless antics and capers around the rude fort, and then whooping a wild applause after their own peculiar style, all of which signified that they liked good rum, took their departure for the St. Lawrence.

Captain Stevens bolted and barred his fortress and posted a stronger guard that night, and the next day, finding that all was quiet, sent off a dispatch to Governor Shirley, of Massachusetts, informing him of the remonstrance and declaration on the part of the Arosagunticooks.

The honorable governor heard the message with astonishment. Rather than the "tufted-headed salvages," should rush down upon the frontier settlers, as the wild clansmen of Scotland did upon merrie England, or as the Nipmucks who lived with their dear French friends had been accustomed to do for the past hundred years, the governor thought they had better be allowed to retain the garden-patch at "Cowas."

With great haste he sent a messenger to Governor Wentworth with the news, who, after considering it for some time with his council, came to the sage conclusion that whereas it was going to cost a large sum of money to make the road, and also as it was going to make the dire and dreadful "salvages" exceedingly wroth, and furthermore as there was a great prospect that a terrible war would shortly break out between France and England, they concluded to abandon the very plan that, in any event, was so necessary for their protection.

Thus the two forts were not built, the four hundred men never went to Coos, the bayonets never gleamed over the still water, and the tramp of the soldier-guard was never heard. The happy land of Warren also bid fair to have grown greener in her mountain solitudes, the white man's footstep to have awoke no echo, his cattle to have browsed in no valley, the bleat of his flocks to have enlivened no hillside for the next half-century, had not an additional train of circumstances, which we shall mention in our next chapter, just now commenced.

H

CHAPTER VI.

HOW SABATIS AND PLAUSAWA FARED IN THE HANDS OF PETER BOWEN, TOGETHER WITH THE MIRACULOUS OPENING OF THE JAIL, CONCLUDING WITH A CAPTIVATING ACCOUNT OF A WHOLE FAMILY, WHO WERE POLITELY INVITED TO GO TO CANADA BY THE GENTLE SALVAGES.

EVERY man admires courage. Marshal Ney, "the bravest of the brave," was the envy of the world; but even his daring feats have many a time been equalled. Unfortunately, the heroes acting on a more obscure stage, unlike the favored French, had no historians, and are consequently forgotten. We do not pretend that every savage is a hero; but many an early pioneer of New England can attest to deeds of fortitude and bravery that can scarcely find a parallel. King Philip, civilized, would have stood beside a Hannibal or an Alexander. Even our friend Sabatis, who stole the negroes, furnishes us with a notable instance of physical daring and moral heroism, or as a latter-day Yankee would express it, of cheek, of brass, of impudence, truly astounding.

That kidnapper, that "brave," who wheedled away the poor "darkies," the great and distinguished Sabatis, accompanied this time by a new friend—Plausawa by name—without even a blush on his red face, but with an assuming air, dared to walk into the highly peaceable and prosperous settlement of Canterbury, the very next June after stealing the negroes. Hunters and trappers, farmers, men from the woods, and men black from the "burnt-piece," with their wives and innocent children, were alike astonished. When they had somewhat recovered from their surprise, they upbraided Sabatis with his treachery.

With a haughty air he said, "Me not to blame; St. Francis Indians no make treaty with the English. No harm to steal niggers; white men steal niggers in Africa! Red men same right to steal niggers in 'Merica." This was an irrefragible argument, equal to that learned from the great Socrates by one Strepsiades, and the white settlers would willingly have allowed him to be a keen logician if they could only have had the pleasure of seeing him cantering fast away from Canterbury.

But Sabatis would not go. He put on airs. Like other men who think they have performed great feats, he became insolent in his conduct, boasted in bragadocia style of what he had done, threatened to butcher the inhabitants, flourished a glittering knife, and like another Jack Falstaff, brave where was no danger, brandished his tomahawk over the head of a defenceless woman.

But worse than this — some keen-eyed settler discovered that he carried, secreted about his person, a collar and lines, nice contrivances with which to fetter captives, and then the whole settlement was alive with the kidnapping affair again. "It might do to steal negroes," said an old farmer, "but 'pon honor it will never do to steal white folks." Brag was a game that two could play at, and some old soldier-citizens of Canterbury, who had seen service at the siege of Louisburg, believed that they themselves would be yet good for blows and even bullets. So when Sabatis commenced his insolence again, he heard something that he had never heard before in that settlement. Gleam of steel shone on steel, and the cry of "Blood for blood!" greeted the ears of the tawny brave. The frontier hamlet grew too hot for the St. Francis men, and one July day they quietly decamped, this time without any prisoners, crossed the bright Merrimack in a beautiful birch canoe, and took up their residence in Contoocook, now Boscawen.

But they had not yet learned to be civil; they were just as insolent as ever. Plunder, captives, and scalps were continually on their tongues, and the whole settlement soon grew heartily sick of them. They were the guests of two men, Messrs. Morrill and Bowen. The first was a farmer, but Peter Bowen was a wild borderer. He knew every trait of Indian character. A hunter and trapper, he had passed half his life in the woods. He was well acquainted with the two Indians and their misdeeds, and knew that they were hated by every settler. For years it was reported how Bowen fought them in self-defence — but this was an idle tale got up for effect. Bowen reasoned in this wise: "The Indians have murdered a great many white men. They say they will murder more. Only last year they stole the negroes. At any moment my neighbor or myself is liable to be killed. Now to protect them and my family, and to get a rich lot of furs — for the Indians in question have two hundred pounds worth — I will put the pestilent serpents out of the way. Every one will justify the deed, and I shall be the gainer."

So when Sabatis and Plausawa were about to leave the settlement, Bowen invited them to have a treat at his house. Both Indians got drunk, and Bowen drew the charges from their guns. Then, when they departed, they went into the woods towards the Merrimack. The Indians got separated some distance apart and then Bowen attacked Sabatis. The drunken brave snapped his gun at him, but Bowen sank a hatchet to the helve in his brain, cut him with it several times in the back, and plunged a hunting-knife into his heart. Plausawa coming up begged for his life. Bowen answered not a word, but killed him on the spot.*

That night he left them by the path-side. The gibbous moon looked through the trees upon their upturned, ghastly faces. The wolf howled on the mountain as he scented their blood afar, and the solemn owl hooted in harsh, discordant notes — nature's requiem over wild spirits departed, whose earthly delight had been human butchery.

On the morrow Bowen returned with his son, scooped a shallow hole and threw the bodies in, slightly covering them with earth and leaves. But wild animals and dogs dug them up, and for years afterwards their white bones bleached by the road side in the woods.

Indian hunters, who had come to the settlements to traffic, heard of the murder of the two Indians, and bore the news to the St. Francis.

The New Hampshire authorities also heard the story. As in duty bound, the government officials clapped a legal hand upon

---

* Potter's Hist. of Manchester, 281.

Morrill and Bowen. Like Paul and Silas they were borne away to prison, yet for a very unlike cause. They were incarcerated within the walls of the old jail at Portsmouth. That they might not attempt the role of Jack Shepard, their limbs were placed in iron manacles. They were indicted for murder, and were to have their trial March 21st, 1754.

Telegraphic operators sometimes send messages without the aid of a battery. The air, overcharged with electricity, produces an almost magical effect upon the wires, and with hardly an effort the thoughts of the operator leap thousands of miles away. Although there was no telegraph at that time, still a subtle and mysterious agency, almost as wonderful, seemed to be at work. It pervaded every settlement. An almost unexplainable attraction seemed to impel men, and on the cold night of March 20th, as the story is told, hundreds were threading their way through the dark and the storm. Down by Dover Neck, along by Squamscott's snowy banks they came, and up by the ocean shore, where the waves were " roaring on the rocks."

At midnight scores of dark forms crouched under the walls of the jail, and then simultaneously rushed at the gate, broke it in, knocked the irons from the limbs of Morrill and Bowen, and set them free. In the morning a thrill of excitement ran through the community. Law-abiding citizens demanded their recapture; but the larger number rejoiced at their escape. The two men were generally justified. The best men in New Hampshire had aided them. Governor Wentworth offered a reward for their recapture, but no man troubled himself to apprehend them. In a short time they went wholly at large, and an arrest could not easily have been made. If it had been, as in the case of James the Second, every body would have been displeased with the captors, and would have given the Indian killers a chance to run away again as fast as they were able.

But something must be done to appease the Indians, who were not so readily satisfied. New Hampshire therefore sent presents to the relatives of Sabatis and Plausawa, and with them the blood was wiped out—but not so with the St. Francis people. They were enraged; they muttered threats of vengeance. The retaliating blow was planned, and "like a thunderbolt it fell on the

infant settlement, but a kind Providence partly averted its effects."
It was May 11th, 1754, one of the brightest days of spring.
A party of thirty Indians, every one of them painted like a circus
clown, and with scalp-locks dancing in the wind, had come down
from Canada. Nathaniel Meloon and William Emery, who lived
in Stevenstown, now a part of Franklin, discovered them the night
before. Emery was a wide-awake man, and he immediately took
his family to a garrison-house near by. But Meloon was dilatory,
and like the Mr. Slow mentioned in Mother Goose's melodies, was
given to procrastination. His family were all at home in unconscious innocence, except one son, Nathaniel, Jr., who was at work
in a field near by. They were taking a hearty breakfast of bean
porridge, when they were startled by the wild whoop of the
Indians, who had captured the elder and slow Meloon, as he was
returning from the garrison.

The capture of the family was also but the work of a moment,
and then the painted demons, to speak in the respectful language
of earlier historians, brandished their tomahawks and flourished
their scalping-knives, as they proceeded to rip open feather-beds,
for the sake of the ticks, and to steal all the clothing and provision they could lay their hands upon.

In a wonderfully short time they served Emery's house in the
same manner and then, before the sun was very high, were all on
their way to Canada.

Meloon, junior, who had seen the Indians approach, fled five
miles as fast as his legs could carry him, to Contoocook, raised
eight men, and hurried back to the rescue. But he was too late.
Father, mother, sisters, brother, had been gone for hours.*

The people of Stevenstown and Contoocook were terribly
aroused by the Indian depredations. It was necessary to do something, and so Stephen Gerrish was dispatched to Portsmouth. On
the 17th of May—quick time in those days of tote-roads and
bridle-paths—he laid a petition before the Governor and Council,
signed by all the inhabitants, praying for assistance.

"Oh! how we wish the forts at Coos intervals had been
built," said one; "And the four hundred stout men with mus-

---

* Meloon and his family, with the exception of one child, Sarah, who died in
Canada, all got safe home about four years afterwards, having experienced numerous hardships and many strange adventures.—Potter's Hist. of Manchester, 283.

kets," added another; "Then our settlers would have been secure," said all. But it was of no use to wish that. The next best thing, however, could be done. What that was it took a long time to determine. But finally, with great wisdom and foresight on the part of His Excellency the Governor, and his council, it was ordered that *twenty mounted men*—good cavalry soldiers—should be sent to the woods of Contoocook and Stevenstown, riding through underbrush and over windfalls, across marshes, bogs, and fens, with what effectiveness must be very plain to every one familiar with the north woods of New Hampshire.

CHAPTER VII.

HOW CAPTAIN PETER POWERS MARCHED GALLANTLY THROUGH THE PEMIGEWASSETT COUNTRY TO THE LAND OF THE COOSUCKS, OF A BRAVE EXPLOIT AND A HEROIC RETREAT.

THE wild moss-troopers—brave cavalry soldiers as they were—scouted valiantly in the shaggy woods of Contoocook and Stevenstown. For a month they galloped up hill and for a month they galloped down. Not a red-skin was discovered, for with their prisoners and plunder they had all gone to Canada. Yet we would not detract a particle from the merit of the brave English scouts. Captain John Webster was leader, and a bold man was he. James Proctor was lieutenant and Christopher Gould was clerk. But their month's term of duty soon expired and they returned home, having done good service in beating the bush without catching the bird.

But the high functionaries of the royal province of New Hampshire, so loyal to George the Third—for the reader must recollect that our worthy ancestry once lived under a king— were not satisfied with the results of the expedition. They had been frightened out of the plan of building strong fortresses at Coos, and now they believed it necessary to hold that territory with companies of scouts and rangers. So another expedition was immediately planned, and Captain Peter Powers, of Hollis, N. H., was put in command. James Stevens was his lieutenant, and Ephraim Hale, ensign. Both these latter were from Townsend, Massachusetts.

And here, by the way, we must acknowledge our obligations to the first historian of Coos, the Rev. Grant Powers, in most respects truthful, yet not without family pride. This is plainly exhibited when he tries to exalt Captain Peter, his grandfather or great-uncle — no matter which — into a distinguished traveller, like Marco Polo of former times, or a Humboldt of later days; or into a great military hero and explorer, like John Charles Fremont, who rode a woolly horse over a mountain 18,000 feet high! But we honor the historian for wringing from oblivion so many important facts of history that would soon have been lost forever.

Captain Powers was an active man. His company immediately rendezvoused at Rumford, formerly Pennacook, now Concord, N. H. It was June 14th, 1754, when the last man of the party arrived there. On Saturday, the 15th, they proceeded to Contoocook, where they tarried over the Sabbath and went to meeting, as good Christians should.

Let us now pause here for a moment. It is no holiday excursion upon which these stout hearts are entering. No one of all the gallant heroes who had formerly headed expeditions against the bloodthirsty Arosagunticooks, had ever penetrated much farther north than the White mountains; but now Captain Powers was going to eclipse all the historic deeds of previous brave Indian fighters, to plunge further into the wilderness, and perform deeds of glory that should render him immortal.

We have said they were all ready for a brave dash into the northern wilderness, and so on Monday morning, the 17th, at the first dawn, they put their baggage into their canoes. By nine o'clock A. M., a part on the shore, a part in their light barks, they were hurrying up the Merrimack. The painted salvages were in the upper country, and Captain Powers' men were eager for the fray. They passed the forks, or "crotch" of the river, where the "dark Aquadocta" mingles with the bright Pemigewassett, pushed up the latter stream, toted their baggage and canoes round the falls and camped the first night at the head of "the hundred rod carrying place."

Beautiful weather greeted them in the morning, and they shot rapidly up the winding stream, shut in by green woods. The winds piped in the foliage, and the wood-thrush mingled his sweetest melody with the roar of Sawheganet falls. Here they saw great fat salmon shooting up the rushing waters. They looked into the dark opening from whence came Squam river, flowing from the most beautiful New England lake; gazed with delight on the broad intervals of Plymouth, and saw in the distance the sharp Haystacks, yet white with winter's snow.*

They turned up the Asquamchumauke, otherwise called Baker river, which came down from the west, and paddled their light canoes rapidly along its crooked and sluggish course. The fourth day, the setting sun half an hour high, saw them camped at the foot of Rattlesnake mountain,† the most bold and precipitous peak in the valley, and its towering cliffs echoed to the report of their muskets, as they shot a moose for their supper. They left their canoes in the shoal head water of the river, thought they would try the west route to the Connecticut, and that night they camped between the two Baker ponds in the present town of Orford.

Storms of "haile" and "heavy showers of raine" kept them here for two days. This detention very much tried the patience of the Captain and his trusty scouts. They were eager to cope with the brave salvages, whom they expected to find at the head of the long river towards which they were hastening.

But Captain Powers managed to while away the time, watch-

---

*"*Wednesday, June 19th*, 1654.— We marched on our journey, and carried across the long carrying place on Pemigewassett river, two miles north-east, which land hath a good soil, beech and maple, with a good quantity of large masts. From the place where we put in the canoes we steered east, north-east, up the river about one mile, and then we steered north-east one mile, and north six miles, up to Sawheganet Falls, where we carried by about four rods; and from the falls we steered about north-east to Pemigewasset interval, two miles, and from the beginning of the interval we made good our course north four miles, and there camped on a narrow point of land. The last four miles of the river was extremely crooked."

"*Thursday, June 20th.*— We steered our course one turn with another, which were great turns, west north-west, about two miles and a half, to the crotch, or parting of the Pemigewasset river at Baker river mouth, thence from the mouth of Baker river, up said river, north-west six miles. This river is extraordinarily crooked, and good interval. Thence up the river about two miles, northwest, and there we shot a moose, the sun about a half an hour high, and there camped."

[This must have been in the town of Romney.]

"*Friday, June 21st.*— We steered up the said Baker river with our canoes about five miles, as the river ran, which was extraordinarily crooked. In the after part of this day there was a great shower of 'haile and raine,' which prevented our proceeding further and here we camped: and here we left our canoes, for the water in the river was so shoal that we could not go with them any further."

"*Saturday, June, 22d.*—This morning was dark and cloudy weather, but after ten of the clock, it cleared off hot, and we marched up the river, near the Indian carrying place, from Baker river to Connecticut river, and there camped, and could not go any further by reason of a great shower of rain, which held almost all this afternoon."—Capt. Peter Powers' Journal, Hist. of Coos, 18.

†Powers says the inhabitants of our valley can without doubt fix upon Capt. Peter's several encampments with tolerable accuracy, and that it must be very interesting to mark out the places which were thus occupied by swords and bristling bayonets in 1754, whilst the whole country around remained an unbroken wilderness.—History of Coos, 19.

ing the clouds whirling around the summits of the lofty eastern mountains, and writing in his journal of the broad and fertile intervals, the beautiful white pine that grew upon them, and how "back from the intreval is a considerable quantity of large mountains" which he looked upon with much admiration.

Reader, think of the forest stretching a hundred miles away, unbroken by a single white man's clearing; of the bright lakes, the silver rivers winding through the woods; of the wild and savage beasts that roamed and howled and bellowed therein; of the great shaggy mountains, "daunting terrible;" of the numerous cruel murders committed on the frontiers by the Indians; of this company of stalwart hearts, camped in storm of "haile and raine and thunder," beside these exceedingly solitary ponds in the basin of the great mountains, each man eager with trusty "Queen's arm" to hurry further away into the wilderness, to fight what were to them veritable "painted, red demons;" perchance to be slain, to be scalped, to be devoured by wolves, or to rot in some cold swamp—and you have the romance of Captain Powers' expedition. Truly one might expect heroic deeds from such brave men.

On Tuesday, June 25th, they struck Connecticut river. Proceeding up the east bank they crossed the Oliverian, swollen by the great rain, and pushed rapidly forward until they came to the mouth of the Ammonoosuc. Here they tarried a day, built a canoe with which to cross the latter stream, and there dismissing four of the men who were lame, sent them in it down the Connecticut to "Number Four."

From Ammonoosuc river they went tramping through the woods northward, over John's river and over Israel's river, to the beautiful interval of upper Coos. On this interval the brave Captain left his soldiers to mend their shoes, and with two men proceeded up the Connecticut "to see what they could discover."

Five miles on he met with an Indian encampment—a sight that gladdened his very eyes—and found where not more than two days before they had constructed several canoes. Like every other great military hero, he was now eager for the contest; so, musing on this sight for a few moments, he returned to his men. They were soon mustered in battle-array. A council of war was held. That their shoes were worn out, that their provisions were nearly gone, that they were foot-sore and lame, and that their hail-pelted bodies were rheumatic — was all true. But notwithstanding this, now was the time, and they determined to make a vigorous campaign after the Indians, and if possible to eclipse the renown of the bold cavalry troopers in the woods of Stevenstown and Contoocook. To do this it was necessary there should be a change of base. Strategy must be used, and this should be the great plan: They would advance towards home on the double-quick; the "painted salvages" of course would pursue them; the bold strategists would then make a deadly ambuscade, and there shoot and capture the whole Arosagunticook army.

And here some skeptical reader may ask us where we got our information. We can only reply, if this was not the "plan," what was it?

But the Indians, obdurate pagans, did not pursue, although Captain Powers advanced homeward most gallantly. We are sincerely sorry they did not, for we are thereby prevented from recording a most fierce fight, wherein Captain Peter and his men would have won immortal renown, and some hallowed spot on "the long river of pines" would have been as celebrated as the mouth of Baker river or Lovewell's pond.

The last we hear of the war-party they are hurrying on through the gap of the eastern mountains — the Oliverian* notch — to their canoes waiting in the Asquamchumauke. No doubt they reached home in safety, for we never heard anything to the contrary, told big stories of their brave exploits to the day of their death, relating how they enjoyed themselves killing moose and deer, and eating the same, how they saw the pleasant lands about Moosilauke and the head waters of the Asquamchumauke, and how they got well paid in "old tenor" money for these important services.

In all probability the Governor thought this expedition would aid materially in keeping off the Indians; indeed, much more than

---

* *Saturday, July 6.* — Marched down the great river to Great Coos, and crossed the river below the great turn of clear interval, *and there left the great river, and steered south by east* about three miles and there camped. — Powers' Hist. of Coos, 31.

Powers says he knows no more of the homeward march. The journal ceases at the point where he left the river. — Do. 32.

the two forts which were to have stood on the Coos intervals, or the four hundred armed men who were to have held them, or than even the two score of moss-troopers at Contoocook and Stevenstown. But how great must have been his surprise at the shocking deeds committed by the Arosagunticook braves in a very few days after Captain Powers' gallant change of base, as will be truthfully set forth in this brief history of Indian wars, in which the armies marched and countermarched through our much loved territory of Warren.

CHAPTER VIII.

OF A GALLANT EXPLOIT ON THE NEW HAMPSHIRE FRONTIER, OF AN EXCITED CAMP ON THE SHORE OF WACHIPAUKA POND, WITH OTHER ENTERTAINING AND CURIOUS MATTER, VERY INTERESTING TO KNOW.

EVERY child of New England has heard of the old French war. It had much to do with the settlement of our mountain hamlet, Warren — almost as much as the creation of the world, or the discovery of America by Christopher Colon. The narration of all its great and important events would be decidedly foreign to our purpose, and we prefer to place ourselves immediately *in medias res*, and only describe those extraordinary occurrences that served to make the Indian corn-fields and pumpkin patches, fishing waters and *hunting grounds* under the shadows of bald Moosilauke, so well-known.

War was declared in Europe in 1753. A colonial congress met at Albany, New York, in 1754, to devise means of defence. Canada roused the Indians to further hostilities, and the New Hampshire frontier bled again.

Like a wolf skulking about a sheep-fold, or a thief crawling down chimney at night, thirty brave Indian fellows, armed cap-a-pie, guns on their shoulders, scalping-knives in their belts, plumes in their tufted scalp-locks waving like the white feather of Murat, bright uniforms in the shape of dirty breech-clouts, and moose-hide moccasins, came down for open war.

'Twas the morn of August 15th. Jolly Phœbus had just cooled his hissing hot axletrees in the cold currents of the Atlantic, and was driving pell-mell up the eastern sky, when the above-mentioned war party boldly marched into a little clearing in Stevenstown. A one-story log cabin, with a cow pen and pig sty near by, stood on one side of the small field. Mrs. Call, her daughter-in-law, wife of Philip Call, and an infant of the latter, were there. Mr. Call, and young Call, and Timothy Cook were at work on the other side of the clearing.*

The braves made directly for the house. Mrs. Call, like a Spartan mother or a Roman matron, bravely met them at the door. Without a word the foremost Indian with a blow of his tomahawk felled her to the earth, and her warm blood drenched the threshhold. Kicking her dead body aside they rushed into the house. The young woman crept into a hole behind the chimney, kept her child quiet, and escaped.

The father and son, and Timothy Cook, attempted to get into the house before the Indians but did not succeed. They heard the blow that knocked down Mrs. Call, her scream and death groan, and the wild war whoop, and then, as the savages rushed towards them they fled. Cook, like Horatius Cocles, leaped into the river; but unlike that Roman swimmer, did not reach the opposite shore. The Indians shot him from the bank. Dragging him from the water they peeled off his scalp, served Mrs. Call's head in the same manner, rifled the house, and then took to the woods.

The flying Calls notified the garrison at Contoocook, and a party of eight immediately went in pursuit. The Indians as yet had taken no prisoners, and without these to sell to the French the expedition would be unprofitable. So one Indian got beside a stump, another under a windfall, a third behind a greenwood tree, and whole squads lay down beneath thick clumps of bushes or the deep green branches of the fir copse. In other words, they made a regular ambuscade.

But somehow the keen-eyed settlers discovered them at a distance, thanks to their good fortune, and ran away as fast as they could, with the Indians in full pursuit. But one Enos Bishop, who was not very nimble-footed, had the ill luck to be captured. The rest of the party escaped. The captured man was then compelled to go with the enemy, and was that day marched a long way towards the captive's happy land, Canada.

---

* Potter's Hist of Manchester, 291.

Now it chanced that one Samuel Scribner and one John Barker—we won't accuse them of laziness—had left their haying and clearing, and were looking after beaver meadows near Newfound lake. It was a hot afternoon and they were sitting in the shade of a wide-spreading maple, by the shore of the bright, sparkling water, when the Indians suddenly came upon them. They were so completely taken by surprise that resistance or escape was hopeless, and much against their inclination they were compelled to leave the crystal sheen, low set among the dark brown hills, and grace the captors' train.

Tradition has it that the war party feared pursuit, and hurried rapidly forward by the shortest route.* The second night they halted by a little lake called in the Indian tongue, as we have before said, Wachipauka,† but by modern civilians, Meader pond. They built their camp and kindled their fire on the rocky beach. On the opposite shore a precipitous peak shot a thousand feet into the clear blue sky. During the evening hours the stars glimmered on the cool night-air, the full moon shone brightly on the dark water, and its rays glinted from the granite mountain. At midnight a black cloud spread across the sky, darkness grew grimmer, and a thick fog from the Connecticut, that had crept up the gorge of the Oliverian, settling dank and heavy on the craggy mountain brow, made the night still more black. At this moment John Barker rose silently among the sleeping Indians, glided over them like a pale ghost, unbound Bishop, and gently endeavored to wake him. Just then a wolf howled on the mountain top, a great owl in a lofty hemlock answered back the wild cry, and a sudden gust of wind whirled a shower of sparks into the dark shadows of the woods. An Indian, dreaming perhaps of the land of shades, was startled. He caught sight of the dim form of Barker bending over his companions. Leaping to his feet he uttered the war whoop. Across the lake the echo-god returned the wild battle-shout, and every brave sprang for his musket and his tomahawk. Barker was seized and doubly bound, the other captives were made more secure, and thereby a second Mrs. Duston tragedy was

---

*The Indians had a route by the lake, north, and they knew the shortest paths as well as the white men.
Acteon often told this story.

†Wachipauka is from Wadchu, mountain, Sipes, still water, and auke.

prevented. There was no more sleep in the Indian camp that night, and at the earliest dawn they were threading their way down the wild, roaring Oliverian, to the Connecticut.

In thirteen days they arrived at St. Francis village. Bishop and his good friends rejoiced, for they were leg-weary, foot-sore, and half-starved. Where Bishop was placed is not told, but Scribner was sold to a Frenchman at Chamblay, and the valiant Barker to a jolly man of the same race, who lived near the Indian village.

Enos Bishop practiced with his heels that year, and one night ran away, as any other white man would have done under similar circumstances.* But he had a hard time of it. After toiling for eighteen days through the wilderness, suffering intensely from fatigue and hunger, he reached Number Four, from whence he returned to his family at Contoocook. Barker and Scribner were shortly after redeemed.

Precisely in the same manner as when Meloon and his family were captured, the inhabitants on the frontier were all terribly frightened. Andrew McClary, of Epsom, a descendant of the Scotch covenanters, was deputed Mercury. Like the swift son of Maiæ, with winged feet he flew to Portsmouth and narrated to the Honorable Governor and the worthy council the sad deaths of Mrs. Call and Timothy Cook, the probable capture of the missing men, and the great fight of the renowned eight, who went out to see the Indians, while only seven returned, and that every family on the frontier, to the number of eight all told, had left their fields, corn, hay, flocks, herds, and homes, and had come down to the lower towns.

His Excellency was astounded. The council looked aghast. But they proved themselves equal to the great emergency. The trumpet was not immediately sounded, but the decree went forth.

---

*Extract of a letter from an officer in Charleston, otherwise called Number Four, in the province of New Hampshire, dated October 4th, 1756:

"This day arrived here one Enoch Byshop, an English captive from Canada, who was taken from Contoocook about two years since. He left Canada twenty-six days ago, in company with two other English captives, viz: William Hair, entered into General Shirley's regiment, and taken at Osewego, (the other name unknown). They came away from Canada, without guns, hatchet or fire-works, and no more than three loaves of bread and four pounds of pork. As they suffered much for want of provisions, his companions were not able to travel any further than a little on this side of Cowass, where he was obliged to leave them last Lord's day, without any sustenance but a few berries. Six men were this evening sent out to look for them, but it is to be feared that they perished in the wilderness."—[Copied from the New York Mercury of October 25th, 1756, in the library of the N. Y. Hist. Soc., by John Libbey].

But that they might show themselves men of deliberation and firmness, they caused said decree to be entered on the council minutes as follows: "*Whereas*, That the settlers might be encouraged to return to their habitations and secure their cattle and harvests, and to encourage other frontiers in that quarter, His Excellency be desired to give immediate orders for enlisting or impressing such a number of men as he may think proper, and dispose of the same."

Governor Wentworth acted. A detachment of Capt. Odlin's troop of twenty horse, with an officer in command, also a like detachment of Capt. Stevens' troop, were ordered to Stevenstown to guard the inhabitants on the frontier.

But Governor Wentworth was no fool. The idea did creep into his head that a few foot soldiers, fitted out in the Indian style, would be about as effective in fighting the painted red-skins as good cavalry troopers. Whereupon he immediately issued a further order to Colonel Joseph Blanchard, that he forthwith enlist and impress fifty, or more men, if he thought that number insufficient, that he put them under an able and brave officer, one in whom he could confide, and order them to march immediately to Contoocook and Stevenstown. Then he added—and may be the framers of the great constitution of the United States copied this illustrious example when they inserted the clause whereby Congress should vote supplies for the army,—"I have convened the General Assembly. It will vote pay and supplies. The soldiers shall not want."

Colonel Blanchard was a brave officer. He immediately performed his duty. Our brave Captain John Goffe, of Amoskeag, marched to the scene of action. He behaved valiantly. For many a hot summer day he scouted through all the wild border, far up the Merrimack towards our beloved land, but not an Indian did he encounter.

And here a great historian, a lover of that race whose council fires have gone out, whose war songs are no longer heard, whose name only is chronicled by their destroyers, exclaims with much dignity and self-congratulation, that "the promptness of Governor Wentworth in this emergency, and the effective force detailed, preserved the inhabitants of the Merrimack valley from any further molestation," when in fact there was not an Indian within a hundred miles of the place, and there did not choose to be. They had accomplished their purpose, and laughing in their moccasins, with dangling scalp locks and groaning captives they had gone to Canada.

Men frequently buy a padlock for the stable door after the horse is stolen. So New Hampshire afforded protection after the blow was struck.

But if Governor Wentworth did protect the Merrimack valley he did not the Connecticut, and he would have displayed his promptness to better advantage if he had also sent a "scout" to the latter place for a "preventive," as we shall immediately proceed to show.

CHAPTER IX.

ACCOUNT OF THE MANNER THE BRAVE AROSAGUNTICOOKS OF ST. FRANCIS PASSED CAPTAIN GOFFE; THE CAPTURE OF THE JOHNSON FAMILY, WITH OTHER INCIDENTS NO DOUBT VERY INTERESTING TO THE PARTICIPANTS; TOGETHER WITH THE FIRST CAMPAIGN OF THE OLD FRENCH WAR.

THE St. Francis Indians, the great nation of the Arosagunticooks, were cunning men. Whether, like the Spartan youth, their understanding was cultivated in order that they might successfully practice craft, shrewdness, and honorable deception in war is not recorded, but we rather suspect it was. Like the Spartans also they had a terse brevity in their speech that might well be termed *laconic*. But, unlike the Spartans, they were fond of rough romance and poetry. There is no doubt of this. Many a wild legend could their medicine man recount; many a plaintive air did the Indian lover sing, as with palpitating heart he wood his dusky mate; and they always went forth to battle with the war-song pealing high. But the modest souls would never sing when they came near the enemy.

Captain Goffe scouted up the Merrimack. He paddled his canoe in the bright Pemigewassett and turned its prow up the Asquamchumauke. He snuffed the winds laden with forest sweets, as over bending woods and rustling leaves they came frolicking on their way from the Haystacks. And on the very morn of the day of his return, when Aurora stepped blushing like a modest damsel into the eastern sky, and the sunbeams were kindling in purple and gold on Moosilauke's bald crest, about thirty mighty savages were over the highlands in the Connecticut valley, and already were hurrying down "the long river of pines." Two days afterwards, August 29th, they were at Number Four. Downy couches on the bosom of mother earth did not woo their slumbers long. They were early risers. They leaped over the hedge on the border of the woods before a white man was stirring or a blue smoke curling from a cabin chimney. But a white family did stir quickly in James Johnson's house two minutes afterwards. Johnson, wife, three children, and Miriam Williard, Mrs. Johnson's sister, together with Peter Larabee and Ebenezer Farnsworth, who were lodging there that night, with all the household provisions and furniture to which the "war-hawks" took a fancy, constituted the *spolia optima*. These captives and this plunder were about as much as the war party could conveniently manage, and so they concluded to instantly decamp. As their appearance had been sudden, their disappearance was more so. Not a white settler knew of the dire catastrophe for a long time afterwards.

But the spoils were cumbersome, the children were young, and Mrs. Johnson in a very critical condition, so they did not travel very far that day. On the morrow, in the deep wilderness, fifteen miles from her home, Mrs. Johnson gave birth to a daughter. The sailor boy, born on the deep blue sea, has Neptune beating time with foamy trident to his own deep basso of thanksgiving and praise at the christening, so that ever after the boy loves the crested waves and the music of the winds piping in the shrouds. So Ceres, the earth mother, assisted at the birth of the forest child, and all the sylvan nymphs danced for joy, as they crowned the little cherub with garlands of wild-flowers, kissed dimples into her rosy cheeks and covered with nectar her glowing lips.

The mother called the daughter "CAPTIVE." But whether in after life she loved the wild woods, its cool dells and shaded grottos, its deep green foliage, its singing birds, its wild wind sighing through the branches, or its deep and awful roar in the storm—like the voice of the distant ocean—we cannot say. All we do know of her further is that she lived to be married like other women, and found a kind husband in one George Kimball. He was a colonel of foot-soldiers, but whether serving in the militia or in the wars we were never informed.

The Indians may be called cruel savages for carrying off this family and plundering their dwelling; but this time they can not be called human butchers. As our readers must already know, they did not dash out little Captive's brains against the nearest tree; on the contrary, they kindly cared for her, waited a whole day for Mrs. Johnson, carried the unfortunate mother on a litter, and afterwards it is said, though we somewhat doubt it, furnished her with a horse. Like a man who would keep his ox well, or like the master who would have fat sleek slaves, this was not all done out of pure kindness of heart. On reaching Canada the Indians sold all the big captives—and little Captive also—to the French for a good round sum. But an early historian of this sad tale says that they met with great difficulties and experienced great suffering at the hands of these polite descendants of the noble Franks. After two long years, Mrs. Johnson, her sister, and two daughters returned home. Where went Larabee and Farnsworth is not recorded. Mr. Johnson did not behave in a manner satisfactory to the hospitable sons of Gaul, and so for three years he was kindly suffered to pine in a Canadian prison. At the end of that time he with his son had the good fortune to return to Number Four by way of Boston.

But the eldest daughter had a different fate. Like many another giddy damsel, she became deeply enamored of the things of the new country. She became either so exceedingly wise or foolish, we can hardly tell which, that she fell in love with a shaved head, a straight gown, a white veil, a string of beads, a Latin prayer-book, and a chapel bell, and in a nunnery concluded to spend a portion of her days in the enjoyment of "those religious festivities in which some priests, certain shaking quaker elders, and not a few ministers, so much delight."*

If a messenger went to Portsmouth to tell of this hostile inroad of the enemy, we are not informed of the fact. At any rate no particular notice was taken of it. Settlers in the Connecticut valley might take care of themselves or look to Massachusetts for aid. New Hampshire could not now attend to them. The times were pregnant with great events. Even the shrieking

---

*Thus wrote certain historians long ago; but it must be remembered that they hated all religions except their own.

autumn blast portended horrid war. Mars, hot and fierce, leaped across the Atlantic on an angry visit to the New World. All the gods buckled on their armor and put themselves in battle array. The mighty deep was lashed in fury, as hostile fleets swept over it; the pent-up fires in the earth beneath blazed anew under the tramp of hostile squadrons, and the awful bolts of Jove thundered at mid-winter in the heavens.

Three armies, such as the western world had never before seen, were put in rapid motion. General Braddock, accompanied by Washington, penetrated the southern wilderness. His destination was Fort Du Quesne, on the Ohio river. But he never reached it. He perished, with three-fourths of his gallant soldiers, in the dark forests of the Alleghanies. Governer Shirley led a second army against Fort Niagara. With his cannon he was to batter down its strong walls. But their roar never mingled with the thunder of the mighty cataract near which stood the fortress. The expedition was a failure. General Johnston led a third force against Fort Edward. And here fortune favored the hero. New Hampshire furnished a regiment for his army, commanded by Colonel Blanchard, of Dunstable, now Nashua.

How they rendezvoused at Stevenstown, and marched and countermarched through our beloved Pemigewassett country, up the Asquamchumauke, and across the land now called Warren and so to the Coos country, we shall endeavor most faithfully to narrate.

CHAPTER X.

TREATING OF THE ASSEMBLING OF THE REGIMENT AND THE BUILD-
ING OF THE LOG FORTRESS AT COOS, WITH OTHER INTERESTING
ADVENTURES IN THE COUNTRY ABOUT LAKE CHAMPLAIN.

THE call to arms was sounded. Mars' messengers went forth and New Hampshire was quick to respond. In the style of the old Scotch poets it is related how from Strawberry Bank, Boar's Head, and Dover Neck, came a company of hardy ship builders, cod fishers, and fur traders,—men used to hard knocks, to ocean's battling storms, and cunning wiles of Indians. From Squamscott's winding valley, Newichannock's bright stream, and Pautuckaway's deep indented shores, came a company of stalwart farmers, full fifty strong. From Massabesic's blue waves, the twin Uncanoonucks, and the falls of Amoskeag, came Fraziers, McKenzies, Campbells, and Grants, Scotia's descendants, amounting to two full companies. The latter were potato-planting men, linen spinners,—besides numerous shad, eel, and salmon fishers — all good tough fellows, used to shillalah fights, and not a few had taken many a bout in the woods after the Indians. From the pebbly-bottomed Nashua, the cloud-capped Monadnock, and the frontier about bristling Kearsarge, came farmers, hunters, trappers, and wild borderers. Captain Goffe and Captain Moore, both brave Derryfielders, men who never quailed beneath the Indian's eagle eye (to put it grandly), and who loved the music of the whirring tomahawk and the singing shot, each commanded a company.

Captain Robert Rogers, of Starkstown, now Dunbarton, whom the war-cry of a thousand braves could not move a hair, marched at the head of seventy jolly bruisers, who were accustomed to fish at Amoskeag falls. Noah Johnson was one of his lieutenants and John Stark was the other. The latter was now a long, lank young man, with a frame not encased in a coat of mail, but in iron muscle, with a physique which could endure without a moment's sleep a march of a hundred long miles through the snow when four feet deep. With these lieutenants, Rogers had the bravest company of the old French war. They were known as the "Rangers." They carried but little baggage and were lightly armed; and as the French employed the Indians, so were these employed by the English to scour the woods, to waylay the enemy, or to obtain supplies.

As Xerxes rendezvoused at Capadocian Critella, or the Greeks of Cyrus the Younger at Sardis, so all these great companies, fully equipped, with knapsacks on their backs, canteens and haversacks at their sides, and old queen's arms on their shoulders, debouched from the deep wilderness upon the broad Merrimack intervals at Bakerstown, alias Stevenstown, now Franklin, N. H. Colonel Blanchard, of Dunstable, as we have before stated, was the great generalissimo or commander-in-chief.

There was a log fortress in the centre of the black stump clearing at Stevenstown. The said clearing was afterwards a fine field, owned by the Hon. Daniel Webster. Around the above-mentioned fortress Colonel Blanchard mustered his regiment, while all day long was heard the din of preparation, as the sappers and miners and artisans were engaged in building bateaux on the river bank. With these they were going to transport their baggage along the navigable waters.

Governor Wentworth, as we have before shown, was an exceedingly learned man in the arts of war. He had sent good cavalry soldiers, jolly moss-troopers, to scout through the windfalls and tangled thickets. He was also a man of taste and fond of artistic beauty. This was very commendable, and he exhibited it by building for himself a beautiful rustic residence on the shore of Lake Winnepisseogee, from the silver surface of which as he glided along in his sailboat he could see the gaged hackmatack mountains in the great wild north. He now showed himself a greater geographer than Ptolemy or Christopher Columbus himself, for he verily believed that Albany, the place to which he was to send the regiment, lay in the path of a direct line drawn from Stevenstown to the north pole. Besides, all his council and confidential advisers believed the same. So the order was issued to Colonel Blanchard, and that gallant officer in turn commanded Captain Rogers to proceed with his rangers due north one degree west to the upper Coos meadows, and there construct a fort for the accommodation of the little army when it should follow.

The rangers left the old garrison house in the before-mentioned field and followed the trail up the Merrimack. With their trusty queen's arms on their shoulders, their hunting knives in their belts, their wolf-skin caps, their bright red shirts, buttoned close about their throats, their short sheep's-gray frocks tucked within their moose hide or sheep-skin pants, and with real Indian moccasins on their feet, the rangers presented even a more picturesque appearance than their painted foe, with tufted scalp-locks, dirty breech clouts, and long-haired leggins.

They pushed up the Asquamchumauke, camped one night on the shore of the cold mountain lake, Wachipauka, under the shadow of precipitous Webster Slide, and in six days reached the upper meadows. They built the fort on the east bank of the Connecticut, just below the mouth of the upper Ammonoosuc river, in the present town of Northumberland. It was constructed of huge logs from the dense wilderness and the summer winds now sighed through the thick leaved trees and anon moaned around the picketted palisades of the wooden fortress.

After they had completed the work of course there must be a christening. So each ranger took a good swig of old West India from his canteen—thus pouring a libation to the sylvan deities. Then an old soldier, mounting the topmost timber, delivered himself of a short speech, this being a part of the ceremony of "naming the building," as was the old time-out-of-mind custom, in which without doubt he remarked what a good geographer the governor was, and ended by calling the stronghold, Fort Wentworth. Then the orator descended from the rostrum, and the whole company joined in three lusty cheers, which awoke all the bats, owls, and similar drowsy gods for many a league around. They then sat down to a bountiful feast of corn cakes and 'fresh moose meat, of which last they had taken care to secure an ample quantity.

On the morrow a messenger came. His Excellency had discovered a slight mistake in his reckoning. He had come to the sage conclusion that Albany lay nearer a line drawn due west from Stevenstown to China than that to the north pole. Captain Rogers received a different order. With his rangers he left the ungarrisoned fort to slowly rot away under the shadow of the white summits of Percy peaks, and marched directly to Number Four. From thence with the rest of the regiment they struggled through the wilderness over the Green mountains and joined General Lyman, who commanded the New England troops.

In the campaigns about Lake George, Crown Point, and Ticonderoga, the whole New Hampshire regiment, by their endurance and daring, won an enviable reputation. But Rogers—who soon rose to the rank of Major—far exceeded all the rest with his bold rangers. They fought like heroes every man, when at the capitulation of Oswego the savages butchered the captive English by scores. They were the bravest of the brave, when at Fort William Henry the butchery of Oswego was re-enacted with additional scenes of horror.

The heroes of Charles the Twelfth never won brighter renown than the New Hampshire contingent, when Rogers with only one hundred and eighty of his rangers fell into an ambush of over seven hundred French and Indians. At midwinter, with the mercury below zero, in a dense forest, and with the snow four feet deep, they fought all day long. The blood of many a poor fellow stained the crystal snow, and at night the moon gleamed on the crimson crust. In the twilight Rogers at the head of his few comrades charged up the hill against the line of the enemy, broke it, and escaped. A mile away over the ridge they met John Stark coming to their relief.

He who fought at Trenton, the hero of Bennington, left his blanket, his provision, and his soldiers to protect Rogers, and alone pushed back on his trail forty miles through the wilderness to Fort Edward. He reached it a little past midnight, obtained a company of soldiers, also handsleds for the wounded, returned on his track, and burst in upon Rogers' camp at a little past noon. *John Stark had travelled a hundred and twenty miles in less than two days, without rest and without a moment's sleep.*

But the crowning achievement of the rangers was their destruction of the St. Francis village and their retreat through the wilderness to the meadows of Coos, lying green beneath the shadows of lofty Moosilauke. As this was the effective stroke that opened our northern paradise, Warren, to the white settler, we shall endeavor to faithfully narrate all its most interesting details.

CHAPTER XI.

A LONG MARCH THROUGH THE WOODS; A TERRIBLE ATTACK ON AN INDIAN VILLAGE; A BLOODY BUTCHERY—AWFUL TO THE PARTICIPANTS—BUT WITHAL VERY PLEASANT TO READ ABOUT.

LIKE Robin Hood's forest, like the villages of the Norman freebooters, or in later times like Algiers, the rendezvous of the Algerine pirates, numerous war parties for more than half a century had continually been dispatched from the little village of St. Francis to harass the English pioneers. Located at the confluence of the St. Lawrence and the St. Francis rivers, it was of easy access. From it they could proceed to Lake Champlain by the river Sorrel, or ascend the river St. Francis, cross the highlands to the Connecticut, and drop down the latter stream. Then, hanging like a black cloud over the border settlements, they would hurl their fury upon the defenceless inhabitants, and fly back with scalps and captives, to receive their reward from the French. In this manner they had made the Pemigewassett territory a dangerous abiding-place, and kept new settlers far away from the historical land of Warren.

A long continued warfare had enriched the St. Francis village, and forty dwellings, thrown together in a disorderly clump, presented a strange contrast to the ancient Indian wigwams. A small Catholic church stood in the midst. In its steeple hung a bell brought from France, whose clear tones summoned the villagers to matin hymns and holy vespers. Within its walls waxen candles shed their flickering light on golden crosses. Pictures of patron saints hung on the dingy columns. In a niche behind the altar stood a large silver image of the Virgin Mary, while in the low gallery was a small but beautiful organ of excellent tone.

Their worship here, as Lord Macaulay has perhaps unjustly remarked, was what the Catholic religion ever is to the ignorant and superstitious—an appeal to the senses and the passions rather than to the understanding. Pictures, crosses, gorgeous altars and images, charmed the eye. The beautiful strains of the organ, now soft and delicate as the notes of an æolian harp, now rushing and wild as the storm on the mountains, anon deep and heavy as the muttering of distant thunder, enraptured the ear, while burning incense in the censer of the French friar who officiated, his mystic words and chant accompanying, and the tolling of the concealed bell, made the Sabbath worship most impressive, and cast a strange spell over the wild spirits of the savage braves. But the very pious French friar of St. Francis had other duties besides ministering to the religious wants of the red men. It is said that he was the modest, meek, and holy tool of the very honest and peaceable French government. With his keen perception of human nature, and his "good Jesuitical qualities," he was to the Indians what the legislative branch is in a civil government. He voted war, and stirred up his devout church members to fight the English, while the grand sachem, a brave chief—once personated in the heretofore mentioned and renowned Acteon—was the executive. For he, like most good Catholics, implicitly obeyed the priest and led the war-parties.

As the conquest of Canada now appeared quite probable, it was thought good policy to make peace with these Indians. Accordingly the British commander sent Captain Kennedy with a flag of truce to arrange a treaty. But they seemed to have forgotten how politely Captain Stevens had received them, and how they had been entertained with sundry mugs of flip, when their own flag of truce was presented at Number Four. With a sort of Punic faith or Roman honor, they seized the gallant captain and made him their prisoner.

This proceeding enraged General Amherst. He resolved to chastise them and teach them a short lesson in the law of nations that seemed to have escaped their memory. For this purpose he issued, September 13th, 1759, the following order:

"Maj. Rogers: This night join the detachment of two hundred rangers yesterday ordered out. Proceed to Mississqui bay.

March from thence through the woods. Attack the settlements on the south side of the St. Lawrence. Effectually disgrace and injure the enemy. Let honor and success attend the English arms. Remember barbarities committed by the enemy's Indian scoundrels. Take deep revenge—but spare the women and children. Neither kill nor hurt them. When you have performed this service, join the army again."*

This order was worthy of a Spartan Cleomenes or Agesilaus, and the way in which it was executed was equal to a feat of old Scotch McIan, or the sally of a horde of Tartars from their fastnesses on the steppes of Asia.

Rogers and his men struck camp that very night. Embarking in bateaux, for ten days they kept directly down Lake Champlain. The weather was delightful. The hardy rangers vigorously plied their oars. When the wind was favorable they rigged a sail in the prow. The stirring strains of a solitary bugle, echoing from the indented shores and dying away upon the dimpling waves, cheered them on. Night and day they kept on their course. No sleepy Palinarius fell from the high-pointed stern. Each bark followed that of Rogers, and every man, trusting him as a guiding star, faithfully discharged his duty. But as they approached the outlet they grew more cautious. At times they would hug close to the shore, and then again would strike boldly across from headland to headland, carefully avoiding the French cruisers that hovered about the foot of the lake.

At Mississqui bay they left their boats and provisions in charge of two trusty Indians and struck into the wilderness. There was no road. They struggled through thickets, over fallen trees, and forded streams now swollen by the autumn rains. At night of the second day the boat guard overtook them. Four hundred French and Indians had captured their bateaux, and two hundred were now on their trail. This caused much uneasiness. Their mission was before them. To abandon it would be disgrace. They must escape from the French who were hanging upon their rear to fall upon and chastise the St. Francis Indians. Like the ten thousand

---

* It must be borne in mind that several hundred of the frontier settlers of New Hampshire had at different times been killed by the savages, and the people of our State very naturally hated this St. Francis friar. The Puritan writers of that day gave him a very poor character.

under Xenophon they must fly before one enemy to fight and conquer another.

Lieutenant McMullen was dispatched across the country for supplies, and then, as related by an early historian, like Charles XII dashing across the marshes of the Baltic, the rangers hurried through the forest. For nine days they marched in a spruce bog. Many a mile it was covered a foot deep with water. At the first dawn they would breakfast, and long before the sun had chased the shadows from the woods were far on their way. They scarcely halted for dinner, but ate as they marched. When the twilight faded and the stars came out, they would stop and construct a kind of hammock to secure them from the water, and lay down to sleep in their pole and bough beds, rocked by the winds that sighed and soughed through the evergreen spruces.

The fifth day Captain Williams was accidentally burnt with gunpowder, and returned with the sick and hurt. The little party, reduced to one hundred and forty-two men, now pushed on with vigor, and in five days came to a river fifteen miles from the St. Francis. It was several rods in breadth, and flowed with a strong swift current. A raft could not be pushed across it, and the men must struggle through by fording. The tallest were placed up stream, and holding by each other that rope of human beings, writhing and swerving in the rushing torrent, toiled across. The remaining distance was good marching ground, and on the evening of the twenty-second day, a scout having climbed a large hemlock, discovered the church spire of the village gleaming through the tree tops.

Rogers writes in his journal that he ordered the rangers to encamp and refresh themselves, and at eight o'clock, taking with him two officers, he reconnoitered the town. He found the Indians celebrating a wedding. There was feasting on the village green. The old forest-arched canopy resounded to the merry song. The sprightly dancers with jokes and laughter kept time with nimble feet to the wild music of an Indian drum, blending with the quicker notes of a half-civilized violin. Like the exultant Trojans, when they had drawn the wooden horse within their walls, they seemed to celebrate their own destruction.

At two o'clock in the morning Rogers says he returned to his camp, that he found it buried in slumber, and that before waking his command he sat down a moment to rest. The fires of the village had gone out; the shouts of the Indian revellers had died away, and not a footfall disturbed the silence. To him the moment was impressive and awful. He could almost hear the solitude creeping down the St. Francis river, only broken by the water kissing the pebbly shore, or by the mournful howling of the Indian dog upon the bank, sending his monotonous cry after the cloud shadows, as they flitted like phantoms over the starlit water.

But duty forbade delay. Rousing his men at three A. M., he advanced within five hundred yards of the village. Ordering the rangers to halt and lighten their packs, he formed them for action. In the manner of true Indian warriors they wait for the most favorable moment. The stars glimmer less brightly through the trees, and the rosy dawn of morning tinges the eastern sky. It was the time when deep sleep bound the limbs of the tired Indian fastest, when Rogers gave the signal, and those hundred and forty-two men, in three divisions, rushed forward with horrid yells, hurled the blazing fire-brands into the dwellings, and shot down alike men, women, and children.

The lurid glare of the blazing habitations showed more than six hundred human scalps, with hair fluttering in the fire-made breeze, stretched upon poles—savage trophies of the border war. The sight filled the men with rage, and they rushed with redoubled fury to the slaughter. Some of the Indians, leaving their dwellings, fled to the river and leaped into their canoes. The rangers pursued, sank their frail craft and shot or drowned those endeavoring to escape. Others concealed themselves in the cellars and lofts of their dwellings and preferred to perish in the flames. Two of the strongest rangers, Bradley and Farrington, came to the door of the wigwam where the wedding had taken place. They threw themselves violently against it, burst it from its hinges, and Bradley fell headlong among the sleeping inmates. The Indians were filled with consternation, but seizing their arms fought bravely for a few moments, when the rangers pouring in overpowered and slew them.* Rogers writes that the first beams of the morn-

---
* History of Concord, N. H., 194.

ing sun pierced the mingled smoke and fog that rolled slowly down the valley of the St. Francis; that the spire of the blazing church glistened for the last time in the bright sunlight, then, tottering for an instant, fell with a loud crash, the bell uttering a mournful peal—the last sad requiem over the doomed village of St. Francis.

At seven o'clock in the morning the work was done. Like Ilium, the Indian hamlet smoked to the ground. Two hundred Indians lay half consumed in the embers of their dwellings, or stained the noble river with their blood. Of all the inhabitants but twenty women and children were alive. Retaining five of these as guides, Rogers suffered the remaining fifteen to depart.*

Only one of his men had fallen and but five or six were wounded. Five English captives who had been sometime with the Indians escaped during the fight. They reported that three hundred French and Indians had encamped the previous night four miles down the river, and were already moving to the scene of action.

Rogers had retreated before them to fall like a thunderbolt upon the St. Francis, had accomplished his purpose, and with the enemy more than double his number still following him like a blood-hound, must now plunge into an unbroken wilderness. Ordering his men to secure the small quantity of corn which they found in three remaining outbuildings, for there was no other provision, he began to retreat. As the forest closed around the rangers, hiding the smoking ruins from their view, the shouts of the enemy coming rapidly up quickened their flying footsteps.

---

*We have not been able to learn with certainty the fate of the St. Francis friar. It is probable, however, that he made good his escape.

CHAPTER XII.

THE RETREAT AND ITS HORRORS, THE CAMP ON THE COOS INTERVAL UNDER THE SHADOW OF MIGHTY MOOSILAUKE, CONCLUDING WITH A BEAUTIFUL AND GOLDEN TRADITION, THAT HAS BEEN REPEATED AROUND THE FARMER'S FIRESIDE FOR A HUNDRED YEARS.

MARSHAL JUNOT defeated and dispersed the Turkish army at Nazareth, and Mount Tabor saw the Musselmen flying before the gallant Kleber; yet famine and the plague drove Napoleon's brave soldiers from Palestine. So the hardy rangers, who never quailed before any human foe, now met in the deep forest an enemy more terrible than the half-blood Frenchman or the maddened savage. True it was that three hundred of the latter still hung like ravenous wolves upon their trail, joining additional horrors to ghostly famine. Yet the starving rangers hurried on through the pathless woods, over rugged mountains, with no landmarks to guide them, while the old forest roared and rocked in the cold October storm. Nor did they always advance. Their guides were treacherous. For three days, as the record reads, they wandered about in an almost interminable swamp. The fourth day they returned on their retreat so much that they struck the trail of the enemy that was following them.

The French and Indians were well provisioned. The rangers were worn down; famine preyed upon their emaciated forms, and at any moment they were in danger of falling into the deadly ambuscade. There was but one hope. The famishing party divided itself into nine small companies, each with a leader.* It was

---

*Rogers led one of the parties; Lieuts. Philips, Campbell, Cargill, and Farrington, Ensign Avery, Sergeant Evens, and Dunbar and Turner, led the others.

agreed that the one which should encounter the enemy should, like a forlorn hope, fight till the last moment, while the others, warned by the contest, might escape. Having separated, in half an hour volley after volley told that one of the companies was sacrificing itself for its companions.* Hurrying forward to meet death in a more terrible form, they left their brave comrades to waste away in the damp mosses of the swamp.

Memphremagog lake, sparkling like a gem in its forest setting, saw them boiling and eating their powder-horns and shot pouches. When these failed their moccasins furnished another tough morsel, from which they gathered strength to drag on with bleeding feet through the wilderness.

At the end of the eighteenth day one party struck the Connecticut river at upper Coos, mistaking it for lower Coos. Bradley, he who was so brave in the fight at St. Francis, was among them. He was a native of Concord. He said if he was in full strength he should be in his father's house in three days. He took a point of compass which at lower Coos would have brought him to the Merrimack, but in fact led directly over the White mountains. A ranger and a mulatto man accompanied him. The next year a party of hunters found in one of the deep mountain gorges a man's bones; by them were three half-burned brands piled together. Silver brooches and wampum lay scattered about—plunder from the St. Francis—while a leather ribbon, such as Bradley wore, bound the long black hair to the whitening skull. No arms were by him and no signs of companions.†

The remainder of the company made a hurried march down the river, for the current was too wild for rafts. Where the Ammonoosuc, coming from the south, and seeming to beat back the dark waters of the Connecticut as they surge through the "Narrows," Rogers had appointed a rendezvous. Here they expected to find relief. General Amherst had indeed dispatched

---

*It was the party led by Ensign Avery which was overtaken by the enemy. Besides those killed, seven of his men were taken prisoners, but two of them escaped. Lieut. George Campbell's party, and Sergeant Evens' party saved their lives by eating Avery's dead soldiers, who had sacrificed themselves that the others might escape. This act of Ensign Avery's men, yielding up their lives that the others might live, is one of the most noble recorded in history.

†Tradition has it that Bradley started with two or three men, but they never reached home. It is supposed they all perished with hunger and cold amid the snows of the wilderness.—History of Concord. 194.

Lieutenant Stevens with provisions, directing him to remain till the rangers arrived, but reckless of his duty he returned at the end of two days, carrying everything with him. He had been gone but a short time when the first party came upon the interval and found his camp-fires still burning. They discharged their muskets to bring him back. He heard them, and thinking it was the enemy, hurried on the faster. Despairing, they eat their last morsel of food, and then laid down in Stevens' deserted camp and awaited their fate.

That night Lieutenant Philips brought in his party. Philips was a half-blood Indian, his mother being a wild Mohawk. The Earl of Loudon commissioned him lieutenant, and throughout the whole seven years' war he was a gallant leader of the rangers. Yet his party suffered terribly. Day after day, as the story is told by himself, they continued to retreat without a morsel of food. As they reeled through the woods it seemed as if the dry limbs of the trees shrieking in the wind was the voice of ghostly famine croaking over them like the boding owl of destruction. When their emaciated forms seemed just ready to sink down they determined to kill a St. Francis prisoner who was with them. A draft of human blood and a feast of human flesh, or death—this was the dreadful alternative. But that afternoon they killed a muskrat, which they divided amongst themselves, and human life was spared.*

Sergeant Evens, another leader, came in with his company on the following morning. Their sufferings if possible were even more terrible. The sergeant used to tell how for days and weeks they wandered through the woods. Birch bark, gnawed with ravenous teeth, and roots dug with long bony fingers, only kept away death. In the cold swamp, through which they staggered delirious, they stumbled upon the mangled remains of their slain companions. Almost every man, as if he were a ravenous beast, gorged himself upon human flesh. Evens' feelings revolted and he refused to eat. But his soldiers laid in a supply, and a few nights afterwards, when the chills of death seemed creeping over

* Philips did not remain long on the Coos intervals. He took the old Indian trail up the Oliverian, reached the Asquamchumauke, and followed down the river home to Concord, N. H.—History of Concord, 200.

him, he took a steak of his comrades' flesh from the knapsack of a sleeping ranger, roasted it upon the coals, and years afterwards pronounced it "the sweetest morsel he ever tasted."

Lieutenant George Campbell, who led another company, said that his men suffered severely. For four days not a particle of food passed their lips. Without a guide and ignorant of the country, they wandered they knew not whither, like a ship upon a stormy ocean, without compass or star to direct. The weak in mind were driven mad by despair and suffering; the weak in body laid down and died. Eating leather straps and the covers of cartouch boxes, tough food, did not appease the dire hunger that consumed them. At length their resources were all gone, and not a ray of hope gleamed through the bars of their forest prison. Death had laid his fearful grasp upon them, and it seemed as if the last man must perish. October 28th but half the party were alive. A few hours more and these must die. But a ghastly relief came to them when they least expected it. A ranger crossing a stream slipped from a log. His foot disturbed the leafy covering that had fallen upon the water and he caught sight of some human bodies scalped and horribly mutilated. The furious hunger of these famishing men knew no restraint; they did not even wait for a fire with which to prepare their ghastly banquet, but ate like beasts of prey. Then, collecting carefully the remnants, they pursued their journey.

At this time Rogers also came with his party. During the whole retreat he had shown himself a hero, and now when his men were perishing he constructed a rude raft, and with Captain Ogden and an Indian boy started to float down to Number Four and obtain supplies. The famishing rangers saw him disappear around a long sweeping bend of the river, and then lay down to wait ten days, at the end of which he had promised to return. The hours went slowly by—a week passed—and those men sat in the smoke of their fires and listened to the wind sighing about their camp. As their forms grew more attenuated, their faces more haggard, and their eyes and cheeks more sunken, they would reel into the woods to gather roots and bark, coarse food to keep the last spark of life from going out.

Across the open meadow was a lofty mountain, and the early

snows of autumn glistened in the sunlight upon its summit. Old settlers tell the story how two of the rangers, one of them by name Robert Pomeroy, had hunted on the streams beyond that mountain in bygone days. With their companions dying around them and death staring them in the face they resolved to cross it and go home. One night, when the rest of the band were asleep, they took from a knapsack a human head, cut off pieces, roasted them upon the coals, satisfied their hunger, and at the earliest dawn departed.*

Late in the afternoon they were standing upon the summit of Moosilauke mountain. They stopped to rest and to gaze upon the wildest scene that ever met their eyes. Mountains like mole hills were scattered through the great northern country. To the east, peak after peak shot thousands of feet into the clear ether. Looking south, the mountain upon which they stood seemed the wild head of the deep wilderness. Scattered through it were gleaming rivers, flashing ponds and silver lakes, while at its foot, a hundred miles distant, a bright line on the horizon showed where the blue sea was dashing. Westward, range after range of lofty wooded mountains stretched far away, like the rolling billows of a tempest tossed ocean. And then all the forest for a hundred miles around was one glorious blaze of brilliant colors. Every autumn hue and tint imaginable shone resplendent, as though the hand of the Divine Artist had woven together myriads of gorgeous rainbows with which to mantle this hitherto unseen solitude.

Half an hour later they saw the sun sink slowly down and gild every range of mountains with golden rays of glory. The clouds that lay along the horizon sparkled in roseate tints, while the horizon itself, appearing like a golden plain in continuation of the earth, changed soon, first to green, and then to a cold ashen gray. As the crescent moon, at first pale but with growing brightness, together with a single star of large magnitude, appeared over the summits of the snowy eastern mountains, Pomeroy, be-

---

*David Evens said that one night, while the men of his party were asleep in the camp, his own cravings for food were so unsupportable that he awoke from sleep, and seeing a large knapsack belonging to one of his comrades, opened it in hopes to find something to satisfy his hunger; that he found in it three human heads; that he cut a piece from one of them, and broiled and ate it, while the men continued to sleep. But he said he would sooner die of hunger than do the like again. He observed that when their distresses were greatest they hardly deserved the name of human beings.—History of Concord, 195.

numbed with cold, sank down saying he must sleep.* His companion tried to rouse him but in vain, and fearing for his own life hurried down the mountain. The wolf howled in the great gorge that night and the wild echoes were roused by the panther's cry. But the ranger heeded them not, and when the last twilight had faded from the western sky he in turn sank down exhausted at the foot of the Seven Cascades.

The legend further relates in a beautiful manner—and surely this can be nothing but a legend—how the ranger seemed to be dying; and when the stars shone bright above him and the moon looked in through the trees and lighted up the white foam of the cascades, distant music coming nearer seemed to mingle with that of the water, and his quickened senses heard fairy harps joined with fairy voices, and saw fairy feet dancing in the silver spray. Elfin kings and fairy queens whirled in the mazy dance for a moment and were gone. And then came a troop of nereids, with long dishevelled hair and eyes lustrous as the stars that shone above them, to bathe in the clear crystal fountain. For an instant they seemed to hold sweet dalliance with the sparkling water and then floated away in the thin mist that hung over the great wood and turbanned the distant mountain. Day seemed breaking, and the bright sun looked in from over the eastern hills upon a crowd of mountain genii, who chanted their matin hymns in their wild rock-hewn temples, and then mounted up on viewless steps to offer incense on their rainbow altar, golden in the flood of rosy light, and glistening in the diamond drops of the waterfall.

As a dark cloud stole across the sky, veiling the moon, the scene changed. The shrieks of the dying Indians at St. Francis, the mournful peal of the chapel bell, the retreat, the famine, the terrible feast upon human heads, the dying comrade upon the mountain top, himself perishing by the torrent,—and then, seen for a moment, the picture of a dark form bending over him—and the famishing ranger was unconscious.

The next morning the sun, glorious in his splendor, gleamed on the seven cascades of the gorge. There was no wind, and the

---

* Robert Pomeroy, a ranger from Derryfield, * * * perished in the woods * * * during the Indian wars * * * and his bones were found years after about the sources of the Merrimack. They were identified by his hair and some personal effects that had not decayed.—Potter's Hist. of Manchester, 336.

THE LONE HUNTER. 153

bright flashing waters as they leaped down seemed to hymn a lofty pæan of praise in the solitude. It was a far, wild country, one in which seemingly no human foot had ever trod. Yet there was one being even here. An old hunter from the frontier had penetrated this wilderness to trap otter, beaver, and sable. He had constructed a rude camp for himself by the side of Gorge brook. In the great meadow over the ridge he set his steel traps for beaver, and built Indian culheags for sable by his spotted line on the mountain side. It chanced that he was visiting the latter that morning. He discovered the footsteps of the ranger who had crossed his line, and following them found him almost insensible at the foot of the cascades. Bearing him to the camp he nursed him back to life, and for a few weeks he assisted the hunter in his duties.

One day, as the early settlers relate the golden tradition, the ranger stopped to quench his thirst at a little mountain rill. As he kneeled to sip the sparkling water he saw shining in the sand at the bottom what appeared to be bright grains of gold. Picking up a handful of these he tied them in a corner of his handkerchief and after heaping a small monument of stones on the bank, departed. The particles thus collected, on being shown to a jeweller, proved to be pure gold, and he received for them fifty dollars. But although careful search has since often been made neither the monument nor the golden stream has ever again been discovered. When the snow began to fall in the valley the hunter, accompanied by the ranger, returned to the settlements.

The remaining companies of the rangers came straggling in upon the intervals. As one by one they died—the allotted ten days not yet passed—despair seated itself on the countenances of all the living, and they prayed once more that Rogers might return.

CHAPTER XIII.

HOW THE SURVIVING RANGERS ALL GOT SAFELY HOME, AND HOW THENCEFORWARD THE PEMIGEWASSETT LAND, CONTAINING THE PLEASANT LITTLE TERRITORY OF WARREN, BECAME VERY SAFE COUNTRY IN WHICH TO SOJOURN.

ROBERT ROGERS' journal, written by himself, gives a succinct account of his exploits in the old French war. It relates how at his departure from the intervals to obtain help he laid down with his two companions on their rude craft, by far more primeval than that on which sailed Jason and his mythical companions in search of the golden fleece, and for hours floated swiftly down in the rapid current. Yet he fails to narrate the fact—for it is presumed that every one should know as much—that the river was swollen by the autumn rains, and that the streams from the highlands on either hand poured in their turbid floods. Neither does he mention the bright hues spread over all the woods; nor the wild geese which, noting the strange craft on the water, cackled at them from the sky; or that at night bears halloed from the hills and muskrats swam splashing along the shores.

Even Ompompanoosuc, a western stream, heaving with its muddy tide, was unnoticed, and they were only roused from their lethargy by a dull but fearful roaring ahead. Starting up they saw a thin mist rising from the falls which their raft was rapidly approaching. Their oars were too small to manage their unwieldy craft in the now eddying and boiling current. A few moments more and they must go over. Death stared them in the face. But they had met it in a thousand forms and though famishing they would not yield. Leaping into the water, after a hard struggle they gained the shore. Their raft, pausing a moment on the brink, leaped like a thing of life into the wild vortex, and was dashed in pieces.

Wet, cold, and starving, with much difficulty they reached the foot of the falls. To proceed by land was impossible; yet Rogers' indomitable spirit never sank. Bidding his men hunt for food, he went to work in true Indian style and kindled a fire. In three days he had burned down and burned off trees sufficient for a raft, and bound them together with withes. In the meantime his companions had procured a red squirrel and a single partridge —just sufficient to keep soul and body together—and on the morning of the fourth day they placed themselves upon the new raft and once more glided swiftly on. The genii of the waterfall seemed to scream after them through the mist, bidding them make no delay, for the famishing rangers were roasting human flesh far back in the cold shadows of Moosilauke mountain.

White river was passed, and in another hour they heard the roaring of Wattoqueche fall. Rogers this time was on the watch for dangers ahead. Paddling their raft ashore, Ogden guided it over the falls with a long withe-rope of hazel bushes, while Rogers swam in and secured it. This raft was their only hope; with it lost their fate was death. All night without food they floated down the stream. Morning showed them a clearing. Shortly after men came to cut timber on the river bank, who discovered and assisted them.

Rogers' first thought was for his rangers who were dying one by one at Coos. Several canoes were immediately fitted out, and manned by strong arms they shot like arrows up through the forest that shut in the Connecticut. In four days the suffering rangers saw them pull round the headland where ten days before their leader had disappeared. Resting for a day only, Rogers went up the river to meet his men and again share their fortunes. It was a strange sight, that silent voyage down the blue stream; those rude boats, freighted with men whose matted beards, sunken eyes, and hollow cheeks told of the horrors they had endured.

On the fifth day of November the last living ranger had arrived at Number Four. Gathered around their leader at the fort they seemed more like ill-dressed corpses than like human beings. Delaying a few days to recruit their exhausted energies, Rogers placed himself at their head and hurried away across the Green mountains to Ticonderoga and Crown Point to take part in the closing scenes of the war.

Perhaps some would like to know the subsequent history of Major Rogers. To narrate all of the events of his after life would be altogether foreign to our purpose. When Wolfe defeated Montcalm on the plains of Abraham, and the flag of old England was unfurled above the battlements of the strongest fortress in America, the major went to the far west. He scouted sometime in the woods about Detroit, searching for Indians, and then made an expedition on the ice up Lake Huron, towards Michilimackinac. At the close of the war he went to Europe, and thence to Africa, where he fought two battles under the Dey of Algiers. For a further account of his life we would refer to "Rogers' Journal," published by himself, a very old and rare work, the author of this veritable history never having met with but one copy.

Rogers himself and his rangers never forgot their memorable visit to Coos, and years afterwards many of them found a home in the scene of their suffering.

The work was now all done. There was no more fear of the Indians, and our beloved Pemigewassett land, including the town of Warren, the history of which we are trying so hard to write, was now destined to undergo a great change. A more glorious era was about to dawn upon the great wild north of New Hampshire.

As this second book was designed only to treat of the border wars by means of which the old hunting grounds of the Pemigewassetts became known and opened up for settlement, we shall here necessarily put an end to our narrations of bush-fights, captivities, and explorations, and shall endeavor in our next to tell how our own Warren — one of the wildest of the northern hamlets — was established and occupied.

BOOK III.

OF THE BIRTH OF A MOUNTAIN HAMLET, OR THE PRECISE AND ACCURATE HISTORY OF THE ACTS OF SIXTY-SIX DISTINGUISHED MEN, OTHERWISE KNOWN AS THE PROPRIETORS OF WARREN.

CHAPTER I.

CONCERNING A GREAT SHAGGY WOOD AND NUMEROUS HUNTERS THEREIN, AND THEN OF A SWEET LITTLE FEUD BETWEEN THREE ROYAL GOVERNORS AND HOW ONE OF THEM POLITELY EUCHRED THE OTHERS, MUCH TO THEIR DELIGHT.

THE old French war was ended. The Indians were no longer feared. Rogers had crushed them. A vast extent of forest country now lay open to the colonists. Our little mountain hamlet—not yet called Warren—was in this mighty wood, in which there were no openings save those made by the hurricane, the flood, or the Indian's fire. Camel's Hump and Mt. Mansfield looked down upon the lesser heights of the Green mountains; the White hills rose out of the woods like islands in a sea, and Mts. Aziscoos and Katardin stood high above Umbagog and Moosehead lakes, which had mirrored them for centuries. Otter creek, Onion river, and the Lamoile, flowed from the wilderness to the west; the Connecticut, the Merrimack, and the Saco came down from the mountains of New Hampshire, and the Androscoggin, the Kennebec and the Penobscot from the bright lakes of the east.

The Indians, as we have before shown in this most veritable

history had nearly all left this umbrageous wilderness; but the "wild beastes," so accurately described by that early, celebrated, and very chaste historian, John Josselyn, Gent., such as bears, wolves, panthers, moose, deer, loupcerviers, and sweet-smelling "squnckes," remained.

My gentle reader, without doubt you know already that the little tract of territory at the head of the Asquamchumauke valley and surrounded by lofty mountains was in the very heart of this great, wild, beast-filled wilderness. The far-sighted glance of the eagle, soaring aloft above the crests of its mountains, scarce penetrated to the distant confines of civilization. The nearest far apart settlements in New England were mostly along the seacoast and on the banks of the largest rivers. Up the Merrimack the clearings had crept as far as a place called Bakerstown, afterwards Stevenstown, and now Franklin, N. H. On the Connecticut river the most northern settlement was around that little log-fort which we have known in the book preceding as Number Four, at present the town of Charleston. For a hundred and fifty years the French had lived in the St. Lawrence valley and their settlements branched off into this wilderness on the banks of the Chaudiere, the St. Francis, and the Sorelle. To the east, Frenchmen lived on the river St. John, and westward were scattered openings beyond Champlain and by the great lakes. It was hundreds of miles across this forest, east and west, north and south.

Yankee men of that heroic age were as fond of hunting as any who live at the present day. Even those not quite so brave spirits who had hitherto been compelled to stay at home through fear of the Indians, could now take up their march with perfect impunity into the woods, to hunt and to trap all that wild ferocious game which John Josselyn, Gent., has so particularly described to us in his veracious history.

The last of September—in this climate the most delightful month of the year—now saw hundreds of men, old and young,

---

"The *wild-cat*, lucern, or luceret, or ounce as some call it, is not inferior to lamb. Their grease is very sovereign for lameness upon taking cold."

"The *squncke* is almost as big as a raccoon, perfect black and white, or pye bald, with a bushtail like a fox, and offensive carrion. The urine of this creature is of so strong a scent that if it light upon anything there is no abiding of it. It will make a man smell though he were of Alexander's complexion, and so sharp, if he do but whisk his bush which he pisseth upon in the face of a dogg hunting of him, and if any of it light in his eyes, it will make him almost mad with the smart thereof."—John Josselyn's 2 Voyages to New England.

leaving their wives and sweethearts and journeying to those pleasant solitudes in the wooded valleys beside the sylvan brooks, rivers, and lakes. They were accustomed to go in boats up the streams as far as possible, often following the same routes that Capt. Peter Powers sailed, rowed, and poled over, or that Col. Joseph Blanchard, Maj. Tolford, and Capt. John Goffe traveled. We can imagine them leaving their canoes, gun in one hand, axe in the other, and a great pack made up of steel traps, spare shirts, feeting, and provisions, in all more than a hundred pounds weight strapped upon their backs, and toiling through the woods and over the mountains in search of beaver meadows and sable ranges. They would build for themselves pleasant little cabins beside some musical stream, and here they would hunt till the snowflakes flew. Then, toting their traps and rich peltries back to their canoes, they would paddle rapidly down the swift current of the now swollen streams to their homes again.

Such were the human inhabitants of our very interesting forest just after the closing of the "Seven Years War;" and such were the only visitors of our mountain bounded valley. By these hunters every stream of the wilderness was explored, every meadow and valley noted, mountain gorges traversed, and even the mountains themselves ascended.

Hitherto the propensity of the Yankee people to emigrate and take up new lands, to clear farms, build log cabins to be succeeded by pine board palaces, had been restrained as we have already hinted by a terror of the Indians. But now a new instinct seemed to have taken possession of the multitude. Like the mutterings preceding the destruction of Jerusalem, an ominous voice seemed to say, "Let us depart hence," but the departure was for a very different reason. The wild lands of the north were on every tongue. All the hunters we have mentioned, all the wild borderers, all the explorers, and all the seven years war men who had marched and campaigned through that section, told almost fabulous stories of its richness and fertility.

The world has seen many an exodus. But the flight of the Jews from Egypt was very unlike that about to be seen in southern New Hampshire and Massachusetts. The wild Asiatic hordes, hurrying from the northern table-lands to the south and west, furnished hardly a parallel case. There they moved as a vast army, conquering the lands they coveted and making serfs of the original dwellers of the soil. Here, however, they seemed desirous to go one by one into the wilderness; fathers with their families, and young men without families, each for himself, caring for nobody, thinking only of future fields and meadows full of black stumps and logs, rich pastures with the same attractive features and no end of cobble-stone pyramids added, out of all which should come great gains and much happiness.

But we would not detract one iota from the merits of our forefathers. Let no one think they resembled the squatters of the present day, or that they occupied the lands without leave or license. They had great respect for law, order, and the rights of property. Much as they desired rich homes for themselves, not a family would move into the wilderness until they had acquired a title to the lands they wanted. But who owned the lands? Who could give them deeds? Who could insure them a perfect immunity from being considered trespassers, and protect them from writs of ejectment and perplexing lawsuits in which some men so much delight? These were very interesting questions, and upon them a great discussion arose. All the provinces began to talk of the great discoveries of Christopher Columbus, of the seizure of the different portions of America by the several nations of Europe, of the portion old England modestly took, that of the Virginia company, the Dutch West India company, the Massachusetts Bay company, and the grant of that famous little tract of land, made by the last named company to John Mason, and then about the entertaining lawsuits instituted by said Mason's heirs against other claimants of the soil of the province once known as Mariana, otherwise Laconia, and finally New Hampshire.

At last the very wise conclusion obtained possession of men's minds that the land belonged to the crown, and to the crown they began to look for grants. Then came the question, "Through what channels?"—and upon this the distinguished rulers of New Hampshire, Massachusetts, and New York each set up their claims to the land in question, and each announced to the people that he was the person to issue grants.

It is said that three proclamations were put forth by the rival governors stating this fact, and by this means all the people of the several provinces were clearly enlightened. The dilemma waxed more difficult. The law-abiding citizens became more and more impatient, and like the ass between two bundles of hay, they might wait forever.

To relieve the public mind of the great suspense that was now hanging over these mighty provinces, embassies were dispatched to England to obtain a settlement of the great question. Who went on this important mission, and when they went or returned, it is not for this veracious history to chronicle. Suffice it to say that they did return and made so satisfactory a report that the whole matter seemed more befogged than ever, and things did not advance a particle.

The several royal governors grew more belligerent than before. They eyed each other like dogs watching a bone, each jealous of the other. So furious did they become that even grim visaged war with its horrid front seemed portending. An old historian said the moon looked like blood, that a comet appeared in the heavens, and meteors flashed across the sky. Provinces hitherto peaceful among themselves, content to fight only a common foe, Indian or French, now seemed ready to gird on their armor for internecine strife. Of the two methods of settling boundary lines — one by arms, the other by compromise — it seemed at one time highly probable that the former might be chosen.

But the fates decreed otherwise, and determined that neither method should be followed. While the royal governors of Massachusetts and New York were contending with high words, and seemed almost ready to come to blows and broken heads, New Hampshire's greatest and best ruler continued to add fuel to the flames of contention now brightly burning, and also *sub rosa* took time by the forelock, boldly cut the gordian knot for himself, and before a rumor of what he was doing had gone abroad, made hundreds of grants to actual settlers, leaving his two dear friends the governors nothing to fight about, and so shot far ahead of them in worldly riches and gubernatorial fame. How this was accomplished we shall immediately proceed to show.

CHAPTER II.

OF A FINE OLD GOVERNOR OF YE ANCIENT DAYS AND OF HIS ROYAL SECRETARY. HOW THESE TWO WORTHIES BUILT GOLDEN CASTLES IN THE AIR AND FINALLY GREW QUITE RICH.

BENNING WENTWORTH, whom we have many times before mentioned, was the son of John Wentworth, one of the former royal lieutenant-governors of the province of New Hampshire. He was installed in office with great ceremonies and rejoicings on the 13th of December, 1741. It is recorded how a mighty cavalcade escorted him into that great seaport town, Portsmouth, and how he was received amid the joyful acclamations of thousands of people who assembled to welcome him. This is probably the partly truthful and the partly poetical language of the distinguished historian; but we can well pardon his veneration for one of the most honorable governors of his loved State.*

Had our royal ruler consented to have lived till the present time we might have presented a faithful portrait of his character, appearance, and habits; as it is, we shall be under the necessity of giving him but a passing notice.

Governor Wentworth was a fine gentleman, "all of ye olden time," and in the matter of dress was fastidious. On state occasions he appeared in powdered wig, three-cornered hat, blue coat with buff facings and bright buttons, breeches rather broad in the

---

* Benning Wentworth was a descendant of Elder William Wentworth, of Dover. Lieut. Governor John Wentworth had fourteen children : 1st, Benning, afterwards governor; 2d, John, Judge of Probate of Portsmouth; 3d, Hunking; 4th, William; 5th, Samuel, father of Mrs. Gov. John; 6th, Mark Hunking, father of Gov. John; 7th, Daniel; 8th, Ebenezer; 9th, George; 10th, Hannah, married Samuel Plaisted and Theodore Atkinson; 11th, Sarah, married Archibald McPhedris; 12th, Mary; 13th, Elizabeth; 14th, Rebecca, married Thomas Packer. Benning Wentworth was councillor from 1732 to 1741, when he became governor, and remained in office till May, 1767.—History of Chester, 54.

seat and tight around the leg, long stockings, sharp-pointed shoes, silver knee and shoe-buckles, an immense frizzle around the neck, and a shirt bosom set forth with enormous ruffles.

In education he was superior to most men of his time, having spent several years at Harvard University and received all the honors of that renowned institution. Probably geography was not then taught, or he never would have made those lamentable mistakes in reckoning latitude and longitude, which as we have before shown in this most delectable history cost so much blood and treasure.

He made but few laws, but he took great care that these should be well understood and executed, as we have seen in the case of Peter Bowen and his friend, when they went scot free on account of public opinion.

As a warrior he was peculiarly great and fortunate, although we have no knowledge that he ever fought a battle in his life. He preferred rather to plan mighty campaigns and trust to his distinguished generals to execute them. Cavalry soldiers were his favorites, and the desperate charges of his bold wild horsemen through the dark woods of the north are facts well known in history.

Governor Wentworth reigned long and well, much to the satisfaction of his loyal subjects, and bid fair to have held his position till the day of his death but for his love of wealth and that his great gains excited the envy of other ambitious and avaricious men of the province.

The governor had a worthy secretary, who had been a friend and acquaintance of his boyhood, they having attended the same school and hunted birds' nests and stole apples together on holidays. At a later day his honorable secretary—the "Right Honorable Theodore Atkinson, Jr.,"—had married Benning Wentworth's sister, and the governor having an eye for the advantage of his relations—like many another high in office before and since his time—had given his brother-in-law an appointment. They pulled together kindly, and Secretary Atkinson held his place till the honorable governor was obliged to retire.

We have been thus particular in mentioning these two men, high functionaries of the royal province of New Hampshire, because to the bravery of the one and the faithfulness of the other is due the creation of our little dependant democracy—Warren. They stood godfathers at the birth of our mountain hamlet, and must not be forgotten.

Some men act from principle and sink self, the motive that actuates them being purely philanthropic; but like angels' visits they are few and far between. Selfishness is generally the ruling motive. Thus Governor Wentworth and his precise secretary saw a golden opportunity before them and interest whispered that it must be improved. Dreams of how they could make a howling wilderness blossom as the rose; broad intervals and rich hillside pastures covered with flocks and herds; nice farm houses, great barns filled with hay and grain, and an industrious population exceedingly eager to pay a large sum in quit rents, burst upon their vision, and they were not slow to take advantage of the opportunity.

While the discussion was going on, and the governors of New York and Massachusetts were considering the case, Governor Wentworth, as we have already intimated, commenced the grand work of giving titles to the land. He secretly gathered together all the surveyors of the surrounding country and set them at work to survey the richest portions of our great wilderness. On each side of the Connecticut river three tiers of townships were laid out, and before the worthy rulers of the neighboring provinces were aware of it the sections had nearly all been granted to intelligent and enterprising men, who were making every effort to settle and cultivate the same.

We cannot stop to tell of the mighty wrath that waxed hot in royal bosoms when the acts of Governor Wentworth were reported; how Massachusetts finally relinquished her claim, and how New York by fraud established hers; nor how the rough backwoodsmen on the borders and among the Green mountains contended with the avaricious "Yorkers," who were encouraged by old England, for long years, until they established their independence and Vermont became a State by itself. We leave such things to graver and more prosy historians.

Governor Wentworth, thrice happy, thrice blessed, now made himself a great favorite with all his people—for a short time. All the wild moss-troopers, all the heavy infantry that had served in the old French and Indian wars, all who had money in their pockets wherewith to pay good round fees, were now suddenly enriched by the good governor. All they had to do was to draw up a petition, get the requisite number of signers, go to the governor with a nice bag of gold, and a charter was sure.

Our respectable secretary had a hard time of it, writing out all the charters and recording them in the book kept for that purpose, but many a weary day he toiled on for fees which were great and for reservations which were greater. Their coffers were well filled, their purses were heavy, and their broad domains extended on every hand. Our royal governor reserved for himself five hundred acres of good land in every township, and his diligent secretary's name always appeared in the list of grantees. Then there were the quit-rents of money and numerous ears of corn, stipulated to be paid in all coming time. And the governor and his worthy secretary longed for the day when they should revel in their palaces on the shores of the silver lake Winnepisseogee, and with fleet horses and baying hounds follow the deer, or with costly equipage roll along busy and prosperous thoroughfares. What vistas of joy and grandeur opened on their delighted vision.

Wild contentions with the "Yorkers," and the envious avarice of others, destroyed their bright air castles. But all these and many other things were necessary to bring our little mountain hamlet into existence.

CHAPTER III.

WHAT JOHN PAGE, ESQ., DID, OR HOW HE PROCURED A ROYAL CHARTER OF OUR MOUNTAIN HAMLET, WARREN, CONFERRING MANY GLORIOUS PRIVILEGES, AND ONLY A FEW CONDITIONS, VERY EASY TO BE COMPLIED WITH.

NOT far from Portsmouth, the residence of "Old King George's" royal governor, Benning Wentworth, is the little town of Kingston.* One of the most prominent persons of the latter town was John Page, Esq. He was a man of intelligence, of extensive acquaintance, and always prompt to take advantage of the times. In personal appearance he was nearly six feet tall, broad, square-shouldered, and would weigh one hundred and eighty pounds. He had a square-set face, keen grey eyes, light hair and sandy whiskers. His dress was neat and he wore short breeches, long stockings, and on Sundays silver shoe and knee buckles.

He had served as selectman, had represented his town in the general court, and had also engaged in trade and speculation. He was a man who would act when occasion presented itself, and now when speculation in land was rife he was wide awake for his share of the profits. It was an easy thing for him to draw up a petition, and it did not bother him much to get sixty odd men possessed of means to sign the same. No less than eight men of his own name—including John Page, Jr., a son of course; Colonel Jonathan Greeley, mine host who kept the village inn, with his relatives, Jonathan Greeley, 2d, Andrew Greeley and Joseph Greeley, Esqrs., also Moses Greeley, of Salisbury, Mass.; Trueworthy Ladd, who kept the country store; the Hon. Dr. Josiah

---
* Since divided into Kingston and East Kingston.

THE CHARTER GRANTED. 167

Bartlett,* afterwards a member of the Continental Congress; John Hazen, John Parker, George Marsh, and Thomas Pierce, four valiant captains who had commanded companies in the old French war, were among the petitioners.

Armed with this petition, and carrying in his saddle-bags a little purse, containing a hundred pounds or more in gold, he mounted his dark bay horse one fine morning, just as many other men at that time who wanted grants of land were doing, and rode to Portsmouth. He had no difficulty in gaining access to His Honor the Governor, and when he had shown his petition, signed by the best of the king's subjects who lived in Kingston, and had jingled his little purse of gold in the gubernatorial ear, His Excellency, was delighted to grant a charter. He could not find it in his heart to refuse such honorable men, and withal so brave soldiers. How wonderfully does gold grease the wheels of all enterprises.

"My secretary shall write you a charter immediately," said His Excellency, and the Hon. Theodore Atkinson, Jr., was called and directed to proceed with the work. Theodore, the secretary, smiled as he said to John Page, Esq., that he would be delighted to place his own name among the list of the honorable grantees. Esquire Page could only reply that he would be most happy to have him, and then the governor rang the bell and directed the servant to bring three bowls of rich punch, in which they were all very much pleased to drink each others' health.

In the meantime the charter was duly written out, signed by Benning Wentworth, the great seal affixed, handed to a clerk to be recorded, and John Page, Esq., bidding the governor and his secretary good day, mounted his horse and went home.

Warren then had a legal existence. It had been marked on the map and named nearly two years previous, and was then politically conceived. *The 14th of July,* 1763, *was its birthday.*

John Page, Esq., told his friends the grantees what he had done and promised them, as the governor had him, that they

---

*Josiah Bartlett was a physician, born at Amesbury, Mass., in November, 1729. He commenced practice in Kingston, N. H., became an active politician, a member of the provincial legislature, also of the committee of safety, in 1775, and at the close of that year a member of the continental congress. He was afterward a judge and then governor of New Hampshire, and died in May, 1795. He was at one time a Colonel.

should have the charter in a few days. But they were destined to wait. They could not hurry the governor, and his secretary, "The Rt. Hon. Theodore Atkinson, Jr.," had so much business on hand that neither he nor his clerks could possibly find time to complete the work of recording the charter of Warren until the 28th January, 1764. The original was then forwarded to John Page, Esq.

That night he met his friends the associate grantees at Colonel Jonathan Greeley's inn.* He showed the prize, and they all seemed exceedingly well-pleased. It was written in a nice round hand, the parchment was excellent, a blue ribbon was attached, and the great seal of the royal province gave it regal dignity and legal consequence.†

---

* Four roads meet in East Kingston, N. H., one pair running north and south, the other east and west. On the latter, one-fourth of a mile west of the four corners was the Colonel's hotel. It stood on the north side of the road. In front undulating fields sloped up to the top of the low wooded hills in the south, while to the north they gradually declined a mile away to the low bottom land. For fifty rods in front of the house the road is level, beginning to descend to the eastern valley by the great rock on the left, and to the western by the old burying-place. On this road our old proprietors tried the speed of their horses after town meetings. West of the house was the orchard. The house itself was a large two-story building, eaves to the road, built in the style peculiar to those days. Two square rooms in front—the south-east one the bar room—a long dining-hall or kitchen in the rear, and behind was a dairy and cook room. There was a long unfinished hall up stairs, over the dining room, filled with beds for lodgers, and in front two furnished chambers. The bar room and dining hall were ceiled with white pine boards, but the parlor and chamber walls were " hung with rich paper." The house was built over about twenty years ago, but the same materials were used, and to-day the doors, the windows, the casings, are all the same as when Colonel Greeley, John Page, Dr. Bartlett, and Jeremy Webster first assembled at the proprietors' meetings. In the back room is an old chest of drawers, and a cupboard; also the "Dairy" used by Colonel Greeley's family.

† CHARTER :

Province of New Hampshire, George the Third, by the Grace of God, of Great Britain, France, and Ireland, King, Defender of the Faith, &c.

To all persons to whom these presents shall come, greeting : Know ye that we of our special grace, certain knowledge, and mere motion, for the due encouragement of settling a new plantation within our said province, and with the advice of our trusty and well beloved Benning Wentworth, Esq., our governor and commander-in-chief of our said province of New Hampshire in New England, and of our council of the said province, have upon the conditions and reservations hereinafter made, given and granted, and by these presents for us our heirs and successors do give and grant in equal shares unto our loving subjects, inhabitants of our said province of New Hampshire and our other governments, and to their heirs and assigns forever, whose names are entered on this grant, to be divided to and amongst them into seventy-two equal shares : All that tract or parcel of land situate lying and being within our said province of New Hampshire, containing by admeasurement twenty-two thousand acres, which tract is to contain almost six miles square and no more; out of which an allowance is to be made for highways and unimproved lands by rocks, ponds, mountains, and rivers, one thousand and forty acres free; according to a plan and survey thereof, made by our said governor's order and returned into the secretary's office and hereunto annexed, butted and bounded as follows, viz: Beginning at the northwesterly corner of Romney, thence running north twenty-four degrees east five miles and three-quarters of a mile; thence turning off and running north fifty-eight degrees west, six miles and one half mile to the southeasterly corner of Haverhill; thence south twenty

In the manner of the most standard novelists we would here pause and invite the gentle reader to look with us over the shoulders of John Page, Esq., Col. Jonathan Greeley, and their numerous friends the grantees, at this mighty instrument:

Province of New Hampshire:

George the Third, *by the Grace of God, of Great Britain, France, and Ireland, King, Defender of the Faith, &c.*

Such was its heading; and we must remember that they lived in good old provincial times and that George III was their king. How glad they are that Governor Wentworth has been so good to them. He has given them thirty-six square miles of territory, and

degrees west five miles and three-quarters of a mile; then turning off again and running south fifty-nine degrees east six miles to the corner of Romney begun at; and that the same be and hereby is incorporated into a township by the name of WARREN, and the inhabitants that do or shall hereafter inhabit the said township are hereby declared to be enfranchised with and entitled to all and every privilege and immunities that other towns within our province by law exercise and enjoy; and further, that the said town as soon as there shall be fifty families resident and settled therein, shall have the liberty of holding two fairs, one of which shall be holden on the [   ], and the other on the [   ], annually; which fairs are not to be continued longer than the respective [   ] following the said [   ]; and that as soon as the said town shall consist of fifty families a market may be opened and kept one or more days in each week, as may be thought most advantageous to the inhabitants; also that the first meeting for the choice of town officers, agreeable to the laws of our said province, shall be held on the second Wednesday of February next, which said meeting shall be notified by John Page, Esq., who is hereby also appointed the moderator of the said first meeting, which he is to notify and govern, agreeably to the laws and customs of our said province; and that the annual meeting forever hereafter for the choice of such officers for said town shall be on the first Wednesday of March annually: To have and to hold the said tract of land, as above expressed, together with all privileges and appurtenances, to them and their respective heirs and assigns forever, upon the following conditions, viz:

1st. That every grantee, his heirs or assigns, shall plant and cultivate five acres of land within the term of five years for every fifty acres contained in his or their share or proportion of land in said township, and continue to improve and settle the same by additional cultivation, on penalty of the forfeiture of his grant or share in said township and of its reverting to us our heirs and successors, to be by us or them regranted to such of our subjects as shall effectually settle and cultivate the same.

2d. That all white or other pine trees within the said township fit for masting our royal navy be carefully preserved for that use; and none be cut or felled without our special license for so doing first had and obtained, upon penalty of the forfeiture of the right of such grantee his heirs and assigns to us our heirs and successors, as well as being subject to the penalty of any act or acts of parliament that now are or shall hereafter be enacted.

3d. That before any division of the land be made to and among the grantees a tract of land as near the centre of said township as the land will admit of shall be reserved and marked out for town lots, one of which shall be allotted to each grantee, of the contents of one acre.

4th. Yielding and paying therefor to us our heirs and successors, for the space of ten years to be computed from the date hereof, the rent of one ear of Indian corn only, on the twenty-fifth day of December annually, if lawfully demanded; the first payment to be made on the twenty-fifth day of December, 1763.

5th. Every proprietor, settler, or inhabitant shall yield and pay unto us our heirs and successors yearly, and for every year forever from and after the expiration of ten years after the above said twenty-fifth day of December, namely, on the twenty-fifth day of December which will be in the year of our Lord, 1773, one shil-

divided it into seventy-two equal shares. The number of acres is twenty-two thousand, all good and excellent land. By the way, they have never seen it yet, but then certainly most of it must be good, for has he not made an allowance for highways and unimproved lands, by reason of rocks, ponds, mountains, and rivers, one thousand and forty acres free? How accurately it is bounded. Romney is its southeast corner, and Haverhill its northwest corner; so we know that both Romney and Haverhill have been already located and surveyed.

ling proclamation money, for every hundred acres he so owns settles or possesses and so in proportion for a greater or less tract of the said land, which money shall be paid by the respective persons abovesaid their heirs or assigns, in our council chamber in Portsmouth, or to such officer or officers as shall be appointed to receive the same, and this to be in lieu of all other rents and services whatever.

In testimony whereof we have caused the seal of our said province to be hereunto affixed. Witness Benning Wentworth, Esq., our governor and commander-in-chief of our said province, the 14th day of July, in the year of our Lord Christ one thousand seven hundred and sixty-three, and in the third year of our reign.
[L. S.]   B. WENTWORTH.

By His Excellency's command, with advice of Council —
                                      T. ATKINSON, JUN., Secretary.
Province of New Hampshire, Jan. 28th, 1764.
  Recorded in the Book of Charters, No. 3, pages 78, 79.
                                      T. ATKINSON, JUN., Secretary.

THE NAMES OF THE GRANTEES OF WARREN:

John Page, Esq.,
Jona. Greeley, Esq.,
James Graves,
Joseph Blanchard, Esq.,
Capt. John Hazen,
Ephraim Brown,
Joseph Page,
Belcher Dole,
Reuben True,
Stephen Webster,
John Darling,
Capt. John Parker,
Jona. Greeley, 2d,
Enoch Chase,
Lemuel Stevens,
Abel Davis,
Capt. George Marsh,
Ebenezer Morrill,
Trueworthy Ladd,
William Whitcher,
Ebenezer Collins,
Ebenezer Page,
James Nevins, Esq.,

Samuel Page,
Moses Page,
John Page, Jun.,
Ephraim Page,
Enoch Page,
Benj. French, Jun.,
Aaron Clough, Jun.,
Silas Newel,
David Morrill,
Nathaniel Currier,
Benjamin Clough,
Henry Morrill,
Jacob Hook, Esq.,
Josiah Bartlett,
Joseph Whitcher,
Reuben French,
Samuel Osgood,
Thomas True,
David Clough,
Daniel Page,
Peter Coffin, Jun.,
William Parker, Jr., Esq.,
Capt. Thomas Pierce,

Ebenezer Stevens, Esq.,
Dier Hook,
Philip Tilton,
Nathaniel Fifield,
Andrew Greeley,
Jacob Currier,
Samuel Dudley,
Joseph Tilton,
Francis Batchelder,
Joseph Greeley,
John Batchelder,
Jacob Gale,
Abraham Morrill,
Jeremy Webster,
"The Rt. Hon. Theodore Atkinson, Jun., Esq.,"*
Nathaniel Barrel,
Samuel Graves,
John Marsh,
Moses Greeley, of Salisbury,
Andrew Wiggin, Esq.,

His Excellency Benning Wentworth a tract of land to contain five hundred acres, as marked B. W. on the plan, which is to be accounted two of the within shares. One whole share for the incorporated society for the propagation of the gospel in foreign parts. One share for a glebe for the Church of England, as by law established. One share for the first settled minister, and one share for the benefit of a school in said town forever.

Province of New Hampshire, Jan. 28th, 1764.
  Recorded in the Book of Charters, No. 3, page 80.
                                  T. ATKINSON, JUN., Secretary.

*1 N. H. Hist. Col. 282.

The next fact that meets the eye is, "That the same be and hereby is incorporated into a township by the name of

WARREN:"

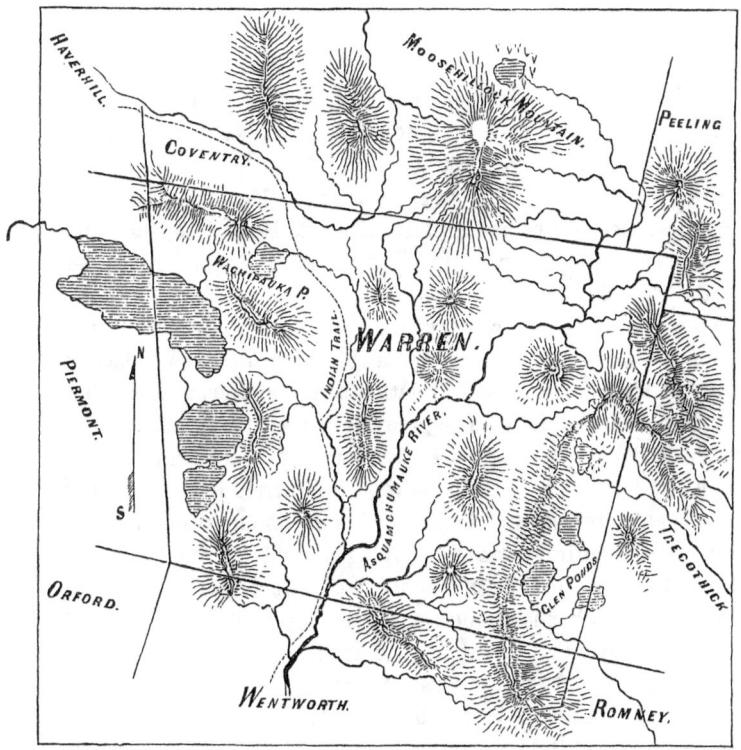

John Page, Jr., must here have asked his venerable sire why it was so called. Tradition has it that John Page, Sr., replied that he had conversed with the governor about the origin of the name, and that His Excellency informed him that the surveyors of the "King's Woods," who had visited the township to establish the lines, reported that it was a beautiful land, full of rabbits, where nature had seemingly appropriated a piece of ground to their breeding and preservation.

Dr. Josiah Bartlett, who was learned in Indian as well as medical lore, interrupted and said he supposed it must be a place granted by the Gitche Manito, the Indian god who had his home on the summits of the lofty mountains round about, to the red sons of the forest in which to keep all their "beastes," fowls, and fish; "For," said he, "all the jolly hunters say that the woods are full of moose, deer, bear, and other game, that wild ducks swim on the rivers and ponds, and that every stream is alive with the speckled trout and golden salmon."

John Page, Esq., further said that His Excellency told him that he was also influenced to bestow the name, Warren, upon this tract of wild, mountainous country, out of respect for his friend, Admiral Warren, of "Louisburg notoriety." He wished to honor the admiral, because he had greatly aided the New Hampshire and Massachusetts troops in wresting that almost impregnable fortress from the French.

Now we desire to caution our readers against putting too much faith in the above very plausible traditions. We have a pretty theory of our own in relation to the matter, and it is but natural that we should want to give it a place in this most ambitious history. It is this: Old England has a borough named Warren, and there was then a town of Warren in nearly every other royal province, and it was and is extremely fashionable to bestow this beautiful name, signifying a rabbit borough, upon a handsome and fertile tract of country; therefore His Excellency, imitating the mother-land and the royal governors of other loyal provinces, named this beautiful and fertile grant, given to John Page, Esq., and sixty-five others — Warren.

We cannot conclude this subject of etymology without noticing the opinion of the learned Deacon Asa McFarland, so long the able editor of the New Hampshire Statesman, and a member of the New Hampshire Historical Society. He gravely asserts that the town is named for and after General Joseph Warren, who fell a martyr for his country at Bunker Hill.* But as General Warren was but a stripling in 1761, and probably unknown to our good governor, and as the battle of Bunker Hill was not fought until fourteen years after Benning Wentworth had retired from office, and even his loyal successor had taken French leave of his most royal province, we can but conclude that our most wise editor was entirely correct in the matter, and would enjoin upon our

* See files of the New Hampshire Statesman.

readers to put the utmost confidence in the learned deacon's opinion.

Having thus profoundly shown how the name of our little hamlet originated, we will proceed to examine with John Page, Esq., and the numerous other grantees, into the further mysteries of their great and mighty instrument, the charter.

The next fact learned is that the future inhabitants of said township—once called in the charter "*a new plantation*"—are hereby declared to be enfranchised with and entitled to all and every privilege and immunity that other towns within "our province" exercise and enjoy.

This was kind. But His Excellency, the geographer, was determined to do more for John Page, Esq., and his friends than was customary. The governor loved them exceedingly; they had been so good as to bring a larger bag of gold than was usual. He therefore ordered "The Rt. Hon. Theodore Atkinson, Jun., Esq." to insert the provision, "That as soon as there shall be fifty families resident and settled in town they shall have the liberty of holding *two fairs*." This would make the land sell better.

It was a glorious privilege, and all the grantees imagined—and some of them had excellent imaginations—how like old Derryfield or the fairs of England and Ireland, or like the Olympic, Pythian, Isthmian or Nemean games of classic Greece, their semi-annual gatherings should be held, when the farmers could sell and swap horses, run horse and foot races, wrestle and box, climb slippery poles, and pursue greased pigs; while at even-tide the youths and maidens should dance on the village green, or witness the wild acts of improvised athletes, and listen to the sweet songs of wandering minstrels.

That there might be no doubt concerning the governor's sincere friendship he also caused to be inserted the authority "That a market may be opened and kept one or more days in each week, as may be thought most advantageous to the inhabitants."

What a happy idea was this: The village green should be alive with horses, beeves, sheep, and hogs, with loads of hay and grain and wood, and long rows of stalls where marketmen and marketwomen, carrying well filled baskets, could buy and sell poultry, fish, meats, and vegetables of every sort and kind.

But there must be a few conditions. The privileges must not be all on one side. If the grantees do not hasten, the town will not flourish with a rich and teeming population, and the quit-rents, ears of corn, and proclamation money will not come in fast enough, and the royal governor and his secretary cannot ride in their coaches and build their palaces on the shore of the smiling lake as they would like. So it was stipulated:

1st. That *every grantee* for every fifty acres he owns shall within the term of five years *plant* and *cultivate five acres* of land.

2d. That all *pine trees* fit for masting *our royal navy* shall be carefully preserved.

3d. That a *town lot* one acre in size shall be laid out near the centre of the town for each grantee.

4th. That for ten years each grantee shall pay the *rent* of one *ear of Indian corn* annually.

5th. That after ten years each grantee shall annually pay for every hundred acres owned *one shilling proclamation money.*

We are thus particular to put all these conditions into our most important history because it must be remembered that the governor put them all in the charter.

Then in the most gracious manner possible the governor reserved for himself only one lot containing five hundred acres, and he was very particular to have it marked on the little plan of the town accompanying the charter. But he had the misfortune to locate it in a very poor place, owing no doubt to his great skill in geography. Wachipauka pond, the precipitous face of Webster Slide mountain, and the blueberry patch on its summit, constituted the good gentleman's reservation.

Governor Wentworth was an excellent man. He belonged to the high church of England, and withal was piously inclined. So he told his brother-in-law the honorable secretary to reserve one whole share "for the incorporated society for the propagation of the gospel in foreign parts," "one share for a glebe for the Church of England as by law established," and "one share for the first settled minister."

But not an acre did he give to the witch-hanging, ear-cropping, cheek-branding, bundling puritans, as he called them, nor to the Scotch covenanters. Not he! He did not believe in them.

But he did believe in education, and was very willing to do something for coming generations, especially when other people paid the expenses; and so he ordered in addition that "one share should be appropriated for the benefit of a school in said town forever."

How satisfactory were all these conditions, provisions, and reservations, and how well John Page, Esq., Colonel Jonathan Greeley, and all their friends felt that night. Visions of broad acres and riches without limit, accruing from great sales of land and from rents, floated before them. The entire brood was reckoned up before a single chicken had burst the shell, and with characteristic liberality drinks and viands were ordered up. Bowls of hot punch and mugs of good old fashioned flip circulated freely, and with song and jest and shout the time flew fast. The moon had gone down in the west and the stars were dimming when these future lords of the soil separated for their homes.

CHAPTER IV.

OF EAGER MEN — HOW THEY HELD SEVERAL MEETINGS — ALSO OF A GAY AND FESTIVE CORPORATION DINNER — CONCLUDING WITH A POWERFUL EFFORT TO OBTAIN A SURVEYOR OF THE "KING'S WOODS."

NOW there shall be no more delay. The long summer and autumn had passed, and part of the winter had gone, since the visit of John Page, Esq., to Portsmouth, and it did seem to the anxious grantees that the Rt. Hon. Theodore Atkinson, Esq., had not the slightest regard for their feelings and desire for gain, else he would have recorded and forwarded the charter sooner. No more time should be lost; a meeting must forthwith be called. At the gathering at the inn of mine host, Colonel Jonathan Greeley, the grantees one and all had importuned John Page, Esq., to make all possible haste, post the notices, and let them, the eager grantees, immediately assemble.

John Page, Esq., did so, agreeably to the provisions of the charter, and in just ten days after it was recorded, on February 8th, 1764, Colonel Jonathan Greeley's lively inn was honored by the great initiatory meeting.

The proprietors of our little mountain hamlet assembled in full numbers. Even Moses Greeley, of Salisbury, was present. At ten o'clock A. M. they were ready for business, and John Page, Esq., as directed by the charter, called the meeting to order.

It was held in the long dining hall back of the parlor and the tap-room. A bright fire was blazing on the open hearth, there were benches around the hall on which the men were to sit, while some of the more chilly gathered standing about the fire. An old

THE FIRST PROPRIETARY MEETING. 177

table was placed upon a little platform at one end of the hall, and by it sat John Page, Esq. Rapping upon it with his knuckles he called the meeting to order and immediately the hum of conversation ceased. From the time of his return from Portsmouth he had kept close possession of the charter, and now drawing it forth he proceeded to read it at length. When he had finished a buzz was heard about the room, as is usual at town meetings, but Esquire Page again rapped upon the table and proceeded to remark that the first business in order would be the choosing of a *town clerk;* and the proper way to proceed would be to elect him by ballot. He therefore requested that written ballots might be prepared and forwarded. Upon counting them it was found that Jeremy Webster had received the whole number, and it was declared that Jeremy Webster was unanimously elected. In a like manner Jeremy Webster, Colonel Jonathan Greeley, and Lieutenant James Graves were chosen *selectmen*. It was then voted that the annual meeting of the proprietors of Warren should be held on the first Wednesday of March, and that the next one should be held at the inn of mine host, Col. Jonathan Greeley, on the 7th of March, 1764, that date falling on the said first Wednesday. The meeting was then dissolved.

But the proprietors did not disperse. It was the first corporation meeting and there must be a corporation dinner. John Page, Esq., himself says that two long tables were set in the very hall in which the meeting was held. The plates, knives, spoons, pewter-platters, mugs, and service, all brought from England, were arrayed with mathematical exactness. Roast beef, spare ribs, turkeys, and chickens; chicken pies, plum puddings, mince pies, apple pies, cakes, sauce, and savory viands of all kinds, including without doubt sundry pots of baked beans contrasted with huge loaves of Indian meal bread, fairly caused the festive board to groan.

John Page, Esq., also says that he himself sat at the head of one table, and Col. Jonathan Greeley at the other, and that each man carved for himself, as was the fashion in "ye ancient time." As beef, pork, and fowl rapidly disappeared, what cheer was there—what jokes they cracked—how rich they felt—and how

L

fast flew the time. And then the hissing hot punch was brought in, and first of all, every one standing, they drank King George's health. Then the song, the jest, the laugh, and the health of our good governor was not forgotten. To each other long life, happiness, and riches were drank, and the short hours flew swiftly by until one by one our worthy proprietors had drank themselves sober and had departed their several ways. The expense of this and all other meetings was paid out of the proprietors' stock.*

It was a worthy company that took supper at Col. Greeley's inn. The presence of the Rt. Hon. Theodore Atkinson, Jun., the Hon. Josiah Bartlett, afterwards governor of New Hampshire, Col. Jonathan Greeley, a man of much influence, John Page, Esq., and a host of other good and notable men, made a most respectable meeting.

Of course not many plans were made, for according to the vote another meeting was soon to be held, at which a programme was to be fully discussed and adopted.

Consider for a moment this first meeting of our forefathers. All northern New Hampshire was then a wilderness. The little hamlet of Warren was chalked on the map, but there was no road to it or through it; nothing but an Indian trail. A few settlers had just set themselves down by the Connecticut river, at the Coos intervals, and twenty miles away the Hobarts and the Websters were building the first camps on the Pemigewassett. King George ruled the British empire, and the western world but composed his royal provinces. The king's head ornamented all the coin of the realm, and even on Jonathan Greeley's sign was painted the English coat of arms. No dreams of independence flitted through their brains then; all were loyal subjects.

Riches were what the proprietors wanted, and so when the first Wednesday of March, 1764, came they were nearly all present and eager for action. How avarice will spur men on.

The meeting being called to order in the same old hall, John Page, Esq., was chosen *moderator;* Jeremy Webster, *clerk;* Joseph Whitcher, *constable;* Capt. Ephraim Brown, Col. Jonathan Greeley, and Jeremy Webster, *selectmen;* Capt. Stephen Webster, Joseph Page, and Ebenezer Stevens, *surveyors of highways*; and

---

* See Proprietors' Records.

SCARCITY OF SURVEYORS.

that there might be no delay they determined to choose a committee to run the lines round about the township and view the land. For this purpose they chose John Page, Esq., Lt. James Graves, Col. Jonathan Greeley, Capt. John Hazen, and Captain Stephen Webster. They were authorized to procure a surveyor and other necessary assistants and to proceed immediately to the business. Our first annual town meeting, at which these fourteen men were immortalized by being elected to such important offices, was then adjourned. Every one now believed that the work would go bravely on and that soon the land would be all sold and settled — and then how rich they would be.

Our valorous committee, chosen to run the lines and view the lands, did indeed go to work in a bold and enterprising manner. They made application to every trusty and skillful surveyor in the country, but to no purpose. They were all engaged running town lines and lotting lands for other proprietors. The committee even made sundry and divers journeys across the border to the land of Massachusetts Bay to see if they could find one, but without any better success. The whole summer went by, and when autumn came they were thoroughly convinced that among other requisites a considerable sum of money was necessary to secure the services of so important a personage as a surveyor had now got to be.

Accordingly a third meeting was called and held on the 17th of September, 1764, when it was voted, "That a dollar (or its equivalent in paper currency,) be paid upon each right in order to furnish and pay the fore-mentioned committee when they should act for running the lines about the township." That there should be no mistake this time, Col. Jonathan Greeley was chosen treasurer, to collect and pay out the money for that purpose.

But prosperity did not smile upon them. Although the honorable committee labored with all their might, still no surveyor was procured. The year went by and nothing was done.

Consequently when the selectmen, as in duty bound, on the 19th of February, 1765, warned another meeting to be held on the 6th of March following, they inserted an article in the warrant, "To vote what the proprietors will further do relative to the committee chosen last year and the business they were to transact."

This was the mighty question. Every grantee considered it most thoroughly. At the 6th of March meeting, held at the inn of Col. Jonathan Greeley, they voted unanimously "That the proprietors' committee run the lines about the township as formerly determined; they are to begin the work about the first of June next, and to proceed in the business as fast as possible, and if they need assistance they are hereby authorized to get it."

Now they will surely act—no, gently, not yet. They cannot get a surveyor any more than last year, although the most strenuous efforts are made. The summer again goes by and the lines are not run. Some of the proprietors who had paid liberally were indignant, and said this would not answer.

The last of August the rulers of the proprietary, otherwise the distinguished selectmen for that year, call another meeting. It is to be held on the second Tuesday of September, 1765. The proprietors were alarmed. They had contributed to the little purse of gold for the governor, they had paid for corporation dinners, they had been assessed for contingent expenses; these had all been outgoes, but not a penny had they received. Besides, the conditions of the charter, especially that one requiring that the town should be settled in five years, had not been fulfilled, and if much more precious time was wasted all would be lost. The proprietors met as directed, this time at Jacob Currier's inn, in South Hampton, and not at Col. Greeley's; but they did nothing but talk. After a long discussion they adjourned to meet again in one week at the same place.

Being met again and the meeting called to order, John Page, Esq., said that he had some good news to communicate. He then announced that by good fortune the proprietors' committee had secured the services of an excellent surveyor and assistants. This piece of information was greeted with applause, and the whole proprietary felt so good that both flip and punch were ordered up and every one drank to his heart's content.†

It was then voted that when the meeting adjourn it be to meet on the third Tuesday of October, 1765, to hear the further report of the committee. Some one then suggesting that they had better

---

* See Proprietors' Records.
† Proprietors' Records.

meet at Col. Jonathan Greeley's again, a motion to that effect was passed with almost an unanimous vote, only a few of Jacob Currier's friends dissenting, as they wanted him to have the profits of the meetings. But the majority remembered the good things in Col. Greeley's larder and bar; they believed also that the good will of his place had much to do with success. Thus the hope of gain combined with a longing for the flesh-pots of Egypt succeeded.

There shall be no more delay. The committee, no longer furnished with excuses, must act at once, and we shall now have the pleasure of accompanying the valiant little surveying party far to the north for a delightful stroll in the great wilderness of the future town of Warren.

CHAPTER IV.

HOW THE LINES WERE RUN ROUND ABOUT WARREN—A CAMP IN THE FOREST—A ROARING, RAGING EQUINOCTIAL STORM WORTH SEEING, AND A REPORT OF THE WHOLE AFFAIR BY SURVEYOR LEAVITT.

AND now John Page, Esq., and his associates move in their work, and Benjamin Leavitt, the excellent surveyor whom they had hired, together with his assistants, are soon ready.

The committee accompany him, and one bright morning we find the little surveying party breaking camp beside Stinson pond, on the east side of Mount Carr, and wending their way by the blazed line to the northeast corner of the town of Romney.

They found and established that point of our little mountain hamlet. Its lines had before been chalked on the map, but now its bounds were to be set up, and the trees blazed to show the course.

They first traced the east line, following along upon the eastern slope of Mount Carr. At noon they halted for dinner on the shores of Glen upper pond. No clearings were visible. There are none to be seen to-day. The same wildness, the same solitude witnessed by John Page, Esq., Benj. Leavitt, and their associates, when they stood by that little circular pond a hundred years ago, exists there now. The deer and the bear then came to drink of its water. The bear drinks there to-day, and the mottled fawn and the antlered buck now crop the grass upon the moist shore the same as then. There were moose there then, but there are none there now.

THE BOUNDARY LINES RUN.

At night they camped on the side of Mt. Kinco. The morrow saw them across Cushman mountain to the northeast corner, saw them traveling down the slope of Mt. Waternomee, on the north line, to the Asquamchumauke river. That night they camped by the roaring torrent. The third day they crossed the spur of Moosehillock, passed the head waters of Berry and Oliverian brooks, climbed the precipitous Webster Slide, and sundown found them camped by a little stream that flowed down into Tarleton lake. Across the lake or around it, down over Piermont mountain, leaving Eastman ponds to the east and including them in Warren, to the southwest corner, and there they camped the night of the fourth day. Eastward over Sentinel mountain, across Martin brook, then so called from a hunter who had trapped upon it, and over the spur of Beech hill to the Asquamchumauke river again. Here the quick eye of Surveyor Leavitt noted the old Indian trail. It was about two o'clock in the afternoon. Leaving their surveying instruments in a safe place they followed the trail up the river for two miles, crossed the mouth of Black brook— the Mikaseota—and at the end of the ridge between the brook and the river they camped for the night.

Tradition, that most trustworthy historian, has it that while they were cooking their supper John Page, Esq., followed up Black brook a few rods to where there was *a little white fall* leaping over the mica slate rock, and shot a deer which had come there to drink, the sun being about half-an hour high. The surveying party had an extra supper that night. Flashing knives carved out the choicest morsels, and by their campfire that gleamed through the woods they sat for long hours telling old legends and bloody tales of Indian wars.

The next morning they crossed the valley and climbed the hill, came back and followed the trail to Runaway pond, then back and up the valley to Berry brook. At night they had returned to their camp again on the end of the ridge. The land in the valley was good, and the great pine trees on the plain, where the common is now, some of them more than two hundred feet high, in whose cones they heard the autumn wind sighing, were the objects of their especial admiration. But they could only admire them. The surveyor of the *king's woods* had marked them with the *broad arrow*, and they could only be used for *masting the royal navy.*

They had gone to sleep, their camp-fire burning brightly in the darkness. Hours of quiet went by, when suddenly John Page, Esq., started up. What was that? Was it the howl of the wolf, the cry of the catamount, or the well-nigh forgotten but terrible whoop of the savage? He listened for a moment but heard nothing save the murmer of the brook and the river, which united just below them. Soon a flash of lightning lighted up the forest, followed by the low deep rumble of thunder behind the western mountain. A moment more, others having been aroused, and a sharp flash blinded their eyes, followed by another, which in turn was succeeded by a crash of thunder louder and more stunning than any they had ever before heard. Mount Carr echoed back the terrible peal, and then the rain poured down in torrents.

Our little surveying, land-locating, fortune-hunting party were now all wide awake. Their fire was out, their camp leaked, and almost in less than no time they were drenching wet. For the rest of the night they sat there in a delightful condition of shiver. They thanked their lucky stars for their good fortune, that they had only got a good wetting and nothing more, and without doubt they said their prayers and made sundry pious ejaculations during those luminous and happy hours. But they did not swear.

When the morning dawned they found that the wind was blowing from the northeast, that black clouds were hurrying across the sky from Moosehillock to Mount Carr, and that the thunder shower was but the prelude of the storm. It was no use to break up the camp then — everything was too wet. They made a fire, dried their clothes, breakfasted on the remains of the venison, longed for a dish of delicious punch to wash it down, and then tightening the camp and gathering more firewood waited as best they might for what could not be helped.

By ten o'clock A. M. the wind was howling in the woods and the rain fell fast. All day long they sat there, managing one way and another to pass away the time, while Surveyor Leavitt made notes in his journal to assist him in writing his report.

A STORM AMONG THE MOUNTAINS. 185

When the sun went down a new sound arose. As the evening hours wore on it seemed as if all the storm spirits had leaped from the waterfalls in the ravines of Mount Carr, and were joining in one grand pæan, louder than the mightiest roar of the ocean. The Indians' god, Gitche Manito, with the whole host of lesser aboriginal divinities, assisted by Jupiter Tonans, Vulcan, Pluto, and every other heathen god, seemed mingling their voices in one continuous roll of thunder through the huge mountain forests. John Page and his companions had heard the roar of the ocean in a storm, but never a sound like this. People of Warren sometimes hear the same now, when the equinoctial storm of autumn comes late, or when the winter breaks up suddenly and the melting snows and warm rains turn the mountain streams to torrents.

In the morning the storm was over. A bright fire made them comfortable, the last of the venison was cooked for breakfast, and when the white mists from the waterfalls were climbing out of the ravines and chasing each other over the wooded crest of Mount Carr, and the wind had shaken the rain from the trees and bushes, they hurried back down the trail to the spot where they had left their surveying instruments. They crossed the now roaring Asquamchumauke and climbed over the eastern mountain. The line was finished that day, and night found them back in their old camp by Stinson pond. Four days more and they were at home making up their report.

On the third Tuesday of October, 1765, the proprietors met again. Col. Jonathan Greeley's long hall and cosy tap-room seemed like home to them. The meeting having been called to order, John Page, Esq., chosen moderator, and Jeremy Webster, clerk, they passed the following vote: "That we receive and accept the report of the committee we sent to the township, and give the committee, Jeremy Webster, Esq., Col. Jonathan Greeley, and John Page, Esq., the sum of sixty-four dollars for their time and expense in going up to Warren to run the lines about the township and viewing the land." *

The report of the committee has not come down to us in form, but tradition says that the committee told the proprietors that our beautiful little hamlet was located among great mountains "daunt-

---
* See Proprietors' Records.

ing terrible;" that to all *sound* appearances "loud roaring divels" lived among said mountains; that silver rivers and streams ran through it, and upon the borders around it were sparkling lakes and ponds. They might also have stated that on Patch brook (not then having a name) was an old beaver meadow where the grass grew wild, and that there was another meadow larger and better, at the outlet of Runaway pond.

Perhaps they might have further made mention of the fact that on the slopes of Beech hill and Picked hill were immense maple groves where sugar might at some later day be made, but this we can only conjecture. Suffice it to say that the committee made an exceedingly interesting report, that the proprietors were mightily well-pleased thereat, and immediately took other and more determined steps to accomplish the settlement of the town.

CHAPTER VI.

CONDITIONS HARD AND TERRIBLE — A ROAD MADE OF AN INDIAN TRAIL — RICH LOTS OF LAND DRAWN BY LOT, AND HOW MEN FELT RICH BUT ANXIOUS.

"1ST, *That every grantee for every fifty acres of land he owns in Warren township shall within the term of five years plant and cultivate five acres of land.*"

LIKE the sword suspended by a hair over the head of terrified Damocles, so the above condition of the charter was forever hanging over our worthy proprietors. The very first condition — it must be fulfilled. A failure, and the little hamlet of Warren was lost to them. The other conditions could be easily complied with. The pine trees fit for masting our royal navy could be preserved; the town lots could be laid out; the rent of one ear of Indian corn only could be yielded; and the one shilling proclamation money could be " deposited in our council chamber at Portsmouth " without difficulty. But in performing our first condition — there was the trouble.

What shall be done? . It must be planted and cultivated in the space of five years. This not done and the charter is forfeited.

We have seen how the lines were run and went with the committee to view the lands. It was necessary to set up the boundaries so that the proprietors of other towns should not trespass upon our woody territory. That the proprietors, owners, and would-be settlers might journey thither without difficulty, a road must be cut. But two years had passed already and one had not as yet been begun. Perhaps the worthy proprietors waited for those of other townships on the river below to cut out their roads, so that it might be more easy to get to the boundary of Warren to begin theirs; perhaps they had no money in the treasury to pay for the work; perhaps they thought there would be such a spontaneous rush to buy their lands that there would be no need of their doing anything. But time dispelled the first and last of these illusions.

The year 1765 was nearly passed; almost half the time given for the settlement was gone, when at a proprietors' meeting held late in autumn it was voted to pay for clearing a public road through the township, and a committee was chosen to attend to the same. It consisted of Col. Ebenezer Stevens, Col. Jonathan Greeley, Jacob Hook, Esq., Samuel Page, Esq., John Page, Jun., John Page, Esq., and Capt. Ephraim Brown.* The road once cleared, and then emigrants would flock to the land of the hills. Our mountain hamlet would certainly be settled, and the first requirement of the charter fulfilled.

But that there might be no failure in this matter of cultivation and settlement, they determined to divide a portion of the land into lots and distribute them among the several grantees. Then each one would have a separate personal interest, and would labor with more energy for the settlement. Accordingly at the annual meeting in 1765 it had been voted that a division of home lots should be made by the above-mentioned road committee, to contain eighty acres each, respect to be paid to quality as well as quantity.

But this vote was all for nought. The season went by, and late in autumn, the proprietors being again met, they voted to lay out a home lot to each grantee, containing one hundred acres to the lot, as convenient as may be. That there might be no repetition of failure they further voted to raise money to defray the charges of laying out the same, and also instructed the road committee to lay out said lots. The vote to raise the funds to pay for the work was the best vote passed. The work must now move. Something will surely be accomplished.

We have seen how difficult it was for our former committee to procure a surveyor. The one headed by Col. Ebenezer Stevens

---
* See Proprietors' Records.
1765. The proprietors voted to raise money to defray the charge of clearing the public road now about to be laid out through the township of Warren.

AN INDIAN TRAIL MADE USEFUL.   189

encountered the same obstacle. Procure a surveyor they could not. The year 1766 passed, and *nothing* was done. The grantees waited for their committee to act, and did not even call a proprietors' meeting. Individually they exhorted the committee to work — but all to no purpose.

As we have before said, and as every wide-awake proprietor knew, the time for fulfilling the first condition of the charter was fast flying, and their claim to the little mountain territory seemed slipping from their grasp. The spring of 1767 came. Only one year of the five given was now left. The work must be done at once or all would soon be lost. At this critical juncture of affairs John Page, Esq., rallied. A meeting of part of the committee was held at the usual place, Col. Jonathan Greeley's inn, at which it was emphatically redetermined to run the lines, locate the road, and lay out the lots.

To accomplish all this a surveyor must be had, and John Page, Esq., said he was happy to inform the committee that Benjamin Leavitt, who had formerly run the lines, could be procured. Samuel Greeley, Fry Bayley, Abraham Morrill, Samuel Page, Joseph Eastman, and Jacob Morrill were to be his associates. They were to perambulate the boundaries and lay out the first division of lots.

It was spring time when the surveying party and the committee chosen to clear the road came to Warren. They established themselves in the old camp on the end of the ridge between the Mikascota or Black brook and the Asquamchumauke or Baker river, and while Surveyor Leavitt went over the lines again and was laying out the lots, the road committee attended to their duties.

And now our worthy readers will naturally inquire what kind of a road they made and where it was located. We have no doubt concerning the truthfulness of the reply we shall give, for we have the facts vouched for by many of the ancient settlers and also recorded by history itself. Our indefatigable committee did not locate any new road — they simply cleared out the old Indian trail, and made it into a tolerable bridle path.

This Indian trail was a very ancient way, about as much so as the old Roman roads. For centuries back the Indians had followed it. Wonalancet and his friends had journeyed over it nearly a hundred years previous to the little improvement undertaken by our committee. Waternomee knew every rod of it. Arosagunticook warriors had led their captives on it northward to Canada.* Capt. Baker's "marching party" had hurried down it to fight the Indians at the mouth of the Asquamchumauke. Capt. Peter Powers† made use of it in his glorious retreat, and along its windings Robert Rogers had marched his whole company of rangers. It was the shortest road to the sea board, and those in a hurry to reach the lower country have always traveled it.

Many a hunter, trapper, and explorer journeying northward in those primitive times availed themselves of its facilities. The Rev. Grant Powers, a most truthful historian, narrates how the very first settlers who came up the Merrimack valley to Coos employed it. In April, 1762, he says that Col. Joshua Howard, Jesse Harriman, and Simeon Stevens engaged an old hunter at Concord to guide them through the wilderness. They came west of Newfound lake, in Hebron, followed up the northwest branch of the Asquamchumauke or Baker river into Coventry, and down the Oliverian to the Connecticut. They performed the journey in four days from Concord.‡

Most of these things happened when the Pemigewassetts, the Coosucks, or the Arosagunticooks had a right of way over it. But this very summer, after our committee had so much improved it, a lady, solitary and alone, took a romantic journey along its woody windings. The story is this—a simple tale—told in an ancient record: Thomas Burnside and Daniel Spaulding were journeying with their families to settle at the upper Coos. At Plymouth one of Mr. Spaulding's children was so badly burned as to be unable to proceed, and Mrs. Spaulding was left behind to attend to it. Her husband and friends having gone she became lonesome and resolved to follow them. A friend living at Plymouth had agreed to accompany her through the woods with a horse thirty-four miles to Haverhill, but he left her at a house in Romney, the last one, nine miles on, and turned back. Mrs. S. was not discour-

---

* Acteon's Narrative.
† Powers' History of Coos, 46.
‡ "Some of the early settlers of Haverhill and Newbury took the same route to Plymouth, kept on the north side of Baker river into Coventry, and then down the Oliverian."—Powers' History of Coos, 169.

aged; with her child in her arms she proceeded. She waded through Baker river, which was low from drouth, and all day long toiled up the blazed path to Warren. Across Black brook and up the meadow she met two men, whom she tried to avoid by stepping out of the path. They saw her and endeavored to persuade her to turn back, and among other things told her that she must "wade through a part of Wachipauka pond where there was nothing to direct her." But she still persisted. In the course of the afternoon a heavy thunder shower passed over and thoroughly wet both mother and child. She continued travelling until in the darkness the track could be no longer followed. Then quietly seating herself by the side of a tree she leaned against it with her child in her arms, and there rested without sleep till morning. It was a lonely night. The rumble of Oak falls echoed through the leafy wood, the whippoorwill sang in the alders by the brook, and the bullfrogs in the neighboring pond croaked and "chugged" the whole night long.

At early dawn she continued her journey and soon arrived at the pond, through part of which she waded waist deep. Fortune favored her and she found the path on the opposite shore without difficulty. She also waded the Oliverian which, to use her own language, "looked wild and terrifying," being probably swollen on account of the shower of the preceding day. Pushing rapidly on at eleven A. M. she reached the settlements on the Connecticut.*

Where through Warren did the Indian trail run—that most ancient way over which Indian kings and princes of mighty tribes had travelled, and where Mrs. Spaulding took her romantic journey? It followed up the west bank of the Asquamchumauke to the mouth of the Mikaseota or Black brook, crossed the latter stream and followed up its east bank, going some of the way just where the road is located now, to the neighborhood of Beech hill bridge, where it crossed to the west bank and continued along the same to its source in Wachipauka or Meader pond. Crossing the pond at the outlet it continued round the east shore to the head, over the little summit, down the slope of Webster Slide mountain to the Oliverian, and down the latter stream to the Connecticut.

The surveyor and his party did even better than our road

---

* 1st Farmer & Moore's Historical Collections, 85.

committee. Benj. Leavitt with his assistants, as we said before, perambulated the old lines and then proceeded to lay out the lots. They began on the south side of the town and laid out the first division. The crest of Mount Carr, where the hackmatacks grow, they did not think worth spending any time upon, but Surveyor Leavitt spotted his lines across Hurricane brook, and washed down his dinner one day by a draft from "Diana's bowl," which is carved in the rock at the top of Wolf's Head falls.

They made nine ranges in the first division, and as high as eleven lots in a range, as can be seen by looking at any old plan of the town. The land was lotted as far north as the "*Eleven mile tree*," so called, which stood beside the Indian trail, and is often spoken of in the proprietors' records. This work accomplished the whole party, road clearers and surveyors, returned to the southern country.

Benj. Leavitt, Esq., took his time. He made up his report carefully, drew an accurate plan of his survey, and when the committee to notify proprietors' meetings notified said proprietors to meet on Tuesday, Nov. 17, 1767, he was ready to hand it in. The meeting was called for that purpose. Art. 2d of the warning was, "To hear a report of a committee returned from running the lines of said township, and as they have laid out part into lots, to see if the proprietors will vote to accept it." At the meeting held on said day it was voted to allow the committee for their services in the sum of twenty-one pounds and four shillings.*

Thus the lots were laid out, the report made and accepted, and it now remained to divide the land. After due consideration it was voted that it should be distributed by lot, and that one man should draw the lots for the whole proprietary, and also voted that the moderator was the man to draw said lots. The meeting then adjourned for half an hour, the slips of paper were prepared, and being again met the lots were drawn.

At the drawing Thomas True got the first lot in the first

---

*1767, Nov. 17. Voted that we allow the committee above mentioned in full for their services, as followeth, viz:

To Fry Bayley, 4 days at 5 shillings per day,	1*l* 0	0
" Benj. Leavitt, Surveyor, 14 days at 6 shillings per day,	4*l* 4	0
" Abraham Morrill, 14 days at 5 shillings per day,	3*l* 10	0
" Samuel Page, 11 days at 5 shillings per day,	2*l* 15	0
" Joseph Eastman, 11 days at 5 shillings per day,	2*l* 15	0
" Jacob Morrill, 14 days at 5 shillings per day,	3*l* 10	0
" Samuel Greeley, 14 days at 5 shillings per day,	3*l* 10	0

range, Ebenezer Stevens got the second lot in the first range, and so on until all were drawn. The names of the drawers were then entered respectively upon the original plan and this constituted their title to the land. It was real estate which did not come to them either by descent, purchase, escheat, forfeiture, execution, or directly by grant. The land was granted to the proprietors as a corporate body, divided by lot, and when so divided each grantee had a good title, which he could alienate either by deed or devise. In the old proprietors' records are recorded the drawings, the divisions, the ranges, the number of the lots, and the names of the proprietors by whom they were drawn. Thus was the land in our beautiful mountain territory most equitably divided.

At an adjourned meeting, held November 26th, 1767, it was voted "that we will raise nine shillings on each right in addition to what has been already voted to be raised, to defray the charges that have arisen on account of laying out the lots." Our worthy proprietors, now severally rich in lands, were yet compelled to pay somewhat for the privilege of being considered rich land owners. But the distinguished grantees were now perfectly certain that the town would be settled and cultivated and the first condition of the charter fulfilled. So much were they of this opinion that they passed by without notice an article in the warrant of the meeting to be held in November, 1767, which was to vote "what encouragement they will give to any person who will undertake to build a *saw mill* in said town the next year." There was no need of spending their money for such a thing. They also passed by without action another article in the warrant, as they did a similar article at the meeting the previous spring, which was "to vote what encouragement they will give to forward the settlement of the township." There was likewise no need of this—the condition would be fulfilled sure.

But there were some not so sanguine; the time was almost out. If terms could not be made with His Excellency the Governor, then time, taxes, treats, dinners, and purses of gold would all be lost, and they would get no profit whatever from their speculation. Something, thought the wiser, must be done, and upon this thought they acted. What they did we shall proceed to show in our next chapter.

M

CHAPTER VII.

HOW THE PROPRIETORS' PROSPECTS GOT DESPERATE, SO MUCH SO THAT THEY WERE WILLING TO GIVE AWAY SOME OF THEIR LANDS; HOW PHILLIPS WHITE CAME TO THE RESCUE — GOT THEM OUT OF A TERRIBLE DIFFICULTY, AND FINALLY PROCURED A NEW CHARTER — WHICH ENDS THIS BOOK AND INTRODUCES US TO AN ALTOGETHER NEW LIFE IN WARREN.

LONG and faithfully have we toiled over the Proprietors' Records, extracting therefrom, as a bee honey from a flower, everything sweet and beautiful. Our duty as an accurate and truthful historian compelled us to do this — as a sample of which witness the disagreeable passages of the last chapter — and our most comprehensive history would never be complete without such conscientious regard for facts.

John Page, Esq., and the most energetic of our venerable proprietors, were now very anxious about the township. They must work or the charter would be forfeited, and all the line-running, lot-locating, and road-making would go for nothing. Accordingly at a proprietors' meeting held the 2d Tuesday of May, 1767, the question of what should be done came up, and among other things it was determined to send a committee to the new governor to obtain if possible a longer time in which to fulfill the first condition of the charter. Col. Jonathan Greeley and the Hon. Dr. Josiah Bartlett were chosen as the committee.

We have said they were to treat with the *new* governor. His Excellency Benning Wentworth had been compelled to resign, and his nephew, John Wentworth, had been commissioned in his place, under date of August 11th, 1766, as "Governor of New

A NEW GOVERNOR.

Hampshire and Surveyor of the King's Woods in North America." He had been installed in office with even more pomp and ceremony than Benning Wentworth himself. On the morning of his entrance into Portsmouth—we have it on the authority of one of the best historians —all the bells rang a regular double-bob-major, the cannon of the forts and batteries thundered till their brazen throats were hoarse, and the numerous ships anchored in the stream and at the wharves flung out all their bright bunting, flags, and streamers to the harbor breeze.

Col. Greeley and Dr. Bartlett found no difficulty in gaining access to His Excellency. He was a jolly soul and loved to welcome company, especially when he could see a fee in prospect. The committee laid their case before him in the prettiest manner possible; told him of the great difficulties which they had met; that there were no roads, that it was far in the wilderness, and that men could not be found to settle all the towns which had been granted.

Governor Wentworth sympathized with the committee and sought to console them by ordering up three bowls of " creature comfort." After drinking enough to remove their melancholy, Governor Wentworth told them to go on as well as they could, just as though their time was not out and would not be out, and he would do what was right in the matter. But His Excellency, like his uncle Benning, was exceedingly fond of the root of all evil, and so he told the committee that he thought that by and by they would need a new charter, gently intimating that considerable expense generally attended the granting of such new instruments.

Our committee were exceedingly well pleased with their reception by the young governor. They went home and reported their success to the proprietors individually, no meeting being called, and as the season was nearly passed—the fall rains had come and the winter was coming soon—they concluded they had better wait until the next annual meeting, and not try to do anything that year. But when the winter was gone then they would act. There would be three beautiful spring months before July 14th, 1768, and in that time they could accomplish wonders. Besides, they would send the committee to the governor again, and they had no doubt but that they could get excellent terms from him.

During the early part of the winter they discussed numerous plans, and when the annual meeting of 1768 came they adopted one very much in vogue among the proprietors of various other townships and were thus prepared to act most efficiently. As a preliminary to their grand plan they passed the following votes:

1st. To give to each family, to the number of twenty-five, that shall settle in said township before the first day of October next, 1768, fifty acres of land.

2d. That the first settler shall take his first choice of the fifty acre lots and so each in their order.

3d. That each family that shall settle agreeably to the above vote by the first day of October next shall have six pounds lawful money.

And they did not stop here. To show their decided determination to clear and cultivate the land, and not forfeit their title as grantees, they chose another committee to finish clearing the road through the town. It was a strong committee chosen for that purpose, and consisted of Mr. Samuel Page, Col. Jonathan Greeley, Lieut. Joseph Page, Phillips White, Esq., Ensign Jacob Gale, Jacob Hook, Esq., and Mr. Enoch Page. This committee really worked sometime on the road, and also laid out the land as above voted for the settlers, and at another meeting they were allowed five shillings a day for their time.*

All that men could do by voting was now done. They shall surely succeed this time. Everybody is going to work. So each one thought as he waited for his neighbor; but as is usual in such cases, where each depends upon the other, nothing at all was done. Our committee did not even go again to the mountain territory of Warren before the fatal day of July 14th, 1768.†

That day came and the charter was forfeited. All legal right was gone. The only hope of the proprietors now lay in executive clemency. Col. Jonathan Greeley and the Hon. Dr. Josiah Bartlett had got encouraging promises from the governor, and on these they relied.

---

*Feb. 6th, 1769. "Voted to give those that worked clearing the road thro' Warren five shillings a day for the time they worked on said road."
See Proprietors' Records.

† But the committee did go to Warren, where they worked sometime during the season of 1768.

Yet our proprietors had done as well as most of those of other townships. Benning Wentworth had granted towns and made himself rich in so doing. John Wentworth's great plan was to regrant them and make himself equally rich.

The committee saw His Excellency again. This time as before he promised them fair things, and again gently hinted at the great expense which usually attended the regranting of charters.

Again they went home encouraged and determined to work. Another proprietors' meeting was soon called. They paid those who had worked on the road. They voted six shillings a day to those who had been engaged laying out the lots. They further voted to those who should settle in said town lands and money. They agreed to give "ten more settlers" who should settle in said township fifty acres of land and six pounds in money to each, or one hundred acres of land without any money, which the said settlers shall choose; and further voted that said land "*shall be laid out on the road which is cut through said town.*"* At a subsequent meeting it was voted that Col. Jonathan Greeley, Lieut. Joseph Page, and Mr. Enoch Page be a committee to lay out said lots and agree with settlers.

These several things were done as an earnest of their good intentions, and they then voted that Col. Greeley and Phillips White, Esq., go to the new governor and treat with him for a new charter.

Phillips White was not one of the original grantees. We first find his name in the Proprietors' Records, March 14th, 1768, as having been chosen one of a committee to get the road cleared through our mountain territory. He had become possessed of a certain portion of the lands by heirship; he had bought out the rights of a few of those grantees who had become discouraged in the enterprise, and afterwards, for meritorious services, the grantees themselves gave him several large tracts of land located east of the *new reservation*, and upon the side of Waternomee mountain. Next to John Page, Esq., he had become one of the most prominent men among the grantees. He held all the important offices of the proprietary, was entrusted with all the funds, served on all the principal committees, and during his long life frequently

---

* See Proprietors' Records.

came to Warren to look after his own interests and those of the other proprietors. He had much wealth and good common sense, and therefore much influence. He was just the man to go to the governor with mine host, Col. Jonathan Greeley.*

Col. Greeley had learned the way to the governor's heart. He told Phillips White, Esq., what must be done, and Phillips White, Esq., was prepared to do it, and to become the saviour of the proprietors' inheritance. How?—by his gold. If Benning Wentworth liked the musical jingle of the filthy lucre, so also were the ears of John Wentworth delighted with it.

It was on a cool September day that our new committee rode their two strong saddle horses to Portsmouth. They had no difficulty in gaining access to His Excellency, and the latter was glad to see the proprietors' committee. Well he might be—for he knew that when Phillips White, Esq., came something was certain to be accomplished. The governor rang his bell and a servant appeared. He ordered four bowls of punch just as before, and as was always the custom called in his secretary, the Rt. Hon. Theodore Atkinson, Jun., Esq.,—who was not dead yet nor out of office either—and they then began to discuss the subject of a new charter.

All the difficulties which the grantees had encountered were enumerated; how a mistake had been made in surveying the grant, whereby the proprietors of other towns had claimed a considerable portion of the lands; how much difficulty they had experienced in cutting roads in such a far foreign land, and how

---

* He was a member of the Continental Congress, 1782, 1783. Also a member of the Committee of Safety, from Jan. 20, 1776, to Jan. 20, 1777, and from Dec. 27, 1781, to the autumn of 1782.

"In
Memory of the
HON. PHILLIPS WHITE, ESQ.,
Who departed this Life
June 24th, 1811, in the
82d year of his age."

The above was copied from his gravestone, a plain slate stone slab, April 20, 1865, in South Hampton, N. H. The following is on the gravestone of his wife:

"MRS. RUTH WHITE,
Comfort of
THE HON. PHILLIPS WHITE,
Died July 9th, 1797,
In the 69th year of her age."

much trouble they had found in getting settlers for the township. "Hundreds of other towns," said Phillips White, Esq., "have been granted and all of the other proprietors have met with the same difficulties as the grantees of Warren; in fact," said he to the governor, "have we not succeeded as well as nine-tenths of the proprietors of other townships, and have you not given them new charters? Will you not treat us as well as you have them?"

The governor acknowledged the fact, ordered his secretary to make a minute of what was required, and then in the blandest manner possible suggested that the surveyor-general would be under the necessity of making new plans, the secretary would have a great deal of writing to perform, and of course a small amount of funds would be necessary.

Col. Greeley and Phillips White, Esq., both had the same thought and assured him the money should be forthcoming. The governor was much pleased and said, "You shall have the new charter, and that soon."

His visitors thanked him and went home. They thought they should get the charter in a few days, but they were again destined to wait. The year went by, the winter and spring of 1770 passed, and the summer was nearly half gone before they were notified that it was ready for them.

Phillips White went to Portsmouth for it. Like John Page., Esq., he carried a bag of gold. He counted out the yellow sovereigns to the governor, to Col. Atkinson, to the surveyor, and to the surveyor-general — in all for the procuring of a new charter the sum of seventy-eight pounds one shilling. It also cost the proprietary for the further expenses of its committee the sum of seventeen pounds four shillings.* The governor was happy to

---

April 29, 1773. "Voted to give Col. Greeley for services done the proprietary one hundred and twenty-five acres of land in the northeast corner of the township to begin at the said northeast corner and to run southerly on the line of said town 290 rods, thence westerly 69 rods, thence northerly 290 rods to the northerly line of the town, thence easterly on said line 69 rods to said northeast corner."

Also, "Voted to give Phillips White, Esq., for services done the proprietary, 400 acres of land in the northeasterly part of the township, to begin at the northerly line of said town adjoining the land voted to Col. Greeley, thence southerly by said Greeley land 290 rods, thence westerly 221 rods, thence northerly 290 rods to the north line of the town, thence easterly 221 rods to the bound first mentioned."
See Proprietors' Records.

*For obtaining the new charter: "Voted to pay, March 25, 1771, to Phillips White, Esq., 7*l* 18*s*; to Col. Jonathan Greeley, 6*l* 14*s*; to Josiah Bartlett, Esq., 2*l* 12*s*. See Proprietors' Records.

welcome Phillips White, Esq., a second time. His were golden visits.

This second charter was not so long as the first. It recited the difficulties the proprietors had met. It included the prayer for more. land, and then prescribed the bounds of the township, stating that they were made by actual survey by "Isaac Rindge, our surveyor-general of our lands within the province of New Hampshire." But the great point gained by the charter was that the proprietors should have four years more in which to clear and settle our wild mountain hamlet. All the remaining conditions were the same as before, and the young and gallant governor was very careful to stipulate that all the rents due to us in our council chamber in Portsmouth shall be paid. The great seal was affixed, the charter signed by His Excellency, and Phillips White, Esq., returned with it to the proprietors.

How great was their joy! They were saved. Col. Greeley's little taproom and long dining hall saw a merry time on the night 'Squire White returned with the charter from Portsmouth. The health of everybody in general, but of P. White in particular, was drank. Influence and gold had been their salvation. Now they were sure there would be no failure on their part. Individuals went to work on their own responsibility, and some of the land was actually cleared and cultivated. *But they never succeeded in fulfilling the first condition of their charter.* True they accomplished much; but when four years more had passed they incurred another forfeiture. They would undoubtedly have again lost the township—or have been compelled to pay roundly for a new title —had not the Revolutionary war, which was their salvation after the year 1774, providentially occurred.

But we will here put an end to this third book and now proceed to more congenial themes in the fourth. To continue further the history of the proprietors, separate from that of the settlers, would only serve to involve everything in inextricable confusion.

BOOK IV.

WHICH RELATES HOW OUR WILD MOUNTAIN HAMLET WAS CULTIVATED AND SETTLED.

CHAPTER I.

OF DIVERS AND SUNDRY SOUNDS HEARD ON THE HEAD WATERS OF THE ASQUAMCHUMAUKE, AND OF TWO HOTELS IN WHICH NOT A DROP OF "GROG" COULD BE GOT, EITHER FOR LOVE OR MONEY.

THERE are a few great eras in the history of all civilized communities. The entrance of the Israelites into a land flowing with milk and honey, their deliverance from Babylon, and their dispersion by Titus, are some of the distinguishing epochs of that people. The founding of Rome by Romulus and Remus, the sacking of Troy, the destruction of Carthage,—are extraordinary events in the history of other nations. So the year **1767** is one of the most distinguished in the chronology of our little mountain hamlet.

Its position was chalked on the map in 1761. It was granted to John Page and sixty-five others in 1763, and the year 1767 is the date of its actual settlement.

The old year 1766 is dying. Let us pause on the threshhold of 1767. During all the time of Queen Anne's war, of Lovewell's war, of King George's war, of the Seven Years' war, when scalping parties hastened along the Indian trail down the Asquamchumauke, and drafted men were hurrying through the woods in search of their red foe, and further back than the memory of man runneth, Warren was a wilderness. It is in this case on the last night of 1766. There is no clearing, no house, no human being. It lies a cold, crisp, terrible solitude in the heart of a vast forest.

The low winter sun, the last of the year, has gone down in a blaze of glory; the twinkling stars are glowing in an ebon sky, and Venus, just on the edge of the horizon, is hastening down the impearled pathway of the sun. The evening hours fly swiftly by. It is chill, freezing cold, and the very silence is oppressive. No sound comes up from the Asquamchumauke; it is ice-bound. Waternomee falls, on Mount Carr, and the "Seven Cascades," between the two peaks of the mountain, are silent. They are ice-falls, frozen as they leaped, and the moon gleaming on them makès them glorious, as though their mighty columns were pillars of ruby, amythyst, jasper and gold. Moosehillock — king of the mountains — stands up in awful silence amid the lesser peaks around him.

But hark! — the howling of a pack of wolves comes sounding down the valley, and no human ear is there to hear it. At night they will feast upon one of their own number. Another sound! The moose and deer in their yards tremble as they listen to it, and the old crow who has lived for a century amid the thick hemlocks of this unbroken forest nearly topples from his roost. It is the terrible, almost human cry of the catamount. But even this lion of the American forest is soon stilled, — it is so cold. There is a moaning in the air. Is it the wind sighing in the leafless branches of the forest? Is it the aurora borealis snapping its electric streamers and crackling its flaming pennons athwart the sky? Is it a troop of pale ghosts, shades of departed Indian warriors, charging through the air across the valley to the distant mountain side? But it is still now for a moment and you see only the gnarled trunks of the trees standing like grim sentinels in the shadows of the great mountains, and the cold snow shroud of mother earth.

Listen again — for it is never long silent in this mighty wood. Hear the cry of the wolves once more, the terrible voice of the catamount, the bark of the fox in the spruce swamp, and then at intervals again that strange, unearthly noise, coming from one cannot tell where. The wind perhaps?—may be the sound from the polar light, perchance the troop of ghosts, the spirits of the departed.

What a terrible solitude it is; never broken, an ocean of woods full of dark streams, wild torrents, shaggy hills, and great mountains. But there shall never be another new year's night like this in our mountain hamlet. Before 1767 passes a change will come. Be easy for a moment, most critical reader. We have written the above that you might have some faint idea what a place Warren was just before civilization came to it. But we will now come down from our lofty stilts and plod along at our usual pace.

The Indians had taken French leave of the Asquamchumauke or Baker river valley nearly fifty years before, and had gone to Canada. The era of border wars and savage ambuscades, of scalping knives, war-whoops, and "pow-wows" had passed. Even hunters and trappers were not so numerous as formerly, as game became less and less plentiful. The time of proprietors, surveyors, line-markers, lot-locators, and road-clearers had arrived, and treading close upon their heels would come the frontier settlers.

Did it never occur to our readers during their progress through the third book of this most delectable history that our venerable proprietors might have been a little too avaricious for their own good? The first four years after the granting of the charter by Governor Wentworth passed rapidly away without their even so much as making an offer of either lands or money to any one who would settle in their mountain territory. The proprietors of other townships were shrewder by far, and offered both lands and money to those who would locate on and improve their "grants." The consequence was that many towns further in the woods had numerous settlers, while our lovely little hamlet remained a howling wilderness. Perhaps John Page and the associate grantees thought the land was so fertile, the woods so beautiful, the hills so inviting, the mountains so sublime, the game so plenty, and the streams and ponds so well stocked with the speckled trout and golden salmon, that there would be a mighty rush of settlers eager to occupy our woodland paradise, and that they should make an immense amount of money by the sale of their lands even before they were lotted. But they were most thoroughly disabused of this idea about the time they lost everything by forfeiting their charter. They learned to their great cost that in order to sell any portion of their land they must first give away some of it; and they also got another "cute idea" through their heads—that they would have to pay a good smart bounty to any man, to induce him to receive a portion of the land even as a gift, and engage to settle on it. The reason of this was that there was much more land to be settled than there were settlers in all New England.

But experience, that high-priced schoolmaster, taught them the above lesson, and in 1767 they went to work in a more common sense manner. At two consecutive meetings this year the subject of bestowing lands and bounties was discussed, but it was not fully determined whether they would give them or not. Yet the rumor of what might be expected to be done went abroad, and as a portion of the lands had already been laid out into lots by the proprietors' committee, a few enterprising young men began to turn their attention to them.

But before proceeding further we must consider briefly what took place on the king's great highway which the proprietors had caused to be cleared through Warren. We should not record this slight jotting of history, but that we consider it will prove a great benefit to posterity, and so we piously note it down.

The first human habitations in Warren, of which we have any correct knowledge, were the wigwams of the Indians; the next the rude camps of hunters and trappers, and following them the camps of our former surveying parties.

But when the spring of 1767 came, when the sun ran high and the warm showers descended, when the buds on the trees expanded, and the speckled adder tongues pierced up by the snow banks through the moist mat of leaves on the ground; when millions of flowers were developing, and the delicious yellow dandelion grew blooming so sweetly on the grassy river bank,—then it was that travelers journeying to the lovely Coos country through the land of the Pemigewassetts, built beside the committee's road, or rather the Indian trail, two exceedingly fine and hospitable hotels, even before a single white man had moved into the township. One of them was located beside the trail, on the west bank of the Asquamchumauke, and the other upon the shore of our little mountain pond, Wachipauka.* They were only one-story high, a low one at that, and were built in the most economical manner. Two crotched stakes, each about six feet long, were driven in the ground about seven feet apart; a pole was placed horizontally in the forks for a "plate;" two others some twelve feet long each were then placed with one end on the horizontal pole and the other on the ground, serving for rafters; on these were fastened the ribs for the roof, and then the top and right angled triangled sides were covered with spruce bark. Before the open front, which generally faced the southeast, the fire was built.

Although there was neither landlord nor landlady, chambermaid, cook, or waiter, hostler or errand boy about these one-roomed hotels, still they were most welcome inns to the weary traveller. If he could not find provisions in them, still they afforded him comfortable shelter, with a soft bed of moss and hemlock boughs, and the dry punk, flint and steel, could always be relied upon with which to kindle a cheering fire. Whether or not the bar was well stocked with the good creature we are not succinctly informed; but we have no doubt the guests would have raised the most congenial spirits, provided their own backs had been stouter. Their dispositions were certainly good enough, and their stomachs sufficiently strong, to have brought the requisite store of "old rum" that distance into the wilderness. Pocket pistols of approved construction were not unknown even in those days, and the canteen or bottle-shaped gourd slung to the side of the sturdy woodsman who set his face towards the mountains contained often a more potent restorative than pure spring water. Who knows but that these "first hotels" of Warren saw many a night of jovial revelry in the year 1766?

---

* "It may be proper for me to state in this place that our forefathers had taken the precaution to build camps on the route from Haverhill to Salisbury, one camp in every twelve or fifteen miles, and each was supplied with fireworks and fuel, so that a traveller could soon kindle him a fire, and he had the boughs of hemlock for his bed."—Powers' History of Coos, 72.

They had two camps on the Height-o'-Land, one on the very summit and one by the brook running from Eastman pond into Tarleton lake. The camp by Eastman brook was in Piermont.—History of Coos, 117.

Taverns then there were, two of them, by the old Indian trail in those early times; but who cleared the first land, erected the first cabin, and brought civilization to Warren, we will tell in our next chapter.

CHAPTER II.

ABOUT JOSEPH PATCH, THE FIRST WHITE SETTLER OF WARREN, AND HOW HE HAD A FEW HUNGRY VISITORS WHICH ATE UP ALL HIS PROVISIONS.

ADAM was the first man, Eve the first woman; Noah and his sons peopled the earth after the flood; Columbus discovered America; Captain John Smith explored New England,* and

JOSEPH PATCH

was the first *bona fide* settler in the township of Warren.

Some men are born great, others achieve greatness, and some have greatness thrust upon them; and thus it is the good luck of Joseph Patch, by happening to be the first settler of our mountain hamlet, to be immortalized in this delightful history.

It was in the autumn of 1767 that he first came to Warren to live. He had imbibed a passion for hunting in his earliest boyhood and it was to gratify this taste that he built for himself a hunter's camp, the last of September, beside one of our wildest mountain torrents, Hurricane brook.†

He was a young man not yet twenty-one years old. He had brown hair, blue eyes, light complexion, a pleasing expression of countenance, and was very agreeable in conversation. He was of a middle stature, well formed, muscle hard and compact, would weigh about one hundred and fifty pounds, and was capable of great endurance. He had courage, and was cool and collected in

---

* New England is that part of America which, together with Virginia, Maryland, and Nova Scotia were by the Indians called (by one name) Wingadacoa.—III Series Mass. Hist. Soc. Col. Vol. 3, 239.

† Jacob Patch's statement. He was a son of Joseph Patch.

the hour of danger. It is told how he lay sleeping upon his bed of spruce boughs one dark night in his half-open camp, when the low growling of the dog at his side awoke him. The fire, which he had left burning when he went to sleep, had gone out, and all was black darkness in the woods. Only the rustle of the leaves overhead and the low murmur of the brook on the smooth-worn stones disturbed the silence. Looking cautiously out he could see nothing. His dog continuing to growl, he put his hand on the hound's back and found that the hair was as stiff as bristles. Again he looked out, and happening to raise his eyes he saw gleaming in the branches of a low maple what seemed two balls of fire. He knew what it was; only the eyes of a catamount could glow like that. He felt the cold sweat creeping over him, but realizing his danger he recovered himself, coolly picked up his gun, took deliberate aim and fired. There was a wild howl, a dead fall, a terrible struggle for a moment, biting the earth and rending the bark from the trees, and the ferocious animal was dead. The hunter's courage had saved his life. The catamount was preparing to spring upon him, and had he done so Patch would have been torn in pieces. He built a bright fire for the remainder of the night and in the morning had the pleasure of skinning the largest catamount he ever saw.*

In personal appearance he was the real backwoodsman. He had a cap of wolfskin, the hair considerably worn off; no vest or coat, but a short sheep's gray frock, which he tucked inside his moosehide breeches; a coarse tow shirt, no neck-tie, woollen stockings, and the real Indian moccasins on his feet. His dress was stout and would not easily be torn among the trees and underbrush through which he hastened.

Patch was "born of poor but respectable parents" in Hollis, N. H. His father's name was Thomas Patch. His early education was much neglected, he having attended school but a few months in his life. His boyhood had been passed on his father's farm, and he had been in the habit of gaining a few pence in autumn by building culheag traps on the banks of his native streams, to catch mink and muskrat, and he was also skillful in setting steel traps for foxes.

---

* Mrs. Hobart Wyatt said she heard Mr. Patch frequently relate this adventure.

When the mania for occupying northern lands first came on he accompanied the Hobarts and Websters, his townsmen, into the wilderness. He at first resided in the family of Mr. Hobart, in New Plymouth, of whom he bought some land. But avarice and cupidity got the better of his employer's morality, and he cheated Patch out of it. In after years Hobart repented and to ease his own conscience gave our first settler two cows in payment.* Patch afterwards worked for David Webster, inn keeper, a short time, and was often employed as a guide through the woods to the Coos intervals.

Just west of the main carriage road now running through the town, just east of the railroad and on the south bank of Hurricane brook, Joseph Patch built his hunter's camp. Game was plenty. Great fat salmon were swimming in the river, and trout that would weigh several pounds apiece sported in the brooks. There were partridges in abundance, and thousands of rabbits had here a *warren*—so that there need be no lack of something to eat. One might hunt, trap, or fish at pleasure. Wolf, bear, moose, or deer could be shot, and beaver, otter, sable, fox, mink, or muskrat captured for a rich store of peltries. These were the inducements that brought Joseph Patch to Warren.

Could you have stood by his camp a hundred years ago you would have felt that you were a long way in the wilderness, that you had somewhat of a rural house to stop at, that there was plenty of wood to burn and that there was a great chance for clearing before there could be any very fine farms. You would have seen hanging upon or fastened to the great pine trees around the skins of all the various animals above mentioned, drying with the flesh side out, the many-colored tails pendant presenting a gay and attractive appearance.

Joseph Patch had seen, at Plymouth, the proprietors' committee, that came to Warren the previous spring, and he had heard them say that in all probability land in Warren would be given by the proprietors, either in the fall or the next spring, to any one who would settle upon it, and that the first settler would have his first choice of lots. He had lost what he had purchased at Plymouth, and one day, as the story goes, recollecting what the com-

---

*Jacob Patch's statement.

mittee had said, he thought it might be an excellent idea to select the lot where he had built his camp. After thinking of the subject for some time he finally concluded as he had possession — which by the way is esteemed nine points in law — that committee or no committee, gift or no gift, he would have it if possible and remain where he was.

The next step was to choose a spot for clearing, and *the first week in October* he fell an acre or more of trees. The Indian summer dried them, and setting them on fire he got an excellent burn. Before snow fell he had cleared the ground ready for planting the next spring. This first opening in the forest — the initial acre clearing — was just east of the "Forks" school-house, sometimes called Clough school-house. It was in the corner of this lot that he planted the first apple tree that ever grew in Warren. Patch next cleared a small piece of land a few rods southwest of his camp.

It now became necessary to change his hunter's camp into a cabin, so he dug himself a cellar, stoned it, built over it a log shanty, covered it with spruce bark and tightened it with moss. A chimney of flat stones was built on one side, over a capacious fire-place; his door was made of rifted boards, hewed down with his axe, and an opening in the wall, closed at will with a shutter made in the same manner as the door, admitted the light.

On the top of a great pine stump, cut smoothly for the purpose, he built of stones and earth a tolerable Dutch oven. Thus furnished he was ready for the winter.

The remains of the apple tree which he planted, the old cellar fallen in, and the stump on which he built his oven, are yet to be seen.*

In addition to these labors he had good success in hunting. He found several beaver meadows, one on Black brook, one on Berry brook, and one on Patch brook. There was a beautiful pond on the latter stream, formed by a dam built of poles and mud, as only beavers can build a dam, and on the shores were numerous

---

*Jacob Patch's statement, 1857.
Jonathan Clough's statement. Mr. C. showed likewise the apple tree, the cellar, and the pine stump on which Patch built his oven. A ruler from the trunk of the apple-tree he first planted is in existence. It was made by Amos F. Clough, in 1856. The trunk is nearly all gone, but new sprouts have grown up, marking the place of the old tree.

picturesque, conical little mud domicils, full of various apartments opening only into the water, in which the beavers lived. It seemed too bad to destroy the habitations of these almost half-human and industrious villagers. But such thoughts never enter the head of a hunter, and Joseph Patch was very successful and took great pleasure in trapping these diligent animals. His mink and sable lines were also very productive. Thus he passed his time till the streams froze up and the snow flew.

Then he constructed a sled and took a journey "down country" to sell the rich product of his hunting. Necessaries purchased and he returned to his cabin in the wilderness.

It is winter now. Joseph Patch is alone in a great forest. His nearest neighbor is a Mr. Davis, who lives in that notable tract of country, since inhabited by a proud, good-feeling people, called after our royal governor, Wentworth. Alexander Craig* lived in Romney — now called Rumney on account of the immense amount of "good rum," said to be "excellent for sore eyes," kept and drank by the jolly roisterers who have inhabited that fair region. There was quite a settlement at Plymouth — not the Plymouth of Cape Cod Bay, where pious ministers with vinegar faces preached to witch-hanging congregations — but Plymouth,

---

*Ephraim Lund built the first saw and grist mill in Plymouth, near where Cochran's mills now are. Mr. Dearborn says that in 1765 James Heath, from Canterbury, Daniel Brainard, Esq., and Alexander Craig made settlements in Romney. Soon after a Mr. Davis moved into Wentworth, and Joseph Patch into Warren. He says that he knows that these were the first settlers in these towns, but will not be positive as to the year they made their entrance.—Powers' Hist. of Coos, 172.

"March 1, 1775. This may certify that Joseph Patch is entitled to one hundred acres of land in the township of Warren, by his settling in said town, agreeably to a vote of the proprietary of said township in the year 1773. We agree that he shall have lot No. 19 in the 9th range in the second division in said township for the same.
P. WHITE,
EBENEZER STEVENS,
Committee in the year 1774 to lay lots for settlers."

Jan. 18, 1787. "Voted that Joseph Patch have liberty to pitch one lot in lieu of that he formerly pitched in said town for a settler's lot, which happens to be in Coventry by the running the last lines."

June 28, 1787. "Voted that Joseph Patch have lot No. 14 in the third range of lots laid out for settlers' lots, and for lots taken into other towns by a new line; it being in lieu of one that was taken into Coventry that was given him for settling in said town."

See Proprietors' Records.

JOSEPH PATCH'S FAMILY RECORD.

He married *Anna Merrill*. She was born Dec. 28, 1756.

Daniel, born February, 1778.
Joseph, Jr., born April, 1780.
David, born 1782.
Anna, born 1784.
Thomas.

Jacob, born August 13, 1786.
William. [He was a lame man and taught school on Pine hill.]
Stephen, born August 2, 1796.

N. H. Daniel Cross and Mr. John Mann had founded the mighty town of Orford, sometimes vulgarly called Oxford, owing probably to the huge oxen raised there. The Roots, Crooks, and Daleys had set down in the territory named Piermont, which extends westward quite to the Varsche, or fresh, or Connecticut river, as the Dutchmen call it. There were numerous families squatted on the rich meadows of the Coosucks, but not a human being lived in old Coventry—the land where blueberry hills abound—or in Peeling, or in Trecothick, great wilderness regions beyond the eastern mountains. Patch was veritably alone. Yet the solitude was not so terrible as it was a year before. True he heard the howl of the wolves every night, except when the tempest was so loud as to drown it. Catamount tracks were seen in the snow, and he bolted his door and fastened his one shutter tightly when in the darkness its terribly human cry, freezing the blood, came sounding through the forest. There were yards of wild deer on the hills and in the ravines from which the spring torrents rushed, and Joseph Patch also saw yarded by the Asquamchumauke great wild beasts, or moose, which John Josselyn, Gent., describes as "Creatures, or rather if you will, Monsters of superfluity." "A full-grown moose," to use his own language, "is many times bigger than an English oxe, their horns, as I have said elsewhere, very big, (and brancht out in palms), the tips whereof are sometimes found to be two fathoms assunder, (a fathom is six feet, from the tip of one finger to the tip of the other, that is four cubits), and in height from the toe of the forefoot to the pitch of the shoulder twelve foot, both of which has been taken by my sceptique readers to be monstrous lyes. If you consider the bredth that the beast carrieth and the magnitude of the horns you will be easily induced to contribute your belief." One of these "monsters of superfluity" our first settler killed for the sake of the meat, and a shot now and then furnished delicious venison, equal to any procured from an English park. He buried the greater part in the snow, to remain frozen for future use, and dug it out when wanted. One night his dog, lying by the fire on the hearth, barked. He listened and heard out in the woods the howl of a pack of wolves coming. They were famished and food they must have. They growled about the house, snapped at the closed door, and mounted by the snow bank upon the bark roof. Patch thought there was danger they might come down the chimney, so he piled his morning wood on the fire, making the smoking flue a difficult place of ingress. All at once there was a sharp bark, a howl, then a hurry, then growling, snapping, snarling like hungry dogs, and the man in the cabin knew that his visitors were making most free with his moose meat and venison. He was content, for he was aware that when that was gone he would get a clean riddance of his ravenous friends, the wolves, and then with his long barreled gun he could easily replenish his stock of provisions. The next day however, as a matter of precaution, he strengthened his roof.*

Thus the weeks went by, with plenty to eat and nothing to do but chop his firewood, or hunt up the valley or on the mountains for a day, accompanied by his faithful dog, or a trip to Plymouth now and then, to learn the news and to obtain supplies, which he drew to camp upon a hand-sled; with an occasional visit from his distant neighbors in the wild bordering regions, or a call from some northern traveller,—thus passed the winter. The spring came with its warm sun, melting snows, wild mountain torrents, roaring river, expanding buds, green grass, bright woodland flowers, and then—road-committee, surveying, lot-locating party, and last, though best of all, cheering neighbors, as the next chapter will show.

---

*Samuel Merrill's statement; said he had heard Patch tell this story often.
Joseph Patch moved to the north bank of Patch brook and had his house on the east side of the old Coos road. His son, Joseph Patch, Jr., built the house now [1870] occupied by Jonathan Eaton, and lived in it until he sold it to Mr. Eaton.

CHAPTER III.

HOW EIGHTEEN FAMILIES AND TWO SINGLE GENTLEMEN CAME TO WARREN TO RESIDE AND AMUSED THEMSELVES BUILDING CABINS, CLEARING LAND, HUNTING MOOSE AND DEER ON THE HILLS, AND FISHING IN THE CLEAR RAPID TROUT STREAMS.

AND now the solitary places shall be made glad, and the wilderness shall blossom like a rose. How it all happened, who came to do it, the order of their coming, and the time when they came, will constitute the unity of this most welcome chapter of Warren's history.

We have seen how our worthy proprietors in the spring of 1768 began to put forth the most prodigious efforts to save their well-timbered lands up among the hills. We remember how at the annual meeting it was voted to give each individual who should settle in town prior to October 1st, 1768, fifty acres of land and six pounds in money; how the road-clearing committee came up to Warren, how they were to lay out the twenty-five lots of land in such place as they thought proper, and how each family who should settle as above should have one of the lots, the first settler to have his first choice, and so each in his order.

This was the tempting bait. It had the desired effect. Danger of losing everything was why it was thrown out, and persons wishing to become real estate holders as well as pioneers on the frontier, eagerly caught at it.

I have heard my uncle[*] say, and he was well versed in such matters, that the first family that settled in Warren was from Portsmouth, N. H. He said that in the spring of 1768, before the

---
[*] Benjamin Little.

snow was hardly gone, Mr. JOHN MILLS, with his wife and their son John, several other children and Mr. Mills' sister, with one horse on which they rode by turns and on whose back was borne a decidedly small stock of household furniture, and also driving a cow along with them, came journeying up the bridle-path to Warren. The proprietors had offered the land and Phillips White had persuaded Mr. Mills to come on as a settler.

His was the first choice of lots. He chose one that was bounded west by the Asquamchumauke, and through the meadow on the east flowed Patch brook. On the ridge which once formed a part of the second of the three geological terraces in the Asquamchumauke valley, just south of the river bridge in the lower village, and east of the great railroad bridge, he selected the site of his cabin. It was a frail habitation, erected on the very day of his arrival, but it served as a shelter during the summer. Upon one side he built a stone fire-place, and a chimney of small sticks and mud. Household furniture he had next to none, and he was under the necessity of manufacturing some.

He made a rustic table, but a good one as my uncle testified, by splitting a large ash tree into several thin pieces, smoothing them with his axe, and then pinning them side by side to two other pieces which ran in opposite directions in the form of cleats. This he fastened to one side of the cabin, supporting it by small posts driven into the ground for legs. But he had a more novel method for making chairs, and it was the one generally practiced by the first settlers. The top of a spruce or fir tree was selected, upon which several limbs were growing; this was split through the middle, the limbs cut off the proper length for legs, and after smoothing to suit the fancy the chair was complete. Sometimes the body of the tree was cut nearly off, and then quite off at a proper distance, the wood split down and quite a comfortable back left. These made durable chairs, and the instances were rare in which it became necessary to send them to the cabinet maker for repairs — especially to have the legs glued in.

Bedsteads were made by boring two holes into the log walls of the cabin, about six feet apart. In these were driven two sapling poles, the ends of the same being supported by posts. For cords elm bark was used.

A little, hard-meated, leathern-sided, wiry man, with gray eyes and grizzly hair, was John Mills. His son John also was as tough as tripe, and taken both together they were just the men to make a settlement in the wilderness.

Almost the first thing they did after erecting their rude cabin was to tear out the logs in the beaver dam and drain the pond. Here wild grass grew, which, together with a few turnips, eked out with birch and hemlock browse and such other rough fodder, was sufficient to keep the horse and cow during the winter. All summer their little stock pastured on the banks of the river or browsed in the woods. Then the men cleared a few acres of land to the south and east of their cabin, where they planted corn, turnips, and pumpkins, and a large quantity of beans, which served as the basis of that favorite dish, bean porridge, with which they so often regaled themselves. The seed was almost all obtained at Plymouth and Haverhill.

John Mills was proud of his little farm. His field was then, and is now, a place of beautiful springs, of swift and crystalline brooks. Above them dances in the fresh June breeze, frisky and festive,—warbling, chirping, singing — the little black-backed, white-breasted, gay and jolly bob-o'-lincoln, making all the time music sweet and loud enough to burst his slender throat. In the trees that hang over the waters, and upon the banks, the thrush and the robin build their nests, and send out over the green sward the merry song, or at evening their long plaintive carol, while in autumn the hill and mountain eastward burst into a crimson blaze of beauty.

Mr. Mills also changed work with Mr. Patch, by helping the latter clear and plant, while our hunter-settler, with a rifle which he bought the last winter, paying for it in furs, procured moose meat and venison for his neighbor.*

Now it so happened that there was journeying northward to find a home in the forest a certain Irishman recently from the Emerald isle, named James Aiken. With his wife and two children, one night in May, he stopped at our public hotel on the west

---

*The old settlers used to tell how the wolves howled about John Mills' house the first winter he lived in town, and looked into his only window, putting their noses against the window-pane, and staring at the family as they sat by the great fire-place in the evening; but Mills' folks were not to be frightened by such visitors.

bank of the Asquamchumauke. The next morning the sun came up hot and the weather was sultry. Nevertheless the family shouldered their packs and began their journey. For a time they got along well, for the tall trees through which the path ran afforded an agreeable shade, and the rippling of the river and Black brook—the Mikaseota—made mellow music in their ears. But when they arrived on the ridge between the brook and the river the trees were more scattered, and the sun, which had got higher, shot his vertical rays directly upon their heads, making the day intolerably hot. "Be jabers," said James Aiken, " in faith I can't stand this;" and the rest of the family being somewhat of the same mind, and also slightly foot-sore, they came to a halt near the present site of Warren depot. The river looked pleasant and the meadow beyond inviting, and our traveller thought he might journey to the world's end and not find a better place or a more pleasant home. But the fact that he did not own a foot of the land made him hesitate. But in a moment it was all right, "For," said he, " an' surely we shan't be seen here in the woods, if we only get a good distance from the path."

Resuming their packs, they left the old Indian trail, crossed the river, climbed out of the meadow half a mile to the east, and on the second plateau or terrace, just beside a clear babbling brook, they chose a spot for their cabin. It was built that very day of posts and bark, and served as a shelter till the frosts came and the leaves fell, when they erected a strong cabin of hewed logs, better than any they had ever had in old Ireland. The cellar that they dug, though now nearly filled up, is yet to be seen.

The next morning Aiken climbed up on to the ledgy hillside east of his cabin, as my old uncle* told me, where he could get a good prospect, and was greatly surprised to see a blue smoke curling lazily out of the forest, and floating away above the trees half a mile to the south of him. "Be jabers! I have got neighbors," said James Aiken, and being a genial soul he was not long in making their acquaintance.

A foot-path blazed through the wood to the proprietors' highway, and another to John Mills', were the only roads ever built to the Irishman's cabin.

---

*Benjamin Little.

JAMES AIKEN was thus the third settler in Warren; and Mr. John Mills had still another neighbor just to the north of his own location.

JOSHUA COPP, ESQ., the fourth settler, came to Warren from Hampstead, N. H., the last of May, 1768. He chose a lot laid out by the committee, and built his cabin on the southerly slope of Red Oak hill, forty or fifty rods north of Martin brook, which runs at its base.

Copp was broad-shouldered, square-built, with an open, intellectual countenance, and was always a man of much influence. He was energetic and hard-working, and that summer would often come home to his dinner of bean-porridge, from the woods where he had been burning a piece, with his short frock and long-legged breeches crusted with ashes, and his face smirched with coals. His table, around which gathered his wife and five children, besides himself, was made of a single board, which he hewed from an immense pine tree. Often there was but one dish upon it, a large wooden bowl, which he also made, and it would hold ten quarts. This was filled with bean porridge—the best meal of victuals in his shanty. Furnished each with a wooden spoon, the whole family would eat out of it at once.*

In Mr. Copp's house Joshua Copp, Jr., was born, February 25th, 1769,—Warren's first white son. But we never heard that Mrs. Copp, his mother, ever received a lot of land or other bounty, as was customary in those times.†

---

*The settlers made bean porridge by boiling the beans very soft, thickening the liquor, and adding a piece of salt pork to season it. A handful of corn was sometimes put in. It is said—I do not vouch for its truth—that when the good man was going away with his team the woman would make a pot porridge and freeze it with the string in, so that he could hang it on his sled-stake, and when he wanted to bait he might cut off a piece and thaw it.

† JOSHUA AND SALLY *(Poor)* COPP'S FAMILY RECORD.
He was born in Hampstead, May 11, 1741. She was born in Rowley, Oct. 27, 1741. Married, Sept. 19, 1758.

Molly, born July 15, 1759.
Elizabeth, born April 14, 1761.
Moses, born Feb. 22, 1763.
Eliphalet, born Feb. 27, 1765.
Sarah, born March 25, 1767.
Joshua, Feb. 25, 1769.
Susannah, born March 29, 1771.
Benj. L. died November 23, 1798.

Mehitable, born May 15, 1773.
George Washington, born August 26, 1776.
Samuel, born Aug. 9, 1778.
Benjamin Little, born Sept. 12, 1780.
Nathaniel Peabody, born June 23, 1783.
William Wallace, born April 3, 1786.

Oct. 19, 1797. "Voted that Phillips White, Esq., have a lot marked on the plan, 'Phillips White, N,' adjoining on lot No. 13, laid out to the right of Belcher

ANOTHER BEAVER POND DRAINED. 219

Esquire Copp drove a cow into the wilderness. During the summer she could live well enough, feeding by the brook and in the woods, but in the winter she must have hay. His neighbor, Joseph Patch, told him there was a beaver pond on the Mikaseota or Black brook, and around the sedgy shore wild grass grew in great abundance.

It was a June day when he went to the valley of Runaway pond, where was the little tarn of the beavers. He left the proprietors' road, which ran some forty rods to the west, and proceeding noiselessly through the woods came to the water's edge. A wood duck with her brood was swimming on its surface; sandpipers, uttering their querulous "weet, weet," ran through their reedy haunts; a blue heron was watching for fish at the outlet, and by the head of the pond, on the blasted peak of a great pine, an eagle stood out against the sky. He saw the long row of beaver huts opposite, and a single beaver, watching him, sank in the water and disappeared, leaving scarcely a ripple. Following along the shore a wild-cat sprang across his track; the blue heron at the outlet flew away; the duck with her brood dove and rose farther off toward the head of the pond, then dove and rose again still further away, and the eagle screaming soared aloft in mighty circles till lost in the deep blue. For a moment only he paused; then with his axe he cut a lever, pried out some of the logs in the dam—the gurgling water rushing through assisting him—and before night the beaver pond was gone forever. In August he cut a large quantity of grass upon this made meadow, stacked it, and with the help of his neighbors drew away upon handsleds the ensuing winter what the moose and deer did not eat.

Mr. Ephraim True came from somewhere down country, but from what town never could be learned, even from the oldest

---

Dole, with a gore of land lying near unto said lot; and a lot No. 17, in the first range of lots laid out, for those lots which were cut off by the late lines, and drawn to the right of William Parker, Esq., for a lot he the said White gave to Joshua Copp, Esq., for settling in the town."

Joshua Copp died in Warren about 1804. He was buried near the outlet of Runaway pond, beside the old Indian trail. The precise spot is unknown. There let him rest in an unmarked grave "till the last trump shall call him back to life."

William Wallace Copp, youngest son of 'Squire Joshua, was a very smart man. He became a merchant in Montreal and imported his goods. He went on a sailing vessel to England and no tidings were ever received from him afterwards. He is said to have been the best-looking man in the country, had a fine intellect, and was given to theological discussions. He wrote a powerful pamphlet on predestination and free agency. His death has always been a mystery.

inhabitants. He settled a short distance north of Mr. Aiken, in a place long known to the villagers of our mountain hamlet as "over the river." Mr. True was a strong, stalwart man, and had a large family, his wife being much more prolific than the red-headed spouse of his neighbor Aiken. I have heard my grandmother say that her mother told her — and there is no doubt of the truthfulness of the story, for my great-grandmother was a most excellent woman — that once upon a time she went to Mr. True's a-visiting. On her arrival she found no one at home, Mr. True and his good dame being at work in the woods clearing. Seating herself upon a stool she soon heard a slight noise, and looking carefully about she saw some half a dozen flaxen, towy heads, peeping from under the bed watching her, but not one could she coax to come out. Mrs. True coming in shortly after, excused herself and children, saying, "Lor! they see people so seldom they are as wild as partridges." One man, after listening to this anecdote, was heard to say that the fact afforded food for the contemplation of serious and pious persons, as to whether man, like the ass, kept in solitude, would not quickly return to his naturally wild state. We may add that these children afterwards made smart men and women.

This season the proprietors' committee was in town, clearing the road, and also running the lines about the lots. Travellers journeying to and from the northern settlements were plenty, and our five settlers often travelled to Plymouth or Haverhill for supplies, carrying them to their homes on their backs. Thus passed the time, and this year no more settlers came.

In the winter of 1769, at a meeting of the proprietors, it will be remembered that a vote was passed to give to each of ten settlers "who shall move into town this year fifty acres of land and six pounds in money, or one hundred acres of land without the money, as they may choose," each making his selection in the order of his settling. A committee, consisting of Col. Jonathan Greeley, Lieut. Joseph Page, and Mr. Enoch Page, was chosen to lay out the lots and agree with settlers. The proprietors also began to talk much about building a saw-mill, to supply the inhabitants with boards, thus making them as comfortable as possible. This had the desired effect, and two more brave men came to town.

JOHN WHITCHER, the sixth settler, came from Salisbury in the spring of 1769. He was unmarried, and was travelling about the world in search of his fortune. Some say that Moses Greeley, of Salisbury, persuaded him to come on and make a settlement in order that the most possible might be done to fulfil the first condition of the charter. But this don't matter; all that we care for is the fact that he really came. He was a red-haired man, with light blue eyes, muscles of steel, a heart as brave as a lion, and just the fellow to fell trees and commence a wilderness settlement. He located himself on Pine hill, built a cabin, and in the fall went back down country to see his sweetheart, Miss Sarah Marston.* The proprietors afterwards gave him the lot he chose by direct vote.

JOHN MORRILL was a friend of Mr. Whitcher, and he came to Warren along with him. Mr. Morrill had a family, and being of a speculative disposition, he bought out 'Squire Copp. The latter had procured the lot containing his beaver meadow, and he immediately erected a cabin there and moved into it, being the first settler in the valley of Runaway pond. John Morrill was a lively genius, and was sure to create a wide-awake neighborhood. In short he was a sturdy, obstinate, bustling little man, and it was lucky he moved into the woods, for he always managed to keep every one about him on the *qui vive*. He also had a good store of worldly goods, which he contrived to bring to Warren by making sundry down country journeys. This property was well taken care of, for he was of a saving turn, as evidenced by his always wearing an old greasy pair of moosehide breeches for the sake of economy. As we have before intimated he was continually given to trade, and before he had been in town a year he swapped farms with another settler.

And now came the tug of war — the great struggle of life and death for the proprietors, whether or not they should get a new

---

*JOHN AND SARAH *(Marston)* WHITCHER'S FAMILY RECORD.
He was born at Salisbury, Mass., June 19, 1749. She was born October 14, 1748.
Married, Dec. 6, 1770.

Joseph, born Nov. 10, 1772.	Obadiah, born Oct. 11, 1784.
Reuben, born Dec. 30, 1773.	Batchelder, born Aug. 3, 1787.
John, born Aug. 10, 1775.	Obadiah, 2d, born April 23, 1789.
Betty, born Oct. 3, 1778.	Jeremiah, born Jan. 29, 1790.
Sarah, born Oct. 17, 1779.	Rebecca, born Dec. 19, 1795.
Henry D., born Oct. 30, 1782.	

charter, as we have before shown. To succeed they must make strong, desperate efforts; settlers must be procured faster and other improvements for a new settlement must be pushed rapidly on. Accordingly the grantees of Warren made the king's highway broader; laid out a new road over the Height-o'-land to Haverhill Corner, and discontinued the old route by Wachipauka pond; a new division of lots was located; large bounties* were offered for settlers, and even to those who would only "fall trees" in town; and it was proposed to give thirty pounds to any one who would erect a saw-mill and supply the inhabitants with boards. But all this was to no purpose, for the settlers did not come. Three years went by before another family sat down in Warren.

OBADIAH CLEMENT came from Sandown, N. H., in the year 1772, and settled on the northwesterly side of Runaway pond valley. Mr. Clement, in after years a militia colonel, was a large, stout man, about five feet ten inches in height, would weigh one hundred and eighty pounds, and was as quick-motioned as a cat. He was born at Kingston, N. H., the 19th day of February, 1743, O. S., and married Sarah Batchelder, Aug. 27th, 1765.† He was

---

*March 25, 1771. "Voted to give each family that shall settle in town this present year sixty acres of land, agreeably to the vote of last year."
At the same meeting, "Voted to give to each person as shall fall trees in the township of Warren this year half a dollar per acre."—See Proprietors' Records.
"Voted that Phillips White and Mr. Samuel Page be a committee to agree with settlers."—Do.

---

† OBADIAH AND SARAH *(Batchelder)* CLEMENT'S FAMILY RECORD.

He was born at Kingston, Feb. 19, 1743, O. S.   She was born June 30, 1747. Married Aug. 27, 1765.

Anna, born at Sandown, Apr. 19, 1767.
Job, born Dec. 13, 1768.
Mehitable, born Feb. 27, 1771.
Daniel, born March 7, 1773.

Obadiah, born in Warren, Feb. 28, 1775.
Obadiah, 2d, born Feb. 10, 1776.
Batchelder, born Feb. 15, 1782.
Moses H., born Feb. 12, 1784.

Married *Sarah Baker*, of Suncook, Sept. 9, 1788, who was born Aug. 26, 1750, O. S.

Sarah B., born Sept. 9, 1789.
Batchelder, born June 30, 1791.
Lovewell, born April 13, 1793.

Joseph B., born May 8, 1794.
Joseph, born Oct. 25, 1798.

Col. Obadiah died, aged 87, in 1829.   Sarah Batchelder, his wife, died Jan. 1, 1786.

Obadiah, first child of that name, died March 25, 1775.
Batchelder, died Jan. 24. 1786.

Lovewell, died May 22, 1793.
Joseph B., March 26, 1795.

April 20, 1772. "Voted to give every man that moves into town this year one hundred acres of good land."
"Voted to give half a dollar per acre for every acre of trees that shall be fell in Warren this year."
"Phillips White, Esq., Col. Jonathan Greeley, and Ebenezer Tucker were chosen a committee to agree with settlers."
"Voted to defend the proprietors or others who may settle under them in making improvement on the disputed lands in said town."
See Proprietors' Records.

a cooper by trade, and worked at the business more or less during his whole life. He lived for a short time in Sandown, N. H., and while there speculated somewhat in saw-mills, as a sort of recreation. He bought his land of Col. Jonathan Greeley, and by him was induced to come to Warren. He built a large cabin at the forks* of the bridle paths, where one ran west over the Height-o'-land and the other north by Wachipauka or Meader pond. He took great pains building it, hewed the logs down smooth, made it twice as wide and twice as long as any other cabin in town, had two good large rooms, with bedrooms, cupboard and pantry alongside, and in the rear a shed made of poles and bark. The chimney had two capacious, cavernous fire-places, all built of stone, one in each room. There were four bed rooms in the garret, parted off or separated from each other by a frame-work of poles covered with spruce bark. The house itself was covered with long, shaved shingles. It had doors of hewn boards, a floor of square hewn logs, firm and solid, and each room on the ground floor was lighted by a small window, the five-by-seven glass for the panes having been brought up from down country on the back of a horse. When the cabin was finished and furnished a hotel was opened, and Obadiah Clement was Warren's first landlord.

My great-grandfather† used to tell what a mighty fine building Col. Clement's hotel was, which grew up so suddenly in the wilderness. The old gentleman related how he travelled up the bridle-path one afternoon to see the landlord and get some of the good things with which his bar was always well stocked. Entering the little clearing, which seemed a sort of island in the woods,

---

*At first they only had a spotted line over the Height-o'-Land to Haverhill Corner, and Col. Chas. Johnson and others lost it one night, as they attempted to follow it through by feeling the spots on the trees, and had to lie in the woods until morning. Rev. Grant Powers says: "It was not the expectation of the people of Coos that they should ever have a road through to Plymouth for loaded teams, but their hopes rested on Charlestown for heavy articles; and the first time an ox-team went through it was effected by a company who went out expressly for the purpose with Jonathan McConnell at their head. The expedition excited much interest with the inhabitants at home, and the progress of the adventurers was inquired for from day to day; and when they were making Haverhill Corner upon their return, the men went out to meet and congratulate with them, and as they came in the cattle were taken possession of in due form, and conducted to sweet-flowing fountains and well-stuffed cribs for the night. Their masters were served in the style of lords, and their narration of the feats of 'Old Broad' at the sloughs, the patient endurance of 'Old Berry' at the heights, and the stiff hold-back of 'Old Duke' at the narrows, were listened to by their owners with the liveliest demonstrations of joy."—History of Coos, 118.

†Joshua Copp, Esq.

he sat down on the trunk of a tree to cool and rest himself. Even to him, a rough backwoodsman, there was much of beauty in the place. The green fields lying so peacefully in the forest, which in one place pushed forward its scattered trees, in another retreated, here sprinkling them out thinly, and there hanging their masses of dark foliage over the low-roofed buildings. The cabin, so quiet too; a few wild-flowers, crane's-bill, and honeysuckle growing by the door and open window; a flock of geese cropping the grass, and the cows coming home out of the forest to be milked, the bell on the leader, slung to her neck with a leathern strap and buckle, sounding so quaint and woodland-like, made all resemble some bright land of the poets, full of Arcadian beauty. Then there was a ringing of steel-shod hoofs, and as two travellers on horseback winding out of the woods by the bridle-path proceeded across the field, he looked up and saw the low stone chimney of the cabin smoking, and the shadows stretching out longer from the top of the mountain across the grain and the grass land and over the forest. "But the best of all," said the good old man, "Obadiah Clement treated me handsomely that night."

Col. Clement had the most fertile farm in town, and on his open meadow, which gave evidence that the Indians had burnt it over and planted it long years before, he cut hay enough to keep his cow and yoke of steers. He got corn at Haverhill, and salt and such other necessaries at Plymouth. These he brought home on his back. Fortune favored him in procuring a supply of meat. Opening the door one morning before the rest of the family were stirring, he saw a moose feeding among the black stumps of his little clearing. He had a gun, plenty of powder, but not a bullet in the house. Yet he did not hesitate long. An old military coat that some friend had worn in the French war furnished great brass bell buttons, and he rammed home three of them. Priming the old "queen's arm" he took deliberate aim and fired. One of the buttons pierced the heart and the moose running a few rods fell dead. Col. Clement was standing in his door at the time, and the loud report woke up in great fright the whole family, till then sound asleep; but they soon ascertained what was the matter. That morning they had the choicest morsel, the under lip, for breakfast, and all winter long they rejoiced over the happy shot.

Col. Clement's younger brothers came on and worked for him during the summer, and the next year, 1773,—

JONATHAN CLEMENT* came to Warren as a settler. It was Enoch Page, one of the proprietors, that furnished him a home in our mountain hamlet. He gave Mr. Clement the lot of land lying between Col. Clement's and 'Squire Copp's, and he built his cabin a short distance northwest of the spot where the road from Pine hill *did* intersect with the old turnpike. In September Mr. Clement went down country, got married, and moved his young wife home. Dolly, his first child, was born Nov. 4, 1774, in Warren.

REUBEN CLEMENT, the other brother, lived with Jonathan many years. Reuben was the tallest of the three, standing six feet in his stockings, and was an active, athletic man, but sometimes a little crazy. When the fit was on him he would stalk through the woods from cabin to cabin, carrying a cane as high as his head, stout enough for a lever and with the branches partly left on, for all the world like the one borne by the witch Meg Merillies. On such occasions he would dress himself in his best, a suit brought

---

*JONATHAN AND HANNAH *(Page)* CLEMENT'S FAMILY RECORD.
He was born Jan. 3, 1753, at Sandown, N. H.   She was born Dec. 23, 1756.   Married Sept. 24, 1773.

Dolly, born Nov. 4, 1774; died Nov. 18, 1779.
Jonathan, Jr., born Aug. 23, 1776; died Sept. 23, 1777.
Hannah, born Feb. 20, 1778; died Oct. 30, 1779.
Jonathan, 3d, born Oct. 12, 1780.
Hannah, born Jan. 27, 1783.
Ephraim, born Feb. 12, 1785.

Page, born May 1, 1787; died Aug. 11, 1789.
John, born April 30, 1789.
Page, born Aug. 29, 1790.
Dolly and Eleanor, July 25, 1792.
Sally, born June 20, 1794.
John, born July 17, 1796.
Benjamin, born Nov. 25, 1798.
Daniel, born Dec. 3, 1801.

"Wentworth, Oct. 21, 1796. This may certify that Jonathan Clement, of Warren, is entitled to Lot No. 8 on which he now lives, for settling the same, according to former votes. Accepted and allowed.   PHILLIPS WHITE,
ENOCH PAGE,
Committee."

Oct. 20, 1786. "Voted that Enoch Page, Esq., have Lot No. 2, laying south of the No. on which Jonathan Clement now lives, in consideration of a lot he drawed for said Clement to settle on."
See Proprietors' Records.

April 29, 1773. "Voted that such private ways as Phillips White, Esq., Capt. William Hackett, and Ensign Enoch Page shall think proper to be cleared this present year, shall be done at the charge of the proprietary."

"Voted to give 100 acres of land to each of ten families who shall actually settle in town the present year."

Joseph Patch claimed his land under the above vote, as it was the best offer that had been made.

"Voted that the said committee to clear out private ways be a committee to lay out lots for settlers, and the family that first moves into town to take his first choice, and so as they move in."

See Proprietors' Records.

Joseph Patch did not settle on and never lived on the lot of land he got, as will be seen by examining the Proprietors' Records.

from down country. His glittering knee-buckles, which fastened his short tight breeches to his long stockings, his bright silver shoe buckles, his coat slung on his arm, his long jacket unbuttoned, the collar of his linen shirt loose and flowing, his long hair streaming in the wind, and his bright eye, restless and flashing under his cocked up hat, made him seem some weird man of the woods. Reuben Clement had a friend and familiar companion who came to Warren along with him.

SIMEON SMITH was the man,—and all of his neighbors as long as he lived believed that he was an adept at the black art. Of him it was alleged, "That some gloomy night, like those chosen by magicians to invoke spirits, he had called up the devil at the cross roads where four roads met in his native town, and to obtain superhuman powers had sworn to be his liege man, and had then kissed Satan's cloven hoof." Wonderful were the feats he could perform. Sometimes, from sheer malice, he would saddle and bridle one of his neighbors, and ride and gallop him all over the country round. Then turning jack-o'-lantern, with counterfeiting voice he would call some loitering person through woods, around marshy ponds into tangled thickets, and leave him lost in the cold damp swamp. The butter would not come, and he was in the churn; the cat mewed and jumped wildly about the house, and he was tormenting her; the children behaved strangely, and he had bewitched them. Smaller than a gnat, he could go through the key hole; larger than a giant, he was seen at twilight stalking through the forest. He could travel in the thin air, and mounted on a moonbeam could fly swift as the red meteor over the woods and the mountains.

Without doubt all this was pious scandal, worthy of the old Puritans, for Simeon Smith was a good man, and in spite of their superstition compelled the respect of his neighbors. He came to Warren in February, 1773, bringing his family and worldly effects in a one-horse vehicle, known among farmers as a "jumper." He settled on Red Oak hill, and lived for a time with that restive little backwoodsman, Mr. John Morrill. Mr. Smith was likewise a small-sized man, smart to work and quick-motioned. He had a large family, two or three boys old enough to help, and before another winter he had a comfortable cabin of his own.

EPHRAIM LUND was the next settler. He came from Plymouth, N. H., where he had built the first saw-mill for the proprietors of that township, and he erected a cabin and cleared a few acres on the south shore of Tarleton lake. The place where he lived was long known as Charleston, but why it was so called no one has ever been able to tell. It rained a few days after he first came to Warren, succeeded at night by a thick fog. A little past sunset he was startled by the wildest cry he ever heard. It seemed as if some one lost in the woods was hallooing in despair. He got his gun and starting towards the lake discharged it several times, that the report might guide the lost one to his cabin—but no person came. Who was it? What had happened? A few days after he heard the hallooing again, and going through the woods to the rocky shore he learned that the sound that startled him so was the cry of "the great northern diver." He had never heard or seen the bird before, and was now perfectly satisfied that when told that any one could "halloo like a loon" that such person's voice must be most loud and terrible, especially if it was heard by a man solitary and alone, on a foggy night, and in the dark woods.

JOSEPH LUND, his brother, came shortly after, and settled near him. He was a good-natured, kind-hearted man, and it is said that he was of middle stature, broad-shouldered, rather bandy-legged, brown-complexioned, carroty-bearded, hairy-bodied, big-bellied, and fiery-red-nosed. Dame Rumor has it that he loved good milk toddy and was not averse to whisky punch. He wore a long, home-made frock, coming down half-way from his knees to his heels, and he was accustomed to girt a half-inch rope, twice drawn tightly around him, as some said to keep his well-filled belly from bursting. Then he talked loud on some occasions, but at times his tongue was rather thick, and it bothered people to understand him. He was a good shot, and when he travelled in the woods always carried his gun with him.

It is told how returning home from Wentworth one day in the fall he saw a large bull moose drinking from the river, near the foot of Red Oak hill and not far from the present south line of the town. He immediately fired at the animal, but the ball only staggered it. Instantly recovering itself it dashed out of the water, leaped up the opposite bank, and disappeared in the thick woods. Mr. Lund hastily reloaded, rushed through the river, saw that it was stained with blood, and following the easy trail for a few rods met the moose, which had turned to face him. Again he fired and again the animal fled. This continued till he had lodged six bullets in its body, when he succeeded in dispatching it. It was a prize, and supplied meat for both of the Mr. Lunds all winter.

Mr. Lund was also an excellent trapper as well as hunter, as the following strictly historical anecdote will show. Tradition relates that he drove a few sheep to Warren, the first ones ever kept in town, but he found it rather an unprofitable investment, for the reason that the bears killed so many of them. They had to be yarded every night, and during the daytime they would frequently come running to the house pursued by these black-coated gentry. One afternoon he found the remains of one that had been killed, and wishing to take revenge he gathered and placed them by the end of a hollow birch log. Inside the log he set the gun in such a manner that when the bear began to eat the mutton he would discharge the gun and receive the contents in his own head. Mr. Lund heard the report of his old queen's arm in the night, and rising early the next morning he went to learn the result. He found a very large bear lying dead a short distance from a heap of half-roasted mutton, while the log was a pile of burning coals. Among these was the gun, minus the entire wooden fixtures, with the barrel, lock, and ramrod essentially ruined. This was a great loss to him, but he often recounted with much glee the manner in which he swapped his gun for a bear.* South from the Lunds, and on the eastern shore of Eastman ponds,—

THOMAS CLARK† began a settlement. He was tall of stature, fair-complexioned, with black hair and a keen black eye, his aspect between mild and stern; of few words, slow in speech, not easily provoked, and soon pacified. Another man, just his opposite in appearance, for contraries love companionship, came to Warren with him.

---

*Mr. Stephen Lund's statement.
†Voted, Oct. 19, 1797, that Phillips White have a gore of land running on Piermont line, marked on the plan "Phillips White," in consideration of his settling Thomas Clark.—Proprietors' Records.

ISAIAH BATCHELDER was broad-faced, of a ruddy complexion, rolling eyes, with a large belly, and a lover of fat living. He built a log hut for himself south of Mr. Clark's, but did not move into it with his family till the next season. These two men received their land from Warren's most energetic proprietor, at that time living, Mr. Phillips White.

CHASE WHITCHER came next. He was born in Salisbury, was a relative of Mr. John Whitcher, who was as yet our only settler on Pine hill, and although a mere boy he took possession of a lot of land in the north part of the town, fell a few acres of trees, and built himself a log camp covered with bark. He was sent by the proprietors, they observing that he was a resolute youth, that they might if possible fulfill the to them terrible first condition of the charter.

Chase, the boy settler, was a tall, bony, raw-built fellow, with a spare face, red hair, and a hard head, and he could hunt as well as the best of them. Mink, muskrat, and otter he caught by the foamy, roistering Oliverian;* beaver he trapped at Beaver-meadow ponds, the head waters of the wild Ammonoosuc, and his sable lines ran here and there upon the sides of the mountains. Then it is said he was fond of the occupation indicated by his given name—that in autumn he loved the chase. The cry of his old hound-dog in the woods was music to him, and following a moose one day he climbed over Moosehillock, being the first settler that ever stood on its bald summit.

At another time he was chasing a wild buck, which ran down on the rocky crest of Owl's Head mountain. Whitcher heard the baying of his old bloodhound in the distance, at regular intervals, each time coming nearer, and cocking his rifle got behind a rock, thinking to shoot the stag as he passed. He did not have to wait long. The deer burst out of the thin woods fifty rods away, too far off for a shot, and bounded towards the edge of the precipice. He whistled to the old dog following closely behind, whose three wild yells rang out regularly upon the clear mountain air, but could not make him hear. Neither deer nor hound

---
* "In regard to naming Oliverian brook I have no legal knowledge. Tradition says that in early times a man named Oliver and another person were crossing the stream, that the first fell in and the other gave the alarm by crying 'Oliver's in.' Hence the name, *Oliverian*."—Hosea S. Baker.

heeded where they were going, and when they reached the brink of the mountain, in the excitement of the moment the hunter held his breath, as he saw the buck unable to stop, and the great black hound, intent only on his prey, both leap far out over the edge of the precipice, then falling swift as lightning disappear in the abyss a hundred fathoms down.

In an hour the young man had climbed down through the woods by a roundabout way to the foot of the mountain, where he found the deer dead, and his hound with one leg broken and otherwise terribly bruised. The dog had lighted on the top of a great pine, which broke the force of his fall. In time he got well, but could never again be induced to run another deer on the top of Owl's Head mountain.

Mr. Whitcher lived in his camp but a portion of the time. The rest he spent at Mr. John Whitcher's, and down-country, till 1777, when he married Miss Hannah Morrill,* built him a nice cabin of hewn logs, and moved his young bride home.

WILLIAM HEATH lived in town about this time, but had no particular place of residence. He was one of those curious, nondescript sort of persons, to be found in every back settlement, and there is no country village but has his prototype. He would work out a few days here and a few somewhere else, and then would fell trees on a lot he had selected, saying he was going to settle down. He delighted to hang round Obadiah Clement's bar-room, and he would spend a whole day at any place where he thought they would give him a drink. He had sharked it about the world picking up a living without paying for it, and by long fasting at times had become a tall, lank, hungry looking sort of fellow, swift of foot and long-winded. He had the wolf-skin cap and

---

*CHASE AND HANNAH *(Morrill)* WHITCHER'S FAMILY RECORD.
He was born Oct. 6, 1753, at Salisbury, Mass. She was born June 19, 1758, at Amesbury. Married July 6, 1777.

Levi, born Sept. 22, 1779.
Dolly, born Jan. 22, 1781.
William, born May 23, 1783.
Molly, born April 16, 1785.
Chase, Jr., born Sept. 5, 1787.
Levi, 2d, born Aug. 31, 1789.

Jacob, born June 22, 1791.
Miriam, born March 18, 1794.
Hannah, born March 16, 1796.
Martha, born July 18, 1798.
David, born Jan. 15, 1803.

William Whitcher, son of Chase Whitcher, was the father of Ira Whitcher, Chase Whitcher, Daniel Whitcher, and other sons, all now living at North Benton. His family were all tall in stature, of more than ordinary intelligence, and the sons active and influential business men. "There were more than a hundred feet of Whitchers in William Whitcher's family."

short frock of the settler, but his belt, leggins, and moccasins, gave him an Indian look, and his hair hanging straight in gallows locks made him look more sharky, so that in appearance he was an ugly customer to deal with. It is told however that he chanced one day to meet at Col. Clement's tavern our mettlesome little settler, Mr. John Morrill, and being well pickled—or in plain English drunk—he managed to get up a fight, and Mr. Morrill being sober gave him a good beating as he deserved.

When William Heath sobered off his chagrin was great to think he had been vanquished, and he immediately left the settlement and buried himself for a month in the deep woods. When he came back, to take off the edge of his absence, he said he had been a hunting. But the two combatants were soon friends again. Thus William Heath passed his life, and when the Revolution broke out he was one of the first off to the wars.

Mr. STEVENS MERRILL* was the father-in-law of our first settler, and before coming to Warren lived in Plaistow, N. H. Mr. Patch had called at Mr. Merrill's house when he had been down country to sell his furs and get supplies, had fallen in love with young Miss Annie Merrill, and when she was a trifle more than sweet sixteen they were married. He moved his young wife home and she was the prettiest flower in all the wilderness. She had sparkling black eyes, rosy cheeks, cherry lips, raven tresses in abundance, and in form was light and agile as a doe.

In 1775 Mr. Merrill, who did not like the political complexion of the country, concluded to go where he could find peace and quiet,

---

* STEVENS AND SARAH *(Chase)* MERRILL'S FAMILY RECORD.

Jonathan, born Dec. 13, 1752, at Newbury, Mass.
Sarah, born Sept. 23, 1754.
Anna, born Dec. 28, 1756.
Susannah, June 4, 1759, at Plaistow, N. H.

Mary, born May 13, 1762.
Joseph, born Sept. 24, 1764.
Ruth, born March 6, 1767.
Caleb, born April 4, 1769.
Betsey, May 15, 1772.
Hannah, born Oct. 9, 1775.

Sarah, the first wife, died April 30, 1794. Mary, the second, died August 24, 1804.
Hannah, died Nov. 21, 1806. Caleb, died June 8, 1808.

Nathaniel Merrill and his brother John came from England and settled in Newbury, Mass., 1635. Nathaniel married *Susannah Gordon*.
Nathaniel, Jr., born 1638, married *Joan Kinney*.
Peter, born 1667, married *Sarah Hazzelton*.
Abel, born 1697, married *Ruth*.
STEVENS, born June 10. 1731, married, 1st, *Sarah Chase*; 2d, *Mary Noyes*.
Joseph, born Sept. 24, 1764, married *Sarah Copp*.
Susan C., born July 30, 1808, married *Jesse Little*.

Stevens Merrill was born in Atkinson, N. H., lived at Newbury, Mass., then at Plaistow, N. H., then settled in Warren as above.

and so moved to our woodland paradise. He bought the lot of land on which James Aikin lived, and built a log house on the river bank, a few rods southeast of the present depot, and just south of the west end of the Bixby bridge.

Stevens Merrill was a straight, medium-sized man, had a lean face, a thin straight nose and blue eyes. Mr. M. was a Quaker, did not believe in war, and had no sympathy with the colonists. He was stern of aspect and slow in speech, and the children were afraid of him. He was inflexible, had a mind and will of his own, and could not be bent from his purpose. Courage he possessed to a remarkable degree, and neither man, wild beast, nor devil could frighten him. His cattle used to run in the woods. One day they got lost, and after hunting a long time he found all near Hurricane brook, except one ox and a heifer. Driving them up the bridle-path he heard the ox lowing in the woods on the right. He knew there was trouble. Going back to his son-in-law's he procured a stout pitchfork, then followed through the woods till he found the ox in the meadow near Patch brook, guarding the heifer, which a large bear was trying to kill. The heifer was very badly scratched and bitten. Assisted by the ox, Mr. M. attacked the bear, the largest one he ever saw, and after a hard fight succeeded in driving it away, but did not kill it. The same bear killed cattle in Romney and the towns below, and was itself eventually killed by a hunter.

JONATHAN MERRILL, ESQ., a son of the above, came to Warren with him. He lived for a time with his brother-in-law, and his son Stevens, afterwards the richest man in town, was born in Mr. Patch's cabin. 'Squire Jonathan Merrill was one of the smartest men that ever lived in Warren. He was six feet tall, of a lordly mien, straight as an arrow, and had an eye like a hawk. He was perfect in the science of human nature, knew when to drive and when to coax, and had a large stock of soft soap, which he generally dealt out with a liberal hand. Like his father, he was a Quaker of the straightest sect; wore a broad-brimmed hat, and a long drab coat ornamented with great wooden buttons, called by some "matheman buttons." As soon as his father had finished his large log cabin he moved home with him, where he lived through life.

JOSHUA MERRILL, ESQ.,* followed his friends and relatives into the wilderness. He bought the lot of land immediately south of 'Squire Copp, and built his log hut at the foot of Beech hill, a few rods north of the bridge over Black brook.

He was small-sized, straight, lithe, and agile, and withal was an excellent horseman. "As straight as Uncle Joshua," was a speech common among the settlers. He was also a tough, sturdy, weather-beaten, mettlesome, leathern-sided, lion-hearted, generous-spirited little man. He would never give up when he had entered a contest, and he battled for five-score years with Old Father Time, only yielding when the snows of more than a hundred winters had whitened his head. He was the best dressed man in town, and it would have done you good, kind reader, to have seen him, could you only have lived in those times. He would frequently dress himself in his best on some week day, when nothing particular was going on, and then would call round on all his neighbors to show how pretty he looked. Perhaps he wanted to advertise his wares, for report has it that he was once a tailor by trade.† On such occasions he wore a very short-waisted coat of dark color, with short tail-flaps, a wide-rimmed hat—

JONATHAN AND SUSANNAH *(Eaton)* MERRILL'S FAMILY RECORD.

Samuel, born Feb. 28, 1774, at Plaistow; died Dec. 14, 1815.
Stevens, born Mar. 15th, 1776, at Warren; died May 12. 1843.
Isaac, born Aug. 4, 1778.
Hannah, born May 24, 1781.
Sarah, born Jan. 28, 1784.
Susannah, born April 2, 1786; died April 28, 1813.
Ruth, born June 4, 1788; died Feb. 9, 1790.
Betsey, born Nov. 21, 1790.
Mehitable, born Sept. 6, 1792.
Polly, born March 10, 1794.
Susannah, wife of 'Squire Jonathan, died Dec. 26, 1813.

---

*JOSHUA AND MEHITABLE *(Emerson)* MERRILL'S FAMILY RECORD.

He was born May 27th, 1739, in Newbury, Mass. She was born Aug. 28th, 1741, in Hampstead, N. H. Married Feb. 19, 1760.

Ruth, born Nov. 23, 1760, in Hampstead.
Abigail, born Nov. 6, 1762.
Mehitable, born June 1, 1764, at Sandown.
Ruth, born April 8, 1766.
Hannah, born April 28, 1771.
Joshua, born July 17, 1776, at Warren.

Abigail died April 1, 1764. The first Ruth died June 18, 1764.

At a proprietors' meeting held July 8, 1789, "Voted that Maj. Joseph Page have a hundred acre lot of land, which was surveyed by Mr. Josiah Burnham on the 16th August, 1787, in consideration of his settling Mr. Joshua Merrill in said town." Joshua Merrill was a brother of Stevens Merrill.

† Nearly all the cloth he made up in those good old days was homespun. The sheep kept by the settlers were of a coarse-wooled kind. This wool was carded with hand-cards, which was a very laborious work for the women. Sometimes, to make it more cheerful, they would have a *bee*, or *wool-breaking*. It was nearly as much work to card as to spin it, and a woman's "stent" for spinning was five skeins a day, for which the usual price was fifty cents and board per week. The

rim full ten inches wide—hip breeches fastened at the knee with buckles, color dark; long stockings, blue and white, and fastened by a loop to one of the breeches buttons, and buskins of wool or leather, tied with sheep-skin strings over his thick, double-soled ox-hide shoes. His jacket was of the same material as his coat and breeches, with large flaps over the pockets, and for cold weather he had a great coat with very long cape and no waist, buttoned with four or five "mathemau buttons." The sleeves had very wide cuffs, eight or ten inches at least, and two great buttons on each. When he had this suit on, and was mounted on his great black stallion which he used to ride, he would dash through the woods along the stony bridle-path like a wild Arab. He was known all over the country round, and everybody would say, "There goes Farmer Joshua, the politest and best dressed man in the State."

Mr. William Butler was employed by the proprietors to come to Warren to perform a piece of work which we shall be most happy to mention hereafter. He was born in Brentwood, April 24th, 1757, and married pretty Mehitable Mills,* Mr. John Mills' sister. William Butler was a handsome man, with round features. He was five feet eleven inches tall, straight, well-pro-

---

wool spun, and it was woven in the old hand-loom. The most common cloth was "sheep's gray," the wool of a black sheep and a white sheep spun and woven together. Then they had fulled cloth, dressed by a clothier down country. Sometimes they made heavy waled cloth and dyed it with bark at home. The women in winter wore "baize," dyed with green or red, and when it was pressed it was called pressed-cloth.

Nearly every good housewife would have a blue vat in the form of a "dye-pot," in which, instead of dissolving the indigo at once with sulphuric acid, it was put into a bag and dissolved gradually in urine. What a beautiful smell when our grandmothers wrung out from the dye-pot. Here stockings and aprons and the yarn for blue frocking was dyed.

Our first settlers began to raise flax almost as soon as they moved into town. After the flax was "pulled" the seed was thrashed off, then it was rotted, and about the first of March, before sugaring, "got out." First the flax was broken in the "flax-break," then it was "swingled" on the swingling-board; a very smart man would swingle forty pounds a day. "Combing" came next; the "tow" was got out and then the flax was ready to put on the "distaff." The buzzing linen-wheel made music in the old kitchens, and "two double-skeins" was a day's work for a smart woman. When the cloth was woven it was bucked and then belted with a maple beetle on a smooth flat stone. Shirts, sheets, pillow-cases, and nice dresses were made of the cloth. Small girls spun the "swingling-tow" into wrapping twine and with it bought notions down country. Older girls made "all tow," "tow-and-linen," or "all linen" stuff to barter for their "fixing out."

Farmer Joshua made all the fine clothes our early settlers had.

* WILLIAM AND MEHITABLE *(Mills)* BUTLER'S FAMILY RECORD.

He was born April 24, 1757, in Brentwood. She was born Jan. 23, 1756, in Portsmouth. Married Feb. 15, 1779.

Betsey, born Feb. 15, 1780, in Warren.   Stephen, born Aug. 23, 1785.
Mary, born April 1, 1782.   Sally, born May 8, 1787.
William, Jr., born May 11, 1783.   Dolly, born Aug. 30, 1788.

portioned, and would weigh more than two hundred pounds. Like Chase Whitcher, he was very young when he came to Warren. He was a gentleman farmer, lived several years with Mr. Mills, did not like to work very hard, preferred to oversee his hired help, and spent much of his time buying and selling cattle and trading horses. He was a good calculator, made money, and eventually got rich.

There was another man came to Warren about these times, but no one can precisely fix the year.

JOHN HINCHSON was Warren's first hermit. He built a hunter's camp for himself southwest of Mr. Patch and on the easterly bank of Patch brook. The life he led was that of a wild Indian. A hound-dog, named Wolf, was his only companion. In the summer he spent the time fishing, catching salmon and trout, with which the river and brooks abounded. One fall it is said he went over the mountains hunting — catching beaver by Glen ponds, in Fox Glove meadow, and on Moulton brook — and other seasons he travelled far away across the Pemigewassett valley to the head waters of the streams among the White mountains. In the winter he hunted moose and deer, which afforded an abundance of provision. Sometimes he would be gone a year or two, no one knew where, and then would come back to his old haunts again.

Thus Warren was settled; and living in the fairy realms of her antiquity, these were her first settlers. Laws, churches, schools — they had none; and from all restraints or taxation they were wholly free. Happy days were theirs; plenty to eat and drink, work enough to do, keen appetites, seldom sick, and with neither doctors, lawyers, nor ministers to support. How delightful to dwell on their history, abiding in a woodland town, surrounded by great mountains, and beyond them trackless forests, that seemed to shut out all the cares and vanities of the wicked world. But all this is too beautiful to last long. Dame Fortune, ever blowing a shifting gale, lively, changing scenes are soon to come. How the lives of the settlers checkered up, and Warren right merrily, like bursting flowers dancing into life to the music of spring birds, changed about into a fine old country town, where ambitious men lived, is most interesting to know.

CHAPTER IV.

OF HOW THE EARLY SETTLERS OF OUR MOUNTAIN HAMLET TOOK GREAT THOUGHT ABOUT THE MANNER THEY SHOULD BE SHELTERED, AND WHAT THEY SHOULD EAT, AND OF THE BUILDING OF MILLS; CONCLUDING WITH THE MIGHTY LEAPS OF THE SALMON AND A DELECTABLE SWIM BY THE BOYS.

OUR dignified, worthy, and aristocratical body, the distinguished proprietors, had done pretty well, but had not obtained the fifty families as settlers. There was great danger of their again losing their charter, but the political troubles with the mother country for a time removed attention from themselves, and as we have before remarked, in the end the Revolution proved their salvation. In its turmoils they were forgotten and they saved their lands.

In our mountain hamlet the twenty settlers, constituting the eighteen families, made a most agreeable but a very rustic neighborhood, and they had a most rustic style of living. The rude hunter's camp, the log cabin,—often without glass windows, the rough opening that admitted the light closing sometimes with a wooden shutter—the door of rifted boards, the floor of rough poles frequently covered with bark, the chimney a cob-work of sticks, plastered with mud, the great fire-place built of stones, and all the furniture as plain and simple as the house,—such were the homes found by our early settlers in the days long ago.

Think of these frail tenements, growing up like wild flowers in the wilderness, in the latter half of the eighteenth century. There is no road north or south, only a bridle-path, and that not half as good as the one now running to the summit of Moosehil-

A SAW-MILL IS BUILT. 237

lock. But few of the cabins were located even beside the bridle-route, and a blazed path led through the woods to them, and for years the forest trees locked branches above them. Neither yard in front, nor fence nor wall behind, nor garden gate. The honeysuckle grew sweetly by the door, and wild sumach and blackberry bushes flowering in their season, and the golden-rod, and white birch intertwining with the mountain ash, sprang up by the open window. Near by the cabins were the little clearings—one, two or five acres, no man more than ten acres. But few sheep were kept then; a cow, a yoke of steers, sometimes a horse, constituted the settler's stock. Often bears broke down and ate the corn, or a moose or a deer were seen feeding on their little improvements, and at night, when the gibbous moon shone in the sky and looked in upon the cabin among the trees, the early settlers retiring to rest would hear the wolf* howling on the mountain, and the solemn owl hooting in harsh discordant notes,—wild music heard in the solitudes which had been but just invaded.

All this is now very pleasant to contemplate, but the good men of Warren did not then exactly like it. They longed for something better,—something like what they had left in old Hollis, Hampstead, Sandown, Atkinson, Plaistow, and Salisbury, the towns from which they had emigrated. Framed houses, covered with sawn boards, was one of the requisites to satisfy the heart's desire, but they could not be had without a saw-mill. The proprietors had offered a bounty for building one, and Mr. Stevens Merrill was the man energetic enough to undertake the work.

At the "little white fall" on Black brook, where John Page, Esq., once shot a deer, he chose his mill site. The dam was built of great pine logs, and a pretty pond of five or six acres gleamed in the woods at the foot of Beech hill. Three great rocks stood out of the water among the trees on its western shore, and a green wooded cape shot far down towards the centre. The mill itself was simply a heavy frame of hewed logs, unboarded of course, and the roof was covered with long shaved shingles. Then there was a pause in the work,—the mill irons must be brought up from

---

* *Wolves.*—The year 1786 was a remarkable year for wolves. They swarmed down from the north through all the country. Moses H. Clement used to tell how his mother took him to the door one night to hear the wolves howl. They would come round the barn after sheep but could not get in. Many were killed.

lown country and a saw must be procured. Col. Obadiah Clement went on foot to Boscawen for the last, and brought it all the way fifty miles to Warren on his back. He made the journey through the woods over the rough bridle-path in three days. Another settler brought up some of the smaller irons, but the crank could not come till winter. Mr. Merrill, Col. Clement, and his brother Reuben went for it and drew it to Warren on a great wide-runnered, frame-work handsled, made for that very purpose. In the spring the mill was finished, and the music of its wheel driven by fourteen feet waterfall, the click of the cogs on the log-frame, and the clip of the saw gnawing through the pines, which the settlers sawed up regardless of the " broad arrow mark" upon them, sounded for the first time through the pleasant woods of Warren.

There is a stirring little anecdote connected with the old mill which the kind reader may believe or not, as the highly veracious gentleman who related it said he was not quite sure but that it occurred somewhere else down east after all. It is told by him how one spring 'Squire Jonathan Merrill was at work sawing, and every morning he would miss the lard with which he greased the machinery, and sometimes it would be gone at noon. One day he brought down a large quantity of it, and thinking he heard the thief prowling in the thick swamp woods that grew by the bog a few rods east of the mill, he placed the dish on the long log he was sawing, hoisted the gates and started towards home. Looking back he caught sight of something crossing the logging path, and stealing round so that he could look into the mill himself he saw a great black bear sitting upon the log, back to the saw, eating the grease. Presently the saw came so close it scratched his back, but Bruin only growled and hunched along. Again it bit him, and this time smarting with pain he turned quickly round, reared on his hind feet and clasped the impudent iron intruder on his dinner with his fore-paws, to give it a death-hug. But now he caught a tartar; he gnawed a file. Down came the saw, stroke after stroke in rapid succession, till the black-coated thief was literally sawn in two. It is proper to inform the reader that the bear died, after having given the saw blade a coating of very excellent oil from his own greasy carcass. Over all which, like the boy pelting the frog, 'Squire Merrill shed no tears; and whether true in whole or in part the incident has more than once served to "point a moral and adorn a tale."

High up in the northeast corner of Warren is situated a pretty little sheet of water. As we have somewhere hinted, the Indians called it Wachipauka, but the later generations of our mountain hamlet delight to term it Meader pond. It is yet right in the heart of the woods, and from its eastern shore springs a handsome forest-covered cape. On the north Webster Slide shoots sharp up a thousand feet, its top crowned by silvery birch and waving pine; the crannies of its rocks radiant with the blueberry, harebell, lichen, and other mountain flowers. On a warm summer day the water reflecting the rich foliage of the yet undisturbed forest, is ruffled only by the great speckled trout jumping or the wild duck swimming; but when the autumn winds come the blue water curling smiles upon the mountain-face and laughs at the bald head of Mooschillock, looking in from the distance over the great wood.

Black brook — the Mikascota — comes down from Wachipauka pond. Its waters turn the wheel of our first saw-mill, and the logs cut up furnish the inhabitants with lumber.

And now the great naked log walls, the massive, lumbering doors, the floor of logs hewed down, the rude style of constructing bed and board shall disappear, and the second generation of settlers' houses come. One story high, and a low one at that; a great stack of a chimney of stone — then afterwards containing brick enough to build a modern brick house — right in the centre; two square rooms in front, a long kitchen behind; at one end of this, bedroom and entry; at the other, buttery, stairway, and cellar way; an unfinished attic where the children slept, parted off sometimes by blankets, oftener by spruce bark, one portion for the boys the other for the girls. These were the palaces our forefathers were anxious to get.

One of these stands just at the foot of that steep hill known as the Blue Ridge, and is probably the oldest framed dwelling house in town. This was the dwelling built and occupied by Joshua Copp, Esq., and formerly stood a quarter of a mile west of its present location, near the spot where he first erected his humble cabin. The first framed dwelling, as we have before stated, was erected by Mr. Joseph Patch, by the roadside on the northerly bank of Patch brook.* Latterly the more aristocratic well to do among our fathers built large, double, two-story houses

*THE OLD BARN AT THE HOMANS PLACE, BUILT BY JOSEPH PATCH ABOUT 1768.

of which the old red house built by Stevens Merrill and now standing near the depot is a sample.

For this great enterprise, the building of a saw-mill, the proprietors, Jan. 15th, 1784, long after, voted to allow Mr. Merrill twelve pounds,* to be paid him as soon as collected, in money or in certificates, and so much did our mountain pioneers rejoice that for several years they excused Mr. M. from paying taxes on his mill.

A tight roof to cover their heads was exceedingly nice, but good corn cakes and wheaten loaves were also what they craved; these were difficult to be obtained. It was hard to travel to Haverhill or Plymouth for a grist, and the proprietors realizing that this was an important thing for the town, offered a bounty for building a grist-mill. William Butler accepted the proposition. Across the Asquamchumauke, just below where the great railroad bridge now spans its waters, he built a huge dam. The mudsill is still to be seen, an object of wonder to the boys who go to swim in "the old deep hole," as it is termed; and the holes drilled and

See Proprietors' Records.

cut in the great rock on the western shore show where were the fastenings of the dam. One at a time the rude millstones were drawn up from down country by William Butler, with four men to assist him, just as the crank of the saw-mill came, and early in 1776 the first settlers brought their grains, products of a virgin soil, to be ground, and waited for their grists listening to the buzz of rude mill stones mingling their music with that of the wheel which now for the first time vexed Asquamchumauke's waters.

The proprietors were well satisfied with William Butler's work and afterwards voted to allow him eighteen pounds for building the mill, to be paid him as soon as collected. *

We have said the boys go to swim in " the old deep hole." A great historical fact would be lost to all the coming countless generations did we fail to record that young John Mills, Jr., and Joseph Merrill, Stevens Merrill's son, and Moses Copp, son of 'Squire Joshua, and other boys also went to swim in " the old deep hole," now made doubly deep by William Butler's mill dam. The woods were very thick all around it and not a house was visible, so no delicate sensitive nerves could be shocked. Jumping out of their moosehide breeches and tow shirts the boys ran over smooth pebbles of mica slate and shining quartz, green hornblende and fragments of porphyritic trap, little dreaming of the virgin gold lying concealed beneath them which would only be discovered a hundred years later, and plunged into the clear sparkling water. John Mills, Jr., could swim the whole length of the pond to the dam. Here he would rest himself and look over into the foaming pool below, where the salmon congregated and out of which they would leap up through the falling water, swift as the rush of Indian arrows through the sky, nine perpendicular feet into the pond above. William Butler said he had seen the salmon shoot up over the dam many a time.

Swimming ashore young Mills and his companions would sit down in the shadow of the great hemlocks and wide spreading beech trees and watch the white fleece-like foam, formed where the roaring Asquamchumauke lost itself in the pond. It was a pleasant place to pass a summer afternoon. The wood thrush and the robin were singing overhead, the partridge drummed on an

*See Proprietor's Records.

P

old decaying log up in the pines by Indian rock; a blue jay was ducking its crest and hustling the water with its wings; on the shore a sand piper crying weet, jumped up on a great stone, then ran fast by the water under the bending grass; hoar hound, cranesbill and honey suckle lent a delicious fragrance to the air and bright clouds mirrored in the clear water were floating away and losing themselves in the deep blue beyond old Mount Carr and Moosehillock mountain.

But these were only the beauties of the pond fit for the boys to look at; the utility of the grist mill joined with that of the sawmill constituted one of the mighty agents which wrought such great changes in our mountain hamlet.

CHAPTER V.

NARRATING HOW TWO MEN, STEVENS MERRILL AND JAMES AIKEN, LOVED EACH OTHER,—HOW THE LAWS WERE EXECUTED AND A HOUSE BURNED UP, CONCLUDING WITH A PIOUS INQUIRY WORTHY OF ALL GOOD CHRISTIANS.

WE have said lively changing scenes are soon to come. But let us not be in a hurry to enter upon them. Pause a moment! These are the halcyon days of our little mountain hamlet. Eight beautiful summers have come and gone since it was settled. Our pioneers are living all this time in the most rustic simplicity. There is nought to disturb them, nought to make them afraid. There were no doctors to physic them to death, no ministers to preach war and bloodshed instead of peace and love, and no pettifogging lawyers to send caitiff scouts, catch-polls, and bum-bailiffs to distrain, to attach, and to arrest. In fact there was not a lawyer, sheriff, judge, court, or jailor within sixty miles of our little hamlet among the hills. Neighbor loved neighbor, the golden rule was observed, and peace, happiness, and good will prevailed, and all was harmony serene. It was a place of which poets loved to sing—of old woods, clear rushing streams, wild and lofty mountains, where even the gods would dwell.

But wait, perhaps everything is not quite so nice after all. Men are human even here. Either civil law or club law must prevail in every community, and we shall soon see that in the absence of civil law they sometimes used the club right freely in our good old mountain town.

James Aiken, as previously described, was a lusty Celt from

the Emerald Isle, and Stevens Merrill was a medium sized man, a Quaker of the straightest sect, stern in aspect and slow in speech. We have before said that they both settled on the same lot of land; the first a gentle squatter, the second had purchased it of the lordly proprietors and had a good warrantee deed of the premises. It was natural that one having a good comfortable cabin and a few broad acres nicely cleared should want to stay; and that the other having an excellent title bought with his own hard cash should want the first to leave. Consequently there would be a dignified reserve between the two lords of the soil.

When they first met the Quaker gently hinted to the Celt that he had no title to his land. He did not take the hint. At the next cordial interview Mr. M. said, "Thee must leave." Aiken " did not see it." Next time, a week or so later, Stevens Merrill told him, " Thee have got to go, and if thee do not," said he, " I will serve a process on thee, a writ of ejectment." At this Mr. Aiken laughed politely, then said decidedly, " D——d if I will go." Quaker blood, so peaceful, now boiled like a little pot on hearing this so profane, so unchristian reply, and he inwardly determined to have his rights, legally if he could, by hook or crook if necessary. They did not speak at the next meeting, only eyed each other askance.

Aiken knew by the appearance of things there was trouble brewing and so kept close at home to protect himself and property.

But in process of time it became absolutely necessary for him to go down the valley to the neighboring land of Wentworth, where his brother had settled, for supplies. He went very quietly one morning, away round through the woods down on the east side of Patch brook, next to the foot of the hill, so no one would see him. But he was not so fortunate as could be desired. Our keen eyed hunter, Joseph Patch, was looking about his premises and by chance saw him. He knew what his father-in-law wanted, how hard he had tried to get a writ of ejectment, but could not very well do it on account of distance, bad roads, and expense, so he hurried away to tell him that this was the time for the strategy devised, the opportunity to execute a splendid flank movement.

Stevens Merrill made no delay. He forded the river and crossed the meadow. 'Twas a bright autumn day. A lagging wind blew over the plain, rustling the beeches and maples. On the edge of the clearing he stopped to reconnoitre; the cabin stood in the centre, a little brook was babbling beside it, three children were playing at the door, and the buzz of a linen wheel was heard within.

"It is a bad job," he said to himself, "but it will be worse if it is delayed." Entering the cabin he told Mrs. Aiken she must leave. "An faith I won't," said she. "But thee will," said Mr. M. "I'll see about it," said she, and sprang for an axe that stood in the corner. But Stevens Merrill was too quick for her. He wrenched it from her grasp and then affectionately ejected her from the cabin. The children screamed and Mrs. A. threatened vengeance. But it was no use. Mr. M. began to pitch the things out, and seeing his determination they picked up their extra clothing and trudged away down the bridle path to John Mills' as fast as their legs would carry them.

He moved all the rest of the furniture out carefully, even the linen wheel and the pots and kettles that hung on the stout lug pole* in the great fire place, carried them to a safe distance and then set fire to the cabin. The wind freshened, the smoke curled up and floated away over the woods, the flames roared and leaped about, and in an hour the pleasant dwelling was a mass of blackened ruins.

When James Aiken came back they told him the news at John Mills'. He was terribly mad and swore that he "would have revenge—that old Merrill had committed arson—that he should be locked up between the four walls of a prison—that he was the devil's own and the regular son of a dog mother." to speak politely what the Celt said plump and plain.

Stevens Merrill kept a watch about his own cabin every night, himself, sons, and son-in-law, by turns, until their friend had

---

* In the chimney, across the flue, was the lug pole, made of green beech or maple from two to four inches in diameter, and on which were hung hooks and trammels of wrought iron, so constructed as to be raised or lowered to suit the convenience of the pots and kettles suspended thereon for culinary purposes. These lug poles were liable to be burnt by the fire which blazed beneath and broken by the weight suspended on them, and in due time gave place to the crane which was constructed of iron and fastened on one side to the chimney jamb, while the end swung over the fire with the hooks and trammels on it.—Jacob Patch's statement.

Stevens Merrill drove Aiken off and burnt his cabin.—Deacon Jonathan Clements' statement.

moved his goods away and had gone to his brother's in Wentworth. Even then he did not feel quite safe, for he knew he had not done just right taking the law into his own hands.

James Aiken afterwards went back down country. When people came down he would ask if " Stevens Merrill had gone to hell, for if he had not," said he, " hell no need to have been made;" a pious remark, showing the deep love he had for his gentle friend.

Our Quaker settler from this time forward cultivated the Irishman's field and took pains to obliterate his memory. But the old cellar, now almost filled up, yet remains to mark the spot where this dire calamity happened, and the little brook running down on the second of the geological terraces and near which stood the Irishman's cabin, bears his name and is called Aiken brook even to this day.

CHAPTER VI.

MOUNT CARR, ITS ANCIENT INHABITANTS; AND THEN OF THE GRAND OLD HUNTINGS THAT WERE HAD ABOUT IT, WITH A BEAUTIFUL MOOSEHILLOCK DESCRIPTION THROWN IN FOR VARIETY.

MOUNT CARR is a grand old mountain. It rises 3,506 feet above the ocean, is covered with a dense forest even to the summit and occupies a part of the following four townships: The ancient Trecothick, now Ellsworth, Romney, now called Rumney, as aforesaid, Wentworth, and our own mountain hamlet.

It derives its name from the following circumstance, which we prefer to tell as it was told years ago, and the reader without doubt will think it a "delectable tale." "When the country was first settled and its geography but little known, a certain Mr. Carr, wishing to proceed from Trecothick to Warren, attempted to cross the mountain. At the time he started the sky was free from clouds, and every appearance gave sign of pleasant weather But soon after he entered the woods there arose a terrific shower, common to mountainous regions, and when it had rained a short time, instead of clearing away, a thick fog set in completely enveloping the mountain.

At the commencement of the shower Mr. Carr crept under the trunk of a large tree that had fallen across a knoll, and as the rain continued to fall more violently he concluded he would be compelled to remain there over night. The log above his head was an immense hemlock, and peeling some of the loose bark from the trunk he sat it with sticks of rotten wood against the sides of the tree, more effectually to shield himself from the falling water. He had no means of lighting a fire, and as he had gained a considerable elevation when night came on, he felt cold. He had only taken provisions enough for his dinner, and as he sat, hungry and shivering, the scene to him was a solitary one. The rain as it fell upon the green leaves or sifted through the boughs of the hemlock and spruce, kept up a confused pattering, sifting noise, and as it grew dark he laid down and tried to sleep, listening to its doleful music. But this was almost impossible, for as a drowse would steal upon him some great owl overhead would hoot ominously, and as its rough music died away the other inhabitants of the forest took up the strain, and he heard the hoarse howl of the wolf, and the long-drawn halloo of the bear echoing in the forest.

Thus the night passed away, its long hours seeming like weeks, until at last the dark misty light of morning began to dawn, and the huge, gnarled trunks of the trees appeared through the thick fog. Numb with cold, he arose and resolved to make an effort to find his way out of the woods. He started up the mountain, and traveled, as he thought, until he had reached the top. He then descended until he arrived at the foot and began to have hope that he should find the settlement, but he was doomed to disappointment, for he had traveled but a short distance before he began to ascend again. He then tried to retrace his steps but it was of no avail, and after wandering about for a long time he found himself standing upon the shore of Glen pond. It still rained, and the descending drops made strange music as they struck upon the smooth surface of the little mountain lake.

He now made up his mind, as it was near night, to remain here until the following day, and building a light camp by the side of a rock, passed a much more dreary night than the first. Cold, wet, shivering, and sleepless as he lay by the side of that sheet of water, he heard the hoarse croaking of the frogs mingling with the voices of his serenaders of the previous night. When the morning broke it had ceased raining and although foggy he was able to distinguish the position of the sun when it rose, and thereby learn his points of compass.

Two nights had now passed, he had not tasted food, and hunger was oppressing him. To satisfy it he tried to catch some fish, but after a few ineffectual attempts he gave it up. As he stood looking at the water he saw swimming about and hopping along the shore numerous frogs. A hungry man will eat almost anything. Carr caught a number of them, cut them up with his knife, and made a hearty meal upon the raw flesh or fish.

Feeling now much refreshed he attempted again to find the settlement. Taking a westerly course he once more found himself upon the top of the mountain. The clouds hung thick around making it impossible to distinguish any object a few feet distant. But proceeding cautiously he began to descend, as he believed upon the opposite side. For a number of hours he slowly went down, crossing in his course several streams now swollen with the rain until he reached the level country. Here after wandering about some time he began to think that he should be obliged to spend another night in the woods, but as he was looking around for a convenient camping place, the sharp ringing of a settler's axe greeted his ear, and proceeding towards what was to him the joyful sound, he soon emerged into a recent clearing. In the centre stood a snug cabin and he quickly found himself within its hospitable walls, where he was generously provided for, and after somewhat recovering from his fatigue, related his adventures in the woods. Gradually the story circulated through the neighboring settlements and the people gave his name to the mountain upon which the adventure happened."*

Dr. Jackson says the mountain is composed of granite, which having been erupted through the mica slate lying upon its sides forms a cap on its summit. But after the most diligent search by several very distinguished geologists the granite is as yet undiscovered. Nevertheless, it is a most singular formation. A hundred different kinds of rock are found upon it, and some most interesting minerals, among which are tourmaline or schorl, garnets, quartz crystals of a lovely hue, amythyst, beautiful as the summer rose, and last but not least are scattered all over it small particles of pure virgin gold.

---

*Carr was a friend of Alexander Craig who settled in Romney and who had relatives living at the time in Piermont.

Samuel Knight related how two boys from Ellsworth in these early times came over Mount Carr in the winter, barefoot, and camped one night near Batchelder brook, before they reached the settlements in Warren.

A dozen beautiful, white foamy streams come rushing down its sides, among which may be mentioned Martin brook, branches of Stinson brook, Moulton brook, Batchelder brook, Patch brook, and that most beautiful of all streams, Hurricane brook. On the latter are those little, white tumbling waterfalls which for so many years were almost unknown but are now so much admired.

By these it is said in old times lived the fairies. It was here on the rich carpets of green moss they danced in the moonbeams and sang an accompaniment to the falling waters. The deep, mossy-rimmed basin, set with gems, and carved in the rock high up on the mountain side might have been their bathing font, and in it even Robin Goodfellow and Queen Mab might have performed their ablutions. The Indians had a beautiful tradition how the fairies stole the children away and gave them fairy bread to eat which changed them into fairies. Then said they there was joy for the little folks as they revelled in the green embowering woods; and the elfin king and the fairy queen ruled long and well in the old centuries. But the period when they existed has melted into the mellow twilight of ages and all these joyous revellers are gone forever.

Now it is said there are some so skeptical that they don't believe the fairies ever lived there at all, that the whole story is but a pleasant myth told to please the children. Be this as it may their reputed haunts were frequently invaded about those times. Our rustic pioneers loved fresh meat and a store of rich peltries, and the woods of Mount Carr were scoured for the supply.

When the autumn came and the maples, birches, poplars, and ash were clothed in all their crimson splendors in the glens and on the mountains, the gun was roused from its slumber, the dogs howled in ecstacy on the hills, and the time for partridge shooting, mink, beaver, and sable trapping, and deer and moose hunting had come. Joseph Patch " was in his element then." Chase Whitcher was on the hunter's path, Obadiah Clement's gun resounded in the woods, and even fat William Butler joined in the profitable pastime.

Patch is a happy hunter. He is threading his way along the Asquamchumauke towards the wooded mountain. He steps from hummock to hummock in his little pasture, brushes the blue and gold flowered hardhack aside, and rustles the fallen leaves with his heel in the woods. He shall hear the roar of the torrent, the music of the waterfall; shall wind around the reedy shores of the fir skirted Glen ponds, and at night lie down to sleep on his bed of soft boughs by his camp fire. His youngest son relates that at one time he came home with fifty-three mink, sable, fisher-cat, and beaver skins, caught in a single week in his Indian culheags and steel traps. Old Deacon Jonathan Clement said that Chase Whitcher caught in one season a hundred and forty dollars' worth of beaver, on the head waters of Black and Berry brooks. The old beaver dams and little grass grown meadows where their ponds were are still to be seen. Obadiah Clement could shoot more partridges than any other man in the hamlet. He had a brisk little dog to scare them up and then shot them on the wing.

Joseph Patch also had a good supply of steel traps and there was not a man in the whole country who could catch more foxes than he. He baited them on a bed, as it is called, and late in the fall was sure to get one almost every morning. But once he found an old fox almost as cunning as himself. When he would go to his "bed" he would find his bait gone, his trap sprung, but not a fox to be seen. This happened many times even though his trap was set in the most careful manner. But there was one thing he always noticed,—his trap invariably had a stick in its jaws. One day he set it very carefully and then picked up and carried away every stick more than two inches long he could find in the vicinity. His plan proved successful. The next morning he found a handsome silver gray fox caught by the nose. The stick with which it attempted to spring the trap was too short. Reynard seemed to realize his situation. He looked up in the hunter's face imploringly, as much as to say, "please let me go this time." But Patch could not think of it. With one blow he dispatched him though he often said afterwards he never regretted the killing an animal more in his life.*

---

*This story was told the author by Mr. David Smith. He said Patch related it to him with his own lips. Benjamin Little's statement also.
Anson Merrill said that Patch once saw a bear in his corn, near Patch brook: got within twenty rods and then could not see his game well, so he stood on a hill of corn and raised himself on tip-toe and fired. The bear ran but Patch found that he had drawn blood and following along beside the brook lost the trail. A week later, it being warm weather he scented him and found his game dead on the banks of the stream.

John Hinchson, his neighbor, had two beautiful fleet-footed deer hounds. One of them was named Wolf. Patch prevailed upon him to sell him the latter and then he could rival his friend Whitcher in the chase. My uncle who remembered the history of John Mills so well, said that early settler got a good supply of venison one day, the would-be product of Patch's hunting. He heard the sonorous yelling of the old hound coming down the ravine by Rocky falls, on Patch brook; soon the antlered buck burst from the woods, flew across the little clearing and made for the mill pond on the river. Mills was ready with his gun, and as the stag swam rapidly down across the pond he lodged a charge of buck shot in its throat and before Patch came up the game was hid in the grist-mill, while the hunter was left to infer that the deer had crossed the river and escaped, John Mills all the time maintaining a pious silence, somewhat after the manner of the Quakers.

Pause here, gentle reader! drop a tear for the fate of Patch's fleet deer hound, Wolf. As the years rolled on he grew old. His baying was heard no more on the hills, his feet bounded no more through the woods. Gray with age he could only lie on the hearth by the warm fire. One day Patch said half in earnest to his boys, "I guess you had better take old Wolf out and shoot him, he is no use to any one." The dog looked up sorrowfully, seeming to understand what was said and then slowly left the house. That night they hunted for him, and called him in vain. The next day they found him in a deep pool of Patch brook, drowned.

If Patch suspected his friend Mills of appropriating the venison he could easily forgive him as he sometimes practised such things himself. Strangers from a distance would come to hunt and wantonly destroy large quantities of game much to the annoyance of the good settlers of the hamlet. These marauding parties, lossel scouts, shouting would often come rushing down from the hills with guns and deep-mouthed baying hounds, waking every echo in the old wood. It was then that the Merrills, William Butler, Mills, Patch and Hinchson, hastening would intercept the deer or moose, and kill and conceal it before the fierce intruders could come up. Then there would be a sharp contention, threats, and sometimes blows, but the invariable result was that the game loving invaders would be sent fast flying back across the border with huge fleas in their ears.* Romney men and the sojourners among the hills of Trecothick were thus taught to feel a deep love for the "honest Warrenites," as they most respectfully termed our early pioneers. Chase Whitcher, while following a moose, was the first settler who visited the summit of Moosehillock. It is said that Joseph Patch also, while hunting one bright, clear autumn day climbed the mountain. He had no companion save his dog. Stillness and solitude were there, hill and ravine, sky and valley, everywhere magnificent, the outline everywhere bold, grand, and sublime. No animal life was to be seen, only two fearless, strong winged eagles were soaring over the great gorge down which roars Tunnel brook. White quartz rocks and gray slates, among which bloom the harebell and lichen, and to which the mosses cling, cropped out all around him; then there was the graveyard of the stunted skeleton trees killed by the frost and the fire and bleached white; beyond was the rich green of the mazy, impenetrable hackmatacks; in the zone below the deep brown of the spruce and hemlock, and in the deep valleys at the mountain foot, the bright yellow, the flashing crimson, the purple and gold of the forest, while above was the azure sky, and in the far distance the blue water of the ponds, the lakes, and the ocean. It was a wild scene, " crags, knolls, and mounds confusedly hurled " far as the eye could reach. In the east the highest of the Waumbecket Methna, the Indian name for the White mountains, gleamed white with the first snow, while in the west the sharp peaks of the Adirondacks shone bright above the flashing waters of Lake Champlain. But he hurried away for he felt a strange indescribable awe at a sight such as he had never witnessed before, and the hackmatacks were thick and the way over them long and difficult.

But it was only in the winter when the snow lay four feet deep in the woods of the valley and on the mountains that the moose could be hunted successfully. We have it on the authority of Jacob Patch, son of Joseph Patch, that our hunter on snow shoes was following the Asquamchumauke, otherwise Baker river, high up on the side of Moosehillock mountain. It had snowed that day and

---

* Esq. Jonathan Merrill once whipped a gallant Romney hunter with his ox goad, "making him yell good," when said hunter accused him of stealing a deer.
Stevens Merrill by good luck got a moose once in the river behind his house which somebody's dogs had chased down from the mountains.

the way was slow and heavy. Late in the afternoon he discovered a yard of moose. Trying his gun he found it so damp he could not use it. This was a great disappointment but he was not to be cheated of his game so easily. Cutting a long pole he lashed his hunting knife to one end of it, cautiously approached the moose and cut the ham strings of three of the best of them. This done he found no difficulty in dispatching them. The rest escaped. Of course he dressed them, hung the heavy quarters high up in the trees, and then hauled them home at his leisure.

But the most historical of all the grand old huntings that have come down to us was one that happened that very winter of these primitive times. Chase Whitcher had been across the mountains to Glen ponds to fish for trout through the ice. Coming home he found a great yard of moose. There were more of them than any one man wanted, and he generously told his neighbors of the discovery. Then they began to plan the way of capture and a day to put it in execution was set when every man should be ready for the work.

Simeon Smith, and Morrill from Red Oak hill, Hinchson, Patch, Mills, and Butler, all the Merrills, Joshua Copp, and Obadiah Clement, both the Whitchers and others started for the yard early one bright morning. It was up the side of Mount Carr in the glen through which Patch brook flows, and over the northern mountain spur, like Bonaparte over the Alps, more than 3,000 feet up, in the mid winter snow. There was a hard crust and the sunlight streaming through the trees flashed on the myriad icy particles. A partridge whirred away from before them into the snow covered firs, a rabbit that was eating spruce burrs leaped past, and both were unheeded either by hunters or dogs. It was ten o'clock when they reached the yard. The first sight showed them that it was no ordinary one. It was on the mountain side, on the Black hill beyond, and ran down by Glen pond, across the valley to the side of Mt. Kineo. The Black hill had been crossed and recrossed a hundred times from base to summit. A hundred parallels girdled the hill around, intersecting the perpendiculars, and all were hard and deeply trodden paths, so hard a moose could not be tracked in them, so narrow a man could not run in them. It was a mazy labyrinth and to attempt to thread it was to give the animals an opportunity to escape. The moose could run ten to fifteen miles an hour through the devious windings, browsing and eating as they ran, and neither dogs nor men could come up to them. Therefore this little army of hunters, out on this grand hunting excursion, immediately separated. They went round on either side each leaving the other at a considerable distance, then they cautiously entered the yard; when a gun was fired they let loose the dogs; their yelling was wild music in the woods, accompanied by the noise of the moose pounding away at a hard swinging trot, their broad antlers resounding as they sometimes hit a tree, their wide-spread hoofs crackling at every step as they fled from their pursuers.

And now all are on the tip-toe of expectation. Each man believes he is sure of his game. Captain William Butler is determined to bag one. But when the mightiest animal he ever saw went swinging by he found he had the moose fever, and instead of stopping his game, the old bull answered the crack of his gun with a bellow and bounded out of sight in a moment. It did not even leave the trace of blood on the snow, much to our excellent marksman's delight. Simeon Smith halloed with exceeding joy at the sight of one and forgot to fire at all. Morrill called him a fool and forgot to fire himself, and Stevens Merrill was so greatly pleased, or had the fever so bad that he fired in the air, probably philosophically thinking the ball might strike one when it came down. But Chase Whitcher brought down a moose the first time trying, Joseph Patch had the same good luck, and Obadiah Clement had the good fortune to shoot two. The others did not succeed in getting a shot.

Four moose were as many as they cared for, or could well take care of. So the dogs were called and the rest were suffered to escape. The work of skinning and dressing was quickly accomplished, and the product loaded on the light, broad runnered handsleds which they had brought with them.

It was hard work coming over the mountain, and before they arrived at the summit William Butler's rotund body was too heavy for his legs, and he laid down in the snow from exhaustion. His good friends rubbed him smartly, placed him upon one of the sleds,

John Marston, who lived at the Summit, first house up High street, once went on one of these grand moose hunts. He was pretty hungry and drank two quarts of moose marrow. It made him terrible sick, liked to have killed him, and the party had to build a fire and stay in the woods all night. The next day they drew him home on a hand sled.—Nathaniel Richardson's statement.

covered him warmly with their frocks and drew him home too, the heaviest moose, as they said, of the whole lot. Going down the mountain he playfully asked Stevens Merrill if a moose lived in the moon? a stupid joke that Mr. M. could not see.

There was feasting and merry making in the settlement after that, and the grand hunt known as "the one when Captain Butler's legs gave out," has not yet been forgotten.

CHAPTER VII.

OF A PROVISION FOR RELIGIOUS MEETINGS; GRANDILOQUENT DESCRIPTION OF ONE AND HOW IT CLOSED WITH A CUP OF SWEET COMFORT AND PEACE, AS WAS THE CUSTOM IN ANCIENT TIMES.

LIKE one of the old knights of the middle ages hurrying abroad to avenge the wrongs of a wicked world, but at times pausing under the cool embowering shades, and by babbling brooks in green meadows to enjoy the delights of life, so we hastening to the bustling confusion and the turmoil of the great events of our immortal history, are fain to pause a few moments to revel in the halcyon sweets in this the twilight age of our mountain hamlet, before plunging into the wild scenes of the coming troublesome times that are sure to follow.

Benning Wentworth, peace to his ashes! had a pious respect for the Church of England, a Christian desire for propagating the gospel in foreign parts, and a right good will for the support of preaching. Consequently he inserted in the charter that a certain portion of the lots among the hills should be set apart for the support of the church, preaching, and the missionary cause.

Our excellent proprietors were prompt to second the good intentions of the ancient governor. At the very first division of the lots, No. 2 of the 4th range was drawn for the support of a minister; No. 2 of the 8th range for the society for propagating the gospel; and No. 1 of the 9th range as a glebe for the Church of England, as by law established.*

---
*In the subsequent divisions of land other lots were drawn for the above purposes, for a list of which see appendix.

And the first settlers on the hillsides and in the pleasant valley of the hamlet were just as desirous of a little religious food as the royal governor and the lordly proprietors were to impart it. Therefore they began to cast about for a minister to expound the scriptures and break the bread of life to them.

It is told how the first religious meeting was held one Sabbath out in the broad open air, and the Rev. Mr. Powers, of Haverhill, N. H., preached the discourse. He and the Rev. Mr. Ward, of Plymouth, were the only ministers who resided in the wild regions round about our beloved valley for many years, and a minister and public Sabbath worship were rare in those primitive times.*

It was summer when the meeting was held. Spring is gone, when the corn was planted and the children set to scare away the crows that came to pull up the tender shoots. The snow drop, the primrose, the cowslip, and the violets are gone; but the wild rose has come, the elder is in blossom, the raspberry is red in the hedge by the brush fence, and the unripe blackberry is turning to a rich, luscious, and jetty black. Haying time has come, the mowers have been at work among the stumps and logs cutting the heavy burden of grass. The green swaths have been spread to dry by the merry boys and girls, the haycocks have been heaped high, and upon the rude sled to which the steers have been yoked it is drawn to the barn. But the scythes, rakes, and forks had been laid aside, the steers unyoked and turned away in the pasture that Saturday night and all made ready for the Sabbath.

My grandmother said that Sunday was a bright, beautiful day. When the sun rose over the great mountains and the mighty wood, all the world seemed hushed and still. As the hours crept on the people began to assemble. The spot chosen for the meeting was on the ridge of land that formed the barrier of Runaway pond, and west of Black brook, the Mikaseota. They came by the blazed paths through the woods from every little clearing. Nearly all walked then; there were but few saddle horses and no carriages. Some of the men and the boys and girls are barefoot. They are

---

* When Mr. Powers saw young men felling trees   *   *   *   he would call to them and say if Providence favored him, he would preach to them in that place on such a day and at such an hour. These were welcome propositions generally, and if there were other settlements near they were informed of the appointment, and Mr. Powers at the hour specified would find his hearers seated on stumps and logs all ready to receive the word.— History of Coos. 77.

dressed in their everyday garments; Sunday clothes they have none. The men are in their shirt sleeves, their frocks slung across their arms in case it might rain. You would particularly notice Stevens Merrill and his intelligent black eyed wife. He was a man advanced in years, dressed differently from most of the rest, for he had his Quaker suit on, and was in the habit of speaking out in meeting if the sermon did not suit him.* There was Mr. Simeon Smith, from Red Oak hill, also somewhat advanced in life. He was always noticed to be a little nervous at meeting. His wife had heated the large Dutch oven that morning, and put in an iron pot of beans and an earthen dish of Indian pudding, to bake in their absence, and be ready for supper when they returned. His neighbor John Morrill comes along with him, and his wife, a fleshy woman, has on her arm, as do nearly all the rest, a bag filled with nut cakes and cold meat for a luncheon. You will see coming up from Hurricane brook, Joseph Patch and his young wife, the daughter of Stevens Merrill. His neighbor, Mr. Hinchson, who lives alone in the woods, the hunter and trout and salmon catcher, accompanies him. William Butler also comes, the young man fat and portly. His wife, Mehitable, and John Mills, Sr., and John Mills, Jr., are all on hand, as the saying is. 'Squire Jonathan, as he was known in latter days, is there also with his wife and children. Ephraim True comes from " over the river." He has waded across for there is no bridge. Along with him is his wife and half a dozen small children, the latter still shy and wild just like young partridges. Joshua Merrill, who lived to be a hundred years old, who was a tailor by trade, was there with his family, from the foot of Beech hill. He wore a three-cornered cocked hat on that day, small clothes, neatly fitting, and tight stockings, with huge knee buckles and silver shoe buckles. He was an exception, as we have said before, and was always the best dressed man in town. Joshua Copp, dignified and grave, with his wife and several children was there. Obadiah Clement, always religiously inclined, with his

---

* Some one was once preaching at Jonathan Clement's inn. Mr. Clement sat inside the bar with his hat on. The minister suddenly changed his discourse, from preaching to the saints, and began to talk to the wicked. Mr. Clement jumped up, shouted amen! and said he thanked the Lord that the minister was preaching to the sinners. John Abbott rose at once, and in pious accents advised the minister not to dwell long on that subject, as there was only one sinner present, and that one was shut up in the liquor bar, where he couldn't do any hurt.— Miss Hannah Knight's statement.

brothers, Jonathan and Reuben,* and their families was present. Isaiah Batchelder, the Clarks, and the Lunds, with their wives and children were down from Tarleton lake, a long journey for them. And even Mr. Chase Whitcher, from his home in the basin of mountains at the north part of the town, had traveled all the way down and was present with his relatives Reuben and John Whitcher, from Pine hill, and the families of each.

Parson Powers in those days wore a black kerseymere coat, silk breeches and stockings, three-cornered hat and fleece-like wig, a white band and white silk gloves. With what dignity did he walk among that little crowd of rough backwoodsmen. How meekly they stood aside to let him pass, although Stevens Merrill was'nt much afraid of him. What was his pulpit? No high box like those of ancient days; but it might have been a large pine stump cut smoothly on the top for the purpose. It might have been a platform of poles placed evenly upon two logs. Above his head was no pyramidal sounding board, but in its stead were mighty columns of towering trees, surmounted by capitals of wavy splendor. There were no lofty walls supported by Doric or Corinthian columns around him; no windows painted with images, but in their stead were archivolts of leaves rustling and sighing in the wind; architraves of mighty branches that rocked in the grand chorus of storms, arches of blue with heavenward opening windows painted with rainbows and the golden glories of sunset. There were no cushioned pews nor altars gaily decorated and set with precious stones, but their seats were cushioned with forest flowers, their chancel was of flowering banks with balustrades of evergreen; their altar was gemmed with pebbles and crystals of mica and spangles of emerald moss. Such was the temple in which the first settlers, perhaps blind to the beautiful, worshiped.

Did they have singing at their meeting? Of course they did; but who took the lead it is impossible now to tell.† Whether as was the custom of the day, some one acting as deacon read the

---

* Reuben Whitcher was a new comer about these times.

† "One of the first choristers of Warren was Captain Stephen Richardson. He always wore to meeting short hip breeches, and long white stockings with silver shoe and knee buckles. He had a watch pocket exactly in front, in the waist-band of his breeches, and a long heavy silver chain, key and seal at the end, attached to his great 'bull's eye watch,' hung dangling atwixt his legs almost down to his knees. He used his pitch pipe freely, beat time lustily with his feet, swayed back

first two lines, and another tooted on the pitch pipe and then led off with his voice, or whether as in our prayer meetings now, they all joined in one of those wild, religious hymns, such as the old Scotch Covenanters were wont to raise in their mountain fastness, or the persecuted Christians sang in the catacombs of Rome, it is also impossible to tell. They had no musical instruments then, but if they had listened they might have heard the winds sighing an accompaniment in the woods, the murmuring anthem of the neighboring brooks and distant river, or perhaps if it were a hot summer afternoon the grand diapason of thunder peeling in the gorges of the mountains.

The noontime of that Sunday must have been an interesting occasion for our settlers. Their luncheon eaten and they sat down in knots and groups to talk over the events of the day. The state of the country was discussed then the same as now. The old French war, the tyranny of King George, the Stamp Act, the Tea Party, all came in for their share. Perhaps some of them went to Joshua Copp's cabin, for that was then the most central part of the settlement, and there sat down and drank of his nice cool water from the neighboring spring. Mrs. Copp was a neat woman, her floor ever nicely sanded, her pewter on the open dresser bright and glistening. They talked of the weather, of the births, of the marriages, engagements, health, sickness, and deaths, those among themselves, and particularly of those among their friends down country; the land from which they had emigrated, for which they yearned, and to which they made frequent pilgrimages.

After the services Parson Powers went home with Obadiah Clement to enjoy the hospitality of his house and spend the night, and he did it right merrily. As the story goes, and such was the custom in those days, a good glass of the dear creature was brought forward, just as soon as he had crossed the threshold, to clear the reverend throat. When night came he had a different kind of beverage to make him slumber quietly and induce pleasant dreams.*

and forth as he sung, the watch chain vibrating in unison with the tune, while all the little boys and girls present tittered and laughed at the comical sight."—Miss Hannah Knight's statement.

Colonel Stevens M. Dow said that he had sung with Captain R., and that the Captain was an excellent singer.

*Elder Currier who lived in Wentworth sometimes preached in Warren during the last years of the eighteenth century.

In the morning the best the house afforded was served up for breakfast, then an excellent glass of punch was quaffed and away rode the divine of these wilderness settlements on his strong little horse over the Height-o-land, round Tarleton lake, across which a light winged breeze was blowing, through Piermont woods, to the Coos intervals, as they were known in those times.

CHAPTER VIII.

WAR! HOW IT REARED ITS HORRID FRONT AND ITS DIN RESOUNDED EVEN ACROSS THE BOUNDARIES OF WARREN, TOGETHER WITH WHAT PART OUR EARLY SETTLERS TOOK IN IT.

IT was a bright June day. Joseph Patch was at work clearing a little pasture on the ridge that forms the western foot of Picked hill. It was hot; the sun hung high in heaven, and Patch, pausing to rest, sat down on a long hemlock log to eat his luncheon and quaff a draught of spruce beer. Suddenly there was a strange sound in the air — was it thunder behind the western mountains, the faint rumble of a pent up earthquake, or was it only a partridge drumming in the thick pine woods? He listened and again and again heard it. It was not the partridge's drum, not the thunder, nor the earthquake — what was it?

At noon he spoke to his family about it, but they had not noticed it. At night he talked with his neighbors; John Mills had also heard it, and so had Stevens Merrill, but none could tell what it was.

A week went by and a stranger journeying through the valley northward told them that a great battle had been fought at Bunker Hill, and that thousands of men were hurrying to join the rebel army under General Washington.

Before night every settler in the hamlet had heard the news. It is a hundred and twenty miles as the crow flies, to Bunker Hill. There could be heard the booming of cannon all that distance. Now in a clear day the granite shaft which commemorates that event can be seen from the bald peak of Moosehillock mountain.

The settlers had heard of the battle of Lexington, had seen a few men marching south, through the woods, with their queen's arms on their shoulders, to join the army as they said, but they had not minded much about it. But now a thousand men had died on the battle field and the settlers were all on fire at the news and for weeks talked of nothing else.

There were two parties in town, one favored King George, the other the rebels. The latter were much the stronger, numbering twice as many as the former. Frequent discussions arose. But these soon ceased, the last one taking place at Obadiah Clement's bar room, where mine host and Stevens Merrill had a pleasant little talk about the war which resulted in their hating each other cordially ever after.

But there were some who did not wait for discussion; William Heath, as aforesaid, Reuben Clement, Joseph Whitcher, a new comer, and Ephraim Lund were ready to serve their country. They scoured up their old hunting pieces, mended their clothes and shoes and were soon prepared to leave.*

They all went away together on that summer morning. There was no rail car in which to ride, no jolting stage coach to carry them, no wagon of any kind. A long, weary march on foot was before them. They had said good-bye to their families and friends, and as they journeyed down the Asquamchumauke they stopped to take what might be to them a last look. In their hearts they felt that it was "farewell ye great woods and mountains of Warren, ye moose and deer, and ye bright streams of the hills. We may return no more, our graves may be in other lands." Then all day long they hastened down the river. The hills melted away in the distance and the great forest shut the mountains from their sight. A week later they were soldiers in John Stark's regiment, and a part of Washington's army.

Hold! says some incredulous reader now living in our mountain hamlet. How do you know all this? Be easy for a moment. When we began the great work of writing this immortal history we could not find a single person who knew anything about those

---

*John Hinchson was in Captain John Parker's company in 1775. He went to Canada and got home Dec. 31, 1775. He printed his name thus, "JOHN HINKSON." Vol. viii. page 218.—Records in the office of the Secretary of State, Concord, N. H.

who served in the war of the Revolution. But in the process of time the whole subject gradually unfolded itself. One of the first steps was the finding the census of 1775.* Then Warren and Piermont were classed together for enumeration. The population of both towns was at that time one hundred and sixty-eight persons, and of these, although the war had but just commenced, fifteen men were serving in the army. Now there were about twenty families in Warren, and allowing five persons in a family which is nearly the average, one hundred of the above population belonged in Warren. We can safely say one half of it did and by the same rule can claim half the soldiers. But we are modest and don't claim but five as that is all that we can hear of. Perhaps there were more.

And now excitement prevailed throughout the land; the notes of preparation, the din of arms, the clangor of the strife resounded to our hamlet among the hills. Speculators and sutlers were abroad, and Daniel Gilman came to town buying all the moose skins he could find, which he manufactured into moosehide breeches and sold to the Continental Government at eighteen shillings a pair.† The quartermaster was abroad, and the great Committee of Safety appointed for the whole State of New Hampshire contracted with Joshua Copp, Esq., our settler on the banks of Runaway pond, to notify the various towns of Grafton county and collect their quota of beef for the use of the Continental army.‡ Something to drink for the soldiers was necessary, and as there was no distillery in Warren, Phillips White, the good, kind hearted proprietor we have mentioned so many times before, generously advanced the amount to be furnished by the settlers of his township, which was "*nine garlins and two quarts of West Indea rum.*"** But the strangest thing that happened this year was the appointment of John Balch "*to ride post*" through all the northern country and through our

---

*The following is the entry under the head of Piermont and Warren, in the census report of 1775, viz: Males under sixteen, 52; Males from sixteen to fifty, 28; Males above fifty, 4; Males in the army, 15; Females, 69; Negroes and Slaves, 0. Total, 168. Firearms fit for use 1; do. wanting, 31; pounds public powder, 16; do. private powder, 0.— N. H. Hist. Coll. Vol. 1, 235.

†Thursday Oct. 31st, 1776. Agreed with Mr. Danl Gilman for 100 coarse Moose Hide Breeches, at 18s.—N. H. Hist. Coll. Vol. vii. page 63.

‡ "March 6, 1783. Ordered the Treas to pay Joshua Copp, Colt. of Beef, Grafton, five pounds fourteen shillings, for time and Expences, &c., to notify Towns of the time to receive Beef."—N. H. Hist. Coll. Vol. vii. page 317.

** See Vol. i. Town Clerk's Book.

mountain hamlet of course. He was appointed by the aforesaid Committee of Safety, and was to set out from Portsmouth on Saturday morning and ride to Haverhill by way of Conway and Plymouth, thence down the Connecticut river to Charleston and Keene, and to Portsmouth again in fourteen days, and was to receive seventy hard silver dollars, or their equivalent, for every three months' service. For the whole seven long years of the revolutionary war John Balch rode post.

We are told how one night the storm and darkness overtook him in the woods this side of Plymouth. All the long, black hours he stopped in one of our old "hotels," and only came riding past Stevens Merrill's just as the rising sun was flashing among the waterfalls and sending the night mists down the glens. But most often he came to Warren in the bright forenoon, when the woods were cheerful and the rough clearings inviting. As he dashed along the stony bridle path he would blow a blast on his post horn, rousing the old wood and waking the echoes. Then he would laugh to see what a turn out there would be from the log cabins; the good man and his wife, all the flaxen headed children, and even the cat and dog, the geese, turkeys, and chickens, and sometimes the old horse, cow, and hog, each seeming eager to know why

"Johnny Balch, blowing a blast both loud and shrill,
Dashed through the woods and galloped down the hill."

But most generally the family wanted to hear the news and the jolly post rider was nothing loth to give it.*

But the summer went by and the autumn came, and our settlers learned that Schuyler and Montgomery with a small force had advanced by lake Champlain against Montreal, and Arnold at the head of a thousand men had tramped through the wilderness to the St. Lawrence. Then during all the winter hardly anything was heard from the boys in the army.

In the spring of 1776 there was another call for troops, and news came, after Arnold failed, of a threatened invasion from Canada. All the frontier was in excitement at this, and there was a great demand for arms. The Committee of Safety endeavored to furnish a supply, and they let Chase Whitcher, our boy settler,

*For an account of John Balch's riding post, see Vol. vii. N. H. Hist. Coll.

have money enough to buy thirteen guns, for that number was needed in the hamlet. He gave security to pay for the same when called for, and then loading them upon his horse trudged behind his faithful beast, and brought them all safely to Warren.*

These guns were faithfully distributed among our settlers. Even Stevens Merrill was offered one, but he said he did not believe in war and would not fight on either side and so would not have it. Jonathan Clement and Joseph Patch also refused to take a gun even as a gift.

It is told, with how much truth we cannot say, that Joshua Copp and Simeon Smith went away to the regions of upper Coos about this time to serve with Captain Eames, a renowned military chieftain, said to have once resided in the neighboring province of Wentworth. Captain Eames, with his company, had built a fort at Coos, and was ordered in the autumn of 1776 " to engage ten men through the winter as scouts." Copp and Smith, tradition has it, served on this scout. They had seen the supplies, consisting of two barrels of gunpowder, eight hundred pounds of lead for bullets, six hundred flints, and blankets for forty soldiers, and all other necessaries sent by the Committee of Safety. They were loaded on the backs of a train of pack horses which journeyed along the rough bridle path northward, " and were for the use of the troops on the western portion of this colony at Coos." † They rendezvoused one night at Obadiah Clement's little tavern, at the foot of Height-o-land, and the next morning as they marched away Copp and Smith resolved that they would see before the snow flew what kind of service they would have in the wild upper country.

The folks at home had heard from John Balch, the post rider, all the news of the years' campaigns. The disasters on Long Island and the losses along the Hudson made everything seem black enough; but in the midwinter word came of the great victory of the battle of Trenton and the rebels took heart again.‡

---

* " Aug. 5th, 1776. Ordered the Receiver General To pay Mr. Chace Witcher of Warren, Twenty-four pounds to buy Arms and Ammunition, he Giving Security to pay the Same when Demanded."—N. H. Hist. Coll. Vol. vii. 55.
A gun cost 36s.

† See Vol. vii. N. H. Hist. Coll.

‡ In 1776, Colonel William Tarleton who once lived in Warren, was a sergeant in Edward Everett's company.
The same year, Joseph Lund was in Captain James Osgood's company.— See Records in the office of Secretary of State, Concord, N. H.

The next year war came to our frontier in earnest, and the dwellers in the land of the Coosucks got a slight taste of it. Even our pioneers snuffed the battle from afar. Burgoyne began his invasion from Canada, proceeding by Lake Champlain, and the greatest excitement prevailed through all the wild border. Hitherto there had been only a Committee of Safety for the whole State, but now danger was so imminent that a committee of safety, inspection, vigilance, or correspondence, whatever it might be called, was formed in nearly every town. These co-operated with the State Committee rendering it efficient service. The towns thus became, in a measure, separate provinces, or rather independent democracies, each contributing all the aid it could to the great cause.

The Committee in this northern country, as elsewhere, met at stated intervals and acted in a legislative, executive, and judicial capacity. The conduct of all suspicious persons was inquired into; numerous arrests were made, and imprisonments and banishments frequently followed. They even took the subject of confiscation in hand and the property of many individuals who were not "truly loyal" escheated to the State.

We never could learn that the great committee of Warren ever did much in these matters, but the committees of Plymouth and Haverhill, neighboring democracies, were often terribly exercised. For instance we find it recorded that the State Committee this year received a letter from the committee at Plymouth "informing that several strangers, well dressed, had been discovered at a very unfrequented place in the wood, whom they supposed were engaged in a bad design." The State Committee immediately ordered search to be made and the strangers apprehended if possible. Whether they were arrested or not we never learned.

It is also written down that at Haverhill, in the "Cohass" region, was a great tory, Mr. Fisher by name, who was compelled to exile himself to some foreign land. His farm on the intervals the said committee gently took into their possession, cultivated it with the soldiers stationed at the Cohass, and eventually sold the land and devoted the proceeds to the "rebel cause," as King George was pleased to term it.

But if Warren's Committee of Safety did not do much in the

direction we have indicated, there were some in town who worked for the "patriot cause" in a private capacity, and some who worked for the good of their own pockets.

In the journal of the Committee of Safety it is also written — "Friday July 4th, 1777. Ordered the R. G.* to let John Mills have out of the Treasry £25, to pay bounties to men he enlists, for which he is to be acctble." †

How many men John Mills enlisted we never learned, but report has it that Jonathan Fellows, who had just come to town and John Mills, Junior, went away to the war about these times, perhaps stimulated to patriotic deeds by this very £25. And it would not be at all unlikely that John Mills enlisted men in the regions round about, as many another recruiting officer has done at a later day. Fellows, and Mills, Junior, it is told, were at the battle of Bennington, the latter being first lieutenant in the fifth company of Colonel Nichol's regiment.‡

But it is not written in the Committee of Safety's book, and perhaps that honorable body never found out, what Stevens Merrill and his son Jonathan did. When the cry, "the British are coming," was heard, Mr. M. and his son, who were always true to the royal government, scented gold from afar and prepared to put a fair proportion of it in their own pockets. They quietly went to work and bought up a considerable number of beef cattle of the settlers and obtained others from the wooded pastures in the neighboring lands, and then when they had learned from the well dressed strangers "discovered in the very unfrequented place in the wood," at what time a British guard would be at the rendezvous, over beyond the Connecticut river among the Green mountains, they set off one bright night with the whole herd. They drove the beeves to Haverhill by the old Indian trail, now an unfrequented way, a path in which there was no danger of meeting any one, and when the gray of the morning came on, halted in a secluded glen two miles or so from the mouth of the Oliverian.

---

* R. G. means Receiver General.
† See N. H. Hist. 'Coll. Vol. vii. 104.
‡ John Mills was first a 2d Lieutenant in Colonel Timothy Bedel's regiment, fourth company, in 1776. This regiment was marched to Canada, and at a fort called "The Cedars" was disgracefully surrendered; then in 1777 he was 1st Lieutenant of the fifth company, in Colonel Moses Nichol's regiment, and was present with his company at the battle of Bennington, and last was Captain of the fourth company, in Colonel Daniel Reynold's regiment, in 1781.—See Records in the office of the Secretary of State, Concord, N. H.

All day long they kept the drove together and on the second night, with some assistance, swam them across the Connecticut. Morning found them in the yards of the rendezvous. Fat cattle were valuable then, and on the fourth day our loyal settlers were safe at home again, with their pockets well lined with British gold. Obadiah Clement and others wondered what became of the cattle, but years went by before they learned of the profitable and somewhat wild adventures in which their neighbors were engaged.

Some folks are ready now to cry out; Cowboys! Tories! Traitors! Devils! they ought to have been hung! and a good many other like pious ejaculations. Be easy for a moment; Stevens Merrill, from the manner in which he viewed the great questions of that day, from his own stand point, was a true patriot. He believed the colonists were wrong, that King George was right, and that the war would ruin the country. He himself loved his native land, and was loyal to his king. He firmly believed his opinions were correct, his conscience pointed out the path of duty, and then as always through life he endeavored to follow it. Had the result of the contest been different the rebels would have been in the wrong, deserving the halter, and himself the true patriot. Success makes the hero, failure the traitor.

But if our tory friends performed a night march to the Connecticut, at the head or tail of a horned cavalcade, many another body proceeded through the woods to the same destination, but for a far different object. There was hurrying to and fro throughout all the country, and a large number went marching to the land of Coos. Captain Eames took up squads of men, but Captain Bedel marched at the head of a whole company along the rough bridle path.* He had a fife and drum, and the musicians made exceedingly pleasant music, sweet to hear among the woods of Warren. Then he had a continental flag, carried sometimes in the centre of the column, which fluttered most beautifully in the leafy forest. All the men as a general thing camped near Obadiah Clement's inn, marching the whole distance from Plymouth in a single day, and the train of pack horses used to carry supplies and ammunition, almost eat our poor landlord out of house and home. Sometimes he got his pay, but oftener he did not, and when he did

---

* See N. H. Hist. Coll. Vol. vii.

it was the old Continental currency, that eventually proved worthless. But he kept good natured and always rejoiced at the success of the colonies.*

Captain Eames and Bedel did good service guarding the rich meadows on the "long river of pines," otherwise Dutchman's Varshe, or fresh river. But they never had a fight; not a red coat came to disturb them. Still they kept the town quiet, and made friends with the Coosuck Indians, as they were instructed by the great Committee of Safety.

All this happened right at home, but our hardy mountaineers were exceedingly anxious all this season, 1777, to hear the news from the army. When they learned of the battle of Bennington, Stark, to them, was the greatest man living, and joy was unbounded. There were some who did not like the news, but they were shrewd, and said nothing. Again when word came of the surrender of Burgoyne, most of the good settlers almost went into ecstasies; our silent friends were inwardly as mad as March hares.

At the close of the year the prospects of the colonists were not so good. Another winter passed, the winter of Valley Forge; the spring came, and with it the darkest year of the war. News from the army was scarce; what they did hear was bad, and the inhabitants of Warren seemed divided and estranged.

And now in the colonists' darkest hour happened the greatest event of the war—to the Warrenites. Hostility came to the dwellers of the hamlet. It transpired in this wise. The soldiers who guarded the "Cohass" frontier were enlisted for short periods. Consequently discharges followed rapidly, the veterans returned home, and raw recruits hurried to the log forts, stockades, and block houses, so valorously guarded by Captains Eames and Bedel. There was a continual passing of troops, and as these soldiers, as before mentioned, never found a FOE in the front, being anxious to achieve some deed of greatness, looked sharp for ONE in the rear.

Some folks never can mind their own business, and no man, who is a man, is without his enemies. Joseph Patch, our first settler had his, and to the valorous soldiers, who marched and countermarched along the bridle path, they reported that Patch was a tory. When he was at home no passer by dared meddle with him. But

---
* James Clement's statement.

work must be done, and in autumn he was often away hunting. At such times Mrs. Patch with her children would go for a day or two to her father's, Mr. Stevens Merrill's. On one occasion when her husband was looking after his sable traps and exploring for beaver meadows over Mount Carr, Mrs. P. saw two or three soldiers hurry across her father's clearing, and disappear in the woods towards her own dwelling. Their appearance made a strong impression upon her mind, so much so, that half an hour afterwards she went out, and looking towards her own home, saw a dense black smoke rising like a cloud above it. Screaming, she gave the alarm, then hurried down the bridle path. But she was too late. The fire had burst from the roof; the flames leaped up hot and fierce, and the smoke, a great black column, towered hundreds of feet above and then floated away over the great forest and disappeared beyond the mountain. Twenty minutes later and the house, which was the best one in town, was almost wholly consumed. One of the soldier boys had set fire to it with his pipe, as was afterwards learned, and then they valorously marched on. Mr. Patch had a large quantity of provisions, including several barrels of moose meat, also a considerable store of rich peltries, all which were totally destroyed. Nothing was saved from the house except "*a little iron picking pan,*" partly melted by the fire, which the family kept for many years as a memento of one of the great events of the war.*

Lumber and materials were plenty, there were willing hands to aid in the work, and before winter set in another house rose like the phœnix from the ashes. The barn with its contents did not burn and Patch was nearly as comfortable as before.

Now many people will cry shame. But we would say as before, wait a moment. Don't blame the soldiers. Such things must be expected in time of war. They always happen — and for our own sake and your pleasure, Christian reader, we are almost glad that they do. Without such a dire catastrophe we should not have had this brilliant episode for our most entertaining history.

But we must pause here. A new era dawns upon our mountain hamlet. Hitherto the lordly proprietors had cut all the roads,

---
* Jacob Patch's statement.

fought out all the boundary feuds, had sent men to build mills, had made appropriations for preaching, and had looked after all the interests of our little State just as a parent watches his child. Not a farthing for taxes, not a day's labor on the highways, hardly anything paid for the broad acres in the valley and on the hill-side, not a soldier furnished for the war we have been describing, except such as went from pure patriotism with poor pay, and most often no bounty; the early settlers were free as the wind.

But our little town was fast expanding into strength and beauty; and the former royal province, at present the Republic of New Hampshire, which as yet had paid no attention to the smiling hamlet, now believing that a good revenue might be derived without much trouble, like a fond lover began to pay court and commence suit to the bright and happy township among the hills.

How our pioneer settlement thus suddenly became an ample democracy in which the citizens made sundry laws and appointed the judicial and executive officers, but still acknowledged a slight allegiance to the State, composed like the Amphictyonic council of the great association of democracies, will be told in the most entertaining manner in our next.

BREAKING AND SWINGLING FLAX.

BOOK V.

CONCERNING THE MIGHTY MARCH OF EVENTS IN THE GREAT CIVIL HISTORY OF WARREN.

CHAPTER I.

OF THE ORGANIZATION OF THE HAMLET, AND HOW CERTAIN MEN ACHIEVED IMMORTAL GLORY BY GETTING ELECTED TO TOWN OFFICE.

WHEN in the course of human events one certain body feels a regard for another, there immediately begins to be made sundry strong efforts to inform the regarded party of the remarkable feelings experienced. Smiles, sighs, tender glances, and little gentle pressures of the hands are given if the parties are in the immediate neighborhood of each other. But if distance intervenes or extreme modesty prevails, then fond missives are indited and borne by the fleet post, communicating the heavenly passion,—all which is intensely interesting to the immediate parties but decidedly ridiculous to outsiders.

The latter method—the tender missive—was the one adopted by our young and vigorous republic; but not from any feeling of modesty. It was distance that forced the sending of a tender epistle to our coy little hamlet that hitherto had nestled so quietly and almost unnoticed among the hills. A go-between in the person of the great Committee of Safety, and a few other patriotic agents* had whispered the information that the young hamlet was beautiful and fertile, and growing in wealth, and thus the interest was excited.

What was the tenor of the exquisite billet-doux forwarded? "To the right about face, forward march — wake up, quick-step — take your place in the great family of small States." Short and sweet! But such was love's language in the war times of which we write. Every thing then had to bend and every nerve be strained, that the great Committee of Safety might have money and the soldiers be armed, equipped, and fed. Warren must do her part, must show her love for the young republic, although she might be a little shy and backward, by contributing her mite to the patriotic cause.

Representations, therefore, were made to the Great and General Court of New Hampshire, that it was their duty to attend to the matter, in order that a generous revenue might be forthcoming.

That honorable body acted. The machinery of legislation was immediately put in operation and a statute manufactured. It is very interesting, and reads somewhat like a romance; thus —

"*In the year of our Lord one thousand seven hundred and seventy-nine.*"

"An Act to ascertain the proportion of public taxes upon several towns and to enable them to collect the same."

Thus it opens in a heroic strain. Then follow the several whercases, *to wit:*

"Bath, Canaan, Wentworth, and Warren, have not paid their proportion of taxes.

"This has been represented by agents.

"It is owing, 1st, to the unsettled state of the country; and, 2d, that some of the towns have no town officers.

"Therefore that it may never happen again,—

"BE IT ENACTED.

"1st. That the State Treasurer issue his warrant for the whole tax, State and Continental.

---

* Obadiah Clement was the principal of these.

"2d. That it be assessed the same as on the first day of April last.

"3d. That the town of Warren pay twenty shillings for each £1,000 raised in the State.

"4th. That Samuel Emerson, of Plymouth, is commanded to call a town meeting in Warren, and preside until a moderator shall be chosen."

This bill was passed to be engrossed, June 22d, 1779. It was signed by John Langdon, Speaker of the House; Meshech Weare, President, approved it, and it was examined by Ebenezer Thompson, Secretary of State.

Samuel Emerson, who dwelt upon the east bank of the Asquamchumauke, where it runs a slow and lordly river, felt highly complimented when he heard of the great honors thrust upon him, and he promptly began his duties.

July 12th, 1779, he posted a notice warning the inhabitants of our pleasant township to assemble;* and on the 28th of the same month, the true men of Warren were on hand at the inn of mine host, Obadiah Clement, ready for business. Our tory friends did not attend; they forgot that the meeting was to be held that day.

But steady here—with great dignity and profound gravity! The mighty events of history should not be hurried over. How important is the first assembly of the hamlet. It is an auspicious moment, a new birth for the town; an entrance upon a higher life. A web of circumstances is to be woven about the citizens that shall change the whole course of their aspirations and ambitions; that shall furnish a field on which they may achieve distinction, as legislators, executive officers, and judges.

Did the wise men as they went to that meeting from their

---

*NAMES OF THE LEGAL VOTERS OF WARREN FOR THE YEAR 1780.

Isaiah Batchelder.	Joseph Kimball.	Joseph Patch.
William Butler.	Ephraim Lund.	Simeon Smith.
Daniel Clark.	Joseph Lund.	Ephraim True.
Thomas Clark.	John Marston.	Moses True.
Jonathan Clement.	Jonathan Merrill.	Chase Whitcher.
Obadiah Clement.	Joshua Merrill.	John Whitcher.
Reuben Clement.	Stevens Merrill.	Reuben Whitcher. (1)
Joshua Copp.	John Morrill.	
Gardner Dustin.	Nathaniel Niles.	

(1) JULY 8, 1787.—*Voted*, That Mr. Moses Page have one hundred acres of land laying northerly on Josiah Bartlett's Esq., in the sixth range, first division to be laid out in the same form as other lots in said range, in consideration of his settling Mr. Reuben Whitcher in said town.—Proprietor's Records.

fields where they had been haying among the charred stumps and logs, realize its importance? Did they know as they assembled in Obadiah Clement's old log bar-room, where the soldiers of the Revolution hastening to the camp or journeying home from the war, were wont to stop; where good milk-toddy, whiskey-punch, flip, and egg-nog, could always be had, and where in winter the old fashioned loggerhead was always kept at a white heat, that this was the beginning of a long series of meetings that should continue even down to our time? Did they think that in that identical bar-room, varnished and painted by the smoke of pitch knots and tobacco pipes, would arise those celebrated political parties — the Patch party, the Merrill party, and the Clement party — which always existed in town, down to the era of the "Know Nothings;" that it would be here that they would learn to love office, its honors and emoluments, to spout and talk and wrangle about the laying out of roads, the constructing of bridges, the clearing of training fields, the locating of school houses, and the building of meeting houses? Perhaps they realized it, and perhaps they did not.

But certain it is, that when the hour of ten was shown by the sun-dial which Obadiah Clement had fixed by his door, 'Squire Emerson in the most dignified manner, called the meeting to order. He knew his business, and he thought he knew himself. A moderator, as commanded by the statute, was first to be chosen. "Please forward your ballots, gentlemen," said he. But not a man moved. They hadn't a ballot. Then the 'Squire explained and some one asked Col. Clement for paper and a pen. He had the pen, but said he did not think there was any paper in the house. Some one suggested there was birch bark by the fire-place, and ye dignified chairman said *that* would do. It was cut in little slips, the names written, and the ballots forwarded. It did not take long to count them, and the chairman declared Joshua Copp unanimously elected. 'Squire Emerson, after administering the oath of office, whispered in Mr. Copp's ear that a clerk was necessary, and 'Squire Joshua, in the style of his great predecessor, said, " Please forward your ballots, gentlemen, for town clerk." This time they knew how to do it, and Obadiah Clement having every one, was also declared unanimously elected.

Then there was a pause; no one knew exactly what was wanted, or who would be suitable for the offices; and after a little general discussion, and considerable private talk, they concluded to adjourn to the twelfth of August next, as the day to finish the business of the meeting, and obey the requirements of the great statute so kindly passed for their benefit.

The morn of August 12th came. The patriots of Warren assembled, and even a few of those loyal to King George, who were not in the habit of saying much, looked in upon the meeting. But every thing was cut and dried beforehand, as is often the case for town meetings of later years, and it took but very few minutes to elect Obadiah Clement, Joshua Copp, and Israel Stevens, another new comer, selectmen; Simeon, Smith, constable; and William Butler, Reuben Clement, and Thomas Clark, surveyors of highways. Then, as this was all the business that could legally come before the meeting, they adjourned without day.*

Another thing might also be established, and as it was immediately done, it is proper to mention it here. *It was the opening of a Court.* In it Judge Joshua Copp † presided for a long time with dignity, and dispensed exact justice. As he grew in years Judge Jonathan Merrill succeeded him, and was noted for firmness and the energy with which he enforced his decisions. This is well illustrated in the celebrated case, Isaac Clifford *versus* John Morrill. Clifford sued Morrill for the value of a hog which he had sold him, and the case was returned before his honor Judge Merrill. Each had a lawyer from some distant land, and after a full hearing, the case was decided for the defendant. The first time afterwards the Judge met Mr. C. the latter would not speak, but grunted like a hog at his honor. The same thing happened the next time they met; whereupon Judge M.‡ turned short about,

---

* See Vol. I. Town Clerk's Records.

† *First Marriage in Warren.*—Esquire Joshua Copp performed nearly all the marriage ceremonies while he held office. He married John Marston, the first marriage in town. The latter had no money and was to pay a bushel of beans in advance. He only carried half a bushel, got married and trusted too for the other half; and would not pay because he said his wife kicked him out of bed, and he had to lie underneath. Marston moved to Romney and was a drunken man. Weld, who kept store, paid him in rum to run naked through the street. Weld's wife horsewhipped Marston, making the fur fly good, and then whipped her husband too.

‡ Esquire Jonathan was a man who could shake folks, if he was smiling and smooth as oil. When he and his father with their families were moving to War-

seized uncle Isaac by the collar, shook him nearly out of his boots, got an apology out of him in double quick time, and only released him when he had promised to behave well in the future.*

But more often when the parties were not satisfied with the decisions of our distinguished jurists, they took an appeal and carried the case to a court of higher powers and broader jurisdiction, established by the great Republic of New Hampshire, in some place far across Warren's borders.†

But the highest of all the rights and privileges that could now be exercised, was that of sending a minister, ambassador, or plenipotentiary extraordinary, commonly termed the *representative*, to the Great and General Court we have mentioned, which like the aforesaid renowned Amphictyonic council, made the general laws which were for the government of the numerous proud little democracies of the republic. By so doing they secured the high honors thus conferred, and had a voice in equalizing the light burdens of taxation imposed.

Thus the work was done. The assemblies, otherwise called *town meetings*, were short but they answered the purpose, and our grand little hamlet was organized a healthful State. It was to pay a light tribute, as we have seen, in the shape of State and Continental taxes, for protection, to the great Republic that had such a kind regard for it, but in other respects was wholly free.

Still there was no danger, even if it had not been compelled to pay a farthing. Its mountain boundaries were a safeguard and a barrier against neighboring territories, and the wild mountain-

---

ren, they met a man who wouldn't turn out. High words ensued, and then the 'Squire and the stranger took off their coats and went at it. The stranger got a thrashing, and Stevens Merrill whose religion forbade him to fight, turned the stranger's horse out of the road, and they went on their way rejoicing.

* Isaac Clifford of Wentworth, was in Col. David Hobart's regiment from Dec. 7, 1776, to March 1777. He was the son of Isaac Clifford of Kingston, N. H., who married Sarah Healy and then moved to Romney. Isaac Clifford, of Romney, was the ancestor of all the Cliffords in the Asquamchumauke valley. Hon. Nathan Clifford, one of the Judges of the United States Supreme Court, is one of the family.—See Hist. of Chester, p. 493.

† *Whipping Posts and Stocks.*—Warren never had these useful machines for preserving the peace and inculcating good order. But our friends down at Plymouth did. At the latter place, Col. William Webster, "the old man of all," had charge of them, and it is said he could lay on twenty lashes as handsomely as any man that ever lived. By an act passed in 1701, a penalty was inflicted for profane swearing, of sitting in the stocks not exceeding two hours, and for a second offence, not exceeding three hours; for drunkenness, to sit in the stocks three hours. Theft might in some cases be punished by whipping, not exceeding twenty stripes. The stocks and whipping were legal penalties, by an act passed in 1791 and in force in 1815.

eers of old Peeling, and the land of Trecothick and the other surrounding regions, seldom durst venture across them.

Yet it was a high honor as we intimated before—worth a thousand times the small pittance rendered—to have all the machinery of State running within its territory. As in old Rome the consuls, so in our mountain town the *selectmen* were the high functionaries and rulers, taking precedence of each other in the order of their election. And then, afterwards elected or appointed the *judges* who presided in the courts, the great ambassador or *representative*, the *treasurer* who kept the money in a ponderous "safe"—his pocket,—the custodian of the peace, the mighty *constable*, the superintendents of the great public roads, the *highway surveyors*, the conservators of the royal game, called *deer keepers*, the *tythingman* who kept order on the Sabbath, the gatherer of the revenue or tribute, styled the *tax collector*, the *hog constables*, politely termed *hogreeves*,* who put yokes upon the necks, and rings in the noses of swine—each well filled his subordinate place and helped continue the State.

Of course now the citizens of our beautiful hamlet, especially those loyal to King George, fondly appreciated the efforts of the kind go-between, the great Committee of Safety, and the other patriotic agents, who had contributed so much to bring about this healthful organization, and gently reciprocating the fond affection of the young and vigorous Republic of New Hampshire, exerted every energy to become a great and powerful democracy, much to the benefit of themselves and their neighbors round about.

---

* *Hogreeves.*—Charles Bowles was the first hogreeve in Warren. By an act of George I, 1719, it was enacted that no yoke shall be accounted sufficient that shall not be the depth of the swine's neck, and half so much below, and the sole or bottom three times as long as the thickness of the swine's neck. The ringing was to insert a piece of iron wire through the hog's nose, bring the ends together, and twist them so that it should project about an inch above the nose, which would prevent rooting.

CHAPTER II.

HOW THE REVENUE WAS RAISED TO CARRY ON THE WAR MUCH TO THE DELIGHT OF SEVERAL PATRIOTIC GENTLEMEN CALLED TORIES, AND WHAT SOLDIERS WERE FURNISHED TO FILL WARREN'S QUOTA; AND OTHER VERY INTERESTING AND ENTERTAINING MATTER.

THE young Republic wanted money; the good citizens of Warren knew it; Samuel Emerson, of Plymouth, had instructed them how it must be raised; the selectmen wanted to try the new democratic machine, and they immediately called a town meeting for that purpose. August 28, 1779, it was held. Gardner Dustin having been chosen moderator they refused by vote to accept a plan of government sent them by the Continental Congress and then voted to raise one hundred and fifty pounds to lay out on highways and one hundred pounds to defray town charges.*

And now the selectmen, as assessors, went to work immediately. They traveled from clearing to clearing, the little islands in the woods, for the forest was the rule and the openings the exceptions in these bright primitive days; they counted the horses and neat cattle, and estimated the broad acres of arable, mowing and pasture lands, and then carefully calculated each man's proportion. The lists made out, they were placed in the hands of Simeon Smith, constable, for collection, he filling the office of tax collector as well.†

Simeon Smith was a man of perseverence, but he found his

---
* This was depreciated currency—the old Continental money.
† For the first inventories of Warren, and tax list, see Appendix.

task a difficult one. Some paid willingly, and some resolutely declared they would not pay at all. He coaxed and flattered, but all to no avail. Then he determined to try what virtue there was in law. In right good earnest he went to work. He took the hardest cases first. Stevens Merrill, the stern, silent man, was the toughest customer. His whole tax was 29*l* 15*s* 11*d*, and he declared he would not pay it. So Simeon Smith took his cow by distraint, and advertised it for sale by posting a notice in Obadiah Clement's bar-room. It read as follows:—

"TO BE SOLD AT A

PUBLIC VANDUE

at the highest bidder, at the house of Mr. Obadiah Clement, an innholder in Warren, the 21st day of December, at six o'clock, P. M., One Cow. Artical of sale to be seen at time and place by me the subscriber.
          SIMEON SMITH, Constable.
Warren, Dec. 18, 1779."

Then the conditions are set out at length, something as follows:—"A cow to be sold; no man to bid less than a pound; if two persons bid at the same time, then the cow to be set up again; cash or money to be all paid down: if the buyer won't pay, then he shall forfeit the cost of the vandue. Obadiah Clement apinted vandue master and clark of the sail."

But Simeon Smith had to look sharp or he would not be able to keep that cow to sell. Stevens Merrill was on the watch to retake her. Three nights the constable had her in possession, and each night he had to post a guard over her. The first night two men at the price of ten shillings each, stood sentry; next, one man performed the duty through all the dark hours for the same amount, and the third night two strong men mounted guard, and also had a large force at convenient distance, who would come at call to assist them if necessary. There was great danger, and people were afraid of Stevens Merrill, for he was brave as a lion, and his son Jonathan as cunning as a fox. In the still hours of night they might come and steal the cow away. And so they watched, but the "terror" of the mountain hamlet did not come.*

December 21, 1779, the cow was sold, being struck off to Reuben Whitcher, the "hiest" bidder, for ninety pounds. Mr. M. received all the money except what was necessary to pay taxes, costs, and charges.

Jonathan Clement was as obdurate as Mr. Merrill. He was determined not to pay, and there was also a special "vandue" for the sale of some of his property.

All the rest of the few contrary citizens now saw that our constable was in earnest, and so paid up. But such things often happened afterwards. The very next year Jonathan Merrill and Joshua Merrill had some of their ewe sheep sold, and a little after, Joseph Patch had "so much of his good inglish hay sold as would pay his taxes," and somebody else had the exquisite pleasure of seeing their two "puter platters" auctioned off for their rates.†

The next year Col. Clement was himself constable, having taken the place of Joshua Merrill, who backed out of the honor. Col. C. collected and paid over an immense sum of money to Maj. Child, for supplying the troops to the westward, and also furnished a large sum to the Committee of Safety.‡ Thus the sinews of war

---

* SIMEON SMITH'S ACCOUNT.

	£	s.	d.	f.
The acompt of my feeas for distraining	0	10	0	0
To two keepers one knight	1	0	0	0
To one keeper one knight	0	10	0	0
To two keepers one night	1	0	0	0
To one knight	0	10	0	0
one keeper one knight	0	10	0	0
To evidences to tendering the Overplus money that is due to the said Merrill	1	16	0	0
To expenses of the cow & under charges and expenses for keeping	18	10	0	0
	24	6	0	0
Tax	14	17	11	2
	14	17	11	2

† For account of these sales, see Town Clerk's Records, Vol. i. 311 to 314.

‡ "Thursday March 8th 1781. Ordered the Treasr to Discount with Obadiah Clemens, Constable for Warren, One thousand and five hundred pounds, old Emission, being so much paid to Major Child by order of the Committee of Safety, agreeable to his Receipt of the 10th of Octo 1780 for surplying the Troops at the Westward, £1500."—N. H. Hist. Coll. Vol. vii. 252.

Cold Winter.

The winter of 1780 was terrible cold. There were forty days, thirty-one in March, that it never thawed on the south side of the house.

Dark Day.

May 19, 1780, was the dark day. The sun was seen at rising, but it was soon obscured by clouds and smoke, and it became so dark that fowls went to roost and candles were lighted.

were procured and the Continental Congress and the young republic satisfied.

But something else beside money must be had. Men to fill up the army were absolutely necessary. We have seen what a number, considering the whole population, had gone voluntarily, but now, though the will was good, the country was weary and drafts must be made. The soldiers had got to come, and the citizens in their democratic capacity were ready to furnish them.

The selectmen also called a town meeting for this purpose. It was held July 10, 1780. They all felt very patriotic in Obadiah Clement's old bar-room. The good "old west endea rum" made them stomachful and brave, and they voted without a dissenting voice "*that the soldiers shall be raised by a rate for that present time.*" Also voted *Obadiah Clement, Joshua Copp to be a committee to provide soldiers for the town,* "AND TO EXEMP THOSE THAT HAVE DONE TURNS IN THE WAR, TILL OTHERS HAVE EQUILL TO THEM."

This was done in the selectmenship of Joshua Copp, Thomas Clark, and John Whitcher, and our committee assured by these high rulers that all their expenses should be promptly paid labored bravely to hire a soldier, for only one was wanted then from the town. They succeeded and Caleb Young* went as Warren's levy into the Continental army. He was but a youth who happened to tarry a few days at Obadiah Clement's inn, and a few pounds for a bounty and several mugs of flip, in which the hissing loggerhead had been thrust, made the young man exceeding brave and caused him to greatly desire " to hear drums and see a battle."

Next year the town had to furnish another man. March 7, 1781,† " Voted, that the selectmen be a committee to provide one soldier for three years, or during the war." This time the task was more difficult, but Col. Clement who was now the first " in the triune of mighty governors " yearly chosen, called selectmen, bent all his energies to the work and accomplished it.

CHARLES BOWLES, a young stalwart man, of dark complexion,

---
* Caleb Young enlisted July 11, 1780.
† The new voters in the year 1781, were—

Charles Bowles.	Amos Heath.	Henry Sunbury.
Jonathan Foster.	John Hinchson.	William Tarleton.
Joseph French.	Peter Stevens.	William Whiteman.

having some of the blood of Ham flowing in his veins, and his hair slightly "kinky," had just settled on the top of that fertile ridge over which wound the Height o' land road towards Tarleton lake. He had also made another opening in the woods in the north part of the town, near the line of old Coventry. He was a good man, religiously inclined, somewhat given to preaching, and when his patriotism was roused, as only Obadiah Clement knew how to rouse it in those days, was decidedly in favor of the war. In the time of the town's sorest need, he came to the rescue, pocketed a good fat bounty, as is the custom in all times when it is to be had, and as many another had done, shouldered his musket and went marching away to the wars.

When the contest was over, he came back, got married, settled down, labored hard week days, preached with unction on the Sabbath and raised up a large and respectable family of children. It was his boast through life that he fought his country's battles bravely.*

---

* CHARLES BOWLES was at the battle of Bennington, in Col. David Hobart's Regt. His Captain was Jeremiah Post. He enlisted July 24, 1777, and was discharged Sept. 25, 1777, having served two months and three days. He received in all 9 pounds and 9 shillings, and traveled to No. 4, 72 miles, and from thence to Bennington, 142.

Col. David Hobart was from Plymouth.—See Sec. State's Records.

CHARLES BOWLES' CERTIFICATE.

"in the year 1781 i, charles bowles, made a pitch of one hundred aker lot of land by order of the Committee of Coventry which lot was Savaid by Josiah Burnham by order of said Committee in the aforesaid eighty one i went to work and fall trees and made me a house on said lot—then i was called into the army in 1783 i went to work with some hands with me and cleared and soed one bushel and half of grain and in october 1780 i moved my family thare whare i have made my home ever since till i sold my enterest to Obadiah Clement and said Lot hath never been claimed by any other person till this day as I have ever heard
CHARLES BOWLES."

Charles Bowles was claimed by the town of Andover, N. H., as a part of their quota, May 8, 1782, but that town did not get him.—Sec. of State's Records.

FAMILY RECORD OF CHARLES AND MOLLY (*Corliss*) BOWLES.

He was born Oct. 20, 1760, at Hanover, Mass.
She was born Mch. 3, 1768, at Salem, N. H.
Married Apr. 14, 1784.
James, born Dec. 19, 1784, at Warren, N. H.
Molly, born Dec. 12, 1787 at Warren, N. H.
Charles, born Jan. 24, 1789, at Warren, N. H.
Elenor M., born May 18, 1792, at Warren, N. H.
Jesse, born Feb. 26, 1795, at Warren, N. H.
Euna, born May 17, 1797, at Warren, N. H.
Hannah, born Mch. 3, 1799, at Warren, N. H.
Jonathan, born Jan. 12, 1801, at Warren, N. H. Died Aug. 23, 1803.
Sarah, born May 20, 1803.

Charles Bowles afterwards became a Free-will Baptist minister, and is now one of the saints of that church. A volume of some 300 pages printed matter has been published, giving a history of his wonderful powers and eloquence as a minister. He was a mulatto.

ADDITIONAL SETTLERS.   287

In 1782 * the same thing happened to the town again, and HENRY SHAW,† a new comer who paid the great tax in town that very year, of three shillings and nine pence, also went to the war from our hamlet. He got a snug little bounty of sixty-nine pounds fifteen shillings, lawful money, for enlisting. What became of him we are not informed; but it is certain he never returned to Warren.

Now this was all on account of the organization—what the town was obliged to do according to law. But a hundred other things were done about these times, many of which are exceedingly interesting to us, who live in "this latter and degenerate age."

MOSES COPP,‡ son of 'Squire Joshua Copp, though a mere boy, had been in the army a great deal, and was noted for his daring and bravery. He was at West Point when Arnold sold himself to the British. DAVID MERRILL, a strong muscular man, who married 'Squire Joshua's daughter, but did not then live in town, assisted in rowing Arnold to the hostile man-of-war that received him. He was paid a large sum of gold for his services,— not very meritorious ones as most folks think at the present day.

The great Committee of Safety admired William Heath, our lank rawney hunter of fighting proclivities, and paid him £18 for depreciation.**

---

* The new settlers in 1782, were,—
Jonathan Harbord.   Gordon Hutchins.   Henry Shaw.
Barnabas Holmes.   Moses Noyes.   Nicholas Whiteman.

                                              WARREN, August 26, yr. 1782.
† "HENRY SHAW. Received of the selectmen of Warren Sixty Nine pound fifteen shillings Lawful money as a Bounty for inlisting to serve in the Continental army three year for the town of Warren from the time he pass muster I say received per me
                                                               his
test   JOSHUA MERRILL   HENRY ⋈ SHAW
       JOSHUA COPP   mark
                A true copy Exmd
                       Attest JOSHUA COPP,   ⎫ Selectmen
                              WILLIAM BUTLER,   ⎬   of
                              STEPHEN RICHARDSON,⎭ Warren."
Henry Shaw.   Warren, 1782, Aug. 28th.
1787 Recd an order on the Treasurer for twenty pounds.
                                                    JOSEPH PATCH.
                                           —See Sec. of State's Records.

‡ Moses Copp married a daughter of John Mills, and after the war, moved away to Canada. He had several sons. One settled in Iowa, (Burlington,) and at his death left a property of more than one hundred thousand dollars. Moses Copp was entitled to a pension, but never got it because he lived in Canada. He was accustomed to scold about it.
** See N. H. Hist. Coll. Vol. vii.

Right at home Mrs. Joseph Patch had another pleasant adventure in which she exhibited the pluck of her father, and the shrewdness of her sharp brother Jonathan. One day when her husband was away, an old soldier called at the house and walked in without ceremony. Mrs. P. and her children were at dinner, and the stranger helped himself. Then he became saucy and impudent, and when he was proceeding to offer her some personal indignity, saying he would burn the house if she resisted, she drew herself up firmly and said to her little boy, " Go to the barn and tell your father to come in instantly. I'll see if I am to be abused in my own house." The ruse worked admirably. The son started on his errand, and the old straggler, who had heard of Patch and did not care to meet him, rushed out of the house and disappeared in the thick woods in the shortest time possible.

But the saddest thing was the death of *Ephraim Lund*. He had served three years and then re-enlisted during the war. It was in a battle in the south, shortly before Cornwallis' surrender, that he met his death. He died bravely; a comrade placed the green turf above him, and dropped a tear on the new made grave. The spot where he is lying is unmarked and forgotten; and his little clearing where he lived, the green woods upon Mt. Mist, and on the shore of Tarleton lake, know him no more forever.

Many other men who came to Warren shortly after the contest closed, also served in the war. Of these, Joseph French and Samuel Knight, who were at the battle of Bunker Hill, are perhaps the best remembered.*

While the town was thus gallantly raising men for the army, other great events were transpiring in the wild but pleasant regions beyond the western mountains. When Burgoyne had marched down by Lake Champlain, the inhabitants on the long river of pines, the Connecticut, had been terribly frightened, and leaving homes, crops, and cattle, had hurried away into the eastern inte-

---

* Other revolutionary soldiers who lived in Warren, are Asa Low, Jacob Low, Luke Libbey, the latter served seven years and six months, was taken prisoner, carried to England and kept there fourteen months. John Abbott, he served seven years and was a drum-major, and Reuben Batchelder. Mr. Batchelder never got a pension. He would tell in his old age how he suffered in the war, and then cry about it. He was a prisoner, and came so near starving that he had to eat the very leather breeches which he wore. Henry Sunbury who lived on the Height-o'land, was a Hessian in the British army, and was taken prisoner at the surrender of Burgoyne.

rior, where buried in the fastnesses of the mountains, and in the deep woods, they felt that they were safe. But in the closing days of the war when many of the Green-mountain boys were away fighting bravely under Washington and Greene, frights came oftener to the dwellers of the New Hampshire Grants, as they were known in those days. To understand these terrors fully it will be necessary for us to write a few dignified pages.

New Hampshire, Massachusetts, and New York as we told in the history of the old proprietors, each laid claim to the Vermont territory. The people of that hilly country wanted to be admitted into the confederation, and the Continental Congress did not dare do it for fear of offending these other important States. The would be State of Vermont was slightly discontented at this; the British government knew it, and now when the prospect of failing in subjugating the rebels was every day becoming more apparent, it was thought to coax her away along with the "Canuck" country and the land of the "Blue-noses," and continue her a pleasant British province.

For this purpose agents with British gold in plenty in their pockets, travelled the whole country through. The few who were venal, they bought, but the most were faithful to the rebel cause. To capture the leaders of the latter class and to give the tories who were frequently rather roughly handled, revenge, marauding parties consisting of French, Indians, and loyalists, hurried to the Connecticut valley. Then there were the wildest kind of panics, and men, women, and children, ran away. Nearly all would go, and at times the Coos country would be nearly deserted.

The Committee of Safety made every effort to render assistance. A large number of soldiers were raised to defend the land of the Coosucks, and Captain Absalom Peters* who chose the neighbor-

---

* Captain Absalom Peters graduated at Dartmouth College in 1780. His health failed him and he settled on a farm in Wentworth, N. H. In Oct. 1780, a great alarm was occasioned by the destruction of Royalton, Vt., and from a report that 4,000 British troops had crossed Lake Champlain with the intention of proceeding to the Connecticut river. At this time Captain Peters marched at the head of six companies from the northern part of New Hampshire to Newbury, Vt., the place appointed for the rendezvous, and on his arrival was aid to Maj. Gen. Bailey which he sustained till the close of the war.—N. H. Hist. Coll. Vol. iii. 245.

Captain Peters lived in Warren in 1793, and had at that time living with him a "little nigger boy" named Prime. One very rainy day he told Prime to get the cows; but "young sooty" wouldn't, and unbeknown to Captain Peters, hid under the barn. About dark the Captain went after them himself and hallooed for Prime all over the pasture. He drove them up and hallooed "little nig" in the barn-yard, but got no answer. While milking, Captain P. happened to turn his head and saw

ing land of Wentworth for his home, went marching through our hamlet to the rescue, at the head of six companies. Hundreds of pounds of powder and balls, a thousand flints and more, tin kettles, borax, New England rum, files, and a screw-plate, were forwarded to "Cowass," to the care of Col. Charles Johnson and Maj. B. Whitcomb. They put all these munitions of war and men to good use, and did guard duty most valorously.

But they could not do every thing; they could not prevent a panic, and to provide for that, our township of Warren went to work bravely. The citizens enlarged their houses, increased the number of their beds, raised more provisions, cut more hay to put in their barns, and then last of all called a town meeting to provide for emergencies in case of "great alarums."

Without a dissenting voice they determined March 22, 1780, in order to receive their neighbors properly, who generally came pretty much out of breath, "*to lay up a stock of provisions to be delt out as it appears to be wanted.*" "*Voted to raise two hundred wait of flour and two hundred wait of beef for this present year, to be dealt out in case of alarum.*" "*Chose Joshua Copp and Obadiah Clement a Committee to provide the towns stock of provisions.*"*

Having thus handsomely provided for their friends, then, if the terrible foe should pursue across the highlands by Tarleton lake or up the wild roistering Oliverian, our mountaineers were also prepared to receive him in a manner which would not be quite so agreeable. They procured a good stock of lead, powder, and flints, scoured up their muskets, and bloodshed would have followed had the Britishers only ventured within the border. The Coos neighbors often came to Warren; but King George's troops and allies, never.

And now Warren had a different kind of warlike excitement.

Prime's white eyes and teeth looking out from under the barn. Peters was mad. He took Prime into the house, stood him on a case of drawers and told him to answer in the same tone he used. First, Peters whispered the word "Prime," and Prime answered back in a whisper. Then he raised his pitch until he shouted so that he could be heard half a mile, and "little sooty" strained himself so much trying to answer, that he looked white in the face and was well punished. The neighbors who heard were greatly amused, and it is said that Prime was a good boy and never hid under the barn again.

Captain Peters generally went barefoot. When elected to the legislature by the town of Wentworth, he wore shoes; but he said it made his feet so tender it took more than six months to toughen them.

* Town Clerk's Records, Vol. i. 7.

COLONEL GREELEY ARRESTED. 291

When the tide of battle was rolling through the south and Gen. Greene was winning glory, fighting with Cornwallis, John Balch, who still rode post, brought the news that our great Committee of Safety were trying Col. Jonathan Greeley, one of the old proprietors "for practices inimical to the United States." Our citizens were greatly roused by the intelligence, for Col. Greeley had been one of their best patrons. But when they learned that he had been found guilty and sentenced to give a bond for his behavior to Gen. Folsom, and was confined to his own house and a certain portion of the highway, eighty rods or so in length, limited by the flag-staff on the east and the old burying ground on the west, they were almost as much excited as when they heard of Gen. Stark's great victory at Bennington. But Col. Greeley did not long remain in confinement. He had good friends on the committee and they well remembered what a fine fellow he was as mine host in old East Kingston, and they soon let him off easy.*

But in nine days this affair was an old story, so fast did events hasten in these troublesome times. Something new came almost every day and when the fortune of war hung trembling in the balance and victory inclined first to one side and then the other, away up in this northern country, in the wild forests of the New Hampshire Grants, discontent was fomenting, treason to the young republic of New Hampshire was hatching, and a power in the west, almost like Satan in Heaven, was trying to draw off one-third of New Hampshire's beautiful towns, Warren among them, lying in the vicinity of Connecticut river. Who did it? It was the delightful-would-be-Green-mountain State; that could not get admitted to the Union, that was determined not to go with old England, and so was planning how a free and independent republic she might set up for herself.

All the territory and the greatest population possible was essential in the highest degree, and so, as has been softly insinuated, in imitation of the fond mother country, agents from west of the Connecticut crossed that bright stream and labored in all the bordering eastern towns. Their logic was powerful, and their tongues persuasive, and a score of young democracies were almost influenced to cast their lot with that of the young empire to the

---
* N. H. Hist. Coll. Vol. vii.

west. So much progress was made that a convention was called to meet at Charleston, N. H., and the townships agreed to send delegates.

Warren was wide awake. Still business must be performed in a manner that should comport with the solemnity and dignity of the occasion. A town meeting was called. It was held Jan. 3d, 1781, and was " *to see if the town will send one man to attend on the convention to be held at Charlestown on the third Tuesday of January, inst., at one o'clock afternune, according to an ennotification sent from the county of Chester.*"*

After a long discussion chose Obadiah Clement to attend the convention at " Charlestown, No. 4," and as it was very important whether they should belong to the great " Amphictyonic council," of the east or to that of the west, a committee consisting of the most dignified and influential men of the hamlet, was chosen to instruct the delegate elect how he should act. It consisted of Joshua Copp, William Butler, John Whitcher, Thomas Clark, and Isaiah Batchelder.

They performed their duty faithfully, and in mid winter Col. Clement mounted on his strong black stallion, rode away through the woods, over the mountains, down the Connecticut to " Charlestown, No. 4."

Col. Clement attended the Convention thoroughly. What transpired has never been fully written in any history. Like the transactions of the old Hartford Convention, or the mighty mystery of the Iron Mask, its acts will never be known.

Suffice it to say, our delegate heard all that was to be said, pondered upon it deeply, and then came home. He was not pleased, and plainly said so. To cross the mountainous Height-o'-land, to ford the Connecticut, to climb the Green mountains that they might reach the future capital of the would be empire, was not so easy as to ride down the banks of the delightful Asquamchumauke and Merrimack, to the bright lands from which they had emigrated, to the homes and pleasant associations of childhood, and the happy intercourse of those with whom they had done business for years, and with whom by far they had rather be united as members of a great Amphictyonic Council.

---

* Town Clerk's Records, Vol. i. 8.

THE FIRST REPRESENTATIVE. 293

So our grand little hamlet among the hills gave her western friends the go-by and determined to remain as she was. But Col. C. did not feel quite right in relation to the "Charlestown No. 4," Convention. He felt he was not aiding the cause in the least which of all others was most dear to him. So, to ease his conscience, he went to work, like a true lover of office, to get elected Representative to the Great and General Court of New Hampshire. Warren, Wentworth, and Coventry, were then classed together, and Dec. 11, 1782, the free and independent voters of these several towns being met at the house of our friend Joshua Merrill, familliarly called farmer Joshua, Obadiah Clement was chosen Representative. That night "he felt complete." He was the first man in Warren to enjoy this high and immortal honor.

The Great and General Court met at Exeter, N. H., in those days, and at the opening of the session, Col. C. was as usual promptly on hand to attend to his duty. And he did it faithfully. The war of the revolution, although rapidly drawing to a close, was not as yet finished; much remained to be done, and our patriotic Representative was not behind hand in voting men and money. He was for pushing on until independence was fully secured. His constituents sustained him in this, and afterwards gave him a triumphant re-election.

And now what a proud satisfaction our citizens possessed if they could only see it. They had done their duty, and were more than ever prepared to move on in the grand march of democracies, well knowing that the taxes were all raised promptly, the men for the army all furnished and more too, supplies of provisions, moose-hide breeches, ammunition, and West India rum, always forthcoming, and herself and representatives loyal to the core, and as true to the New Hampshire republic, her lover, as the needle to the pole.

Soldiers in the Revolution.—The following men served in the war of the Revolution, going from Warren at or about the date given:

William Heath, 1775; Reuben Clement, 1775; Joseph Whitcher, 1775; Ephraim Lund, 1775; Joshua Copp, 1775; Simeon Smith, 1775; Chase Whitcher, 1776; John Marston, 1776; (1) John Hinchson, 1776; Joseph Lund, 1776; Jonathan Fellows, 1777; John Mills, Jr., 1776, 1777, and 1781; Moses Copp, 1779; David Merrill, 1779; Caleb Young, 1780; Charles Bowles, 1781; Henry Shaw, 1782; William Tarleton, 1782. (2)

(1) John Marston was in Captain Joshua Hayward's Company in 1776. He settled in Warren before 1780. Alex. Craig was Lieut. of a Company.

(2) William Tarleton was Captain of the 8th Company of Col. Timothy Bedel's regiment, raised in 1778, and doing duty on the northern frontier.

CHAPTER III.

THE FIRST FUNERAL OF A WHITE MAN IN WARREN; OR HOW JOHN MILLS DIED AND WAS BURIED.

JOSHUA COPP, Jr. was the first white child born in Warren. John Marston was the first man married; but eleven years went by after the settlement, before old father Time on spectral wings, with hour-glass and scythe, lighted down in our Asquamchumauke valley, and claimed a victim.

It happened thus: John Mills, the first settler, who brought his family to Warren, was engaged " falling a piece" on the west side of the river by Indian Rock, near old Coos road. He was a very smart chopper, and his son, Captain John Mills, who was at home from the war on a furlough, was helping him. They had notched or partly cut more than two acres of trees, but had not brought one to the ground. Then they fell a great pine upon a clump of spruces; this broke them down, and they falling broke down their neighbors, and so, like boys setting up bricks the whole forest that had been notched was driven to the ground. This was called " driving a piece," and two smart men would fell several acres a day.

But unfortunately a large pine had not been sufficiently notched, and it stopped the drive. John Mills, Senior, ventured under to cut the pine; it fell before he could escape, a limb struck him on the head, and instantly he was dead.

The son bore his father home on his shoulders, laid him upon the bed and summoned the neighbors. They came and tried to console the grief-stricken family. But they almost refused to be comforted. There was sorrow and sadness, and wretchedness, and tears in that humble log cabin, and they felt that now the father was dead, the world was hardly worth living for, and that they too, might as well die. Captain John Mills, Jr., had seen a thousand men dead on battle-fields, but never had death come home to him so terribly before.

The third day was the funeral. How long and lonely and terrible were the hours of waiting. But the time came at last, and all the neighbors began to assemble. There was no minister in town, no church, no tolling bell; but 'Squire Joshua Copp read a chapter in the Bible, a hymn was sung, and then he offered a prayer.

The coffin was brought out and placed on a bier under the trees. Sunlight and shadow, fit emblems of the hour, flickered over the scene, not more breathless, hushed, and solemn, than were the voice, step, and heart of those sympathizing neighbors.

The rough coffin lid was turned back and they approached one by one to take a last look of the remains; then sunk away into the silently revolving circle. The mourners presently came out and indulged a tearful, momentary, final vision, and the lid was closed. Col. Obadiah Clement took the charge. The bier, carried on the shoulders of four men, was followed by the relatives, and then the friends — every family in town were friends then — came two and two abreast.

There was no graveyard in our hamlet, and they carried John Mills down the bridle-path, the road was on the other side of the Asquamchumauke then, to the cluster of hard pines on the river bank.* Here beneath the deep shade, the first grave of a white man in Warren had been dug, and here was the first burying ground of the settlers. There was no fence, no tomb stones, nor turfy mounds, no choir, no singing at the burial, but the wind sighing in the scattered pines, and the voice of the murmuring river seemed a requiem to the departed.

---

* The little woods where John Mills was buried was used for a graveyard for more than twenty years. Then Pine hill burying ground was laid out, and the place where John Mills and his kindred lie sleeping, fell into vandal hands. To-day, few persons know or dream that the unsightly spot on the river bank, where wild brakes and bushes are growing, and gravel is dug for the roads, is the last resting place of Warren's second settler. The graveyard was on the east bank of the river, about thirty rods below the old deep hole.

As they approached, the men took off their hats, the four biermen lowered the coffin by leathern straps, and then all looked in. 'Squire Copp, as the last obsequiel act, in the name of the bereaved family, thanked the people for their kindness and attention to the dead and the living, and the procession returned to the house.

Mrs. Stevens Merrill, Mrs. Joseph Patch, and other women, had cooked a plain dinner of pork and beans and Indian pudding for all. The mourners had a little spirit to take, but Stevens Merrill went to the well for pure water for the others to drink. They had no pumps then, and he found the long sweep piercing the skies; the bucket swinging to and fro in the wind. He reached up and caught it, and grasping the pole drew it down hand over hand until the iron bound vessel almost touched the limpid water. He paused; the mouth of the well was shaded and narrowed with green mosses and slender ferns, which bore on every leaf and point a drop of water from the waste of the bucket. Below the calm surface of the water appeared a reversed shaft, having its sides begemed with the moss-borne drops which with a singular effect of darkened brilliancy, shone like diamonds in a cave. Through a small green subterranean orifice he could look into the nethermost, luminous, boundless space, a mysterious, etherial abyss, an unknown realm of purity and peace below the earth, the mirror faintly revealing the bright heaven above, the place to which, as he believed, the pure spirit of John Mills had gone. Then he drew up a bucket full of clear water, spattering on all the rocks, and returned to the house where dinner was waiting.

The meal over, each friend tried to say a comforting word and then went mournfully home, fully realizing that there was no spot on earth where men could live forever, and that death swift and sudden, had stricken down one of their number in Warren. How solitary and dreary was that house of mourning when all the friends had gone away home from the funeral.

A week later and Captain John Mills' furlough was out, and he went away again to the wars. Captain William Butler had married a sister of the deceased man, and henceforth he was the head of the family.

CHAPTER IV.

ABOUT A GREAT ARMY IN WARREN; HOW IT MARCHED AND COUN-
TER-MARCHED; OF THE PRETTY NAMES IT WAS CALLED, AND
HOW IT WAS SUBSISTED.

IN these troublous times when all was dire consternation along the border, and the sounds of war came from every quarter, it was necessary to keep up a powerful military force throughout the country. Measures, therefore, were immediately taken to organize the whole people into companies, regiments, and divisions, and the citizens of Warren must become soldiers, of course.

The scenes and experiences of the old French war and the Revolution gave a martial turn of mind, and when the order came to form a military company in our mountain hamlet, they went at the work with alacrity.

February 8, 1780, Obadiah Clement was commissioned Captain of the 9th Company of the 12th Regiment of militia, at this time commanded by Col. Israel Morey. No sooner was the document placed in his hands than he immediately began with his usual energy to organize his company. He quickly procured commissions for Lieut. William Butler and Ensign Ephraim True, and then when the time arrived he warned the good inhabitants of Warren, who had much increased in numbers, to meet for May training, armed and equipped as the law directs.

The place where they were ordered to assemble was in the dry little field situated about half way between Farmer Joshua's and 'Squire Copp's; and on that third Tuesday of May, familiarly known as "Little Training Day," every man, woman, and child, almost, came together to execute and witness the mighty military evolutions that were to be performed.

It was one of the brightest of May mornings, a sunshiny breezy day, balmy in hollows and dells, and on southern uplands, but fresh blowing on the ridges and along the northern mountain slopes. There was music in the air, for the robins sang in the maples, and the blackbird and the wood thrush warbled the sweetest melody in the white flowering sugar plum and the wild cherry trees. Then the red squirrel chattered in the spruces, and the hairy woodpecker rat-tap-tapped on the hollow beech tree, or on Farmer Joshua's sap-buckets, not yet gathered; the partridges drummed on the hill-side, and the little chipmonk — the striped squirrel — sunning itself by its burrough, startled by the children, uttered the sharpest notes. Overhead the swallows, on twittering wings, skimmed along the blue sky, or diving down with arrowy rush, laved for an instant their wings in the cool water of Black brook — the Mikaseota — and flew away to their nests in the log barns of the settlers. There were flowers opening by the path, violets springing up by the hedges, dandelions growing on grassy banks, moosemissa, white and odorous, skunk cabbage, addertongues putting out in the shadows of the trees, making the air so fresh and sweet smelling, while the children, shouting and laughing, chased the first golden butterfly, hunted birds' nests and snail shells, and turning over stones and old logs, explored the haunts of thousands of ants, just thawed out into life. Then they found the blue-tailed skink, the salmon colored salamander and the crimson-spotted triton, along the high, warm banks of little runnels, and by the loud rill that comes down from Beech hill woods.

But hark! the drum-beat is heard in the little training field, and the shrill notes of the fife go piercing through the forest. Captain Obadiah Clement is giving the note of command in clear ringing voice, and every loiterer is hurrying to see the company drill.

It is a beautiful training field, full of charred stumps, and here and there a great black log heap not yet wholly burned up. But Captain Clement managed to find a clear space to draw up his whole company in single file, and then the work commenced in good earnest. The lieutenant and the ensign took their places, the sergeants and the corporals were properly posted, care being taken not to select too many, as it was necessary to have some privates as well as officers; for the whole company did not number more than forty men, though every man and boy old enough to do military duty was present, except those who were away in the army, and Stevens Merrill and Jonathan Clement, who declared "they would not train in such a string-bean, slam-bang, flood-wood, light infantry company as Col. Clement had; they would pay a fine first."*

Captain Clement told his grandson, Jim Clement, all about what beautiful uniforms they wore. Some had cocked hats, and some woodchuck and wolf skin caps, with the fur well worn off; one or two had nice straw braided hats which their wives and mothers had made them. And then there were all kinds of coats; some of which had been in the army; many had short frocks of every day wear, and some did not have anything over their rough tow shirts. Their breeches were almost invariably of one kind,— moosehide, home tanned,— a kind not easily worn out, untorn and no holes in the seat. Moccasins were worn on the feet, but some of the men, as it was a warm day, were barefoot; their tough soles being less liable to be hurt than the moccasins themselves. They had belts of every sort and kind, canteens of various patterns, priming wires and brushes, and well worn cartridge boxes that had seen service in the old French and Indian wars, and some in the Revolution now going on. Their guns were of almost every pattern, muskets, fowling pieces, one or two old match locks, queen's arms, and some were the very guns also that Chase Whitcher had procured from the Committee of Safety.

Captain Clement said he was better dressed than the rest. He had prepared himself for the occasion. His hair was not powdered, and he had no wig on his head. But a white cockade glistened on his three-cornered cocked hat, silver epaulettes rounded off his shoulders, his coat was faced with blue, a scarlet sash ornamented his waist, and his yellow buckskin breeches were

---

* A poor excuse was better than none. It was not safe for them at that time to say they would not train with rebel soldiers, and so they called the company all manner of names, and said it was so mean they would not be seen in it.

graced with silver lacings. He made a fine appearance, and as his said grandson, "Jim," well expressed it, "He felt complete."

"To the right face," was one of the first commands, and the men looked "every which way." "Eyes right," the Captain sung out, and they all looked at him. "Shoulder arms,"—the accoutrements rattled and jingled, and up went musket, rifle, fowling-piece, match lock, old queen's arm, and the three or four bayonets, gleaming "like rotten mackerel by moonlight," flashed in the bright spring sun. "Shoulder arms," he shouted again in a sharp tone, for some had hold of the breech, some by the small part of the stock and some by the lock; but every man looked blank, and did not shoulder arms. Then he showed each man how to do it, and soon they could carry arms and present arms, ground arms and arms aport, without the least difficulty.

"Music!" ordered the captain, and the drums beat again and the fife flourished wonderfully. "Mark time!" and their feet moved up and down in the most remarkable manner. "To the right face"—"To the left face"—"Forward,"—"File in platoons," "Into sections," "Into divisions!" And then they marched and countermarched in single file and double file, and four abreast in quick time, in slow time and in no time at all. Then they wheeled round the log heaps, and flanked the stumps, and circled round the edge of the clearing next to the woods, where stood the trunks of the old trees that had been killed by the fire. For four long hours they thus manœuvered, until all were convinced they understood the whole thing perfectly, and could go through every sort of tactics ever thought of since by Scott or Hardee.

Oh! how brave and valorous they all were! Captain Clement was lord of all he surveyed. The mighty rulers of the town, the selectmen, in their official capacity, had nothing to do with this training. Even Simeon Smith, the great constable from Red Oak hill could not interfere, and Judge Joshua Copp was a sergeant in the ranks. The men from Trecothick and the neighboring regions of Romney, Wentworth, and "Pearmount," said to be present as visitors, had nothing to do about it. Only the great Committee of Safety, and Col. Israel Morey, the superior officer, could command our brave and valiant captain in any manner whatever.

And now it was high noon and very warm; and the company

being tired, they were dismissed for dinner. This consisted of corn-cakes, boiled moose meat, nut-cakes and such other fixings in great store, which wives, sisters, and sweethearts, had brought. The huge repast finished with a relish, and washed down with a "little good west endea," they sat down to rest and became spectators themselves. The women gathered in knots and groups under the trees, chatted and gossipped as only women can, and the boys and girls, enjoying themselves, played "goal" and "tag," and "pizen," and "hide and seek," and "blind man's buff," and "'igh spy," and "wolf," and shouted, and yelled till the woods rang with echoes.

The music struck up again, the drum-call was beat, and each man sprang to arms. Once more all the evolutions were gone through with, and then they thought they would see how they liked the smell of powder. The guns were loaded, the command was heard, "Make ready, aim, fire!" and bang went the whole of them. Again they loaded, and again they fired, greatly to the joy of themselves and all the rest of the people assembled.

Captain Clement would tell the pleasant story how young Moses True, a new comer, and some relation to Ensign Ephraim, who lived "over the river," inspired by extra potations of good grog, was filled with exceeding valor and wanted to show what he could do. So the company halted and he loaded up his great musket with a mighty blank cartridge. Turning away his head, he fired most intrepidly into the air; but the blundering weapon recoiled and gave the valiant Moses an ignominious kick which laid him prostrate with uplifted heels on the lap of mother earth. The company seeing that he was not much hurt, applauded him with the most uproarious laughter, much to his great delight, of course. But the discharge made an immense noise; great echoes came back from all the wooded hills around, and even the green heads of Moosehillock and Mount Carr, and the other neighboring mountains, looked in with wonderment on the scene.

When the shadows were lengthening, and the old trees on the edge of the clearing began to seem distant, withered, and dark, with not a leaf to shake in the breeze, Captain C. halted his company again, and in a short speech invited them up to his house for refreshments. They accepted his invitation with a loud cheer, and "single file, forward, march," was a pleasing command. Captain Clement with drawn sword takes the lead; the music follows; the fifer first, the tenor drummer second, and the bass drummer next, all playing as loud as they can. Then Ensign Ephraim True marches by the colors, a red silk bandana handkerchief upon a pole improvised for the occasion, near the centre, while fat Lieut. William Butler brings up the rear; the children running before shouting as usual; the women and visitors following behind. Up the bridle path by Joshua Copp's, across Ore-hill brook, and up Black brook, in half an hour they are at Warren's little hotel, Captain C.'s inn.

The Captain's entertainment was plenty of pudding, pork and beans, with an abundance of the good creature to wash them down. Pails of toddy were passed about. Old and young men and the middle aged all drank that day, for it was the fashion, and even some of the boys tugging at the slops got fuddled and tight.

As they went in, their spirits got elevated, and they made bar-room speeches and sang patriotic songs, which were greeted with shouts of applause. Then their courage increased and their strength came and they "pitched quoits" and tossed great logs, and lifted at "stiff heels." Lieut. Butler was the strongest man, and he picked up every person who would lay down. A ring was formed and they wrestled "to backs," at "side holts," and at "arms length." Joseph Patch, our first settler, was the spryest, smartest man. They could not kick his shins nor tread on his toes, and he succeeded in laying every one who dared step into the ring squarely on his back; making both shoulders touch the ground at the same time. He was great at "the cross buttock play" as it was called.

When they had ate all they possibly could, and drank all the punch they could carry, Captain Clement formed them in line again, thanked them for their excellent behavior as soldiers, and then they broke ranks in the common form, which is well understood by military men.

At home safe, they were all much pleased, with their captain especially, also with the other officers, said they had had an excellent time, and wished "little training day" might come every month in the year.

So much were they rejoiced that at the very next town meeting, held July 10, 1780, they determined to put a merited compliment on record, which stands even to the present time, and is as follows:—

"*Voted*, That when the officers of the mility belonging to the town are called up on that thay bee paid equill from the town. In thare rank as soldiers highered by the town for that year."*

An excellent vote, exceedingly grammatical and well spelled.

---

* Town Clerk's Records, Vol. i. 7.

CHAPTER V.

THANKSGIVING DAY; OR HOW THERE WAS FEASTING, DANCING AND MERRYMAKING IN OUR HAMLET AMONG THE HILLS.

AND now the war is over, and the piping times of peace have come.* How glad all the people are! From the poorest man that trapped in the woods and fished in the streams, farmers, mechanics, merchants, ministers, doctors, lawyers, Committee of Safety, and even President Meshech Weare himself, all rejoiced exceedingly. Such an occasion must not be passed by without appropriate celebration, and President Weare appointed a thanksgiving day to be observed in all the little democracies of the State.

The proclamation† went forth; copies were sent to every town and the one that came to Warren was posted in Obadiah Clement's little bar-room, so that all could read it. Thanksgiving days had come before; but the occasion had never been so great as now, even since the first one, which took place June 13, 1632, and the good people of our mountain hamlet, like all the rest of the country, resolved to celebrate it with the utmost eclat. The Warren folks did not nor never have kept Christmas or Good Friday or Easter, and they had no "goodings nor candles, clog, carol, box or hobby horse," neither did they ornament their places of worship,

---

* The final definitive treaty of peace between the mother country and colonies was signed Sept. 3, 1783, at Paris.

† Thanksgiving day was on the 2d Thursday of December, 1783.—See Proc. in Sec. of State's office.

for they thought all such things to be "Heathenrie, Devilrie, Dronkensie and Pride." Yet they must have some sort of festival, when they could celebrate in the most festive manner; they must pay some fealty to the universal gala sentiment.

The morn of that day was waited with expectation, and the greatest eagerness. What mirth and hilarity should prevail! Col. Clement sent a rude ox team clear down country for supplies, and a stock of the good creature for the occasion. Capt. William Butler was determined to have a grand turkey shoot and a raffle, and the young men and maidens of the hamlet planned to have something else that should please them as well.

Every thing was just so through all the towns in the State and even the clerk of the weather, as the old tale runs, grew amiable and determined to introduce a novelty for the occasion; accordingly long before the dawn of the happy day, he marshaled the snow makers who live, it is said, somewhere in the neighborhood of Greenland, and set them about their business. From midnight till morning they were actively engaged in sifting a delicious whiteness upon the gray autumnal bosom of our mother earth. They whitened the trees and the fields; they covered the long shingled roofs; they sprinkled it like feathers upon the log walls of the cabins and against the four-by-six panes of glass, introduced just about this time into the settlement. In fact they worked like heroes all night to make everything look bright and beautiful as possible for the morning. Everybody felt when they woke up in happy surprise that,

> "The fairies all bright
> Came out that night,
> As of a season long ago:
> And their feet on the ground,
> Had a tinkling sound,
> As they scattered the milk-white snow."

The little boys and girls clapped their hands with delight, and marshaled out on the hill-side for a grand snow-ball and coasting frolic. In the woods the tracks of the wild game were beautifully distinct and the delighted sportsman hurried away in the early morning to get his share of the partridges, joyfully listening to the "deep-mouthed blood hounds' heavy bay, resounding" in the distance, and the echoes of the fowling pieces as they brought down the birds on the wing, to make partridge pies for dinner.

About nine o'clock in the forenoon, all the men and boys were hurrying away to William Butler's turkey shoot. It was out in the little field that John Mills and son cleared, by the bubbling sand-rimmed springs northeast from his house. The captain had a fine lot of turkeys reared with great care, to keep them from the foxes, and he set them up twenty-five rods away for shot guns, and forty rods for rifles. The hunters of that time were better marksmen than those of the present day. A sixpence a shot, payable in silver or its equivalent — a high price — was what each had to pay. If he had not asked it he would not have made much, for Chase Whitcher, Joseph Patch, and Obadiah Clement were there, and they seldom fired without bringing down a bird. They did not have to lie down and sight slowly over a rest, but brought their guns rapidly up to their eyes and fired.

Simeon Smith was there also, making dry remarks, and Reuben Clement, the weird man, now rather taciturn, was seated on the top of a great stump watching the scene. Before him was the crowd, a jargon of voices, and an occasional shout. There was the report of rifles, the running to and fro of men and boys, disputes about shots, wrangling and wrestling, the smell of gunpowder, and the blue smoke curling away among the trees. He saw the brooks which rippled and murmured as they ran from the springs through their white and shining snow-covered banks, and the river that tossed and heaved as it hurried on among its snow-capped boulders and sent a dull sullen roar to the neighboring hills. On his right, blue forest-covered Mount Carr shone white and glistening under the morning sun as a frosted cake, while in the north, above the huge trees of the almost interminable forest, old Moosehillock in snow rears his rugged forehead. Every one before him seemed to feel well, and many a man who could not shoot a turkey, carried one away which he had won at the raffle.

At home the wives and comely buxom daughters were making mighty preparations for the feast. The door-yards had been picked up and set in order, the house had been cleaned, the floors scrubbed white, the beautifully ceiled walls were of spotless purity, and the newly scoured pewter on the open dresser gleamed and flashed in the bright light of the great kitchen fire-place.

The turkeys and other barn-yard fowls were killed and pulled yesterday; the partridges brought in this morning are made ready. And then, what a mixing of puddings of the richest composition; what pies are made; pumpkin, custard, apple, and mince, minus the raisins, but plenty of sweetening, for they made maple sugar then as now in great abundance; the chicken and partridge pies, the best of all. What cakes of transcendent brilliance, and bread of the most exquisite fineness, from flour ground at William Butler's mill. The oven door opens and shuts, well stuffed turkeys, and pies, and cakes, and bread, go in, and odors most delicious and mouth-melting, inexpressible, fill the house. What glowing looks were there. What speculations, contrivances, and anticipations in those milk-and-honey flowing kitchens. They have found the richest cheese in the whole cheese-room by tasting, and the purest and sweetest butter is moulded in small cakes, and imprinted with patterns of the most elegant figure. In fine, what efforts are made that all should experience the wonders and delights of this our delicious little mountain Canaan.

It is told how on that day there was visiting and merry-making, that Joseph Patch went home to his father-in-law's. Mr. Stevens Merrill's and that Joshua Copp and Joshua Merrill, also went down there to eat thanksgiving supper. Then all the Clements assembled at Col. Obadiah's, all the Whitchers at John's on Pine hill; Simeon Smith and his friends were social on Red Oak hill, and the Clarks and the Lunds had a merry-making over at Charleston,* and down by Eastman ponds.

The good man and his wife went to these hilarious meetings of families, parents and children, grand-parents and grand-children, uncles and cousins, riding double on the good old horse that had done them so much service in the woods; often carrying the youngest children in their arms, while the elder children trudged along the rough bridle-paths on foot. What a welcome they got: what lively salutations. The horse went to the barn,—" Come in!" —off came hats, caps, bonnets, shawls, and great-coats,—" Sit

---

* *Charleston.*—Mr. Nathaniel Libbey, on reading the advance sheets of this work, said he knew why Charleston was so called, that it was named after Charles Bowles, who once lived in that delectable region. Bowles only stopped there a short time, and said he was frightened away by the immense bull-frogs which inhabited Tarleton lake; that every night he could hear them singing out, " Charles Bowles! Charles Bowles! We are a coming, we are a coming! Don't run, don't run!"—and that he would not stay there for the whole district. His friends laughed at him and called the place Charles' town—Charleston.

down!" — chatting and talking and asking after the health of this one and that one all the time.

The men go out for an hour while the table is being set; they go about the little clearings — the arable land, the mowing and pasture are shown, and the questions, how much they can raise; how many trees they shall fall next year; how the young apple and plum trees flourish; and whether or not the climate is too cold for them; what huntings they would have this winter; what fine steel traps and guns and smart powder they had got, and a host of others were all freely discussed.

In the house the hostess shows the women folks round — to the cheese and butter room; to the weave room where such nice cloth is made, and then they talk about fattening calves and rearing poultry; the growing of vegetables, of fruit, and flowers, and of the nice things they would get from down country, when their husbands went down to Portsmouth and Newburyport with the ox teams, carrying the butter, cheese, and wheat, the sheep's pelts, moose and deer skins, and all the rich peltries, the product of their husbands' hunting in the woods.

In an hour the settlers, (joking that they are afraid of their wives' tongues if they did not come back in season; that they did not want any dinner, not a bit; they were only afraid of getting a scolding,) make their appearance.

And now all are seated around the table. What a dinner! The great mealy potatoes are smoking hot, the fat turkey carved in the most admirable manner, the rich gravy steaming beside it, and the venison on Stevens Merrill's board, furnished by Joseph Patch, a most tempting dish. How excellent is the stuffing, what cool crystalline water to drink, and what good "old west endea," out of the stone bottles furnished by Col. Clement, so exhilerating to set them all aglow.

How much they eat; how fast the bounteous store disappears! One would think no respect could be paid to the chicken and partridge pie, the plum pluddings, sweet cakes, pies of all kinds, most delicious sauces, maple honey, butter and cheese, the nicest and richest. But he would be greatly mistaken. They share the same fate as the first course, disappearing amid the most hearty laughter, sharp jokes, and "mother wit of the keenest kind."

Supper over, the hours fly swift, passed with pleasantries and glowing conversation. By sunset they are all safe at home again. Every body in the township has enjoyed this thanksgiving; all have feasted to their heart's content; there is not a poverty stricken cabin in the hamlet.

In the evening the young boys and girls of neighboring families get together and pass a pleasant hour, playing "blind man's buff," "run round the chimney," and "button, button, who has got the button?"

But the older youths and blushing maidens, and the young men and their wives, as we said before, had determined to spend the evening in another way. It was dark when they began to assemble in Obadiah Clement's great kitchen and little bar-room, the only inn in the hamlet. The windows were all bright-lighted, as they came out of the woods in the little clearing. Entering they found a great fire burning in the cavernous fire-place. A huge green back-log, five feet long, a great forestick of half the size, and a "high cob-work of refuse and knotty wood," blazed and roared, and crackled, sending up a bright and golden flame,— the black smoke hurrying away out doors all the time through the great flue of the immense stone chimney. They sit down to warm themselves. The wood sings, the sap drops on the hot stones hissing and crackling and great red coals roll out on the hearth, glimmering, sparkling, glistening.

Moses Copp and his handsome sister, Sarah, with several other brothers and sisters, came first; and Joseph Merrill and some of his sisters, Captain Butler and wife, and pretty Anna Mills who lived with them, Joseph Patch and wife, two sons of Simeon Smith, and others from that neighborhood; some of Ephraim True's grown up children, who used to be as wild as partridges, Chase Whitcher and his wife, from the Summit, and numerous others came, for unity and harmony once more prevailed now the war was over.

Reuben Clement, who could not keep away from the turkey shoot, must also attend the ball; but all the evening stubbornly refused to dance, for he was an odd genius, as we have gently intimated before.

The hall was the long unfinished kitchen, having its naked

timbers overhead ornamented with boughs of spruce and hemlock and festoons and wreaths of evergreen. Tallow candles in wooden blocks were placed in the distant corners, that every part might be well illuminated.

How pretty they were all dressed! What a variety there was too. There were styles that had come into being in the backwoods, and old styles, and new styles, and no styles at all. There were flashy prints, bought down country, good blue woolen dresses, and tow and linen skirts of beautiful colors, and striped and checked linen waists. All had necklaces of gold, glass, or waxen beads. Their head-dresses were simple and plain, oftenest their hair neatly arranged without ornament. Their shoes were of the best pattern, sometimes striped with a white welt.

The belles of the evening were Anna Mills and Sarah Copp. The latter wore a bright blue woolen dress, a little short with a red border at the bottom, a white linen apron, with flowers elaborately wrought with her own needle on the lower corners, pure white woolen stockings, a pair of neatly fitting moccasins, tight laced about the small, well turned, delicate ankles; her plump arms bare, a golden clasped bracelet on one of them; on her neck, a string of gold beads; her dark and shining hair close braided and only ornamented with a sprig of evergreen twined in one of the heavy plaits. Her complexion was clear, bright blue eyes that sparkled, white regular teeth, lips of cherry red, and plump rosy cheeks. Anna Mills was also plainly but neatly dressed. She was light and agile in form, as the wild doe; had flashing black eyes, and a wealth of raven tresses. Both were much sought after, and they never lacked a partner for the dance.

The young gentlemen of the settlement were also dressed in the most remarkable manner for a ball. Moses Copp had on a portion of his old Continental uniform. Col. Clement, mine host, wore his military coat, and Jonathan Clement kept on his hat, an immense one, through the whole occasion.* Then the short frocks

---

* *Wearing a Hat.*—Jonathan Clement almost literally *always* wore his hat. He kept it on at meal times, at town meetings, in religious meetings, and in presence of every one he met, high or low. It was the first article of clothing he put on in the morning, and the last he took off at night. N. Libbey went to Mr. C.'s tavern at midnight for a pint of rum, rapped at the door, and when said landlord came, the only article of dress he had put on was his hat. But the sheriff knocked it off for him in high Court one day, to his infinite disgust, and Mr. C. had a fearful hatred of courts ever after.—Nathaniel Libbey's statement.

were present, tucked out of the way inside of the moosehide and buckskin breeches. There were long stockings and many a pair of silver shoe and knee buckles, and the tough moosehide moccasins were the easiest things in the world to dance in. Their hair was not powdered, they had no wigs; our settlers did not take to such things; but Col. Clement, as did some other elderly men at the time, wore a queue, handsomely tied with an eel skin.

But they were a happy company if they were rather oddly dressed. There were smiles and jokes, and bright sayings, and when Moses True, the youth who made such a heroic noise on "little training day," took his seat upon a high bench in the back entry-way, at the farther end of the kitchen, violin in hand, the whole party leaped up at the wagging of his fiddle-stick, and took their places on the floor. Then soft music arose in Obadiah Clement's old kitchen, and happy hearts and nimble feet kept time to the merry strain.

By-and-by they had a slight refreshment, and the "milk toddy" and "egg-nog," mild drinks, were passed round and disappeared in vast quantities. On this their spirits rose. The young men shuffled and kicked most vigorously, and now and then gave a hearty smack, in all honesty of soul, to their buxom partners. Then they used the step called "shuffle and turn" and "double trouble," and cut many a lively fantasy as the short hours wore rapidly away.

Late in the night some of the dancers got tired and two young gentlemen, Jonathan Harbord and Nicholas Whiteman, who had recently come to town, laid down by the bar-room fire to rest themselves. Reuben Clement, who had watched them all the evening, said in a quiet way that he "knew they must be fatigued, exceedingly weary, they could not be tight, nothing of the kind. for they had not drank more than a quart of good rum, each."

The cock crowed in the barn; the shrill cry was answered from the nearest farm-yard, down at Jonathan Clement's, and then the dancing ceased, for Moses True, the good fiddler, was more tired than all the rest.

Some who resided farthest away, resolved to stay all night and go home by daylight. But those who lived down the valley towards Red Oak hill, were off in the shortest time possible.

Some rode on horseback, but the most walked; and Joseph Merrill waited upon Sarah Copp, and Moses Copp went home with Anna Mills. Now and then they were startled by the cries of the wild denizens of this new country. An owl hooted from a great hemlock by the path, there was a wild-cat crying over by Black brook, the Mikaseota, and a wolf howled in Beech hill woods. Yet it was only Nature's music to the settlers. They did not fear; they loved the beautiful night, for the crescent moon was not yet set behind Sentinel mountain in the west; the dark vault above them was powdered with stars, and they saw Aldebaran, Lyra, Orion, and the Pleiades, holding their silent course through the heavens.

There was not much labor performed in the settlement next day, for nobody got up very early that morning. Yet every one was content, and always maintained that this was the happiest Thanksgiving ever known in Warren.

CHAPTER VI.

THE FIRST SCHOOLS OF WARREN; OR HOW THE YOUNG IDEA WAS TAUGHT TO SHOOT; AND OF A CERTAIN OIL MUCH USED IN YE ANCIENT DAYS.

VENERABLE and much to be respected are ye worthy men of ancient times, who had the public good, the prosperity of the State at heart. Benning Wentworth and the honorable proprietors of our mountain hamlet, next to the cause of religion, as we have before mentioned, believed in public education. So in addition to the other reservations in the charter for great and good purposes, the excellent governor provided that one share in the township of Warren should be reserved " for the benefit of a school in said town forever."

The proprietors, as before, seconded the governor's good intention, and in the drawing of the lots, No. 3 in the 9th Range, 1st Division, and No. 15, in the 7th Range, 2d Division, were devoted to the cause of education.*

Yet it was many years before any revenue could be derived from the lands thus appropriated, and the children of the hamlet would have grown up in the most lamentable ignorance if they had waited for an education till the lots got productive.

Our sturdy settlers, before whose strokes the forest bowed, could all read and write, as is well attested by the old documents that have come down to us, and they could not bear the thoughts that their darling offspring should be deprived of a good education.

---

* Other lands were set apart for school purposes, for account of which see Appendix.

Yet they went at the work in rather of a negligent and dilatory manner; now and then supporting a private school in some settler's cabin, and then letting whole years go by without any school at all. But now the town being so well organized, they began to agitate the subject of opening a *public* school. But it was only agitation at first, and then an attempt which was a failure. At the annual assembly of the citizens, otherwise called the town meeting, for 1781, held March 22, it was " put to vote to see if the town would raise money to *higher* schooling, and it passed to the contrary."* The same thing happened at the town meeting held March 6, 1782. The inhabitants felt as though the burdens of taxation were heavy, and they could not afford to raise money in addition to what they had to pay to build roads, to furnish soldiers, to raise town supplies, and pay the State and Continental taxes. Some said — and there are always a few of that sort in every enterprise — " O, why can't we have private schools? We have always got along well enough so far with those."

But next year, when they could see the war drawing to a close and peace beginning to dawn, they voted almost unanimously to raise six pounds sterling " to higher schooling this year." At a subsequent meeting held May 5, 1783, " voted to lay out this money that is raised this present year, in hiring a *woman school*;" also " voted to begin said school the twentyeth of May enstant." And finally, " voted to keep said school at Stevens Merrill's for this present year."

In those times the selectmen were charged with the duty of hiring a schoolmarm and providing her a suitable boarding place. They immediately commenced their labor. First they looked over the hamlet, but found no one qualified whom they could engage. They then journeyed in the neighboring lands — to Wentworth — where they met with no better success, and thence on horseback to the region called Oxford, now Orford. There they hired Miss Abigail Arling, and she promised to be on hand at the appointed time, May 20. Returning home, they fitted up the school room in the most substantial manner. It was in one end of Mr. Merrill's barn, — a rough school house but good enough for the hot summer.

---

* Town Clerk's Records, Vol. i.

A rude table and chair for the schoolmarm was set on one side by an open place where a window should be. There were no desks for the scholars, and the seats were planks placed upon rough logs. First day of school in the country—who does not recollect it? The scholars are up bright and early in the morning, faces washed, hair combed, dinners and books packed up ready to be off the moment they can get permission, so as to get the first choice of seats. It is so now; it was so then; and from the Height o'land, Pine hill, Runaway pond, and the Summit, the children that morning trudged merrily along the bridle paths and tote road. They did not think so much of traveling a short distance then, as now, and they could walk by the paths easier than the settlers in the land of Trecothick, now Ellsworth, could come up by Glen ponds and over Mount Carr, as they often did, visiting. What if a moose was killed that very summer near the mouth of the Mikaseota, and Joshua Merrill shot a wolf by Cold brook, that came howling along down from Blue ridge, and they themselves tracked bears in the muddy path; they did not mind it much, for they were used to such things. They were born in the woods; the hills and the valleys, the wild flowers of summer, the mottled fawns and young rabbits that lived among the evergreens, and the swift waters of the glens were their live-long-day companions, and they went happily home to their bean-porridge supper and a bed as simple as their garments. The young Copps, the Clarks, and the Lunds, the Whitchers, Trues, Patches, Clements, and Merrills, made a numerous school, and they liked the schoolmarm, for she was gentle and good and did not anoint their backs much with the oil of birch, to sharpen their wits.

They did not have many visitors nor any superintending or prudential committee; but one day when the golden rays of the sun streamed through the great cracks of the barn, reflecting the myriad of particles ever floating like things of life in the air, and the swallows were twittering in their nests on the ribs of the roof, Stevens Merrill, who had been swingling flax in a shed near by, followed by his dog, looked in. An involuntary murmur of surprise and gladness went round the school-room, for the children could see through the netted tow and whitcish down that covered his hat, clothes, and face, like a thin veil, a happy smile of approval, which they did not always get from him. Their studies were as simple as their school-room. It did not require "much book larning" to teach school in those days. The *Psalter* and *Primer* were the only books used, and "readin', ritin', and 'rithmetic," the latter learned by rote, were the only accomplishments required.

Abigail Arling received three pounds for teaching that school twelve weeks. William Butler was paid two pounds fourteen shillings for boarding the schoolmarm, and Stevens Merrill got six shillings rent for his school-room.*

Once begun our settlers did not falter in the work. The next year they formed themselves into a union district, voted to build them a school-house in which to teach the young idea how to shoot, chose a building committee who called upon each man for labor and lumber as fast as wanted, and in less than six months the house was finished and furnished.

It was a framed building with rough benches and desks for the scholars. A huge stone fire-place occupied one end, and the walls were sealed with white pine boards, instead of being plastered. It was located by the tote road, a little above the present railroad crossing, north of the depot, and was right in the heart of the wilderness.†

Nathaniel Knight taught the first school in it; and to him three families sent twenty-five scholars. He was an excellent teacher, a splendid penman, and the most authentic tradition has it that he applied the birch in the most magnificent manner, as was common in old times. Yet he had a pleasant winning way with him, and the scholars liked his school and its surroundings.

He commenced in the autumn; but before the term closed the snow came, and then the boys took their sleds of broad runnered, frame work pattern, along with them, often giving their

---

* Aug. 28, 1783. Paid to Abigail Arling, three pounds for twelve weeks' schooling 3 0 0
Paid to William Butler, two pounds fourteen shillings time for boarding school mistress 2 14 0

JOSHUA MERRILL, } Selectmen.
WILLIAM BUTLER, }

David Craig once got three shillings room rent for a school.—Selectmen's Records, Vol. i.

† The windows were of mica or isinglass, which was obtained, as tradition has it, on Beech hill. Good isinglass or mica is now worth $12,000 per ton.

little sisters a ride, and at noon-time, just as the boys go to Beech hill now, they went out on the hill-sides,—the sharp pitch down to the *moat*,* or to the long declivity down to the bank of Black brook, for a coasting frolic.

When the crust was hard and sparkled in the winter's sun, then boys and girls together enjoyed the exciting sport. Up hill nimbly climbing; down hill flying swift as an arrow, scranching and goring the frozen snow. The wind whistles by their ears, their hair streams far back as they come down on their light-winged sleds, and the fine grail craunched and scored by the runners, glances up in their faces and furzes their clothes and hair. They leap the hollows and mount the swelling ridges, gliding on swifter, faster, surer, than the snug trimmed yacht before a spanking breeze flies through the troughs and over the crests at sea.

Nathaniel Knight also taught the following summer, and the children loved besides the school the pleasant woods full of sweet sounds, and dancing brooks, and cold crystalline springs, all about.

It is very interesting for young persons to know — elderly people need not read this — that in these ancient times, just the same as now, the scholars often went up at the nooning to the foot of Mt. Helen, sometimes called Keyes ledge. Here they traveled beside Cold brook, which made music with the mossy rocks in its bed; and they crossed by the tree bridge, from under which a pewee flew, chirping as it left its nest. They saw flies and spiders and long legged creepers dancing and jumping on the surface as though their feet were cold in the chill water, and down near the bright sandy bottom were half a dozen shy, speckled trout, their bright eyes glancing as they lay almost motionless in the current. Tall birches grew on the banks, and poplars and maples, and here and there great pines shot out, like tall sentinels, a hundred feet above them.

The scholars came up here to get the young checkerberry, its red plums and flowers. It was a cool nice place for a summer noon, full of birds. A wood thrush sang sweetest by the edge of

---

* The moat is a cold spring situated down the bank, and a little south and east from the town house. James Dow named it the moat, and for many years got his water to drink there. Owing to recent freshets which have changed the river's course the spring is now in the river bed.

the clearing; clinging to the breezy top of a white birch, a robin chanted its sweetest madrigal; a little yellow poll, perched on a rustling beech tree, whistled, and chattered, and chanked, as though it would burst its throat; a blue jay in a cluster of sapling pines screamed sharp and shrill, then itself flew away up the steep hill-side, as an old owl, disturbed in the shadows, hallooed and whooped in affright.

They got great handsfull of checkerberry, tied up with a little root of the gold-thread, a pocket full of red berries and bunch plums that grew under the pines. They also found partridge berries on evergreen vines, and unripe blueberries. Then they made a nice bouquet for the teacher, gathering the beautiful purple cranesbill from where the fire had newly burned in the woods, bright purple twin flowers and star of Bethlehem from a cool grassy recess in the forest, and from Joseph Merrill's new field red clover, yellow buttercups, white daisies, and deep blue violets. Then they wove in blue-eyed grass, mosses that grew together family like, star grass and brown sorrel.

One day, as the story goes,—and it is an important bit of history that should not be forgotten,—the larger boys and girls started for the summit of Mt. Helen. They wound slowly along among the stately three-leaved ferns that overhung the flowers like elm trees, through blueberry bushes and beds of yellow brakes, a music box where numberless crickets and grasshoppers keep up a perpetual lulling murmur, following sort of a path trod by hedgehogs, wild deer, and bears, till they came to the open ledge upon the summit. Around them were scattered red oaks, a few hemlocks, great pines, and among the rocks, blueberries, thistles, and bind weed were growing.

The woods shut out the view of the mountains to the northward; but east and west the sky seems resting on the lofty crests, and adown the valley where Black brook, the Mikaseota, flashes in the sunlight, and Baker river winds like a silver line through the forest, far in the south is seen the round, bald top of old Mt. Cardigan. The clouds floated away in the mellow sky above it; and it is here through the rifts the sun first shines, and the first bit of blue sky appears after a storm.

Farmer Joshua had a pasture then, cleared at the foot of the steep precipice on the right, and from it came the music of the well remembered cow-bell, mingling with the lowing of cattle, and the bleating of sheep. Then there was the cawing of crows in a clump of hemlocks, where they had their nests, the whimpering of hawks overhead, and their sharp shrill scream at intervals; by them swarms of flies wheeling in circular squadrons buzzed a lullaby; the tree-toads and hylodes chimed in with trilling chirup; the locusts made melody in the branches, and the flying grasshoppers with trapsing, quivering wings, gave out a pleasant note like mowers sharpening their scythes in haying time. A robin by tiny Cold brook, sent up to them "his long, sweet, many-toned carol." From the warm swamp near by, came the clubbing, grumming, croaking, crooling, trilling melody of the frogs, and through the woods, just audible from the farthest distance, the voice of Asquamchumauke's waters. And then all the time odors sweet smelling, and perfumes magnificent, from the blooming swamps, the flowering trees, the brakes and the ferns, the millions of wild flowers and grasses in the pastures and fields came floating up on the gentle breeze to regale and delight the senses. Amidst all these charms of nature, perhaps unnoticed but felt, the scholars made a sort of pic-nic, eating their dinner under the shade of the wide-spreading beech trees, and quenching their thirst from a pail of pure sparkling water brought up from Cold brook.

One of the numerous other visits which has been made to the ledge since that olden time, deserves especial mention in this history, for it then got a new name which seems most likely to cling to it. The scholars begged an afternoon as a holiday, and then all marching two and two, wound their way to the summit. Here they gathered flowers in the woods, sang songs, told stories, and played plays. On the large flat rock the older boys and girls formed for one of the simple country dances, and to the merry music of their voices kept time with nimble feet. When they were tired of this, as some tell the story, they feasted on the abundant collation which they had brought. Then a rude stone altar was erected; the fragments gathered up and placed upon it, a rustic throne built, and on it was seated the most beautiful girl of the party, named Helen, crowned as queen, with a garland of evergreen and wild roses. All the youths and maidens joined hands in a circle around her; the master of the ceremonies lighted the fire, the flames leaped up devouring the offering, a libation of pure Cold brook water was poured and then all dancing around in the circle sang:—

> " The hill shall be called Mt. Helen,
> The hill shall be called Mt. Helen,
> The hill shall be called Mt. Helen,
> Henceforth and forever more,"

until the offering was consumed, the fire went out and the blue smoke from the white down-like embers and ashes no longer curled away in the summer breeze.

Long years passed before a new school-house was built to take the place of this first one, and then another was erected only because number one was too small. James Dow moved Warren's oldest school-house away to Pine hill, where it did good service for a whole generation.

From this first union district, the germ sometimes called the *" Centre District,"* sometimes the *" Village school on the Green,"* have sprung first *Runaway pond district,** otherwise known as the *Weeks district,* in the school house of which for many years the town meetings were held; and then in their order came the now defunct *Charleston district,†* *Beech hill district, Pine hill district,* the *Summit, Height o' land, East-parte, The Forks,* sometimes called *Clough district* in *" Patchbreuckland," Streamy valley* or *Sawtelle district,* and *Mooschillock district* on the south-western mountain spur.‡

---

* " Uper scholl house," first mentioned in 1792, in Town Clerk's Records Vol. i.

† Nathaniel Merrill taught school in Charleston in 1795, at old Mr. Lund's. Nathaniel Merrill was the son of Rev. Nathaniel Merrill, and settled on Beech hill.—Selectmen's Records, Vol. i.

‡ *School Districts.*—" *Voted*, March 26, 1793, to have two districts. Voted at same meeting to begin the public school the first of Aug. next."

June 2, 1794.—" Voted that all to the east and south of Mr. Batchelder's 'Squire Copp's and Col. Clement's shall belong to the loer school house, & the rest to the uper one, as far as it did extend last year."

" Voted to begin the public school the first of September, at the upper school house, & the first of August at the Loer school-house in said town."

School districts were as follows in 1806:—" *Voted*, The first district begin at Wentworth line, thence north as far as outlet of Runaway pond, thence on Pine hill road as far as Mr. Batchelder's, and on East-parte road far enough to include Mr. Knight, Mr. Ramsey, and Timothy Clifford. The second district to take all on Beech hill. The third to take all upon the main road to Piermont line, including Mr. Batchelder. The fourth district to take all Charleston. The fifth district to take from Mr. Batchelder's on Pine hill to Coventry line. The sixth district to take all the inhabitants on East-parte road east of Mr. Ramsey's. The inhabitants of this town are divided and defined accordingly."

1812.—Paid James Williams for building a school house in the East-parte, $94,00.

EARLY SCHOOLMASTERS.

In these primitive school-houses, Nathaniel Knight, before named, Nathaniel Merrill, David Badger, a wandering pedagogue, Josiah Burnham,* (sad was his fate for he was hung at Haverhill jail,) and master Abbott, not yet quite forgotten, all knights of quill pens and the birch and ferule, to make the young idea shoot quick, taught with marked success. Then came Lemuel and Joseph, Benjamin and Moses, Nathaniel 2d and Robert E. Merrill, Jesse and Jonathan Little, and David Smith, keen witted, shrewd, and long headed, and each did honor to the profession.†

From these schools,— *and may they continue forever* — have gone out some who were brilliant, and some who were dull, of course; yet none but who could read, write, and cipher, and all sharp and keen enough to compete with the best and smartest of this whole shrewd, swapping, peddling, jockeying, guessing yankee race.

---

* Josiah Burnham took his pay for teaching in produce. He taught in 1795. This unfortunate gentleman was not born in Warren.

† *Schoolmasters.*

Thomas Whipple.	Ezekiel Dow.	John French.
Robert Burns.	Stevens M. Dow.	Calvin Sweat.
Luke Aiken.	Job E. Merrill.	Michael P. Merrill.
George W. Copp.	Isaac Merrill.	Russell K. Clement.
Master Newell.	Russell F. Clifford.	James M. Williams.
Anson Merrill.	William Merrill.	Horatio Heath.
Levi B. Foot.	Moses Davis.	Ira Merrill.
Jacob Patch.	Joseph Fellows.	Ira M. Weeks.
Wm. B. Patch.	Reuben B. French.	Albe C. Weeks.
Stephen Batchelder.	David C. French.	William Merrill.
John L. Merrill.		

U

CHAPTER VII.

HOW SARAH WHITCHER WAS LOST IN THE WOODS; WHAT HAP-
PENED AND HOW THEY HUNTED FOR HER, TOGETHER WITH A
REMARKABLE DREAM, AND HOW A BUSHEL OF BEANS SUD-
DENLY DISAPPEARED.

IT was the most beautiful Sabbath of June, 1783. Quiet pervaded the haunts of men. The clatter of the mills had ceased, no rude cart rumbled along the stony path, the voice of the ploughman was not heard, and the woodman's axe was hushed and still. A mellow softness pervaded the air, the woods, and the waters, and a thin haze of the most delicious and tender blue, rested upon the mountains. All nature seemed in worship. The leaves murmured melody in the light breeze, the brooks sent up the gentlest music from the mosses of their stony beds, the clouds like silent nuns in white veils worshipped in the sunbeams, and the birds sang psalms.

And yet there was no religious meeting in our mountain hamlet. The settlers with their families sat down in their homes or reclined in the shade of the trees about their dwellings, reading their bibles or engaged in silent meditation.

On Pine hill, Mr. John Whitcher dreamed the morning hours away, and then suggested to his wife that they pay a visit to Chase Whitcher, their relative, who lived by the wild roistering Oliverian at the Summit. The idea was agreeable to Mrs. W., and in a few minutes they were ready for the pleasant walk along the bridle-path through the woods.

Their little girl, Sarah, not yet four years old, lispingly asked her mother if she could go, but was told she must stop at home with the other children, and they would bring her something nice on their return.

And then they walked rapidly away across the ridge, and down toward babbling Berry brook, admiring not a bit the dewy wild flowers in the path, and hardly noticing their delicious perfumes as they crushed them beneath their feet. In an hour they were at Chase Whitcher's by the Oliverian.

The day was spent most agreeably. The new fields of full blown clover and honeysuckle, and on the borders of which the bright purple cranesbill was just blooming, were alive with the music of the vireo, blackbirds, and the wood-thrush, and the mild fairy-like hum of the myriads of wild bees sipping their nectar from the delicious flowers. Among the grasses they found the sweetest wild strawberries, and they passed the hours talking of the wonders of the deep forests where they would go hunting in autumn, speculating how high was the mighty precipice of Owl's head, and what an abundance of blueberries were growing on its summit.

It was only when the sun was sinking behind Webster-slide mountain in the west, that they said good by, asked Chase Whitcher and wife to come and see them and then hurried for home.

It had hazed up in the afternoon, and as they climbed the gentle slope of Pine hill night overtook them, and the few stars that shone out struggled through the rifts of the rainy clouds and the moon was scarce seen at all. But the bright light that streamed from their cabin window was cheerful and made their home doubly inviting.

"What made you leave Sarah up at the Summit?" said one of the older children almost as soon as they entered.

"We did not leave her," instantly replied the father, astonished.

"She is certainly not at home. Where can she be?" each one exclaimed, and then the dread reality burst upon them in a moment. Lost! lost! Sarah is lost in the woods!

Mr. Nathaniel Richardson tells that the ruddy face of Mr. Whitcher turned pale, but he said, "Trust in the Lord;" that Mrs.

Whitcher's countenance lighted up with afright, and the other children gathered closer to them, not knowing what to do. Reuben Whitcher who was present, seized the dinner-horn and started instantly for the woods. Mrs. Whitcher followed him, then came back and with the older children went to Mr. Stephen Richardson's to spread the alarm. The father seemed as if smitten down, then agitated paced to and fro in front of the house, then hurried away in the woods alone. The nearest neighbors came, shouting and hallooing in the forest; then built great fires that gleamed through the trees. Thus passed the night.

When her parents were gone little Sarah followed after them, then missed the path and wandered away in the woods.

As she —"Mrs. Dick French"—told the story in after years, it was a new world for her; the giant forest extended itself interminably, and the huge old trees looked as if they grew up to the skies. Among their roots was the young wood sorrel, its beautiful white flowers with brown spots about the stamens; then she gathered handsful of wild peony with deep red flowers, with leaves that curled over the purple and yellow flowers of the adder tongues, like Corinthian capitals. In the branches above were strange birds that she had never seen before. The Canada jay, called sometimes carion bird, because it robs the hunter's traps almost before his back is turned, with slate colored back and white breast, sent its strange wild note deep in the forest. Large owls in hooded velvety sweep, flew by her. Squirrels chattered and scolded one another, and their companions the partridges clucked before her, or flew away with heavy, rumbling flight. Once an eagle screamed above her; and she started back affrighted as a wild cat sprang past.

All day long she wandered on; her little hands full of flowers, her mind filled with a strange indefiniteness, hoping continually to find her father and mother. But she did not meet them, and no cart tracks, no cow paths, no spots or blazes on the trees were to be seen.

Despairing, at last exhausted, her feet scratched and bleeding by the underbrush, she sank down on the thick moss by the great rock that stands by the old beaver meadow, at the foot of the Cascades on Berry brook. "It is night now. Darkness has come down on the woods. She is alone. The wind is heard on the mountain. The torrent pours down the rocks. No hut receives her from the rain, alone in the thick woods of the valley. Rise moon from behind thy clouds. Stars of the night arise. Give light to her, sitting alone by the rock of the mossy stream."

Something is coming. She hears a strange sound; the underbrush is crackling, a black form appears in the darkness. Frightened the tears roll down her cheeks. It is a great shaggy black bear. He came close to her, smelt of her face and hands, and licked the blood from her feet. She was no more afraid of him than of her own great dog at home, and dared to stroke his long, brown nose, and put her arm about his neck. Then he lay down beside her, she placed her head upon his shoulder and alone in the thick woods, with the dark clouds of the sky for a covering, she was quickly asleep.*

Two days afterwards the foot prints of the child and the bear were found in the sand and mud of the brook.

None slept in John Whitcher's house during the long hours of that terrible night. The father was out in the woods, the children sat down with woe pictured on their faces, while the mother would not suffer a door or a window to be closed, but listened to every sound, and started at every leaf.

In the morning, the exciting rumor of "John Whitcher's child lost and supposed to have perished in the woods," seemed to speed itself, on the wings of the wind, sounding along the borders of Beech hill, startling the wild solitudes of the East-parte region, arousing the rugged yeomanry of the Height-o'-land, the brave boys of Runaway pond and Patchbreuckland, charging them all to pack up their dinners and hurry away to the search in the woods.

In an incredible short time all the dwellers in the hamlet were moving towards Pine hill. Col. Obadiah Clement left his oxen yoked, mounted his horse and galloped swift away up the bridle path, passing Jonathan Clement and 'Squire Copp, with their sons, who, leaving their hoeing, were hastening in the same direction with tin dinner horns in their hands. Joshua Merrill, Joseph Merrill, Stevens Merrill, and 'Squire Jonathan, seized their axes and

---

* Sarah Whitcher's, otherwise Mrs. Dick French's, own statement.

ran. Joseph Patch, with his long barrelled gun, and his neighbors, came up at a rapid pace, and a little later in the day, Lunds, Clarks, and Tarletons came over the mountain.

All day long they hunted. Col. Clement and his friends went down through the maples to Black brook, and Kelly pond, then climbed up by Oak falls, and beat the woods as far as Wachipauka pond under Webster slide. 'Squire Copp blew a loud blast with his horn on the shore. "No response came from the far glimmering passionate sound but its own empty echo," hurled back from the mountain face.

Stevens Merrill and others, with Joseph Patch crossed Berry brook and went through the darkest forest to the very foot of Moosehillock mountain.

Chase Whitcher, Stephen Richardson, and a host of others hunted along the bridle path, and then explored the Oliverian up what is at present High street, as far as the dark passes on either side of Black mountain. The women and children hunted for long hours, but in vain.

The night came, and one after another the parties returned empty from the search. Despair seemed to have taken possession of the grief-stricken parents, and a feeling of sadness pervaded the whole settlement.

On Tuesday morning the entire town renewed the search. As the day wore away, people began to arrive from the neighboring lands. They came from Wentworth and Romney, from Orford, Piermont, Haverhill, and Newbury. At night, one of the last men to come in, reported that he had found the track of a child and of a bear on Berry brook. "She is torn in pieces!" "She is eaten up!" every one said, and Mrs. Whitcher was nearly frantic.

The next day they searched on the Summit, going over the ground thoroughly; but night brought no success. "She is hopelessly lost." "She will never be found." Yet at the earnest request of the agonized mother they promised to continue the search one day more.

Thursday the woods were alive with the people hunting. The long hours slowly wore away, when about noon a Mr. Heath who had walked the whole distance from Plymouth, came to the house. Mrs. Stephen Richardson who was cooking a bushel of beans for the people's supper, and Mrs. Obadiah Clement, were alone at John Whitcher's. Mrs. Whitcher was still searching in the woods. "Give me some dinner," said Mr. Heath, "then show me the bridle-path to the north, and I will find the child." While he was eating, he stated how he heard last evening that little Sarah Whitcher was lost, and that three times in the night, he dreamed that he found her lying under a great pine top, a few rods to the south-east of the spot where the path crossed Berry brook, guarded by a bear.*

The women smiled, but partly believed it might be so, for people had different notions then from what they entertain now. Some believed in witches, ghosts, and goblins, and all had a certain kind of faith in dreams; at any rate the women wished his dream might prove true; they felt so sad at the loss of the child; they wished so much it might be found.

Just then Joseph Patch came into the clearing, heard Mr. Heath's story, and said he would accompany him.

An hour went by; the sun was going down on the last afternoon of the search, which would be given up that night, and every one felt that little Sarah was lost forever.

Suddenly a gun was heard; every soul in the clearings and the woods listened. Another report, then another. It is the agreed signal of success. "Thank God! the child is found." "Is it dead or alive?"

They found her just where Mr. Heath said they would; but no bear was to be seen. When she woke up, she said, "I want to go to mother. Carry me to mother." When asked if she had seen any one, she said "a great black dog stopped with her every night."†

Joseph Patch took up the half famished child in his arms and carried her home. On the bridle-path they met many people, and they ran before, hurrahing, waving their hats and green boughs to tell the good news, how all on account of a wonderful dream the child was found alive. Some said the bear guided her to the path.

---

* Samuel Merrill, who resided at the East-parte, and lived to be 84 years old, often told about the lost child. He believed in Mr. Heath's dream as much as in his own existence. There were hundreds of people in Warren of the last generation who believed implicitly in Mr. Heath's dream.

† Nathaniel Richardson's statement.

Mrs. Whitcher was so overjoyed that she fainted. Mr. Whitcher could not say a word, but smoked his pipe as hard as he could, to keep his feelings down, and the rest of the children were so glad that they cried and laughed by turns.

Tradition has it that the Rev. Mr. Powers was present and offered a prayer of thanksgiving, and then all the people sang Old Hundred. However that may be, we know that they ate all the baked beans * that Mrs. Richardson had prepared, and everything else they could find cooked on Pine hill. Then they blew their tin horns as though the 4th of July had come; shouted and hurrahed again and again, while those who had guns fired volley after volley till all the powder in the settlement was burned, so much did they rejoice that the lost child was found.

---

* Nathaniel Richardson, son of Stephen Richardson, also gave many incidents about the search, and told of the beans.

CHAPTER VIII.

OF A MIGHTY BATTLE FOUGHT BETWEEN TWO AMBITIOUS OFFICE SEEKERS, AND HOW EACH GAINED THE VICTORY MUCH TO HIS GREAT DELIGHT.

At the organization of our little democracy, Warren, Col. Obadiah Clement, being in sympathy with the government, immediately took the lead in town affairs, and held it for several years. But when the war was over, others began to aspire for the honors of place and position, and naturally envied the Colonel. The most prominent of the aspirants was 'Squire Jonathan Merrill. For five years he had sought office, but in vain, for Obadiah Clement knew well how to kill him off — only having to tell what a tory he was in war times, to sink him out of sight in every election.

But this would not last always, and 'Squire Jonathan, who as we said before, was as cunning as a fox, went shrewdly to work to beat the Colonel and gain the honors of office. "I'll fix him," said he. "I'll make him hate the town, and the town will then hate him." This is the way he did it:

Colonel Clement had a bill against the hamlet for services. It was for a journey to Exeter to get the town incorporated; for drafting and notifying "Grand Jurors," and for recording in the town books. In all it amounted to nine pounds eleven shillings and three pence.

'Squire Jonathan heard of it and slyly whispered round telling every body in a confidential way that it was too large; that the town was too poor to pay it. In other words, he appealed to the avarice of the people most effectually.

Col. C. was first in the mighty triumvirate of town governors for that political year, 1785–'6, and it was the third year of his selectmenship.* Likewise he was and had been for the last six years, the great scribe or mighty town clerk, and having been ambassador or Representative to the Great and General Court, and also a high commander in the military forces, he naturally felt himself to be the most important man in the hamlet.

'Squire Jonathan labored with Col. Clement's associates in power, and they being near relatives to the 'Squire, the first the father, and the second the brother-in-law, he succeeded most effectually in making them think the same as he did about the bill.

So when the day of settlement of town matters came, they refused to allow the Colonel's account. The latter labored with his associates sometime, but with no effect, for he had two stubborn men to deal with; and then when he could not succeed, parted from them in a huff; in other words he was exceedingly wroth. "Pay, you must," said he. "Pay, we won't," said they; and so the matter waxed worse and worse.

This was what the cunning 'Squire wanted. He was pleased, and openly expressed his delight. Col. C. heard of his adversary's remarks, and his anger was fiercer than ever.

One more effort was made, one more meeting was held, but with no better success than before.

The Colonel had all the town books, both the selectmen's and the clerk's, and he was determined to hold them until he should get his pay. If he could not have his rights, he would make a storm in the political sky. He would hold on to all the records and prevent an assembly of the people. If he could not rule, no one else should.

'Squire Jonathan made a few more aggravating remarks, and the storm burst. When asked to call a meeting on the Ides of March, Col. C. raged, stamped his foot, and then with a look of fierce determination, cried, "Pause!" and there was a pause. The wheels of government in our mountain hamlet stopped. The proud ship of State no longer sailed on. She was foundered on

---

* Stevens Merrill and Joseph Patch were the other Selectmen.

AN INTERREGNUM. 331

the rocks of that discord to which 'Squire Merrill had so cunningly directed her. The waves of destruction beat over her, threatening to rend her in pieces.

And now occurred an interregnum* similar to those which happened in the early days of the mighty Roman Empire. There were no powerful rulers, no great scribe, no superintendent of the public roads, no gatherer of the revenue, and no taxes. Every thing seemed to have returned as it was at the time when the revolutionary war was raging.

What should be done? It was a great question, powerfully discussed by those interested, but months went by and no action was taken.

At last the matter was brought to the attention of the Great and General Court, and the Legislature took the question in hand.

The great mother of towns could not see any of her children commit suicide. So after a long time spent in solemn consideration, a resolution was framed and passed, going through both houses of the legislature the same day, June 24th, 1786, whereby Absalom Peters, the barefooted military captain who marched at the head of six companies, to the Coos intervals, was empowered to call an assembly in Warren, for the choice of town officers, and preside therein during the whole election. †

But the wise legislature forgot one thing, taxes, and had to pass another resolve, Sept. 24, in order that the State might get her share of the revenue.

A. Peters called the meeting, and presided therein in the most proper manner.‡ But the spirit of the citizens ran high. They marshaled around their leaders, and fought for victory. Each side marched up to the ballot box in solid column. On counting the votes, it was found that Obadiah Clement and his friends had won every time; electing Joshua Copp, Stephen Richardson, and William Butler, great rulers or selectmen, Joshua Copp, scribe or clerk, and Jonathan Clement, conservator of the peace or constable. 'Squire Jonathan and his friends felt cheap enough, and

---

* It happened in 1786.

† Town Clerk's Records, Vol. i. 21.

‡ The meeting was held July 19, 1786.

silently went home.* But Jonathan Merrill did not give up even in the hour of his seeming defeat. He went to work twice as hard as ever. So persistently did he talk upon the subject of Col. Clement's bill, that even the new selectmen, the Colonel's friends, did not dare to pay it, for fear they should be indicted for mis-spending the people's money, and the Colonel was more enraged than ever.

This was just what the 'Squire wanted, and although he was defeated again at the annual election in 1787, still he managed to have a meeting called July 27th of that year, and succeeded in getting himself, with Joshua Merrill and Lieut. Ephraim True, appointed a committee to settle with Mr. Clement, and procure from him all the town records. That every thing might seem fair, it was "Voted, that a settlement might be made, if it could be done consistently with justice." The meeting was then adjourned to August 6, to hear the report of the committee.

'Squire Jonathan went to work as slick as "ile." But he did not get a settlement; he did not want to.

At the adjourned meeting he reported as follows: *First*, not to allow anything for going down to get the town incorporated; and —

Second, to pay eighteen pence for legally drafting and notifying jurors.

But they knew Col. C. would not accept this, and so they chose Stevens Merrill and Lieut. Ephraim True a committee to settle with him, or to follow suit or suits at law, if he commence one or more against the town, to final end and execution. "Now we will teach him how it is done," said 'Squire Jonathan. Col. C. heard of the remark, and how mad he was.

By chance they met. One to have seen them would have said "surely they do love each other." Determination seated itself on their countenances. Rage flashed from their eyes. "You miserable tory," growled Col. C. "You old thief and extortioner," hissed 'Squire M. through his teeth. Then Col. C. shook his cane threateningly. 'Squire M. doubled his fists belligerently. And now grim visaged war smiled approvingly, and Saultenbattery,

---

* Old men used to say that it was the toughest fight they ever saw at town meeting.

one of the ancient goddesses, grinned with malignant satisfaction. Blows would have fallen swift, and the battle waxed hot had not Stevens Merrill, the man of iron firmness, and Joshua Copp, who had been watching the impending conflict, interfered and said, " Gentlemen, thee must stop, thee can't fight in this town."
This rencountre only made matters worse. But the Colonel did not plunge heels over head into lawsuits. He had more shrewdness than that; he quietly went to work and induced some one else to get up some pleasant little suits against the town; to wit, he got all the public highways indicted, and thus raised the d—l generally.*

With so much avidity did the Colonel prosecute his schemes, so many suits did he institute, that the town was perfectly sick, and was glad to cry, hold, enough. At a regular town meeting, it was " Voted to dismiss the committee appointed to fight Col. C., and that Captain William Butler and Joshua Copp, friends of the Colonel, take the certificate that is in the selectmen's hands, and lay it out discretionary if wanted in carrying on the lawsuits commenced against said town for the repairing of roads, and to pay Col. Clement's demands on said town." Thus they were going to come a flank movement on road suits, by making friends with the prime mover of them.†

This ended the war, and Col. Obadiah, in one sense, gained the victory. But it accomplished all that 'Squire Jonathan desired. It made Mr. Clement exceedingly unpopular, and he never could get elected to any office of consequence again; the only one he ever held afterwards being that of moderator at some special meeting.

---

* Nov. 27, 1790.—" Voted to pass over the 4th article in the warning, which was to see what the town will do on account of being presented."—Town Clerks' Records, Vol. i. 43.

† Allowed constable Copp fifteen pounds sixteen shillings, new emission, it being for three pounds nineteen shillings silver money, which said Copp paid Obadiah Clement that was due to him from the town.

JOSHUA MERRILL, } Selectmen.
WILLIAM BUTLER, }
—Selectmen's Records, Vol. i.

" May 10, 1791.—Voted that Capt. William Butler and Joshua Copp should take the certificate that is in the selectmen's hands, and lay it out discretionary if wanting in carrying on the lawsuits commenced against said town, and to pay Obadiah Clement's demand on said town."—Town Clerk's Records, Vol. i. 45.

Names of the legal voters who had come into town from 1782 to 1788, inclusive:

Nathaniel Clough.	Samuel Knight.	John Stone.
Caleb Homan.	Levi Lufkin.	Elisha Swett.
Enoch Homan.	Stephen Lund.	Aaron Welch.
Nathaniel Knight.	Stephen Richardson.	

Yet this contest was prolific of mighty results. From it sprang two great parties, the Clement party, and the Merrill party, that fought each other with powerful tenacity for more than two generations. When the sons of Joseph Patch became voters, a third party sprung up that achieved some success, and was called the Patch party. It frequently held the balance of power.

'Squire Jonathan was now able to succeed, and by striving, in the course of years, held all the important offices in the gift of the people, although Col. Clement at the head of the Clement party often said that he frequently had the pleasure of giving the 'Squire and his friends a sound drubbing at the polls.

CHAPTER IX.

CONCERNING A GREAT BOUNDARY FEUD, AND WHAT CAME OF IT.

AND now when the wilderness blossoms like a rose and good settling lands begin to be of some consequence, the proprietors of the grants made in Provincial times under Gov. Benning Wentworth, having many of them survived the Revolution, commenced to bestir themselves and look sharp after their interests. Mighty boundary feuds began to arise, for neighboring peoples set on by their patrons the proprietors, did not always observe the old maxim of "cursed be he who removeth his neighbors' land-marks," and the citizens of Warren found that their friends across the frontiers began to show an inclination to trespass on their fertile possessions.

In fact they had some excuse for so doing, for in laying out the townships, in 1760 and in 1761, "the surveyor of the King's woods," employed by the Governor, had not been very careful to make the lines of townships correspond. Consequently settlers upon them did not know exactly where the lines were, nor in what town they lived, and so did not scruple to conduct themselves in rather a lawless manner.

In a short time, great complaints began to arise, and the town of Warren thus finding herself encroached upon, by means of the selectmen, mighty rulers, and the lordly proprietors, who of course took a lively interest in the matter, immediately entered into negotiations with the neighboring powers round about. It is a tradition often related that by dint of numerous diplomatic [missions a meeting of many of the town proprietors and numerous boards of selectmen was held at Plymouth, about 1778.

It was a jolly old meeting. They treated themselves on grog, and swallowed all the various kinds of liquors mixed in those days, and then, when pretty well fired up, proceeded to business. A chairman and clerk were chosen, and then charters, surveys, and

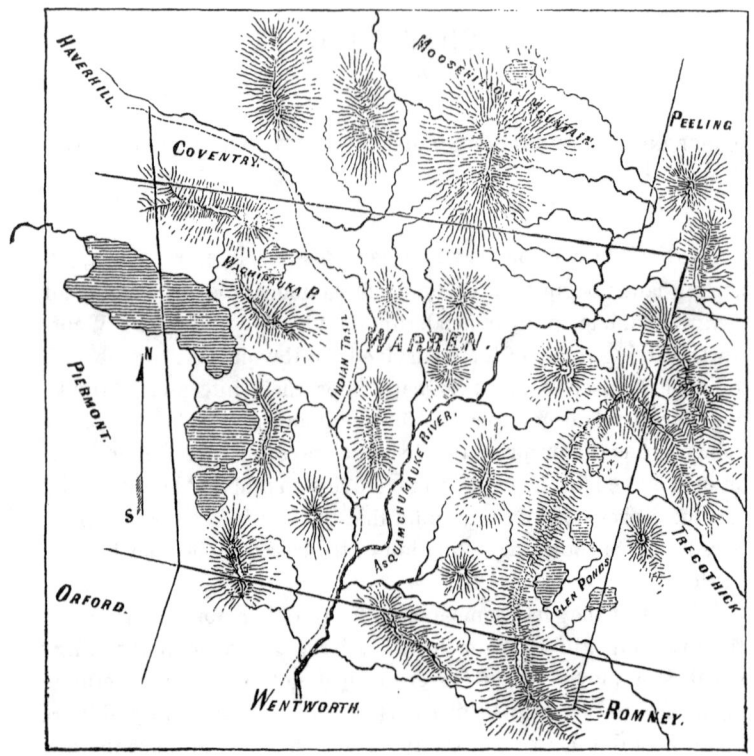

OLD BOUNDARY LINES.

plans of townships, were produced. Each delegation had a speaker of its own and wanted to be heard first, and cried out, our lines run so and so, our charter says so and so, our lots are located so and so, and so on, *ad infinitum*. The chairman called to order, but it was no use. Confusion, a goddess, got confused. Babel seemed to have arrived, and when all was clatter-and-bang, the meeting broke up in the most dignified and wonderful manner.

THE LEGISLATURE INTERFERES.

But it is a historical fact, on record, that the delegates went home and considered. Some of the wiser ones drew up a petition to the legislature, to have a committee appointed to settle the boundaries, and circulated it. It was extensively signed, and when presented to the Great and General Court, that body immediately acted, and appointed a committee for that purpose.*
Said committee were nearly four years performing their duties, and they had numerous meetings at which many boards of selectmen and proprietors' committees appeared. They also employed several surveyors to run the lines and set up the bounds, and only made their report to the Legislature, Sept. 24, 1784, which report was approved and the bounds thus established.†

Strange work the Court's committee as they were called, made with our young and vigorous township. They actually pushed it up a considerable distance to the north and east. Think of it. A whole township moved. Piermont and Wentworth on the west and south, got large slices of territory. But Warren got more — clipping of large portions of old Coventry, Peeling, and Trecothick. But Warren gained no settlers. Wentworth and Piermont did. Warren lost on the west, Isaiah Batchelder and Thomas Clark, and on the south, Simeon Smith, Peter Stevens, Joseph Kimball, and Lemuel Keezer. Besides it lost of unsettled land four lots into Coventry, eight into Wentworth, and fifteen into Piermont. The four taken by Coventry were on the north-west corner; but Warren got far more land from Coventry on the north-east boundary than it lost.

And now that the lines were changed, the losses and gains must be settled. This was not easily done, and a war about payments arose hot and earnest. Blows did not come for they feared

---

* The Committee was appointed by an act of the Legislature passed Oct. 23, 1780, and it consisted of Ebenezer Thompson, Joseph Badger, Ebenezer Smith, Levi Dearborn, and John Smith, Esquires, and they, or the major part of them, were authorized to survey Romney, Wentworth, Warren, Plymouth, Campton, Piermont, and Orford.

† BOUNDS OF WARREN.

"*Warren.*—Beginning at a bass tree, being the north-west corner bound of Romney, thence north, 2¼ degrees east five and three-fourths miles to a maple tree; thence north about 74 degrees west, eight miles to a beech tree, being the south-east corner of Haverhill; thence 5½ degrees west, five and one-half miles to a beech tree, the north-east corner of Orford, thence on a straight line to the bound began at."

These are supposed to be the present boundaries of Warren.

the great central power, the mother of towns; but litigation, such as the old Greeks loved so well, was rife. Warren did not resort to it, but entered into negotiations with the far lands of Wentworth, Piermont, and Orford.

Meeting after meeting was held by the proprietors to settle up the difficulties. Committees without number tried their hand at the matter. The first chosen June 17, 1785, consisted of Enoch Page, from down country, and our citizen, Captain William Butler; but they did not accomplish anything. Then Major Joseph Page, another down country gentleman, was associated with Capt. Butler. They went into a minute investigation of the whole matter, and made a full report, much to the satisfaction of the proprietors. Oct. 20, 1786, Capt. William Hackett was chosen a committee to settle with Gen. Moulton, agent for the Proprietors of Piermont, on account of land given to Messrs. Batchelder and Clark. But he did not succeed, and afterward Major Joseph Page, by order of Warren Proprietors, laid out two hundred acres on Green mountain, now called Sentinel mountain, to satisfy the claims of our western power.*

Then other settlements had to be made. The town of Wentworth got more than four hundred acres in Warren, on account of what Warren's Proprietors had given of Wentworth lands to settlers. A goodly lot in Warren had to be given to Orford, on account of the pretty quadrilateral on the south-east corner, which the proprietors had also given away to a settler, but which belonged to Orford town. Perhaps some may maliciously think Warren was more to blame about boundary feuds than her neighbors, but we must positively assure them that it was not so.

In the matter with Coventry, now Benton, the conclusion was arrived at that the changes or swops were about equal, although there was some difficulty in relation to the Bowles lot, so called from Charles Bowles, who served in the war and afterwards was a celebrated revivalist, that Coventry's Proprietors had given away, but which actually belonged to Warren.

Now that the boundaries are set up with stability, the proprie-

---
* "June 28, 1787.—Voted, That Capt. William Hackett give Gen. Moulton, agent for Piermont, immediate notice to make his pitch of 200 acres of land in Warren, in consideration of that quantity taken into Piermont, settled by Thos. Clark and Isaiah Batchelder, by the 10th of October next, and that if he doth not

tors came to the conclusion that a new survey of the whole territory was actually needed. The Leavitt survey, running as far north as *the eleven mile tree*, the Cummings survey, the Rindge survey, would not answer at all, and they immediately contracted with Josiah Burnham, school-master, to make an accurate plan of the town. He entered upon the work, but it was a long time before he finished it. He re-run the lots, established the range lines and surveyed the divisions, making everything harmonize as much as possible with the old surveys, the proprietors' drawing of lots and the former sales by deed.

But he did not lay down the roads and brooks, nor trace the course of the river; neither did he indicate the locality of the ponds, and the mountains. He had no taste for such things.

But he was accurate as far as he went, and his plan has been the foundation of every map of the hamlet made since. May 4, 1795, the proprietors accepted his work and paid him a vast sum for doing it.

Thus the lines were settled and peace prevailed once more along the borders. It continued for more than fifty years, and was only disturbed by old Peeling and Trecothick, who grew jealous of our vigorous democracy, and raised another boundary feud, as will be related in a subsequent book of this history.

---

make said pitch by said time, then Capt. Hackett to lay 200 acres of equal goodness as near the line of Piermont as conveniently may be, and make return thereof at the adjournment of this meeting."—Proprietors' Records.

* See Proprietors' Records for full notes about lands taken into other towns.

CHAPTER X.

OF THE MIGHTY REQUISITES NECESSARY TO MAKE A PERFECT DE-
MOCRACY; ALL GRAPHICALLY PORTRAYED IN THE MOST ATTRAC-
TIVE MANNER.

DOES any one wish to know what are the *requisites* to make a perfect community, a complete town organization, then let him in addition to what we have already stated, read this chapter of our no less great than modest history, and a tolerable idea can be obtained.

And first of all, after houses, mills, and cleared lands, good roads were greatly needed and our valiant citizens went bravely to work to build them. The old proprietors' highway, partly following the route of the Indian trail, did not suit them, and so they surveyed a new road over Red Oak hill, through "Patchbreuckland," across the Asquamchumauke or Baker river, through the centre district, over the Mikaseota or Black brook, along the basin of Runaway pond, and winding away over the Height-o'-land by Tarleton lake to Piermont. It was four rods wide, and afterwards was a great thoroughfare, the first ox teams from Coos passing over it soon after it was built, to the sea-board, a circumstance most pleasingly narrated by Rev. Grant Powers, the distinguished historian of the "Cowass country."

And then a road, now discontinued, was laid out on the west side of the Asquamchumauke, following the old Indian trail and the proprietors' first highway from Wentworth line to the mouth of Black brook, for the accommodation of Nathaniel Clough, who had just settled on that side of the river.

From Black brook bridge over Beech hill to Wentworth line another was cut for the benefit of 'Squire Abel Merrill,* a new settler on the hill among the beeches and maples. Leading from the last at a point where now stands Beech hill school-house, a fourth road ran away to the west high up on the side of Sentinel mountain, to accommodate Mr. Amos Little,† who was at this time clearing a beautiful and fertile spot in the woods, a delightful breezy sunshiny nest on the hill, from which he could overlook the valley and out upon the panorama of great eastern mountains.

The selectmen also hurried to lay out a road over Pine hill from Chase Whitcher's by John Whitcher's down to the "Society school-house,"‡ as it was sometimes called, in the Centre district.

For several years Aaron Welch,** who lived near where the ceme-

---

* ABEL AND TAMAR (*Kimball*) MERRILL'S FAMILY RECORD.

Benjamin, born Oct. 19, 1784.
John, born Mch. 4, 1786.
Daniel, born Mch. 24, 1788.
Sally, born Mch. 9, 1790.
Polly, born Mch. 28, 1792.
Betsey, born June 9, 1794.
Samuel L. born Apr. 10, 1796.

Joseph, born Feb. 16, 1798.
William, born Apr. 10, 1800.
Ira, born July 17, 1803.
Tamar, born Mch. 9, 1805.
Hannah, born Apr. 3, 1807.
John L. born May 8, 1810.

Names of those voters who moved into town in 1789:—
John Abbott.
John Badger. (1)
Samuel Fellows.
Jonathan Fellows.

Ebenezer Hidden.
John Hidden.
Amos Little.
Silas Lund.

Abel Merrill.
Richard Pillsbury.

(1) John Badger was a curious genius. He once ran away to avoid his creditors, and they went after him and brought him back. Then he acquired considerable property, ran away again, but his debtors did not got go after him to bring him back. He scolded and said he thought it was a poor rule that would not work both ways.

† AMOS AND BETSEY (*Kimball*) LITTLE'S FAMILY RECORD.

Sally, born May 31, 1787, at Plaistow.
Tamar, born Aug. 25, 1789, at Warren.
James, born Sept. 6, 1791.
Benjamin, born Sept. 22, 1793.
Betty, born Aug. 31, 1795.
Amos, born Dec. 15, 1797.
Jesse, born July 4, 1800.

William, born June 19, 1802.
Jonathan, born June 8, 1804.
John, born Mch. 7, 1806.
Judith and Dolly, twins, born Feb. 25, 1810.
Kimball, born Jan. 8, 1815.

‡ I. "Voted to allow Stevens Merrill £0-4-6, Capt. Wm. Butler 5 shillings, and Ensign Copp 3 shillings, for their services as a committee, laying out a road from Coventry line to the Society school-house, on Coos road."

"Voted to lay out the road through Mr. Aaron Welch's land, near the bank of the river, direct as is convenient from his house to the Society school-house."

** AARON AND BETTY WELCH'S FAMILY RECORD.

Moses, born Dec. 10, 1788, at Warren.
Aaron, born Sept. 8, 1791.
Judith, born May 19, 1793.
Betsey, born Apr. 18, 1795.
Samuel, born May 15, 1797.

Oliver, born April 15, 1799.
Thomas, born Aug. 18, 1801.
Lois, born May 19, 1804.
Sally, born Feb. 20, 1807.

tery is now, by vote in public assembly, was allowed to have two gates upon it.

Then one was laid out for Christian William Whiteman round the east side of Tarleton lake; another from Height-o'-land road across Runaway pond valley to Pine hill road, and yet another from said Pine hill road across Berry brook, through Streamy valley, far into the East-parte regions. Samuel Knight, who had served in the wars, built his cabin beside it.* It was a frail dwelling, and through the crevices of its roof blew the summer winds, and the stars shone in at night. Knight was a man of pleasant adventures, and a narrator of wild and startling traditions. He found where the Indians lived in the valley and turned up their stone arrow-heads with his plow. He had been a brave man in his country's battles, and exhibited nerve in his encounters in the woods.

These were the principal highways, but as the years went by, roads were laid out up into Moosehillock district, to accommodate James and Moses Williams, Caleb Homan,† and Samuel Merrill, who had settled in that section; up Patch hill, towards Glen ponds, for the benefit of Mr. Reuben Batchelder and Capt. Stephen Flanders, who had settled in the East-parte country; round the foot of Moosehillock to the Summit; up High street, through the North woods; from Pine hill road, up towards Webster-slide Mt. by Wachipauka pond, to convene Mr. Paul Meader, a new settler in this part of the hamlet; down Height-o'-land road by Eastman

---

* SAMUEL AND SARAH (*Bradley*) KNIGHT'S FAMILY RECORD.

He was born in Plaistow, Feb. 21, 1757. Sarah Bradley, his wife, was born in Plaistow, Aug. 23, 1760. Married Aug. 20, 1778.

Susannah, born May 25, 1779.
Abigail, born Apr. 7, 1782.
Married Mary Merrill, Aug. 26, 1784.
Nathaniel, born Apr. 29, 1785.
Stevens, born May 9, 1786.
Sarah, born Feb. 3, 1788.
Abigail, born Apr. 16, 1790.
Polly, born Oct. 21, 1792.
Betty, born Apr. 30, 1795.
Ruth, born July 17, 1798.
Hannah B., born July 16, 1801.

New voters in 1790:—
Amos Clark.   James Little.   Thomas Pillsbury.
John Gardner.   Daniel Pike.   C. William Whiteman.

† CALEB AND RUTH (*Merrill*) HOMAN'S FAMILY RECORD.

Married, Jan. 18 1789.
Sally, born Aug. 10, 1789.
Joseph, born Apr. 23, 1792. Died June 29, 1794.
Susanna, born Apr. 29, 1795.
Joseph, born Oct. 11, 1797.
Mary, born July 14, 1800.
Ruth, born Feb. 26, 1803.
Mary, born June 6, 1806.

New voters in 1791:—
David Badger.
Joseph Knight.
Enoch Page.
Dr. Joseph Peters.

ponds to Piermont, and up Patch brook on to Picked hill, where a son of Joseph Patch had built a cabin and commenced a clearing. These roads were gems in themselves, being so much better than none at all; but however good, they were often presented to the grand jury by indignant men, who jolting over them thought they ought to be indicted and thereby made better. Then an attempt was made to lay out a road to old Trecothick, now Ellsworth, across the depression between Carr and Kineo mountains, and by Glen ponds; but it was never accomplished, much to the detriment of fishermen who wish to visit those beautiful sheets of water.*

On these roads have happened many a strange adventure worthy of record in this remarkable history. Ox teams, as we have said before, drawing ponderous freights to and from the Cowass country; great canvass covered teams, drawn by eight horses, coming all the way down from the traditionary land of Canada; riders upon horseback, like Johny Balch, who carried the mail and blew a horn in the woods, and long trains of pungs and two horse sleds with jingling "coffee bells" and shouting drivers, coming from the high north country in winter, used them.

Once Mr. Samuel Flanders slew an enormous wild cat that was devouring a goose on the Height-o'-land road by Tarleton lake. The hungry beast was too fond of poultry to have a prudent regard for its own safety, and Mr. F. not having a thought of danger, with a large goad stick attacked the cat and with a single blow killed it.

Races have been run upon them, when they were not in so good a condition as they now are. When the East-parte route†

---

* Paid Abel Merrill and Joseph Patch $1.00 each for meeting selectmen of Ellsworth and examining a route for a road.—See Selectmen's first book.

New Voters.—In 1792, Uriah Cross, Josiah Magoon. In 1793, Abram Alexander, Thomas Boynton, John Chase, David S. Craig, Daniel Welch. In 1794, Stephen Badger. In 1795, Stephen Flanders, Barnabas Niles.

† John Low lived on the East-parte road. He was a very neat farmer, and would follow the man who reaped for him and cut up the stray stalks of grain which the reaper would leave about the stumps and rock heaps, with his jack-knife.

He had the very economical habit of laying in bed all day, winter times, and at dark would yoke up his team and go into the forest after a load of wood. He would often work all night at his business. My uncle Anson one bitter cold night saw him starting out with his cattle at 9 P.M., for a load of wood.

John Low, one winter, found two bushels of swallows in a hollow birch tree. They were torpid when found, but were lively enough after they had laid before the fire a short time. John Libbey and Nathaniel Merrill saw these swallows.(?) 'Squire George Libbey affirmed that he saw these swallows.(?)

was first cleared, Mrs. Samuel Knight, Mrs. Caleb Homan, accompanied by several other women, and a young man by the name of Webster, who was from Landaff, went to Mr. Stephen Flanders' to pay the family a visit. On their return home when they arrived near the bridge over what is sometimes called Moosehillock falls near East-parte school-house, Mistresses Knight and Homan challenged young Webster, who was mounted on a very fleet horse, to a race. At first he did not like to consent, but they strongly urged him and he acquiesced. Whipping up, they went over the rough road for the distance of a mile and a half, at almost lightning speed, when Webster who had the fastest horse proved the winner, much to the chagrin of the racing ladies. Mr. W., when an old man, remarked in telling the story that he had rode over that piece of road many times since, but never a quarter so fast as then.

Soldiers have marched over them. Many a time on little training day, flood-wood, slam-bang and string-bean companies, and others that were entitled to more respect, have right-wheeled and left-wheeled upon them. Col. Moses H. Clement,* son of Col. Obadiah, marched a whole regiment along the Height-o'-land, or old Coos road, the first one that ever mustered in Warren.

Battles have been waged upon them. The fiercest one was fought one night when it was "dark as pitch," by Samuel Knight and a terrible foe. It had lightened, thundered, rained, and hailed, "like great guns," and Mr. K. who was dripping wet in his camp by Silver rill, resolved to go home to his boarding place at Joseph Merrill's inn. At the foot of the hill, near Berry brook bridge, something stopped him. There was a low deep growl and directly before him, seemingly, two balls of fire flashed in the blackness. He shouted, and the bear, for such was his enemy, leaped upon him grasping him with its fore paws and scratched him fearfully. It was a critical moment, but Knight's right arm was free, and quick as thought he pulled a knife from his pocket, opened it with his teeth, and thrust it with desperate force into the

---

MOSES H. AND TAMAR (*Little*) CLEMENT'S FAMILY RECORD.

Russell K., born Apr. 19, 1809.
Hazen, born Dec. 14, 1811.
Elizabeth, born Feb. 28, 1814. Died Jan. 27, 1815.
James, born Nov. 10, 1815.
Joseph, born Apr. 3, 1818.
Amos Little, born Dec. 12, 1820.

Sarah, born Dec. 29, 1822.
William, born Jan. 26, 1825.
Daniel Q., born May 31, 1826.
Eliza, born Jan. 20, 1828.
John, born Aug. 12, 1830.
Tamar J., born Dec. 4, 1832.

side of the bear. Luckily it pierced its heart, and instantly relaxing its hold, it fell upon the ground and expired. Knight was severely torn by the claws of the bear, and sitting down by his dead enemy concluded to remain there during the night. But the clouds shortly broke away, the stars came out, the moon shone brightly, and changing his mind, he hurried home.

Returning the next morning with his friends, he found a bear of the largest class which gave evident tokens that she was engaged rearing her young. This probably induced her to attack Mr. K., something she would not have done under any other circumstances.

Men have died on them. Richard Pillsbury, who lived in Wentworth, had been to Haverhill on foot one cold stormy winter day. Climbing Red-oak hill at night, on his return, he became chilled through, lay down in the road and died. In the morning his dog came to the door of his home and howled, then seemed to look towards the road on the hill. They followed and found him there. Friends and neighbors carried him home, then buried him in the grave yard by the mossy stream,—" down on the east side." To-day he is almost forgotten, and soon would be lost to the memory of men forever, did we not here record his death.

In order to make these roads really serviceable, bridges were wanted and must be had over the little meadow streams, across the mountain torrents, and spanning the river. Most of these were easily built; but the great work of that time was the building of the large bridge over the Asquamchumauke, near the mouth of Black brook, the Mikaseota. The citizens of Warren had sent a letter to the proprietors, praying for aid, and the godfathers of the hamlet generously voted nineteen pounds ten shillings and seven pence to build the bridge. On the third of March, 1784, at a public meeting, Jonathan Merrill, Joshua Copp, and Joseph Patch, were appointed a committee to perform the work, and authorized to proceed as far as the money would go. They commenced the work at once. They labored themselves, they paid Stevens Merrill three pounds for plank to put on it, and Obadiah Clement two pounds seventeen shillings and one penny, for labor, besides vast sums paid to other individuals.

That the work might go on bravely, they purchased at the

price of sixteen shillings, a little old rum "to wet their whistles and strengthen their muscles." Moses True, it is said, once carried the great stone jug to Stevens Merrill's, who kept the pure "west endea," to get it filled. Mr. M. was away, and he went into the kitchen. It was a sight that met his eyes not often seen in these degenerate days. Mrs. Merrill was mounted on the loom, which stood in one corner of the room, smoking and weaving with all her might, the fumes of her tobacco pipe mingling with the whiz of the shuttle, the jarring of the lathe and the clattering of the treadles, while buzz, buzz, went the rapid wheel, and creak, creak, the windle from which run the yarn that her grandchild, daughter of 'Squire Jonathan, was quilling.

But Moses True was a dauntless youth. "Come down," said he, showing the jug. At first she was not inclined to accommodate him; but he persisted, and she put up a gallon of the good creature that was so much needed in those days.*

How they worked when they got the exhilerating drams of good grog. How the axes flew in the great pine timbers, how the mallets resounded as the mortices were made, how the augurs bit as they gnawed through the wood, turned by strong arms, and how the shovels went as they dug great trenches in the bottom of the stream in which to place the mud sills on which the bridge would stand.

They drank better rum in those days than now. There was not so much strychnine in it. Besides, there were no temperance societies then; the ministers drank themselves.

But when the bridge was raised they drank lots of the good creature. The great rulers of the town, the selectmen, paid Joshua

---

* 1784.—Paid Stevens Merrill for plank to build the bridge over Baker river, three pounds.
Paid Stevens Merrill for rum to raise the bridge, eight shillings.
" Obadiah Clements, two pounds seventeen shillings one penny, in full pay for work done on the bridge over Baker river.
Ordered Constable Butler to pay Ephraim True eight shillings, it being for rum that he found to build the bridge, which sum is to be taken out of his note that he gave to the town.

OBADIAH CLEMENT, } Selectmen.
SAMUEL KNIGHT,

Paid to Joshua Merrill sixteen shillings, it being for two gallons of rum that he found for the town to be spent in raising the river bridge, which is to be allowed to him on the former account.
March 27, 1786.—Paid Obadiah Clement two pounds two shillings and eleven pence, it being due to him for work done on the bridge over Baker river.

JOSEPH PATCH, } Selectmen.
WILLIAM BUTLER,

Merrill sixteen shillings for two gallons that he furnished, and eight shillings to Ephraim True for one gallon found by him; all for the purpose of raising. Three gallons! Wonderful to relate, with this powerful assistance, they got the bridge up without difficulty, and then the work stopped; the funds were all spent.

July 6, at a town meeting, the report of the distinguished committee was accepted, and then, that the enterprise might go on, voted to finish the bridge at the town's expense. That the work might be done at reasonable rates, "Voted to let the finishing of the bridge to the lowest bidder," and Col. Clement having bid five pounds, it was struck off to him. There was some planking and considerable grading to be done, but before the summer was over the great work was complete.

But the building the bridge over Patch brook was a greater work than the one over the Asquamchumauke. A mighty freshet happened about these times; somebody said "a cloud broke on Moosehillock," the river overflowed its banks and spread out across all the intervals. Of course a portion of the river water ran down the valley of Patch brook, and the shrewd citizens thought a bridge would certainly be needed from high bank to high bank, and they proceeded to erect one immediately. It reached from the Forks school-house twenty rods away to the spot where the little bridge now spans the rill at the foot of the northern bank. Twenty pounds sterling the town appropriated March 18, 1790, to commence the work, and chose Joseph Patch, Stephen Richardson, Stevens Merrill, and Joshua Copp, a committee to lay it out.

It only made a beginning. Next year in meeting assembled the citizens enacted, after the manner of other great legislative bodies, that they would appropriate "as much of that money as was raised to lay out on the highways as will finish the bridge near Joseph Patch's house."

Then the work glowed and the mighty structure advanced; the money was all laid out. There came a halt, and the bridge was not finished. The year 1792 came. Not a drop of river water had flowed down Patch brook valley for three years. The warrant for the assembling of the democracy that year contained the following article:—"To see what method the town will take to finish the bridge."

At the meeting when the article came up to be acted upon, some shrewd citizen who was given to doubting suggested that he doubted very much if the bridge was needed at all; that he guessed the ground where the water did not run " was safer to travel upon than planks, and a mighty sight cheaper." He was heard by the assembled wisdom in silence, and the projectors of the long bridge looked grave and wise as owls. Some one suggested that the matter better be postponed to a future day, and thus it was disposed of. The half completed bridge stood all summer a silent monument of the great freshet and the sageness of men. Next year it is recorded that " Long Patch bridge " is yet unsettled for, but no action was taken in the matter. By some mishap, while the citizens were deliberating what to do with it, in the hot summer a spark of fire fell upon the work; the flames leaped up devouring sills, posts, stringers, and planks, and the noble work was gone forever.

Two short bridges were afterwards erected in its place which are continued to this day.*

And now, roads and bridges complete, travel through our hamlet much increased as was hinted before, and the business of taverning grew to be the best in town. Lemuel Keezer,† who lived on the southern border, immediately opened a hotel and kept it for a long time. Stevens Merrill had accommodations for man and beast; his son, Joseph Merrill, opened a hostelrie on the plain

---

*The river flowed under Patch brook bridge again in 1858; also in 1866 and in 1869.

† LEMUEL KEEZER'S tavern sign had a dove painted on one side and a serpent on the other. When asked why he had such a sign, he replied that it represented himself; that sometimes he was a serpent, but more often he was a heavenly dove.

Keezer was a most remarkable man, and very keen withal, as our readers will learn in a subsequent part of this history. He once had two of his relatives stop with him over night. They had a gay time, and when they harnessed up in the morning they thanked him for his hospitality, but he never minded them and said we will settle the bills at the bar, gentlemen. They were surprised and said they thought they were cousins. Keezer's eyes twinkled, and he said just pay the money, gentlemen, and then we will be cousins.

Keezer set scythes in his orchard to cut the boys who stole his fruit. One Amos Clark, a cunning youth, found " the man trap " on a moon-shiny night, and drove it to the heel into the ground, Keezer piously forgave the trespasser, and spent two hours digging the scythe out.

Keezer hired Peter Martin and Albert Hogan to fall trees for him. He took Martin aside, gave him a bottle of rum, and told him Hogan was going to sweat him. Then he took Hogan aside, gave him a bottle of rum and told him the same story. Martin mistrusted, but Hogan put in terribly all the forenoon. In the afternoon Martin explained Keezer's little game, and then the men drank their rum together, and had a sweet time, much to the landlord's delight.

where the common is now; Jonathan Clement kept an inn at Runaway pond; Obadiah Clement continued in the same business just above him, and Col. Tarleton kept an excellent house high up on the western marche by the shore of Tarleton lake. These taverns flourished wonderfully, and the proprietors all arrived at considerable wealth. The landlords had comely daughters for waiting maids; strong armed sons to attend the great ox teams that stopped to bait or rest over night, or to groom the saddle horses of gentlemen who patronized them.

Then the bar-room, furnished with the best of drinks, milk-toddy and egg-nog, and numerous other kinds, with its great wood fire and loggerhead at white heat, was an excellent loafing place for the nearest neighbors. They assembled here to learn the news from travellers, hear the gossip of the country round and discuss politics. The Merrill party and the Clement party had each hotels of their own, and there they held their caucuses.

These inns of those old days were good ones, the table was always well set, the cream the sweetest and richest, the butter and eggs always fresh, vegetables and everything else nice, clean white beds, snowy linen sheets, well swept floors, all was bright and neat as strong hands could make it.*

With good roads, bridges, and hotels, population began to increase, and a hundred clearings shone bright in the woods. Beech hill, Height-o'-land, the Summit and East-parte, were alive with settlers.

Better mills were other most important requisites, wanted to accommodate the inhabitants. And Moses H. Clement, son of Col. Obadiah, bought out Stevens Merrill and William Butler, and moved the grist-mill where the sons of Joshua Copp long had tended, up to the mouth of Black brook where Stevens Merrill first built a dam. He also had a saw-mill, and afterwards put in a wool carding machine. That he might have a good supply of water, by leave of the town he cut a canal from Baker river to Black brook, and built a stone dam across the former stream. His canal went under the highway just at the railroad crossing above the depot.

---

* Some of the teamsters, especially the Scotch from Vt., would carry their own victuals and drink, and eat by the bar-room fire, much to the disgust of the landlord.

The new comers wanted town affairs well conducted; they considered it a great requisite. So they bought new town books, Ephraim True purchasing some for the selectmen, paying therefor five pounds and two shillings; and Obadiah Clement bought a town clerk's book in which he made the first records. He gave for it two pounds ten shillings " lawful money."

Then that justice might be done and no mistake, they purchased a " law book " as a legal requisite. Horrid thing, many a defeated client has said after having become satisfied that a little law, as well as a little learning, is a dangerous thing.

Out of the law book and from ancient tradition, common law, they learned that for troublesome estrays and trespassing cattle, a Pound was an excellent institution, a very requisite thing; and straightway they went to work to obtain one. For the first few years they used the best barn yards of the settlers, voting to have it first in one and then in another, until at last they were tired of that style and were determined to build a real genuine Pound. And first a plan was necessary, and an admirable one was soon furnished. It is included in the following "enactment" of the democracy. "Voted to build a Pound on the '*Parade*' near Joseph Merrill's inn, of good suitable pine logs locked together, thirty feet square within walls, eight feet high, the upper logs hewed triangular, underpined with stone six inches high, with a good, suitable door, hanging with iron hinges with a staple, hasp, and padlock, and furnished to the *exception* of the selectmen." Said Pound was bid off to Joseph E. Marston, at $19.50. But strange to say, it was never built. The whole thing flashed in the pan, and in despite of good intentions, law-book and all, the citizens have gone on as they begun, using somebody's barn-yard for a Pound every year since.

That every body might be honest, and that there might be no cheating in weights and measures, which by the way is the meanest kind of cheating, our little State among the hills, deeming it necessary to make a perfect State, voted to purchase a standard of weights and measures, a very necessary requisite. We are accurately informed that one dollar and twenty cents was paid for the measures, and thirty dollars for the weights.

Also that the roads might be well cleaned out, paid one dollar

ARRIVAL OF A YOUNG PAUPER. 351

and fifty cents for a set of drills. With these a little blasting was frequently done.

Then for the sake of some heraldry, pomp, and ceremony, a stamp, seal, or device, was procured as an absolute and grand requisite for the good of the State. But it was as plain as Democratic institutions generally are, a simple W^n With this, every thing belonging to the town should be accurately marked as well as known; besides, the sealer of weights and measures should stamp it upon every thing he inspected, that people might know they were exactly correct, and that he had done his duty.

In the town were some gamesome fellows, as we have often hinted in these interesting pages, and in our most historic times they were greatly afraid that all the game would be destroyed. So that they might enjoy the pleasure of hunting in after years the same as formerly, they deemed it an absolute requisite to choose in 1791 Joseph Patch and Jonathan Clement "deer keepers."*

Tradition has it that for long years they did their duty faithfully, keeping the game all to themselves, and outside hunters far away from the goodly land of Warren.

With the abundance of inhabitants came some who were wretchedly poor. But the first pauper in Warren was not a very aged person. Every body said this was not a requisite to make a perfect community; that it was very unnecessary; but they could not help themselves. In fact a certain young, marriageable damsel, worshiping the goddess of love, without the aid of a shower of gold, or the machinations of a river god, all of a sudden saw fit to enrich the world with a bantling, whom no fast young man was willing to father. It created an immense sight of talk all over town. The knowing young folks tittered when they heard of it; the old ones looked grave and indignant. "Who is the father of it? Who will support it? What will become of it?" Such were the remarks heard every day.

The child was born; the mother called on the town for help.

---

* *Deer Keepers.*—By an act of 14th of George II., it is enacted that no deer shall be killed from the last day of December to the first day of August, annually, under the penalty of ten pounds; and in case of inability to pay, to work forty days for the first offence, and fifty days for subsequent offences. Any venison or skin newly killed was evidence of guilt.

In 1758, towns were authorized or required to choose two suitable persons

"What in the world shall we do?" said the selectmen. "Call a town meeting," said 'Squire Jonathan Merrill; and one was called to consider this momentous subject.

The following articles were in the warrant for the meeting, posted up Nov. 10, 1788, at Jonathan Clement's inn:—

"*Secondly*, to see what measures shall be taken for the maintainance of the child which is cast on the town's charge."

"*Thirdly*, to see what measures best to be taken to prevent others from being chargeable to said town."

At the meeting the subject was gravely discussed by the elderly gentlemen present, much to the delight of Moses True and a few other young bucks, and then they voted to choose a committee to see whose right it is to support the child which is become a town charge. This was followed by the following extraordinary vote, viz:—"Voted that William Butler, Stevens Merrill, and Master Nathaniel Knight, (he was a school master,) for a committee to take care of the child above mentioned till they *peruse the law* and make a return to the town — at the adjournment of this meeting — whose right it is to support the child."

The committee did "peruse the law," and at the adjourned meeting reported that after enquiry found the grand-parents' right to support the child.

Then there was a pause. 'Squire Joshua Copp took the floor and after a few grave and pertinent remarks moved that the whole matter be postponed fourteen days, and it was postponed. Whether or not it was ever taken up again, or what became of "the stray child pauper," neither record nor tradition has told us.

But certain it is that nearly two years after, the following action was taken that may throw some light on the matter. March 18, 1790.—"Voted to allow Constable Whitcher's account for conveying Dorathy Clifford through town, which is £0-18-10, five shillings of which sum to Mr. Jonathan Clement for expense at his house, and four shillings and two pence to Ensign Moses Copp for his trouble with said Dorathy Clifford."

Oh! the charming fair young Dorathy! How grand you must

---

annually, whose peculiar office it shall be to prevent as much as may be the breach of this act. They shall have full power of search, and may break locks or doors of any place where they may suspect game is concealed.—History of Chester, 448.

have felt, being conveyed "thro' town" by Constable Whitcher! Who was there to see! Did you, peerless one, ride on a gaily caparisoned charger, or were you conveyed in a lordly, dignified ox cart, the only vehicle in the hamlet? This latter fact has also passed from the memory of man.

But the citizens of Warren were not to be served in this manner again. They acted upon the third article in the warrant. At the first meeting they voted to warn out — which was the fashion in those days — such persons as appear liable to become a town charge, and that there might be no danger voted to warn out Reuben Whitcher if he appears likely to become an inhabitant. At the adjourned meeting, "Voted to warn out the widow Mills' two children, now resident at Ensign Moses Copp's."

This had an admirable effect for several years; but in process of time another pauper came, and poor Betty Whittier had to be maintained by the young democracy. Mr. Enoch Davis, who lived by Davis brook, in the East-parte regions, influenced by the nice little sum of one hundred and thirty silver dollars, generously took her home, and gave his bond to the selectmen to maintain her as long as she lived.*

Warren as an independent State has ever treated her poor in the kindest manner, getting the best of homes for them by humanely setting them up at auction, and striking them off to any one that would keep them cheapest, and at the least expense to the town.

That they might not seem barbarous and heathen, they felt that one of the solemn requisites of civilized life was a proper observance of the forms of paying respect to the dead. That their funerals might be conducted with the highest degree of propriety, they determined in a public assembly of the citizens to purchase a pall or grave cloth.

The rulers of the town were entrusted with the duty of obtaining it. They procured a very nice one for sixteen dollars and fifty cents, silver money.† Obadiah Clement, ever public spirited,

---

* 1805.—"Voted to choose a committee of two persons to settle with Mrs. Stone [widow Joshua Copp,] about the maintainance of Betsey Whittier, or prosecute as they shall think best for the town. Chose Dr. Ezra Bartlett and Lieut. Abel Merrill for the above committee."—Town Clerk's Records, Vol. i. 167.

† March 17, 1803.—"N. B. John Abbott is not to be taxed for said pall."—Town Clerk's Records, Vol. i. 134.

with the aid of his brother Jonathan, had anticipated the action of the people by buying a small burying cloth or pall for their friends and neighbors, and the next year the town purchased theirs also, at an expense of five dollars. For several years these emblems of funereal pageantry were kept at the inn of Mr. Joseph Merrill.

But that the pall might not often be wanted, and funerals be rare, the good citizens of Warren thinking it of the greatest necessity, induced Dr. Joseph Peters, a relative of Captain Absalom Peters, to move into town and have a care after the physical health of the people. Warren's first physician came to town in 1791, and took up his residence with Mr. Stevens Merrill. He was a well educated man, of genial temperament, and was much beloved by almost every body, particularly the women. But being also of a roving disposition he did not abide long in the valley among the hills. Whence came Dr. Peters the Lord only knows ; where he went, the men said, " perhaps the d—l can tell."

He was succeeded by Dr. Levi Root, another eminent practitioner, who remained in town about three years, from 1795 to 1798.

Then Dr. Ezra Bartlett* came, and being a college bred young gentleman, of great promise as a physician, and withal a son of Dr. Josiah Bartlett, one of the old proprietors, a signer of the Declaration of Independence, and a member of the Continental Congress, he easily rooted out Dr. Root, and had the whole township, with all the country round, as a field for practice. He settled on the fertile uplands of Beech hill, just to the southward of Amos Little.

---

*FAMILY RECORD OF EZRA AND HANNAH (Gale) BARTLETT.

Laura, born Oct. 20, 1799, at Warren.
Josiah, born Oct. 25, 1801. Died Sept. 25, 1802.
Josiah, born May 3, 1803.

Hannah, born Jan. 7, 1805.
Levi, born Oct. 4, 1806.
Mary, born Aug. 22, 1808.
Sarah, born Apr. 23, 1810.

New voters in 1796 :—
  Nathan Barker.
  James Harran.
  Olney Hawkins.

Joseph Jones.
William Kelley.
Dr. Levi Root.

John Weeks.

New voters in 1797 :—
  Benjamin Kelley.

Jesse Niles.

Joseph Orn.

New voters in 1798 :—
  Dr. Ezra Bartlett.
  James Dow.

Asa Low.

Abial Smith.

New voters in 1799 :—
  Benjamin Brown.

Benjamin Gale.

James Williams.

New voters in 1800.
  Daniel Davis.
  Job Eaton.

Samuel Jackson.
Luke Libbey.

Jacob Low.
Abel Willard.

Dr. Ezra Bartlett was a distinguished man in his day, often representing the towns of Warren and Coventry in the Legislature. He was a side justice in the Court of Common Pleas, a Senator in the New Hampshire Senate, and a member of the Governor's council. No man for fifty miles away could compete with him as a physician, and he was an excellent surgeon, as well. The children loved him, but they looked upon his house with a sort of dread, for they had heard the strange story how he had the body of Josiah Burnham, who was hung at Haverhill jail, there preserved in alcohol in a glass case. It was said by the knowing ones that he bargained with Burnham for his body, giving him for it all the liquor he could drink before the day of execution. Be that as it may, Dr. Bartlett always had medical students, for he had excellent facilities for study, and some of them afterwards ranked high in professional life. Two of them, Dr. Thomas Whipple and Dr. Robert Burns, were members of Congress. the first holding the office for eight years.

The doctor gave a mighty impetus to town affairs, showing what were the necessary requisites for a perfect democratic community; the roads were better; the schools were better, the farms were better; and he set a good example by building a nice house for himself, after which every man in town aspired to pattern. So much was he admired that many children born at this period were called Ezra Bartlett.

Dr. Bartlett also considered that it was one of the much desired requisites that there should be no boundary feuds among the good citizens of Warren, and perplexing lawsuits arising therefrom. That they might not be harrassed with these evils, he determined that the bounds should be well kept up, and shrewdly went to work to accomplish it, and obtain a plan of lots for the town. The proprietors, as already related, had one. How much good a man of refined tastes and education can do in any community. He quietly went to work and got an article inserted in the warrant for town meeting, to see what the citizens would do about procuring a plan. At the annual assembly of the people it was determined to elect a committee to provide one, and chose Joseph Patch, Nathaniel Clough, and Samuel Knight for that purpose.

Under his guidance they immediately went to work and obtained copies of all the old surveys and plans, (particularly that of Josiah Burnham,) which were so admirably made during the time of the old proprietors' boundary war. With this material for a basis, Dr. Bartlett lent himself to the task, and produced the beautiful and excellent plan of Warren that now stands as the frontispiece in the Proprietors' Records. He worked a week making it, and then,— what do you think!— he only charged the town one dollar for his services. Cheap enough most people would say; but then some grumbled about it even at that, as is always the case. The committee received twenty-eight dollars and thirty-eight cents for their services.

To accomplish all these necessary requisites and make Warren a flourishing democracy, required money, and as we have gently intimated, the town contrived each year to raise a fair amount, easily from the most, by process from a few.

Sometimes it was paid with paper bills, the old continental currency, once or twice in new emission money — a sort of promissory notes founded on real estate and loaned on interest; but these run down and became worthless sooner than the old continental currency,— and frequently in *produce;* the citizens in the selectmenship of Joshua Copp, Ephraim True, and Nathaniel Knight, voting that the town charges be paid in wheat at *five*, rye at *four*, and corn at *three* shillings per bushel. The selectmen were likewise paid in this way for their services, and it was the commonest of things to purchase their English and West India goods, by bartering their produce.

For the first three years of the town organization taxes were reckoned in depreciated currency, raising £500 in 1781, then they were computed on a specie basis, assessing in 1782 but £4 1-2 silver money, to pay town charges, and in 1797 taxes were made up in dollars and cents.*

Simeon Smith was the first collector, as we have said before, and then they had a different one almost every year, and all conducted in the most faithful manner. But Daniel Patch did not do quite so well. He was fond of fine clothes and fast horses, and

---

* Aug. 25, 1794.—"Voted to let the certificate money lay on interest, unless it will turn for fourteen or fifteen shillings in specie on the pound."—Town Clerk's Records, Vol. i. 58.

when he got the town's money he was not very careful to keep it separate from his own. When pay-day came he found himself in hot water. He tried to borrow and could not; he was afraid they would call on his bondsmen; that his own property would be attached; that he would be indicted by the grand jury and mulcted in damages or imprisoned.

He did not want any of these things to happen; but he could not see how to escape. The days went by and the clouds were thickening, and the storm howled in his political sky.

There was but one way; he must fly before the sarcasm, the jeers, the maledictions, anathemas, and curses — the people's whirlwind.

At the winter's sunset, Patch harnessed his team. "He drives two thin-maned, high-headed, strong-hoofed, fleet-bounding horses of our hills. Harnessed to the sleigh, they champ the iron bits, and the tight checks bend on their arching necks. They fly like the wreaths of mist over the streamy vale. The wildness of deer was in their course; the strength of eagles descending on their prey." A day — and they are a hundred miles away.

A long time afterwards the citizens learned that Daniel Patch was seen late the next afternoon driving through the streets of old Haverhill, Mass. That was all the tidings of him.

But his bondsmen had to pay up, much to their great delight, what the faithful collector had spent, and then they levied on his goods and chattels, and got their own pay. After this, Mr. P.'s friends settled up the whole affair, and he returned, paid every dollar like an honest man, and became one of the best of citizens.*

Such things never come single, and Abel Willard, another collector, following the above illustrious example, absconded with the town's money. He went to the west of the Green mountains, and the town did not succeed in getting it back from him quite so well as from Daniel Patch.

That there might be tranquility with all the world without,

---

* Daniel Patch was a man of fine intellect, was agreeable in conversation, though somewhat given to metaphysics.

DANIEL AND BETSEY (*Hall*) PATCH'S FAMILY RECORD.

Joseph, H. born May 27, 1809.
Daniel, B. born Jan. 20, 1812.
Betsey, W. born Jan. 29, 1816.
Mahala, born Aug. 23, 1817.
Louisa M. born Nov. 15 1819.
Marinda F. born June 8, 1822.
William D. Mc. Q. born March 31, 1825.

and peace within our mountain hamlet, our young democracy took a lively interest in political affairs. They voted for Gen. Washington for President, for members of Congress, and all the other foreign officers, helping to maintain a republic without as well as a democracy at home.

But that which interested them most, creating profound discussions and calling for the exercise of the discreetest statesmanship, was the adoption of, first, the articles of confederation, then of the Federal Constitution, and frequently afterwards of whether or not it should be amended.

Warren's citizens, on mature deliberation of these momentous subjects, generally voted nearly unanimously either one way or the other, always believing that the destiny of the whole country hung upon their action. They were thus called upon to save their country some twenty times in the course of a few years.

But we cannot close the final chapter of this book, and let down the curtain upon the last years of the eighteenth century, without recording as a faithful historian what our good citizens of Warren thought to be the highest and grandest REQUISITE to make a perfect democratic community.

They early made great efforts to accomplish it. In the selectmenship of Jonathan Merrill, Thomas Boynton, and Aaron Welch, they chose a committee consisting of Joshua Copp, Reuben Batchelder, Joseph Patch, Thomas Boynton, and John Whitcher, to report where it would be convenient to set a meeting house, and what measures were best to be taken to erect the same and procure the preaching of the gospel. But the committee, living in different parts of the town, could not exactly agree where the best place was. It took them so long to find a spot that they spent all their energies upon that part of the subject, and the whole thing fell through.

But such a subject could not slumber long, and as a result of deep thought, 'Squire Joshua Copp, in March, 1798, made a liberal proposition to the town. The citizens were much pleased, and voted to accept a piece of land from him, situated on the easterly side of his farm, and on the north side of the highway leading to Haverhill, for the purpose of erecting a meeting-house thereon, which was to be of the same size as the one in the neighboring province of Romney, and for a burying ground and training field.*

Chose Joshua Copp, Esq., Joseph Patch, Stephen Richardson, Obadiah Clement, and Levi Lufkin, a committee to provide timber for the meeting-house, to be drawn the ensuing winter. Each individual was to pay for the house according to his proportion of taxes, and all should hold themselves ready to work on the building after three days' notice from the committee.

And now the very town sweat with the work *in prospectu*. What a splendid house we shall have; soon it will be all complete.

But too many cooks spoil the broth. Things did not go on any better this time than before. There was a hitch. The committee did not work well together. Another town assembly was called. The citizens assembled. A great discussion arose. It waxed warm. The meeting broke up, nothing was done save to dismiss the subject, and the fire of religious enthusiasm seemed to go out.

But it did not; it only slumbered. How it kindled afresh and burned with a steady flame until all were tried and purified, or ought to have been, and the mighty work accomplished, we will show in the first chapters of our next great book.

---

* This was the same spot where the first little training was held.

OUR GRANDMOTHERS' PASTIME.

BOOK VI.

IN WHICH THE MIGHTY MARCH MENTIONED AT THE BEGINNING OF BOOK V. IS CONTINUED.

CHAPTER I.

HOW SEVERAL RELIGIONS CAME TO WARREN, OF TYTHINGMEN WHO FINED MEN FOR TRAVELING SUNDAY, THEREBY MAKING THEM EXCEEDINGLY HAPPY, CONCLUDING WITH AN ACCOUNT OF A CAMP-MEETING WHERE SEVERAL PIOUS YOUTH SOUNDED A HORN IN THE NIGHT, AND DISTURBED THE SLUMBERS OF THE GODLY.

ANOTHER century has come. One generation of white men, the Indians' successors in the Asquamchumauke valley, has passed away. A second is stepping upon the stage. Many things are being left behind, and new fashions and ideas are making their way to our settlement among the hills. A different pattern of dress has been adopted, the style of cooking and living has somewhat changed, new houses have been constructed, and the blazed path, bridle path and tote road have given place to the broad, beaten way, as we wrote in the last book, upon which rumble the wheels of Obadiah Clement's little Dutch vehicle, the first four wheeled wagon that had ever come to town.

Something else is coming. We hinted at it in the last chapter. It is told as follows:—

One day in July, 1799, a solitary horseman was seen riding up the road. He stopped at Joseph Merrill's inn, baited his horse, and while he was eating his own dinner casually dropped a few words upon religious matters. They seemed to make but little impression, and saying something about stony ground and hardness of heart, he rode away over Pine hill to the Summit. That horseman was the Rev. Elijah R. Sabin, a missionary of Methodism. Hundreds of them were riding the country through, preaching in the houses, the barns, in the forests or out in the broad open air, anywhere they could get a congregation to hear them, bringing new religious ideas to the people.

That night he stopped with Mr. Chase Whitcher by the wild roistering Oliverian. The morrow was the Sabbath, and after the morning meal a meeting was suggested. Mr. Whitcher was pleased with the idea. A messenger went to the settlers on Pine hill; down on old Coventry meadows, and to Mr. Eastman's, the first settler of High street.

By ten o'clock, quite a congregation had assembled, and under the maples — they grow there now — by the laughing stream, the first religious meeting was held on the Summit. They had no choir; but the reverend man sang in clear sweet voice, one of those wild revival hymns of John Wesley, which were then waking men's souls through all the land.* His discourse took powerful hold on his little congregation, and before he left this valley, hollowed between five peaks of the mountains, he had laid the foundation for a society, and formed a class consisting of three members — Chase Whitcher, Dolly Whitcher, afterwards the widow Atwell, and Sarah Barker. When he was gone his words were not forgotten. Many believed his doctrine was true and before the year passed more than thirty persons had joined the class.

Out of this mountain valley, over the hills, spread the religious enthusiasm, great numbers getting converted. It even went

---

* *Singing.*—The singing of the early Methodists was glorious, heavenly. Then the music was adapted to the words, and every word could be distinctly understood, and the ideas came home to the listener with spiritual power. Now-days the words are stretched and strained to fit the music; not one of them can be understood; the ideas are lost, and the whole, as a general thing, is a senseless jargon painful to hear.

"BEHOLD A MIRACLE." 363

over the Height-o'-land, and a large class was formed in Charleston, near Tarleton lake. So firmly was Methodism planted that it has survived in Warren three-fourths of a century.

During the summer season for many years the Methodist meetings were held in a barn belonging to Mr. Aaron Welch, and in the winter in his house or in the houses of the neighbors in the immediate vicinity.*

It was at Aaron Welch's† barn people loved to assemble; not to show their fine clothes so much as now, for they then dressed in homespun, but the most to worship. Sometimes the boys went to see the girls; but the girls never to see boys. A few went for fun, and a very few for mischief. One time they had a quarterly meeting there. Old John Broadhead, a powerful preacher, and Rev. Messrs. Felch and Hedding were present. Rev. Mr. Felch was preaching; somebody had been "cutting up shines," and Mr. F. was mad. He began telling how mean the people were, how some were fornicators, and some thieves and drunkards, and how one was so mean as to even steal the snapper of his, the reverend's whip. Capt. Wm. Butler immediately interrupted and said, "he wanted to hear him preach, and not blackguard." Another man sarcastically remarked that " he, Felch, no business to be a horse-jockey, and have a fine whip, if he didn't want the snapper stolen,"— a mean remark, as all good christians can testify. At any rate Rev. Mr. Felch heeded Capt. Butler, immediately changed the subject of his discourse, and preached Christ and him crucified, with such excellent effect that several were converted that very

---

*The Devil's Doings.—One winter they had preaching in Deacon Welch's house. Quite a lot of folks were sitting on the trap-door, and they got to shouting, Glory! Hallelujah! Amen! Good! Just then the Devil broke the trap-door, and half a dozen men and women fell into the cellar. Mrs. Samuel Knight went into a fit, and several of the sisters rolled on the floor in the most wonderful manner. Some wicked youth present smiled, the Devil was pleased, and the minister preached no more that day.—Miss Hannah Knight's statement.

A Miracle.—There was a meeting at farmer Joshua Merrill's in the early times, and Mr. Isaac Merrill, son of 'Squire Jonathan, crawled up the stairs and sat over the heads of some of the congregation. The preaching was so powerful he got to sleep, and while dozing lost his balance and fell down amongst the people. He struck plump on his head, his feet in the air; then in about a minute he pitched over, jumped up quickly and ran out of the house uninjured, all the folks following him. Every one believed it was a miracle, and so great was the awe that they had no more preaching till next Sunday, when a new and more powerful minister arrived in the settlement.—Miss H. Knight's statement.

† Mr. Welch lived near the present village cemetery, where Mr. Samuel Merrill, Capt. Joseph Merrill, and Robert E. Merrill, have all lived. Said house was once occupied by the town's poor.

day. Ministers of the present time would do well to imitate — preach religion rather than politics — and seek to plant more of a christian spirit in the community.

But there were some who would not join the Methodists. Opposition is a good thing for any enterprise, if there is not too much of it. Certainly it helps a church along and always exists where men are left free to think for themselves. We almost believe opposition is a divine institution, and Stevens Merrill, the man who did not believe in the revolutionary war, was now the person to exercise it in Warren. He was a Quaker, and had no faith in those whining, canting Methodists, as he impiously termed them. He "shouldn't jine no how!" But still he loved preaching when it suited him, which was not often the case. He was blunter than Capt. Butler. "You lie, Nat!" "What is the use of your lying that way?" were exclamations that once greeted his own brother, Nathaniel, a Congregationalist, who was preaching to the people that had assembled in the bar-room and kitchen of Mr. Merrill's tavern. The Rev. Nathaniel was as determined as his brother, and such exclamations did not disturb him.

In the year 1802 a minister came to town of a different faith, and by chance he stopped at Stevens Merrill's. He was a missionary of a new religious order; the Free-will Baptists, one of the products of the western world. Sunday following, he preached in the house of his host, to the great delight of Mr. M. He was highly pleased with Mr. Boody and his doctrine, and as he was an aged man, and thinking he might die when Mr. Boody was far away, he resolved to have his funeral sermon preached before Mr. B.'s departure. Accordingly he signified his intention to the Rev. gentleman, who, complying, a day was appointed, and the sermon preached from 2 Timothy, 4th chapter, 6th, 7th, 8th verses: "For I am now ready to be offered, and the time of my departure is at hand. I have fought a good fight, I have finished my course, I have kept the faith; henceforth there is laid up for me a crown of righteousness, which the Lord, the righteous judge, shall give me at that day; and not me only, but unto all them that love his appearing." From this text it is said the Rev. Mr. Boody preached an excellent discourse, and Mr. Merrill and his friends were well pleased. It is handed down that Mr. M. smacked his lips with delight several times as the reverend gentleman drew a vivid picture of his host entering the portals of heaven and taking a seat among the blest, and after the services were over, as they did not have any corpse or coffin, he treated his minister and the whole congregation to the very best his house afforded, not even omitting to furnish good flip, punch, and egg-nog; a generous custom in those days, which laid many a man low. Mr. Merrill died two years after, in 1804, aged seventy-seven years.*

No religious society of the Free-will Baptist order was formed at this time; but Rev. Joseph Boody and other ministers of like faith continued to visit Warren, and about 1810 a society was organized under the charge of Rev. James Spencer. The first members consisted of Samuel Merrill and wife, of the East-parte, James Dow and wife, Caleb Homan and wife, Aaron Welch and wife, True Stevens and wife, Mrs Betsey Ramsey, and Mrs. James Williams. Elder Spencer labored with the society for many years.

And now religious enthusiasm filled the town and all the regions round about. Stricter laws were passed for the observance of the Sabbath, and tythingment were appointed in almost every hamlet to compel the people to keep the Sabbath holy. Many were the instances when pious hands were laid upon wicked travelers. Old Deacon Jonathan Clement had been traveling down country; returning, the tythingman of Boscawen arrested him traveling on the Sabbath, and fined him Monday morning, costs

---

* James Dow and Samuel Merrill, both heard Stevens Merrill's funeral discourse.

† By an act passed in 1715, it was enacted that no taverner or retailer should suffer any apprentice, servant or negro, to drink in his house; nor any inhabitant after ten o'clock at night, nor more than two hours; nor suffer any person to drink to drunkenness, nor others than strangers to remain in his house on the Lord's day; under a fine of five shillings.

The second section provided that the selectmen should see that at least two tythingmen should be annually chosen, whose duty it was to inspect all licensed houses, and inform of all disorders to a justice of the peace, and also inform of all who sell without license, and of all cursers and swearers. Each tythingman was to have a black staff two feet long, with about three inches of one end tipped with brass or pewter, as a badge of office. The penalty for not serving when chosen was forty shillings, and in default of payment or want of property was imprisonment.

By an act passed Dec. 24, 1799, for the better observance of the Lord's day, and repealing all other acts for that purpose, all labor and recreation, traveling, and rudeness at places of public worship on the Lord's day, are forbidden. Taverners are forbidden to entertain inhabitants of the town. The tythingmen had power to command assistance, and forcibly stop and detain all travelers, unless they could give sufficient reason. The tythingmen were required to inform of all breaches of the act, and their oath was sufficient evidence unless invalidated.—History of Chester, 450.

and all, eleven dollars. He came home with religious enthusiasm tingling on every nerve of his body. Some maliciously said he was madder than a March hare. James Dow, then a young and vigorous man, for many years was chosen tythingman of Warren. Old Mr. Page, of Haverhill, was desecrating the Sabbath by driving his horse and wagon through the town, and said Dow gently laid his hand upon him and stopped, seized, and detained him, and prevented him from traveling, as aforesaid. Monday, Page was fined, and he went home feeling complete.

John Varnum was chosen to this high office, and he arrested some Scotchmen, teamsters from Vermont, and had them fined, and then all the tavern keepers were mad, for it hurt their business to have travelers thus waylaid. Tavern keepers with nice bars had influence, and henceforth only those who lived in the most remote parts of the town, were chosen "grab-men," as they were facetiously termed.

One year "Old Potter," who lived by the road leading to Wachipauka pond, was chosen; but the town clerk, Mr. Anson Merrill, tried to cheat him out of his high honor, by neglecting to make a record of his election. Many men were indignant on account of Merrill's official malfeasance.*

With two rival societies in the full tide of success, and the tythingmen well preserving the peace, meetings without number were held. In Merrie England, and on the low lands of Holland, and along the banks of the Rhine, it had been the practice for centuries to hold meetings in the suburbs of old cities, by neglected grave-yards and among shady mountains. This practice must needs be revived in America, and the Methodist brethren established "Camp-meetings." One must be held in Warren, and the pleasant pine woods near Pine hill school-house was selected for the occasion. Inspiring woods! They thought they could worship better there. There, Adam and Eve enjoyed their pastime and sought repose; there, the Amorites and Assyrians learned to pray; there, Hertha the Goddess of the Angles, had her lovely residence; there, the Druids thought everything sent from heaven that grew on the oak; there, Pan piped and satyrs danced; the

---

* Potter was for many years a town pauper, and Mr. Merrill only tried to prevent him from gaining a residence.

fawns browsed, Sylvanus loved, Diana hunted, and Feronia watched; there, the stately castle of the feudal lord reared its head, the lonely anchorite sang his evening hymn, and the sound of the convent bell was heard; there, Robin Hood and his merry men did their exploits, and King Rufus was slain; there, the ward of dryads, the scene of fairy revels and Puck's pranks, the haunt of witches, spirits, elves, hags, dwarfs, the Sporn, the man in the oak, the will-o'-the-wisp, the opera house of birds, and the shelter of beasts. The green, sweet-smelling, suggestive, musical, sombre, superstitious, devotional, mystic, tranquilizing woods, was the place of all others for the camp-meeting.

It was early in the cool September that it was held; delegations came from nearly every society in the whole conference, and white tents in good numbers sprang up beneath the pine trees. There were booths outside the circle of tents for the sale of candy, gingerbread, more substantial eatables, and withal, in sundry jugs, kegs, and spiggots, was a good deal of "the good creature," to keep out the cold from the hearts of the lukewarm, and to raise the spirits generally. On a smooth plat of ground were long rows of seats made of boards, plank, and slabs, placed on pins driven into the ground, for the congregation, and on a little knoll in front, was a raised platform, with a box around it, for a pulpit. Above this were the thick, dense branches of several large pine trees, which served as a canopy to keep off the sun and rain. At night, in front of the tents, great fires were kindled for cooking and to keep the worshipers warm.

More sinners than saints came to these meetings, and one of the great objects was to convert the ungodly class. The more converted, the greater the success of the meeting. In the morning came early prayer-meeting, then breakfast, then two sermons in the forenoon, dinner, two sermons in the afternoon, supper, then evening prayer meeting and to bed. Joseph Boynton led the singing. He sometimes gave out the tune, read two lines, the choir and congregation sung them, then two lines more were deaconed off, and so on through the hymn. Sometimes the choir sung by itself. Boynton, who was class leader for many years, a great man in the church, and lived on the turnpike, first house up the hill beyond the Cold brook, had a pitch-pipe made of wood, an inch or two wide, something like a boy's whistle, with which he pitched the tunes, much to the delight of all who heard. The presiding elder summoned the brethren to each exercise by a loud blast on an old fashioned tin horn. One night some " wicked " youth, among whom, it is said, though we do not vouch for it, were Robert Burns, Thomas Whipple, Nathan Clifford, Joshua Merrill, Anson Merrill, and Jacob Patch, besides numerous others, stole the horn and went sounding it through all the woods, first on the north, then on the south, then east, then west, while for long hours the presiding elder, several ministers and a whole host of deacons went chasing through the forest, trying to find the vile thieves, as they piously termed them, who were disturbing the slumbers of the godly. But they did not catch them.

One day elder John Broadhead had preached. He was a powerful man of more than ordinary eloquence. Then there was a call to come forward for prayers. The choir sang one of their sweetest hymns, then paused. Just at that instant a flock of blackcap titmice with their white sides glowing in the sun, alighted in the green pines overhead, and appearing to take up the strain, sang so sweetly that they seemed bright messengers from heaven. The electric current was complete, excitement filled every breast. Glory to God! said elder Broadhead. Amen! shouted the whole congregation. The hymn was taken up again, and when it ceased a hundred rose for prayers. And then there was praying and shouting, and singing, such as never was heard in the woods of Warren before. One young female was so wrought upon that she fell down and rolled upon the ground, kicking up her heels towards the blue sky. Some said she was in a trance seeing

---

Accident.—Lemuel Keezer, innkeeper. went to this first camp-meeting on horseback. When he had nearly got there, his horse threw him off and hurt his shoulder badly. At the meeting, one of the ministers asked Keezer if he wanted to see God, and he only answered that his shoulder pained him badly. The minister repeated the question the second and third time, and got precisely the same answer; but when he put the question the fourth time, Keezer got mad and very imprudently and impiously replied that he " didn't know the gentleman, and didn't care a d—m either."

One day Captain Daniel invited Elder Wood, a minister, to share the hospitalities of his house, and introduced him to Mr. Keezer. " Elder Wood, Elder Wood," exclaimed Mr. K., snuffing his nose, " that is the stinkingest wood I ever saw;" much to Captain Daniel's delight, for he was very pious and had great respect for his minister.

Keezer was gifted in prayer. When the minister put up with him, he would pray at night and the minister in the morning, or *vice versa*, and when the reverend was gone he would ask the women folks if he didn't beat the minister at praying? K. was proud of his gift and liked to be praised.

heaven; but young Dr. Whipple wickedly held hartshorn to her nose to her great delight, and quietly said she was only a little "hysterica."

Thus the meeting went on for a week, more than two hundred were converted, and when it broke up each went to his home thanking the Lord that he had prospered him so much. Several other camp-meetings have been held in Warren since, the last being in the young maple woods on the river island just east of the depot.

X

CHAPTER II.

OF GRAND HUNTINGS, FOWLINGS, AND FISHINGS, CONCLUDING WITH HOW A 'SQUIRE, A DOCTOR, AND A MINISTER, WERE PERFECTLY DELIGHTED TRYING TO CATCH EVERY FISH IN WACHIPAUKA POND.

THE learned Puffendorf says all animals were wild; Grotius says all were tame. Common law takes middle ground, and leaves it to the judgment to say what were wild and what were tame. Certain it is that all the animals, birds, and fishes of Warren were wild enough before the advent of the white settlers, and many were the exciting times had capturing and destroying them, as we have before remarked.

The most formidable of all these animals was the panther, otherwise called painter, and sometimes catamount, whose cry would make the Indians' blood feel cold; the wolf and bear came next, then the two wild cats known as the loup-cervier and the bay lynx. Of deer, as John Josselyn, Gent., would say, there was the stately moose, the caribou, — hard to catch, — and the common red deer. Others, and they are all interesting, are the raccoon, wolverine, otter, sable, mink, muskrat, fisher-cat ermine or weasel, black or silver-gray fox, red fox, beaver, hedgehog, woodchuck, gray, black, red, striped and flying squirrels, rabbit, rat, mouse, — several kinds — four varieties of mole, bat, and last and sweetest of all, the skunk.

The panther was a rare animal, only one ever having been killed in town, and that by Joseph Patch one night as he lay in his camp by Hurricane brook. Wolves were for years more plenty. Our first settler once started one in Stephen Richardson's field on Pine hill, and followed it down near Patch brook, where he killed it. Old 'Squire Burns, of Romney, caught the mate to it in a trap. This pair had killed many sheep.

But years before the town was settled, an adventure with the wolves took place in the East-parte regions of a far more startling kind. Long before the country was settled, a hunter by the name of Cushman was trapping upon one of the eastern mountains. One day, after being busily engaged in his labor, he entered his camp, and night had scarcely begun to come over him, when the melancholy howl of the wolves struck on his ear, the mournful echoes of which were repeated through every part of the forest. Every moment they seemed to approach nearer, and soon his camp was surrounded by a pack of the hungry creatures. Snatching his gun, he scrambled up a small sapling near by, just in time to save himself from their jaws. Being disappointed of their prey, they howled and leaped about in mad fury. Cushman now thought he would treat them with a little cold lead, and aiming at the leader of the pack, fired. The wolf gave a wild howl, and leaping several feet into the air, fell to the ground and was torn in pieces by his hungry companions. Loading his gun, he fired at another which shared the same fate. Again he fired and killed a third, when the wolves seeing their numbers decreasing, and having satisfied their appetites upon one of their own species, fled, and Cushman was no more annoyed by them that night. The mountain upon which this happened took the hunter's name, and is called Mt. Cushman to the present time.

Bears were more plenty than wolves, and for thirty years after the settlement of Warren, they were seen almost every day. Stephen Richardson had a fine flock of sheep, but he had to yard them every night. Yet this did not always save them. Once in early evening a large bear, known as "old white face," carried away two sheep, leaping with them over a wall five feet high. "Old white face" was the terror of the whole country and traveled up and down the valley oftener than any hunter or fisherman has ever done. John Gould, who lived in the East-parte, had been out to "the road," as it was called. Coming home in the early evening, at the mouth of Batchelder brook, in Sawtelle district, he thought he met this bear. He was terribly frightened, threw his little white dog at the ferocious creature, and with his teeth chattering, ran back to Mr. Samuel Knight's as fast as his legs would carry him. Here he stopped all night, slept on the floor by the fire, and in the morning in company with Mr. Knight, went to the spot. They found on the place where he said he saw the bear, only a great hemlock stump. Knight laughed at him; Gould felt exceedingly fine. But two days after, Knight and a man named Ramsey killed a bear, and Gould claimed that as the one he saw.

Daniel Patch, son of Joseph, had been down to deacon Stevens' blacksmith shop, on Red-oak hill, to get a three-year old colt shod. Coming back at evening down the hill, the bear called "old white face," jumped into the road behind him and gave chase. The colt scented him, pricked up his ears, and, frightened, ran. Young Daniel clung to the colt's mane and there was a wild race on Red-oak hill road. The steel shoes of the colt rang on the rocks, the sparks of fire flashed in the darkness and it was only when the boy passed Hurricane brook bridge and came into Warren's first clearing, that the bear gave up the chase. When Daniel Patch got home it was hard for the father to tell which was the most frightened, the boy or the colt.*

About this time occurred the last moose hunts in Warren. A Mr. Webster, who lived over the Height-o'-land, one autumn was out hunting for moose. He started one in Piermont, and followed him by Tarleton lake into Warren. Here he took an easterly course, evidently designing to cross over the lower ranges of mountains and make for Moosehillock. When he reached the summit of Webster slide the dogs came up with him and pressed him so hard that he took a southerly course upon the top of the mountain till he arrived upon the edge of the precipice. The dogs were close upon him, and as he turned they made the attack.

---

* *Bears.*—Mr. George Bixby once killed a bear on Beech hill, with a good stout cane. It had been an excellent season for berries of all kinds, and the bear was so fat that it could hardly walk.

A bear followed Mr. Samuel Knight and his wife as they were going home. There was a figure-four trap near where is now Levi F. Jewel's mill. The bear looked into it and got caught, Mr. K. and wife being not six rods away at the time.

Bears, more or less, are caught every year in Warren, even at the present time. The principal bear catchers now living in Warren are Joseph Whitcher, E. Bartlett Libby, Amos L. Merrill and Isaac Fifield.

It was a hard fight. As they leaped at him, the antlered monarch of the New England forest tossed one upon his horns, and when he fell it was over the precipice. Another dog caught the moose by the throat, and a third seized him on the flank. Round and round they went, the noble animal in vain trying to shake them off. They neared the very edge of the precipice. The rock on the brink was slippery, and the hoofs would not cling to it. Back! Back! A hoarse panting, a dire swinging to and fro, and then the rock was standing naked against the sky; no living thing was there, and moose and hounds lay shattered far below.

Webster followed to the edge of the precipice and saw the place of encounter. He was not long in determining the result, and half an hour later he found them all dead at the foot among the boulders and debris. From this circumstance the huge cliff rising sharp from Wachipauka pond received its name — Webster slide.*

Early in the spring of 1803 the last of these animals ever known in this section was killed. Joseph Patch's supply of moose beef had run short, and he tried his grown up sons, Joseph and Daniel, to go with him after more: but as they refused, he took his son Jacob, then about seventeen years old, who wanted to go. At the East-parte Stephen Flanders joined them, and the three on snow shoes, for the snow was four feet deep, proceeded through the forest, up the Asquamchumauke on the north bank. They crossed the Big brook near where the bridle-path up Moosehillock crosses it now, and half a mile beyond on the plain through which rushes Gorge brook, they found where moose had browsed. Following the trail they crossed the latter stream, now buried in snow, and Patch sent his son and Captain Flanders around the spur of the mountain† after more browse, and following on they all came together on the crest where they found "floats."

It was now late in the afternoon, and the little party stopped to consult. They were far in the woods, and young Jacob thought it was a lonesome place to spend the night. Looking about he saw rabbit tracks in the snow; he heard black-cap titmice sing "chick-

---

* Mr. George Libby says that the above story is not exactly correct, that Mr. Webster came very near falling down the mountain face himself, and afterwards gave a gallon of rum to have the mountain named for him.

† Sometimes called Black hill.

adee" in the leafless branches, the sweet note of the brown creeper, as spirally he climbed the huge trunks of the great spruces, and a hairy woodpecker rattling on an old dead hemlock. Just then a flock of pileated woodpeckers flew by, screaming as their scarlet red heads flashed over the snow, and then it was still for a moment.

From the appearance of the "floats," Joseph Patch knew that they were in the immediate vicinity of the moose, and for fear of frightening them they did not dare to build a camp nor light a fire. So they made a large bed of evergreen boughs, thick and warm, and when night came on, they wrapped their blankets about them and with their dogs lay down to sleep. Nice bed, beautiful place, and splendid night. What if it had happened to snow or a southern rain come on? But it did not, and the hunters lay on their sweet smelling couch, and listened to the wind singing through the leafless branches and the evergreens and saw the northern lights flash blue and red up to the zenith, pouring their crimson dyes upon the frozen snow. As the night wore away the north star looked down upon them, and Andromeda, Cassiopea, and the Great Bear, wheeling around the pole, shone bright through the crisp, frosty air. Jacob Patch said in his old age that he never enjoyed a night's rest better in his whole life than that one in the winter snow, and that he ate his breakfast from their almost frozen provisions with as keen a relish as he ever knew.

At the earliest dawn they started on the trail, keeping their dogs quiet behind them, and traveling two miles they found the moose in a large yard beside a little mountain stream. There were three of them, a bull, a cow and a calf. Patch shot the calf, Flanders fired at the bull and missed, when Patch fired again and killed him. The cow started off at a fast trot down Baker river. The dogs followed, a bull dog and a hound,* yelping, yelling, and baying, till the woods rang with echoes, and the men running after

---

* They used to have good dogs in those days. Esq. Abel Merrill once had a dog and a pup, and wanted to sell one of them. A man came to buy, and Abel said the old dog, Bose, was as good a dog as ever was in the world. Then said the man, I will take the puppy. "But, but," said 'Squire Abel, "the puppy is a little mite better."

"*Bose is the best dog in the world, but the puppy is a little mite better,*" was a byword in Warren for a long time after.—Anson Merrill's statement.

as fast as they could. A mile away, and the old moose turned to fight the dogs and Patch coming up first, shot her.

As they were dressing them, three other men, who by a singular coincidence were hunting in the valley, came up and claimed the moose. Patch was a little covetous, and as his neighborly hunters from over the mountain were exceedingly saucy, he would not give them a bit of the meat. But our hunter and Captain F. had to stay and watch their captured game while young Jacob went for sleds and help with which they brought home the product of their morning work. Thus perished the last of that race of animals in our mountain valley, so many of which at one time lived about Moosehillock mountain.

In old times it was a common thing for the best hunters to station themselves behind a tree or rock by Rocky falls on Patch brook or Waternomee falls on Hurricane brook. Then they would send men with their dogs sweeping across the sides of Mt. Carr to start wild animals, and often deer and moose would come flying down the beds of the streams, when the hunter in ambush would shoot them.

Chase Whitcher once got behind the great rock at the foot of Waternomee falls, and sent John Marston with a hound on to the mountain. The latter, on snow shoes, climbed up near the very top of Mt. Carr, and there started his game. But it was only for a moment that he saw it,— a giant deer, beautiful beyond anything he had ever seen before.

That deer was of the variety called the American Caribou,* the fiercest, fleetest, wildest, shyest, and most untameable of the deer tribe in the whole world, and are only shot by white hunters through casual good fortune. The hound bayed and followed; but it was a useless chase, for the Caribou's feet were like snow shoes, and he ran as no other animal could. One might as well think to pursue the hurricane as to follow him. He seemed like the ship of the winter wilderness outspeeding the winds among his native pines and firs.

Whitcher heard the baying of the hound far up the mountain.

---

* The Caribou averages from fourteen and a half to fifteen hands high, is taller than ordinary horses, and is more than a match for a wolf or a panther in a fight. (?)

then crouched close behind his rock. As he waited the sun shone out clear, lighting up the frosting of ice on the great rocks, and making the fantastic icicles hanging pendant on the birch and spruce to throw forth a thousand brilliant shades and hues, and to sparkle like gems.

Soon he heard the mighty beast flying down the bed of the torrent, and he involuntarily cocked his gun, and a moment after held his breath as he saw the great antlers of the bull flash through the trees.

The Caribou paused on the cliff, hesitating to jump; then catching the fresh scent, snuffed the air, dilated his flashing eyes, shook his branching horns, and gathered himself up to bound away on the right.

It was too late, the sharp crack of Whitcher's rifle awoke the echoes, and the Caribou shot forward far over the brink, and fell dead at the foot of the falls.

Whitcher had seen tracks of this fleetest, wildest deer, on other occasions, but never before or since has a white hunter shot a Caribou in Warren.

Deer have always been more or less plenty in Warren, and hardly a winter passes, but that a few are caught. In early times they were seen in the fields almost every day. Joseph Patch† used to relate how as he was coming home from the East-parte soon after the road was built, a deer stood drinking by Silver rill at twilight, a will-o'-the-wisp playing around his branching horns. Patch gave a low whistle, the buck snuffed the air for a moment then bounded away in the darkness.

Of the other four-footed beasts that have lived in the Asquamchumauke valley, many have been hunted for their furs. The fox has generally been esteemed the best; and the music of baying hounds has been the delight of many a hunter's heart. Trappers in the forest have built culheags and set steel traps for sable, otter, mink, martin, ermine, and muskrat, and old Mr. Vowell Leathers, a gipsy descendant, who lived on Beech hill, used to catch skunks

---

† Joseph Patch, when advanced in years, followed a deer on snow shoes, all one day, as fast as he could, then at night laid down on the snow without a fire, and got cold. It settled in his hips, and our hunter was lame ever after. He could stand up and swingle flax all day long. He learned the shoemaker's trade, and was good at it; but he never could run on snow shoes in the woods afterwards. Yet he was good at "still hunting" as long as he lived.

to obtain their pleasant odor. He thought it decidedly superior to musk, cologne, or otto of roses, and he once placed one of these sweet smelling creatures under a certain lady town pauper's bed, kindly remarking that it smelt far better than she did, and was much to be preferred by all refined people,— a remark highly complimentary to the lady.

Of all the birds that abound in Warren, the black-cap titmouse, sometimes called chickadee, is deservedly the greatest favorite. Why? Because he has a beautiful song, does a great deal of good and no harm, is very plenty, and stops with us all the year round. His feathers are as warm as wool, are immensely thick as compared with his whole body, and he is so sprightly that he could not be cold, no matter what might be the weather. A whole flock, clinging, backs down like pirouetting fairies to the breezy tops of the pine trees, swinging in the wind on the outermost end of the slenderest boughs of the birch, singing all the time, chickadee, chickadedee, in the sweetest notes, making a lively party, and music that causes us to love the bright days of winter.

When the low southern sun is hid in murky leaden clouds, and the snow flakes begin to spin round in the freshening gale and the storm spirit is roaring on the mountains, then the white flashing bodies of the snow-buntings, who were hatched on the snowy isles of the frozen ocean, in nests of reindeers' hair, lined with soft down of sea ducks and the warm fur of the white foxes, hurrying before the storm, bring a weird feeling and a sort of a superstitious awe to the chilly traveller. Along with them come the goshawk, light winged, from Greenland; the snow owl and the Acadian owl, his companions, and the Bohemian chatterer, that incessantly sings when the sun shines on his home, the eternal snows and glaciers about the pole. On mild winter days, in our hamlet, the shrike, cross-bills, mealy red polls, lesser red polls, pine grosbeaks, Arctic woodpeckers, brown creepers, nut hatches, make busy parties in the spruce swamps, while on the borders of the fields, and about the barns, is heard the screaming of jays and the cawing of crows.

Spring brings a host of eagles, hawks, owls, woodpeckers, cuckoos, thrushes, wrens, kingfishers, humming birds, warblers, swallows, orioles, blackbirds, sparrows, finches, buntings, and many others, among whom is the red-eyed vireo, one of the most welcome of the summer singers, for he sings all day long, no matter how dark the weather or hot the sun.

For the sportsman, the beautiful wood duck, the black duck and sheldrakes swim in the ponds and river, and in autumn the wild goose crying " hawnk-honck-e-honck," as he flies through the sky, often lights in Tarleton lake. But never yet has sportsman lived in Warren who knew how to hunt upland plover, or the woodcock that breed every year in the meadows of Runaway pond, and along the shores of some of the sedgy streams. That kind of shooting belongs to another generation.

Among the dark firs and thick hackmatacks of the mountains is found the spruce grouse, sometimes called the Canadian grouse. They have a beautiful plumage, but are not considered good eating. They are very remarkable for their manner of drumming. They leap up from the earth and beating their wings rapidly against their sides, rise spirally some fifteen or twenty feet into the air, then slowly descending in the same manner, they all the time produce by the rapid motion of their wings a low rumbling sound like distant thunder which in a still day can be heard nearly a mile away.

The ruffed grouse is a larger bird, much more plenty, is more sought after, and affords the most savory dish for the table. This bird is generally known as the partridge, is very numerous, and in fact cannot be exterminated. Their drumming, which every one has heard, is the call of the male bird to his harem of attendant wives, and is beautifully done. Standing up proudly on an old prostrate log, or flat rock in a spruce copse, he lowers his wings, erects his expanded tail, contracts his throat, elevates the two tufts of feathers on the neck, and inflates his whole body, something in the manner of a turkey-cock, strutting and wheeling about in great stateliness. After a few manœuvres of this kind, he begins to strike his stiffened wings in short and quick strokes, which become more and more rapid until they run into each other, resembling the rumbling sound of very distant thunder, dying away gradually on the ear. Morning and evening in the spring of the year is their favorite drumming time. Warren has had a host of good partridge hunters, from Obadiah Clement down to Benjamin Little,

Russell Merrill, Benj. K. Little, and Amos L. Merrill, who lives in the East-parte region.

Some years wild pigeons are very plenty, and at the commencement of the present century flocks miles in length and breadth, darkening the sun, would fly for days over our valley. In autumn when beech-nuts abounded, our hunters and their friends feasted on wild pigeons.*

Warren's streams and ponds abound in fish, and fishermen have always been more plenty than hunters, trappers, or fowlers. Minnows, dace, eels, suckers, pout, pickerel, and trout, swarm the waters in great numbers; but pickerel and trout are the most sought after. The latter were much larger formerly than now.

Mr. Samuel Merrill, familliarly known as "Uncle Sammy," a man beloved by every body, was one of the first fishermen in the head waters of the Asquamchumauke. He had settled high up on the side of Moosehillock mountain. The woods were thick about his clearing, shutting out the view back of his cabin; but Moosehillock looked in upon him from the north, and east, the crests of the mountains swept round him in a circle to the south-west. Morning and evening he could hear the roar of the river in the gorge just beyond the eastern edge of the clearing.

He used to tell how a July night of those early times had been showery, and in the morning, rising early, he saw a faint blue line of mist which hovered over the bed of the long rocky ravine, floating about like the steam of a seething cauldron, and rising here and there into tall smoke like columns, probably where some steeper cataract of the mountain stream sent its foam skyward. As the sun came up the mists rapidly dispersed from the lower regions, were suspended for a short time in the middle air in broad, fleecy masses, then melted quickly away in the increasing brightness of the day.

"The fish will bite this forenoon, and I will see the river," he said, "and the land beyond." He had bought his hooks down

---

* Anson Merrill said he saw pigeons, year after year, so thick flying over Warren that they looked like a black cloud.

Fowling Anecdote.—Joseph and Orlando, sons of Joseph Boynton, who lived on the ridge above Cold brook, once found a partridge sitting on her nest. Orlando got the gun and he and Joseph went out to shoot the bird; but their father thinking it too bad to shoot a sitting bird, run ahead and scared the partridge up. Orlando saw him and heard the heavy flight. He was mad and hallooed to Joseph what his father had done. Joseph, he was madder still, and with the most filial

country, his wife had spun him a linen line, and he had buckshot for a sinker. Digging some worms by the path that led to his house, he traveled away over the brook to the northeast, through the thick hemlock woods, a mile and more, to the river bank. At the base of this descent, four hundred feet perhaps below, flowed the dark arrowy stream — a wild perilous water. As clear as crystal, yet as dark as the brown lichens, it came pouring down among the broken rocks, with a rapidity and force which showed what must be its fury when swollen by a storm among the mountains; here breaking into a wreath of rippling foam, where some unseen ledge chafed the current, there roaring and surging white as December's snow among the great round headed boulders, and there again wheeling in sullen eddies, dark and deceitful, round and round some deep rock-rimmed basin.

Going down the bank two beautiful spruce grouse, their scarlet feathers gleaming in the morning sun, clucked, clucked, chur-r-red, and then disappeared in heavy flight down among the great trees of the ravine.

At the water edge he cut a beautiful birchen pole, fastened his line upon the end and adjusted a worm upon his hook. Delicately, deftly the bait danced in the clear water across the foamy, crystal eddy to the hither bank, then again, obedient to the pliant wrist it circled half round the limpid basin, then stopped for a moment in a little mimic whirlpool, where it spun round and round just to the leeward of a gray granite boulder. It was only for a moment, and the gay tail of a trout flashed in the sunshine, then a swirl on the surface, a quick turn of the wrist, the barbed hook was fixed and the most beautiful fish of the northern waters spun round and round for a moment in the air, then quickly unhooked was strung on the forked birch twig cut for the purpose. The hook was rebaited, another and another were caught, then down stream leaping on the great round boulders, he stopped again at a second edying basin, adjusted his bait, and hurrying now in the wild excitement, caught brace after brace, taking no note of time till the shadows crept out over the deep gorge and a heavy rumble up

---

affection, and in the most pious manner, shouted out, "*Shoot, shoot the d—d old cuss.*" His father heard him and mildly said, "Orlando, if you do I'll take your hide off;" and Orlando didn't shoot.—Russell K. Clement's story.

in the great basin of the mountains told that a thunder shower was coming on.

A hedgehog had come down by the stream to drink, but he heeded him not. A winter wren, darting quick as a mouse in and out among the roots of a fallen tree, had warbled a trilling fairy song to him; a white throated finch had sung soft and sweet from the top of a beautiful green spruce that shot up like a cone at the head of a little island where the stream divided and rushed rapidly down on either side, and just then a great shaggy black bear came from the woods and laying down in the cold water lapped his fill, and sozzled and tossed the clear crystal fluid to his heart's content. Merrill never disturbed him; but with fish, as many as he could conveniently carry, scrambled up the steep bank and hurried away home. In his old age he would tell what a wetting he got going home from his first fishing excursion in the Asquamchumauke.

Fish have been caught in Glen and Wachipauka ponds, and Tarleton lake, that would weigh over four pounds each,* and I have seen them myself, caught from the Joseph Merrill pond, that would weigh three pounds. Who does not like to fish? In my youth I fished in the dear old mill-pond and tiny Cold brook; but in after years in the wild mountain stream and on the sylvan lake.

There are more than fifty miles of trout streams in our mountain hamlet,† any mile of which can be reached and well fished any day, in the season, from Warren common. Patch brook, Hurricane brook, Batchelder brook, Davis brook, Libby brook, East-branch brook, the Asquamchumauke, Gorge brook, Big brook, Merrill brook, Berry brook, Black brook, (the Mikaseota,) Ore hill brook, and Martin brook, also the Oliverian, afford more than fifty thousand genuine red-spotted trout with pink sides and silver belly and tri-colored fins, white, black, and red, each year. Who does not love to follow the clear streams running over sandy bottoms

---

* Wm. H. Fisk, of Manchester, N. H., once caught a trout out of Patch brook that weighed over four pounds. A fish hawk sat on a neighboring tree looking at him and evidently had been watching the same game. When Mr. Fisk bagged the beauty the hawk flew away with a scream, seeming much disappointed.

† Cyrus C. Kimball, in his day, fished a portion of the Asquamchumauke so much that the fish were spring poor all the year round. He amused himself chasing them over the rocks when they wouldn't bite.

where they abound. Your trout delights in cascades, tumbling bays and weirs. Generally he has his hole under roots of overhanging trees, and beneath hollow banks and great boulders in the deepest parts of the stream. The junction of little rapids, formed by water passing round an obstruction in the midst of the general current is a likely point at which to raise a trout; also at the roots of trees, or beside great rocks, or in other places where the froth of the stream collects. All such places are favorable for sport, as insects follow the same course as the bubbles, and are there sought by the fish. Generally they lie head up stream, not even wagging the tail or moving a fin. Thousands of pounds of fish are also taken from our ponds each year, yet they never seem to grow scarce, and each season brings its accustomed product.

Warren has known some pot fishers, real murderers of the finny tribe; and once upon a time, as the fairy stories begin, several lovers of fat trout resolved to capture every one in Wachipauka pond. Dr. Alphonzo G. French, Rev. A. W. Eastman, and Absalom Clifford, Esq., were the principal actors. But they invited their friends John S. Batchelder, Newell Barry, Newell S. Martin, and several other less important personages, to go with them and share in the spoils. Accordingly, armed with washtubs, mackerel kits, and syrup holders, one bright summer morning they all repaired to the pond.

The plan was to fill a large stone jug with powder, attach a fuse and sink it in the water; one of the number on a raft should light the fuse, and the others with a rope, should pull him ashore. The explosion would kill every fish in the pond; they would float on the surface and the greedy fishermen could pick them up at their leisure. Absalom Clifford was to touch off the fuse, and Dr. French and Rev. Mr. Eastman were to land him before the explosion. The others would get behind great trees in the woods.

The plan is perfected; the raft is floating on the still water and the rope extends to the shore.

Absalom Clifford touched off; a light smoke curled up from the burning fuse.

Pull, shouted the man on the raft, and the doctor and the minister pulled. "Pull! Pull! or I shall be blowed up," screamed the fuse lighter, and the man of physic and the man of the gospel pulled,— pulled with all their might. But alas the rope broke; a terrible explosion was soon to follow, they could not die there, and the doctor and the reverend fled far into the deep woods.

A. Clifford knew his danger, there was no escape, and taking one last lingering look of mountains and green woods around, lay down on his raft, closed his eyes and resigned himself to his fate.

Soon the powder burned; but there was no terrible explosion, only a few bubbles on the surface and then all was calm and still.

A long time after, the doctor, the minister, the hotel keeper, and the farmers, came creeping back. Absalom sat bolt upright on his raft. He was now as brave as a lion, and spoke many gentle words to the bold rope pullers who had left him to die alone.

They felt "cute enough."

Absalom, with a piece of board paddled himself ashore, and the party gathering up all their tubs, kits, and holders, and covering them with green boughs in their wagons, wended their way to their homes, exceedingly delighted with the many congratulations of their friends over their success, and the almost miraculous escape of A. Clifford.

CHAPTER III.

HOW THE TURNPIKE WAS BUILT, AND OF DIVERS THINGS THAT HAPPENED THEREBY.

NEW things came fast to our hamlet among the hills, at the beginning of the present century. In the last chapter of the preceding book, we enumerated many of them, and at the commencement of the present, told of the new religions that came to town. In the land of the Coosucks, far to the northward, the people were similarly blessed, and having a great desire for a further supply of useful commodities, began to make efforts for the building of better roads on which they might come.

About this time a mania had arisen for turnpikes, throughout the whole land; people believed they would be profitable. investments, and every body knew they would help develop the country. Nearly twenty of the roads had been chartered and built in New Hampshire, and December 19, 1805, a charter of the old Coos turnpike was obtained. The enterprising people of Haverhill Corner — they don't live there now — were mainly instrumental in procuring it, and the corporation* the ensuing spring, engaged the services of Gen. John McDuffee, a distinguished engineer of those times, and the survey was immediately commenced.

---

* The turnpike corporation consisted of Moses Dow, Absalom Peters, Joseph Bliss, David Webster, Jr., Asa Boynton, Charles Johnston, Alden Sprague, Moody Bedell, William Tarleton, John Page, and Stephen P. Webster. The first meeting was called by Col. William Tarleton and Stephen P. Webster, by publishing a notice in the Dartmouth Gazette.

The "Coventry turnpike" was chartered December 29, 1803, but it was never built.

There were two points at which it must terminate. Haverhill Corner on the west, and Baker river, the Asquamchumauke, "near Merrill's mill" on the east, and it must be the straightest and shortest line, if it did run plump over the mountain long known as the Height-o'-land. Surveyor McDuffee looked over the route first, and then commencing at Haverhill Corner, ran southeasterly towards the Asquamchumauke in Warren. He was all summer performing the work, getting the bearings, estimating the grade, driving the stakes, and cutting bushes. Thomas Pillsbury of Warren was one of the surveying party, and helped carry the chain. Then the general made up his plan, and in the autumn of 1806 advertisements were posted for proposals to build sections of one hundred rods each, on the whole line.

Joseph Patch, Jr., and his brothers, contracted for and built from the commencement at the narrow point between Baker river and the Mikaseota or Black brook up to the Blue ridge. Joseph Merrill took the job cutting through the high embankment of Runaway pond. It required a great amount of labor and much time, and before it was finished the people thought it was a *blue* job for Mr. Merrill, hence the name *Blue ridge*. Amos Little built the hundred rods above Blue ridge, over the Mikaseota, and one of the Clements the section above that. Captain William Butler also built a section.

In 1808, the turnpike approaching completion, a toll-gate was constructed and located where the road crosses the outlet of Tarleton lake. Here was a narrow ravine and there was no way to proceed except through the gate. Nine pence was the toll for a horse and rider, one shilling for a horse and wagon, one and six pence for a two horse wagon or sleigh, and three shillings for large teams.*

The people who lived beside it were permitted to travel upon it at a small cost; they working out their highway taxes upon it in part payment.† Joseph Merrill was superintendent of repairs for the south division. Several roads not being longer needed were now thrown up.‡

---

* For an extended table of tolls, see charter in office of Secretary of State.
† Each man had to work a day and a half on the turnpike to pay for what he used it.—Gen. M. P. Merrill's statement.
‡ Voted to discontinue from *Bowles'* to the old Potash, (so called,) near Mr. Weeks' so long as the public can pass on the turnpike, free from "towl."

And now, when the road was opened, how the people rejoiced! It would bring new life to the town! Their property would be of higher value, and the world at their doors.

These bright expectations were fully realized; travel greatly increased. Great teams, as they were called, canvass covered wagons, drawn by eight or ten horses, went rumbling by every day in long trains, almost like caravans in the East. Going north they invariably hired all the horses and oxen at the foot of the Height-o'-land that could be found, to help them up. My uncle, Anson Merrill, said that when a boy, he had been to the top of the Height a hundred times or more to take back the oxen or horses. Four shillings or four-and-six-pence was the price of a yoke of cattle or a span of horses over the mountain. The highest point on the road where they dismissed the boy, was about two thousand feet above sea level, and a barn now standing on the turnpike summit is a real water-shed, the rain and melting snow running from one roof flowing into the Connecticut, that from the other roof into the Merrimack. In winter two-horse pungs, with jingling bells and shouting drivers, came from the fertile hill-sides of Vermont, and made trains miles in length on the winter road. Numerous pod teams, or one-horse sleighs, also joined the great caravan to the seaboard.

It was a romantic trip these pungs had to Dover, Portsmouth, and Newburyport. Mr. Samuel Merrill,* "Uncle Sammy," who lived in the East-parte regions, used to narrate his adventures "going down by the sea." When the deep snow had come and the weather was cold, he loaded up his great steel-shod, — shoes of steel more than an inch thick,— market pung. Whole hogs, frozen stiff, apple-sauce, butter, cheese, poultry, feetings, mink, fox, sable, fisher-cat, and bear skins, caught by his boys, sheep's pelts, and all the various articles of country produce, make a heavy load. Then he would take a whole trunk full of pies, cakes, cold

---

Voted to discontinue the old road from the north side of Coventry road to the turnpike above Mr. Swett's as above.
Voted to discontinue from Joseph Merrill's to the saw-mill as above.
Voted to discontinue from Captain Craige's house to Jonathan Clement's inn. Captain Craige lived in Joshua Merrill's house on the west side of the Mikaseota. —Town Clerk's Records, Vol. i. 190.

* Samuel Merrill was the son of Rev. Nathaniel Merrill, a very able Congregational minister. Nathaniel was a brother of Joshua and Stevens Merrill, early settlers in Warren.

meat, cold fowl, and cheese, for himself, and several bushels of oats for his horses. He did not like to pay much money to the thousand and one landlords who kept hotels and furnished drinkables all along the road to the markets, which were known as places down country. Just think of the little man mounting the semicircular step behind the sleigh for the start, amid the tender goodbys and kind wishes of those who were to stay behind, and who must now pass days and perhaps weeks, if drifting snow or a "January thaw" should intervene, before the old mare and her four year old colt should make their appearance, coming up the hill home again. "Out to the road," and he joined the throng coming down the turnpike, and was lost in the hurrying caravan. At the market towns he bought salt, spices of all kinds, steel traps, powder, shot, fishing tackle, and a host of coveted luxuries, and then he was off for his home again. The old mare and the four year old colt turned out of the throng and off the turnpike road instinctively, and was there not joy in the household that night when he unloaded his treasures. James Williams, his neighbor, had a two-horse market sleigh, as did Joseph Patch, Jr., Captain Butler, Obadiah Clement, and several others. There were likewise numerous pod teams owned in town, that made annual pilgrimages down country with the rest.

Freighting and travel to the seaboard so much increased, on account of the turnpike, that one or two new taverns were opened in town. Mr. Nathaniel Clough* had one near the south line of Warren, Captain Butler and Jonathan Clement each kept one in the valley of Runaway pond, and Col. Tarleton, Joseph Merrill, 'Squire Jonathan Merrill, and Lemuel Keezer,† still continued their hostelries and bought hay and grain of all the farmers in the country round.

The old turnpike road had a lively history for a quarter of a

---

* FAMILY RECORD OF NATHANIEL AND BETTY (*Keezer*) CLOUGH.

Jonathan, born Dec. 28, 1790, at Warren.
Nathaniel, born Aug. 17, 1792.
William, born Sept. 5, 1794.
Amos, born May 12, 1797.
Sally, born Apr. 28, 1799.
Betsey, born Feb. 15, 1803.
Juliana, born Oct. 6, 1813.

† Lemuel Keezer in his old age got Captain Daniel Merrill to live with him and take care of him. Captain Daniel among other things agreed to furnish Mr. Keezer a pint of good rum a day during his natural life. Captain Daniel was also a deacon, and Keezer used to say of him, "Now then Daniel always hangs up his deaconship on a peg at home, when he goes out buying cattle, and don't take it down again till Saturday at 4 P. M."

century, and on it has happened many a fond adventure. The Height-o'-landers were in old times a jolly, jovial, hilarious set of roisterers. The Days, especially, who once lived there, were fond *lovyers* of good grog, and many a break-neck ride they took with bottle and bag, a stone in one end of the bag to balance the bottle, to the hotels in the valley of Runaway pond, and on the banks of the Asquamchumauke, to obtain the " good creature." It is told by superstitious people that they used to see ghosts on the road going home o' nights.

But the wildest adventure, a terrible ride, happened on the turnpike about the year 1812, soon after the road was first opened. A teamster of short and stout frame from northern Vermont, used to drive four powerful black horses, freighting to the seaboard. In the hot summer he would travel nights and rest daytimes. He left Tarleton's hotel by Tarleton lake one evening to go over to the Asquamchumauke valley. He came through the Tamarack swamp by the pond, climbed the highest summit and went down to the top of the sharp pitch where commence the cascades of Ore-hill brook. Here he chained his wheel, mounted his load and started down. He had not proceeded a rod when the chain broke. The horses could not hold the heavy load and it forced them into a run down the hill. It was dark as pitch, he could not see to rein his team, he could not hold them, and their speed accelerated every moment. The sparks flew from the steel-shod hoofs, and long trails of light flashed back in the darkness as the wheels rumbled over the rocks. As the speed increased, ghosts seemed to shriek out to him from the murky air, and he could almost see their eyes flashing like meteors,— in fact he did see stars, although the whole sky was covered with thick clouds, for just at the foot of the hill where the road turns to the right before crossing the stream, the wagon struck a rock, breaking nearly every timber in it. The leaders cleared themselves and ran, the hind horses were thrown down and one of them killed, while the driver was thrown from the load against a stone, and one of his legs was broken in three places.

He shouted for help, but there was no house within a mile of the spot, and no one came to his assistance. To stay there was to die in agony, and to move did not increase his pain. On his hands

A TERRIBLE RIDE.

and knee he crawled to his team, cut the harness of the living horse and got him up. Mounting him he rode to Jonathan Clement's inn, a mile and a half away, roused the family, and was assisted into the house. When a light was brought, his hair, dark before, was found to be white as snow.

The horses that ran were found standing quietly under the tavern shed. Dr. Bartlett set the teamster's broken limb, and every thing possible was done for the unfortunate man, but it was four months before he was able to walk a step.*

For a whole generation the turnpike corporation flourished and paid good dividends to the stockholders. Then the feeling became prevalent that a road should be built by which the steep hills and mountains might be shunned. After a long contest one was built and travel ceased over the Height-o'-land. The tavern-keepers in the valley of Runaway pond and on the shore of Tarleton lake† then took down their signs, and the places once bustling with the activity of teamsters, stage-drivers, and travelers, became almost solitudes.

Still the old turnpike did good service for the dwellers beside it of a second generation; but to-day, riding over it, it seems like a monument of a people past and gone. Especially did it seem so when in the spring of 1868, in company with my esteemed friend, Mr. James Clement, we came down from Cross' iron mine, through the Tamarack woods by Tarleton lake. It was a cloudy, wet evening the last of May; the lonely farm house beside the road was deserted, not a human being was to be seen, but from the swamp and dripping wood came the warbling melody of the winter wren, the sweet song of the white-throated sparrow, and trilling sweeter, richer, and far more beautiful than all the rest, the mellow, flute-like notes of the wood thrush.

Reader, riding over the old turnpike, remember that once this solitude was the busiest and most traveled thoroughfare in all northern New Hampshire.

---
* Dr. Jesse Little's statement.
† The old sign of Colonel Wm. Tarleton, that creaked for more than half a century in the winds that blew over Tarleton lake, is still (1869) in existence. When taken down it was nailed upon an inside stable door, where the writer saw it in 1839. It was made of a broad oaken board and was beautifully painted. On the top of the visible side is the name of William Tarleton, and the date 1774 at the bottom. Between the name and the date is an excellent likeness of Gen. Wolfe with drawn sword and full uniform. Wolfe was the hero at that time, and Washington and his generals were hardly known.

CHAPTER IV.

ABOUT THE 1812 WAR; OF DRAFTING AND VOLUNTEERING, CLOSING WITH A GRAND MUSTER WHEN WARREN'S HILLS HEARD LOUDER MUSIC THAN EVER BEFORE.

IN the selectmenship of Jonathan Merrill, Benjamin Merrill, and Joseph Merrill, high functionaries of Warren, the second war with Great Britain broke out. It originated in a series of aggressions made upon our commerce by British naval commanders, they claiming the right to search our ships and of impressing our seamen. This presumption having been carried on with a high hand, a number of our vessels having been fired into, the United States made a declaration of war.

In New Hampshire Gov. Plumer, by order of the President and the Secretary of War, commanded five companies of soldiers from the first brigade of the New Hampshire militia to proceed to Portsmouth for the defence of that seaport, and upon representations of the people in the north part of the State that there was danger of predatory incursions of the enemy from Canada, and that contraband trade was rife on the frontier, defrauding our government of its revenue and furnishing the enemy with supplies, another company was ordered to the north to be stationed at Stewartstown, N. H. Brig. Gen. John Montgomery was commanded to furnish the company from the sixth brigade, and he immediately ordered each company of the several regiments composing it to furnish its respective quota.

By his order the military company of Warren was compelled

THE 1812 WAR. 391

to furnish ten men to serve six months. They were to be drafted July 27th, 1812, and each member of the company having been notified, they met on the parade in front of Joseph Merrill's inn, for that purpose.*

It was a day of great interest to all the people of Warren. There was not much sleep in town the night before, and every military man was up bright and early.

But they did not find fair weather. Those who were up before the sun said they saw the rain gathering around the head of Moosehillock, and the red stars trembling between the flying clouds. At day break it was evident a great rain was coming on. The wind was north-east and the echoing woods of the valley even seemed to foresee the storm. Soon its spirit was heard roaring in the dark forests of Mount Carr; and men at their breakfast saw the ragged clouds hurrying across the heavens, their edges tinged with lightning; saw the winds roll them along the mountain sides, and heard the deep thunder echoing over the crests. By eight o'clock it was pouring in torrents and the brave members of the Warren military company looked solemn as they assembled on the parade amid the rain that came down on the north-east wind.† War was something new for that generation, and the men who should go might be killed on the battlefield, or die of lingering disease in the hospital.

Still, at ten o'clock the company was formed in line at the beat of drum, the command of forward march was heard, and they marched to the floor of the great barn connected with the inn.‡

Here they were paraded in line. The captain made a short speech, telling them that volunteers were better than drafted men,

---

* 1809.—" Voted that the selectmen be a committee to provide powder and ball as the law directs, the ensuing year."—Town Clerk's Records, Vol. i.

† Paid Nath. Clough and others for labor, timber, and plank, for repairing highways in the Forks district. No. 1, after the great freshet, $29.85.
Joseph Merrill and wife went to James Williams' at the East-parte just after the volunteering. It rained two more days; all the bridges were carried away and he had to leave his wife, horse, and wagon, and come all the way home on foot, keeping on the north bank of the river.

‡ Stephen Richardson was a captain of militia about this time. He was an excellent officer, and his son, Nathaniel Richardson, relates what a fine appearance he made when dressed in his uniform. The son says his father was a gay feeling man, and when he stepped on training days he was so light eggs would not break under his feet.

and that it would be more honorable to the company for the requisite number to volunteer. Then the tenor drum played for volunteers, and eight men immediately stepped forward. Two others were soon obtained by the offering of small bounties, and George Libbey, Richard Whiteman, Nathaniel Libbey, Nathaniel Richardson, Ephraim Lund, Daniel Pillsbury, Joseph Pillsbury, Jacob Whitcher, Obadiah Whitcher, and Jonathan Weeks, were the ten men who constituted Warren's quota.*

Addison Patch, Anson Merrill and several other boys, sat on the hay-mow that day, listening to the music of the company band mingled with that of the rain rattling on the long shingles of the roof, and witnessed the volunteering.

Captain Ephraim H. Mahurin of Stratford, N. H., commanded the company, John Page, Jr., was Lieutenant. Perkins Fellows was ensign, and George Libbey of Warren was one of the sergeants, while Richard Whiteman who lived and died at Warren summit, was first corporal. The whole company was raised from the old 13th regiment, which at the time of the breaking out of the war was commanded by Lieut. Col. John Montgomery, John Kimball of Haverhill, Major of the first battalion, and Daniel Patch, of Warren, Major of the second battalion.

The company immediately proceeded to its rendezvous by Indian stream, in Stewartstown. But as good fortune would have it, they saw no bloody fight, and achieved no high honors on the battle-field. Yet they had lively times building block-houses and chasing after smugglers, whom they never caught. Part of the company under Lieut. John Page, who was afterwards governor of New Hampshire, went down through Dixville notch to Errol dam, ostensibly to protect the settlers of that locality from the Indians, of whom old Metalic was chief and the whole tribe, but in fact to prevent a few enterprising Maine men from driving cattle up the Megalloway river to Canada, and there selling them to the British forces.

The party had exciting times performing their duties, and the

---

* John Abbott went for Haverhill as a drummer, and Perkins Fellows, calling himself from Piermont, went with Warren's volunteers. Perkins Fellows married a daughter of Jonathan Clement, inn-keeper.

"Let Richard Whiteman have when he went as a soldier, $5.00."—See Selectmen's Records, Vol. i,

brave commander, Lieut. John Page, got so terrifically lame, Sept. 12, 1812, chasing Maine cow-boys through the woods, that he did not get well during the remainder of his term of enlistment. But Sergeant George Libbey said he had the best time catching the great five pound trout on the falls of the Androscoggin river, and shooting wild fowl that congregated in great numbers on the clear waters of Umbagog lake. Jan. 27, 1813, the time of their enlistment was up and Warren's men, if they did enlist on a terribly rainy day, all came home safe and sound, well pleased with their exploits on the northern frontier.

Warren had some ambitious men. Tristram Pillsbury went into the western army, John Abbott went away, joined some regiment and died while in the service.* Major Daniel Patch was a private and fought at the battle of Bridgewater, where he was wounded. But David Patch gained more distinction as a soldier than any other native of Warren. He enlisted in some other State, got a commission, fought in several battles, got promoted for bravery, and commanded a regiment as a colonel, at the battle of Sackett's harbor.† Here he was taken prisoner, carried to Halifax, and was so badly treated that he was attacked by consumption. When peace was declared, he came home, and shortly after died. To-day, he is lying in an unmarked and almost forgotten grave in the village burying ground.

In 1814, numerous British men-of-war appeared off the coast of New Hampshire, and so great was the panic they created, that Governor Gilman ordered the entire body of the New Hampshire militia, infantry, cavalry, and artillery, "to hold themselves in readiness to march at a moment's warning."‡ Many companies were immediately ordered to Portsmouth, and a draft was once more to be had in Warren. Four men was the quota of our little hamlet this time, and the mighty rulers who were elected this year in our little democracy, Jonathan Merrill, Abel Merrill, and Joseph Patch, Jr., were ordered to see that the men were forthcoming.

Again the company which bore such euphonious names as the slam-bang company, the string-bean company, and the old flood-

---
* John Abbott died of scarlet fever, April 13, 1813, at Concord, N. H.
† David Patch was wounded at the battle of Sackett's harbor. It is doubtful about his ever having held a commission as colonel.
‡ Adjutant General's Report, 1868, part 2d, p. 130.

wood company, was warned to appear on the parade in front of Joseph Merrill's inn. It was a bright day this time, Sept. 27, 1814, when they assembled, and the men were drawn up before the tavern door. Once more there was a harangue for volunteers, once more the drum rolled out a patriotic strain, and when it ceased, four men, Moses Ellsworth, Stephen Whiteman,* Cotton Batchelder, and another,† all "little runts of men," a little over four feet tall, stood valiantly forth, each anxious to be one of his country's defenders.

'Squire Jonathan and his companions in office were indignant. "To send such soldiers will be a disgrace to the town," said they; "They shall not go, the draft shall proceed." Accordingly the name of each man on a slip of paper was placed in a hat, and when well shaken up, Joseph Patch, Jr., drew forth four of them. Stephen Whiteman was in luck. He, with John Copp, William Merrill, and Obadiah Whitcher, were drafted to go. But William Merrill, son of Joseph Merrill, inn keeper, would not be a soldier, and Daniel Pillsbury went as his substitute.

Perkins Fellows, who lived over the Height-o'-land, was also on hand again and went with the quota of Warren. They helped to make up a company which was commanded by Captain John D. Harty, of Dover. Perkins Fellows was first Lieutenant, and by his influence Daniel Pillsbury was first corporal, and Obadiah Whitcher third corporal. These men had gay times down at Portsmouth, by the side of the "deep blue sea," where they went fishing, catching sheep's heads and cuttle-fish, and the only hazardous service they saw was when some shiney nights they made raids upon pig-styes and hen roosts. John Copp and Stephen Whiteman were great on a raid. At the end of sixty days they were all discharged and came safe home.

When peace had been declared, and the war was over, there

---

* FAMILY RECORD OF WILLIAM AND MEHITABLE (*Merrill*) WHITEMAN.
Stephen, born Aug. 12, 1784.   Betsey, born May 24, 1792.
Richard, born June 24, 1786.   Hannah, born June 17, 1794.
Levi, born Apr. 8, 1789.
Mrs. Whiteman died March 29, 1798. She was a daughter of Farmer Joshua. William Whiteman was a Dutchman.

† John Copp was the fourth little man who volunteered.—Stephen Whiteman's statement.
Mr. Whiteman said John Copp was not so tall as he was. Jesse Eastman who lived a long time in the East-parte regions, went from Coventry and carried his own gun.

was great joy in all the land, but the military spirit did not die out. Little training day in May, and muster day were more anxiously expected than ever, and great was the enthusiasm on such occasions.

The old 13th regiment, composed of the companies of Warren, Benton, Haverhill, Piermont, and Orford, was now in all its glory. Moses H. Clement, of Warren, was Colonel, James Rogers, Lieut. Colonel, and James R. Page, Major. Col. Clement had been a captain of infantry, a captain of cavalry or troop, as it was generally called, and now he had got to be a colonel of a whole regiment. What a high honor, thought he, and Warren shall share it. So when the annual muster-day came, all the troops were commanded to meet on the "parade," in front of Joseph Merrill's inn, in our little democracy.

Who of those who lived in the last generation, does not remember what a time they had going to muster. It was the great day of the year. Every body was up by one o'clock A. M., on that morning. All the country round was alive; men, women, and children, hurrying away by thousands over the hills and through the valleys in the morning dawn, to muster. What shouting, what running of horses, what a caravan of peddlers, traveling through the country, going through a whole brigade of musters.

Every one must be on the ground at sunrise at the beating of the reveille, when the companies would be formed. All around the parade, booths, victualing tents, and showmen's tents had sprung up in the night like Jonah's gourd. These would reap a harvest on that eventful day. The whole field north of the parade was thrown open for the muster, and the line was always formed where the railroad embankment is now. What rivalry was there to be the color company, to be the escort company. How gay was the troop, and what splendid uniforms some of the infantry companies had.

The whole regiment with colors flying marched that day with its dashing colonel at its head, along the broad turnpike road. Two dozen drums were beating all at once, a dozen fifes were shrilly playing, the brass band joined its inspiriting strains and the two cannon of the artillery company on the field, helped make music for the regimental march. The forests awoke in echoes, all the hills gave back the sound, and the wooded mountain crests taking up the melody of war, bore it far across the borders to the dwellers beyond Glen ponds in the ancient lands of Trecothick and of old Peeling, along the banks of the Pemigewassett. Those kind neighbors of ours over the mountains, who come to Warren about as often as the Chinese, never forgot the music of the regimental muster, and even now on winter evenings, tell their grandchildren of it.

Col. Obadiah Clement, father of Col. Moses, looked on with ambitious eyes, and a fatherly pride, and said it reminded him of the time when they had the first little training on Blue ridge, by the bank of the Mikaseota, now called Black brook. Besides many of the soldiers of the Revolution were also there; Col. Stone, an old pensioner who had married the widow of Joshua Copp, and was engaged making a perpetual motion, Samuel Knight, Jacob Low, and Asa Low, and many others, together with the soldiers of the 1812 war, all said it was the finest muster they ever saw.* Especially were they pleased when at the review and inspection the General of the Brigade came upon the field, and every soldier stood up straight and did his prettiest.

In the afternoon they had a sham fight, and the side that had the artillery company won the victory, and then even Moosehillock's bald head echoed back the fray. There were also several smaller fights where there was not much noise, but a few broken heads and black eyes, all induced by good whisky; but we won't say much about these as the actors did not want any record made of their glorious achievements.

Thus passed the day. The children and spectators eat gingerbread, nuts, candy, honey, and drank new cider and something stronger, bought wares of the peddlers, watched the march, reviews, and drills, and looked at the shows.

At night they went home, and all the peddlers who had sold at auction, and hallooed and yelled till their throats were sore, all

---

* Jacob Low would twit his brother Asa Low of stealing his money, and when he would ask for it to buy tobacco, the latter would say, "Chaw tow, Jake, chaw tow." Jacob would then piously call Asa a d—d traitor, and said he no business to draw a pension, if he did go to the war. Asa had property and could not get his pension for many years. Jacob Low was at the battle of Bunker hill, and helped fire a cannon thirteen times at the British, and then run with the rest. He said he, himself alone, moved the cannon back and forth behind the breast work with a "handspike" as he called it. He was once a member of Gen. Lee's body-the show-men and victuallers, had pulled up stakes and were off to the muster that would be held somewhere down the river next day.

The soldiers too, all hurried away as soon as they got their silver half dollar, and the drums and the fifes, and the bugle of the troop was heard no more for several years in Warren.*

One man was certainly happy on the night of the muster,— Joseph Merrill, inn-keeper, for he had made $200 clear profit that day, a large sum for those times.

Many musters have been held since in Warren, but none better or more successful than the one when Moses H. Clement was Colonel.

---

guard. In Warren he lived with Amos Little several years, but died at Jo. Boynton's, just above the Cold brook on the old turnpike. Gen. Joseph Low of Concord, once Adjutant General of N. H., was a nephew of Jacob Low.

Jacob said Asa deserted once, then got ashamed of himself and came skulking back.

* Paid Abel Merrill for what he expended for the soldiers on regimental muster day, with adding twenty-five cents for each soldier belonging to the cavalry and artillery companies, $12.10.—Selectmen's Records, Vol. i.

CHAPTER V.

HOW THE FIRST COVERED STAGE ACCOMPANIED BY SWEET MUSIC RAN THROUGH WARREN, WITH AN ACCOUNT OF THE FIRST POST-OFFICE, AND WHO DELIVERED THE LETTERS.

GREAT eras happen in the histories of all nations. They may not be fully realized, they may be hardly perceived at the time, but the consequences are felt and appreciated through the whole life of the State.

Our little democracy had experienced important events, and its discovery by white men, its name, its settlement, its first town meeting when the people assembled to choose rulers, raise revenue, and make proper enactments, were all turning points in our hamlet's existence. Now was to come another. What was it? says our expectant reader. Be patient and we will relate it.

The first post-rider up the Asquamchumauke, through Warren, as we have told, was John Balch of revolutionary times. Several others followed him in rapid succession, whose names and memories are now forgotten. Then at the commencement of the present century, Col. Silas May carried the mail through town,— on horseback with his good horn slung at his side, a worthy successor to Johnny Balch, he "dashed through the woods."

When the turnpike was built he drove a small Dutch wagon, like that Obadiah Clement first brought to town, and then he blew his horn louder and more than ever. He also commenced a new business in addition to carrying the mail. For a ninepence he would do small errands as far away as Portsmouth, and would

Rev. Joseph Merrill

carry small bundles and distribute them all through the country, where he went. For the agreeable part of these small jobs, the pay, he blew his clear, ringing horn as he passed every dwelling. Twice a week the inhabitants saw him climbing up the turnpike, twice a week they saw him disappearing down the valley of the Asquamchumauke.

Once he got snowed in at Warren, and was obliged to stop at Joseph Merrill's inn over the Sabbath. Let us stop there with him. 'Twas a neat bar-room, Joseph Merrill's. The floor was white, the old clock ticked in the corner, and the very attractive bar stood in the north end, its long row of decanters on the shelf behind, clean tumblers and mugs, nice toddy-sticks, and bright drainer. But the crowning glory of that bar-room is not the white floor, not the neat bar with its attractive contents, nor yet the clock ticking so musically in the corner; but it is the old-fashioned fireplace with its blazing embers, huge back-log, and iron fire-dogs, that shed glory over the whole room, gilds the plain and homely furniture with its light and renders the place a true type of New England in "ye olden times." Joseph Merrill's boys, and he had many of them, roasted apples, which swung round and round upon strings before the bright fire of that Saturday evening. Potatoes so rich and mealy, buried deep, were drawn from the ashes on the hearth for the colonel's supper, and Sunday afternoon the wife of our host turned the spit before the golden hue of the blazing embers, on which the turkey roasted, filling the room with delicious odors so suggestive of a dainty repast. Other farmers all over town had a kitchen fire just as beautiful.

There was no meeting-house in town then, no meeting that snowy Sunday. For a long hour Col. May sat gazing in silence into the fire, and conjuring up all sorts of grotesque, fanciful images from among the burning coals. No fabled genii, with magic lamp of enchantment could build such gorgeous palaces or create such gems as one could discover amid the blazing embers of the old fashioned fire-place. How pure was the air of that bar-room! The huge fire-place with its brisk draught, carried off all the impurities of the atmosphere and left it life-giving and healthful, not such as we breathe now as we huddle around the air-tight stoves.

When the colonel got tired of this, he got up, walked about, then went to the little crypt like hole in the wall, just to the right of the blazing hearth, where he found some half-dozen books,— the Bible, Baxter's Saint's Everlasting Rest, Pilgrim's Progress, Robinson Crusoe, and Gulliver's Travels, well read books of the last century; but how entertaining on a snowy day. These served to while away the long hours, and make his stay pleasant.

It was hard climbing the Height-o'-land Monday, and Col. May got through to Haverhill, only after great ox-teams had first broke the road.

But carrying the mail in a one-horse Dutch wagon was not what the people in this northern country wanted. They had heard of something better, and they longed for the rumbling old thoroughbraced coach, such as Merrie England had possessed for a hundred years, such as were becoming the fashion down country. In all the towns from Concord to Haverhill, the matter was talked about, and in the spring of 1814, Robert Morse, of Romney, led off in the enterprise. In each town a subscription paper was circulated, and a considerable sum having been raised, a coach and horses for the route were bought.*

A change of horses were stationed at Franklin lower village, another at Newfound lake, and another at Morse's village, in Romney.† When all was arranged the coach, four horses attached,

---

* *First Stage.*—One was put on in 1811, but it only run a short time, and then "bust up." Lemuel Keezer, Benjamin Merrill, Abel Merrill, Amos Little and Colonel William Tarleton, took stock in this first enterprise. Philip Smart drove the stage. Caleb Merrill got in debt to the line, $1.20, for carrying bundles from Warren to Plymouth. This stage was "to run from Haverhill to Concord *via* Plymouth Court House."

† Lemuel Keezer once kept the stage horses at his tavern. To save work, he had some wooden harrows made and would put them under the horses at night, teeth up, so that they could not lie down and get dirty. This saved a great deal of work, and withal was very kind to the horses—so Keezer told his hostler.

Keezer once had the toothache—very painful. It made him "holler." He went to old Doctor Thos. Whipple to have it pulled. Dr. Whipple commenced to cut round it. With the terrible aching and the pain of cutting, Keezer could not restrain himself, and he shut his teeth down on the doctor's fingers till the blood run. The doctor with a struggle got free, and then applied his old fashioned cant-hook tooth-puller. With a turn of the wrist he held Keezer's head for a minute so tight he could not move, looked him square in the face and exclaimed, "Now Keezer bite! d—m ye, bite!"

Keezer used to compliment Captain Daniel Merrill with whom he lived,—said the captain was born in the afternoon, that he never got round with his work till afternoon; that he never got to meeting till afternoon, and that he wouldn't go to heaven till afternoon. He also said Captain D. was the best farmer in town, for in the fall he always left the plow in the furrow, ready to hitch right on to in the spring.

Captain Daniel used to plague Keezer about going to see the widow Pudney as he called her. Keezer didn't like it, and said he would come it on the captain. So one day he came running into the house all out of breath, and told him that his son John, who was up in the woods after a load, was tight between two trees,

left Concord for Haverhill. Robert Morse, the father of this enterprise was on board, and also some of his friends, as invited guests. It was a romantic ride for those passengers who first " deadheaded" it free, through this upper country. The intervals in Salisbury, now Franklin, where Daniel Webster spent his early years, were delightful. The Pemigewassett roared through the deep ravines of Bristol, Newfound lake shone bright as when Samuel Scribner and John Barker, hunting beside it, were carried away by the Indians, and the Asquamchumauke wound calm and clear, kissing the pebbles on its shore, around the foot of Rattlesnake mountain, as when Captain Tolford's men or Captain Powers' men killed moose on its banks.

But where the mountains, their lofty peaks lost in the clouds, sloped down to the very river, which had now become a wild and foamy stream, where the green woods covered all the hills, and the clearings in the valley grew rare, there the beauties of the ride were fully appreciated.

Col. Silas May was a great horse man. His coach rattled over the bridge on the southern border of Warren, and when he crossed Hurricane brook and hurried over Patch brook, he came by Joseph Patch's, reining his mettlesome team with one hand, while with the other he held the bugle on which he played strains so wild and exhilerating that all the echo gods in the ravines of the hills and mountains, woke up and answered back the music. Nearly the whole of the inhabitants in town turned out to see the strange sight of a covered coach, for it was something new; perhaps they would have turned out any way, for all loved the beautiful airs played by Silas May. All the way up over the Asquamchumauke again, past where the depot is now, it was a fine young apple-orchard then, he played martial airs; Napoleon over the Alps, and Washington's March, till he reined in his horses before Joseph Merrill's inn. The latter was greatly pleased to see the stage: he had worked hard for the enterprise.

Again on the way, they passed the Blue ridge, crossed the

Daniel with a bottle of rum, jumped on to his horse bare back, and run him all the way up there; found John all right, and went back mad enough, and asked Keezer what he meant lying so. Keezer said he didn't lie; winked his eye and asked Daniel where John could be in the woods, if he wasn't between two trees. As the captain went out Keezer meekly said, " *How do you do, Mrs. Pudney.*"

Z

Mikaseota, or Black brook, and climbing the Height-o'-land by flashing Ore hill stream, our driver enlivened the broad and beautiful turnpike road with Lady Washington's reel, Money-musk, and Blue Bonnets over the Border. The Summit passed, they saw a light winged wind blowing across Tarleton lake, and heard the roar of the brook at the outlet. When within half a mile of Haverhill, by some accident a linch-pin was lost from the end of one of the wooden axles; but as the wheel did not come off, owing to May's skill in driving, they succeeded in reaching Haverhill Corner without replacing it.

Another stage route had been established from Concord to Haverhill, *via* Lebanon, this same season; but the route through Warren was so much shorter that Col. May could easily reach Haverhill Corner three hours earlier than the other stage.

Numerous drivers have since been employed on this route, all genial good fellows whom the whole community liked. The names most familiar and not yet forgotten by the old men of Warren are, Caleb Smart, Archibald McMurphy, George S. Putnam, Peter Dudley, Sanborn Jones, Thomas P. Clifford, Jabez Burnham, Eleazer Smith, William Wright, Peabody Morse, John Sanborn, James Langdon, Samuel Walker, Wm. Wash. Simpson, Seth Greenleaf, and H. B. Marden. Twice a week each way the stage run at first, then three times up and three times down, and finally up and down every day, and sometimes two or three stages both ways a day, when there was a rush of travel.

With the stage a love of news increased, and the people desired a post-office and a post-master of their own. For a long time they had to send to Plymouth to mail a letter; then the people of Wentworth had a post-office, and our fathers went there for their mail matter. But this was a great inconvenience, letters frequently laying in the Wentworth post-office a whole month at a time before the owners got them. But now the stage ran so regularly there was no reason why the desire for a post-office should not be gratified. So a petition numerously signed was forwarded to the postmaster-general at Washington. The prayer of the citizens was granted at once, and our little democracy became a post town.

Amos Burton, who had a store near the southern termination

FIRST POSTMASTER. 403

of the turnpike, was the first post-master in Warren. Anson Merrill succeeded him, and then Dr. Jesse Little held the office of postmaster nine years. Dr. David C. French, Levi C. Whitcher, Asa Thurston, George W. Prescott, Charles C. Durant, and numerous others have held the office.

With the stage an easy means of travel, the mail with its letters and newspapers coming and going every day, our little democracy among the hills felt as though it had got out among folks. At any rate it grew rapidly and became a State of great importance, particularly in its own estimation, —a condition especially to be commended, for if a person don't think well of himself, he may be pretty sure no one else will.

CHAPTER VI.

THE BLACK PLAGUE, OTHERWISE CALLED THE SPOTTED FEVER OR
THE GREATEST HORROR WARREN PEOPLE EVER HAD.

IT was a cold year, 1815. Winter lingered in the lap of spring. The summer was damp, cloudy, and cheerless, and the sun's rays seemed sickly. For two years pestilence had been abroad in the land, although not as yet had it come to Warren.

But now old people said everything appeared to bode something wrong. Strange sounds hurtled in the air, the owl hooted hoarse at midnight, a portentous red meteor fell down with a long trail of blood in the great gorge of Mooschillock, and the frogs croaked ominously; the whip-poor-will sang a mournful strain in the dusk of evening, and comets flashed like troops of ghosts through the sky.

Silently came the pestilence. Whence, no one could tell. But its first victim was found in the family of Mr. George Bixby, on Beech hill.* A young son of Mr. B. was suddenly taken alarmingly ill. A physician was sent for, he came, and not discovering the nature of the disease, gave as he thought a simple remedy, and took his departure. In a few hours the young man was dead. The corpse was laid out and two sons of Amos Little came to

---

* FAMILY RECORD OF GEORGE AND SARAH (*Annis*) BIXBY.

George, Jr. born Oct. 14, 1788.
Benjamin, born Apr. 6, 1790.
Anna, born Feb. 8, 1792.
Joseph, born Mar. 2, 1794.
Samuel, born Mar. 13, 1796.
Sarah, born May 28, 1798.

Elizabeth, born Dec. 9, 1802.
Dudley, born Dec. 6, 1804. Died Aug. 24, 1808.
Asa, born Feb. 7, 1807. Died Nov. 13, 1808.
Hannah B. born Feb 7, 1809.

watch by it the succeeding night. The next day one of them, James Little, was taken sick and five hours after was a corpse. Amos Little, Jr., the other watcher, also died.* Then Dolly Little, a sister of James and Amos, Jr., died.

The disease came down from Beech hill, spread rapidly and soon all was consternation. There was no physician in town and the inhabitants were obliged to send to Piermont and other places for one. Dr. Wellman came, also Dr. Whipple of Wentworth, and Dr. David Gipson of Romney. They visited a patient and while they were consulting, he died under their eyes. Cold, feverish, spotted, they said it was the spotted fever. A few hours after death the corpse turned black, hence in other countries the disease was known as the black plague. It has been more dreaded than the cholera or the yellow fever, because it comes without warning, lighting down on noisome pestilential wings, like a foul bird of prey for its victims.

That night the three physicians were discussing the disease in a sort of undertone at Joseph Merrill's inn. Suddenly Dr. Wellman felt cold, chilly. Dr. Whipple† and Dr. Gipson gave him some stimulating medicine and went home down the valley. Joseph French nursed Dr. Wellman, but at night, twenty-four hours after, the doctor was dead. They buried him in the grave yard on Pine hill road, and only carried his corpse to Piermont when the frosts of winter came. Dr. Whipple had the plague, and Dr. Gipson would not come to Warren again.

Families soon got so reduced they could not get a physician. Physicians in neighboring towns were so frightened that they would not come. The selectmen, Jonathan Merrill, Abel Merrill, and Moses H. Clement, came together and called an informal meeting of the citizens. It was agreed that the town should procure physicians. Dr. Robert Burns‡ had studied medicine with Dr. Bartlett on Beech hill. He was attending the medical school at Hanover, and the town in its distress sent for him. Daniel Pillsbury went on horseback to Hanover for Dr. B. But he could

---

* Amos Little, Jr., died in three hours after he was taken sick.

† Dr. Whipple when he lived in Warren, resided first opposite the Abel Merrill house on the west side of the Mikaseota, and afterwards in the house built by Joshua Merrill, Jr., now occupied by Ezra W. Keyes.

‡ Dr. Burns lived in the Ezra W. Keyes house.

not attend to all the sick, and Jonathan Clough immediately went to Hanover for Dr. Amasa Scott. Jonathan Merrill boarded Dr. Scott, and the latter had excellent success treating cases of spotted fever.* Some got well under his care, but the plague did not abate.

At first they had funerals, then they hurried the corpse away to the grave before it was hardly cold in the house. Many were buried in the night, no mourners, and the village cemetery saw in the darkness two or three men digging a grave, the sickly moon looking down upon them, saw the coffin made of rough boards hastily lowered, and heard the falling of the cold clods upon it as the grave was hurriedly filled up. Then they would drive away as though ghosts were screaming after them, and the graves were soon forgotten. Men found weeks afterwards that their nearest friends were dead and buried, no one knew where, whom they thought alive and well. The sexton often digs up those rough coffins even at this late day.†

Some had great courage and lived even in spite of the plague. Joseph Merrill the innkeeper, went wherever he was asked, to the sick bed, to the coffining the black and loathsome corpse, to the graveyard—and never got sick. His wife had the plague, but she got well. On the contrary, Mr. Samuel Merrill who lived next house to the burying ground would shut all his doors and windows when they came to bury the dead. When they brought Tristram Low dead, from the East-parte, he was particularly careful; but it was no use. The grim spectre death was after him, and in two days they carried him out upon the hill-side and buried him without a psalm or a prayer.‡

---

* Pillsbury was paid $1.34 for going to Hanover after Dr. Burns.
Clough received $1.50 for going after Dr. Scott.
Dr. Scott was paid for his services $182.50.
Jonathan Merrill received for boarding Dr. S. and horse, $10.75.
Dr. Burns received $2.00 for carrying money to Dr. Scott.
Paid Col. Clement for his wagon to Hanover, $2.20,—probably the little Dutch one.—Selectmen's Records, Vol. 1.

† 'Squire George Libbey says he dug twenty-eight graves in one month during the spotted fever time, and did not dig them all either. He also worked for a month taking care of the sick.

‡ Samuel Merrill was taken sick in the morning, and at ten o'clock at night was dead.

Lemuel Keezer, Jr., father of Ferdinand and Fayette, kept store in Warren in 1815. He was afraid of the spotted fever, very. One day the fire went out and he went to Joseph Merrill's for live coals. Dr. Wellman was sick there then, and Keezer would not go in, but sent a man in after them. Four days after, Keezer was dead, died of spotted fever.

The town suffered terribly from spotted fever. One third of the inhabitants on Beech hill died. Some families in the valley, like that of Mr. Frederick Brown, almost all died. Half a dozen members of Mr. Jonathan Clement's family died of spotted fever, and are lying in the almost forgotten grave-yard of Runaway pond. On the Height-o'-land, by the ponds near Piermont line, on Pine hill, the Summit, in the East-parte district, and the Forks district — all parts of the town suffered.*

When cold weather came on, the disease grew less malignant, and gradually disappeared. Those who recovered were almost invariably deaf, and there was a good deal of loud talk in town for years after.

Since 1815 but very few cases of spotted fever have been known in Warren. But the neighboring land of Piermont was since sorely afflicted with it — nearly half the inhabitants in Eastman pond district dying in a few months.

May the like never visit our hamlet among the hills again, for the mind shudders at uncoffined burials, at funerals without a prayer, at midnight grave-digging, at persons buried in nameless graves, unbeknown to their friends. Let the memory of the woes of 1815 never be forgotten. They will serve to chasten us and teach us that in life we are in the midst of death, and that time with his scythe may cut us down when we least expect it.

---

* Abram, Elsie, and Emily Brown, Children of Frederick Brown, died; also Ruth Knight, two children of Charles Bowles, two of Luke Libbey, and Mr. Thomas Patch, died. Three of Joseph French's children died.

CHAPTER VII.

HOW ALMOST A FAMINE, THEN A HURRICANE CAME, AND THEN A HISTORY OF ONE OF THE MOST PLEASANT YEARS WARREN EVER EXPERIENCED.

THE war came first, that of 1812, then the pestilence, the black plague, then in 1816 famine almost looked into our valley among the hills. A venerable writer of that time says that the whole face of nature appeared shrouded in gloom. The lamps of heaven kept their orbits, but their light was cheerless. The bosom of the earth in a midsummer's day was covered with a wintry mantle, and man and beast and bird sickened at the prospect. For several days in summer the people had good sleighing, and it seemed as if the order of the seasons was being reversed. On the sixth of June, the day of the meeting of the Great and General Court of New Hampshire, the snow fell several inches deep, followed by a cold and frosty night, and on the two following days snow fell and frost continued; also July the 9th, there was a deep and deadly frost that killed or palsied most vegetables.*

Then one August day in Warren, the sky was lurid in the west.

---

* DIARY OF WEATHER IN 1816.
May 16, froze hard enough on ploughed land to bear a man.
June 6, snow squalls.
June 8, snow-squalls.
June 10, frost last night.
June 11, frost last night, heavy, killed corn and five-sixths of the apples.
June 22, ice formed on water.
July 10, frost on low ground.
August 20, heavy snow on mountains. Hurricane.
August 22, heavy frost.

The clouds thickened fast, hailstones rattled on the forest, and the wind shook the tops of the trees. Suddenly it grew dark, then in the twinkling of an eye the hurricane leaped like a maniac from the skies, and howling, crashing, dizzying, it came. It lighted down on Mt. Mist at first, and then with a breadth of twenty rods, the whole forest seemed to give way; to have been felled by the stroke of some Demiurgic fury, or to have prostrated itself as the Almighty passed by.

Eastward towards Mt. Kineo, it shot like a flash of lightning. Across Pine hill it left the woods and entered the settlement. Nothing could withstand its fury. Stephen Richardson's barn was blown down, and the long shingles of its roof borne across Berry brook valley, across the Asquamchumauke, three thousand feet above it, to Amos Little's back pasture, two miles away on the side of Mt. Kineo. Nathaniel Libbey's house was unroofed and the furniture was scattered over the whole farm. A looking-glass was blown thirty rods and deposited by the wind on a stone, without breaking it.* The tornado cut a swath through Nathaniel Richardson's oats three rods wide, as smooth as if mown by a scythe. Fences were prostrated, cows lifted from their feet and sheep were killed. In bush and settlement, upland and interval, was its havoc alike fearful.

Thus passed the season. Autumn returns, alas! not to fill the arm with the generous sheaf, but the eye with the tear of disappointment. Winter came, and with it would have come starvation had it not been for the tolerably good crop of rye, the only crop that matured, which supplied the inhabitants with bread. So terrible was the year 1816, that the people grew disheartened, and many sold out and went south and west.

But in 1817 a change came. Everything was lovely, and when the year closed people said it was the happiest one they had ever known. Let us follow it through and see how the citizens spent each season,—how they worked, played, and enjoyed themselves.

As the winter wore away, a warm wind blew from the southwest, and the snow begun to melt early. What joy was there when the spring breathed under sheltering rocks the sweet arbu-

---

* Nathaniel Richardson's statement.

tus into bloom, and sky born blue-birds came down on the air of wondrous morning with throats full of fresh and fragrant melody.

As the days grew still and long in the yards of the quiet dwellings, the sturdy chopper's axe was swung all day long above the winter gathered piles. Dogs basked for hours on southern door-steps, and cattle, turned out from dark stables, tried horns and heads with each other.

In the maple groves of Warren, and on all the hill-sides around the quiet valley, sugar fires were smoking, for it was charming sugar weather; bland and sunny overhead, frosty under foot, the sap racing up from the roots every morning and running back at night for fear of a freeze.

There had been a scalding and soaking of sap-buckets, a tramping through maple woods, augur in one hand and sap spouts in the other, a repairing of arches or the hanging of great five-pail kettles; sap pails and sap yokes to bring the sap, all in order; a crackling of dry beech limbs, a roaring fire, then a simmering and seething of the sweet maple sap in the kettles before it leaped up in white dancing foam only to be kept from overflowing by being wallopped with a stick having a piece of pork on its end.*

Amos Little had a glorious sugar place on Beech hill, and his boys and girls,— for he had a large family,— were determined to have a sugar party. Young folks, Merrills, Clements, Bixbys, Knights, and numerous others came to the beautiful farm where George E. Leonard lives now. They had fun and frolic; rosy cheeked girls laughing as they stamp the mud from their thick boots, charming forms carried in stout arms across the little rill which now swollen leaps laughing down to the Mikaseota, sometimes called Black brook.

The great sugaring-off kettle is hung on a pole placed on two forked stakes, by itself. The syrup, enough for all, is turned in, the fire lighted, and then there is a rustic jubilee over the browning cauldron, as the fragrant steam grows richer and the color deepens from hue to hue of russet, till the syrup clings in double drops on the edge of the skimmer, and the hot fluid changes to delicious gum when poured over the melting ice cake. There

---

* The farmers in Warren often use the last runs of sap to make spruce beer — an excellent and very common drink in Warren.

were pretty lips closing over beech paddle sticks, and young John L. Merrill and Russell K. Clement blistered their tongues and got laughed at for they could not wait for the delicious sweet to cool.

Their hearts were all happy, and what sweet songs were sung in the dusk of nightfall, as the earliest frog peeped from the swamp in the valley below. The sweet songs of that day, alas! what were they? They are gone, they are forgotten, like the smiles and the roses of those who sang them, like the hopes and the affections of the youths who listened to them. The triumphs of the singers of those days and the popularity of the songs, where are they? It is a lesson for us; but let us chase it out of mind. Be happy while ye may. We love the month of March, for in Warren it is the liveliest and most romantic month of the year. No tree does so much for happiness as the sugar maple. It brings more good cheer, more joy and frolic, more money into the pocket and more sweetness upon the table than all the rest of the forest trees put together.

As the sun run higher and the air grew warmer, there was a sound in the earth, as if myriads of fairies were at work preparing juices for the grass and fruits and flowers,— a sound of tiny footsteps, multitudinous bells deep down in caverns and dingles, and here and there a bank smiled back in downy green the sun's radiant favors. And then the leaves come out, at first no larger than a mouse's ear, and thousands of birds are singing in all the fields and woods. Up narrow roads, the one to Red-oak hill, and those to Rocky falls, Beech hill, Pine hill, and the East-parte, between high, mossy banks where the little runnels come rushing and chiming along, through the wild, still, shady woods of Warren, and in fields deep with the greenest grass and bright with the sunshine and glory of spring; all these birds are at work building their nests, each in its own peculiar fashion; the song sparrow, the vesper sparrow, the grass finch and Wilson's thrush, on the ground and under warm hummocks; the robin on nearly every tree, black birds and cat-birds in the hedges; bob-o'-links in the meadows of Runaway pond and the swaley fields by Mooschillock road; vireos and orioles in the ever waving boughs of the elms in the valleys, and the maples on all the hills; warblers among the emerald green leaves of the wild rose-brier, to say nothing of the blue-bird in an old knot hole of a fence post; swallows in the barn, Jennie wren in a box in the apple tree, and martins in the house on the top of a pole.

The men are out in the fields and gardens, the cottage dames and the rosy daughters are engaged in the renewal of flower borders, in the sowing of seeds and the planting of shrubs; old men sit watching them on the steps or wooden benches, on the warm side of the house, while groups of children are scattered here and there over the happy fields, tracing the fence sides or the bright streams or running to secure the first dandelions, their clear voices all the while ringing out from the distant steeps and hill-tops. There they find the sugar plum, the wild-bird cherry and the moosemissa in bloom, their flowers hanging on the waving boughs or fluttering on the earth, a profusion of beauty in which the perceptions are almost lost.

Men went to work with good courage in the spring of 1817. They seemed to feel that good times were coming back. How did they work? How did they live? The farmer of that period was up in the morning by half past four, stoutly dressed in his leather pants and sheeps-gray frock. At five he gets up his help. His wife hurries the girls out of bed, crying, "Up sleepy heads, the sun will burn your eyes out if you lay there." The house is swept, the cows are milked, the hogs are fed. Man and boys go to work, fodder stock, clean out barn, prepare for the day's work.

Then comes breakfast. How some of the old settlers could eat. In olden times huge basins of bean-porridge and loaves as big as bee hives and pretty much of the same shape, and as brown as the backs of their own hands, delighted and refreshed our ancestors. To this fare they would betake themselves with a capacity that only pure air and hard labor can give. A settler would eat as much of these as would answer for a round family now at breakfast, and then he would only be ready for his dish of pork and beans; pounds of pork six inches thick set on the top of a peck of baked beans. What a pile he takes on his plate, how sharp is the vinegar he pours on them, how keen the pepper, and then they vanish as rapidly as if they did not follow that mess of porridge and those huge hunches of bread. Christian William Whiteman, who lived on the top of the Height-o'-land, said he "could eat three quarts of baked beans and also Indian pudding and other 'fixings' suitable to accompany them, at his morning meal." Mr. Pixly, a tall gaunt man who once resided in Charleston by Tarleton lake, said that "many a time he had eaten a six quart pan full of pork and beans and vinegar, at a single sitting and then could make a famine among the pies and cakes and cheese on the table." Mr. Nathaniel Richardson, who has had his home on the East-parte road for more than half a century, has been known to eat two full grown chickens, seventeen large, mealy potatoes, and plum-pudding in abundance along with them, and he said he could always top out such a slender repast with twenty-five cents worth of cracker toast, when he stopped at a hotel. Yet Mr. Richardson never was sick in his life, only a little spleeny by spells, and now at the age of nearly eighty years he is tough as an ox.*

And then what mugs of cider those old settlers could drink. A Mr. Lund could swallow a pint at a draught, without stopping to breathe, and Dr. Ezra B. Libbey, in his day, could easily perform the same feat, while Mr. Obadiah Libbey, who lived in Warren long ago, has often been known to proudly drink a quart and a half of hard old cider without once taking his lips from the mug. Mr. Samuel Jewell, who lived on Pine hill road, often said he "wished his throat was as long as a pine mast, that he might more fully enjoy the good taste of the fluid as it trickled down." These are only a few notable cases where hundreds could be cited, and we can but envy the keen appetites and great capacity of our early settlers. Breakfast eaten and at ten they would take a hearty luncheon of bread, nut-cakes, and cheese, to set their appetites right for dinner.†

There is plowing in the field, there is manure to be carted out, there is harrowing, and sowing, and harrowing again, there is furrowing and dropping potatoes and corn, and covering the hills;

---

* Josiah Burnham, surveyor, had an enviable capacity and appetite. He could eat eight quarts of hasty pudding and milk, at a sitting.—Anson Merrill's statement.
  Rev. Charles Bowles could frequently do something in the way of eating. He once eat a whole quarter of lamb and nearly everything else on the table, at 'Squire Jonathan Merrill's, thereby depriving the 'Squire and his family of their morning meal. Mrs. Merrill had to do another cooking that morning.—Moses P. Kimball's statement.

† Mr. James Clement's stories.

there is picking stones, laying wall, and mending fences to keep the cattle in the pastures. Then there is washing of sheep at the pool in the river, and the shearing of sheep in all the barns.*

At home the wife and girls boil potatoes for the hogs, take turns at the churn, gown sleeves rolled up to the shoulder, kneeling to press the sweet curd to the bottom of the "hoop," to salt and turn cheese, and watch progress of different stages from newness and white softness, to their investment with the unctuous coating of a goodly age. They also see that the calves, geese, turkeys, and barn-yard fowls are properly fed, that the door-yard is nicely picked up and swept. Some had a taste for beauty and were most zealous and successful florists. To select rich and suitable soils, to sow and plant, to nurse, and shade, and water, to watch the growth and expansion of flowers of great promise was an occupation affording much enjoyment to our grandmothers. They had the polyanthus, auricular, hyacinth, carnation, tulip, and ranunculus. Then there were pinks, and poppies, and sweet Williams, and peonies, and lilacs, and a host of others; but the splendid dahlias and pansies of to-day were unknown to them. Mrs. Enoch Noyes and Mrs. G. W. Prescott, daughter of Mr. Isaac Merrill, could boast of having the nicest flower gardens.

At night the farmer sits down with his men and boys by the fire, and they talk over the work of the morrow, how to plant, hoe and sow, and where. His wife has a little work-table set near, where she makes and mends; the girls knit, darn stockings, and fix caps for Sunday.

Now days there is a complaint that the farmer has been spoiled by the growth of luxurious habits and effeminacy in the nation.

---

* *Sheep Marks.*—In those primitive times, when fences were rare, and sheep were nimble, it was found necessary to record the marks by which one's sheep might be known or recognized. Accordingly we are certified that Obadiah Clement's sheep are marked by one-half crop on the upper side of the right ear, and one-half crop on the under side of the left ear. Stevens Merrill's a fork like a swallow's tail on the end of the left ear. Joseph Merrill's, a crop of the left ear. Jonathan Merrill's, a crop of the left ear and a slit on the under side of the same. Caleb Homan's, a fork like a swallow's tail on the end of the left ear, and a crop from off the right ear. Amos Little's, a slit on the end of the right ear. Joshua Copp's, a fork like a swallow's tail on the right ear, and a crop on the left. Joshua Merrill's, a crop from off each ear. This mark is now taken by John Whitcher, May 27, 1814. N. B.—Joshua Merrill has removed from this town. (1)

(1) Col. Moses H. Clement's ram once troubled Mr. Keezer and his sheep. Keezer took the ram in the night, led him to Mr. Clement's house and tied him to the door-latch. When Mr. C. opened the door next morning it yanked his ramship, and, indignant, the brute with a bound and a bunt knocked Col. C. "flatter than a flounder."

Old furniture has been cast out of the houses, and carpets, sofas, and pianos, are to be found where once were wooden benches and the spinning-wheel; that daughters are sent to boarding schools, instead of to market, and the sons, instead of growing up sturdy husbandmen like their fathers, are made clerks, shop-tenders, or some such skimmy dish things. There is some truth in this. But never mind; the farmer should be a rural king, sowing his grain and reaping his harvest with a glad heart, and he can do this by being educated.

How much better the farmer enjoys himself than the merchant. The latter coops himself up in a small shop, and there day after day, month after month, year after year, he is to be found like a bat in a hole of the wall, or a toad in the heart of a stone or of an oak tree. Spring, and summer, and autumn go round, sunshine and flowers spread over the world, the birds sing, the sweetest flowers blow, the sweetest waters murmur along the vales, but they are all lost upon him; he is the doleful prisoner of Mammon, and so he lives and dies. The farmer would not take the wealth of the world on such terms. The bright sun, the pure air, the green meadows, the clear streams, the growing crops, the flocks and herds in the pastures, the keen appetite and good health are far to be preferred.

There were no frosts, no snows, no cold and chilling winds in the summer of 1817. All over town there was bustling life and even over to Charleston district, by Tarleton lake, where times had been the hardest, the hearts of men took courage. Corn grew again, the potatoes were luxuriant, and deep grass overhung the banks of all the little streams, and many a flower nodded above the clear water. Upon the fields was a rich mosaic of colors, and on the edge by the wood were seen the wild sun-flower, ox-eye daisies, tiger lilies, and the purple and gold of the hard-hack. Among the crimson headed clover were honey suckles, buttercups, golden rod, and white top, scenting all the air. The oats were so heavy the farmer was afraid they would lodge; the rye was as tall as a man's head, while shadows fly over the yellow barley, and tumbling waves chase each other on the acres of wheat. Horses stand under the great maples by the road, brushing flies with their tails, the sheep are grazing on the hill-sides, cows are feeding where the grass is shortest and sweetest, while Thomas Pillsbury's spotted bull lows in Mt. Mist's echoing pastures.

They were a happy people over at Charleston. Amos Tarleton, Thomas Pillsbury, Ephraim Potter, Richard Pillsbury, Stephen Lund,* Daniel Day, Hosea Lund, Benj. Bixby, and others, lived there. David Smith was born there. He was a good school-master, was selectman, tax collector, town treasurer, and county treasurer; cool, shrewd, long-headed, he was one of Warren's smartest men. They had a Methodist society, a class, Sabbath school and regular preaching, a good school-house, which also answered for a church; many have taught school in it, and a grave yard was by it, where the early settlers were sleeping. Their buildings were good, their great barns were always well filled with hay, and their sugar places were the best in town.

But alas! all this is changed. The dwellers in the district by the lake are all dead, the houses and the barns have mouldered away, the spot where they stood can hardly be found, and the fields and the pastures are grown with forest trees. Even the old school-house, the church in Charleston, is gone. Nothing but the foundation remains. The burying ground by it is overgrown; the thistle shakes its lonely head by the tombstone, the gray moss whistles to the wind, the fox looks out of its hole by the sunken graves, and the wood-brakes and the birches wave above them.

Whence came this desolation? The great west takes away the young men of Warren: they are gone to cities, the gold mines of California invited some of them; some died on the battle-field. A hundred years may go by before Charleston district shall have such a thriving, happy population again.

The sugar and the wool crop made, the hay crop was the next to be harvested. The farmers of Warren have always raised their full supply of hay, never having been obliged to import any, and grazing and stock-raising has been one of their most profitable employments. Who does not love haying time. True, it may be "hot as blazes," but what a softness clothes those green mountains; what a depth of shadow fills the hollows; how sweet the voice of

---

* Stephen Lund lived to be over ninety years old. He was a cooper, and a red headed man, bony and rawny. He shot a trout that weighed four pounds. He used to catch large quantities of trout from Tarleton lake and carry them to Haverhill and sell them, court time.

the waters rises on the hushed landscape. Magnificent arcades of trees stretch up the sides of the fair streams, their luxuriant masses of foliage shading the limpid coolness below.

What a luxury to follow some rapid stream, or sitting down on a green bank, deep in grass and flowers, to pull out the spotted trout from the bubbling eddy below the boulders or from his lurking place beneath the broad stump and the spreading roots of the alder. A summer day spent beside Patch brook as it runs through the meadows, up Hurricane brook to the cool cascades in the deep woods of Mount Carr, by the Mikaseota, or Black brook, by Ore hill's foamy stream, by Berry brook, by the roistering Oliverian, by Merrill brook,* or East branch, or along the roaring, foaming Asquamchumauke, with the glorious hills and the deep, rich foliage clad mountains around you is most delightful — is grand. The power and passion and deep felicity that come breathing from the mountains, forests, and waterfalls, from clouds that sail above, and storms blustering and growling in the wind, from all the mighty magnificence, solitude, and antiquity of nature, cannot be unfolded.

Sit down by the pond where tiny Cold brook comes in. There the wild rose is putting out and the elder is in flower. The lilies are as lovely as ever, the butter-cups as yellow; harebells, violets, and a thousand other kinds of flowers listen to the tinkling music of the stream.

The May flies in thousands come forth to their day-life, flying up and down. There are horse flies and red flies pestering the cattle on the hill-side opposite; but the king-bird, laughing from the breezy maple top, is after them. Over the water midges are celebrating their airy labyrinthine dances with amazing adroitness looking almost like columns of smoke as they shine in new life and new beauty. Dragon flies of all sizes and colors,— boys call them devil's darning needles, and say, " Look out or they will sew your eyes up," —are hovering and skimming, and settling among the water plants or on some twig, evidently full of enjoyment. The great azure bodied one with its filmy wings darts past with reckless speed, and slender ones, blue, and purple, and dun, and

---

* Joseph Patch used to kill moose near the head of Merrill brook.

black, and jointed bodies, made as of shining silk and animated for a week or two of summer sunshine by some frolic spell, now pursue each other and now rest in sleep.

The bob-o'-link in the meadow up the brook, flies up and down on balancing wings uttering its many toned joyous songs, tittering as if in high glee; swallows are skimming along the fields and over the waters catching flies; the song sparrow sings so sweet in the flowers and grasses, the white throated finch warbles tender and plaintive in the fir copse up by Amos Little's field; the Maryland yellow throat in the alders over the water says "sit-u-see, sit-u-see," in such a winsome way; water-wag-tail repeats its "crake, crake," from the grass in the swamp; the spotted sandpiper says, "weet, weet," from the old log and muddy bank; crows are cawing in the woods across the pond, and the water itself ripples on, clear and musical, and checkered from many a leaf and bent and moving bough. We lift up our heads and in the west above Stephen Lund's where farmer Joshua lived once, what a ruby sun, what a gorgeous assemblage of sunset clouds.

The oats, rye, barley, and wheat, were good this year, 1817, and when they were gathered, autumn with its rich corn harvest, and all its happy human groups, and bright days of calm, steady splendor came. After the first frosts, the Indian summer began, and a soft haze pervaded the atmosphere and settled like a thin gray cloud on the horizon, bringing a delicious, sweet, sleep-like feeling, which seemed to fill the valley. On all sides the sky appeared resting upon a wealth of colors, orange and yellow, purple and crimson, blue and green, and red, and every shade and hue that mantled the forests of the mountains. In the woods on the edge of the clearings, fields and pastures, red squirrels chased one another over crisp leaves on the ground and along the limpid branches of the trees, yelping and chattering like king-fishers. Fox-colored sparrows, nut-hatches and great golden-winged woodpeckers vied in their notes and seemed resolved on merriment while the season lasted. The white-crowned sparrow came down from Labrador where it had spent the summer rearing its young and singing all the day long, and stopped a day or so by the banks of the Asquamchumauke, before it hastened on its journey to its winter home in Florida and the West Indies. Wild geese with their weird hawnk-honk-e-honk, were seen tearing the yielding air with wings fierce and strong, as in harrow-like form they hurried down the valley, and now and then the farmer in his field would hear a strange, wild cry, coming seemingly from mid heaven, as a flock of swans, flying more than one hundred and twenty miles an hour, clove the air thousands of feet above the mountains. As the days went by, the leaves of the trees merging from their bright dappled colors into a dull uniform brown, dropped to the earth and were swept by the winds into dusty, crackling torrents, and borne to unknown resting places on the bosom of every tinkling rill. The turnips were dug, potatoes garnered in the cellar, apples carried to the cider-mill and the corn was stacked for husking.

The cider mill! Who does not have one in recollection. They made cider at Mr. Nathaniel Clough's in those days. Mr. Samuel Merrill built the first and only one in the East-parte; then old Mr. Batchelder and Mr. Foote each had one on Pine hill, and Capt. Joseph Merrill one by the village burying ground. What pleasant memories of bins of russet, red, and golden apples, of the great cog-wheels, of the horse going round and round attached to the creaking crane, the crushed apples in the great trough, the large wooden screws that compressed the cheese that was put on so neatly in fresh yellow straw, the gushing juice that flowed so freely at every turn of the levers, into the great holder beneath, and us boys with oaten straws sucking our fill from the little brooklet running down, better pleased and happier than kings. May the picture of the old cider-mill never fade away.

Husking bees were common then in our hamlet among the hills, they are common in Warren now. Generally they were on pleasant evenings in the early part of October. They had one at Joseph Merrill's this season, the grandest one of the year. The people collected from nearly every district in town, my father and his numerous brothers, the Clough boys, the Patches, the Clements, consisting of several families,— old Obadiah would not go,— the Merrill's, and they were numerous, the Batchelders, Richardsons, Lunds, Pillsburys, Dows, and many others, were there. The corn was piled in the centre of the capacious kitchen, and around the heap squatted the huskers. The room was abundantly as well as spectrally lighted from the immense fire-place briskly glowing with pitch knots and clumps of bark. Boys and girls, young men and their wives, and some old people listened to songs and varied their labors with such pleasantry as was natural to the occasion. Great ardor was evinced in pursuit of the red ear, for which piece of fortune the discoverer had the privilege of a kiss from any lady he should nominate. Stevens Knight was the lucky finder, and people who remember him can well imagine how he stammered and blushed, and refused to kiss any girl, and how one of 'Squire Abel's daughters threw her arms around his neck and gave him a good smack amidst the shouts and laughter of the whole party. Nobody accused Stevens Knight of bringing the red ear in his pocket.

The pile was finished and the hard glossy ears were stored away under the eaves of the garret. Then new cider and old was passed around, and some had something stronger. All now repaired to the hall over the bar-room; the violin sounded and the young folks formed for a dance. Enoch R. Weeks danced with Sally Little, Col. Benj. Clement with Miss Dolly Gove, Nathaniel Copp with Miss Mary Pillsbury, and so on; we have forgotten the names of the others. Billy Brock the fiddler was a grand musician and his very soul seemed breathing in his music.* All gloom disappeared and fun and frolic saw them into the small hours.

For variety came the supper. There were great dishes of beans and Indian pudding, pumpkin pies, pewter platters full of dough-nuts, sweet cakes, fruit and cheese, cider, bottles of native wine and spirits washing it down. And then they danced again. We won't go home till morning, was the way they did at this happy husking.

Who can blame them! Peace, plenty, and health had come,

---

* Billy Brock was of Ryegate, Vt., and was the best fiddler in all the country round. He would balance a tumbler of whisky on his head, dance with it, lie down on the floor with it and all the time be playing the violin for others to dance.

Nathaniel Copp tried to fiddle for a party, could only play one tune, broke the fiddle strings trying to play another, and the party broke up in a huff. They sent over the Height-o'-land to get the fiddle for him.

Mrs. Jonathan Clough, then Miss Pillsbury, danced with Joseph Patch, Jr. Mary Pillsbury with Joshua Copp, Jr. Sally Little and Tamar Little danced. The Patches were all dancers. Joshua Copp, 3d, danced. Betsey, who married Joseph Farnham, Sally, who married 'Squire Weeks, Mary, who married Mr. Clark

A PROSPEROUS SEASON.

and why should not the people of our great history be happy at the close of so fruitful and prosperous a year as 1817.

---

of Landaff, 'Squire Abel's daughters, all danced. Dolly Gove and Betsey Gove, Sally White and Ruth White, Col. Cole, father of D. Quincy Cole, all of Wentworth, used to come to Warren to dance. Also Miss Dolly Page. Jonathan Clement's girls,— one of them married uncle Tom Pillsbury, and the other Lt. Perkins Fellows,— danced. Col. Ben. Clement is the son of Jonathan Clement, innkeeper.— Anson Merrill's statement.

CHAPTER VIII.

WHAT A WOMAN CAN DO AND HOW SHE DID IT; OR THE ACCOMPLISHMENT OF ONE OF THE GREATEST "REQUISITES" OF THE LAST CENTURY, VIZ: THE BUILDING OF A MEETING HOUSE.

REV. PETER POWERS preached the first sermon in Warren, Rev. Elijah R. Sabin brought the doctrines of John Wesley, Methodism, to our hamlet among the hills, and Rev. Joseph Boody founded a society of Freewill Baptists in the valley. These and their associates preached sometimes out in the open air, sometimes in the houses or barns of the settlers, and sometimes in the school-houses; for as yet there was no meeting-house in Warren. The first generation of Warren's settlers had tried hard to build one during the last years of the eighteenth century, but had failed in the attempt and then the enterprise slumbered.*

'Squire Jonathan Merrill's wife had died. He found another lady-love, the widow Chellis, down country, and eventually married and brought her to live in Warren.† She told the 'Squire that it was a shame for so smart a town as Warren to be without a

---

* 1806.—"Voted to choose a committee of six persons for the purpose of appointing another committee of three indifferent persons living out of town, for the purpose of establishing a suitable place in this town for erecting a house for public meetings. Chose Col. Obadiah Clement, William Butler, Mr. Jonathan Fellows, Capt. Joseph Patch, Lieut. Stephen Flanders, and Mr. Aaron Welch, for the above mentioned committee."

Dec. 17, 1803.—"Voted not to build a meeting-house in the town way, but that we are willing it should be done by subscription."

Paid William Butler for money he paid the committee for appointing a place to set a meeting-house, $15.00. For expenses at Clement's, 70c.—Selectmen's Records, Vol. i.

† The widow Chellis was from Amesbury, Mass.

meeting-house. She told it to him twice, and she gave him curtain lectures on the subject; in short she gave him no peace till he came to think as she did about it, and until he had stirred up the whole town about the matter and made them all feel that it was an "abominable shame" for the town to be without a meeting-house.

So in the selectmenship of Joseph Patch, Jr., Moses H. Clement, and Stephen Flanders, 1818, the citizens of our little democracy in General Assembly voted to build a meeting-house, the size to be forty feet by fifty feet within joint. Chose Jonathan Merrill, Nathaniel Clough, Abel Merrill, and James Williams a committee to superintend its building, and for that purpose was appropriated all the money due the town on the leases, including the present year, and also the avails of the wild land belonging to the town. What can't a woman do?

To the building of the house the committee proceeded in right good earnest. The frame, that good old oaken one, which is yet as good as new, was hauled from many a dark recess of the old woods, the inhabitants ready to assist, giving many a long day's work. In the neighborhood of Wachipauka pond where the Indians used to camp the oaks were cut, and the long timbers for the ceiling over head; and the masts in the steeple, nearly a hundred feet high, came down from Pine hill, the first selectman, Joseph Patch, Jr., having taken the job to put them upon the ground. Reuben Clifford was the master workman; he could handle a broad axe better than any man in town, and he could hew almost as smooth as one could plane. Amos Little and James Dow helped hew. James Williams took a job of boring, and Samuel Knight made pins. People loved to come and look on, and the master workman would good naturedly say, "You must bring something to treat with if you want to stop about here." The people were so well pleased with his work and the enterprise, that he got many bottles of old rum to drink.

By the first of July the frame was ready for erection, and the "Fourth" was decided to be the time when the raising should take place. What preparations were made for that day! They must have a grand collation and so the building committee had a table constructed, and rude benches on each side of it across the entire common. All day long the third of July the farmers' wives and their daughters had done their very best cooking for the collation. How anxious they were when they went to bed the night before the raising.

The morning of that expected day at last dawned; but before the sun had kindled a rosy light on the bald top of Moosehillock, or on the green wooded summit of Mount Carr, the workmen were on their way. Few indeed were the sleepy persons found that morning, for a raising was a raising in those days, and every body was delighted to attend; but the raising of a meeting-house was a sight seldom witnessed but once in a life-time.

From every quarter they came; the good man and his buxom dame, and their rosy daughters who had spent a long hour more at the toilet that morning than usual. All were there, and by the presence of those fair faces many a young man was stimulated to perform herculean feats of lifting and mounting giddy heights, every way worthy of his ancestors. All about the destined spot lay strewn the heavy timbers. The old men with shining broad axes were shaping pins, or smoothing the end of many a tenon, while the master builder, Reuben Clifford, with rule under his arm, and feeling the great responsibility resting upon him, was moving hither and thither, now giving directions to one party and then to another, whom drolly enough he had designated his oxen, his steers, and his bulls, in order that they might more readily come at the word. These were tugging, lifting, and straining themselves into very red faces as they carried the heavy timbers over the numerous blocks and chips. The building committee were there also giving instructions to each other, the master builder, and every one else.

And now one huge broadside is ready. The rugged yeomanry of Warren range themselves side by side; the master builder gives the word, "All ready, heave-er-up!" shouting in the most wonderful manner; and creaking and groaning, that old oaken broadside slowly rises. A pause — the stout following poles hold; and now long pike poles are applied, guided firmly by strong arms, and again that broadside goes up, as a hush comes over the anxious crowd, eagerly watching, but who soon breathe more freely as the huge timbers erect settle firmly into their resting places. And now with no laggard hands the remaining broadside and the cross-timbers are put in their places, and long ere the rays of the setting sun had departed, the roof, with its crowning steeple towering above, was in its proper position.

Here succeeding generations must lament the loss of that speech called naming the house, every way worthy of the occasion, which Col. Benjamin Clement delivered from the ridge-pole. The gentle breezes of that summer day wafted it far over the green foliage of the wood to the distant hill-sides, where it was recorded in their beautifully shaded dells; but no man can read their phonography.*

Then True Stevens exhibited a mighty feat of jumping ten feet at a leap on the plates and cross-timbers, thirty feet above the ground, the whole length of the frame, and Samuel Knight stood on his head upon the ridge-pole and made flourishes with his feet up into the clear sky, much to the delight of the assembled multitude who held their breath at the sight.

The oration and the gymnastic feats were each greeted with a great shout, and then all the cider possible was drank and they hurried to partake of the grand collation so bountifully prepared for them. Mrs. James Williams, from the East-parte, took charge of setting the tables, and Aunt Ruth Homan and her beautiful daughters, and Mrs. Daniel Ramsey acted on the committee with her. Mr. James Williams and Mr. Samuel Merrill brought out whole wagon loads of the very best eatables, and the Beech hillites and the dwellers of Runaway pond and those from the Heighto'-land, Pine hill, the Summit, and the Forks, also brought a great abundance. There was an immense crowd, many from the neighboring towns;† and how they ate, for it was a free collation; and

---

* It was customary to name all buildings. Jack Tennant got off this, Jesse Little having composed it for him, on a building Gov. Samuel Flanders framed for Gov. Stevens Merrill:—
" Here is a frame deserves a name,
Here is a frame deserves a name.
It is made of spruce and sapling pine—
It was taken down old and put up new,
And you all can see what two Governors can do."
They were called Governors because each had had a few votes for governor at some town meeting.
Then there was a shout, and they had all the cider they could drink.

† Rice Howard and Mr. Samuel Bennett, both of Haverhill, noted gamblers, who attended all musters and public gatherings, were present. It was wonderful what sums of money they would fleece out of the simple country people. The numerous anecdotes of their exploits would fill a volume.

how happy they were when they went home that night, thinking they would now have such a nice meeting-house.

Captain John Gove, the witch killer of Wentworth, and his two sons, Edward and Winthrop, all excellent carpenters, finished off the house. Captain Gove hired a room at the store Capt. Benjamin Merrill built, and his daughters, Dolly and Betsey, cooked for and boarded them during the time. Messrs. Tucker & French, from Haverhill, painted the outside and inside of the meeting-house, steeple and all, and boarded at Joseph Merrill's inn while doing the work. Anson Merrill, a boy then, raised the money by subscription to paint the inside; but it was not all finished that year.*

George W. Copp, son of 'Squire Joshua Copp, went over the Height-o'-land and got the underpinning near Tarleton lake. He hammered and set it very nicely.

The work progressed steadily, and early in the fall, though it was not fully finished, the meeting-house was dedicated. The widow Chellis, 'Squire Jonathan's second wife, was a Congregationalist, and of course no minister but a Congregationalist was fit to preach the dedicatory sermon. Rev. Edward Evens lived at Wentworth. He was a talented man, preached half the time in that pious town, was a missionary the other half, and during week days attended to the duties of Judge of Probate for Grafton County, which office he held. He was the one 'Squire Jonathan's wife selected to preach, and of course he did it.

But all the people must be pleased, so Rev. James Spencer, a Freewill Baptist preacher, assisted, making the prayer and reading the hymns.

The choir of Warren was anxious that day; but its members did their best. Joseph Boynton† was leader, and an excellent singer was he. Betsey Knight, daughter of Samuel, sung air, Mrs. Joseph Boynton,— Sally Knight once,— sang counter or alto, while Betsey Little, Jesse Little, Benj. Little and others assisted. The critics of those days said the choir did exceedingly well.

---

* Nathaniel Richardson shaved the shingles put on the old meeting-house.

† *Funeral.*—Joseph and Orlando, sons of Joseph Boynton, once had a funeral over a grasshopper. They dug a grave, preached and sang, and then prayed that "the Lord might be merciful to the leastest and lastest remains of ye poor grasshopper." Orlando, it is said, shed tears, and a whole generation remembered that prayer. Iantha, a sister of Joseph and Orlando, was chief mourner.

SALE OF PEWS.

Edward Evens was hired to preach in Warren half the time, for several years, and the town voted in 1819 to appropriate the interest of the minister lands towards paying him.*

After the dedication came the sale of the pews. They were set up at auction as is usual in such cases; the person bidding the highest having the first choice and the next highest the next choice, and so on till all were sold. Amos Little got the best pew, the right hand front one, in the broad aisle. He said he was not going to be second to anybody in relation to pews. 'Squire Jonathan Merrill got the next, the left hand front one. He pretended to be a little mortified because he did not get the first; but shrewd folks said he was sharp and had got the best pew after all — the widow Chellis thought it was the best.

James Williams, Moses H. Clement, and Joseph Merrill, each had pews back of Amos Little's on the right-hand side of the broad aisle, in their order, and Abel Merrill, his son Daniel Merrill, and William Kelley, had them in the same manner back of 'Squire Jonathan's.

Sept. 21, 1819, at a town meeting held for the purpose, the following report of the building committee was read and accepted, viz:—

1st. The meeting-house finished except the painting.

2d. All the pews disposed of and are the property of the purchasers when paid for, otherwise the property of the committee. The purchasers and owners of pews to have the liberty to pass and repass the doors and aisles to and from said pews whenever the doors are open for public worship or town meetings.

---

* *Ministers.*—Paid Edward Evens for preaching in 1820, $40.39.
1823.—P'd Newell Culver, $7.50. Mr. Mills, $7.50. Mr. Washburn, $2.00, all for preaching that year.

Rev. Edward Evens was settled in Enfield, N. H., and was dismissed in 1805. He was quite popular, and collected a church of not far from a hundred members. But Mr. Evens was *not* an orthodox congregationalist, nor was his church an orthodox church of that order. Aged people who knew him well say that in sentiment he was always a Methodist.—Hist. of N. H. Churches, 531.

Rev. Jonathan Hovey, of Piermont, used to preach at Warren, occasionally. He was a congregationalist, and Col. Obadiah Clement and old Mrs. Ben. Brown admired him very much. They used to say they wished he would drive the Methodists all out, and then they would have none but decent preaching.

Pay for Preaching.—Rev. Mr. Haynes occasionally preached in Warren, but lived at Romney. Lemuel Keezer, innkeeper, once told him that he would pay him for preaching in grain. He took a two bushel bag, put in wheat, corn, rye, oats, barley, buck-wheat, India wheat, and a few small potatoes, and carried it to the parson. The latter looked at it and said he could not make anything out of it. Keezer flatteringly replied, "Well, parson, you can make just as much out of it as I can out of your preaching."

3*d*. The other parts of the house to be for the use of the town upon the following conditions, viz: That the town pay over to the committee all the money and land they agreed to give to encourage a committee to undertake to build said meeting-house, which was three hundred dollars or thereabouts.

4*th*. The committee respectfully request the town to unite with them and adopt the best measures or means to finish painting the house and erect door-steps.

JONATHAN MERRILL,
NATHANIEL CLOUGH,*
ABEL MERRILL,
JAMES WILLIAMS,† } Committee.

N. B.—There are demands in the hands of the Committee arising from the sale of two pews, viz: number forty-one and forty-two, to the amount of fifty dollars or more, besides what we have laid out painting said meeting-house.‡

Reader, the first time I ever went to meeting it was in this old meeting-house, and I sat in number forty-one. It was on the right of the pulpit in the body of the house, and was, like all the rest, a very large pew, twelve feet long and eight feet wide. There were banisters in the pew walls, seats on two sides that turned up during prayer and often fell down "slam." My mother used to stand me on the seat when they sang, and I often amused myself turning one of the loose banisters to make it squeak during sermon. What an object of wonder was the sounding board over the minister's head. Once I asked what it was for, and they told me "that it was placed there so that if the minister told a lie it would fall on his head and kill him." The pulpit was a little castle high up. With what veneration I first entered it. In it was a

---

* Nathaniel Clough came from Hampstead, N. H.

† James Williams came from Haverhill, Mass., and was a descendant of Hannah Dustin of Indian fame. He had one of her pewter plates which was marked "H. D." A Mrs. Crook has the plate now.

‡ *Lock on Meeting-House Door.*—Jacob Whitcher moved away up country about this time. It was maliciously said of him that he, like some other folks, would lie when the truth would do a good deal better. He would tell his neighbors what a powerful lock they put on the meeting-house door in Warren. He said it was one of the most remarkable locks ever made in modern times; that it was so large that it required a "hand-speke" to turn the key; that when the bolt snapped back it made so loud a noise that it could be heard a mile.

He would tell the story in such an honest manner that his friends thought it was true, and when they came down marketing in the winter, they would call at Joseph Merrill's inn near the meeting-house, and ask to be shown the wonderful lock.

cricket for short ministers to stand upon, and the window behind with its circular glass was a wonderful piece of architecture. In the north porch was the black table and pall used in burying the dead. How I dreaded the north porch, how shunned it.

At first they had no fires in the meeting-house and in winter the minister used to preach with woolen mittens on his hands and our mothers would carry the old fashioned foot stoves, which they would replenish noon times at Joseph Merrill's inn, to keep themselves warm during service. Stoves were put into the meeting-house in 1830.

Mr. James Dow was the tythingman in the new church. He sat to the left of the minister, under the edge of the long gallery that extended on three sides of the house. One Sabbath, while the minister was preaching, a large yellow dog started from the right and traveled round the whole edge of the gallery till he came to the point over Uncle Dow's head. Addison W. Gerald from the East-parte sat there, and the Devil whispered in Mr. Gerald's ear, " Push the yellow cur off." No sooner said than it was done. The poor beast falling fifteen feet, struck on Uncle Dow's bald head; it hurt; and the " purp " he yelled and he yowled. Uncle Dow, who was dozing, sprang to his feet, stamped furiously and at the same instant sung out in a voice like thunder, " Ahem! Ahem! I hope the owner will keep that dog to home and stay to home himself." Of course the choir never smiled nor the audience either. The minister also preserved his dignity; but one thing is certain, he closed the services in very short metre.*

One Sabbath at meeting, I distinctly remember hearing my father who always sat in the singing seats above, he was town clerk too, cry out, " Hear ye, hear ye! notice is hereby given that Russell K. Clement and Betsey Eames intend marriage." There was a grand sensation, for they all thought Russell was a confirmed old bachelor; but perhaps no more sensation than was customary on publishing the " bans."

In the long row of meeting-house sheds we school boys used to play " I spy," " hide and seek," " tag," and " goal," and sometimes plagued the wrens that had their nests in the braces, or watched the swallows which always built in the old belfry.

---

* Gen. Michael P. Merrill's statement.

Our fathers' meeting-house was used for forty years, then it became too unfashionable for a more fashionable generation. In 1859 it was moved back to the northeast corner of the common, altered to a more modern style, and now within the same walls and under the same roof that Reuben Clifford, Amos Little, and James Dow hewed and framed, the dwellers of Warren worship.

In 1826 the town raised fifty-seven dollars and sixty-three cents in lieu of the avails of the wild land voted to the committee appointed to build the meeting-house in 1818.—See Town Book.

CHAPTER IX.

A GAY LITTLE CHAPTER ABOUT WITCHES.

WE should not perform our whole duty as a faithful historian unless we should depict the thoughts, beliefs, and opinions of this second generation of Warren's citizens. We feel ourselves more especially called upon to be faithful to this period, because a few inventions, of no great wonder now, were to make a radical change in society. We refer to the steam-ship, rail-car, telegraph, friction matches, and the like.

In those good old times when they had none of these, divers superstitions were rife, and our ancestors devoutly believed that if a dog howled in the night some one in the neighborhood was going to die sure; that if the scissors, knife, or any sharp thing fell to the floor and stood up straight, some visitor was coming; that if a looking-glass was broken, the person breaking it or some relative would die before the year was out; that if a knife or pair of scissors was given to a friend without making him give a penny or some amount of money for it, love between them would certainly be cut; that if there were tea grounds or bubbles swimming on the tea, as many strangers as grounds or bubbles were coming; that if one stubbed the left foot they were not wanted where they were going, but if it was the right they would be welcome; that to spill the salt was a bad omen; and the ticking of a little bug in the wall was a sure sign of death, and also forty or more other like superstitions.

But they also believed many other things much more serious,

and among them in witches and ghosts. Every town has had its witch or wizard; but if tradition is correct, Warren has had more than its share. It is told that in olden times, when there were but few clearings in town, a young man, Jonathan Merrill, went to see his lady-love. While there the happy moments flew swift and time had crept far into the small hours before he thought of taking his leave. On his way home he had to cross a stream on the trunk of a fallen tree; and when he arrived at this point, as he was stepping upon the log that was shaded by thick foliage, and through which a few straggling rays of the moon struggled, he saw standing on the other end a white, airy figure which looked to him anything but earthly. He gazed upon it for a few moments and then stepped from the log. As he did so the figure followed his example, and he saw it standing on the water. He now thought he would venture across, but the moment he was on the log again, that light form was there also. Filled with terror, he gave one more look, beheld as he thought, a ghastly visage, then turned quick about and ran with all his might to the house where he had so agreeably spent the evening. Here he waited till day-light before returning home. Young Merrill always believed he saw a witch that night.

Some folks have told the writer that they did not believe this story at all, and one estimable lady, daughter of Caleb Homan, said it happened down country when 'Squire Jonathan was courting his wife. The same lady said witches* used to be plenty down at old Plaistow; and then she told how Nat Tucker, one of Uncle Jim Dow's relatives, once sold some walnuts in old Haverhill, much to the displeasure of a certain elderly lady. That night Tucker and his wife could not sleep; all night long there was a rattling of walnuts on the kitchen hearth. Most wonderful to narrate, the next morning when they arose there was every identical walnut piled up like cannon balls in the form of a pyramid on the hearth-stone. The old woman, the witch, had brought them all back. But stranger yet, the silk handkerchief that Mrs. T. had used as a night-cap, when she went to take it from her head, fell to the floor cut in a thousand pieces.

Foolish and superstitious folks scandalously said that the wife

---
* Old Mrs. Bly was one of the great witches of Plaistow.

of Stephen Richardson was a witch. Her son Stephen was a little out of his head, and he said she bewitched him. When his friends tried to reason with him, he would say, "Good Lord, if you had seen her coming over the ridgepole of the house in the air as many times as I have, in the shape of a hog, you would believe she was a witch." Moses Ellsworth's wife, Susan, took her mother's part, and Stephen Richardson, Jr., used to wish that he had them both harnessed so Nathan Willey could drive them with a good stout stage whip hauling hay out of his swamp.

Stillman Barker's wife, who was a sister of Lemuel Keezer, was wrongfully and maliciously accused of being a witch and we are very glad to here have an opportunity of vindicating her good name. It is said, among other things, she bewitched a calf and it happened in this wise. Joseph Merrill, inn-keeper, was a superintendent of the turnpike, and one spring day when the bird cherry-trees were in blossom, was cleaning out a ditch. When he came down from the Height-o'-land he found that old Mr. Barker had altered the ditch so that the water overflowed and ran across the road. Merrill called Barker out and reproved him pretty sharply. Mrs. Barker was mad about it.*

A day or two after Mr. M. turned his calves out to pasture where the meeting-house stands now, and the next morning went out to see how they were getting along. He found one of them lying on the ground in a terrible tremor, with its eyes rolling and flashing towards the sky as though it could see a hundred old witches there riding on a hundred broom-sticks. Merrill was confident Mrs. B. had bewitched it, and with his knife he cut the calf's ear off, carried it to the house and threw it on the fire. "I'll fix her," said he. The calf from that moment began to mend; but it went on its knees for a while as if doing penance, and only got up

---

* A Scotch teamster, long ago, stopped at the Moosilauke house one winter night. Sitting around the fire with others, he said he was never in Warren but once before, and then it was when he was changed into a horse and ridden there by a witch. He told how they hitched him with other horses at a post by the first house on the right coming up from the Noyes Bridge. The whole party of witches went into the house, and from where he stood he could see all they did there; that they drinked up some wine, ate all the bread, butter, preserves, tarts, and pies, and even devoured some sweet, good-tasting medicine that sat on the shelf. Before they left they cracked the sugar bowl.

These things down at Mr. Noyes' did actually happen, and Mrs. Noyes, who was away from home at the time, was very mad at Miss Sallie Barker who worked for her, for allowing such capers to be cut up in her absence. Miss Sallie would always have been presumed guilty had it not been for the confession of the Scotch teamster in after years.

B*

smart when haying was over and the witch on the Height-o'-land had undergone a fit of sickness. Experienced witch killers say that if he had scalded the calf it would have done just as well.

The wife of Mr. Zachariah Clifford, who was a sister of Simeon Smith, was scandalized in a like manner as Mrs. Barker. She lived on Red-oak hill, and it was perfectly wonderful what awful things she could do. If you stuck a needle down in a witch's track, it was said she would stop and look round; if one was put in her shoe she could not go at all. A shoemaker down at Wentworth made her a pair of shoes, carried them home to her and when she tried them on she said one of them was good for nothing, that she could not wear it and that he must make her another. He had broke off his awl in the sole, but he did not tell her anything about it. He carried the shoe home quietly, took out the piece of the awl and when he returned it she said it was a grand fit and the best shoe she ever had in her life.

John Clifford courted a sister of Mrs. Zack. Clifford, then jilted her and went courting a Gove girl. Mrs. C. was awful mad about it, said she would fix him, and when John went courting after that she would go too as a witch and sit in a spare rocking-chair and rock all night. The young couple were terribly afflicted but finally got married. Dr. Horatio Heath, who kept school down on the "East side," said he knew all about Mrs. C.'s pranks and that the stories about her were as true as the gospel,—a very misguided and mistaken youth.

But gossiping slanderers of that day said that the wife of Mr. Benjamin Weeks, Mrs. Sarah Weeks, had ten times the power that the above mentioned ladies possessed. Invisible on her good steed, a broom-stick, she rode all the country round and was a sort of revenging angel for her husband.

One day, it is said, Joseph Merrill, son of 'Squire Abel, started about the middle of the afternoon to come home from Haverhill. Mr. Weeks was there and wanted to ride to Warren with him. Merrill said there was another man to ride; that he had as much load as he could carry, and that he could not take him. Weeks said if you don't take me you will be sorry for it, and you won't get home to-night. Merrill harnessed up and drove out as far as the toll-gate, when his horse, which hitherto had been perfectly kind, kicked up and absolutely refused to go. Merrill coaxed, whipped, and then coaxed again; the horse laid down and would not budge an inch. After an hour spent in vain effort and night coming on, Merrill put his horse in a barn and walked back to the Corner, where he spent the night. The next morning the horse went home in splendid manner, and ever after was as kind as need be. Mr. M. was perfectly certain that Mrs. W. had bewitched the animal.

One day this lady of excellent reputation was sick and sent her husband to Capt. Ben. Merrill's store for a pint of rum.* Capt. Ben. and wife were away, Miriam Pillsbury, afterwards Mrs. Aaron Goodwin, was keeping house, Levi B. Foot was boarding there and studying, and Capt. Samuel L. Merrill "tended" store. Weeks asked for his rum on trust. Captain Sam. said his orders were not to let him have any on tick. Weeks was mad and said "If you don't let me have it you will be sorry for it," and then he went directly away to his Height-o'-land home.

The night was cloudy and dark, and when the twilight had all gone they heard something going over the roof which sounded like a team hitched to a load of slabs dragging along.

All three were terribly frightened although they afterwards stoutly maintained that they were not. The noise continued at intervals for more than half an hour, then subsided. Captain Ben. always kept a fine stallion and it was in the barn at that time. All at once there was a tremendous noise at the stable. It was fearful! Sam. L. Merrill, then quite young, belonged to the troop, and he went and got his sword and buckled it on and loaded his great horse pistols. Just then a cat jumped up on to the window stool, and he cocked his pistol to fire but the cat jumped down too quick for him. Who shall go to the barn to see the horse? No one dared to go alone and no one dared to stay in the house alone, and so they all went to the barn together. They found the horse all right, not a particle of trouble, and they all returned together. Shortly after the same terrible noise began again and along in the night there was also screeching in the air, and two or three times sharp flashes of light, like the flashing of a witch's eyes, gleamed through

---

* It is said Mrs. Weeks bewitched Mrs. Eunice Pillsbury, also Mrs. McConnell of Piermont. Mrs. McConnell scalded Mrs. Weeks by scalding a calf that Mrs. W. had bewitched.

the darkness. All this continued until the first cock crew and then instantly there was silence. Elderly men and women telling the story in an undertone, always believed that Mrs. Weeks with a crowd of old crones, her chums, were thumping and crashing with their broom-sticks on the roofs that night.

Mrs. Weeks, with her husband, once went down to Mr. Nathaniel Clough's after some flax, but was unable to procure it. She was mad as usual, and went to the backside of the room, laid her head upon the table and closed her eyes. Immediately there was a terrible noise at the barn. The men folks rushed out and found that a two years old colt had reached over into the sheep pen and lifted two lambs out with his teeth and killed them. He was now working hard to catch a third sheep. Weeks went back to the house on the run, shoved his wife on to the floor, then told her to behave herself. To the credit of the colt it is told that he quieted right down and never injured a sheep afterwards. All the old ladies said that Mrs. Weeks was raising the d—l for revenge.

Uncle Tom. Pillsbury, as he was familliarly called, got Mrs. Weeks to make three shirts for him. There was some trouble about the pay. He went down country to work* and when the first one was washed and hung out, it was mysteriously spirited away. The same happened to the other two, not another thing being lost from the line. Mr. Pillsbury said he knew Mrs. Weeks had them all in Warren.

But Simeon Smith, as we have intimated in another book of this history, was the great wizard of this mountain valley. His fame preceded him, and it is said he acquired his powers down country. When the revolutionary war was going on he was in meeting one Sabbath, but all at once he left the house. Out of doors he said he could not stop at meeting for a great battle was

---

* "*Ride and Tie.*"—It was customary in old times for young men in all this upper region to go down country to work during the season. They nearly always "footed it," often a dozen or twenty in a party, away to Newburyport, Salem, and Boston, and would come home again late in the fall with money in their pockets. Sometimes two young men would buy a horse and they would "ride and tie," as it was called. One would ride ahead a few miles then tie the horse beside the road and push on afoot, when the other coming up, would mount the horse, pass his companion, get a mile or two ahead, then tie the horse again and walk on. Thus they would walk and ride, accomplishing the journey in a very short time, and when they had arrived at their destination would sell the horse for a good price.

being fought that day. This statement was afterwards found to be true and Simeon Smith was looked upon as a wonderful man.

One day he mounted his horse to go up town, and before he proceeded a rod got lost in one of his second sights. He seemed to notice nothing around him but sat in the saddle in a strange fit of abstraction as if gazing upon the revels of fiends incarnate in some far off world. The horse seemed to behold the same scene also; and great drops of sweat trickled from every part of its body. At last Mr. S. roused himself and strove by every means in his power to make the horse proceed, but in vain; and finally weary in the attempt, he turned the animal into the pasture and relinquished the journey, much to the surprise of several persons who witnessed the scene.*

Simeon Smith was a great rebel, ardently espousing the cause of the colonists, and hated the British. Stevens Merrill was slightly inclined to favor King George, and was strongly opposed to paying taxes to carry on the war for independence. Simeon Smith was constable and tax collector, and compelled Mr. Merrill to pay as we have before narrated. From that time there was a slight enmity between the two families.

Mr. Merrill had a deaf boy Caleb, and one time after the war was over he began to act strangely. He was hoeing in the meadow one day, over the river, when suddenly there was a terrible noise as of the wings of a mighty bird, then an awful screeching. Joseph Merrill, his brother, who was with him, although he looked everywhere, could see nothing, and deaf Caleb of course could hear nothing: but he dropped his hoe and ran for home in a terrible fright. When interrogated, he replied by signs that Simeon Smith was after him. The enmity between the two families slightly increased.†

A few days after deaf Caleb began to act in the strangest

---

* Simeon Smith once said he wished he possessed the power that his mother and sister Nab had: that he had seen them both on the lug pole in the fire-place over the fire, spinning linen, many a time.

† 'Squire Jonathan, Joseph, and deaf Caleb, all sons of Stevens Merrill, had been over the river digging potatoes. There was no bridge then, and coming home with a load they had to ford the river, which was shoal. The three young men and two women were on the cart, and when they came to the water edge deaf Caleb told them by signs that Simeon Smith would tip up the cart and dump them all into the stream before they got across. To prevent this they sat on the front end so that it could not tip up: but, strange to relate, before they got half way across up it went, and potatoes, men, and women all fell into the water.

manner. He would run up the sides of the house or barn like a squirrel, and would traverse the ridge-pole of the highest roofs with the greatest ease, a thing he was never known to do before. At times he would seem to experience the most excruciating torture, and would writhe for hours in agony. When asked who tormented him, he would go with an individual and point out the house in which he said his tormentor lived, but never in any instance could he be persuaded to enter it.

Thus it continued until at last some of Mr. Merrill's neighbors induced him — although he was incredulous as to believing in witches — to try some experiments upon the boy thinking to make his tormentor cease from troubling him. Accordingly some of the boy's urine was procured, corked up in a bottle and placed under the hearth of the fire-place. Immediately after Simeon Smith was taken suddenly with a violent bleeding at the nose, and for a long time it could not be stopped. It finally was, and upon looking at the bottle the cork was found to be out and the urine had run therefrom. The boy began to cut the same antics as before and his tortures were nearly doubled. Again some of his urine was procured and carefully corked in the bottle. The wizard bled at the nose again, the cork got out again and the bleeding stopped.

Then the boy behaved worse than ever and acted in a manner truly terrible. This could not be borne long and they determined to try a more serious remedy. They procured a quantity of deaf Caleb's blood, placed it in the bottle, and as a precaution against its becoming uncorked, a small, sharp sword was placed in the cork. Samuel Merrill of the East-parte regions witnessed the whole proceeding.

It was evening when this was done, and shortly after deaf Caleb went to bed. In the morning when he awoke he seemed to be in great glee, and immediately informed the family by signs that Simeon Smith was dead. Wonderful that the boy should know it; but it was true nevertheless. Upon examining the bottle it was found that the sword had penetrated through the cork to the blood. Tradition says deaf Caleb was no more troubled.

Simeon Smith had a great apple-tree that stood by Red-oak hill road. It bore excellent fruit and the boys robbed it every year. He often said, "Bury me under that tree and I will take care of the apples." His friends did so, and the boys never stole fruit there again. Henceforth, to the present day, the apples are the crabbedest, bitterest things that ever grew.*

Samuel Knight had a pious belief in witches, but said he was born under such a star that they had no power over him. Elder Peck, a Methodist divine of good sense, once told him a story to illustrate what he thought of such things; but it made Mr. K. very mad.

Said the elder, " A man believed he was ridden by a witch, and the belief affected him so much that he grew very poor. A friend advised the witch ridden man when he was saddled and bridled again, to gnaw the post to which he was tied and ease himself about the same, as a horse would when he had been hitched a long time." The man did so, and when he waked in the morning he found that he had bit the bed-post terribly, and that the bed itself was in a most awful filthy condition.†

Of course the reader can judge, like Elder Peck, how much of these stories of supernatural events is true, and make every allowance for the prejudices of those times. For ages the belief in ghosts‡ and goblins had prevailed; indeed the individuals who did not believe in them were considered heretics. Surely did not the Bible teach that there were witches. For many hundred years England had an established code of laws against witchcraft, and it was considered a capital offence. Thirty thousand persons were put to death in Europe in the sixteenth century for being witches.

---

* Deaf Caleb leaned against the apple-tree while Simeon Smith's grave was being filled up, and when the mound was rounded off, jumped upon it intimating that he would keep him down forever.

† James Dow, like Mr. Knight and a good many others, believed in witches; also that the world neither turned over nor went round the sun. Said he, "If the world did turn over would not my mill-pond spill out?" He would get up and turn his shoes the other side up in the night when he had the cramp. He said that was a cure.

‡ Mr. John Whitaker once believed he saw a ghost on the east side of Warren common. He lived at the time in the East-parte regions four miles away, but had a very bad habit of drinking hard and stopping out late nights. Folks thought it was a shame, and George Bixby and Mr. Gould determined they would scare Whitaker and make him stay at home. So they got Lemuel Merrill, son of Joseph Merrill, inn-keeper, to dress himself up as a ghost and stand behind a large pine tree. When Whitaker arrived at the spot, Lemuel, the ghost, stepped forth. Whitaker had heard that if one asked in the name of the Lord what the ghost wanted, the apparition would immediately disappear. He put the question and his ghostship vanished instantly. Whitaker was terribly frightened, ran back across the common shouting, "Bixby! Bixby! Gould! Gould!" so loud that he was heard a mile. He trembled all over, paid Bixby nine shillings to carry him home and did not show himself at the stores or taverns for months after. But he was awful mad when he found out the trick.

The learned Baxter, who lived in the seventeenth century, considered all persons as obdurate Sadducees who did not believe in it, and Sir Matthew Hale, one of the brightest ornaments of the English bar, tried and convicted several persons for the crime of witchcraft. Even Blackstone, the profound commentator of English common law, swallowed and believed implicitly this great humbug of the church.

But the hallucinations of other generations are passing away and few are the persons at the present time who indulge in the belief of goblins, ghosts, and witches. True it is that the mediums, clairvoyants, and cabinet gentlemen bring to mind the diablerie of old Salem, when our fathers, the good puritans, made fools of themselves and hung thirty old women as witches; but such things don't go for much except as a means of speculation in money matters. They are first rate for that.

The dwellers in a new settlement, far away from the older towns, were just the ones to indulge in the belief of the supernatural. Around them were thousands of old solitudes; and as the deepening shades of night cast her sombre mantle over the forest, it required no active imagination to picture the forms of huge giants stalking away among the trees; to see numerous jack-o'-lanterns gliding noislessly along to guide the lone traveler onward until he was lost in the dark intricate windings of some dismal old swamp; to hear the infernal music of old crones as they charged in huge battalions through the tops of the lofty trees mounted upon their never tiring steeds,— broom-sticks. But they are all gone. No more do we see the individuals who indulge in such fancies, and although there were such, and they still live in history, we have little right to laugh at them. If our ancestors did indulge in them, still they had exalted notions of piety, and did thousands of good deeds which latter it would be well if we would imitate.

CHAPTER X.

THE FIRST STORE IN WARREN AND ITS SUCCESSORS, AND OF A ROARING, RAGING CANAL THAT NEVER WAS BUILT.

THE first store in Warren was built near Joshua Merrill's, sometime in the last century. It was kept by Samuel Fellows,* and after trading a short time in English and West India goods he was taken crazy. He would sometimes leave home and wander to the neighboring towns; and when his friends went for him it would be extremely difficult to influence him to return. At one time he went to Haverhill and a young man was sent after him. He found him at the tavern, and to make good friends, asked him if he would have flip or brandy before going home. Fellows looked up sharply and said he guessed he would have brandy while the flip was making.

To him succeeded first Charles Bowles, then George W. Copp, who traded for several years just at the close of the eighteenth century. Col. Obadiah Clement at this period, 1825, a very old man, used to relate what he saw in this store. He said it was a long building on the east side of the old Coos road, not the turnpike, just at the foot of the Beech-hill and fifty rods south of the summit of the Blue ridge. It had large windows with shutters, and door wide enough to roll a hogshead of molasses through; door and shutters always used as advertising boards for our merchant himself and the public generally. Here, in winter, the people would congregate, and with them he would sit by the old fashioned fire and talk over the news and pass away the hours.

---
* Samuel Fellows came to Warren in 1789.

He said he was there all one day when it snowed so hard that looking out the back window he could hardly see Mt. Helen, much less the eastern mountains. First the flakes came down slowly like feathers shading and mottling the sky. Then the storm increased, the wind blazed and racketed through the narrow space between the house and the hill and catching up the falling snow sent it twirling and pitching skimble-skamble, and anon slowly and more regularly as in a minuet, and as they came nearer the earth they were borne by the current in a horizontal line like long quick spun silver threads far adown the landscape. As he watched he saw a flock of snow buntings, their white sides flashing before the eyes, hurried on by the wind. They had come down to avoid the dark night of the Arctic continent, the place where they were hatched. Black brook, the Mikaseota, was ice-bound, covered with snow, and scarce a murmur was heard from beneath its white mantle.

The post-rider was snowed up that day; he had not got through from Plymouth yet, and 'Squire Abel Merrill was without the little seven-by-nine paper which he took, and the visitors at the store lacked their customary news, which was always months old before they got it.

But late in the afternoon it cleared off, the sun shone out, and in the thick woods beyond the Mikaseota he saw a pair of nuthatches, several golden crested kinglets, a downy wood-pecker, two or three brown creepers, and half a dozen chickadees, birds that bide the New England winter. What pleasant music they make! For a wonder, from the cluster of great hemlocks high up on the side of Mt. Helen, came the cawing of crows as if they were glad to see the sunshine, and that the winds had gone down.

While it snowed that day Col. Clement and his friends amused themselves reading the notices posted on the doors and shutters; one was a sale on execution, another informed them that beeswax, flax, skins, bristles, and old pewter, would be taken in exchange for goods; and another read as follows:—

"WARREN, May 18th, 1799.

SIR:—

I send you the following description of a dark brown gelding horse, taken up by me, damage feasant, he appears to be about six years old, is a natural pacer, mane hangs on the near side, well shod, and is about fourteen hands high—the oner is desired to prove property, pay charges and take him away.

AMOS LITTLE.

A true copy: Attest,

JONATHAN MERRILL,
Town Clerk."

Sitting by the fire, he saw a motley array of dry and fancy goods, crockery, hardware, and groceries. On the right were rolls of kerseymeres, calimancoes, fustians, shalloons, antiloons, and serges, of all colors, purple and blue calicoes, a few ribbons, ticklenburgs, and buckrams. On the left were cuttoes, Barlow knives, iron candlesticks, jewsharps, black-ball, and bladders of snuff. On naked beams above were suspended weavers' skans, wheel heads, and on a high shelf running quite around the walls was cotton warp of all numbers. The back portion of the building showed to him a traffic far more fashionable and universal in New England than it is now; and the row of pipes, hogsheads and barrels indicated its extent. Above these hung a tap-borer, faucets, and interspersed on the wall were bunches of chalk scores in perpendicular and transverse lines. Near by was a small counter covered with tumblers, toddy sticks, and sugar bowl, and a few ragged will-gill looking men, either from old Coventry, "Pearmount," or the land of Wentworth, (of course Warren men didn't drink, they *never* have,) were standing there mixing and bolting down liquors.

The colonel said that a favorite and common drink at that period was flip, which was made in this wise: a mug was nearly filled with malt beer, sweetened with sugar, then a heated iron called a loggerhead was thrust into it, which produced a rapid foam. Instantly a quantity of the "ardent,"—a half pint of rum was allowed for a quart mug,— was dashed in, a little nutmeg was grated on the top, and the whole was quaffed off by two men or more, as they could bear it, which had the effect often to set them at loggerheads. Price, twenty-five cents a mug.

Another drink was toddy, which was made of rum and water well sweetened. A stick six or eight inches long was used to stir up the delightful beverage, called a toddy-stick. Price, six cents a glass.

Another favorite drink was egg-nog, which was composed of an egg beaten and stirred together with sugar. The stick used for this purpose was split at the end and a transverse piece of wood inserted, which was rapidly whirled around backward and forward between the palms of the hands. Skillful men made graceful flourishes with toddy and egg-nog sticks, in those days. Price, a sixpence a mug.*

In the farther end was the counting-room with another large fire-place in one corner, a high desk, round backed arm chairs and a little good wine in a keg.

But good-bye to Col. Obadiah and to the old first store, which is a sample, contents, drinks and all, of all the others down to the time of which we write, viz: the close of Warren's second generation; for Geo. W. Copp sold out to Abel Merrill, who traded in 1804, and then the building was converted into a dwelling-house.

Trade in Warren by no means stopped on account of this sale. Benjamin Merrill, son of 'Squire Abel, built another store at the forks of the road where one ran away north, to Coventry, and the other over the Height-o'-land. Although many families have lived in this second store, and under its roof your humble historian drew his first breath, it is still occupied for trade, and stands nearly in the same place. In it Benj. Merrill traded till about 1812,† although it was much disturbed by witches as we have already narrated, when he sold it out to Lemuel Keezer, Jr. Mr. Keezer, father of Ferdinand and Fayette, died of the spotted fever, and the property passed into the hands of Michael Preston, who traded about three years. Preston having married Mary Merrill, was

---

* Sling was sugar, warm water, and whisky, mixed. Sometimes half a cracker was toasted and put with it. This was called a toad. Price for the whole 6¼ cents.

† Captain Ben. Merrill started to go home one night, after closing up, with a large ham in his hand for family use. Before he left the yard he found he had forgot something, laid down the ham in a feed-box for horses, and went back. He was gone sometime, and when he returned the ham was missing. He never said a word, was as silent as the grave, for he thought the thief would show himself in time. One day, six months afterwards, a neighbor said to him standing in the store door, "Captain, did you ever find out who : tole that ham from you?" "Yes," said Capt. Ben., "I know who it was, you are the very fellow; walk in and pay for it, or you'll catch it." It is needless to say that the money was forthcoming at once, and the culprit acknowledged that he could not keep his mouth quite as close as the captain.

anxious to move away to Canada, and sold out to Amos Burton. The latter having high ideas of living, changed the Benj. Merrill store into a dwelling house, and built another store directly opposite where is now a peg-factory and wheelwright shop by the pond. Others who traded in the latter place are, respectively, Samuel L. Merrill, William Merrill, Anson Merrill, and William Wells, who was famous for building up rousing fires, raising the windows and playing lively airs on his fiddle for the amusement of Mr. Asa Thurston and George W. Prescott, who were making music about this time hammering away in the cooper's shop that stood where the old first school-house was located on the river bank opposite. Wells was succeeded by John T. Sanborn, who traded at or about the time of the chronological order of this chapter. Others who have traded in town we will mention in the Appendix, a very necessary thing for this history, for what would it be good for without one?

Mercantile business was good about this time, for the town was growing, and it cost so much for freight that our traders, and in fact all the others in the regions round about, began seriously to consider how they could get their goods brought to their door at a cheaper rate. Considering culminated in acting; a petition was circulated and signed by our merchants and many citizens and numerous signatures were also obtained down the valley. It was then presented to the legislature asking that a roaring and raging canal might be incorporated. The General Court could not refuse so respectable a request and two canals through the central portion of New Hampshire were immediately chartered. One was to commence at Dover, thence by way of Lake Winnepisseogee to the Pemigewassett at Bridgewater; the other followed up the Merrimack to Bridgewater, and uniting with the first, followed up the Asquamchumauke to Warren Summit, and from there down the Oliverian to the Connecticut. It was fashionable to construct canals in those days, and the great canals of New York, of the West, and of southern New England, were then in the course of being built. The United States government also assisted and sent distinguished engineers to all parts of the country where they were needed.

Gen. McDuffee, who laid out the turnpike, now surveyed the canal through our valley, and spent weeks in Warren trying to overcome the obstructions that the Summit presented. Capt. Graham of the United States army assisted him, and the general, the captain and his lady, with their assistants, boarded a long time at Joseph Merrill's inn.

The chief difficulty which they found in the building of the canal was the inadequate supply of water upon the Summit. Two routes were surveyed through Warren, one up Black brook, the Mikaseota, and the other up Berry brook. If the Black brook route was adopted, water was to be taken from Tarleton lake and made to run winding round the hills to the place required. This would be a costly job. If the route up Berry brook was preferred, the Asquamchumauke river was to be tapped near the East-parte school-house and canalled round Knight hill to the Summit, thus affording an adequate supply of water for the numerous locks needed. Gen. McDuffee reported that with sufficient money all the difficulties could be overcome, and that either route was feasible. Which he preferred we never could learn.

And now the canal would surely be built, goods, wares, and merchandise would come cheap, population would greatly increase, and prosperity would bless the land. Alas! the bright dream was never realized. Money was hard to be got, a sufficient amount of stock could not be disposed of, and we are sorry to tell what every body knows, the canals were never built and Warren's traders were doomed to disappointment.

But before we close this entertaining book and say good-bye to Warren's second generation, we must briefly mention one important event which partly grew out of a desire to trade in Warren and enjoy the benefits of the great canal. The people residing in the south portion of old Coventry, now Benton, having said desire and being very poorly accommodated in town affairs, were anxious to be annexed to Warren and made application to our free and independent democracy for that purpose.

This happened in the selectmenship of Enoch R. Weeks, Moses H. Clement, and Samuel L. Merrill. These rulers called an assembly of the people, otherwise a town meeting, and the question was discussed and voted upon. Maj. Daniel Patch modestly presented the claims of the dwellers of the Summit, and of High street.* Moses H. Clement, one of that year's triumviri, was the chief opposition speaker. He maintained that the legal voters of Warren were now nearly strong enough to send a representative themselves, (they had previously been joined to Piermont and Coventry for that purpose,) that the land to be annexed was very poor, that the people were poverty stricken and inclined to whisky drinking, and that Warren would not be benefited.

His counsels prevailed, although we wish they had not, and Warren lost, perhaps forever, the right of jurisdiction over the fine and luscious blueberry fields of Owl's head, the millions of feet of excellent timber growing upon Mt. Black, and the noble and majestic summit of the lofty Mooschillock, to which so many pilgrims annually journey.

* This section of Benton should be joined to Warren, the Benton Flats should partly go to Haverhill, while North Benton and East Landaff would make a beautiful town of Benton with its centre at " Danville."

East Piermont should also be joined to Warren, where it would be so much better accommodated.

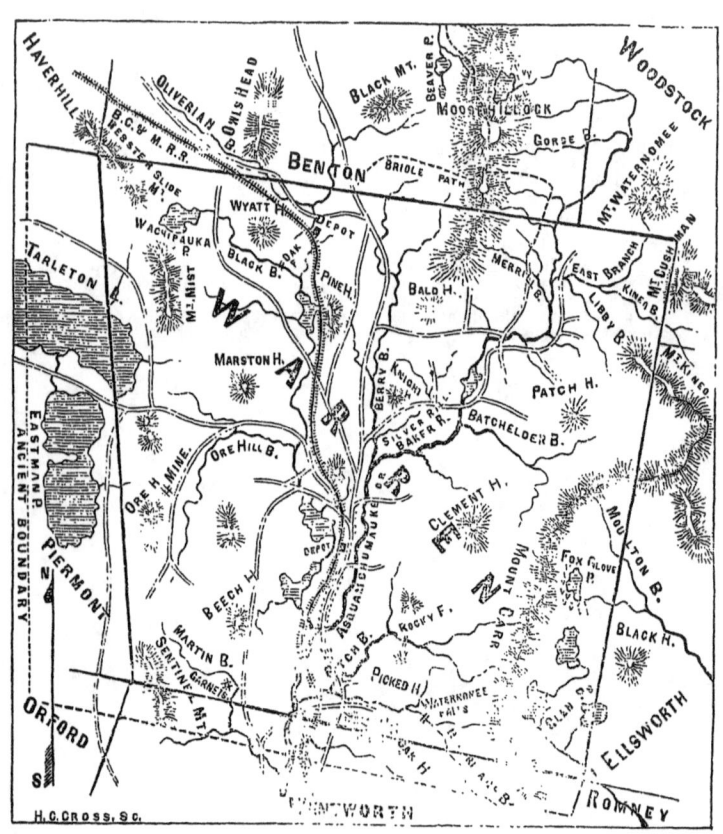

MAP OF MODERN WARREN.

BOOK VII.

WHICH BOOK IS BUT A CONTINUATION OF BOOKS V. AND VI. AND CONTAINS THE HISTORY OF THE THIRD GENERATION OF WARREN'S WHITE INHABITANTS.

CHAPTER I.

HOW GOLD, SILVER, AND DIAMONDS WERE DISCOVERED IN WARREN, AND OF SEVERAL INDIVIDUALS WHO GOT IMMENSELY RICH MINING, ESPECIALLY IN THEIR IMAGINATIONS.

As the third generation of Warren's white citizens are stepping upon the stage, and at the commencement of the period when this last book of our great history opens, a discovery of mighty importance was made in our hamlet. Mr. True Merrill, who lived upon the Height-o'-land, found upon the north bank of Ore-hill brook, what was first known as the "Copper mine," then as the "Warren silver-lead mine," and latterly as the "Warren zinc mine."

It was a rich deposit of minerals. Dr. Charles T. Jackson, a great geologist from Boston, came on and examined it, made a report such as all well paid geologists know how to make, namely a favorable one, and a company was formed, stock sold, and the buyers of the stock it is said were sold too.

Mr. H. Bradford was the head and front of said company.

They worked for a time, made a great hole in the side of the mountain; but not a cent to put in their pockets, and eventually failed up; the usual fate of most great mining companies.

Then as time rolled on for a decade of years several small but terribly enterprising companies wrought the mine on Ore hill. At intervals visions of riches, silvery and golden, would flash before the eyes of individual speculators and operators, only to vanish like a phantom, and as a result every one of the little companies failed.

About 1840 this vein of ore fell into the hands of a certain Mr. Brooks. We never had the pleasure of his acquaintance; but Warren miners say that they knew him, that he was like the dog in the manger; that he would neither work the mine nor let any one else; and that he believed that the property was richer than the silver mines of Mexico or South America.

But after a great deal of diplomacy a heavy company, headed by Mr. Baldwin of Boston, got possession of this wonderful deposit of minerals and ores. They went to work and Ore hill glowed and sweat.

They built half a dozen dwelling-houses — a little village — a mill, put in stamps for crushing ore, set up a steam engine, procured a large number of separators, erected a whim house, sunk the shaft in the copper mine a hundred feet deep, drifted north from the foot of the shaft into the mountain a hundred and fifty feet further in the black blende and galena, raised hundreds of tons of ore, crushed, separated, and sent it to market, and then failed. Too bad! Mr. H. H. Sheldon* was the superintendent, and Captain Samuel Truscott, a Cornwall miner, was the overseer in the shaft. They worked the mine for silver, copper, and lead, but it paid not a cent.

Ore hill slumbered then for a time, and the well wishers of the mine were sad.

Captain Edgar came next. He drove an adit from the new highway a hundred feet into the hill, then abandoned it and the mine too, after sending a hundred tons or so of ore to England to see whether or not it was good for anything.

---

* When H. H. Sheldon, Esq , had charge of the mine, the town built the road from the old turnpike, at the forks of Ore hill stream up to the works. It made a great saving in distance and freightage.

Then the mill and the engine were sold at auction, the shaft and the drift filled up with water; there was no more clicking of hammers nor ringing of drills, and the fires of the forge went out. About five years after, Captain Edgar came back and commenced work again, this time for zinc. He set up a small stationary engine to pump the mine and raise the ore, and put his men to work in the large chamber at the end of the drift. The ore raised was made into a kiln and set on fire by burning a large pile of wood underneath to desulphurize it. This was done to save weight in freight as from every thirty tons of ore about ten tons of sulphur was expelled. After cooling it was put up in bags and sent to Pennsylvania to be worked into metallic zinc. Captain Edgar suspended work, and the mine is now silent and deserted again.* More than a hundred thousand dollars have been expended upon it. We hope a hundred thousand more will be spent, and that somebody will make an immense fortune there.

One good thing has happened by reason of mining on Ore hill. A large and beautiful cavern has been formed, the most extensive in the State, and hundreds of persons visit it when the depth of water will permit.

From Mr. True Merrill's wonderful discovery flowed another result; a mining and mineral fever immediately began to prevail and different individuals discovered first a small vein of copper pyrites, distant forty rods south west from the discovery of True Merrill, then two and one-half miles north east, copper and pyrites in small veins; and one hundred yards north of the first mine an extensive vein of black blende, zinc ore, mixed with copper pyrites and galena. A few years after, copper, beryls, and epidote in large masses, were found upon Warren Summit. Subsequently James Clement discovered copper, iron pyrites, nickel, antimony, arsenic, and beautiful garnets by Martin brook on the south east slope of Sentinel mountain, and Albert M. Barber found gold in Hurricane brook that comes down from Mount Carr. Also James Clement found gold in Martin brook near the spot where the garnets are located. And afterwards the same gentleman found that the Asquamchumauke, the stream by which the Indian chief,

---

* Capt. James Edgar resumed work in the fall of 1869 and suspended business in the winter of 1870. Now at the end of 1870 he has commenced work again.

Waternomee, and Captain Baker fought, and on which Stinson died, was far richer than either in golden sands.

Besides these discoveries others have been made in a most wonderful manner. It is told how a party of tourists from New York, visited Moosehillock mountain. There they fell in with a spiritualist who went into a fit, and looking with shut eyes towards Sentinel mountain saw fourteen different mines upon that green wooded eminence, the best of which was located at a certain clump of spruces. The oracle was believed, a company was organized, and they actually worked a year and a half at the spot indicated.* They indeed found iron and some other minerals, but nothing that would pay, and the undertaking was abandoned after a useless expenditure of from five to six thousand dollars. Another individual, probably a cousin to the tourists, paid one thousand dollars for a worthless piece of land upon which some "golden specimens" had been deposited. It was a regularly "salted claim," and the buyer was out and swindled to the extent of his investment.

So successful have been the gold prospectors and the men with divining rods that a large number of other minerals and precious stones have been found in Warren; the most interesting of which are rutile, plumbago, molybdenum, cadmium, scapolite, tremolite, talc, tourmaline, beryl, apatite, garnet, idocrase, epidote, brown hematite, hyalite, cinnamon stone, quartz crystals in great variety, besides others of less importance and all the rocks common to New Hampshire. It is already known that forty-one different kinds of specimens are bedded in the neighborhood of Sentinel mountain;† but not content with these, several enthusiastic mineralogists, with a wise look and a sly manner, aver that platinum, mercury, tin, and rough diamonds likewise abound, although as yet they fail to produce the samples.

Some also there are who in an undertone will tell you how they know of a mine up in the mountains where they can cut out pure lead with a jackknife or axe just right to run into bullets — Obadiah Clement and Joseph Patch got lead of that kind there

---

* They drove a shaft a hundred feet into the mountain. Capt. Truscott had charge of this job.

† For a list of these see Appendix.

when they were hunting — how they can find mica in sheets a foot square, worth its weight in topazes, sapphires, and rubies, and how they know the very mountain stream and the stone monument beside it, where Roger's ranger picked up nuggets of pure gold as large as robins' eggs. Yet they will not show the places for fear they cannot buy the land, or that they will in some way be robbed of all their hidden treasures. But we will not vouch for their statements, and it is only safe for this history to say that no other spot on earth contains so great a variety of minerals, in so limited an area, as our town of Warren.

But if all the mines in Warren have failed as yet, still it is safe to say that one person has made a profit out of the minerals. Mr. James Clement keeps an abundance of them to sell, and hundreds of people have derived real pleasure in buying and examining them. "Jim" enjoys himself and improves his health, he says, when with basket, cold chisel, and miner's hammer slung on his shoulder, he takes a tramp through the valley and over the hills seeking to find all the metals, minerals, and precious stones known in the books, in this, as he alleges, "*the most wonderful mineral deposit on earth.*"

CHAPTER II.

HOW THE BERRY BROOK ROAD WAS BUILT AND A PATH ON TO MOOSEHILLOCK WAS CUT, WITH A PLEASANT ACCOUNT OF SEVERAL INDIVIDUALS WHO NICKNAMED EACH OTHER IN THE HAPPIEST MANNER.

THE people in all this northern country were disappointed in the failure to build the canal. They wanted an easy route to the seaboard. The old Coos road " was a hard road to travel," and the turnpike which superseded it, although nearly straight and very well made, being over hills and lofty mountains, all known as the Height-o'-land, was a very difficult highway on which to transport heavy freight.

Gen. McDuffee's survey had one important result, it informed the world that there was an easier route than the turnpike and that was the one through the Oliverian notch. Individuals from Wells River and northern Vermont, came down and examined this pass through the hills and went back with a glowing report of the ease with which a road could be built through it. They sent messengers and letters to Warren urging the inhabitants to build it; but our little democracy was violently opposed to the enterprise for the reason that it would subject them to much expense, and as it passed through an uninhabited section it would cost a large sum each year to keep it in repair. Besides, the landlords upon the turnpike knew it would kill them, and they worked against it with all their might.

But something must be done for the clamor came down even

from the boundaries of Canada saying, "Build the Berry brook road." So an assembly of the people was held in the selectmenship of Moses H. Clement, Samuel L. Merrill, and Samuel Merrill, July 22d, 1834, and Nathaniel Clough, Solomon Cotton, and Samuel Bixby were chosen a committee to examine and explore all routes thought proper for a highway through the town.

The committee acted. They went up the banks of the Mikaseota or Black brook, and down Berry brook valley. Whether or not they went over the low pass between Waternomee and Cushman mountains to Woodstock, or climbed the old route surveyed by Abel Merrill and Joseph Patch by Glen ponds to Trecothick, we are unable to say, for the committee made no report and never intended to; the only object was delay.

The people of the upper country waited, then became impatient, finally came to the conclusion that our little democracy did not intend to do anything, and getting mad went before the grand jury at Haverhill, and got Warren's public highways indicted, as Col. Obadiah Clement did once before, and the court ordered a large fine to be imposed upon our modest town, to be paid in work upon her bad roads. The citizens were disgusted and indignant, but they worked out the fine.

The subject of a new road was also presented to the court. After a patient hearing of the matter that august tribunal decided that the road should be built through Berry brook valley, and appointed a committee to lay it out. They immediately proceeded with their work, bushing it through and setting the stakes upon the west bank. Then the court ordered the town of Warren to build it.

When it was evident that the work must be performed, and that they could no longer avoid it, an assembly of the citizens was held on the 8th of December, 1834, and it was voted that the road should be built. They would not fight the court in the matter. So they chose Solomon Cotton, Samuel L. Merrill, and Joseph Bixby a committee to carry the work through, and authorized them to raise five hundred dollars to commence with. But this sum hardly made a commencement, only cutting the trees and digging the stumps, nothing more. Then it was let out in different sections to several individuals, Maj. Daniel Patch and his son Joseph building the one upon the Summit. Carlos D. Woodward, Henry Noyes, Roper Noyes, John Buswell, Stevens Merrill, Winthrop and Roswell Elliott, and Ebenezer Calef, built the sections south. Stephen Whiteman said he was a sub-contractor and cut bushes, and that Rev. Horace Webber did the same thing.

Before it was finished two years of time had passed, more than three thousand dollars expended, and the town was heavily in debt. December 22, 1836, the town voted that although the Berry brook road was not completed, the selectmen should post up notices at each end of said highway, that people might travel over it at their own expense and their own risk.

The debt! It looked like a mountain. Warren hitherto had been an economical town. They were not used to paying big bills. How could they now? The citizens were almost discouraged. But kind Providence, as some of the more pious ones will have it, came to their relief. It happened thus:—

For many years a large amount of money had been accruing in the United States bank. When Gen. Jackson, who was very hostile to the bank, was elected president, that institution was dissolved, and government after paying the debts of the nation passed a resolve that the surplus should be divided among the different States, and then distributed to the towns of which they were composed. By a vote passed at the regular annual meeting, the selectmen were empowered to go to Concord and receive the "Surplus Revenue." They brought home with them eighteen hundred dollars. At first they hardly knew what to do with it; but at a town meeting held for the purpose, voted that the selectmen put the money out at usury, not letting any one individual have more than two hundred dollars. Then in 1838, the town voted that the selectmen call in enough of the surplus revenue to pay up for the building of the Berry brook road,— a very sensible vote — but they coupled on the following rather ambiguous clause, "That Solomon Cotton be an agent to take charge of the money, and that the selectmen hire it of him, giving their notes for the same and pay the town debt with it." What became of the notes we are wholly unable to say. The town certainly never paid them.

With the new road through Berry brook valley built, a hotel must be erected on the Summit. Moses Abbott, the fat man, kept it at first, and then it passed into the hands of Benjamin Little, and he was mine host in that section for many years.*

Travelers who stopped at Mr. Little's inn, frequently suggested that they would like to climb to the bald crest of Moosehillock. To gratify the wish, one summer day he raised all High street by giving them what grog they could drink and they bushed out a path right up the side of the mountain to the topmost peak.

It was a beautiful day when the party of road makers came out upon the bald crest. The wind was blowing strong from the north west, and the little flowers growing upon Moosehillock's bare peak shook their white heads in the breeze.

Our landlord is standing upon the north peak. His friends and their dogs, wild dwellers of the Summit and of High street, are in a group around him. Nathan Willey, playfully called " Mr. Nutter;" Moses Ellsworth, who had the title of " Fortyfoot," on account of the shortness of his stature; Isaac Fifield, a tall man, gifted in prayer in time of revivals, whom the Summit boys facetiously called " Aunt Isaac,"—" Fortyfoot" had " Aunt Isaac's " prayer learned by heart, and could repeat it with unction on occasions when he had put himself outside of two or three beverages;† Sir Richard Whiteman; Stephen Whiteman, with the pious title of " Elder Binx;" John French, the school-master, an early riser, who had the economical habit of lying in bed with his wife till the clock struck three in the afternoon, in winter, to save fire-wood; Welches, father and two sons, Silas and Bartlett; Stephen Martin, Calvin Bailey, Samuel Whitcher, James Harriman, husband of Mrs. Harriman, and others, and Joseph Whitcher, the bear-catcher, wolf-killer, and story-teller, were there — all good men, who thus good naturedly nicknamed each other.‡ Their beards were unshaven, and their long hair streamed out in the pure air that was blowing so steady over the mountain.

The blue sky is above them; no smoke, no haze, no clouds are there. Silver lakes and flashing rivers lay beneath them. A thou-

---

* In early times Chase Whitcher kept entertainment for man and beast on the Summit, Maj. Daniel Patch also, but neither of them kept tavern.

† We once saw Jim Clement burst every button off his vest laughing at "Fortyfoot," when he was repeating " Aunt Isaac's " prayer to " Aunt I." himself, and a crowd of listeners.

‡ Some well bred people have said that it was mean business for the above gentlemen to call each other names.

sand mountain peaks bathing their heads in the bright sunshine are around them. There are peaks sharp and angular, wavy wooded mountain crests, great cones standing alone, dome shaped mountains dark and sombre.

Mr. Nathan Willey wanted to know what that great sheet of water in the south was, and John French, the school-master, said it must be the Smile of the Great Spirit, the beautiful lake Winnepisseogee. Mr. Stephen Whiteman asked what that ragged looking mountain over there to the north-east was, and the school-master told how he had heard Dick French, the hunter, tell about the great Haystacks that had white furrows down their sides, and that they were terrible hard mountains to climb. Capt. Benj. Little pointed out the long river down in the west as the Connecticut and Richard Whiteman said he could see Black mountain, Owl's-head, Webster slide, and Wachipauka pond, — he knew them. Stephen Whiteman stuck to it that he could see Boston; and said it was not a great distance either, only a hundred and forty miles by the road; and that Maj. True Stevens had walked it in less than two days when he came back from Brighton, where he had been with a drove.* Capt. Ben. Little said he could beat that, and then he told how Col. Moses H. Clement went down to Brighton with a flock of sheep, and had a little brindle dog Bose to help drive them, that just at dark in Brighton he lost the dog, and that before night the next day, Bose whined and barked at the door in Warren, and Mrs. Clement let him in, terribly tired and footsore. The dog had run a hundred and forty miles in less than twenty-four hours. Joseph Whitcher said he didn't care anything about such stories, and then he went on to tell that he had been all over the mountain a good many times before, hunting wolves. Said he, " I caught one down there in the Tunnel where you can hear Tunnel brook roaring. Once I followed one down Mooschillock river that rises over there in that dark fir woods and runs down into the Pemigewassett, but did not get him."

"Where does Tunnel brook go to?" said Stephen Whiteman. Whitcher said it ran down into the Swiftwater, and the latter stream emptied into the Ammonoosuc. Then the bear catcher said

---

* John Libbey once did the same thing. He walked from Boston to Warren in two days. He got up to Concord the first day the sun an hour high.—Anson Merrill's statement.

he got two deer once in the meadow where was the little pond which was the head of Baker river, and that once he fished clear down to the East-parte and got more trout than he could lug, and Mr. Fifield said he didn't believe a word of it. But Joseph Whitcher did not care a copper whether he believed it or not, and went on to say that he had a sable line every year on the Oliverian, and that every one of these streams, Tunnel brook, Swiftwater, Moosehillock river, Baker river, and the Oliverian, had its source within a rod of the mountain summit where they stood. Moses Ellsworth said he knew this was a lie for he hadn't had a drop of anything for an hour to wet his whistle with, and he was most choked to death and would like to see the springs from which the streams started.

Just then three eagles rose out of the great Tunnel where the brook was roaring, and came hovering over the grassy mountain crest, hunting for small birds and mice. "See there!" said Mr. Willey. The dogs snuffed the air, erected the hair on their backs, and their ears stood straight. One of them barked. The eagles, one with white breast and tail, the others gray, caught sight and sound. Wheeling in the air, seemingly without moving feather or wing, around and around in great circles, each time higher up, they soared thousands of feet above the mountain peak, until they were almost lost in the deep blue. Then, a speck in the sky, they sailed slowly away eastward over the great Pemigewassett valley. Stephen Whiteman said he would like to know how those birds could get up so high without "floppin" their wings once.

But it was getting cold, the men were dry, and away they went through the matted hackmatacks down the mountain. When they were gone, as great novelists would tell it, the wind still sighed on the rocks, the little birds sang their vesper hymns in the dark firs, the eagles screamed again, and a wolf howled down in one of the great gorges; but no human ear was there to listen. The mountain peak was left alone, a mighty solitude in the great waste of mountains, just as it had been for ages. As the men went home Isaac Fifield said that "the rain might descend, the winds blow, the frosts come, and the snow fall and no human being for years would again gaze upon this wild magnificence." But Mr. Fifield's reflections did not prove true, and scattering visitors from that day forth began to climb Moosehillock mountain.*

This last road cost Warren nothing; the burden of the first the surplus revenue removed. Both brought prosperity and happiness, one by attracting visitors with its mighty grandeur, the other by turning a still larger tide of travel through our pleasant hamlet valley.

---

* Dr. Ezra Bartlett, Samuel Knight and others went on to Moosehillock about the year 1800. They did not succeed in lighting a fire, and it was so cold they had to leave the summit at night. They went down on the north east side over the great ledges in the ravine where they had to let themselves down with a pole. There was snow on the mountain at the time.—Miss Hannah B. Knight's statement.

Explanatory Note.—The substance of the story about cutting the Moosehillock path is true. But our authorities said they would not vouch for all the minute particulars.

CHAPTER III.

OF A GREAT LAWSUIT ABOUT MRS. SARAH WEEKS, WHOM FOOLISH PEOPLE CALLED A WITCH, CONCLUDING WITH PLEASANT RECOLLECTIONS OF A PARING BEE AND A "SHIN-DIG," IF ANYBODY KNOWS WHAT THAT IS.

WARREN in olden times had waged fierce lawsuits. Col. Obadiah Clement, fighting for victory, indignant teamsters and stage drivers getting numerous indictments to cure bad roads, had cost the town many a hard battle. But these old fights buried under nearly half a century were almost forgotten, living only in the memory of the most aged inhabitants. Even the recollection of the would be lawsuit Stevens Merrill might have had with James Aiken, had he not taken the law into his own hands and a house been burned up, had almost faded away forever.

But now when the third generation of Warren's white inhabitants were on the stage the slumbering volcano of litigating wrath once more burst forth and our peaceful hamlet among the hills was tossed from centre to circumference.* It happened in this wise.

---

* *Death by Fright.*—Warren never has had many lawyers, but has been blessed with plenty of law. Joseph Patch, Jr., for a while was deputy sheriff, and he once went on to Pine-hill to arrest one Goodwin on a civil process. Goodwin stood looking at him till the sheriff got within a rod of him, and then fell dead in his tracks. It was said by some that his imagination killed him.

Serious Law Case.—Capt. Samuel L. Merrill once kept store on the turnpike, near the Blue ridge. Some one hitched his horse and sleigh in the store shed one day and went in to purchase goods. While there a person supposed to be tipsy, went up behind the old fashioned, high-backed, blue-painted sleigh, to answer to one of the calls of nature. The sleigh back was five feet high to keep the wind off the driver, and there was a crack near the top of it. The copious flood poured forth by the tipsy man ran through the crack, down on the inside and wet the owner's

Mrs. Sarah Weeks, of whom we have spoken before, and who had the very enviable reputation of being a witch, wife of Benjamin Weeks, Jr., had become chargeable to the town of Wentworth for support as a pauper. She had once lived in Warren on the Height-o'-land, and Wentworth thought our good town should support her. Wentworth requested Warren to do so. Warren refused. Wentworth was indignant—mad—and said she should. Warren was stubborn and a suit was brought.

Our neighbor across the southern border employed distinguished counsel,—Hon. John P. Hale, U. S. Senator, and afterwards minister to Spain, and Hon. Josiah Quincy. Our beloved hamlet engaged the services of Hon. Franklin Pierce, afterwards President of the United States, and Thomas J. Whipple, Esq., to assist him. The case was in the Eastern Judicial District of Grafton county, and was tried at Plymouth. It turned upon this point: Did Benjamin Weeks, Jr., have a residence in Warren? He had never paid taxes there seven years in succession; but on the books was this record: "1817, Benj. Weeks elected hogreeve." There was no record of his taking the oath of office, and unless he had done so, he would not have gained a residence. There was great excitement about the case in both towns, and it greatly increased when the witnesses were summoned. On the part of Wentworth, the following were cited to appear:

Richard Whiteman and Stephen Whiteman, of Warren, William Whiteman, of Canada, Joshua Copp, Jr., of Northumberland, N. H., William Kelley, and Anson Merrill.*

---

dinner, thereby spoiling it. It was a case of trespass; the owner was mad, and swore he would have satisfaction. Moses Ellsworth, sometimes called Fortyfoot, was present, tipsy, and he was at once suspected as the culprit, and taken into custody. There was no judge present, so a "reference" was appointed and they immediately proceeded with the investigation. Fortyfoot plead "not guilty," whereupon a two foot rule was procured and the culprit's legs were measured. They were found to be only two feet four inches long, while the crack in the back of the sleigh was three feet six inches from the ground, consequently the reference after great deliberation, brought in that Fortyfoot could not have possibly done the dirty deed, and he was acquitted. It is said that the accused wept tears of joy over the result of the trial, and that the court, counsel, and spectators, all took a smile at the bar of justice inside the store.

Moses Abbott and Joseph Whitcher once bet on an election. Each staked his hog against the other. Abbott lost but would not give up his hog. After a good deal of discussion they left it out to William Pomeroy. Enoch R. Weeks, and Stevens M. Dow, who brought in that Whitcher should have Abbott's hog; a very proper decision according to the betting code, but decidedly illegal. This case created immense excitement on the Summit.

* ANSON AND MAHALA (*Burns*) MERRILL'S FAMILY RECORD.
Married Oct. 1831. He was born Dec. 4, 1804. She was born Aug. 15, 1815. Their children are Elizabeth, Van, an infant, Ada A. and Ellen L.

On the part of Warren, Moses H. Clement, Jesse Little,* Page Clement, son of old Jonathan Clement, innkeeper, David Fellows, and Nathaniel Clough, were summoned.

William D. McQuestion was agent for Wentworth; Enoch R. Weeks was agent for Warren.

And now the battle began. Wentworth's witnesses testified that Benjamin Weeks, Jr., was chosen hogreeve; but they could not swear that he was sworn in. Warren's witnesses testified that he was chosen, but that he was not sworn in. The lawyers on the trial were very smart as might be expected, and fought tenaciously. They wanted to show their present and future clients what great ability they had.

The evidence was all in; they were about to commence the arguments; silence reigned in the court room. There was a pause. Then Richard Whiteman, sometimes called Sir Richard of Tamarack swamp, again took the stand. His countenance shone, his recollection was refreshed, and he testified as brave as a lion that Benjamin Weeks, Jr., was elected, that he was sworn in, and that he, Whiteman, had helped him on several occasions both yoke and ring hogs. Most satisfactory evidence!

The arguments were made, the Judge delivered his charge, the jury retired, and returning in a few minutes, gave a verdict for Wentworth. Warren's agent and his witnesses went home feeling cheap enough.

That night Wentworth had a jollification. Their old cannon was brought out. It was double charged every time, and again and again it sent the notes of victory up the Asquamchumauke valley, over every hill of our hamlet, even to Warren Summit. Of

---

† JESSE AND SUSAN COPP (*Merrill*) LITTLE'S FAMILY RECORD.

He was born July 4, 1800.
She was born July, 30, 1808.
Married Nov. 18, 1829.
Joseph, born Oct. 28, 1830.

William, born Mar. 20, 1833.
Thomas B. born Sept. 7, 1838.
George A. born May 23, 1847.

GENEALOGY OF THE LITTLE FAMILY IN WARREN.

GEORGE LITTLE, a tailor by trade, came from Unicorn street, London, England. to Newbury. Mass., in 1640. He married Alice Poor.
Moses, 4th child of George, born March 11, 1657, married Lydia Coffin.
Tristram, 2d child of Moses, born Dec 9, 1681, married Sarah Dole.
Samuel, 3d child of Tristram, born Feb. 18, 1713, married Dorothy Noyes.
James, 1st child of Samuel, born Feb. 18, 1737, married Tamar Roberts.
Amos, 3d child of James, born Feb. 28, 1766, married Betsey Kimball.
Jesse, 5th child of Amos, born July 4, 1800, married Susan C. Merrill.

course the citizens of Warren were perfectly delighted with the gentle music.

Wentworth's celebration had a wonderful effect. It waked up the musty recollection of every old man in Warren. They began to remember how the case was. Old Mr. Nathaniel Clough was the first man to recall it. The facts were something as follows: There were in town two men, father and son, by the name of Benjamin Weeks, Benjamin, Sen., and Benjamin, Jr. The son was chosen hogreeve, but as he was not in the meeting at the time, to take the oath, his father, Benjamin Weeks, stepped forward at once and said, "Choose me and I will serve." He was immediately chosen, took the oath, and the record on the town book, "1817, Benj. Weeks elected hogreeve," was correct; but it had no relation to Benj. Weeks, Jr. Many other men now remembered the fact and the town could not give the case up so.

Accordingly at a meeting called and held Nov. 22, 1843, the following vote was passed: "That the agent chosen to carry on the case between Warren and Wentworth, have it tried where they think proper; that the agent ascertain whether the review destroys the decision of the former trial, if it does destroy it, then the agents are to settle with Wentworth, by that town paying the legal cost the town of Warren would recover by law, *and they also support Sarah Weeks;* if they will not settle upon these conditions, then the agent is to proceed with the case."

The facts and the action of the town came to the ears of the agent of Wentworth. At first he was incredulous, then he made inquiries, then went to the old men of Warren and learned how they would testify, and finally after the winter and spring passed, and the summer was far along, he came to Warren, backed down, and paid up. Thus ended Warren's greatest lawsuit; all the citizens felt good and the victory must be celebrated. This was not done by firing cannon after the manner of Wentworth; but parties, junketings, and apple bees were rife, and the people that autumn had a most hilarious time of it.

The young friends of your humble historian, who was a boy then, went with him to two paring bees that fall, according to his recollection. Once we came down by the Forks school-house, where Hurricane brook, a silver stream, falls into Patch brook, after leaping and laughing its way from the summit of Mount Carr, 3,000 feet above us, to Mr. William Clough's. What a pile of apples was worked up that night. Four brave young men were mounted on four old fashioned paring machines, all of different patterns, and with what a buzz they took the skins off the beautiful and many hued apples. A lot of us small boys did nothing but quarter the peeled fruit; the beautiful young ladies and the careful mothers cored them ever so nicely, and a bevy of girls and old Mr. Clough strung hundreds of "strings" and hung them in wreaths and wavy festoons, ornaments like, on pegs about the room to dry.

Ten o'clock in the evening, and the work was done. What a supper we had, fit for a king, and enough for a small regiment. How good it tasted. And the games after supper was over! "Blind man's buff" was glorious, "Button, button," was nice, and "Turn the plate" was so fine. And then the pawns paid and the kisses given. How rosy the lips that gave them. How I envied the boys that got them. A little of superstition must come in; apple peelings were thrown over fine heads to make initial letters of their lovers' names, and several went down cellar backwards holding a mirror in their hands to see their future husband's or wife's face. Then we played "Chase the squirrel," and "Pass the handkerchief," and "Simon says thumbs up," and sombody sang songs ever so beautiful, and it was after midnight when we were going home again by the "Forks school-house," in Patchbreuckland.

We had never been out so late before, and there was a graveyard with white tombstones by the "Forks school-house." But we went bravely past it, and going up by the Patch place where Jonathan Eaton lived, the stars shone above us, and the crescent moon was hurrying down the western sky. Just then there was a strange cry. We listened — heard it again. The older boys said it was a wild hound dog on the eastern mountains. Some said he belonged in Woodstock. How plain I heard him myself on that moonlight night in autumn. Baying at intervals, his three almost unearthly yells would come ringing out through the darkness. What was he pursuing? Was it the bounding deer, the black fox, running straight away for miles, or a shadowy ghost leading will-

D*

o'-the-wisp like through dark ravines and wild gorges. Others said they had heard the old hound in the storm when his baying mingled with the voice of the wind and the roar of the mountain streams.

There were dozens of paring bees that fall, and the numerous parties and festivities provoked by the great lawsuit victory only ended, if we remember right, by a grand ball, where Jim Clement danced his flat-footed double-shuffle so remarkably, and a turkey supper, that came off about Christmas time, at the present Moosilauke house, one of the neat hotels of the hamlet.

May Warren never be perplexed by another lawsuit like the one about Mrs. Sarah Weeks or any other kind; but if she should, may it have a like successful and happy termination.

CHAPTER IV.

A CHAPTER ON FIRES.

WE introduce it here, because the greatest happened about this time, and all the others seem to centre around it. It is worthy of record that they had grand ones when the farms were cleared; but the first dwelling house burned in Warren, as we all well remember, was James Aiken's cabin that stood half a mile east of the depot. Then Joseph Patch's buildings were fired by a brave sojer boy journeying home from the wars, and for more than half a century after not a house was burned in Warren.

Then about the year 1830, Richard Whiteman's house on the Summit went down, followed by the Pine hill school-house, which burned up in the daytime, and shortly after that, the village school-house flashed bright one night and was gone. This was the prelude.

One bright spring day in 1845, the old homestead of Amos Little, on Beech hill, accidentally took fire. All the male members of the family had gone away, while Mrs. Kimball Little, who was unwell, had retired to her chamber. There was a barrel standing in the shed adjoining the house, in which some meat had been placed to smoke, and as the family had smoked their meat here the preceding spring, and no accident having occurred, it was considered safe.

From this the fire took. It was a beautiful day, no wind. An individual standing near the church on the common, happening to look in the direction of the house, saw curling slowly up a thin column of blue smoke. One moment more and the cry of fire rung out rousing every neighbor. The inmates of the school-house near by were dismissed, and the young urchins dispatched in all directions to give the alarm.

When the first individual, a peddler, arrived at the house, with another person to assist him he could have stopped the fire; but in five minutes the roof of the shed was in flames.

Mrs. Little awakened, almost swooned in fright, then with the rest commenced to carry the furniture from the house. In a very short time nearly all the villagers arrived. Some tried to tear down the shed connecting the house with the three large barns; but before it was half demolished the flames and blinding smoke drove them from the undertaking. Every one now worked to save what they could from the burning buildings. But as is customary at all fires, where they seldom occur, people generally lost their wits, and haste, hurry, and excitement prevailed; windows were thrown from the second story to the ground; looking-glasses and other furniture easily demolished, shared the same fate, and there was a delightful scene of confusion.

The fire advanced rapidly, and it was soon evident the building must be abandoned; but one man, Mr. Miranda Whitcher, wishing to save some article of furniture which was in a room on the east side of the house, went thither. He had scarcely entered it before the flames sprung up behind, and firing an unplastered wall made a retreat almost impossible. A dense volume of smoke now filled the room, choking and blinding him; but Mr. Whitcher with a bound shot through the fire, trod quickly along the tottering floor and made for a distant window. The people below saw him and loudly shouted to him to jump out upon the ground; but he seemed possessed of a strange fatality, and did not notice them. The flames creeping rapidly along the floor behind, scorched the poor man, when grasping the window sill he slowly let himself down, but did not relinquish his hold. The fire at that instant bursting from the window below circled up and around him. Individuals entreated him to let go; but he heeded them not, until at last exhausted, his hands slowly relaxed, and he fell. Two persons enveloped in wet blankets succeeded in reaching him, and he was removed to the little field on the west side of the road.

The large buildings were now completely enveloped in fire crowned by an immense column of black smoke. Nearly every person had gathered about the dying man, whose groans mingling with the crackling flames and the roar of the burning buildings, made an impressive scene. In a few moments more, after one convulsive quiver, the fine old house fell a mass of burning ruins. Mr. Whitcher was then conveyed to his home, suffered for an hour and died.

A whole generation had lived in Warren without a fire of any magnitude, and now such a conflagration, with Whitcher's death, following so close upon the heels of "the terrible Parker murder," which had filled the whole State with horror, made a profound impression upon the minds of the people and hardly anything else was talked of for a whole month. The citizens of Warren did what was customary in olden times in New Hampshire; they made a "bee;" a hundred men or so went into the woods with broad axes and narrow axes, and squares, and chalk-lines, and in a week's time almost a frame was raised over the old ruins. Before autumn Kimball Little, youngest son of Amos Little, had moved into the new house and was upon the old farm again.

For the benefit of our readers who are interested in casualties of this kind, we will state that the next fire occurred early in the summer of 1849. Vowell Leathers' house was burned, and in it burned his wife. It was a beautiful summer Sabbath. Mr. Leathers was away at Romney,* attending meeting. His son John,— many yet remember him,—was in the woods listening to the songs of birds and gathering broom-stuff, while Mrs. Leathers, who was old and blind, but an excellent woman for all that, could not help herself in any manner.

About eleven o'clock in the forenoon, Isaac Sawtelle, who lived by Sawtelle school-house, three miles away, saw the smoke curling up from the dwelling, high up on the side of Sentinel mountain. He came to the village on the run, rushed into the meeting-house, and without ceremony gave the alarm, and with the whole congregation hurried away up Beech hill. The house was all in flames when Sawtelle arrived there, and a thin smoke

---

* It is said that the Hon. Josiah Quincy knows how to spell Romney correctly; that instead of R-u-m rum, otherwise "rot-gut," he spells the word, R-o-m-n-e-y Romney, a noble name from a royal English house, that of the Earl of Romney.

was curling through the roof of the barn. Hurrying in and on to the hay-mow, he found it proceeded from a slow match made with great care, and that the hay was not yet burning. He removed the match and the barn was saved. Hardly anything was taken out of the house, and Mrs. Leathers was burned to death.

The next day Dr. Little climbed Beech hill, picked up the charred remains of the poor woman, placed them in a rude box and carrying them to the grave-yard, on Pine-hill road, they were buried.

There was a terrible suspicion in the minds of people. Who set the fire? No one has ever told, and it will probably forever remain a mystery. Still Uncle Leathers, as he is familiarly called, never was considered a bad man, though he descended from the Gipsy race and has many eccentricities, among which is the erecting of tomb-stones with names thereon, for himself and some of his family before their death, and his fondness for perfumes; he being the man, as we have before stated, who persisted in killing, cooking, and eating such sweet smelling animals as skunks, at the town farm, much to the delight of the lady paupers and other persons living there. It is said that he once put a skunk, fresh smelling from the dewy fields, under Mrs. Brown's bed, thereby filling the soul of that chaste and pious lady with great happiness. Uncle Leathers at the close of Warren's first century is still living, a hale and hearty old man.

During the winter of 1854, the buildings of Mr. Amos Clement, together with nearly all their contents, including thirty-three valuable sheep which they could not drive from the fire, a hog and a yearling steer, were destroyed.

Since then a tavern stand built by Mr. Ephraim Clement near the depot, together with Mr. Isaac Merrill's buildings near by, have burned. Moses Ellsworth's little red house on Warren Summit burned up one night. Hazen Clement's house and barn on the side of Mount Carr was consumed one day when all the family were away. Ephraim Clement's house on Pine hill, where Isaiah Batchelder once lived, went down in a night. John Marston's wheel-wright shop blazed like a rocket and was gone; and last, Daniel Marston's house, at the foot of the Height-o'-land, burned up. We had almost forgot to state that George W. Jackson was moving a house from the top of the Height-o'-land one summer. It got stuck in the road and stood there a fortnight. One night some bad person touched a match to it, and the old house never came down to Warren village.*

But the grandest fires we have ever seen, were the fires upon Warren's mountains. Webster slide has blazed like a volcano. Owl's head has burned for months, lighting up the heavens at night; Moosehillock has been wrapped in sheets of flame completely enveloping its twin peaks, and Mount Carr, twice within the memory of the present generation, has flashed from base to summit. It was in the summer of 1854 that the fire roared on Mount Carr. Then a million trees burned to the wind. Then a sound came like the rushing of a tempest; like the mighty voice of the ocean. Its roaring was heard six miles away, and one could see to read fine print at midnight. It was a sight never to be forgotten.

---

* Friday, Sept. 16, 1870, there was a great fire in Warren. Russell Merrill's hotel, the old Joseph Merrill inn, and Henry W. Week's house burned. The fire occurred about two o'clock in the morning. Loss $15,000, insured for $10,000.

CHAPTER V.

HOW AND WHEN THE RAILROAD WAS BUILT, WHICH WILL BE A WONDER TO FUTURE GENERATIONS, BUT IS QUITE A COMMON THING NOW.

THE first railroad steam engine and railway, if we remember right, were built in England. The first railroad in this country was the short line from the stone quarries in Quincy, Mass., to the wharf "down by the sea," to transport stone. Then in New England, the Boston and Providence, the Boston and Worcester, and the Boston and Lowell railroads followed in quick succession, and after these were built, railroads began to multiply wonderfully all through the country.

From Lowell the iron horse crept up the Merrimack gradually to Concord, N. H. Here it paused a short time, but not long. The Northern railroad from Concord to Lebanon, was soon commenced, and then after the most fierce opposition from the Northern and Pasumpsic railroads at the June session of the Legislature in 1844, the Boston, Concord and Montreal was chartered.

The company immediately organized, Josiah Quincy,* of

---

* OFFICERS OF THE BOSTON, CONCORD AND MONTREAL RAILROAD.

Presidents :—
   Josiah Quincy, elected April 8, 1845.
   John E. Lyon, elected May 29, 1860, still in office.

Superintendents :—
   Peter Clark, chosen May 15, 1846.
   James N. Elkins, chosen Dec. 2, 1847. Died June 20, 1853.
   James M. Whiton, chosen June 20, 1853. Died June 20, 1857.
   John T. Coffin, chosen June, 1857, as agent of Trustees.

Romney, being President, and the people along the route freely paid their money for a survey, which was made this season by Mr. Crocker, throughout the whole line. Stock books were also immediately opened, a considerable amount was subscribed, the grading of the road was commenced upon its lower sections, and in about one year was completed eighteen miles, from Concord to Tilton. Then a year more and the cars ran to Laconia, and another year and they got up to Meredith village. Here they stopped a while, for the route by the beautiful ponds of Centre Harbor and over New Hampton summit was a hard one; but late in the autumn of 1849 the cars ran into Plymouth.

But the road was not to stop here; it had already been commenced above on the banks of the Asquamchumauke, and Thomas Piersons was set stoutly to work to find a feasible route over Warren Summit. The first line surveyed by Crocker, came up the west bank of the Asquamchumauke, up Black brook, the Mikascota, the same side to the Blue ridge, thence crossing the valley at the outlet of Runaway pond it passed up the east shore of the latter basin, up Black brook, over the Summit and down the Oliverian. Thos. Piersons took the east side of the valley through Warren, crossed the Asquamchumauke, with a "fill" for half a mile seventy-five feet deep, to the side of Knight hill, and thence up Berry brook to the Summit. Then he tried up the road to Noyes Bridge, kept under the bank on the east side of the lower village, thence across the plain by the place where James Aiken got burned out, and up his old route by Berry brook. He made his report and "the directors considered."

Two years they considered; and then another engineer was procured, T. J. Carter, and he surveyed and located the present railroad route through Warren. He did his work best of all, for

---

Joseph A. Dodge, chosen Aug. 9, 1858, still in office.
Clerk :—
    Charles Lane, chosen April 8, 1845, still in office.
Station Agents at Warren:—
    David Atwood and Mr. Chase.
    Richard Wiggin.
    Marcus M. Lawrence.
    Edwin C Wentworth.
    Morrill J. Sanborn.
    J. M. Parks, at Summit.
—Col. Charles Lane's statement.

no where else in town could the depot have been so satisfactorily located.

The road was already nearly graded to the south line of Warren, and a contract was made in the summer of 1850 with Warren H. Smith, an enterprising gentleman residing at Tilton, to complete it to Warren village. Mr. Smith commenced work the ensuing October, and then Warren glowed with life.

As many men as possible were put into the Clifford cut on the southern boundary, and there were a lot of shanties built at the east end of the bridge over the river near by, for the Irish shovelers to live in. Well do we remember the pleasant little anecdote told of these transient residents here. One of the shanty families sent to Ireland for a friend of theirs. He landed in Boston and then came immediately to Warren. The next Sabbath as alone he was walking out for his health and a little pious meditation, he chanced to find as he thought a spotted cat by the wall. Catching it up in his arms he began to stroke its back saying, "Poor pussy," when suddenly dropping it he grasped his nose and exclaimed, "Howly Mither, what has the crathure been aiten!" Not being particularly fond of sweet perfumes, he quickly returned to the shanty and with religious fervor related his adventures with the cat, much to the delight of all his friends.

The Redington boys, brothers, finished the Clifford cut. Mr. Gipson was "boss" in the "side-hill cut," near the old Nathaniel Clough place. It took all winter to dig this out. William Clement, of Warren, son of Col. Ben., oversaw a gang of Irishmen near the long covered railroad bridge, making the fill above the bridge and the cut through the John Mills burying-ground, down by the Patch place to Patch brook. Old "St. Bowen" graded up about the depot, running his "dump carts" all winter down through the village over the Noyes bridge to the mound just below on the east side of the road. Pity he hauled sand from there, for he left an unsightly cut. All of Clement's and Mr. Bowen's men lived in shanties over by Patch brook where it leaps down Rocky falls. Batchelder of Lake village made the rock cut just west of the Moosilauke house, and the butments, and the great bridge, were built during the winter.

Before the first of April, 1851, the grading and bridges on the whole line from Plymouth to Warren village were nearly completed. As soon as the ground was sufficiently settled, Mr. Smith commenced to lay the track, and on the 24th of May the first steam engine ran into Warren, and on the 25th its bell was rung at Warren depot.

May 25, 1851, was a great day for Warren. It should not be forgotten. With that day came a new life. The great teams and covered wagons, the pungs of winter, driven by the Vermont farmers; the stages, the mighty droves of beef cattle tramping along the road; the flocks of sheep, thousands together; herds of swine more numerous than the one the devils of Mary Magdalene drove into the sea, going to market,—all these shall now disappear from the highways of Warren forever. In their place shall come thundering cars, the iron horse with ribs of steel and heart of fire, screaming with its steam whistle loud enough to be heard far away beyond Glen ponds and Woodstock, passenger trains and freight trains, and telegraph.

The people of Warren did appreciate the day and celebrated it. Mr. Smith gave a bountiful and excellent supper at the Moosilauke house, then kept by Levi C. Whitcher, and mirth, hilarity, music, and dancing prevailed.

On the first Monday in June, 1851, the cars began to run regularly from Warren, no longer a quiet, pleasant hamlet, but now a smart, bustling little town among the mountains.*

At the railroad company's annual meeting, held at Wentworth on the last Tuesday of May, it was voted to prefer six hundred thousand dollars of stock, with which to construct the road from Warren to Woodsville; and early in the fall the grading was contracted for by Mr. Warren H. Smith, and rapidly commenced. Owen McCarthy made the great fill across the plain from Mt. Helen down to the common. Mr. Dolloff cut the ledge near the basin of Runaway pond, called the Dolloff cut; "St. Bowen" made great cuts and fills around Pine hill, and the Redington boys had the deep excavation near Kelly pond. But the cutting through

---

* When they were surveying the railroad, Mr. Nathaniel Clough, 89 years old, who was incredulous about the enterprise, said that he did not want to live any longer than to see the cars run into Warren. He was sick at the time the first regular train passed his house and they sat him up in bed to look at it. Two weeks after he was dead.

the ledge on Warren Summit was the great work, and it involved an immense amount of labor. For a year and a half a hundred and fifty men, superintended by two brothers by the name of Keyes, from Romney, seventeen horses, with a number of yokes of cattle, were employed. Tons of powder were burned, a man was killed, and more than one hundred and fifty thousand dollars expended before a steam engine ran over the Summit.*

The cut at this, the highest point of our railroad, is nearly three-fourths of a mile in length, and in some places sixty feet deep. Near the north end a little rill of pure, clear water comes dashing down over the huge rocks, and at the bottom, divides itself into two streams; the waters of the one running north emptying themselves into the Connecticut eventually find their way into the ocean, through Long Island Sound; while those running south unite with the Merrimack river which discharges itself into the ocean nearly two hundred miles from the mouth of the Connecticut.

The cars commenced running over this last section in the fall of 1852, as far as East Haverhill, and early the ensuing spring the road was finished to Woodsville, where it connects with the Passumpsic railroad and the White mountain railroad.

Green were the hills of Warren. The mighty spruces and hemlocks still stood untouched upon the mountains, and amongst them the wood-chopper's axe had not as yet been heard. The reason of all this was the inconvenience of getting the timber to market, and the consequent unprofitableness of the business. But now, through the medium which the railroad afforded, a rapid and convenient communication was opened with the large towns down the Merrimack, and thereby the business of lumbering was much more profitable.

Wood also became an object of importance, and the once heavy forests fast began to disappear. Upon the side of Mount Carr, high up in the valley of Patch brook, a large company of French Canadians, honest men every one, made a rural settlement and chopped wood, under the superintendence of Col. Charles Lane. This individual, more easily to facilitate its transportation

---
* C. H. Latham had charge of the engineering. Jonathan Little kept the hotel on the Summit, and made money while the railroad was building; but the tavern was good for nothing after the cars began to run.

from the mountain side, constructed a sluice nearly two and one-fourth miles in length, extending to the valley near the railroad. The sluice was twenty inches in width and sixteen inches in height. In it he turned the waters of Patch brook, the wild mountain stream, and placing the wood in this, it rapidly descended in its serpentine course, now crossing some deep gully, then spanning the torrent, and then creeping rapidly along on the side of some steep bank till at last it reached the valley, falling over a thousand feet.

Mr. Lane also constructed a large canal, half a mile long, through which he turned the water of Baker river into the large mill-pond on Black brook. The cost of the work was about two thousand dollars. It was finished late in the fall, and the water first let in on November 28, 1853.

This made an excellent mill-privilege and a great saw-mill went up in Warren village. Millions of feet of lumber have been manufactured here and sent to market. East-parte also waked up and a mighty mill was erected there. Warren Summit also got enterprising; numerous mills have been built, and the timber comes down from Black mountain, Owl's head, Webster slide, and Wyatt hill.

What was the consequence of all this enterprise? Warren village doubled in size, and the population and wealth of the town much increased.

CHAPTER VI.

A BRIEF ACCOUNT OF TWO MURDERS.

THIS is a chapter we would gladly omit, but we should not be deemed a faithful historian if we did not write it. Within a year and a half of each other, *it was alleged*, two men were murdered in Warren. Antony McCarter and Vanness Wyatt were the alleged murdered men,—Patrick Sweeney and James M. Williams were the alleged murderers.

The first tragedy happened in 1859, and it was a snowy day in March when Antony McCarter was last seen in Warren. He had led a secluded life for years; but that winter had taken up his residence with Sweeny, an Irishman, who had his shanty in the fir woods by the brick-kiln, on the East-parte road. He had quarrelled with Sweeny's wife that morning, and she had inflicted a deep gash in his face with an iron poker. No one saw him after that day.

Sweeny sold McCarter's stove, his clothes, axe, and jack-knife. He told many different stories about where he had gone, and when hints of foul play were thrown out, Sweeny left town suddenly in the night and went to Vermont.

Enquiries were made for the murdered man in all the neighboring towns, and even letters were sent to the other side of the Green mountains by the river Lamoile, where he used to live; but nothing could be heard from him.

The people grew anxious, excited; the summer went by and still nothing was discovered. Wild stories were told, how some boys passed him in the woods where he was just covered in a shallow grave; how a fisherman hooked up one of his ribs from the great pot hole in the river; and how will-o'the-wisps were seen hovering at night over the old cellar of the shanty.

So intense was the excitement that in January people began to search for McCarter. The cellar was dug deeper, the woods were searched where the boys said they discovered him, and the great basin in the rocks was dipped out by more than twenty persons; but no dead man could be found. Where was he? All believed him murdered. Where was Sweeny?

More than two years afterwards, an old man with a pack on his back was seen traveling through the village towards the Eastparte. To the surprise of every one, it was McCarter. He went back to the old shanty again, fitted it up, and to-day, with his hens, his dog, and his cat, he lives alone in the fir woods.*

The second occurred in 1860, and it was far more serious than the Sweeny-McCarter affair, and the dead man never came back to life again.

James M. Williams was a nervous, thin-haired man. Vanness Wyatt was stout and strong; but was loose in his conversation, and did not weigh well his words. Mr. Williams was a man of considerable property. Mr. Wyatt was poor. Mr. Williams had become very unpopular, owing to an alleged improper intimacy between himself and Mrs. Joseph Chamberlain. Said intimacy was stoutly denied by Mrs. Chamberlain, Mr. Williams, and all their friends, and the persons who circulated the stories were prosecuted for slander. Mr. Wyatt was a good natured fellow, and was generally liked; but persons who said they were disgusted with the alleged conduct of Mr. Williams with Mrs. Chamberlin put Wyatt up to "haze" Williams.

But *this* was the real cause of the quarrel between the two men. Wyatt's father owed Williams a debt; the latter sued the father and attached and sold some peg wood and bark which the son, Mr. Wyatt, claimed to own. Mr. Wyatt was mad, made an

---

* McCarter was born in Canada, of Irish parents. He served in the 1812 war, was in several battles, and at Sackett's harbor was severely wounded. He belonged to the British army.

Patrick Sweeny in 1864 lived in Manchester, N. H. He is a thick set, light complexioned man, somewhat given to drunkenness and telling foolish lies.

assault upon Mr. Williams, although he did him no injury, and used very threatening language towards him. He was somewhat encouraged to do this by those persons who disliked Mr. Williams. The friends of the latter advised him to arm himself. He did so with a revolver. Should not the parties who encouraged this bad blood on both sides feel a little guilty? If any one should ask us to express our opinion privately, we should say that the persons who advised Mr. Williams were vastly more to blame than himself for what he did; also, that if those who set on Mr. Wyatt had minded their own business they would have done far better.

The killing took place on the morning of July 27, 1860. Williams had been to Samuel Bixby's, who lived over the river from the depot, to milk his cow. Wyatt was at work loading bark near the railroad track. Coming home in company with William Clement, Mr. Williams saw Mr. Wyatt approaching him with a small stick in his hand. When near the south-east corner of the house Stevens Merrill built sixty odd years before, Williams spoke and said, "Van. is after us." Clement said, "I guess not." They passed along a few steps, when Williams turned again, drew up his pistol and said to Wyatt, " Step another step and I will blow you through," and fired at the same time. He then passed along on the sidewalk about six feet, and by the corner of the fence made a short halt, and as Wyatt came near where Clement stood, Williams started across the street.

William Clement under oath, says in continuation: — " He (Wyatt) then said, ' I have not touched you Mr. Williams, and wasn't a going to,' and Mr. Williams had got out a little ways in the road and said ' I know you havn't, but you followed me with a stick,' and then he passed along across the road. Wyatt then looked up and said, ' Bill. he has killed me.' I saw he was pale, and saw a red spot on his shirt, and he was tottering; went towards the fence and I sat part down and caught him. After I got hold of him I looked around for help, but could see no one; but turned and saw Williams across the street, and called to him to help carry in that man or take care of him, don't remember which, and then I looked back up street and saw Boynton coming out of his door, and called to him and he came, and we carried Wyatt to Knapp's hotel. Wyatt lived from five to ten minutes, and then died."

They had a post-mortem examination of the murdered man, and the following doctors were present: David C. French, A. G. French, Jesse Little, Peter L. Hoyt, and A. A. Whipple. They found that Vanness was shot in the left breast, the ball passing through between the fourth and fifth ribs, above the centre of the breast, through the covering over the heart, through the heart—and it lodged in the right lung. Dr. Alphonzo G. French took out the ball.

There was a terrible excitement in Warren that day; men turned pale when they heard the news, and almost every person in town came to the village. They wanted to see the murdered man, and they wanted to see the murderer too, as they called him. One political party was almost wholly against Williams. The other party with equal unanimity immediately began to stand up for him.

Hazen Libbey, the constable, arrested Mr. Williams. Chas. H. Bartlett, Esq., an attorney at Wentworth, came to advise with him. Hon. Thomas J. Smith came to advise with the citizens. He counselled moderation, and had a coroner's jury summoned. It consisted of Samuel L. Merrill, George E. Leonard, and Samuel Bixby; and after hearing the evidence they brought in the following verdict: "He came to his death by a bullet shot from a pistol by the hand of James M. Williams." Then Mr. Williams was brought before a Justice of the Peace, Col. Isaac Merrill, waived an examination, and was committed to Haverhill jail. At the August term of court he was admitted to bail, and at the January term at Plymouth he had his trial.

Justices Bellows and Nesmith held the court; Hon. John Sullivan, the Attorney General, and Henry W. Blair, county solicitor, were counsel for the State. Hons. Josiah Quincy and Harry Hibbard were assigned as counsel for the respondent, he representing himself as poor. The jury consisted of nine of one political party and three of the other.* The respondent plead, "Not guilty," and set up that the act was committed in self-defence.

Many witnesses were called† and the case occupied several

---

* It was alleged, but perhaps wrongfully, that Mr. Williams' friends, those who advised him to get a pistol, were about the court working for him, and that they log-rolled the jury, &c.

† The State called the following persons as witnesses: William Clement, Wil-

E*

days; the jury were out thirty-six hours, could not agree and were discharged. It was understood that the jury divided politically; the three of one party being for the State, and the nine of the other party for the respondent. The case was continued along for a year or more, and then a *nolle prosequi* was entered.

It is but justice to Mr. Williams to add that no juryman found him guilty of murder. The three who were for convicting him only wished to bring in a verdict for "manslaughter in the second degree."

Afterwards Mr. Williams had a short history of the trial published in pamphlet form in vindication of himself. If any should think our brief chapter does not do him justice, we would advise them to procure the pamphlet and read and judge for themselves.

Vanness Wyatt was buried in the village grave-yard, and on his tombstone is the following inscription:—

"VANNESS WYATT,

DIED

July 27, 1860,

Æ. 28.

He came to his death from a pistol shot by the hand of James M. Williams, in the street at Warren village, at five and one-half o'clock, A. M."

---

liam Caswell, Dan. Y. Boynton, Alphonzo G. French, Hazen Libbey, Henry A. Colley, Isaac Merrill, J. B. S. Otterson, Hobart Wyatt, Veranus P. Drew, George H. Moulton, Ezra Libbey, George W. Merrill, Isaac Sanborn, Benjamin Clement, Damon Y. Eastman, and several others who were not put upon the stand. The defence called Arthur Knapp, Darius Swain, Otis Chamberlin, Joseph Bixby, Adoniram Whitcher, Caleb H. Noyes, Morrill J. Sanborn, George Libbey, Harvey Chamberlin, N. P. Folsom, Ezra B. Eaton, Addison Robinson, Ferdinand C. Keezer, Jas. P. Webster, Nathaniel Merrill, Salmon Gleason, Joseph Chamberlin, and put in the affidavits of George W. Prescott and Mary G. Noyes.

Warren has had two or three other very mean and as some say very dirty cases; but we can't stomach to put them in this our modest. pleasant, and urbane history. The writing the above chapter was about the worst dose of literature we ever took. For a history of said cases we would refer the historian of a hundred years hence to the N. H. Law Reports.—*Author's Note.*

CHAPTER VII.

CONCERNING A GREAT RIVALRY BETWEEN CHARITABLE RELIGIOUS SOCIETIES, WHICH RESULTED IN MOVING AND REMODELLING THE OLD MEETING-HOUSE, IN A TOWN-HOUSE, A NEW SCHOOL-HOUSE, A BEAUTIFUL COMMON, AND IN IMPROVING THE GRAVE-YARD, ALL WHICH IS AN HONOR TO THE TOWN AND THE PRIDE OF THE INHABITANTS.

ABOUT the year 1830, and perhaps at an earlier date, different clergymen of the Universalist denomination preached occasionally to the believers in a world's salvation from sin and suffering; but the first society was organized in the year 1838, under the ministry of Rev. John E. Palmer.

The Methodist at this time was the most prominent society in town, in fact the Congregationalists had nearly all disappeared,* and the Freewill Baptists were but a weak handful of brethren. Consequently it was natural that the followers of John Wesley,

---

* The Congregationalists often tried to make inroads upon the Methodists, but without much success. Priest Davis, (I. S. Davis,) of Wentworth, was instrumental in getting a daughter of Capt. Daniel Merrill converted, and wanted her to join his church. Capt. Daniel's folks were Methodists, but they all went down to the congregational church one Sunday. Davis was a cunning man and he preached a good Methodist discourse to please them. Aunt Daniel heard him through, and after meeting she spoke. Said she, "Mr. D.'s preaching reminds me of Farmer Joshua Merrill up at Warren; when he goes out to catch his old mare, he shakes a nice pan full of oats and calls, 'ker-joh, ker-joh, ker-joh,' holding the bridle all the time behind him out of sight. Just so with the priest; he halloos 'ker-joh,' and shakes a nice pan-full of Methodism; but when he gets 'em caught, he'll put on the orthodox bridle with a vengeance." "The daughter didn't jine that society no how."

Capt. Daniel Merrill once did something that pleased or displeased his wife very much. To recompense him, she made up his new pants wrong side out, seam like a welt on the outside, and the Captain highly delighted wore them to meeting several times, in that fashion.—R. K. Clement's story.

wishing to retain the supremacy, should regard this new sect with suspicion and much jealousy, especially as its members, disciples of John Murray, did not believe in an endless hell at all.

At first the Universalist society had their meetings in the school-house, the one with four roofs that stood in the fork of the turnpike and Beech hill roads, and once in a while they would get possession of the meeting-house on the common. Then the Methodists would be filled with righteous indignation at the sacrilege, as it seemed to them.

But the Methodist society still increased much the fastest, and finally having been disconnected from the Wentworth and Orford circuit, it obtained what it had not before had, preaching every Sabbath; yet as they had no right to occupy the old meeting-house all the time, although they wanted to, they were compelled to use the school-house as often as one Sabbath a month, while the Universalist minister held forth in the pulpit under the great sounding board. This seemed too bad, and the Methodist brethren would steal the Bible away from the pulpit sometimes, and carry it to the school-house with them. David Smith, Esq., a leader in the new society, and withal a good disputationist, often remonstrated with the Methodist brethren, but to no purpose, and much ill feeling was engendered.

At last the feud culminated. The believers in eternal torment came to the conclusion that they would not worship under the same roof with that "damned society," that did not believe in "damnation" at all; that they would give up the old meeting-house entirely for a season, and under the ministry of Rev. Sullivan Holman a new and beautiful chapel was built. Much taste and piety was evinced in selecting the locality for the new house. It was located a short distance from the front door of the old church. Then a school-house committee, from the same good society, with excellent taste, located a new school-house nearly in front of the old meeting-house; building a nice school-house privy close up to the old sanctuary. And now the Universalist society could have as much preaching in the old house as they wished; and some wicked outsider who sympathized with the Methodists said, "They could be damned into the bargain if they pleased."

The two societies being thus now in full blast, and the Free-will Baptists wide awake, there was a great rivalry among them, and as a result the whole town went to meeting with all its might. In winter they came in sleighs from Beech hill, Height-o'-land, Pine hill, Runaway pond, the Summit, East-parte and the Forks, many of the women bringing their mother's old foot stoves to keep their feet warm, and hitched their horses during the services under the new chapel sheds, a long row that the Methodists had proudly stretched more than half way through the very centre of the old common. In the summer time, no matter if it lightened, thundered, rained, and hailed, or the sun poured down its rays with torrid heat, they all turned out to meeting just the same. The ladies on such occasions carried fans and parasols to keep cool, and most every one brought bouquets or bunches of flowers, and alecost, thyme, and southernwood, the pungent qualities of which they found very useful stimulents to keep them awake during drowsy sermon time. The choirs also sang better than ever before, and they had some glorious awakenings and revivals. Everything was lovely and nobody seemed to care a copper how the village, churches or common looked, provided only the societies flourished. Opposition, excitement, and rivalry are grand things in church affairs. For as many as ten years ecclesiastical matters thus went on, and then the fever heat began to cool down a little.

The eyes of the citizens opened slightly, and they could see that the old meeting-house of 1818 was out of repair and fast going to decay; and that the paint was worn off the new Methodist chapel; also the once beautiful parade in front of Joseph Merrill's inn was fondly in the recollection of some of the oldest inhabitants, and the school-house and the new chapel-sheds seemed out of place and unsightly. In short, the whole village looked bad and was an object of remark in the neighboring towns.

Soon a general discontent arose against this order of things on the common. Sundry individuals began to move in the matter. Plan after plan was devised and abandoned; but at last a town meeting was held at which it was voted, the Universalists acquiescing, to sell the old meeting-house to the Methodist society and that the town should buy the Methodist chapel at an expense of five hundred dollars, for a town-house. The village school district No. 2 had a meeting, or several of them, and voted that the district would exchange its lot of land for one to the north, and then it was generally agreed that all three of the buildings should be moved and the common cleared.

There was much opposition and a great fight about the moving and where the houses should be placed; but they finally settled down into their present locations and everybody was delighted.

Ira Merrill gave the lot of land for the town-house; money was raised by subscription to buy of Albe C. Weeks the lots for the meeting-house and school-house. Henry W. Weeks and Levi C. Whitcher paid the most liberally, and Capt. Samuel L. Merrill, more generous than any of the rest, gave most of the land where the common is now.

Ephraim S. Colley moved the meeting-house and town-house, and Janes Glazier the school-house. John M. Whiton managed the remodeling of the old 1818 meeting-house. Columbus Clough, George Clough, Amos F. Clough, and Ezra W. Keyes, did the work. Considerable additions were made, but the body of the old house remained the same, posts, timbers, walls, and roof, and even the plastering overhead is the very same put on in 1818, better than any that can be spread at the present day.

Thus the common was cleared and the looks of the village improved. Our good Methodist society also, after twenty years of effort, had now obtained what they had always longed for, the full control of our fathers' old meeting-house; and that they might be a little more popular, under the pastorate of the Rev. L. L. Eastman they had purchased the beautiful toned bell that has so often enlivened our hills and valleys. At first they had it rung every day at noon, and several times each Sabbath; but the week-day ringing shortly fell into disuse except on funeral occasions, and when it tolls at the deaths of the inhabitants.*

Jared S. Blodgett has always had charge of the bell, and the moment it is heard to toll all know that he is in the church tower and every individual is all attention, hushed, standing in the attitude of profound listeners. The bell, by some signal which all understand, proclaims the sex, the married or single state of the

---

* *Tolling the Bell.*—A man dead and the bell strikes one; a woman and it strikes two; a pause—then if the person is single the bell strikes three times slowly; if married, four times slowly, then the age is counted out.

deceased, and then counts out his or her age. Having ascertained these particulars, the people begin to speculate, for they already know every one that is ill in town, and thus generally discover pretty certainly before any other intelligence reaches them, whose bell it is. That bell is a sufficient text for the discourses of the day. They run all over the biography of the individual and bring up many an anecdote of him and his contemporaries which had long slept in their minds.

After the meeting houses, sheds, and school-house were moved, what an amount of work was done on the common! The stumps of the dark old pines two hundred feet high, that once sighed in the wind and shaded the Indian beneath, were dug out; hundreds of tons of stones were removed, and ploughs and harrows were used day after day. One spring, Henry W. Weeks, Charles Leonard, and others, planted elms and maples all around it, and the good citizens have now in part the village green that Gov. Wentworth wished they should when he so kindly gave the town charter in 1763. It is the pleasantest place in town. The wide spreading trees cast a refreshing shade there. Caravans with elephants, lions, and tigers,—and circuses—pitch their tents upon the greensward, and the great mountains, bright and refreshing, look in upon the gatherings of happy citizens. May the common be forever preserved.

With a new meeting-house and bell, town-house and common, the village cemetery must be improved. Col. Isaac Merrill was the leading spirit in this enterprise, and the wall was re-built, good fences erected, and some trees set out, and to-day Warren has as beautiful a burying ground as almost any country town.*

From our grave-yard a green vale extends far away to the south. Great hills lift their heads around and stretch their old trees to the wind. Warren's first settler, Joseph Patch, lies here

---

* The first grave-yard in Warren was located a short distance below the village on land near the great railroad bridge. It was situated on the west side of the road at the top of a little hill which was once the bank of the river. In this yard about twenty were buried, among the first of whom were John Mills and his son, early settlers. When excavations were made for the railroad, the remains of several bodies were exhumed; but the overseer of the work dug the graves deeper, and in them again deposited the remains.

There were also three other burying grounds which have become almost unknown. One of these was located near the present site of the railroad depots. Another is on Blue ridge, where Joshua Copp was buried. It was the piece of land which the town voted to accept of him for the purpose of erecting a meeting

without a tombstone. His grave is beside a rustling tree. The breezes are sighing there. A little streamlet murmurs near and sends its waters to the Asquamchumauke. A great mountain to the northward, Moosilauke, looks in on the turfy mound. " O lay me, ye that see the light, near some rock of my hills! Let the thick hazels be around. Let the sound of the distant torrent be heard."

Obadiah Clement also lies sleeping in an unmarked grave, and Stevens Merrill and Jonathan Merrill are resting near by. Joshua Copp is buried on the Blue ridge by the banks of the Mikaseota. Simeon Smith has his grave under the great apple tree by Red-oak hill road, and John Mills is sleeping on the river bank where the " roaring rips are ever sounding." Who can tell of the others?

Warren's old settlers are all dead now. A life interspersed with joys and sorrows was theirs.

> " Oft did the harvest to their sickle yield;
> Their furrow oft the stubborn glebe has broke;
> How jocund did they drive their team afield,
> How bowed the woods beneath their sturdy stroke.

But now—

> * . * * * * * *
>
> Each in his narrow cell forever laid,
> The rude forefathers of the hamlet sleep.
>
> The breezy call of incense breathing morn,
> The swallow twittering from her straw built shed;
> The cock's shrill clarion or the echoing horn,
> No more shall rouse them from their lowly bed.
>
> For them no more the blazing hearth shall burn,
> Or busy housewife ply her evening care;
> No children run to lisp their sire's return,
> Or climb his knee the envied kiss to share."

How different in effect is the city from the country funeral. In the city a strange corpse passes along amid thousands of strangers, and human nature seems shorn of that interest which it ought,

---

house, and occupying as a burying-yard and training field. The third is in the basin of Runaway pond. In this yard about thirty were buried, the last being children of Jonathan Clement, innkeeper, who died in 1815 of spotted fever. In the pond basin was also the old Indian burying ground.

The old burying ground at Charleston should not be forgotten.

Besides the village cemetery on the Pine hill road, there are used at the present time, the Clough grave-yard, by the Forks school-house in Patchbreuckland; the East-parte grave-yard, as you turn up the Moosehillock road; and the Summit grave-yard, as you go up High street road. The Whitchers also had a grave-yard of their own on Pine hill.

especially in its last stage, to possess. In the country, every man, woman, and child, goes down to the dust amid those who have known them from their youth, and all miss them from their place. Nature seems in its silence to sympathize with the mourners. The green mound of the rural grave-yard opens to receive the slumberer to a peaceful resting place and the maples and the elms which he climbed when a boy in pursuit of bird's nests, moths or butterflies, overshadow as it were with a kindred feeling his grave.

In concluding this chapter let us say that the Methodists and Universalists have had no fights since; the former having the whole control of the old meeting-house, and the latter using the townhouse when they want preaching. The Freewill Baptists have preaching at either place just as they can get accommodated. Sometimes the Second Adventists, a new sect that has seen the world destroyed a half dozen times or more, occupy the town-house much to their great delight. And now at the close of Warren's first century entire harmony among the different religious societies prevails.

CHAPTER VIII.

OF A DELECTABLE VISIT TO MOOSEHILLOCK, AND WHAT CAN BE SEEN THERE — THE WEATHER PERMITTING.

READER, let us go on to Moosehillock. The Indians called it *Moosilauke* from mosi, bald, and auke, a place,—" Baldplace." There are three paths leading to the top of the mountain, one from North Benton, one from Warren Summit, and one from the East-parte region. The last one will answer our purpose best.

Let us start early on the East-parte road. There has been a great storm, but it has cleared off now; the moon is on the full, and the air is clear as a bell. We cross Berry brook where Samuel Knight had a fight with a bear, keep Silver rill upon our left, and come to the Sawtelle school-house. Crossing the bridge over the Asquamchumauke or Baker river, we pass a remarkable flume in the rocks which the waters for ages have been wearing out, leave the " pot holes " where McCarter was said to be hid when he was murdered, to our left, and listening to the white thoated finch, our mountain whistler, as he sings the prelude to the " Wrecker's daughter," in the fir woods, we reach East-parte school-house by Moosilauke falls on the Asquamchumauke.

It is a modest little school-house by the roadside, but it has a history such as few others can boast. Within thirty years, nearly a score of boys have been to school there, who have made preachers of the gospel. Heber C. Kimball, the celebrated Mormon, and Moses H. Bixby, an eloquent divine, are the most noted. Four doctors and two lawyers also got their early education there. Perhaps the great wooded mountains around, the mighty chasms worn in the solid rocks, with pot holes, some of them forty feet deep, and the music of falling waters, had something to do with forming the character of the pupils who have attended school there.

We go up through Moosehillock district, climbing the hill all the time, past a swaley meadow-field on the right, where a hundred bob-o'-links titter, and laugh, and sing all through the month of June, past another school-house and over Merrill brook, and we arrive at Nathaniel Merrill's, the last house high up on the northern marche or boundary of Warren.

What a magnificent place is Mr. Merrill's; green fields up to his very door; rustling maples, the hum of millions of bees, the primitive cheese-press and an old loom in the shed, and pure water to drink. Cattle and sheep are in the rich pastures, there are waving fields of ripening grain, the orchard is filled with apples, cherries, and Canada plums, and the murmuring of brooks and the roar of the distant torrent is heard. Around are the lofty wooded crests of the great mountains, Waternomee, Cushman, Kineo, and Mount Carr, sweeping away in a circle to the southwest.

We will get saddle horses here and go up the mountain slowly that we may enjoy the trip all the better. We open the heavy gate, cross the little rill that comes down from the great sugar orchard where the song thrush is singing, and going up through the pasture, startle a grass finch that skippering to the top of a low waving maple, warbles two soft half plaintive notes, followed by a sweet silvery giggle, as though the bird exceedingly pleased, was laughing at its own rich melody.

As we enter the woods we see the mountain summit rising 4,000 feet above us; the river is roaring in the ravine 500 feet deep, on our right; the red-eyed vireo and winter wren are perpetually singing in the thick forest, and when we cross on rustic bridges two mossy streams, where a pair of solitary sand pipers are feeding, we begin the sharp ascent of the mountain.

The forest is deep and dark. Deer yard in these woods every winter; bears prowl in them all summer long, there are sable-traps beside the path, traps in which wild cats are caught; and it was near here that Joseph Patch, his son, and Captain Flanders killed the last moose that were ever found in this region. Yet no one was ever hurt by these "wild beastes," so terrible, only Jared S. Blodgett once was greatly frightened by a bear by the path, and many a traveler has seen a hedgehog rapidly disappearing in the thick bushes. Hear that great owl hooting away across the table land by Gorge brook. What a dreadful voice he has; but it never injured one yet. There are red squirrels chattering by the roadside,— a pleasant sound.

Climbing, zigzaging up the mountain, the forest changes, the ash, beech, and maple disappear, and the spruce, fir, and silver birch take their places. We have reached a different zone, and the birds change,— the soft, sweet love note of the purple finch is heard up among the cones, the ivory billed snow bird is startled from its nest by the path, Canada jays scream out from the fir shade, and sometimes cross-bills, yellow rumped warblers, pine grosbeaks and lesser red polls, birds that breed in Labrador, are found. The Canada grouse, with their brood of chicks, run from the path. Then there are nut hatches, kinglets, ruby crowned wrens, oven birds and olive backed thrushes far in these woods.

The trees grow smaller and smaller, so short and thick and scraggy that one can almost walk on top of them. Blueberries and raspberries, that are ripening in the valley below, are just beginning to flower here; the bunch plum is white by the path, and a dozen kinds of flowers, new and strange, flora of Greenland, appear.

We will stop at the cold spring just under the southern peak, to drink. It is the coldest water we ever drank; our teeth ache and chatter, and we say with all the rest that surely there is an ice bank near by.

Soon we are out on the bald mountain ridge that connects the two peaks; on either hand are wild and hideous gorges, three thousand feet down into the depths below. Beyond to the west is the bright valley of the Connecticut, garden land, with silver river; to the east the dark ravine of the Asquamchumauke filled with the old primitive woods, where the trees for thousands of years, like the generations of men, have grown, ripened and died.

THE PROSPECT HOUSE. 493

Half a mile further on and we are at the Prospect House on the bald summit of the mountain. The most sensible thing that we can do is to hitch our horses under the ledge on the eastern side, out of the way of the wind, and go in and get a good cup of tea, or something of the sort. The house is a rude structure, built of stone. Darius Swain and James Clement built it in 1860.* Samuel Hoit was master workman and John Whitcher, Nathan Willey, and numerous others, worked there. They had two yoke of oxen up on the mountain for a whole month, and the men all camped over by the cold spring.†

We are out now on top of the mountain, well wrapped up in shawls and quilts. It is a glorious day, but a little colder than when the Indian chief, Waternomee, sat on this summit, yet not so cold as when a century ago one of Robert Rogers' rangers died here. Chase Whitcher, the first white settler who came up here, thought it a cold place. But Mrs. Daniel Patch, the first white woman who ever stood upon this summit, thought it quite pleasant. She brought her tea-pot with her, and made herself a good cup of tea over a fire kindled from the hackmatacks, bleached white, so many of which you see standing like skeletons down on the shoulders of the mountain, just as though a great grave-yard had been shaken open by an earthquake. Mrs. Susan C. Little, wife of Dr.

---

* The persons who worked on the mountain:—James Clement, Darius Swain, John Hoit, Samuel Hoit, John Whitcher, with yoke of cattle; Nathan Willey, drove cattle; Vanness Wyatt, Burgess A. Clement, Jesse Eastman, James S. Merrill, J. F. Merrill, Horatio Willoughby, with cattle; Eben Swain, Chas. Carpenter, Joseph Whitcher, Hazen Libbey, Benjamin Eastman, Daniel Willis.

The Prospect House was opened July 4, 1860, and the day was celebrated on the mountain. More than a thousand people were present; the Newbury brass band furnished the music. Col. Stevens M. Dow marshaled the citizens, a whole regiment of them, marching and counter-marching upon the mountain top, and Hon. Thomas J. Smith delivered an excellent and patriotic oration.

On this occasion Daniel Q. Clement drove two horses attached to a large pleasure wagon on to the mountain; and the celebration concluded with a show by a party of Indian performers, genuine Indians, who danced, sang, and sounded the war-whoop.

† Nathaniel Richardson and Nath. K. Richardson made the shingles high up on the mountain side.

"1860, Aug. 29.—Philip Hadley, 90 years old, came up to the Prospect House. He lives at Bradford, Vt., and he walked all the way from that place to the top of the mountain."—Register of Prospect House, 1860.

James Cutting, 85 years of age, rode horseback from his home in Haverhill, to the top of Mooshillock, and back the same day, Aug. 24, 1869.

Immediately after opening the Prospect House, several citizens of Warren commenced to keep summer boarders; Russel Merrill was the first to open the business; and after him, H. H. Sheldon; the Moosilauke House, now kept by D. G. Marsh, and Nathaniel Merrill, 2d, have followed the business.

Jesse Little, was the first woman who rode a horse on to the mountain, and that was in 1859.

William Little was the first landlord of the Prospect House, then Ezekiel A. Clement kept it for one season, and afterwards James Clement, for years and years, was mine host on Moosehillock. He was really the old man of the mountain. Many a night he has stopped alone up here among the clouds and the eagles. The housewife rocking her cradle of a stormy night, below, would mutter as a gust of storm thundered over the roof, " O then it is poor Jim that has enough of fresh air about his head up there this night, the creature!"

One summer they had, as visitors at the Prospect House, a deer, three eagles, a bear, and a wild cat. Jim said he saw the deer cropping the harebells on the mountain top; that the bear lay in the grass at the foot of the falls; the wild-cat screamed from the hackmatacks at the moon, and the eagles looked in at the window as he was building the morning fire. Jim was a great hand at telling stories of his adventures in the woods, and what he had witnessed on the mountain. He said he had seen the fog so thick that he could bag it up like corn; that he had seen it so cold that it turned into icicles and sailed round like birds; that the wind would blow one hundred and twenty miles an hour; that once a whirlwind lifted a pair of cart-wheels fifty feet into the air, spun them round for a minute and then let them down again uninjured; that he had heard a bear in the night, hallooing over on the south peak so loud that it waked the whole family up; that there was an earthquake that shook the crockery on the shelves; that once a column of smoke and fire issued from the easterly ridge, belching up like a volcano; that the aurora borealis came down on the mountain so thick and so splendid that it seemed like a shower of silver and gold; and that every year, there was one night, about the full of the moon in August, when witches, and ghosts, and spirits, and fairies danced, and yelled, and sang over the mountain peaks by the million. When remonstrated with for telling large stories, he would reply, " What is the use of telling a story at all unless you can tell one that will call the mind into activity."

Let us get up on the deck of the roof. It is the best view of all from here; the grandest and most sublime, far surpassing that from any other peak in New England, because of its isolated position, and of its great height, and no other mountains near to hide the prospect, as is the case at the White mountains. Then standing alone it does not attract the clouds as the White mountains do, and for a whole month in the season it shoots up into the clear heaven when all the eastern peaks are cloud capped.

Just around us, the mountain is green with mosses and lichens, thirty kinds of mosses; and harebells and mountain cranberries, with their millions of flowers, make it seem like a garden, with a green border of firs and spruces and birches below. Purple finches, snow birds, and the mountain whistler are singing in this garden.

The sun is going down and it is cold you say. Let us travel with our eyes round the whole horizon.

Look away to the south first. How the ruby light is gleaming on Lake Winnepisseogee, " The Smile of the Great Spirit;" see that tall shaft just on the horizon beyond. It is Bunker hill monument standing " down by the sea." Carry your eye round to the west; Mt. Belknap is first, then Wachusett in Massachusetts, the Uncanoonucks, and to the right of them, Jo English, Kearsarge, Mt. Cardigan, Monadnock, and Croydon mountains. Close by is Waternomee, Cushman, Kinco, Mount Carr, Stinson mountain in Romney, Smart's mountain in Dorchester, Mt. Cube in Orford, Sentinel mountain in Warren, and Piermont mountain.

Across the Connecticut river to the southwest is Ascutney, and beyond it, farther down, is Saddle mountain, Graylock, and Berkshire hills, in Massachusetts. Then wheeling round towards the north are Killington peaks, sharp and needle like, shooting up above the neighboring hills; farther north and directly west, is Camel's Hump, unmistakable in its appearance; then Mt. Mansfield, towering above the thousand other summits of the Green mountains.

Above and beyond them, in the farthest distance, are counted nine sharp peaks of the Adirondacks in New York, Mt. Marcy higher than all the rest. To-morrow morning at sunrise you will see the fog floating up from Lake Champlain this side of them.

In the northwest is Jay peak on Canada line, and to the right of it you see a hundred summits rising from the table lands of

Canada. Then there is the notch at Memphremagog lake, Owl's head by Willoughby lake, and Monadnock in northern Vermont.

Close down is Black mountain; Owl's head of New Hampshire, and Blueberry, Hogback and Sugarloaf mountains. Then north is Cobble hill in Landaff; Gardner mountain in Lyman, and Stark peaks away up in northern Coos.

To the right, and stretching away to the northeast in Maine, you see a long rolling range of hills, the water-shed between the Atlantic ocean and the St. Lawrence river, said by Agassiz to be the oldest land in the world. East of these is the white summit of the Aziscoos, by Umbagog lake.

Nearest and to the north-east is Mt. Kinsman, the Profile mountain; and above and over them Mt. Lafayette, its sides scarred and jagged where a hundred torrents pour down in spring, its peaks splintered by lightning. South of this, and near by, are the Haystacks. Over and beyond the latter are the Twins, more than five thousand feet high; and just to the right of them Mt. Washington, dome shaped and higher than all the rest. Around this monarch of mountains, as if attendant upon him, are Mts. Adams and Jefferson, sharp peaks on the left, and Mt. Moriah, the Imp, Mts. Madison and Monroe, Mt. Webster, the Willey notch precipice, Double head, and a hundred other great mountains standing to the right and front.

A little to the south is Carrigan, 4,800 feet high, black and sombre, most attractive and most dreaded, not a white spot nor a scar upon it; covered with dark woods like a black pall, symmetrical and beautiful, the eye turns away to return to it again and again. Mt. Pigwacket in Conway, its neighbor, always seems gray in the hazy distance, Chocorua rises farther south, and Welch mountain, Osceola, Whiteface, Ossipee, Agamenticus, on the sea coast; Mt. Prospect and Red hill fill up the circle.

This view to the north and east is the most magnificent mountain view to be had on this side of the continent. The most indifferent observer cannot look upon it without feeling its grandeur and sublimity.

Forty ponds and lakes are sparkling under the setting sun. Two in Woodstock, the little tarn in the meadow where the Asquamchumauke rises; Stinson pond in Romney, Lake Winnepisseogee, Winnesquam, Long bay, Smith's pond, Squam lake, Mascoma lake, two ponds in Dorchester, Baker ponds in Orford, Indian pond, Fairlee pond, and numerous others in Vermont; Tarleton lakes, Wachipauka pond, by which Rogers and his rangers camped, Kelley, and Horse-shoe ponds; two others in Haverhill, Beaver meadow ponds in Benton, and many more with names unknown; how they all gleam and glisten, and look like silver sheens.

The Pemigewassett, the Asquamchumauke, the Ammonoosuc, and the Connecticut, from their wooded valleys are flashing in the setting sun.

The villages with their church spires are gleaming. See Bradford, Haverhill Corner, East and North Haverhill, Newbury, Woodsville and Wells River, down there in the Connecticut valley. A hundred spires are shining on the hills of Vermont. Landaff and Bath are lighted up, and Warren, Wentworth, Campton, Franconia, Lake Village, and Laconia all come distinctly out as the sun goes down.

Now see the sun just touching the Adirondacks beyond Lake Champlain in the west. There is a rosy blush on the White mountains, the Green mountains are golden, while all the peaks behind which the sun is going down are bathed in a sea of glorious light. How it changes! Darkness creeps over the eastern peaks, the Green mountains are going into shadows, the vermillion, pink, ruby, and gold of the Adirondacks, is fading away, and the stars are coming out.

But look! there is a silver line on the eastern horizon. 'Tis the moon rising. But Luna don't come from behind the hills. Her upper limb as she creeps up is distant twice her diameter from the land horizon. That bright band twixt moon and earth is

---

The view is the grand thing of Moosehillock. But if it should happen to be cloudy, as is frequently the case, there is much of interest about the top of the mountain. Garnets an inch in diameter, with perfect faces, are found by the carriage road, forty rods from the house. The best tourmalines in New Hampshire are also obtained in the same locality. Down in the Tunnel are magnificent quartz crystals. On the south peak is a most curious turrow. Mr. James Clement says it was undoubtedly plowed by an iceberg drifting from the north-east to the southwest, when New Hampshire mountains were under the ocean. No person can fail to notice it. "Jobildune" ravine where the Asquamchumauke leaps down a thousand feet at an angle of 80 degrees, is much visited. The Seven Cascades between the two peaks of the mountain on Gorge brook, are also well worth a visit. The stream descends at a sharp angle eight hundred feet over a series of steps, and after a great rain is a most magnificent sight.

F*

the ocean. It is a sight seldom seen from New Hampshire's mountains.

As we come down from the roof, the mountain whistler, well called the northern nightingale, chants its sweet notes in the hackmatacks, an owl hoots over by the old camp at the Cold spring, the wind is soughing mournfully on the mosses of the rocks, and the deep voice of the torrents comes up from the dark ravines below. Let us go in, get supper, listen to Uncle Jim's yarns for a while, go to bed and sleep till the sunrise, which is scarcely less glorious than the sunset.

CHAPTER IX.

HOW SEVERAL INDIVIDUALS GOT RICH MANUFACTURING, OR OUGHT TO, WITH THE GLORIOUS RESULTS OF IT.

WARREN has always been esteemed an agricultural town. Some mining has also been carried on, but we do not now propose to consider either of said branches of industry; but to give a brief history of manufacturing in our little democracy.

Saw Mills.—In the earliest days of our hamlet the manufacture of lumber was the most important of this branch of industry. Stevens Merrill, as we have said before, built the first saw-mill at the "white little falls" on the Mikaseota, Black brook, where once John Page shot a deer.

Joshua Copp built the next saw-mill near the outlet of Runaway pond. What an excellent mill privilege might be made there now by constructing a short dam fifty feet long and forty-feet high and flowing all Runaway pond basin again. The pond would be a mile wide, two miles long and thirty feet deep. What a grand reservoir! Then Kelley pond could be flowed so as to make a reservoir of eighty acres, twelve feet deep, and Wachipauka could be raised some eight feet by a short dam. If it was raised higher than that its water would flow down the Oliverian to the Connecticut.

After Mr. Copp, Nathaniel Clough built two saw mills, the first on the Asquamchumauke near the southern boundary, and the second on that musical stream, Hurricane brook. Joseph Clement repaired the latter and then sold it to John L. Stevens, who moved it away to High street.

My grandfather Joseph Merrill, Jonathan Merrill, and Benjamin Merrill, then built the great saw-mill just at the depot crossing.

Ruel Bela Clifford built on Moosehillock falls the mill standing near the East-parte school-house, and later, Adoniram Whitcher built the old mill now gone to decay, on Berry brook, far up the "New Road."

William Kelley built the saw-mill at Kelley pond.

Joseph H. Stevens, the mill on Oak falls;* hardly a vestige of it now remains.

Mrs. James Harriman, first a mill up High street on the Oliverian, and second another mill lower down on Warren Summit.

Sylvester Merrill and Capt. Daniel Merrill, a flourishing mill high up in the East-parte regions.

Levi F. Jewell, two mills on Berry brook, and Isaac Sawtelle, a mill in Streamy valley district, near the mouth of Batchelder brook.†

What a host of different persons have owned some of these mills. Stevens Merrill sold his to Moses H. Clement, and the subsequent owners are Ebenezer Cushman, F. A. & M. E. Cushman, Philo Baldwin, Hazelton & Eaton, and Whitcher, Merrill & Clark.

Joseph Merrill bought out Jonathan and Benjamin Merrill, and then sold to Anson Merrill. He sold to James Dow; and subsequent owners are Col. Charles Lane, Albe C. Weeks, Whitcher & Weeks, L. C. Whitcher, J. M. Whiton, and last, H. W. Weeks.

At first all the lumber was manufactured for home consumption; but since the railroad was built millions of feet are annually sent to market, bringing thousands of dollars back to the lumbermen and farmers of Warren.

Grist Mills.—The manufacture of all kinds of grain into meal and flour is one of great importance, yet but two grist mills of

---

* Mr. Paul Meader was killed here, Nov. 8, 1835. A log rolled over him crushing his head to a jelly. He was 77 years old.

† Since the advent of the 2d century Col. John S. Bryant built another mill on the Oliverian, at the Summit, and Charles Thompson, a large steam mill by the depot on the Summit.

any consequence have ever been established in Warren; Butler's mill at the old deep hole, and Clement's mill at the mouth of Black brook. For nearly twenty-five years the Butler mill stood on the Asquamchumauke, and sons of Joshua Copp "tended it." Then it went to decay. The Clement mill has since done nearly all the "grinding." Col. Obadiah Clement was the first miller* at the white little falls on Black brook, and old men and women tell how when they were boys and girls they went there "to mill" and waiting for their "grist" whiled away the time listening to the buzz of the old Col.'s rude mill stones, the splash of the water-wheel and the rattling music of the kingfisher, equally familiar, that every year had its nest down the stream in the river bank.†

Carding Mill, &c.—Col. Moses H. Clement established a carding mill for the manufacture of rolls, which the farmers' wives and their daughters spun into yarn, and wove into cloth. It was built beside his grist mill, and he had in connection with it a fulling mill and dye house. Ebenezer Cushman continued the business and employed Moses W. Pillsbury for many years to work for him. Philo Baldwin followed Mr. Cushman, and after him Haselton & Eaton. Hobart Wyatt used to do the dyeing for them.

Clapboard and Shingle Mills.—Moses H. Clement also had a shingle mill. Ebenezer Cushman in Mr. Clement's mill, and Salmon Gleason at the East-parte, have sawed an immense quantity of shingles. Shingles have also been made at the Sawtelle mill, the Joseph Merrill mill, Kelley mill, and at Warren Summit. But very few are now made in town.

Col. Isaac Merrill had the first clapboard mill in Warren. It was located on Patch brook, just below Rocky falls. Then Haselton & Eaton had one at the Stevens Merrill mill, and both together they cut out and sent to market millions of clapboards. Not a clapboard is made in Warren now.

---

* Others who have tended mill there are Moses H. Clement, Joshua Copp, Jr., James Mills,(1) the perpetual motion maker, Ebenezer Cushman, Page Kimball, Robert B. Stevens, John Haselton, E. B. Eaton, Ira Merrill, and George Prescott, miller.

(1) Mills worked on "perpetual motion" all his life, but did not make it go.

† Some grinding has been done where the peg mill is now. Salmon Gleason once had a corn mill at the East-parte. Levi F. Jewell now grinds corn, and long ago the Curriers had a grist mill in the edge of Benton on Warren Summit. True Stevens "named" Moses H. Clement's grist mill. He said, "What came by Hazen's industry was Tamar's delight," and many other things of the same sort.

Pegs.—Barker & French commenced the manufacture of shoe pegs, near the close of Warren's third generation. They made thousands of barrels of them, the very best sent to market, and employed many boys and girls in the manufacture. They carried on business just at the end of the old Coos Turnpike near the Joseph Merrill mill, and had both steam and water power. John M. Whiton succeeded them and had a small pond on Cold brook north east of the railroad, in which to keep his peg timber soaked.

Tanning.—Walter Whipple, brother to Dr. Thomas Whipple who went to congress so many years, built a tannery on the Mikascota, just below the Blue ridge, and a dwelling-house near by. The house was for many years the old parsonage, and Anson Pillsbury lives in it now. Joseph Boynton, the great Methodist class leader, succeeded Whipple in the business, and Joshua Merrill followed him. Col. Isaac Merrill had a tannery on Ore-hill brook, and William Pomeroy bought him out and carried on the business for many years.

Window Shades.—Haselton & Eaton commenced the manufacture of window shades, and carried it on extensively at the old Stevens Merrill mill. The material is got out here, but almost every woman in town has a loom and weaves window shades. Merrill & Clark still continue the business.

Starch.—F. A. & M. E. Cushman built a starch factory at the Stevens Merrill mill. They made the starch from potatoes. Shortly after, Russell K. Clement built another starch factory by Rocky falls on Patch brook, where he manufactured potato starch for a few years. He then moved his mill to the mouth of the Mikascota, where in company with Daniel Q. Clement he has continued the trade, and they have both acquired considerable property.

Bobbins.—Levi F. Jewell built a bobbin mill at the mouth of Berry brook and has made money making bobbins. He uses more than a hundred thousand feet of hard-wood lumber annually, and has usually sold in Nashua. Mr. Jewell made wash-boards for a few years. Nathaniel K. Richardson made bobbins a short time at the Sawtelle mill.

Coopers.—A cooper came to town long years ago, Mr. Asa Thurston. His shop stood exactly on the spot where the first

Very truly yours,
Dr. W. E. Boynton.

school-house in Warren was built. Mr. Thurston employed George W. Prescott, trader, and John Lord, to work for him. Afterwards George Bixby, Sen., and Samuel Bixby and Samuel Goodwin made buckets, kits, and barrels, and Leavitt, on the Height-o'-land, made "leach-tubs" for Anson Merrill.

Shaved Shingles.—Old Antony McCarter, the hermit, made shingles by hand, and Samuel Osborn, Stephen Richardson, Isaac Clifford, on Red-oak hill, William Stearns,* by Kelley pond, Nathaniel Richardson, Daniel Bailey, James Dow, and Stevens Merrill, son of 'Squire Jonathan Merrill, Tappan Craige, Stephen Craige, and numerous others in town, have followed the same business. Nathaniel Richardson and his son Nathaniel, high up on the side of Moosehillock mountain, made the long shingle for the Prospect House. They camped out in the woods while thus engaged. Persons who shaved shingles were called "shingle weavers."

Pearlash.—Capt. Benjamin Merrill, son of 'Squire Abel, made salts and pearlash. His potash stood down the bank from the old first school-house and Thurston's cooper shop. Ashes were plenty then and Thomas Pillsbury and Col. Ben. Clement worked night and day for him, leaching, boiling, and pearling. What hot fires they kept! Preston & Keezer bought out Col. Ben. Merrill and continued the business.

Anson Merrill built a potash just west of the depot "crossing" and did a large business. He always made A No. 1 pearlash, and got the highest price for it. William Wells worked for him a while and then he employed Hobart Wyatt, Daniel Day, Col. Ben. Clement, "Biger" Wright, Nathan Willey, Thomas Pillsbury, Stephen Whiteman and others in the business. Old settlers say "lots of rum used to be drank in the potash premises;" but this must be a mistake, for although all the ministers in those times invariably drank what liquor they could get, yet it is well known that all or nearly all the above worthies were, or ought to have been, good temperance men.

---

* Stearns once stopped at Glines' hotel at East Haverhill. He had in a few glasses and felt good. He called for supper; Glines asked if he had any money. Stearns said "yes." Glines made him show it, then had a good supper prepared. When it was ready he wanted Stearns to walk in. The latter did so, went twice around the table, walked out into the bar-room and told Glines that he had seen the money, and the supper had been seen, and now he guessed they were even. Stearns then walked off, leaving Glines in a very pleasant mood.

Uncle Eben Cushman built a potash at the lower village and worked it a long time. Then Hobart Wyatt* got exclusive control of these important manufactories, and with his son Vanness,† was the last who ever carried on the pearlash business in Warren.

Brick.—Brick making has never been very extensive in our town. Long ago clay was dug in the bottom of Runaway pond, and brick made from it just below Beech hill bridge on the south bank of the Mikaseota; but who did it the oldest inhabitants of the present day have forgotten. Three-fourths of a century ago a kiln was burned at the forks of Orc-hill stream where the road turns off to the mine, from the turnpike, and Dr. French burned several kilns in the East-parte region.‡

Oils and Essences.—Every one has heard of Stephen Whiteman's large essence manufactory, by Berry brook on the Summit. He made peppermint essence, checkerberry essence, hemlock oil, fir oil, spruce oil, pipsissiwa, and others, at his renowned distillery. Mr. Whiteman says Ellsworth and Woodstock will soon be grand places to make spruce oil, for the lazy farmers of those towns are letting their farms all grow up to spruce bushes. Once Dr. David C. French had a large fir oil manufactory on the East-parte road near where old McCarter was not murdered.

Blacksmithing.—The following persons: Joseph Kimball, Samuel Knight, Samuel Gilman, Joseph Rollins, Stephen Whiteman, (he served seven years to learn the trade,) Deacon Peter Stevens, on Red-oak hill, David Colby, Enoch R. Weeks, Moses H. Clement,** James Clement, Joseph Clement, George Libbey, at

---

* Hobart Wyatt once got mad at Moses Ellsworth and chased him all round Joseph Merrill's bar-room trying to kick him; but Moses was too spry for him and kept out of the way. Both were "balmy." The next day Ellsworth was "tight" and went into the potash to whip Wyatt. He "hit him once," when Wyatt, who was a very strong man, seized "Fortyfoot" by the nape of the neck and the seat of the breeches and ducked him in a lye tub. "You are wetting me," sung out Ellsworth. "Then I'll dry ye," said Wyatt; and he held him at arms length before the fire. "You are burning me," screamed "Fortyfoot." "Then I'll cool ye," said Wyatt, and he soused him in the lye tub again. Just then somebody came in and stopped the pleasant fun, much to the disgust of both parties.

† Van Wyatt went to a revival one evening after having collected ashes all day. He was sleepy. One of the ministers approached and asked him if he was looking for religion. Vanness raised his eyes meekly and replied in the most honest manner imaginable, "No sir, I am looking for ashes." The minister laughed in spite of himself, and passed along.

‡ They made a kiln of brick in 1801, near Aaron Welch's on Pine hill road.

** Lemuel Keezer once agreed to pay Col. Moses H. Clement in mutton for blacksmithing. One morning the colonel found two sheep tied in the shop, one very fat and the other awful poor. Col. Clement, the next time he saw Keezer, asked him what he meant by such work. Keezer said that some of the blacksmithing was good, but some mighty poor, and the bad mutton was for that.

the East-parte, Hazen Libbey, Walter Libbey, Moses Abbott, Hazen Abbott, Paul White, George W. Jackson, Moses W. Pillsbury, Emerson Pillsbury, Anson Pillsbury, James Harriman, and others have made horse shoes, axes, hoes, and nails, and shod oxen and horses, and ironed wagons, sleighs and sleds.

Shoemakers.—In later times George W. Jackson, Jared S. Blodgett, John Merrill, son of Capt. Daniel, Ezra B. Libbey, William Weeks, Enos Huckins, Nathaniel Libbey, Coleridge Marston, have worked at making shoes and boots. Long ago Caleb Noyes, (Noyes bridge was so called for him) Joseph Patch, Benjamin Brown, Frederick Brown, Tristram Brown, John Abbott, Chase Whitcher, and Luther Gove, made boots and shoes and mended the same for our ancestors. These good men, knights of St. Crispin, often went about the town "whipping the cat," as it was called. The farmer with his ox cart would go for the shoemaker, load in his bench, lasts, leather, and all the rest of his "kit," and drive him jolting home. A gallon of rum generally went with him. Old men tell us how in one corner of the room the shoemaker sat, in a red flannel shirt and a leather apron, at work on the kit mending and making shoes. With what long and patient vibration and equipoise he draws the threads and interludes his hammer strokes upon leather and lap-stone and pegs, with snatches of songs, banter, and laughter. The next farmer who wanted his services came and carried him away, when his job was done, and thus he "whipped the cat" all over town.

Tailoresses.—Warren has had many of them. They used to go all about, just like the shoemakers, making clothes for the farmers and their families. Hitty Smith, daughter of Simeon Smith, was the first one. She was an excellent workwoman, and after long years of service, married a Mr. Clark, of Dorchester. After her, in order, came Jane Parkinson, who married Adams Preston, of Bradford; Nancy Marsh, Sally Barker, who married Jesse Eastman; Nancy Barker, who married Col. Isaac Merrill, and Sarah Clement, who married George Noyes. There were numerous others, but these are best remembered.

Among the minor manufactures we should not omit to mention that Richard Whiteman, sometimes called "Sir Richard," made *kitchen chairs;* that Jacob Whitcher and George Libbey made *baskets;* that Frank Cushman made *whetstones* and " *scythe rifles;*" that A. L. Noyes made *jewelry;* that J. M. Spaulding and John C. Sinclair made *harnesses*; that Amos Clement, J. M. Williams, Morrill J. Sanborn, and numerous others made *soft coal;* that Ruel Bela Clifford made *rakes;* that Hazen Kimball, Charles Chandler, James M. Hartwell, Damon Y. Eastman, Addison W. Eastman, Joseph M. Little, and Henry N. Merrill made *carriages* and *sleighs;* that Amos F. Clough was a *photographer,** and Chas. A. Fiske, a *painter;* and both made beautiful *pictures.* Mr. Fiske came to Warren about 1863, and afterwards built " Green Lane Studio," with a trout pond by it, the pleasant pine woods near, where the Asquamchumauke bends away to the East-parte.

If the making of maple sugar is a manufacture, then certainly it is the sweetest and largest, and more profitable than all the rest, and every farmer in town is or ought to be engaged in it as we have before mentioned. Don't! don't cut down the sugar places.

Warren has done a great deal more than the average of country towns in manufacturing, and could the reservoirs we have mentioned be built, and the surplus water of Berry brook and the Oliverian be carried down into them, as could easily be done by a skillful engineer, a large manufacturing village could be built up. Two good mill privileges on the Blue ridge, the Joseph Merrill pond, the fall at the depot, the Stevens Merrill pond, the fall at the mouth of the Mikaseota, and the old deep-hole fall would furnish a series of mill sites, such as few towns possess, and water enough the year round.

Progress in manufacturing has made mighty changes in Warren during its first century, as well as everywhere else. No more do we have the rude camp and log cabin, except in the French settlements, stone chimney and Dutch oven outside, and ill fitting windows through which the wintry winds come whistling; but our modern house is a snug and silken nest of delight, rising in some lovely spot light and airy, with heavy carpets, rich curtains, and elegant beds. The rude fashion of furniture and vessels for the table, pewter ware, wooden knives, forks, and spoons, and noggins, and the rude style of cooking, bean porridge hot and

---

* Charles F. Bracey was also a photographer in Warren.

cold, has departed. Now we have a superior grace in fashion of furniture and all household utensils,—silver and gold, brass and steel, porcelain and glass, wrought into beautiful shapes, and for the morning meal China and the Indies send their coffee, tea, sugar, chocolate, and preserved fruits; the West its flour, and our own farms an abundance of rural dainties.

No longer do we have a dearth of books and pictures, with a life of story telling around the hearth, little intercourse with the outer world, roads almost impassable, and hunting and carousing for the chief pleasures and amusements; but to-day on our tables are daily papers from Boston and New York, bringing news from the whole world. There is nothing going on in the Legislature, in Congress, in the courts of law, in public meetings, religious, political, or musical, in any town in the country; no birth, marriage, death, or any occurrence of importance; nothing in the mercantile, the literary, or the scientific world, but they are all laid before us. We sit in the midst of our woods and groves in the quietness of the country, a hundred miles from the capital, and are as well acquainted with the movements and incidents of society as though we were almost omnipresent.

So much for the advancement of one century. Will the next show as much?

CHAPTER X.

OF SEVERAL THINGS THAT HAPPENED; CONCLUDING THIS HISTORY
WITH SINCERE THANKS AND MANY KIND WISHES.

WARREN'S wars have seemed to repeat themselves once in a hundred years.

King Philip's war in which our Indian chief Waternomee, sometimes called Wattanummon, took his first lesson, occurred in 1675, and a hundred years after came the revolution, in which the first settlers of our hamlet distinguished themselves.

Then came Queen Ann's war of 1712, and Capt. Baker's fight, one of its battles, in which Waternomee was slain, and a hundred years after was the war of 1812, with the British, during which in our hamlet there was such lively volunteering.

King George's war came in 1743, with its memorable expeditions through and about our mountain valley, with the capture of Louisburg, and a hundred years after came the Mexican war, when Henry Albert went in Captain Daniel Batchelder's company to Mexico.

The next great conflict was the old French and Indian war, the result of which, with Robert Rogers' great fight,— his rangers against the St. Francis Indians,— made Warren a safe place for white men to live in. This struggle ended in 1760, and a hundred years later happened the war of the great rebellion, just at the close of Warren's first century, and of this great history.

Our citizens took a lively interest in this last conflict. A majority of them said it was all about the negro, as some of the winning party now boast, got up to free their man and brother from slavery, and that it was fought under cover of a lie; the abolitionists loudly proclaiming that it was to preserve the Union and the Constitution, and to maintain the flag, when in fact it was nothing more nor less than a negro crusade. Now it is over they good naturedly suppose it is all right, although some of them think that the result will be very fatal to the " poor darky."

The citizens of Warren, many of them, did not believe in the war, thought there was no need of it; but they had to sustain it as some said "at the point of the bayonet."

At first quite a number of Warren's sons volunteered, some of them from patriotic motives, and some thinking the war would not last long, and they would have sort of a holiday excursion; but the latter soon got disabused of that idea, and when a new quota was called for the town was compelled to offer bounties. One hundred dollars to a man was first offered, the State and the United States each also paying the same men one hundred dollars, and a few young men inspired by patriotism, took the bounty and went. Then when another call for troops was made, the town voted to pay a bounty of one thousand dollars in addition to the State and United States bounty, to each man, and a few more got exceedingly patriotic and went away to the war.

Afterwards when a quota was demanded from Warren, like every other town in the State, her selectmen paid three hundred dollars for her part, filled it up with Canuck substitutes and other foreigners, and these bounty jumpers "skedaddled" or deserted the very first opportunity, as can be seen by any one who will take the pains to look at the Adjutant General's Reports for New Hampshire. Nearly all the persons from Warren in the 4th, 5th, 6th, 7th, and part of the 8th regiments were bounty jumpers and deserters.

The following list of soldiers from Warren, was kindly furnished by George Bartlett Noyes. It was taken from the reports of Adjutant General Natt Head:—

First Regiment:—
Ward C. Batchelder.

Second Regiment:—
Lieut. Andrew G. Bracey.
William Clifford.
Osco H. French.
Aaron Goodwin.
Lieut. Thomas B. Little.

Eighth Regiment:—
John S. Hennessy.
John Ryan, captured at Sabine Cross Roads, La., April 8, 1864.
James Ragan.
John Sullivan.
John O. Sullivan,—deserted.
Walter Veasey.

510   HISTORY OF WARREN.

Thus the war went on past 1863, the year Warren was one hundred years old, and ended in April, 1865; a little more than four years from its commencement. Every body rejoiced when the war was over, and every bell in the whole North rang a jubilee when peace came.

Some of Warren's sons behaved with much gallantry and gained credit on the battlefield. Others did not do so well. Their names and their records are all truthfully preserved in the Adjutant General's Report. Gen. Natt Head* did his work well, " and

Fourth Regiment:—
Oliver R. Counter.
James Dougherty.
Joseph Hartman.
John Kehoe,—deserted.
Michael King,—deserted.
Daniel Sayers.
Henry C. Scott.
Jas. Welch,—wounded Aug. 16, 1864.

Fifth Regiment:—
Alphonzo Brochat,—wounded Apr. 7, 1865.
John Cochran.
Chas. W. Cowen,—promoted to sergt. April 1, 1835.
Edward Jones,—deserted.
Perkins H. Mott,—promoted to corp. then deserted.
John McCarter.
Antoni Robba,—deserted.
Benjamin Varney,—wounded April 7, 1865.

Sixth Regiment:—
Andrew Ballman,—wounded May 12, 1864.
Charles M. Hosmer,—deserted.
Thomas Jones,—deserted.
Edw. Nero,—wounded June 22, 1864.
Edward Saliske,—deserted.
John Saunders,—deserted.
John Smith.
Joseph Tarbell,—wounded June 28, 1864.
Samuel Wilson,—wounded May 12, 1864, died of wounds June 21, 1864.

Seventh Regiment:—
Samuel Allen,—deserted.

Twelfth Regiment:—
Joseph M. Bixby.
Charles H. Caswell.
Rufus L. Colby,—died at Falmouth, Va., Feb. 7, 1863.
Reuben Gale,—killed at the battle of Chancellorsville, Va., May 3, 1863.
Horace W. Gleason.
Charles H. Hinman, corporal.
Jonathan K. Kelsea,—died at Washington, D. C., Jan. 24, 1864.
Ezra Walton Libbey, musician.
George W. Merrill, musician.
James M. Noyes,—wounded May 3, 1863; promoted sergt.; wounded severely May 14, 1864.
Lieut. Charles H. Sheldon,—wounded June 3, 1834; died of wounds, June 27, 1864.

Fourteenth Regiment:—
Fernando Hobbs,—died May 17, 1863.
John S. Varney,—wounded Sept. 19, 1864.
Richard Varney,—died in 1864 of wounds received at Winchester, Va. Killed there.

Fifteenth Regiment:—
John Kimball,—died May 28, 1863.
John Wiggin.

First Regiment N. H. Cavalry:—
Edward I. Robie.

First Regiment Heavy Artillery:—
Leonard Colburn.
Edwin Fifield.
Osco H. French, corporal.
Proctor E. Harris.
Henry T. Latham, corporal.
George M. Little.
Henry D. Noyes.
Darius O. Swain, wounded.
Dr. John F. Willey.

* Gen. Natt Head is the grandson of Nathaniel Head, of Hooksett, who was a captain in the Revolution. He was Adjutant General during the whole war, and had great pride in New Hampshire soldiers, and did more than any other man to preserve their record. Through his efforts we are able to give so complete a list of the soldiers from Warren.

pity 'tis" that our ancestors, soldiers of the revolution, could not have had the memory of their deeds as well preserved. Warren can be proud of her sons.

As one of the results of the war our town is staggering under the burden of an enormous debt; and the millions owed by the State and the nation make taxes high, and the poor to be oppressed. The bondholders are now in the hey-day of their glory.

One of the grand things that happened while the war was going on was the *telegraph* put up in Warren in 1862. Arthur Knapp erected the poles from Plymouth to Littleton. The operator first had his office in W. S. Doggett's store, and then in Jewett & Eaton's, at the railroad crossing.

About this time, although not exactly in chronological order, happened a great boundary feud, like those of ancient time, between our flourishing democracy and old Peeling, now called Woodstock. It occurred in the selectmenship of Jesse Little, Ira M. Weeks, and David Smith. The preceding year, and in fact for several successive years before, the dwellers in the East-parte regions would see the smoke of strange fires curling out of the woods on Mts. Kineo, Cushman, and Waternomee; but no one could tell what they were. Some said they were fishermen, some that they were deer stalkers; and others that they were diamond hunters camping there; but this year it came out that they were parties of land surveyors from Woodstock.

Soon the selectmen got a notice that a hearing would be had at the Moosilauke House. It came off in the summer, and the citizens of Warren then learned what Woodstock claimed. By its charter, Woodstock was granted as nearly a square township, cut-

---

The following persons from Warren served in regiments out of this State, in some capacity:—

Capt. Dudley C. Bixby.
Anson Chandler.
Commodore Clifford.
Rev. Addison W. Eastman.
Martin V. Libbey.
Joseph Noyes.
Delano Prescott.
Charles Merrill.
Albe W. Merrill.
George Miller.
Hazen Libbey.
Newell S. Martin.

Andrew Jackson.
Merrill S. Lund,—died in the army.
Harvey Eames,—died in the army,— brought to Warren for burial.
Thomas Miles.
Charles N. Harris.
George E. Swain.
Daniel French,—died in the army,— brought to Warren for burial.
Charles F. Bracey.
John T. Bailey.
Thomas J. Clifford.

ting a square of about six hundred acres out of the north east corner of Warren. Our democracy was chartered in the same manner, nearly square, and cutting about the same amount of land out of the south west corner of Woodstock. Warren was chartered first, but Woodstock had her charter on *record* first, and hence the controversy — which town should own that six hundred acres of land.

Woodstock's selectmen, agents, and surveyors who had built the strange camp-fires in the woods, and interested citizens, came over the low pass between Waternomee and Mt. Cushman, to that meeting; and our selectmen, Col. Isaac Merrill, Dr. David C. French, and other citizens, met them at the village hotel. They had a long good natured talk which amounted to nothing only that each party got considerably enlightened about the history of town charters, and all were firmly convinced that they had got to go to court to settle the matter. Then Woodstock's officers, surveyors, and citizens went home by the route they came.

At a town meeting held November 7, the representative of Warren to the Legislature was instructed to procure a copy of the charter of Peeling, now Woodstock, and at the fall term of court at Plymouth, after an extended hearing, a commission consisting of David C. Churchill, of Lyme, and Nathaniel S. Berry, of Hebron, the side judges, was appointed to investigate the whole matter.*

The committee came to Warren and looked at the line, examined the charters, looked over the "doings" of the old court's committee, and finally came to the conclusion that as the Legislature in 1784 had established by an act for that purpose the boundary lines of Warren and the towns around it, those boundary lines must stand; and the case was decided in favor of Warren. The court affirmed the report of the commissioners, and Isaac Sawtelle was ordered to re-mark the old line between our two towns, putting on every blazed spot of the trees the cross mark of the court's committee, that the boundary might never more be forgotten. Thus Warren's last boundary question was settled.

Had Woodstock prevailed, all that section of the East-parte regions known as the *reservation*, together with a part of the last

---

* Col. Isaac Merrill's statement.

farm up the mountain road to Moosehillock; on the west side of the Asquamchumauke, now owned by Nathaniel Merrill, 2d, would have been lost to Warren, and many of the inhabitants compelled to go over the mountain on the surveyors' path to Woodstock to do town business.

When the temperance reform sprang up in the country, of course it came to Warren. It was conducive of great good, and appealed to the understanding and moral nature. They had a great many temperance meetings in town; but the one best remembered was held about the close of Warren's first century, by Alfred Dustin, painter. William Weeks, shoemaker, presided, and he had a great bulls-eye watch and copper chain attached to time the speaker. James Clement and Francis A. Cushman were deacons, and sat by the speaker's stand. Uncle Ebenezer Cushman and Aunt Eben, his wife, were present. Cotton Foot was there also, and he furnished applause with his droll and magical laugh.

Mr. Dustin made a good speech, full of fun, pathos, and eloquence; but as there was no short hand reporter present little of it is remembered. He commenced by saying that the terrible effect of drinking intoxicating liquors could be seen in his own case. That he was a living example of the ruin rum could make. Then he showed that in rum-drinking nearly all the vices and crimes of society originated; that it filled the poor-houses, work-houses, jails, prisons, and furnished victims for the gallows. Dispense with rum-drinking and crime would be banished. Rum-drinking, said Mr. Dustin, is the meanest business on earth; and the man or woman, the boy or girl, who engages in it, might as well be damned,— is damned now and eternally.

Rum-selling, said he, is a hellish, damnable traffic. Law don't stop it. It is a traffic that gets the orphans' and widows' curse, and the deepest execrations of the wife and mother. Devils laugh and gloat over it, and hell yawns for the men who engage in it.

At the conclusion of Mr. Dustin's address, Mr. Weeks, the chairman, said he was fully convinced, and that he should not make a swill-tub of his bowels any longer. Said Mr. Weeks, " God help the poor rum-drinker! The Devil will get the rum-seller, for he commits a dastardly crime with his eyes wide open."

G*

Poor men! They talked well; but like a great many other people they could not practice what they preached.

We remember well how about this time four young men, Benj. K. Little, Amos F. Clough, Joseph Noyes, and another, went over Mount Carr to Glen ponds fishing. On their way they passed through Fox-glove meadow and came to the most northern pond first. Standing on the western shore, it appears almost in the form of the letter Q, very deep in the middle, and grassy on the beaches, with some large stones rising out of the water by the outlet. South, one-fourth of a mile, is pond number two, three times as long as wide, very shoal, and containing about ten acres; and east of this half a mile is the third pond, almost circular, very deep, and about half as large as the second.

The little party built their camp on the north shore of the middle water where the forest was dark and sombre, standing just as it has stood for centuries. The valley of the ponds is like a great horse-shoe basin; three lofty mountains on the east, north, and west, while to the south an extended vista over the woods is terminated by Mt. Stinson. It is four miles from the pond through the woods over the mountain to Warren, and further than that to a farmer's house in the ancient land of Trecothick. From their camp our party saw no clearing, no lumberman's habitation, no sign of civilization, no more than when hundreds of years ago a party of Indians camped on the shore, (Indian arrow heads have been found among the pebbles of the beach); or when in the last century John Page and Surveyor Leavitt ran the first lines about the township; or Mr. Carr stood listening to the rain pattering on the water and like a Frenchman dined on frogs; or the party of hunters from Warren crossed the ice and then went after moose in the great yard over and around Black hill. The same great interminable wood was seen, and the same sounds were heard that Moses Abbott the fat man and Capt. Marston saw and heard when they stopped here weeks at a time, and lived on the trout they caught from these ponds.

A bright fire was built, then two of the party went on a raft fishing. The other two sat on a log and watched and listened. As the sun went down an osprey was seen flying over the water, and a great hen-hawk sat on a stub by the shore. Then the laughter of kingfishers and red squirrels was heard, and white throated finches, ruby-crowned wrens, golden-crested kinglets and snow birds, sang as the mellow twilight faded away. Suddenly a flock of black ducks whistled through the tree-tops and lighted down in the shoal water where the reeds and lilies were growing. They had come from the little meadows at the head of Moulton brook, where they were hatched, to stop on the pond all night.

The fishermen came back on their raft at dark; more wood was cut, the fire was replenished, and the flames crackled and flashed, and shone through the trees. One of the party went to the grassy shore for a drink of water. He saw something across the pond, and he never forgot the sight — three wild deer were standing on the rocky beach. They had come down to the pond to feed. How still they are—not a motion; and their eyes, how they glisten as they stand there almost spell-bound, gazing through the darkness at the camp-fire of the fishermen.

Another individual used to tell what a grand hand Amos F. Clough was to keep the fire burning all night long, and how B. K. Little nudged somebody and whispered, "Hear them! hear them!" Half a dozen great owls attracted by the blaze had gathered in the hemlocks, and were giving the grandest concert ever listened to. "Hark! hear that!" he whispered again. It was the long drawn halloo of an old bear far up the side of Mount Carr. Hear it again and again. It was enough to make one's hair stand on end. But it is soon over and the party go to sleep once more, listening to the frogs singing in the pond, and the splash of the muskrats among the reeds.

Hundreds of men have seen and heard these same sights and sounds; but never as yet has a white woman stood on the shores of Glen ponds.

The fish bite well in the morning and when the sun goes down. What beauties they are! Some of them will weigh a pound. One of those fat fellows with a piece of pork inside cooked on a forked stick held over the fire, is the daintiest morsel in the world. As the sun gets high, the fish cease to bite, the "traps" are packed up and the party is off over the mountain home, having had a pleasant experience, never to be forgotten.

Thousands of pounds of trout are caught out of these three

dark little tarns every year. It is said that pot fishers sometimes go there and catch bushels of trout with a net; that they snare large but poor fish on the spawning beds, and lime the waters. We hope that all such persons may get choked to death with fish bones.

Glen ponds, it is alleged, are filling up, and that the next century will see them in the same condition as Foxglove meadow a mile to the north of them. It would be a shame for such a thing to happen. There is no spot on earth where trout grow faster or better. If the fishermen of Warren, Wentworth, Romney, and old Trecothick would but club together and build short earth dams at the outlets of each, they could be made six feet deeper, many acres more of now useless land would be flowed, and Glen ponds with all their wildness, solitude, and piscatorial beauties, would last forever.

Warren people, like other highly civilized communities, have always been fond of amusements, more especially of the higher order of the drama. Many of her sons have cultivated the histrionic art, and arrived at a good degree of perfection. The first exhibition we ever attended was in the old school house at the forks of the turnpike and Beech-hill road. This was followed by a theatrical entertainment at the old meeting house. A stage was erected about the pulpit, without scenery and without curtains. Mr. James Clement was one of the principal actors, and we recollect him in a single act piece, entitled "I think I have been eating sunthin." Jim had padded himself out with pillows till he had a belly larger than Jack Falstaff's and looked comical enough. Col. Thos. J. Whipple had been assigned the post of honor, namely: a seat in the pulpit. As Jim proceeded to tell what he had eat the colonel was convulsed with laughter, and Jim's story and funny look, together with Col. W. behind him stretching his mouth from ear to ear, with his loud haw-haw, made a broad farce, and the whole meeting-house roared. The scene produced made such a strong impression upon the writer's mind, that although very young he never forgot it.

The next exhibition was managed by Col. Isaac Merrill, and Addison W. Eastman was one of the star actors. Miss Tamar J. Clement also took a prominent part. We remember very little about it, only it was considered a decided success, and was the principal subject of conversation in town for weeks after. Then there was a grand combination of performers in Warren one winter; A. W. Eastman being the leading star. Forest was outroared and outdone, and Warren shone with brilliancy. All the surrounding regions came to see the plays that season.

Since, there have been school exhibitions, religious exhibitions, and various other kinds, all successful, and more recently a sort of stock company that gave entertainments for a pecuniary consideration, in addition to the glory they might achieve; and this collection of stars was perhaps the most successful of all.

In addition to these exhibitions by our home talent, traveling performers have sometimes entertained our citizens. What a wonder was Potter, the juggler and ventriloquist. How he made the eyes of the Warren youth stick out when he fried eggs in a gentleman's hat, and returned the hat uninjured; when he smashed a beautiful gold watch "all to flinders," and burned a lady's handkerchief to ashes, and then restored the same whole and entire; also when he suffered himself to be shot at, and cut a man's head off without hurting him. Old Glynn was nearly as wonderful as Potter; and the above named A. W. Eastman was one of his grandest performers. A people's civilization can be judged by the character of their amusements.

In addition to having good schools, Warren has been celebrated for her spelling schools. They were held in winter time in all the districts, and there was a great rivalry to see who could spell down the whole town. One in Runaway pond or Weeks district, that came off about this time, is well remembered. John French was keeping the school, and the little red school-house was packed with youths and maidens. Young Joseph Bixby, a naughty youth, was present, and some wicked person pushed him over the roaring, red hot stove, knocking it down. The schoolmaster, Mr. John French, rushed forward, feeling that his dignity was injured, stamped his foot, and with stentorian lungs shouted, "Cassius! May Brutus and all the other heathen gods preserve and defend us." And then there was a roar of laughter, much to the school-master's delight, the flames belching out and the smoke rolling up. But some resolute boys at once procured two stout levers, carried the stove out into the snow, cooled it, set it up again, aired the house, and then the spelling-school went on.

Two of the best scholars chose sides, taking care to seat the boys and girls who were fond of each other together, and choosing the poorest spellers last, each chooser trying to get the best, that his or her side might miss the least words and thereby win. Then after spelling a while the tally keepers announced the result and they had a recess; such a grand time. When it was over they "chose" again, spelt round a few times and then spelt down. Misses Elsie Ann Bixby and Caroline French could beat the whole town in their day. After the spelling exercises they propounded conundrums, put out hard words, and spoke funny pieces.

Then the school-master made a speech. How well it is remembered. Some believed it. He began by telling the advantages of the common schools, how they had made New England what she is; how, educated in them, the sons of New Hampshire were the representatives and senators in congress, the judges in the courts, and one of them an honored President. That where the common school system did not exist, there ignorance, superstition and priest-craft prevailed, and the people were the slaves of despots. That there was a class springing up in the country that was opposed to our system; would have none of it; would break it up. This should not be allowed. The school system should be preserved. We should stick to it, cling to it. We might as well let our fields and pastures grow up to bushes, burn up our houses and factories, let our ships rot at the wharves, and destroy our railroads, as to give up our school system, and the liberty and the glory it brings with it.

Then some of the citizens in a few words agreed with the speaker, made complimentary remarks, and the exercises closed.

When dismissed, the boys waited upon the girls home, which was the grandest part of the whole performance. No wonder, when the families were large, (what a shame they are not so now,) and district schools were crowded, spelling schools were in high esteem.

The last great occurrence at the close of Warren's first century

---

About these days the citizens procured a hearse, and the town voted to build a hearse-house near the grave-yard. Mrs. Mercy J. Knapp, wife of Arthur Knapp, headed the subscription list, raised the money and bought the hearse. Cannot some lady do as much towards building a receiving tomb?

of white settlers, and with its narration we shall end our entertaining history, was Warren's Centennial Celebration. At the annual town meeting it was voted to have a celebration on the 14th day of July, 1863, just a hundred years after the day the town was chartered.

ENOCH R. WEEKS
was chosen President.

The following men over seventy years of age, were chosen Vice Presidents, viz.:—

BENJAMIN BIXBY.
JOHN CLARK.
WILLIAM CLEASBY.
JONATHAN CLOUGH.
JONATHAN EATON.
DR. DAVID C. FRENCH.
ASA HEATH.
VOWELL LEATHERS.
GEORGE LIBBEY.
SAMUEL MERRILL.
NATHANIEL RICHARDSON.
JOSIAH SWAIN.
STEPHEN WHITEMAN.

All men over sixty years old were chosen as a committee of arrangements. They were as follows:—

JOSEPH BIXBY.
SAMUEL BIXBY.
BENJAMIN CLEMENT.
JESSE EASTMAN.
JOSEPH B. FARNHAM.
SAMUEL GOODWIN.
JAMES HARRIMAN.
EZRA B. LIBBEY.
JOHN LIBBEY.
NATHANIEL LIBBEY.
BENJAMIN LITTLE.
DR. JESSE LITTLE.
CALVIN MAY.
SAMUEL L. MERRILL.
ANTONY McCARTER.
NATHAN WILLEY.

The 14th day of July, 1863, was rainy; but the people in goodly numbers assembled in the town house on Warren Common. Charles Leonard, when the hour arrived, rang the bell, and his father, George E. Leonard, acted for the committee of arrangements. Enoch R. Weeks, faithful to his duties, presided, and the following was the order of exercises:—

  I. Reading the Scriptures, — Isaiah xxxv.
  II. Music, — America, by the choir.
  III. Prayer, — Rev. Josiah Hooper.
  IV. Music, — Auld Lang Syne..
  V. Address, — by William Little.
  VI. Music, — Old Hundred.
  VII. Benediction.

Rev. Josiah Hooper made an excellent prayer. The choir, consisting of Messrs. Amos Clement and Wesley C. Batchelder, Mrs. George E. Leonard, Mrs. Russel Merrill, Mrs. Susan C. Little, and Misses Sarah J. Leonard, Ellen J. Bixby, Sarah J. Merrill and Amelia S. Clifford, sang in their best style, and the address was afterwards published. Any one can express his opinion of that after he has read it. Capt. Daniel Batchelder and others, of Haverhill, were present, and many came from Wentworth and Romney. In the evening they had a ball at the Moosilauke House and the young folks enjoyed themselves. Thus ended Warren's first century. May the next be as prosperous, and have a like happy end.

Eighteen hundred and sixty-three! A hundred years have passed since Warren became a town, and we close our history here. We are happy we have written it, and happy should be the great historian of Warren of the next hundred years, for we believe we have made a good beginning for him. Thrice happy should be our citizens that they have this good history.

We trust all will be pleased, for we have set down naught in malice. Everything has been written in the most perfect good nature, and with the best intentions. We have even taken pains to make some of our friends show off in good style. We have also given every citizen a chance to appear in our book, to immortalize himself by enrolling his name in our subscription list. Many

CONCLUSION.

have availed themselves of the opportunity, and to such we return our heartiest and most sincere thanks. If by our efforts we shall cause any of our friends to feel a tithe of the pleasure in reading the preceding pages that we have in writing them, they will be very happy indeed and we shall be amply compensated.

In closing, we sincerely wish that as long as any trout shall swim in the River Baker, otherwise the Asquamchumauke, and all its silvery, musical tributaries, as long as partridges shall drum in the forests on the mountains, as long as any blueberries shall ripen on the crests of Webster slide and Owl's head, as long as the Mikaseota shall come down from Wachipauka pond, as long as silver and gold shall be found on Sentinel mountain, as long as the sparkling waterfalls shall gleam on Mount Carr, and as long as the bald head of Moosehillock shall whiten with winter snows, so long may our friends and their children live and enjoy themselves in our town of WARREN.

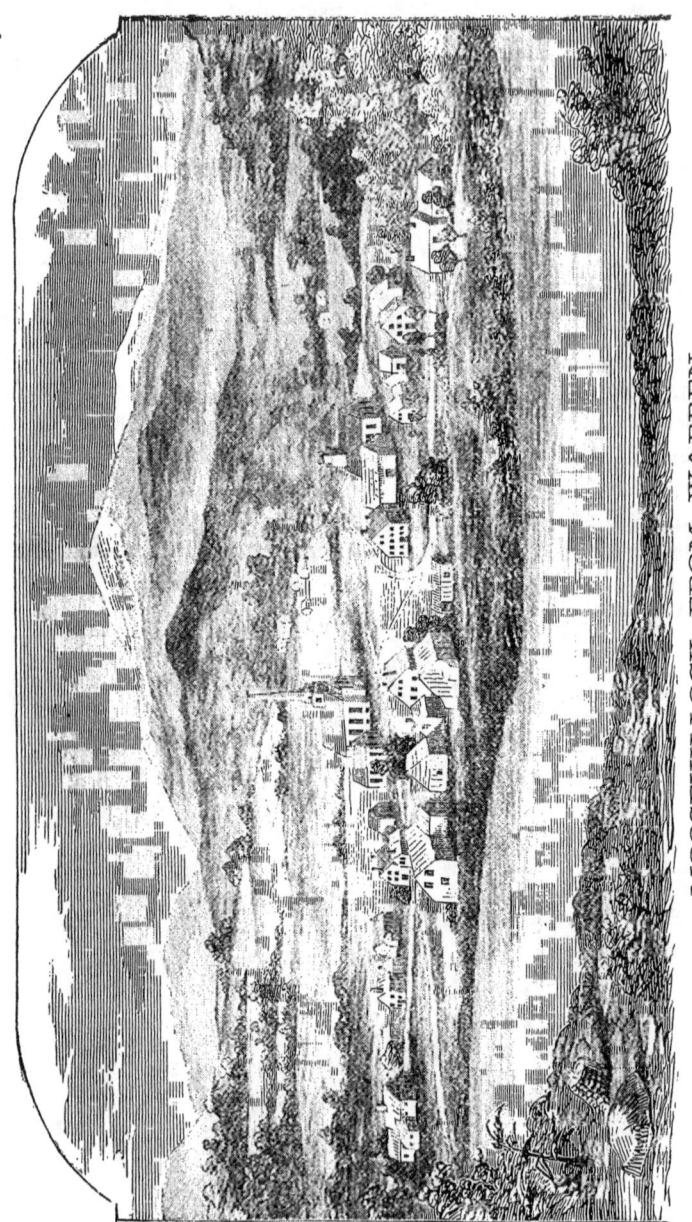

MOOSEHILLOCK FROM WARREN.

APPENDIX.

APPENDIX.

EXPLANATORY NOTES.

PAGE 57.—WETAMOO.

The bride of "Montowampate." Her real name was "Wenuchus."—Hist. of Concord, p. 32.

PAGE 134.—CAPTURE OF THE JOHNSON FAMILY.

The Indians did furnish a horse for Mrs. Johnson to ride. The horse was afterwards killed and eaten to prevent the party from starving. The oldest daughter, who was educated by the French, concluded to return home. Roswell H. Hassam, of Manchester, furnished us an interesting account of the capture of the Johnson family, which we would be glad to see published.

PAGE 152.—ROBERT POMEROY.

There is a tradition that Chase Whitcher and Joseph Patch both told of finding a human skeleton on Moosilauke, and without doubt it was Pomeroy, one of Rogers' rangers.

PAGE 208.—JAMES DOW.

James Dow, tythingman, contributed most of the descriptions of dress and appearance of the early settlers.

NATURAL HISTORY.

ANIMALS WHICH NOW, OR FORMERLY, LIVED IN WARREN.

MAMMALIA.

ORDER I.—CARNIVORA.

Bat.

Shrew Mole.
Star Nose Mole.
Say's Least Shrew Mole.
Brewer's Shrew Mole.

White Weasel, or Stoat, or Ermine.
Little Nimble Weasel.
Tawny Weasel.
Small Weasel.

Sable, or Pine Marten.
Pennant's Marten or Fisher Cat.

Otter.

Mink.
Mountain Brook Mink.

Skunk.

Wolverine.

Cougar, or Panther, or Painter, or Catamount.
Canada Lynx, or Loupcervier.
Bay Lynx, or Wild Cat.

Wolf.

Red Fox.
Black or Silver Gray Fox.

Black Bear.

Raccoon.

ORDER II.—RODENTIA.

Gray Squirrel.
Black Squirrel.
Chickaree, or Red Squirrel.
Chip, or Chipmonk, or Striped Squirrel.
Flying Squirrel.

Wilson's Meadow Mouse.
American White Footed Mouse.
House Mouse.
Leconte's Pine or Field Mouse.
Jumping Mouse.

Black Rat.
Norway Rat.

Beaver.
Musquash.

Porcupine or Hedgehog.

Woodchuck.

Rabbit, or Northern Hare.

ORDER III.—RUMINANTIA.

Moose.
Caribou, or American Reindeer.

Common or Fallow Deer.

BIRDS.

[c means common; r, rare; m, spring and fall migrants.]

ORDER I.—RAPTORES—ROBBERS.

Bald Eagle, r.
Golden Eagle, r.

Broad winged Hawk, c.
Marsh Hawk, c.

APPENDIX. 527

Black Hawk, r.
Fish (or Osprey) Hawk, c.
Goshawk, r.
Pigeon Hawk, c.
Red tailed, or Hen Hawk, c.
Sharp shinned Hawk. c.
Sparrow Hawk, c.
Cooper's Hawk, c.

Great horned Owl, c.
Long eared Owl, r.
Short eared Owl, r.
Screech Owl, c.
Snowy Owl, m.
Acadian Owl, m.
Barred Owl, m.
Hawk Owl, m.

ORDER II.—SCANSORES—CLIMBERS.

Black billed Cuckoo, c.
Yellow billed Cuckoo, c.

Downy Woodpecker, c.
Three toed Banded Woodpecker, r.
Golden winged Woodpecker, c.

Black backed 3 toed Woodpecker, r.
Hairy Woodpecker, c.
Pileated Woodpecker, r.
Red headed Woodpecker, r.
Yellow bellied Woodpecker, r.

ORDER III.—INSESSORES—PERCHERS.

Ruby throated Humming Bird, c.

Chimney Swallow, c.

Whip-poor-will, r.
Night-Hawk, c.

Belted Kingfisher, c.

Kingbird, c.
Pewee, or Phebe Bird, c.
Olive-sided Fly-catcher, c.
Wood Pewee, c.
Chebec, c.

Wood Thrush, c.
Olive backed Thrush, c.
Hermit Thrush, c.
Wilson's Thrush, c.
Robin, c.
Brown Thrasher, r.
Cat-bird, c.

Bluebird, c.

Ruby crowned Wren, c.
Golden crested Wren, c.
Chickadee or Black cap Titmouse, c.
White bellied Nuthatch, c.
Red bellied Nuthatch, c.
American Creeper, c.
House Wren, c.
Winter Wren, c.

Black and White Creeper, c.
Blue, Yellow backed warbler, r.
Maryland Yellow throat warbler, c.
Golden winged warbler, c.
Nashville warbler, r.
Oven-bird warbler, c.
Water Thrush warbler, c.
Black throated Green warbler, c.
Black throated Blue warbler, m.
Yellow rumped warbler, c.
Blackburnian warbler, m.
Pine-creeping warbler, c.
Chestnut-sided warbler, c.
Black Poll warbler, r.
Yellow warbler, c.
Black and Yellow warbler, c.
Yellow Red-poll warbler, c.

Canada Flycatcher warbler, m.
Red Start, c.
Scarlet Tanager, c.

Barn Swallow, c.
Eave Swallow, c.
White bellied Swallow, c.
Bank Swallow, c.
Purple Martin, c.

Cedar, or Cherry Bird, c.
Bohemian Chatterer, m.
Shrike, or Butcher Bird, m.
Yellow throated Vireo, r.
Solitary Vireo, r.
Red-eyed Vireo, c.

Pine Grosbeak, m.
Purple Finch, c.
Goldfinch or Yellow Bird, c.
Pinefinch, m.
Red Crossbill, m.
White winged Crossbill, m.
Mealy Red poll, m.
Lesser Red poll, m.
Snow Bunting, m.
Lapland Longspur, r and m.
Savannah Sparrow, r.
Grassfinch or Bay winged Bunting, c.
White crowned Sparrow, m.
White throated Sparrow, c.
Snowbird, c.
Tree Sparrow, m.
Field Sparrow, c.
Chipping Sparrow, c.
Song Sparrow, or Ground Bird, c.
Swamp Sparrow, r.
Fox colored Sparrow, m.
Rose breasted Grosbeak, r.
Indigo Bird, c.
Ground Robin,—Chewink, r.

Bobolink, c.
Cow Blackbird, c.
Red winged Blackbird, c.
Meadow Lark, r.
Baltimore Oriole, c.
Rusty Blackbird, r.
Crow Blackbird, or Purple Grakle, r.

Crow, c.
Blue Jay, c.
Canada Jay, c.

Order IV.—Rasores—Scratchers.

Wild Pigeon, c.
Carolina Dove, r.

Canada Grouse, c.
Ruffed Grouse, c.

Order V.—Grallatores—Waders.

Great Blue Heron, or Crane, c.
Bittern, or Stake Driver, c.
Green Heron, r.
Night Heron, r.

Woodcock, c.

Snipe, m.

Solitary Sandpiper, c.
Spotted Sandpiper, c.

Upland Plover, r.

Order VI.—Natatores—Swimmers.

Canada Goose, m.
Brant Goose, m.

Black Duck, c.
Blue winged Teal, r.
Green winged Teal, r.

Wood Duck, c.
Sheldrake, c.

Gull, r.

Great Norther Diver, or Loon, c.

Reptilia, or Reptiles.

Snapping Turtle, or Tortoise.
Painted Tortoise.
Spotted Tortoise.
Wood Terrapin, or Tortoise.
Mud Turtle or Musk Tortoise.
Box Tortoise.
Blanding's Box Tortoise.

Striped Snake.
Ribbon Snake.
Water Snake.
House Adder.
Red Snake.
Green, or Grass Snake.
Ring-necked Snake.

Blue tailed Skink or Lizard.

Yellow bellied Salamander.
Violet colored Salamander.
Red Backed Salamander.
Painted Salamander.
Salmon colored Salamander.

Blotched Salamander.
Red Salamander.
Blue spotted Salamander.
Granulated Salamander.
Tiger Triton Salamander.
Crimson spotted Triton Salamander, or Evet.
Dusky Triton Salamander.

Toad.

Bull-frog.
Large Northern Bull-frog.
Spring Frog.
Marsh or Tiger Frog.
Shad Frog.
Wood Frog.

Tree Toad.

Pickering's Hylodes.
Cricket Hylodes.

Fishes.

Trout.
Troutlet.
Pickerel.

Pout.
Roach.
Dace.

Shiner.
Sucker.
Eel.

Spiders.

One hundred and twenty-six kinds, some with six eyes and some with eight eyes.

APPENDIX.

INSECTS.

BEETLES:
Tiger.
Long-horned Water.
Rover.
Flat Boring.
Death-watch or ticking.
Bone.
Carrion.
Short horned Water.
Weevils.
Capricorn.

Cockroaches.
Crickets.
Nocturnal Grasshoppers.
Diurnal Grasshoppers.

Squash Bug.
Bedbug.

Common Harvest Fly or Locust.
Bark Louse.
Oyster-shaped Bark Louse.
Dragon Flies, or Devil's Needles.
White Ants, or Wood Lice.

Saw Flies.

Ants.
Stinging Ants.

Wasps.
Hornets.
Wood-cutter Bee.
Leafcutter Bee.
Humblebee.
Honey Bee.
Butterfly.
Skipper Butterfly.
Humming Bird, or Hawk Moth.
Locust-tree Cossus.
Caterpiller.
Autumnal Web Caterpillar.
Cut Worm.
Apple Worm.
Bee Moth.
Clothes Moth.
Mosquito.
Gnat.
Horsefly.
Flesh Fly.
Bot Fly.
Common Flea.
Louse and many other kinds, together with several species of worms.

TREES.

White Pine.
Hard Pine.
Norway Pine.
Black Spruce.
Spruce.
Red Hemlock.
White Hemlock.
Fir.
Tamarack.
Cedar.
Red Oak.
White Oak.
White Maple.
Birds-eye Maple.
Rock Maple.
Red Maple.
Swamp Maple.
Elm.
Slippery Elm.
White Birch.
Yellow Birch.
Black Birch.
Red Birch.
Silver-gray Birch.
Bass.

Red Beech.
White Beech.
White Ash.
Swamp Ash.
Black Ash.
Mountain Ash.
Prickly Ash,
Red Ash.
Butternut.
Poplar.
Lombardy Poplar.
Horn Beam.
Leverwood.
Balm Gilead.
Choke Cherry.
Black Cherry.
Bird Cherry.
Tame Cherry.
Canada Plum.
Witch Hazel.
Hazel.
Red Alder.
Black Alder.
Thorn.
Willow.

Bog Willow.
Weeping Willow.
Elder.
Ground Hemlock.
Moosewood.
Moosemissa.
Wild Gooseberry.
Currant.
Skunk Currant.
Rose-Bush.
Lilac.
Sumach.
High Blueberry.
Blueberry.
Whortleberry.
Dogwood.
Sweet Fern.
Apple.
Pear.
Wheat Plum.
Damson.
Sugar Plum.
Withe-wood.

PLANTS.

Wild Sarsaparilla.
Parsnip.
Lovage.
Sweet Sicily.
Bane Berry.
Columbine.
Cowslip.
Gold Thread.
Liverwort.

Yellow Wood Sorrel.
Violet.
Chick-weed.
Pig-weed.
Poke-weed.
Joint-weed.
Bind Knot-weed.
Knot Grass.
Field Sorrel.

Mullen.
Vervein.
Pennyroyal.
Hoarhound.
Horsemint.
Peppermint.
Spearmint.
Catmint.
Scullcap.

H*

Buttercup.
Crowfoot.
White Pond Lily.
Yellow Water Lily.
Horse Radish.
Mustard.
Strawberry.
Sweet-brier.
Black Raspberry.
Red Raspberry.
Blackberry.
Hard Hack.
Thorn Bush.
Field Clover.
Red Clover.
White Clover.
Nettles.
White Mulberry.
Red Mulberry.
Grape.
Poison Ivy.
Wood Sorrel.

Dock.
Honey-suckle.
Trailing Arbutus,
Partridge Berry.
Cranberry.
Wintergreen.
Harebell.
Wormwood.
Burdock.
Marygold.
Canada Thistle.
Common Thistle.
Artichoke.
Dandelion.
Fire-weed.
Golden Rod.
Colts Foot.
Tansy. *
Checkerberry.
Twin-flower.
Milk-weed.
Fox-glove.

Forget-me-not.
Mouse-ear.
Plantain.
Yellow-eyed Grass.
Star Grass.
Blue Flag.
Blue-eyed Grass.
Ladies' Slipper.
Indian Poke.
Solomon's Seal.
Bell-wort.
Cat-tail.
Sweet-flag.
Skunk Cabbage.
Hair Grass.
Meadow Grass.
Beard Grass.
Timothy Grass.
Sedge Grass.
Bay Rush.

FLOWERLESS PLANTS.

Horse-tail.
Maiden Hair.
Brake Fern.
Adder Tongue Fern.
Common Brake.

Rock Brake.
Ground Pine.
Liverwort.
Shield Lichen.
Lichen.

Puff-ball.
Smelt.
Frog Spittle.

ROCKS AND MINERALS.

Gold.
Silver.
Iron.
Zinc.
Lead.
Copper.
Nickel.
Cadmium.
Antimony.
Plumbago.
Iron Pyrites.
Iron Pyrites Black.
Molybdenum.
Arsenic.
Brown Hematite.

Garnets.
Epidote.
Idocrase.
Tremolite.
Tourmaline.
Beryl.
Apatite.
Cinnamon Stone.
Massive Garnet.
Rose Quartz.
Smoky Quartz.
Hyalite.
Quartz.
Calcspar.
Porphyritic Trap.

Trap.
Granitic Gneiss.
Feldspar.
Granite.
Mica Slate.
Talcose.
Hornblende.
Scapolite (with the Apatite) Crystals.
Limestone.
Argillaceous Slate.
Clay.
Feruginous Sand.
Alluvial Sand.

TOWN OFFICERS.

SELECTMEN.

1779.
Obadiah Clement.
Joshua Copp.
Israel Stevens.

1780.
Joshua Copp.
Thomas Clark.
John Whitcher.

1781.
Obadiah Clement.
William Butler.
Isaiah Batchelder.

1782.
Joshua Copp.
Ephraim True.
Simeon Smith.
Joshua Merrill.

1783.
Obadiah Clement.
Joshua Merrill.
William Butler.

1784.
Obadiah Clement.
Stevens Merrill.
Samuel Knight.

1785.
Obadiah Clement.
Stevens Merrill.
Joseph Patch.

1786.
Joshua Copp.
Stephen Richardson.
William Butler.

1787.
William Butler.
Joshua Copp.
Stephen Richardson.

APPENDIX. 531

1788.
Joshua Copp.
Ephraim True.
Nathaniel Knight.

1789.
Nathaniel Knight.
Samuel Knight.
Moses Copp.

1790.
Nathaniel Knight.
Jonathan Merrill.
Stephen Richardson.
Abel Merrill.

1791.
Joshua Copp.
William Butler.
Stephen Richardson.

1792.
Ephraim True.
Joseph French.
Samuel Knight.

1793.
Jonathan Merrill.
Joseph French.
Jonathan Clement.

1794.
Jonathan Merrill.
Thomas Boynton.
Aaron Welch.

1795.
Jonathan Merrill.
Thomas Boynton.
Joseph French.

1796.
Jonathan Merrill.
Abel Merrill.
Elisha Swett.

1797.
William Butler.
Jonathan Merrill.
Joseph French.

1798-'99.
Jonathan Merrill.
Abel Merrill.
Elisha Swett.

1800
Jonathan Merrill.
Ezra Bartlett,
William Butler.

1801.
Jonathan Merrill.
Ezra Bartlett.
Abel Merrill.

1802-'3.
Jonathan Merrill.
Abel Merrill.
Elisha Swett.

1804.
Ezra Bartlett.
Abel Merrill.
Elisha Swett.

1805.
Abel Merrill.
William Butler.
Daniel Patch.

1806.
Jonathan Merrill.
Daniel Patch.
Jonathan Fellows.

1807.
Abel Merrill.
Joseph Patch.
Elisha Swett.

1808.
Joseph Patch, Jr.,
Aaron Welch.
Ebenezer Barker.

1809.
Jonathan Merrill.
Joseph Patch, Jr.
Jonathan Fellows.

1810.
Jonathan Merrill.
Abel Merrill.
Amos Tarleton.

1811.
Abel Merrill.
Joseph Patch, Jr.
Amos Tarleton.

1812.
Jonathan Merrill.
Benjamin Merrill.
Joseph Merrill.

1813.
Joseph Patch.
Thomas Whipple.
Stephen Flanders.

1814.
Jonathan Merrill.
Abel Merrill.
Joseph Patch, Jr.

1815-'16.
Jonathan Merrill.
Abel Merrill.
Moses H. Clement.

1817.
Jonathan Merrill.
Abel Merrill.
James Williams.

1818-'19.
Joseph Patch, Jr.
Moses H. Clement.
Stephen Flanders.

1820.
Joseph Patch, Jr.
Nathaniel Clough.
Jacob Patch.

1821.
Nathaniel Clough.
Jacob Patch.
Amos Tarleton.

1822.
Jacob Patch.
Amos Tarleton.
George Libbey.

1823.
Abel Merrill.
Joseph Patch, Jr.
Joseph Bixby.

1824.
Jacob Patch.
Moses H. Clement.
William Clough.

1825.
Moses H. Clement.
Jacob Patch.
William Clough.

1826.
Jacob Patch.
William Clough.
Enoch R. Weeks.

1827.
Moses H. Clement.
Enoch R. Weeks.
Stevens Merrill.

1828.
Moses H. Clement.
Enoch R. Weeks.
Samuel Merrill.

1829.
William Clough.
Samuel Merrill.
George Libbey.

1830.
Jacob Patch.
Benjamin Little.
Samuel Merrill.

1831-'32.
Jacob Patch.
Benjamin Little.
Anson Merrill.

1833.
Enoch R. Weeks.
Moses H. Clement.
Samuel L. Merrill.

1834.
Moses H. Clement.
Samuel L. Merrill.
Samuel Merrill.

HISTORY OF WARREN.

1835.
Jacob Patch.
Isaac Merrill, 2d.
Solomon Cotton.

1836.
Samuel L. Merrill.
Solomon Cotton.
George Libbey.

1837.
Samuel L. Merrill.
George Libbey.
Enoch R. Weeks.

1838.
William Clough.
William Pomeroy.
Jonathan Little.

1839.
William Pomeroy.
Jonathan Little.
Joseph Bixby.

1840.
Jonathan Little.
Joseph Bixby.
Stevens M. Dow.

1841–'42.
Enoch R. Weeks.
Solomon Cotton.
Nathaniel Merrill, 2d.

1843.
Enoch R. Weeks.
William Pomeroy.
Russell F. Clifford.

1844.
Isaac Merrill.
Russell F. Clifford.
Stevens M. Dow.

1845.
Isaac Merrill.
Russell F. Clifford.
James S. Merrill.

1846.
Samuel L. Merrill.
James S. Merrill.
James Clement.

1847.
Jesse Little.
Solomon Cotton.
Ira M. Weeks.

1848.
Jesse Little.
Ira M. Weeks.
David Smith.

1849.
Samuel L. Merrill.
David Smith.
Thomas P. Huckins.

1850.
Samuel L. Merrill.
Thomas P. Huckins.
Albe C. Weeks.

1851.
Samuel L. Merrill.
Albe C. Weeks.
Michael P. Merrill.

1852.
Samuel L. Merrill.
Michael P. Merrill.
Joseph Clement.

1853.
David Smith.
Joseph Clement.
Jonathan Little.

1854.
William Pomeroy.
Ezra W. Cleasby.
James Clement.

1855.
William Pomeroy.
Ira Merrill.
Enoch R. Weeks, Jr.

1856.
Ira Merrill.
Enoch R. Weeks, Jr.
Darius Swain.

1857.
Samuel L. Merrill.
Darius Swain.
Stephen M. Boynton.

1858.
Isaac Merrill.
Stephen M. Boynton.
Nathaniel Merrill, 2d.

1859.
Russell F. Clifford.
Nathaniel Merrill, 2d.
Ezra Libbey.

1860.
Russell F. Clifford.
Ezra Libbey.
Nathaniel Merrill, 2d.

1861.
Ira Merrill.
Nathaniel Merrill, 2d.
Caleb I. Heath.

1862.
Ira M. Weeks.
Caleb I. Heath.
George E. Leonard.

1863.
Stevens M. Dow.
George E. Leonard.
James S. Merrill.

1864–'65.
Ira M. Weeks.
Levi C. Whitcher.
Adoniram Whitcher.

1866–'67.
Enoch R. Weeks, Jr.
George E. Leonard.
Calvin W. Cummings.

1868.
Stevens M. Dow.
Walter Libbey.
Amos Clement.

1869.
Ira M. Weeks.
Walter Libbey.
Amos Clement.

1870.
Ira M. Weeks.
Arthur Knapp.
James M. Bixby.

TOWN CLERKS.

1779—Obadiah Clement, 6 yrs.
1786—Joshua Copp, 1 "
1787—Joshua Merrill, 1 "
1788—Nathaniel Knight, 2 "
1790—Joshua Copp, 2 "
1793—Jonathan Merrill, 10 "
1803—Ezra Bartlett, 2 "
1805—Abel Merrill, 1 "
1806—Jonathan Merrill, 1 "
1818—Joseph Patch, Jr., 2 yrs.
1820—Moses H. Clement, 7 "
1827—Enoch R. Weeks, 1 "
1828—Anson Merrill, 4 "
1831—Jesse Little, 7 "
1838—R. K. Clement, 6 "
1844—Isaac Merrill, 2 "
1846—R. K. Clement, 13 "
1859—Albe C. Weeks, 2 "

APPENDIX. 533

1807—Abel Merrill, 2 yrs.
1809—Jonathan Merrill, 2 "
1811—Benjamin Merrill, 2 "
1813—Thomas Whipple, 2 "
1815—Jonathan Merrill, 1 "
1816—Joseph Patch, Jr., 1 "
1817—Robert Barns, 1 "

1861—Daniel Q. Clement, 3 yrs.
1864—R. K. Clement, 1 "
1865—William Pomeroy, 2 "
1867—Samuel B. Page, 1 "
1868—James B. Eastman, 2 "
1870—Nathan Harris, 1 "

REPRESENTATIVES.

1784—Obadiah Clement, 2 yrs.
1789—William Tarleton, 1 "
1793—Jonathan Merrill, 3 "
1797—William Butler, 2 "
1800—William Tarleton, 1 "
1801—Abel Merrill, 1 "
1805—Ezra Bartlett, 2 "
1808—Abel Merrill, 2 "
1811— " " 2 "
1814—Joseph Patch, Jr., 2 "
1817— " " 4 "
1822—Amos Tarleton, 2 "
1825—Abel Merrill, 2 "
1828—Jacob Patch, 1 "
1830—Moses H. Clement, 1 "
1831—Enoch R. Weeks, 2 "
1833—Jacob Patch, 1 "
1834—Moses H. Clement, 1 "
1835—Jacob Patch, 1 "

1836—Moses H. Clement, 1 yrs.
1838— " " 1 "
1839—Enoch R. Weeks, 1 "
1340—Jesse Little, 2 "
1842—William Clough, 2 "
1844—Russell K. Clement 2 "
1846—Jonathan Little, 2 "
1848—R. K. Clement, 1 "
1849—Levi C. Whitcher, 2 "
1851—William Pomeroy, 2 "
1853—Isaac Merrill, 1 "
1854—R. K. Clement, 1 "
1855—Isaac Merrill, 3 "
1858—James Clement, 2 "
1860—Ira M. Weeks, 2 "
1862—James M. Bixby 2 "
1864—Samuel B. Page, 6 "
1870—George F. Putnam, 1 "

MODERATORS.

Joshua Copp, 1779, '82, '98, '99.
Thomas Clark, 1780, '81.
William Butler, 1783, '84, '87, '88, '91, 94, 1801.
Stevens Merrill, 1785, '89, '90.
Absalom Peters, 1786.
Ephraim True, 1792.
Thomas Boynton, 1793, '95.
Abel Merrill, 1776, 1802, '3, '5, '7, '10, '12, '13 '14, '15, '17, '18, '19, '20, '25.
Anson Welch, 1797.
Ezra Bartlett, 1800, '8, '11.
Obadiah Clement, 1804.
Jonathan Merrill, 1806, '9.
Daniel Patch, 1816, '21, '22, '23, '24.
George Libbey, 1826, '36, '37, '38, '39, '40, '42.
Jacob Patch, 1827, '28, '29, '30, '31, '32, '33, '34.
Anson Merrill, 1835.
Isaac Merrill, 1841, '43, '48, '52, '53.

William Pomeroy, 1844, '45, '47.
Francis A. Cushman, 1846.
Michael P. Merrill, 1849, '50, '51, '54, '55, 56, '57.
William Little, 1858, '59, '60.
Enoch R. Weeks, Jr., 1861, '62, '64, '65, '67.
Samuel B. Page, 1863, '66, '68, '69.
George F. Putnam, 1870.

SCHOOL COMMITTEE.

1829.
David C. French.
Horatio W. Heath.
Robert E Merrill.

1830.
Jacob Patch.
Anson Merrill.
Jonathan Little.

1831.
Isaac Merrill, 2d.
Job E. Merrill.
Russell F. Clifford.

1832.
Jonathan Little.
John L. Merrill.
Nath'l Merrill, 2d.

1833.
Job E. Merrill.
Stevens M. Dow.
Russell K. Clement.

1835.
Job E. Merrill.
Stevens M. Dow.
Anson Merrill.

1837.
Jesse Little.
Moses Merrill.
Russell K. Clement.

1844.
Michael P. Merrill.
David Smith.
James M. Williams.

1845.
David Smith.
Michael P. Merrill.
James M. Williams.

1846.
Michael P. Merrill.
Dudley B. Cotton.
Ira M. Weeks.

1847.
David Smith.
Dudley B. Cotton.
Ira M. Weeks.

1848-'49.
Dudley B. Cotton.
Ira Merrill.
James M. Williams.

1850.
William Merrill.
Albe C. Weeks.
Joseph B. Cotton.

1851.
William Merrill.
Joseph B. Cotton.
James M. Williams.

1852.
Michael P. Merrill.

1853.
James M. Williams.
Ira Merrill.

1854, '55, '56, '69, '70.
Ira Merrill.

1857.
Dudley B. Cotton.

1858, '59.
Russell F. Clifford.

1860.
William Little.

1861.
Alphonzo G. French

1862, '65, '66, '67, '68.
Samuel B. Page.

1863.
Ira M. Weeks.

1864.
Josiah Hooper.

POPULATION AT DIFFERENT PERIODS

1780—(about) 125
1790— 206
1800— 336
1810— 506

1820— 544
1830— 702
1840— 938
1850— 872

1860— 1,152
1870— 960

MONEY TAX.

Year	Amount	Year	Amount	Year	Amount
1779—	£100	1810—	$0.00	1841—	$400.00
1780—	150	1811—	0.00	1842—	800.00
1781—	500	1812—	300.00	1843—	1,000.00
1782—	* 4 1-2	1813—	100.00	1844—	1,200.00
1783—	6	1814—	245.00	1845—	650.00
1784—	5	1815—	0.00	1846—	525.00
1785—	0	1816—	30.00	1847—	425.00
1786—	5	1817—	60.00	1848—	1,000.00
1787—	0	1818—	30.00	1849—	900.00
1788—	3	1819—	75.00	1850—	700.00
1789—	6	1820—	50.00	1851—	800.00
1790—	9	1821—	30.00	1852—	600.00
1791—	6	1822—	40.00	1853—	500.00
1792—	0	1823—	50.00	1854—	550.00
1793—	4 1-2	1824—	75.00	1855—	800.00
1794—	6	1825—	60.00	1856—	1,200.00
1795—	3	1826—	75.00	1857—	1.200.00
1796—	0	1827—	150.00	1858—	1,200.00
1797—	$13.33	1828—	200.00	1859—	1,600.00
1798—	10.00	1829—	300.00	1860—	1,600.00
1799—	0.00	1830—	200.00	1861—	1,600.00
1800—	13.00	1831—	200.00	1862—	1,600.00
1801—	0.00	1832—	200.00	1863—	1,600.00
1802—	15.00	1833—	150.00	1864—	4,000.00
1803—	30.00	1834—	150.00	1865—	4,000.00
1804—	70.00	1835—	400.00	1866—	4,000.00
1805—	160.00	1836—	250.00	1867—	4,000.00
1806—	40.00	1837—	250.00	1868—	4,000.00
1807—	40.00	1838—	300.00	1869—	4,000.00
1808—	75.00	1839—	400.00	1870—	4,000.00
1809—	80.00	1840—	600.00		

* Silver money.

LAWYERS.

The following persons have practiced law in Warren:—

JOSEPH B. HILL — 1855 to 1857.

JOSEPH W. ARMINGTON — 1861, a short time.

SÁMUEL B. PAGE — from 1861 to 1869. Mr. Page was born at Littleton, N. H., June 23, 1838. He was educated at Phillips, Kingston, and Lyndon academies; studied law with Hon. Harry Bingham, of Littleton, and graduated at the Albany Law School in 1861. In 1861 he commenced the practice of law at Warren.

In the course of the next six years he held the offices of moderator, town clerk, and school committee, and also represented the town for seven consecutive sessions in the Legislature.

As a representative he was diligent, worked hard, and was always in his place. During the last two years he was the leader of the House, and as a debater and tactician had no equals.

Mr. Page received the degree of A. M. from Dartmouth College in 1868.

He married Miss Martha C. Lang in 1860. They have had three children, Child L., William H., and Elizabeth Berkley Page.

In 1869 he removed to Concord, N. H., where he had already formed a law partnership with Hon. Ira A. Eastman and John H. Albin, with the firm name of Eastman, Page & Albin, which still continues.

GEORGE F. PUTNAM — 1869 to—. Mr. Putnam, the son of Jo[?] and Almira (*French*) Putnam, was born at Croydon, N. H., Nov. 6, 1841, and is the youngest of a family of eight children. He fitted for college at Thetford Academy, Thetford, Vt., and graduated at Norwich University in 1863. In the fall of that year he commenced the study of law with N. B. Felton, Esq., at Haverhill, N. H., where he remained till the summer of 1866, when he went into the office of Judge C. R. Morrison, and was admitted to the bar at Manchester, Jan. 1, 1867. Mr. P. commenced the practice of law at Haverhill, in the summer of 1867, and remained there until the summer of 1869, when he removed to Warren.

In 1866 and '67 he was superintendent of schools in Haverhill, and in 1868 and 1869 represented that town in the New Hampshire Legislature. In 1870 he represented the town of Warren in the Legislature.

Mr. Putnam married Mary R. Reding, daughter of Sylvester and Ellen D. Reding, Dec. 22, 1868, at Haverhill.

Mr. P. is a young man of fine ability, of genial and courteous manners, and without doubt will make his mark as a good lawyer.

PHYSICIANS.

The following persons have practiced medicine in Warren:—

DR. JOSEPH PETERS was the first. He came in 1791, and lived in town about two years.

APPENDIX.

DR. LEVI ROOT — from 1795, three years.

DR. EZRA BARTLETT — from 1798 to 1812. Dr. Bartlett was the son of Dr. Josiah Bartlett, one of the governors of New Hampshire, and came to Warren in 1798. For a short sketch of him see page 354.

DR. THOMAS WHIPPLE practiced in town from 1811 to 1814. Dr. Whipple was born at Lebanon, N. H., in 1787. He attended the common school of his district, and went to an academy for a few weeks only. In Warren, on Beech hill, he studied Latin by the light of Dr. Bartlett's great fire-place, and also medicine with Dr. B. for about two years. He completed his medical studies with Dr. Nathan Smith, at Hanover, N. H. Attended lectures at the Dartmouth Medical College, and received his diploma Aug. 4, 1810.

Dr. Whipple practiced medicine a short time at Bradford, Vt., and moved to Warren in 1811. While at Warren he held the office of town clerk and selectman. In 1814 he removed to Wentworth, where he lived till his death.

Dr. Whipple possessed great ability, had excellent success in his practice, and living but a short distance from Warren practiced in our town all his life. His face was just as familliar to our citizens as though he was one of their own townsmen. He was free and easy in his manners, and the people were always pleased to see him. His argumentative powers were good, and he was very keen at a joke. Only one man in Warren dared meet him in argument or wit, and that was Stevens Merrill, son of 'Squire Jonathan Merrill. Stevens Merrill was "enough for the doctor," and the latter was often glad to shun our keen, witty farmer. The doctor had a powerful memory and could recite nearly the whole of Virgil and Milton, and much of Shakspeare. Besides his practice in Warren and Wentworth he visited patients in all parts of the county of Grafton and in neighboring towns in Vermont.

At Wentworth Dr. Whipple held nearly every town office in the gift of the people, and for many years represented that town in the Legislature. His greatest triumph was the passage of the "Toleration Act," in 1819. By it all denominations in New Hampshire were placed upon an equality, and every man could support preaching or not, as he felt disposed. In the discussion of the act in the House of Representatives, Dr. Whipple exhibited talents as a debater, equal if not superior to any man in the State.

In 1821, he was elected Representative to Congress, and was re-elected in 1823, 1825, and 1827. He was a prominent, hard-working member, and as a debater on the floor of the House had few equals. He married Phebe Tabor of Bradford, Vt.

Secondly, he married Pricilla Pierce of Royalton, Vt., and their children were Pricilla P., who married Dr. Boney; Phebe T., who married Ben Ayer, of Manchester, now of Chicago, Ill. ; and Celia, who married Mr. Wallace, of Chicago. The latter is a talented lady and a writer of considerable ability.

Dr. Whipple died Jan. 23, 1835, aged forty-eight years, and was buried at Wentworth.

His son, Dr. A. A. Whipple, born in Warren, is now practicing medicine at Wentworth. He is a man of fine ability. Col. Thomas J. Whipple, his second son, is a lawyer of extensive practice, and resides at Laconia.

DR. THOMAS AND PHEBE (*Tabor*) WHIPPLE'S FAMILY RECORD.

Alonzo A., born Feb. 27, 1811.   Walter G., born Nov. —, 1818.
Thomas J., born Jan. 30, 1816.   Caroline B., born Apr. 1, 1820.

DR. ROBERT BURNS practiced from 1816 to 1818, when he moved to Hebron, and from thence to Plymouth. He was a Representative in Congress four years.

DR. JOHN BROADHEAD — from 1818, one year. He was the son of Rev. John Broadhead, Methodist minister.

DR. LABAN LADD — from 1820, two years. He was a native of Haverhill, and died there shortly after he left Warren.

DR. DAVID C. FRENCH — from 1821 to 1870. He was a son of Joseph French, one of the early settlers of Warren, was born in town, and now at the age of eighty years is still in active practice.

DR. JESSE LITTLE — from 1830 to 1865. He was the son of Amos Little, who came to Warren in 1789. Dr. Little studied medicine with Dr. Thomas Whipple, and graduated at the Dartmouth Medical College, Hanover, N. H., in 1828. He practiced

APPENDIX. 539

first at Landaff, and moved to Warren in 1830. He held every office in the gift of his townsmen, and represented the town in the Legislature in 1840 and 1841. He died at Warren, July 29, 1865.

DR. JAMES EMERY — from 1845, one year.

DR. MOODY D. PAGE — in 1849. He lived at the old Homans place, East-parte.

DR. A. BUSWELL — from 1852 to 1854.

DR. ALPHONZO G. FRENCH — from 1853 to 1862. He was a son of Dr. David C. French, graduated at the Medical School at Hanover, in 1853, and died in California, in 1865.

DR. MOSES C. EATON — from 1864 to 1869.

DR. JOHN F. WILLEY, (eclectic)—from 1860 to 1865. He is a son of Nathan Willey, and a nephew of Dr. D. C. French. Dr. Willey returned to Warren in 1870.

DR. CHARLES A. MANNING, (eclectic) — from 1868.

DR. ROBERT E. MERRILL — from 1869. He was the son of Samuel Merrill, and was born in the East-parte district; graduated at the Medical School at Hanover, and after practicing many years at Meredith, Pembroke, and Laconia, moved to Warren.

COLLEGE GRADUATES.

JOSEPH MERRILL, eldest son of Joseph and Sarah (*Copp*) Merrill, was born Oct. 19, 1788. He in a great measure fitted himself for college, and graduated at Dartmouth in 1814; being the first person born in Warren who received college honors. He then engaged a year and a half in teaching in Haverhill, at the same time diligently pursuing the study of law. Thence he removed to Marblehead, Mass., still successfully occupying himself in teaching. Here his theological views and religious character took definite shape, and having made a public profession in 1818, he entered upon the study of theology, under Rev. Samuel Dana. In June, 1820, he was licensed to preach, and was ordained Nov. 15, of the same year, pastor of the Evangelical Congregational Church in the East Parish of Dracut. There he remained thirteen years. He took great interest in the public schools, and special mention is also made of his services to the people of Lowell, in the infancy of that city. As the nearest Congregational pastor he was in constant request for pastoral duties before any minister was settled there. His church in Dracut was blessed during his ministry with three distinct periods of special revival.

Oct. 16, 1833, he removed to Acworth, N. H., where he was settled about five years. While here it is said that "he was favored with the confidence and affection of his people; that he was erect and dignified in person, genial and affable in his manners, and sound and interesting as a preacher." With the assistance of the great revivalist, Burchard, ninety-five persons were converted and added to his church in 1835.

In 1838 he removed to Wellfleet, Mass., and for a considerable time was engaged as a revivalist in different places, with great success. In 1840 he returned to Dracut and was pastor of the church in the West Parish for eight years. He was then elected for two years a member of the Legislature of Massachusetts, and afterwards resided in Lowell.

Mr. Merrill married Eleanor Haynes, of Romney, in 1812. Their children were:—

George Anson, born April 14, 1813. Died May 3, 1835.
Harriet W., born April 15, 1815.
Eleanor H., born Jan. 7, 1818.
Joseph A., born Sept. 13, 1819.
Sarah H., born Feb. 23, 1822.
Mary, born Jan. 22, 1824.
Elizabeth, born March 7, 1826.
Martha, born Dec. 7, 1830.

Rev. Mr. Merrill died at Lowell, Nov. 21, 1856, aged 68 years. In theology Mr. M. was a decided though not an ultra Calvinist. He left behind him nearly fourteen hundred written sermons, a part only of those which he prepared and preached, and a memorandum in his hand writing records that he preached 3,077 times during thirty years of his ministry, from manuscript, besides all his unwritten sermons, lectures, and addresses.

WILLIAM LITTLE, son of Jesse and Susan Copp (*Merrill*) Little, born March 20, 1833; graduated at Dartmouth, 1859; studied law and practiced at Manchester, N. H.

GEORGE LEROY GLEASON, son of Rev. Salmon and Jerusha (*Willard*) Gleason, was born Feb. 25, 1835; graduated at Dartmouth, 1861; studied at the Andover, Mass., Theological School, and preached at Rutland, Vt., and at Manchester, Mass. He was ordained pastor of the Congregational Church at Bristol, Vt., Feb. 1, 1865.

JOHN MERRILL, son of Abel and Tamar (*Kimball*) Merrill; born March 4, 1786; entered Dartmouth 1806. He died while a member of the sophomore class. The following lines are to be found on his tombstone:—

> Behold the blooming youth is gone;
> The much loved object's fled:
> Entered his long eternal home,
> And numbered with the dead.
>
> But he shall live and rise again
> Enrobed in bright array;
> Shall take his part in heavenly strains,
> In Everlasting day.

LEMUEL MERRILL, son of Joseph and Sarah (*Copp*) Merrill; born Nov. 8, 1793; entered Dartmouth College in 1814, but did not graduate. He studied law and practiced with good success, acquiring a large property, at Tuskega, Ala. He died about 1862.

GEORGE ALFRED LITTLE, son of Jesse and Susan Copp (*Merrill*) Little, born May 23, 1847, and entered Dartmouth in 1867.

The following have received college honors:—

MOSES H. BIXBY — the degree of A. M., in 1868, at Dartmouth.

SAMUEL B. PAGE — the degree of A. M., in 1868, at Dartmouth.

GEORGE F. PUTNAM — the degree of A. M., in 1870, at Dartmouth.

The following Methodist ministers have preached in town:—

Rev. Elijah R. Sabin.	Rev. N. W. Aspinwall.	Rev. James Martin.
Thomas Skeel.	C. R. Harding.	J. A. Sweatland.
Joel Winch.	J. W. Morey.	Silas G. Kellogg.
Jacob Sanborn.	Phineas Peck.	S. Holman.
John Lord.	S. A. Cushing.	J. A. Scarritt.
Wm. Plumbly.	Enos Wells.	L. L. Eastman.
John Davis.	R. Dearborn.	Rufus Tilton.
Walter Sleeper.	Moses Merrill.	O. H. Call.
Newell Culver.	J. W. Sanborn.	James Adams.
Charles Baker.	Salmon Gleason.	Charles Smith.
Nathan Howe.	B. R. Hoyt.	Josiah Hooper.
Damon Young.	Kimball Hadley.	W. H. Jones.
Caleb Dustin.	L. D. Blodgett.	
J. H. Hardy.	Samuel Baker.	

The following Free-will Baptist ministers have preached in town:—

Rev. Joseph Boody.	Rev. James Spencer.	Rev. G. W. Cogswell.
Jos. Boody, Jr.	Joseph Quimby.	J. Moulton.
Lewis Harriman.	Amasa Messer.	—— Sargeant.
Thomas Perkins.	Aaron Buzwell.	Horace Webber.
J. Marks.	S. Doane.	J. D. Cross.
John Wallace.	—— Leavitt.	

The following Universalist ministers have preached in town:—

Rev. John E. Palmer, 1838 to 1841   Rev. Chas. C. Clark,1852 to 1853
S. A. Johnson,   1841 " 1845   S. W. Squire,   1853 " 1859
Alson Scott,   1845 " 1849   T. Barron,   1858 " 1861
Macey B. Newell, 1849 " 1851

CHORISTERS.

Samuel Knight.	Capt. Benj. Little.	Gen. M. P. Merrill.
Samuel Merrill.	Joseph Boynton.	Capt. Ira M. Weeks.
James Dow.	Dr. Jesse Little.	William Merrill.
Paul Taber.*	Col. S. M. Dow.	Albert Bixby.

* Taber was a brother-in-law of Dr. Thomas Whipple.

POSTMASTERS.

Amos Burton.	Asa Thurston.
Anson Merrill.	George W. Prescott.
Dr. Jesse Little.	Charles C. Durant.
Dr. David C. French.	Russell K. Clement.
Levi C. Whitcher.	Ezra Bartlett Eaton.

The following are persons born in Warren who afterwards became lawyers:—

Lemuel Merrill, practiced at Tuskega, Alabama.

Joseph F. Merrill, practiced in Port Huron, Michigan.

Benjamin Bixby, practiced in Ohio.

William Little, practiced in Manchester, N. H.

The following are persons once living in Warren, who afterwards became ministers of the gospel:—

REV. JOSEPH MERRILL, Congregationalist. (See biography, page 539.)

REV. FREDERICK CLARK, ordained in Warren in 1817, in the barn at the forks of the turnpike and Coventry road.

APPENDIX. 543

Rev. Horace Webber, Free-will Baptist, ordained in Warren in 1836. Col. Moses H. Clement objected to his being ordained in Warren, unless he would sign acquittance to the minister lands, which Mr. Webber did.

Rev. Charles Bowles, Free-will Baptist. (See sketch on page 286.)

Rev. Moses Merrill, Methodist. He was born on Beech hill, in Warren, June 26, 1802, and is the son of Nathaniel Merrill, and grandson of Rev. Nathaniel Merrill, of Boscawen, who was the brother of Stevens and Joshua Merrill, early settlers of Warren. Mr. Merrill was an excellent school teacher as well as minister, and the writer of this owes much to his teaching and encouragement.

Rev. Ezekiel Dow, Congregationalist. He is the son of James Dow, and was born on Pine hill in Warren, April 9, 1807.

Rev. Charles Bowles, Jr., Congregationalist. He was ordained as minister at Bridgewater, N. H., in 1825, and preached there three and one-half years.—Hist. of N. H. Churches, 515.

Rev. Heber Kimball, Mormon. He was a great high priest in his church, and next to Brigham Young in authority. At his death he left an estate valued at $80,000, and forty-one children, thirty sons and eleven daughters, to share it. When in Warren he used to tend bar for Mr. Anson Merrill, and sell rum to the customers.

Rev. Addison Patch, Methodist. He was the son of Joseph Patch, Jr.

Rev. William Bixby, Methodist.

Benjamin Bixby, Methodist.

George W. Bixby, Calvin Baptist.

Rev. Moses H. Bixby, Calvin Baptist. Rev. Mr. Bixby, the son of Benjamin and —— (*Cleasby*) Bixby, was born in Warren, August 21, 1827. At the age of twelve years he experienced religion, and having a strong conviction that he would at sometime preach the gospel, he entered at once on a course of preparation.

He began his studies at the Literary and Theological Seminary at Newbury, Vt., then attended the seminary at Derby, Vt., two years, and finished his course at the Baptist College, in the city of Montreal, where he enjoyed decided advantages, being instructed by Rev. J. M. Cramp, D. D., and Rev. Dr. Davis, of London.

Mr. Bixby was ordained to the gospel ministry in 1849, at the age of twenty-two years, at Williston, Vt., and was married that year to Miss Susan C. Dow, daughter of Deacon Gilman Dow, of Hardwick, Vt.

After four years of pastoral work in this country he received an appointment of the American Baptist Missionary Union, as a missionary to Burmah.

For four years he labored ardently and successfully in that country, when Mrs. Bixby's health failed, and he was obliged to return home, His wife shortly after died at Burlington, Vt.

He soon after settled in Providence, R. I., as pastor of the Friendship Street Church, and afterwards married Miss Laura A. Gage, who was then and had been for several years principal of the New Hampton Female Seminary.

In 1860 the Missionary Union gave him an appointment as missionary to open a new mission in Burmah, for the Shaus.

With his family he spent eight years at that station, and labored with signal success, when failing health compelled him to return to America.

Mr. Bixby is now settled as the pastor of the Cranston Street Baptist Church, Providence, R. I. He has been a missionary in Eastern Asia twelve years, and a pastor in this country eight years. He has preached the gospel in Europe, Asia, Africa, and America, with a good degree of success; and the denomination to which he belongs holds him in high esteem. The degree of Master of Arts was conferred upon him by Dartmouth College, while he was absent from the country.

Mr. B. has eight brothers, five of whom have been ministers of the gospel. Their names are found in the accompanying list of ministers. His father and mother are still living at Warren, aged respectively eighty and seventy-five years. His grandfather, Wm.

Cleasby, died in Warren, at the age of ninety-five years. We give this extended account of Mr. B. for we regard him as one of the most able and eloquent of Warren's sons.

 Rev. Dudley C. Bixby, Calvin Baptist.

 William Merrill, Methodist.

 Addison W. Eastman, Methodist.

 George Leroy Gleason, Congregationalist.

 Charles W. Cushman, Methodist.

 George C. Noyes, Methodist.

 James M. Copp, Methodist.

 Lafayette W. Parker, Methodist.

 Timothy Clifford, Methodist.

 John French, Spiritualist.

The following are persons once living in Warren who afterwards became doctors:—

 Dr. Eliphalet Copp. He was the son of Joshua Copp, and practiced in New Jersey.

 Dr. David C. French.

 Jesse Little.

 Alonzo A. Whipple.

 Levi B. Foot.

 Dr. William Merrill. He was the son of Abel Merrill, graduated at the Dartmouth Medical School, Hanover, and after practicing a short time at Lisbon, died.

 Dr. Levi Bartlett, son of Dr. Ezra Bartlett.

 Josiah Bartlett, son of Dr. Ezra Bartlett.

 Robert E. Merrill.

 Horatio Heath.

Dr. TRISTRAM HAYNES. He removed to Vermont, opened a great water-cure establishment and home for invalids; amassed a large fortune, and died leaving an estate of over fifty thousand dollars.

Dr. WORCESTER EATON BOYNTON. Dr. Boynton, the son of Samuel H. and Mehitable (*Clark*) Boynton, was born on Beech hill, Warren, March 26, 1824. His early education was acquired at the common schools, and at Newbury, Vt., Seminary. He received a diploma from the Medical University of New York, and also another diploma from the Mass. Medical College, and commenced the practice of medicine at East Hopkinton, N. H., in 1851. He has since practiced in Concord, Nashua, Dover, and Lawrence, Mass., at which latter place he is now located. He is the inventor of the "Electric Med. Lung Flannels," for which he was awarded a diploma; and of a "Lung Barometer" of acknowledged merit. He is also the author of several medical works, of which his treatise on the "Human Eye," the "Medical Instructor," and the "Private Medical Lectures," are the most important. These works were all well received by the public. Dr. Boynton has had excellent success in his practice. He is the proprietor of several kinds of medicine which find a ready sale in different parts of the world. One brother, David M. Boynton, and his only sister, Mrs. Bixby, also reside in Lawrence. Dr. B. married Miss Ada A. Lane, of Nashua, N. H., in 1857.

Dr. ALPHONZO G. FRENCH.

Dr. JOHN F. WILLEY.

Dr. FRANCIS L. GERALD. He graduated at the Medical School in Philadelphia, and is a young physician of much promise. He is now located at Nashua, N. H.

MILITARY OFFICERS.

The following persons who have lived in Warren have held military positions.

GEN. MICHAEL P. MERRILL.

GEN. ABSALOM PETERS. He was a Captain in the Revolution.

Col. Obadiah Clement.
William Tarleton. He was a Captain in the Revolution.
Benjamin Stone. He was a Captain in the Revolution and drew a pension of $216 a year.)
David Patch. He commanded as Captain in the 1812 war.
Moses H. Clement.
Benjamin Clement.
Isaac Merrill.
Stevens M. Dow.

Maj. Daniel Patch. He was also a Quartermaster in the 1812 war.
True Stevens.
Simeon S. Clifford.
Ira Libbey.

Capt. William Butler.
Stephen Flanders.
James Aiken. He was a Capt. in the Revolution.
John Mills. He was a Captain in the Revolution.
David S. Craige.
Joseph Patch, Jr.
Jonathan Ramsey.
Daniel Merrill.
Benjamin Merrill.
Samuel L. Merrill.
Perkins Fellows. He was a Lieut. in 1812 war.
Stephen Richardson.
Joseph Rollins.
William Clough.
Enoch R. Weeks.

Capt. Jonathan Clough.
George Libbey.
Benjamin Little.
John Low.
Hosea Lund.
Russell K. Clement.
Moses H. Clement, Jr.
John L. Merrill.
Joseph Merrill.
Ira Merrill.
Stephen Marston.
Ira M. Weeks.
Isaac Sawtelle.
Dudley B. Cotton.
David Harris.
Nathan Harris.
Nathaniel Merrill.

HISTORY OF WARREN.

The following is the record of the Divisions of Lots in the township of Warren, as they were drawn to their several original rights, and entered on the original plan, viz:—

FIRST DIVISION OF LOTS.

NAMES OF PROPRIETORS.	Range.	No. of lot.	NAMES OF PROPRIETORS.	Range.	No. of lot.
Thomas True	1	1	Capt. Henry Pierce	5	10
Ebenezer Stevens, Esq.	1	2	Moses Greeley	5	11
John Batchelder	1	3	Josiah Bartlett	6	1
Nathaniel Barrell, Esq.	1	4	Ebenezer Morrill	6	2
Lemuel Stevens	1	5	Phillip Tilton	6	3
John Page, Esq.	1	6	Ebenezer Collins	6	4
Samuel Osgood	2	1	Aaron Clough	6	5
Belcher Dole	2	2	Capt. John Hazen	6	6
Peter Coffin	2	3	Reuben True	6	7
Daniel Page	2	4	Jacob Currier	6	8
Capt. Ephraim Brown	2	5	Henry Morrill	7	1
Joseph Whitcher	2	6	James Graves	7	2
Joseph Blanchard, Esq.	3	1	Jacob Hook, Esq.	7	3
Enoch Page	3	2	John Marsh	7	4
Stephen Webster	3	3	Andrew Wiggin, Esq.	7	5
Ebenezer Page	3	4	Jonathan Greeley, Esq.	7	6
Silas Nowell	3	5	Trueworthy Ladd	7	7
Joseph Greeley	3	6	Capt. John Parker	7	8
Minister	4	2	Benj. French, Jr.	8	1
Jeremy Webster, Esq.	4	3	The Society for Propagating the Gospel	8	2
James Nevin, Esq.	4	4
Andrew Greeley	4	5	Nathaniel Currier	8	3
Nathaniel Fifield	4	6	Jonathan Greeley	8	4
Capt. George March	4	7	Benjamin Clough	8	5
Ephraim Page	4	8	Francis Batchelder	8	6
Abel Davis	4	9	Enoch Chase	8	7
Theodore Atkinson, Jr.	4	10	Samuel Graves	8	8
Moses Page	5	3	Dyer Hook	8	9
Wm. Whitcher	5	4	Jacob Gale	8	10
Abraham Morrill	5	5	Glebe for the Church	9	1
David Clough	5	6	David Morrill	9	2
Joseph Page	5	7	School lot	9	3
Samuel Dudley	5	8	John Darling	9	4
Joseph Tilton	5	9	Reuben True	9	5

Samuel Page, John Page, Jr., and Wm. Parker, Jr., their lots being taken into Wentworth, have each two lots in the second division.

APPENDIX. 549

THE SECOND DIVISION OF HUNDRED ACRE LOTS.
[Drawn March 25, 1771.]

Names of Proprietors.	Range.	No. of lot.	Names of Proprietors.	Range.	No. of lot.
David Morrill	1	2	Ebenezer Collins	5	3
Josiah Bartlett, Esq.	1	4	John Page,	5	4
Capt. John Hazen	1	5	Joseph Blanchard	5	5
Aaron Clough, Jr.	1	6	Moses Greeley,	5	6
Enoch Chase	1	7	Ephraim Brown	5	7
Ephraim Page	1	8	P. White, for two settlers	5	8
William Parker, Jr.	1	9	Enoch Page	5	9
Nathaniel Fifield	1	10	Dyer Hook	5	10
Joseph Tilton	1	11	Samuel Dudley	5	11
Capt. John Parker	1	12	Silas Newell	5	12
Phillips Tilton	1	13	Theo. Atkinson, Jr.	5	13
David Clough	2	1	Nathaniel Currier	5	14
Stephen Webster	2	2	Henry Morrill	5	15
Hon. Nathaniel Barrell	2	3	Jonathan Greeley	6	9
Lemuel Stevens	2	4	Joseph Whitcher	6	10
Minister lot	2	5	Daniel Page	6	11
John Marsh	2	6	Hon. James Nevins	6	12
Trueworthy Ladd	3	1	Belcher Dole	6	13
Moses Page	3	2	William Whittier	6	14
Ebenezer Page	3	3	Reuben French	6	15
Jacob Gale	3	4	Jeremy Webster	6	16
Ebenezer Morrill	3	5	Church of England	6	17
Samuel Page	3	6	John Batchelder	6	18
Samuel Osgood	4	1	John Page, Jr.	6	19
Capt. Thos. Pierce	4	2	Samuel Page	7	14
Benjamin French	4	3	School lot	7	15
Jacob Currier	4	4	John Page, Jr.	7	16
Jonathan Greeley	4	5	Peter Coffin	7	17
Jacob Hook	4	6	Abraham Morrill	7	18
Joseph Page	4	7	Andrew Greeley	7	19
Francis Batchelder	4	8	James Graves	8	14
John Darling	4	9	Reuben True	8	15
Samuel Graves	4	10	Andrew Wiggin	8	16
Benj. Clough	4	11	Abel Davis	8	17
Capt. George March	4	12	Joseph Greeley,	8	18
Soc. for Propagating the Gospel	5	1	Thomas True	8	19
Wm. Parker, Jr.	5	2			

Those that have two lots drawn in this division is to make up for their first division lots that were taken into Wentworth.

July 7th, 1789, Joseph Page reported that they had laid out the Governor's 500 acre lot, and also 27 lots on the line of Piermont.

Voted to draw said lots, and they were drawn as follows:—

Names of Proprietors.	Range.	No. of lot.	Names of Proprietors.	Range.	No. of lot.
Thomas True	1	12	Moses Page	3	12
David Morrill	1	13	John Marsh	3	13
Stevens Webster	1	14	Joseph Greeley	3	14
Samuel Osgood	1	15	Minister lot	3	15
Aaron Clough	1	16	Andrew Greeley	4	13
William Parker	1	17	Trueworthy Ladd	4	14
Col. Stevens	1	18	Samuel Osgood	4	15
Lemuel Stevens	2	12	School lot	4	16
Jacob Gale	2	13	John Hazen	4	17
Gospel lot	2	14	John Page, Jr.,	4	18
Samuel Page	2	15	Belcher Dole	5	16
Ebenezer Morrill	2	16	Josiah Bartlett	5	17
Thomas True	2	17	Ebenezer Page	15	18
David Clough	2	18			

At a meeting held Oct. 20, 1796, at Lemuel Keezer's Inn in Wentworth, (formerly in Warren) the following lots were pitched in the

THIRD DIVISION.

Names of Proprietors.	No. of lot.	Names of Proprietors.	No. of lot.
William Parker, Jr.	1	Nathaniel Currier	35
John Darling	2	Andrew Greeley	36
Jacob Currier	3	Samuel Graves	37
Benjamin Clough	4	Trueworthy Ladd	38
Thomas True	5	Jeremy Webster	39
Jonathan Greeley	6	Ephraim Page	40
Daniel Page	7	Capt. Thomas Pierce	41
John March	8	Andrew Wiggin	42
Joseph Whitcher	9	David Clough	43
Francis Batchelder	10	James Nevins, (pitch $40)	44
School	11	Joseph Greeley	45
Jacob Hook	12	John Page, Jr.	46
Joseph Tilton	13	Nathaniel Fifield	47
Ebenezer Morrill	14	Jacob Gale	48
Reuben True	15	William Whitcher	49
Minister	16	Samuel Osgood	50
Aaron Clough, Jr.	17	James Graves	51
Peter Coffin, Jr.	18	Ephraim Brown	52
Moses Greeley, of Salisbury	19	Enoch Chase	53
Silas Nowell, marked 69 on trees	20	Capt. John Hazen	54
John Page	21	Phillips Tilton	55
Samuel Page	22	Moses Page	56
Abraham Morrill	23	Lemuel Stevens	57
Josiah Bartlett	24	Samuel Dudley	58
Reuben French	25	Joseph Page	59
Nathaniel Barrell	26	Enoch Page	60
Ebenezer Collins	27	Ebenezer Stevens	61
Henry Morrill	28	Joseph Blanchard	62
John Batchelder	29	Abel Davis	63
Dyer Hook	30	Theodore Atkinson, Jr.	64
Jonathan Greeley	31	Belcher Dole	65
Capt. George March	32	Benjamin French, Jr.	66
Stephen Webster, (pitch $40)	33	David Morrill	67
Ebenezer Page, (pitch $42)	34	Capt. John Parker	68

TAXES OF THE CITIZENS OF WARREN FOR 1780.

[STATE AND CONTINENTAL TAXES.]

NAMES.	First.			Second.			Third.			Fourth.			Town Tax.			Beef Tax.		
	£	s.	d.	£	s.	d.	£	s.	d.	£	s.	d.	£	s.	d.	£	s.	d.
Thomas Clark	2	13	0	1	6	6	2	13	0	1	6	6	6	12	0	5	6	0
Isaiah Batchelder	5	18	4	2	19	2	5	18	4	2	19	2	5	16	0	7	16	8
Reuben Whitcher	4	14	0	2	7	0	4	14	0	2	7	0	3	4	0	2	8	0
Ephraim True	11	2	8	5	11	4	11	2	8	5	11	4	6	0	0	22	5	4
William Butler	14	1	0	7	0	6	14	1	0	7	0	6	8	8	0	28	2	0
Simeon Smith	8	7	7	4	3	9	8	7	7	4	3	9	13	1	4	18	15	2
John Morrill	2	6	5	1	3	3	2	6	5	1	3	3	1	14	8	4	12	10
Stevens Merrill	21	15	9	10	17	9	21	15	9	10	17	9	12	14	8	43	10	6
Jonathan Merrill	1	2	8	0	11	4	1	2	8	0	11	4	6	16	0	2	5	4
Joshua Merrill	4	3	7	2	4	9	4	3	7	2	4	9	8	11	4	8	19	2
Joshua Copp	8	14	11	4	7	5	8	14	11	4	7	5	15	13	4	17	9	10
Jonathan Clement	4	17	1	2	8	7	4	17	1	2	8	7	11	10	8	9	14	2
Obadiah Clement	7	17	7	3	18	10	7	17	7	3	18	10	13	17	8	15	15	2
Reuben Clement	6	3	7	3	1	10	6	3	7	3	1	10	[illegible]	17	8	12	7	2
John Whitcher	6	2	11	3	1	6	6	2	11	3	1	6	7	16	4	12	5	11
Joseph Patch	4	8	3	2	4	1	4	8	3	2	4	1	10	13	4	8	16	6
Daniel Clark	4	16	0	2	8	0	4	16	0	2	8	0	10	16	0	9	12	0
Chase Whitcher	7	11	8	3	15	10	7	11	8	3	15	10	5	16	6	15	3	4
Joseph Kimball	4	4	8	2	2	4	4	4	8	2	2	4	0	6	8	-	-	-
Nathaniel Niles	0	13	4	0	6	8	0	13	4	0	6	8	4	2	0	1	6	8
Ephraim Lund	0	16	0	0	8	0	0	16	0	0	8	0	4	16	0	1	12	0
Joseph Lund	0	16	0	0	8	0	0	16	0	0	8	0	4	16	0	1	12	0
Moses True	0	4	6	0	2	0	0	4	6	0	2	0	1	4	0	0	8	6
John Marston	0	13	4	0	6	8	0	13	4	0	6	8	0	4	0	1	6	8
Gardner Dustin	1	0	0	0	10	0	1	0	0	0	10	0	0	10	0	-	-	-

INVENTORY OF WARREN FOR 1781.

NAMES.	No. of Polls.	Arable.	Mowing.	Pasturing.	Horses.	Oxen.	Cows.	Three years old.	Two years old.	One year old.	Unimproved land.	Tax in silver.		
												£	s.	d.
Peter Stevens	1	-	-	-	1	-	-	-	-	-	-	0	1	10
Simeon Smith	1	2	8	8	1	2	2	-	-	-	171	0	5	3½
John Morrill	1	1	2	-	-	-	1	-	-	-	47	0	1	11
Joseph Patch	1	2	5	12	-	-	1	3	-	-	77	0	3	5½
William Butler	1	2	2	-	1	2	1	-	-	-	616	0	10	9¾
Jonathan Merrill	1	-	-	-	-	2	2	-	-	-	-	0	1	6¾
Stevens Merrill	1	4	10	-	2	2	3	-	-	-	386	0	7	9¾
Joshua Merrill	1	2	8	4	1	-	2	-	3	-	86	0	3	11
Joshua Copp	2	3	12	4	2	-	3	-	4	1	333	0	8	3½
Jonathan Clement	1	3	8	2	1	2	1	-	-	-	87	0	2	9¾
Obadiah Clement	1	3	12	4	1	-	2	2	2	1	300	0	6	9¾
Reuben Clement	1	-	3	-	-	-	1	-	-	-	150	0	2	10
Thomas Clark	1	1	5	1	1	-	1	1	-	-	45	0	2	7½
Isaiah Batchelder	1	1	-	-	-	-	1	-	3	-	95	0	1	7
Jonathan Foster	1	-	-	-	-	-	1	-	-	-	50	0	3	11½
Daniel Clark	1	2	8	-	1	2	1	1	-	1	90	0	3	1½
Reuben Whitcher	1	1	6	-	1	-	1	-	-	1	93	0	3	1½
John Whitcher	1	3	4	2	-	2	1	1	-	-	141	0	3	10¼
Amos Heath	1	-	-	-	-	-	1	-	-	-	-	0	1	4½
Chase Whitcher	1	2	2	-	-	-	1	-	2	-	196	0	3	10¼
Ephraim True	1	3	4	4	1	-	1	1	1	-	240	0	5	6½
John Marston	1	-	-	-	-	-	-	-	-	-	-	0	0	11½
John True	1	-	-	-	-	-	-	-	-	-	100	0	1	11½
Aaron True	1	-	-	-	-	-	-	-	-	-	100	0	1	11½
Henry Sunbury	1	-	-	-	-	-	-	-	-	-	100	0	1	11½
William Whiteman	1	-	-	-	-	-	-	-	-	-	100	0	1	11½
Joseph French	1	-	-	-	-	-	-	-	-	-	-	0	0	11½
Charles Bowles	1	-	-	-	-	-	-	-	-	-	-	0	0	11¼
William Tarleton	1	-	-	-	-	-	-	-	-	-	-	0	0	11¼
John Hinkson	1	-	-	-	-	-	1	-	-	-	50	0	1	7¾

LONGEVITY.

The two following tables were most of them taken from a record by Mrs. Levi C. Whitcher:—

Year	Name	Age	Year	Name	Age
1808	Anna Bixby died aged	84	1853	Mrs. John Farnham,	85
1810	Mrs. Rebecca Clough,	82	1854	Mrs. Ingraham,	85
1811	Thomas Richardson,	92	1856	James Dow,	81
1811	Phebe Richardson,	92	1856	John Farnham,	90
1826	Jesse Brown,	102	1856	Mrs. Samuel Merrill,	81
1826	Reuben Batchelder,	85	1856	Mrs. Hoyt,	84
1829	Obadiah Clement,	87	1859	Moses Kimball,	80
1840	Joshua Merrill,	100	1859	Mrs. Cross,	82
1842	Mrs. Jonathan Clement,	80	1860	Nathan Willey,	83
1843	Phebe Abbott,	87	1862	Mrs. Clark,	83
1843	Joseph Lund,	92	1863	Samuel Merrill,	84
1843	Joseph French,	84	1863	Mrs. Nathan Willey,	87
1844	Mrs. George Bixby,	80	1864	Mrs. Stephen Boynton,	84
1846	Samuel Knight,	86	1865	William Cleasby,	95
1846	Mrs. John Whitcher,	80	1865	Chase Marston,	80
1847	Elizabeth Merrill,	80	1865	Mrs. R. Whiteman,	81
1849	Mrs. Abbott,	81	1866	Mrs. Stevens Merrill,	86
1851	Mrs. Polly Knowlton,	82	1867	Enoch R. Weeks,	80
1851	Nathaniel Clough,	86	1868	Mrs. Moses Kimball,	82
1852	Mrs. Joseph French,	83	1869	Bijah Wright,	95
1852	Joseph Lund,	85			

DEATHS IN WARREN.

1841— 8 died.	1851—13 died.	1861—15 died.
1842—18.	1852—20.	1862—19.
1843—29.	1853—14.	1863—40.
1844— 9.	1854—15.	1864—16.
1845— 4.	1855—16.	1865—27.
1846—15.	1856—23.	1866—10.
1847—10.	1857— 6.	1867—12.
1848— 3.	1858—18.	1868—16.
1849—18.	1859—15.	1869— 9.
1850—14.	1860—14.	1870—12.

The following persons were living in Warren, A. D. 1870, over seventy years of age:—

Name	Age	Name	Age
Abbott, Anna.	82	Carleton, Rodney.	71
		Clement, Benjamin	71
Barker, Charles	82	Clement, Tamar.	81
Barker, Mary,	79	Clough, L. Mercy.	76
Batchelder, Abigail,	81	Clough, Sally.	75
Bixby, Benjamin, .	80	Colby, David.	74
Bixby, Betsey	76	Cotton, Eliza.	76
Bixby, Joseph	76		
Bixby, Mary,	76	Davis, Ruth.	85
Bixby, Samuel B.	74		

APPENDIX. 553

Eaton, Betsey.	80	Martin, Stephen	70
Eaton, Jonathan	76	Marsh, Mary,	73
		McCarter, Antony.	77
Farnham, Betsey	76	Merrill, Sally.	70
Farnham, Joseph B.	73		
French, David C.	80	Noyes, Orra.	71
Gale, Lydia	80	Osborn, Samuel	70
Glover, Benjamin	83		
Goodwin, Samuel	70	Patch, Betsey.	86
		Perry, Percy.	80
Haines, Susan *	70	Pomeroy, Durocsy.	71
Heath, Asa	80	Pope, Naomi.	87
Kenney, Elizabeth	74	Richardson, Nathaniel	77
Kenney, Hugh	75	Richardson, Sarah.	70
Leathers, Vowell	87	Swain, Josiah	80
Libbey, George	77		
Libbey, John.	73	Warren, Lucy B.	76
Libbey, Nancy	75	Weeks, Sally.	80
Libbey, Nathaniel	75	Whitcher, Ruth	88
Libbey, Sally	76	Whiteman, Stephen	87
Little, Sally	73	Willey Nathan	74

GENEALOGIES.

We insert the following, being nearly all we could find in the town books. Pity 'tis that families do not have their family records recorded on the town books, the same as they did in old times; and a thousand times more pity 'tis that families have no children of any consequence to record. Oh! it is the meanest of all mean things to let our race "play out" by being too mean, too stingy, too lazy to have children.

ABBOTT, JOHN. Ch., Sally, b. Oct. 1, 1793; Nancy, Jan. 31, 1795; Polly, June 30, 1796; Betsey, Oct. 15, 1797; Susanna, Feb. 7, 1799; Ruth, Oct. 6, 1800; Hannah, Jan. 18, 1802; Ruth, Aug. 21, 1803; Cotton, Aug. 12, 1805; Enoch M., Aug. 13, 1807.

BARKER, EBENEZER, m. Anna Clement, July 28, 1800. Ch., Sally, b. Dec. 30, 1801; Abigail, Feb. 1, 1804; Nancy, Dec. 9, 1808.

BATCHELDER, REUBEN, m. Hannah'Merrill, June 22, 1794. Ch., Ward Cotton, b. March 25, 1795; Reuben, Dec. 6, 1796, died Nov. 17, 1797; Reuben, July 14, 1798; Nathaniel, Aug. 25, 1800; Betsey, Oct. 17, 1802.

BOYNTON, SAMUEL H., m. Mehitable Clark. Ch. Louisa, b. Jan. 14, 1818; David, Nov. 2, 1819; Maria, May 29, 1821; Worcester E., Mar. 26, 1824.

BOYNTON, NATHANIEL, son of Sir Matthew Boynton, of Salem, Mass. Ch., Nathaniel, lost at sea; David, Richard, Asa, kept hotel at Haverhill Corner; Thomas, he was grandfather of Dr. W. E. Boynton; Eunice, Polly, Louis. Sir Matthew Boynton, of Old Salem, was a man of estate; owned much land, horses, cows, sheep, goats, swine, &c. He held important offices of trust, and discharged his duties with fidelity.

BOYNTON, THOMAS, son of Nathaniel, and grandson of Sir Matthew Boynton, m. Elizabeth Keezer, 1775. Ch., Betsey, b. Sept. 2, 1777; Elizabeth, Oct. 8, 1778; Stephen, Dec. 21, 1780; Thomas, Jan. 18, 1783; Sally, Dec. 29, 1784; Abigail, Dec. 30, 1787; Samuel H., father of Dr. Worcester Eaton Boynton, Nov. 25, 1790; Mary, Dec. 21, 1792; Joseph, June 10, 1795; Timothy, Aug. —, 1797; Nathaniel, May —, 1800.

CLARK, THOMAS, b. at Hampstead, N. H., m. Hannah Foster, of Hopkinton, N. H., granddaughter of Hannah Eastman, who was captured by the Indians at Haverhill, and carried by them to upper Coos. Ch., Amos, Hezekiah, Joseph, Betsey, Hannah, Sarah, and Mehitable, who was the mother of Dr. W. E. Boynton.

CLIFFORD, TIMOTHY. Ch., Dolly, b. May 9, 1799; Russell Freeman, Feb. 9, 1802; Polly, Sept. 21, 1803; Ruth, Oct. 24, 1805; Timothy, Jr., Sept. 24, 1807; Mehitable, July 30, 1810; Absalom, May 15, 1812; Simeon Smith, Sept. 9, 1814; John C., Nov. 9, 1817.

CLOUGH, AMOS, son of Nathaniel, b. May 12, 1797; m. Orra Jewett. She was b. Jan. 5, 1799, at Rowley, Mass. Ch., Aaron J., b. March 31, 1821; Columbus, May 19, 1825; George M., Jan. 13, 1827; Orra A., July 17, 1830; Amos F., Feb. 24, 1833. Amos Clough died Jan. 7, 1833.

DOW, JAMES, m. Ruth Williams. Ch., Susanna, b. June 21, 1796; Sally, Dec. 24, 1798; Ruth, Aug. 24, 1800. Ruth Williams Dow died Aug. 28, 1800. James Dow m. Hannah Merrill. Ch., Betsey, b. Dec. 5, 1801; Stevens M., Nov. 29, 1804; Ezekiel, Apr. 9, 1807; Jonathan Merrill, Feb. 2, 1809; Lorenzo, Sept. 12, 1811.

FRENCH, JOSEPH, m. Polly or Molly Batchelder. Ch., David C., b. April 21, 1791; Hannah, Mar. 1, 1793; Joseph, Nov. 16, 1794; Polly, Apr. 9, 1797; Mehitable, June 30, 1799; Daniel, Nov. 7, 1801; Reuben B., May 12, 1804; John, Nov. 24, 1806; Benj. M., July 6, 1809; Sally A., Aug. 5, 1811.

JEWELL, SAMUEL, m. Sally Foot, Nov. 25, 1802. Ch., Betsey F., Nov. 7, 1802; David, Dec. 13, 1804; Lovina, July 30, 1807; Fanny D., Mar. 15, 1809; David M., June 4, 1811; Dolly F., Apr. 27, 1814; Samuel, Mar. 15, 1816; Levi F., July 4, 1818; Jacob, ——; Alonzo, ——.

LIBBEY, GEORGE, m. Sally Abbott. Ch., Hazen, b. June 10, 1815; Anna, Nov. 3, 1816; John, Feb. 9, 1819; Mary H., June 21, 1821; John, Nov. 12, 1823; Walter, July 29, 1826; Mary, Oct. 26, 1831.

LIBBEY, LUKE, m. Anna ——. Ch., George, b. Aug. 22, 1792; Nathaniel P., Mar. 2, 1795; John W., June 19, 1797; Stephen W., Oct. 20, 1799; Ezra Bartlett, Aug. 24, 1801; Anna Patch, Feb. 26, 1804; Jonathan M., Mar. 8, 1806; Obadiah Clement, Dec. 15, 1807.

LITTLE, GEORGE, came from Unicorn St., London, Eng., to Newbury, Mass., in 1640, m. Alice Poor. Ch., Sarah, b. May 8, 1652, d. Nov. 19, 1652; Joseph, Sept. 22, 1653; John, July 28, 1655, d. July 20, 1672; Moses, Mar. 11, 1657; Sarah, Nov. 24, 1661. His wife, Alice, d. Dec. 1, 1680. Married Eleanor Barnard, of Amesbury, July 19, 1681. He d. about Nov. 27, 1694, as the Amesbury records say: " Widow Eleanor Little d. Nov. 27, 1694." He lived a few rods from the house now occupied by Silas Little. He was remarkable for strength of mind as well as strength of body, but was not an educated man. The farms which he selected in Newbury contain some of the best land in that town, and are still owned and occupied by his descendants, at Oldtown and Turkey hill, where the houses which he built are in part standing. The farms have been owned and occupied by the Little family for 230 years.

MERRILL, ISAAC, was b. Aug. 4, 1778, m. Anna Blodgett, Feb. 13, 1806. Ch., Benjamin Franklin, b. Dec. 13, 1806; Job Eaton, Nov. 12, 1808; Arvin, Dec. 13, 1810; Mahala, Jan. 25, 1813, d. Nov. 12, 1815, of spotted fever; Esther, Apr. 4, 1817.

MERRILL, JOSEPH, son of Stevens, m. Sarah, daughter of Joshua Copp. Ch., Jonathan, b. Nov. 24, 1786; Joseph, Oct. 29, 1788; Stevens, Apr. 24, 1790; Joshua, Jan. 25, 1792; Lemuel, Nov. 8, 1793; Caleb, June 7, 1795; William, Feb. 28, 1797; Mary, Dec. 4, 1798; Ezra, Sept. 6, 1800; Sally, Dec. 9, 1802; Anson, Dec. 4, 1804; Hannah, July 25, 1806; Susanna, July 30, 1808.

MERRILL, NATHANIEL, m. Betsey Favour. He was b. in Boscawen, Apr. 10, 1769; she in New Chester, Feb. 10, 1773. Ch., David B., b. Dec. 11, 1791; Nathaniel, Jr., Nov. 6, 1793; Sabina, May 27, 1796; Polly, Aug. 7, 1798; Judith, May 18, 1800; Moses, June 26, 1802.

MERRILL, STEVENS, m. Hannah Clifford, Dec. 31, 1802. Ch., Isaac
Merrill, b. Nov. 17, 1803; Stevens, Jr., Mar. 4, 1806; Nathaniel,
Apr. 28, 1808; Ruth, Mar. 4, 1811; Susannah, Mar. 28, 1813;
Mary, Oct. 26, 1815; 2d, m. widow Colby. Ch., Michael P., b.
Dec. 26, 1818.

PILLSBURY, RICHARD, m. Miriam ——. He was b. Feb. 5, 1763;
she Feb. 25, 1768. Ch., Tristram, b. Mar. 19, 1787; John,
Nov. 11, 1788; Thomas, Mar. 23, 1791; Daniel, Feb. 28, 1793;
Polly, Mar. 5, 1795; Miriam, May 7, 1797; Polly, May 12,
1799.

RICHARDSON, STEPHEN, m. Susanna ——. Ch., Stephen, b. Nov.
29, 1779; Anna, Nov. 21, 1784; Phebe, Apr. 24, 1787; Sarah,
Apr. 7, 1789; Dorcas, Feb. 25, 1791; Nathaniel, May 30, 1793;
Susanna, May 17, 1797; Joanna, Feb. 3, 1705.

MISCELLANEOUS.

JOSEPH PATCH.

WALDEN, VT., Dec. 25, 1869.

MY DEAR SISTER HANNAH:—

You ask for information about father and mother Patch. About that I am not so clear. Father Patch died in 1822, I think in August; any way it was in the time of making hay. It was before I united with the family. I have never been able to ascertain his age. However, I think he must have been as old as seventy-four or five. He came to his death passing from the once Meader farm to where he then resided, with his son Daniel, in the neighborhood of Meader pond. All who remember the circumstances know how he was overtaken and carried home dead. Mother Patch was born Dec. 28, 1756. She died March 4, 1835, in her 79th year, on the Summit, where Chase Whitcher, Jr., once kept a house of entertainment. They were both buried in the village graveyard on Pine hill road, near the height of the ground. David, their son, died first, in August, and was buried at the left hand as you stand at the head of the graves looking towards the road; then Thomas at the right of him; his grave was marked with the common stones for the times; then Anna, then William, then mother Patch and father Patch on the right of all. If I were there I think I should not be puzzled to go right to the spot; but it is not at all probable I shall ever stand on Warren soil any more.

Since the death of my son my health has been very poor. I hope you are now better. You asked whether Mr. Hunt's family had moved away; they have moved to his father's.

> Now fare you well, my sister adieu;
> If I no more your face can view,
> O may we hasten to the shore,
> Where we shall meet to part no more.

Yours affectionately,

MRS. BETSEY PATCH.

To Miss Hannah B. Knight.

PAGE 302.—WRESTLERS.

Warren has always been celebrated for her smart wrestlers. They would practice the art at trainings, musters, town meetings, raisings, huskings, piling bees, at all public gatherings, and with the Vermont teamsters that for fifty and more years passed down through Warren to the seaboard. Among those best remembered after Joseph Patch, are Samuel Knight, True Stevens, Ezra B. Libbey, Joseph Merrill, and Samuel L. Merrill, (one of the best,) sons of 'Squire Abel, Joshua Merrill and Anson Merrill, sons of Joseph Merrill, inn keeper; Joseph Pillsbury, Joseph Patch, Jr., Reuben B. French, Beniah Wyatt, Hobart Wyatt, Walter Wyatt, Col. Benj. Clement, Alonzo Gale, Hazen Libbey, Ezra Libbey, Robert E. Merrill, (now in California,) Moses Page, Darius Swain, Reuben Gale, Freeman Gale, Hiram Gale, and E. Walton Libbey. The latter was a member of the 12th N. H. Regt., in the war of 1861, and was the champion wrestler of the whole brigade to which his regiment belonged. He often won as much as $25 "wrestling in the ring."

TOWN MEETINGS.

From 1779 to 1799, the annual town meetings were held on the first Wednesday of March, each year. Then by act of the Legislature, passed Dec. 20, 1799, the annual meeting was held on the third Thursday of March. In 1804 the annual meeting was held on the second Tuesday of March, which custom still continues.

HEALTH.

No person born and living in Warren, has died of consumption for the last twenty-five years. The children are free from it.

But few cases were ever known in town, and those were persons who inherited it and then came to Warren and died, or the children of such persons. The elevation of the land and the purity of the air exempts our citizens from this dread disease.

SUICIDE.

No one has ever yet committed suicide in Warren. "The people are not such fools." Pure air, pure water, and lofty mountainous scenery keep them from having the blues. Dwellers in the region of Wentworth and the land of "Pearmount," sometimes do the foolish thing.

LOST.

MARY ANN GERALD, daughter of Addison W. and Mary (*Merrill*) Gerald, was lost in 1852. They lived in the East-parte. The little girl was gone for two days.* It rained pouring one night. The whole town hunted for her, and they found her drenching wet in the woods near where Seth Jewett Brown once resided.

DANIEL WELCH, who was crazy by spells, started about 1825 to go from Mr. Daniel Ramsey's by Silver rill, to Joseph French's east of Knight hill, where Stephen Noyes once lived, He never reached the place and was never seen again. The old story runs that straying away through the woods far up the side of Moosehillock, he perished in the great gorge, south of the lower mountain peak, and that his spirit still crazed wanders there yet. Old hunters who took their last journeys in the forest about this time used to tell how no one ever stopped in that gorge at night without experiencing a haunted and weird like feeling, and some said they had heard the lost man just at nightfall calling for help from the shadowy gorge, and had seen his white ghost gliding noiselessly through the stunted spruces and dark firs.*

* Welch gave the town much trouble as will be seen by the following from the town records:—
1821.—Due Nathaniel Clough $3.94 for advertising Daniel Welch.
" Paid Joseph Kimball for going after him $7.32.

PAGE 425.—STINT.

Gov. Samuel Flanders once took his stint of Capt. David S. Craige, who lived by Blue Ridge. It was to dig so many potatoes, and he had three days to do it in. The first day he looked at it, said he knew he could do it in two days, and so he put on his boots with red morocco tops and silk tassels and went a visiting. The next morning he looked at the stint again, said he had no doubt but that he could do it in one day, and so went visiting once more. The third morning he looked at it, said he couldn't do it without killing himself; that he wouldn't try; that he might as well die for an old sheep as a lamb, and he went visiting again. That night he set his boots on a red silk handkerchief so they wouldn't get soiled. Such was the Governor's style through life, and he was always poorer than Job's turkey.

LIBRARY.

A Circulating Library incorporated by the Legislature was established in Warren about 1808. The books were kept at the house of Mr. Nathaniel Clough. By vote they were distributed among the library members a few years ago.

The ladies of Warren established another library in 1851. It contains 240 volumes of an interesting and useful character, which are much read.

SALMON.

This fish ceased to come to Warren after the dam at Wentworth was built. In 1866, Joseph Clement hatched a large quantity of salmon eggs, brought from Miramachi river, in New Brunswick, in Patch brook. The young fish did well and went away to the ocean. But as the fish-way was "constructed with a great deal of pig-headedness" over the Lawrence dam, the fish never came back to Warren again.

DEATHS BY CASUALTY.

John Mills killed by a falling tree, 1779.
Amos Eaton, killed " . " 1780.
Capt. John Mills, Jr., " " 1784.
Richard Pillsbury, killed at a raising, 1800.
Reuben Batchelder, " " " 1802.
Joshua Copp, Jr.'s child drowned in a wash-tub, 1808.

Caleb Merrill, deaf and dumb, killed by a falling tree, June 8, 1800.
Joseph Patch, first settler, killed by a fall, 1822.
William Kelley, Jr.'s child drowned in Kelley pond, 1833.
Paul Meader, killed by a log rolling over him, 1835.
Ward C. Batchelder, killed by a falling tree, 1836.
Mr. Merrill, killed by a pitchfork falling on him, 1840.
Miranda Whitcher, burned to death, 1845.
Abigail Weed, killed by falling on pitchfork, 1846.
Calvin Cummings, killed at a raising, 1848.
Mrs. Vowell Leathers, burned to death, 1849.
David Antrine, drowned in Meader pond, 1849.
Calvin May's adopted son, accidentally killed by manure-fork, 1850.
An Irishman killed at work on railroad, by falling tree, 1852.
Mr. Anderson burned to death at a coal pit over to Charleston, 1852.
Bartholemew Welton's child drowned in Lower Village pond in 1860.
Vanness Wyatt, shot by J. M. Williams, 1860.
Cornelius Flynn's child drowned in canal east of common in 1861.
Daniel S. Hoit, killed by the cars in 1862.
No person was ever yet killed in Warren by lightning.

UNITED STATES, STATE, AND COUNTY OFFICERS WHO HAVE LIVED IN WARREN.

Dr. Thomas Whipple, Representative to Congress.
    Robert Burns,   "   "
William Tarleton, Councillor.
Dr. Ezra Bartlett,   "
Abel Merrill, State Senator.
Dr. Ezra Bartlett, State Senator.
Benjamin Merrill, County Treasurer.
David Smith,   "   "
Samuel L. Merrill,   "   "
E. R. Weeks, Jr.,   "   "
Abel Merrill, County Judge.

Dr. Ezra Bartlett, County Judge.
Isaac Merrill, County Commissioner.
William Tarleton, High Sheriff.
Joseph Patch, Jr., Deputy Sheriff.
Stevens Merrill,* " "
Benjamin Merrill, " " .

* Stevens Merrill was the son of Joseph Merrill, innkeeper, of Warren. His son, Hon. George A. Merrill, of Rutland, Vt., was for many years Supt. of the Passumpsic Railroad, is at present Supt. of the Vermont Valley Railroad, and has been a member of the Vermont State Senate.

PAGE 441.—TRADERS IN WARREN.

Samuel Fellows, store on old Coos road in 1789.
Charles Bowles, " " " 1795.
George W. Copp, " " " 1800.
Abel Merrill, " " " 1804.
Capt. Benjamin Merrill, store at fork of Coventry road and turnpike in 1805.
Lemuel Keezer, " " " " " 1814.
Michael Preston, " " " " " 1816.
Amos Burton, store at end of turnpike.
Samuel L. Merrill, store at end of turnpike and on Blue ridge.
William Merrill, " " "
Anson Merrill, " " "
William Wells. " " "
John T. Sanborn, " " "
Asa Thurston, store at end of turnpike, and on road to grist mill.
D. Quincy Cole, " " " " "
Francis A. Cushman, store at end of turnpike, and by Noyes bridge.
George W. Prescott, store at end of turnpike, and near depot.
William A. Merrill, " " " .
Stevens Merrill & Tristram Cross, store in valley of Runaway pond.
F. A. & M. E. Cushman, store by Noyes bridge, 1846.
James & Joseph Clement, store on road to grist mill, 1848.
E. C. Durant, " " "
C. C. & H. H. Durant, " " "
J. & C. C. Durant, " " "
Walter Pike & William Swain, " " " in 1855.
Daniel Q. Clement & Omar Little, " " 1856.
Russell K. Clement, store on " " 1857.
James M. Williams, store near depot in 1847.
E. F. & C. F. Withington, " " 1862.
William C. Webster, " " 1863.
Charles Thurston, " " 1864.
William S. Doggett, " " 1869.
Moses W. Pillsbury, store opposite Moosilauke House in 1855.
George W. Jackson, " " " 1854.
Calvin Getchel, store opposite depot, in 1860.
M. P. Merrill & Levi C. Whitcher, store near railroad crossing in 1853.
Henry W. Weeks, " " " .
J. M. Twombly, " " "
H. H. Sheldon, " " "
Ira Merrill, " " "
J. S. Jewett, " " " in 1868.
E. B. Eaton, " " " 1868.
John M. Whiton & H. W. Weeks, store of Capt. Ben. Merrill in 1868.
Enoch R. Weeks & L. C. Whitcher, " " " 1869.
Ezra Libbey, store on Summit in 1853.
Jonathan Stickney, " " 1853.
Warren H. Smith, " "
W. R. Parks, store on Summit in depot in 1870.
Joseph H. Noyes, store by East-parte road in 1870.
A. L. Noyes, store, jewelry.
Joseph Chamberlain, store at East-parte in 1860.
Russel Merrill, store near Town House in 1847.
True M. Stevens, store by Moosilauke House.

J*

WATERNOMEE FALLS

On Hurricane brook are so called from the Indian chief, Waternomee. Chase Whitcher shot a caribou here, sometime in the last century. Chas. A. Fiske, painter, from New York city, has spent whole summers by these "falling waters." The hottest days are cool and comfortable here.

HURRICANE FALLS

Are on Hurricane brook, above Waternomee falls. Mr. Willard Hamilton, of Worcester, Mass., in 1870, fell down this fall, a distance of a hundred feet, where he caught upon a tree that had blown down and was saved from instant death; as it was, he was very severely bruised and injured. The water jumps down a series of steps more than two hundred perpendicular feet, at this falls.

WOLF'S-HEAD FALLS.

They are just above Hurricane falls. Amos F. Clough once made one of the most beautiful stereoscopic views of these falls that we ever saw.

DIANA'S BOWL

Is a beautiful basin worn in the rocks at the top of Wolf's-head falls. It is situated some 2,600 feet up the side of Mount Carr. The first mention we have of this spot is by Surveyor Leavitt. He ate his dinner there one day more than a hundred years ago.

MIDDLE CASCADES

Are between Waternomee falls and Hurricane falls. The water jumps down sixty feet in the distance of a few rods.

INDIAN ROCK.

The marks on the rock are undoubtedly of Indian origin. They are the most remarkable monument of the Indians now existing in Asquamchumauke valley.

APPENDIX. 563

HEIGHTS OF MOUNTAINS ABOUT WARREN.

The result of calculations by

PROFS. HITCHCOCK AND HUNTINGTON, STATE GEOLOGISTS.

Moosehillock,—feet above the sea,			4,941	Owl's Head,—feet above the sea,			3,357
Mt. Black,	"	"	3,701	Mt. Waternomee,	"	"	3,152
Mount Carr,	"	"	3,652	Mt. Mist,	"	"	2,373
Mt. Kineo,	"	"	3,557	Webster Slide,	"	"	2,320
Mt. Cushman,	"	"	3,456	Mt. Sentinel,	"	"	2,209

THE MOOSILAUKE MOUNTAIN ROAD COMPANY.

This road company was incorporated at the June session of the Legislature, 1870. John E. Lyon, Joseph A. Dodge, Daniel Q. Clement, Samuel B. Page, David G. Marsh, G. F. Putnam, and James Clement were made the "body politic." The corporation immediately proceeded to build the road, and the work thus far has been under the superintendence of D. Q. and James Clement. They have pushed the enterprise with a great deal of energy and the road is nearly completed.—(For charter in full see Pamphlet Laws 1870, page 452.)

DISTANCES ON THE MOOSILAUKE ROAD,

Measured by

NATHANIEL MERRILL, 2D, AND AMOS L. MERRILL.

From N. Merrill, 2d's to	Benton line on west bank of Big brook,		1 mile	25 rods.
"	"	"	Half-way Spring.*	2 "	13 "
"	"	"	Half-way Monument	2 "	62¼ "
"	"	"	Cold Spring	3 "	121 "
"	"	"	Prospect House	4 "	125 "
"	"	"	. . (.	"	

* It is said by thirsty people that Half-way Spring dries up in summer time when it rains.

THE POETS OF WARREN.

The first great poet of our town lived on Pine hill. Only one of his productions has come down to us. It is entitled—

MOTHER CLUCK—A SCARCASTIC POEM.

BY JOHN ABBOTT, FIFER.

The poet was a fifer in two wars, and a schoolmaster in time of peace. He blew a fife through the whole Revolution. Two families on Pine hill had a hot feud about a stolen drag. Abbott immortalized the great family fight by writing the following beautiful stanzas:—

Come all ye false professors,
  Who say you love the Lord,
You always have a hell at home
  And strive for one abroad.

But when the d—l comes for them,
  They will no longer brag,
For he will tote them all away
  Upon the stolen drag.

Come listen to my ditty,
  The truth I will reveal;
You tattle, lie, get drunk,
  And from your neighbors steal.

If you want to know the names
  Of those who stole the drag,
They are Scotch bastard, burnt ——
  And Captain Rennett bag.

When the drag begins to move,
  They will all begin to teeter,
Like mother Cluck with her budget
  Of lies astride of Hipen Peter.

When she had stole the buckle
  And the knife which she surely took,
She said that she had found them
  Down by the alder brook.

You make a noise about a squirrel,
  Your neighbors to abuse,
And then you go to meeting
  With your blackened Sunday shoes.

You kill your neighbors' ganders,
  About the chickens you make a touse,
And then you crop the pigs' ears,
  And lay them up for souse.

You thought your store was rather small,
  That it might quickly fail—
You turned your knife the other way
  And cut off a pig's tail.

When these folks go to meeting,
  They are for singing, red hot;
And if they can't get singing
  They will rattle the —— pot.

Now I will conclude my ditty—
  No longer will I sing,
Though they accuse innocent boys
  Of —— in the spring.

They said they were good judges of ——,
  And that you can't deny,
For one would —— a kernel of wheat
  And another a kernel of rye.

THE MOOGENS.

AN ELEGY.

The Moogens were a strange, nondescript race that lived on the Summit sixty or seventy years ago. They then mysteriously disappeared and none live at the Summit now. A wild sort of tradition alleges that they were last seen going through the notch between Black mountain and Moosehillock, down by Beaver meadow ponds, and that they were all lost in the dark gorge known as the tunnel of the mountain. It is told that, like Hendrick Hudson and his men in the Catskill mountains, their ghosts hold high carnival there every ten years; and the writer of this can solemnly affirm that in 1860, at the time when he spent two months on the mountain top he once heard terrible and awful sounds coming up from far down in the dark depths of the tunnel as though all the lost Moogens were having a grand carousal, or in other words were raising h—l and turning up jack.

Reuben B. French, of the East-parte, wrote a mournful elegy on this lost race. Only one stanza, the following, has come down to us:—

> When God made man they paid the cost—
> The remnants he considered dross;
> He threw this out among the dung,
> And from it the Moogens sprung.

It is much to be regretted that all the other stanzas are lost.

SENTIMENTAL ACROSTIC.

BY OBADIAH CLEMENT.

The following verses were written by Col. C. on the death of his first wife, Sarah Batchelder:—

> Oh me! unhappiest of all creatures,
> Unto you I will relate,
> I am unhappy in every feature,
> I've parted with my loving mate.

> But since to God I must submit,
> And fall upon my bending knees,
> For to his creatures he has a right,
> To call them home when e're he please.

> A thousand thoughts run through my head,
> While I do ponder all alone,
> To think, alas, my wife is dead,
> And gone into the silent tomb.

> Dreadful hard it is to part,
> With one that has been always kind,
> Sometimes I think t'will break my heart,
> Or at least will wreck my mind.

> I hope that I shall learn submission,
> And let my thoughts be cool and calm,
> And never run into distraction,
> Although my heart seems overwhelmed.

> Alas the pains that pierce my heart,
> It seems as though it will me kill,
> But I must learn with friends to part,
> And to obey God's holy will.

How desolate I now must be,
  While I am here upon the stage,
  And from my troubles never free,
  While I am in my pilgrimage.

Come people all, both great and small,
  Why are you hardened in your sins?
  Come, and obey God's precious call,
  And be attentive unto him.

Look back into that Holy Book,
  And there you'll see that all have died,
  But only two, and God them took,
  We never read death on them tried.

Elijah he was carried up
  Into the air upon the wind,
  Elisha he looked after him,
  'Till he dropped his mantle down behind.

Many sepulchres we read were used,
  Our Saviour he was laid in one,
  By ancient people of the Jews,
  And at the door they rolled a stone.

Equal with God, he then arose,
  And took his seat at his right hand,
  Ten thousand angels, as we suppose,
  Ready to obey the Lord's command.

Now let our love to God abound,
  For at the best we are but clay,
  Soon as the dying trumpets sound,
  Oh, then we can no longer stay.

Then under ground we all must rot,
  Beneath the cold and frozen sod,
  Our names and memory soon forgot,
  All to fulfil the will of God.

And now my name can here be read,
  I think I've spelled it very plain,
  And if you read it when I'm dead,
  Pray do not read it with disdain.

THESBIAN LYRIC.

BY "SCHUTE."

"Schute" and a party of friends prepared to visit the summit of the lofty Moosilauke. He invited Eva to accompany him. Her mother objected—would not let her go—on the ground that it would be too much of a task. "Schute" sorrowfully wrote the following lines:—

TO EVA.

Believe it or believe it not,—
  Dear Eva, on the mountain-top
  I found a little toad;
  And it may puzzle you and I
  To know how he could climb so high
  And o'er so rough a road.

His little legs you know are short,
And consequently he is thought
  To be a clumsy climber.
But he has beaten longer legs,
And stronger frames and wiser heads,
  And some who are diviner.

I will not say he's beaten you,
Dear EVA,—that may not be true,
  But he has beaten others,
The fault may not be theirs, I know;
Like you, dear Eva, they may owe
  Obedience to their *mothers*.

To mothers, too, who may have seen
Some of the evil ways of men,
  And hence gave timely warning.
They know too well a tarnished fame
Must end in grief and pain,
And that a pure, unsullied name
  Is woman's best adorning.

And your fond mother, knowing this,
Dear Eva, thought it not amiss
  To keep you nearer home,
Nor trust her darling out of sight
Upon Moosilauke's towering height
With men whose motives might be right,
  Yet still to her unknown.

But Eva, may I dare to hope
The happy day is not remote
  When you will venture up the slope
  With some one whom you'll know;
And may the one who shares with you
The toilsome jaunt, the glorious view,
Not only be a friend to you,
  But may he be your *beau*.

And Eva, whether high or low,
Or up or down life's path you go,
With husband, friend, or lover:
  Whatever be your lot below,—
Remember you will ever owe
  Allegiance to your *mother*.

THE SERPENT.

A SLEIGHING SONG, BY MERRILL BIXBY.

The village school once got up an immense omnibus and made a visit to the East-parte school by Moosehillock falls. The East-parte boys painted up a great four horse sleigh in the most fantastic manner, and labelled it the "Serpent." In this sleigh all the East-parte scholars visited the village school and sang this song both on their arrival and departure, greatly delighting themselves and everybody else:—

Did you ever see a serpent crawling on the snow?
Did you ever see the folks laugh to see the serpent go?
Why 'tis nothing but a carryall to carry us along—
And now if you are willing we'll sing you a song.

We are a little company of jolly girls and boys,
We've just begun to read and spell and make a little noise.
The times are hard, our parents poor, our chance is very small;
But for our own exertions we could not read at all.

We'll continue our exertions, the hill of science climb—
We'll improve upon our talents and not mis-spend our time,
When we have gained the eminence and buffeted the storm,
We'll double our exertions for a common school reform.

Now don't mistake our motive in giving you this call,
Our feelings are quite generous, although our talent's small;
We will tender you our thanks, and will show to you our love,
Though we are not as wise as serpents we'll be harmless as the dove.

We respect and love our teacher, for he is very kind
To impart to us instruction to cultivate the mind.
His task is very hard, his time is very brief,
But the motto of the serpent shall be to him relief.

'Tis "labor vincit omnia,"
The motto of our crew,
By this we can accomplish much,
Although our number's few,
'Tis now we bid adieu to you,
And hope again to meet,
That the Warren Centre omnibus
May the infant Serpent greet.

To return we are now ready
To our homes in the east,
For the child is not a man,
And the serpent not a beast;
For the children they may cry,
And the serpent he may hiss,
But of all the childish concerts
There is none can equal this.

EAST-PARTE SONG.

A BALLARD BY MERRILL BIXBY.

It is said, though some doubt the truth of it, that the poet sang this song, accompanying himself on a harp. We give only two stanzas, the others are all supposed to be lost:—

Ye Warrenites that live in town,
Think this not done to gain renown,
'Tis but a glance that you may see,
What simple fools some folks can be .

Think not I censure every one,
But those who mischief much have done,
I mean those rakes out in the east,
Who out of slander make a feast.

AMOS F. CLOUGH'S DIARY.

KEPT ON MOOSEHILLOCK IN WINTER OF 1870.

1869, Dec. 31.—To-day I got my "traps" to make stereographs in order and started for the mountain. D. G. Marsh brought me out to Merrill's, where Prof. J. H. Huntington, of the Geological Survey, was waiting for me. We started at 11 A. M., "traps" on a handsled, rope to draw by; a string team, Huntington on the lead. We made good progress to where he left his sled; snow was hard and the walking good. Here we divided up, took on some luggage, and then began the ascent in earnest. It was warm and we had to rest quite often. My load became heavy and at the steep part I left off the valise, which had nothing to freeze in it.

When we came on to the ridge the scene was the grandest I ever saw. Large, massive clouds were floating along the base of the highest mountains, and sweeping across the tops of the lesser ones. The White mountains, snow white, were all above the clouds, piercing the blue sky. The Green mountains were dark and frowning. Lake Winnepisseogee was a field of glaring ice. The mountains of Maine, of Canada, and the Adirondacks flashed dazzling in the setting sun.

The wind blew strong as we neared the Prospect House, and we were glad to go in and get some "grub," and prepare for the night. We have made a good fire, and fixed up our room. A cloud has settled down upon the mountain top, it is as dark as Egypt without, and here alone, away from friends and social life, we feel as isolated as though we were in Greenland.

1870, Jan. 1.—Happy new year "to people down on earth." It is a glorious morning up here. The scene is one of wild magnificence. A vast ocean of clouds is below us. Rolling masses, white crested, stretch to the south and east as far as the eye can see; high mountains pierce through them like islands. The White mountains resemble huge icebergs in mid ocean, so white and dazzling is their lustre. As the sun rose higher, breaks began to occur in the cloudy mass, revealing the world below, which seemed a dark yawning abyss.

Went down after my luggage and brought it up. A fox had

the curiosity to follow us up the mountain yesterday. He came to the Prospect House, but never asked to come in. He probably thought it was an erratic notion of ours to come up on this bleak peak at this season of the year. I found rabbit tracks plenty among the firs. A Canada grouse had crossed and re-crossed my path before I returned. White winged cross-bills were at work among the cones. Black capped titmice were as merry as crickets, singing all the time and rattling off loose pieces of bark in search of insects, while Canada jays fluttered before me, now cackling like wild geese, then whistling like a hawk, then barking like a small dog, often uttering a weird and querulous note, and finally dropping with motionless wings soft and silent as a falling snow-flake, out of sight in the dark firs. These are all hardy birds and endure the rigors of our coldest winters.

Fixed up bed-room at end of dining hall, as it presents more chances for comfort than any other room. Shall paper it throughout, top and bottom. The wind is blowing strong from the southeast. "A storm may now be expected," as the almanac makers say. Well, I can't help it, so, "let-er-rip." Huntington is going to make meteorological observations. I am going to make pictures.

Jan. 2.—I was awake nearly all night. Wind blew hard and it began to snow. It makes the old stone house shake. It blows a perfect gale; not in gusts, but a steady pull and a pull altogether. At 9 o'clock A. M. I took the anemometer, stood out and held it five minutes. It registered 75 miles an hour. It was all I could do to stand up against the tempest. The wind increased, and at noon I went out again. The wind caught me and swept me several yards before I could make a stand, and then only by bracing against a rock. I could not hear Mr. Huntington, so had to watch to see when the five minutes was up. He gave the signal and I started to come in. The wind threw me down five times before I reached the door. I clung to the rocks, then crept on my hands and knees, and when I entered the house, my clothing, though of the heaviest kind, was saturated with the rain. I was completely out of breath, and trembled all over with the exertion. We found that the wind was blowing at the rate of 97 1-2 miles per hour—a hurricane— the strongest, fiercest wind ever recorded in the United States.

Well, if it blows much harder, there is a chance that they will have a first class hotel over at North Benton. If we go it will be by wind, house and all. We can go well enough, but how the devil shall we light. Blow and be hanged. I have my boots, coat and hat on, ready for a start. Huntington looks as if he was ready. How it blows! The wind moans, whines, shrieks, and yells, like a thousand ghosts, the house trembles and rocks though the walls are of stone three feet thick, and the roar is deafening. The rain comes in through every crack and crevice. So fierce is the draft of the stove that the wind has literally sucked the fire out and we have had the greatest difficulty in re-kindling it. Crash! every glass in our window is broken, the fire is sucked out of the stove again, the light in our hurricane lantern is extinguished. I speak, but no one answers; I call louder, but there is no response; I shout, but no answer comes; I shiver with cold, and wet, and tempest. Darkness, if not terror, reigns.

Well, we have got the window fastened up. I held the boards and Huntington nailed them. Then we nailed blankets over the crevices to keep the wind out. After 9 P. M. the wind lulled; at midnight it was over and we went to sleep.

Jan. 3.—The storm has passed by. The wind has changed, but the clouds still wrap the mountain top. H. went down to Nathaniel Merrill's, and I have been busy fixing up our domicil. Snow has nearly all gone from the top; icy and slippery. Heard a flock of cross-bills near the house.

4.—The clouds rise up occasionally, giving us a glimpse of the lower world. We hung out a red light to-night.

5.—Some snow has fallen. Wind strong. Our life is very quiet—hermit like!

6.—Snowed all this day. Wind S. W. Am reading geology.

7.—Cold. Thermometer 3 degrees below. Wind N. W.

8.—Weather milder. Clouds have blown away. Snow drift as high as the house, and over our window. We had to shovel a hole through it before we got any daylight.

9.—Cold. Wind N. W. Heavy clouds driving across the mountain. Came down after a barometer. Had tough time getting over the ridge where it was drifted. Snow a foot deep in woods—five inches at Mr. Merrill's.

10.—At Mr. Merrill's.

11.—Left Mr. M.'s at 10:20 A. M. with a haversack well filled—barometer, gun, and snow-shoes—a heavy load, for the Prospect House. Snow grew deeper as I went up the mountain. Could not use the snow-shoes they "loaded" up so. Had to take them off and wallow up to my knees. Shot at two birds; did not get either of them. At last I gained the ridge where the snow was blown off; it was like taking the fetters from one's feet to be able to walk without wallowing. Never was a breeze more reviving in a hot sultry day in midsummer, than the one on the ridge, though it was far below the freezing point. It infused new vigor into my weary limbs, and I pushed rapidly forward to the Prospect House; arrived at 2:30 P. M. having been a little over four hours from Mr. Merrill's. As I came along the ridge, saw rabbit tracks where it had leaped along the path. There were also the tracks of a stoat or ermine, evidently in pursuit; but I lost sight of them where the snow was blown away.

12.—Rains. Wind S. W. No fair weather since Jan. 1.

13.—Snowed nearly all day. Shoveled out our window. H. went down and got the snow-shoes I left. The storm has broken up this P. M., and massive clouds roll along the base of the mountain. Snow squalls are to be seen here and there over the country. Still and calm, more so than usual up here. House is well chinked and daubed with frost.

14.—A remarkably fine day. We are up in a clear, beautifully transparent atmosphere. All below is covered with clouds; a vast ocean of clouds dotted with islands to the east and northeast, the mountains rising through the dense vapor.

I have made some glorious stereoscopic views; frost views and cloud views, and mountains in the distance. How I have enjoyed this day!

15.—A hard storm, snow and rain. Terrible long days and nights up here!

16.—H. went down to-day. Got back at 4.30 P. M.—brought lots of letters. Played boy to-night and went sliding down the side of the mountain on a sled.

17.—Hard storm. Rain and snow. Wind S. E.

18.—Wind shifted to N. W., and blowed hard enough to knock the storm all to shreds. Clear as a bell this A. M. The mountains are gray, snow mostly gone, only large drifts left in the ravines and gorges. Dug out the spring to-day—don't fancy snow water much.

19.—Pleasant. Went over to "Jobildunk" ravine. The falls are ice crags,—splendid! Shall make some views there. Cross-bills and chickadees were plenty in the hackmatacks. As we came up over the brow of the mountain, saw what I took to be a smoke and thought the house had burned. I went a few rods pretty quick; it proved to be a thin cloud, so I was sold cheap.

20.—Pleasant. Got breakfast, took my gun and started down the mountain. Shot some cross-bills; heard a bird whistling away; mocked him, he lighted on a stump to investigate; I fired and he flew "like thunder." Lucky fellow! he was about two thirds as large as a robin. Shot at a large pileated wood-pecker, but did not hit him. Saw an abundance of chickadees. Got to Mr. Merrill's at noon. No letters, no papers, "no nothin,"—a big joke! Sent the birds to a taxidermist. Got dinner, talked with a minister of much religion and but little sense; started, struck a two-forty gait, and came up to the Prospect House on time.

21.—Cold. Five men and a "spotted dorg" came up to see us from North Benton.

22.—Made some pictures—good ones. Cross-bills were plenty about the house to-day. An ermine crossed the mountain last night, about half-way between the house and the spring. They are hardy fellows and pursue their game with a great deal of tenacity. H. is getting lonesome.

23.—Rained. H. went down—brought up two letters. Shoveled snow to keep out the wind.

24.—Made picture of frost feathers to-day. Glorious! Also cloud view over Lake Winnepisseogee,—grand and sublime! The Adirondacks were lighted up to-day, their sharp peaks gleaming in snow with dark clouds for a back-ground—never saw them so magnificent before.

25.—Stormy.

26.—Storm has abated, but dark heavy clouds drive across the mountain, making it almost as black as night. The bushes in the sheltered spots are covered with great balls of ice of a tea green color. On these form the "*frost feathers*." What is very peculiar, these feathers form or build up against the wind, while the side opposite is left bare. The same effect is produced on the rocks, presenting a complete covering of pure white snow feathers. Went down towards the ravine.

27.—Mounted my snow shoes, took an axe and an old iron tea-kettle, and started for Jobildunk ravine. Splendid view there; ice columns a hundred feet high. What a time I had getting down to the foot! First, I sent the axe down on a voyage of discovery and to bush out a path. How it leaped and slid and plunged as it went down to the woods a thousand feet below! Next went the snow-shoes; but the kettle would be smashed and I kept it along with me. Then I slid a little way clinging by the bushes, and holding to a birch got down a perpendicular descent some ten feet. From this I could not get back at all nor down except by jumping. Then I sent the tea-kettle ahead—it went leaping and whirling twenty feet at a bound, smashed in pieces and was lost in the firs. I never saw it again. I looked over the precipice. There was a shelf of the rock twenty feet below and a snow bank on it. It was the only way. I jumped and settled to my knees in it. The rest of the way was easier, and sliding and jumping, I was at the foot in almost no time, It was a wild, grand scene, ice precipices rising one above the other a thousand feet, till the tops are lost in the clouds. Spotted my views, and was two hours climbing home through the woods. The ravine is one of the wildest places in New Hampshire, especially in winter. The Asquamchumauke comes down through it.

28.—Cold. Made some pictures of frost work, and one magnificent cloud view. H. went down to Mr. Merrill's and brought up letters and papers. I am pleased. Two white-winged crossbills came into the house to-day as I left the door open. They were lively and are the only living things that visit us except a few mice who have taken lodgings on the outside of our room, where they can get some heat from the stove. A man by the name of Adams started to come to the house, got lost and stopped out on the mountain all night. He got back, having only frozen his feet. Wonderful that he did not perish.

29.—Storms. Terrible lonesome here to-day.

30.—Wind fifty miles per hour. Snow flies. Dug out the

window three times to let in daylight. The house is snowed up very tight—very monotonous. Clouds and storm, storm and clouds. Not so cold here as I thought it would be.

31.—Cool but pleasant. Ther. stands at 0. Made the best pictures of the White mountains that I have ever got. The mountains are clear and white, and seem brought forward.

Heavy banks of clouds have been hanging on the horizon, south and east, all day. About 3 P. M. they began to come inland like a huge sea, enveloping the hills and valleys. Then the vapor rose up over the high mountains forming dark domes in the sunlight, and at 5 P. M. we were enveloped with so thick and black a cloud that we could scarce see three rods. Such is life on a mountain.

One month has gone since we came up here. It has slipped quickly and quietly away, and I have had about all of this that I want, but shall stay a while longer if nothing happens.

Feb. 1.—Went down on earth. Huntington stops at Merrill's, and is to walk up and down the mountain to get the record of the thermometer and barometer.

15.—Well, after two weeks of sojourn below, I am here in the region of bleakness and storms once more. A dense fog envelops the mountain, shutting out all distance.

16.—Cold; wind N. W. Clouds drove over our mountain peak till about noon, then cleared off clear as crystal,—clearer than I ever saw it before. We can see the ocean plain as the nose on a man's face. It is through the notches of the hills beyond Lake Winnepisseogee, a long bright line of blue.

It is growing cold, thermometer 16 degrees below. Hope it will be cold as Dante's hell, for it gives us a glorious view.

17.—Cold. Made a few pictures, then started for Mr. Merrill's. Slid on sled half a mile down to the ridge. Was one and a half hours getting to Mr. M.'s. Got letters, papers, pail of sugar, and gun, and am now on the road back, snow-shoeing it up the bridle path—am stopping on the ridge now. *Can see the ocean distinctly.* Heavy clouds are coming from it. 5 P. M.—Am at the Prospect House, and the clouds are here too. *They were just one hour coming from the ocean to Moosehillock.* My boots froze stiff coming up. Storms to night.

18.—Storms. Well, I like a storm; it rouses peculiar feelings; excitement, when it goes in strong, and it does that to-day, sure. One incessant roar all day; driving sleet and rain. The house shakes and trembles, though one side is buried in a snow drift to the top of the roof, nearly, with five inches of snow and ice on the roof and walls.

10 A. M.—Went out with the anemometer. We had a barrel set for the purpose, but the snow and ice had filled it up. So I held the machine for ten minutes. Sat down back to the wind astride of the barrel. It was no boy's play. Machine won't weigh five pounds, but it tired me terribly. The wind would ease a trifle, then come with a rush and a roar louder than thunder, that made me cling legs and arms to the barrel. The roar was deafening—I could not hear. Huntington gave signal with his hand and I made for the house. Was thrown flat down by the wind, then crept in. How queer I felt. I reeled and staggered like a drunken man. My head was giddy, my eyes on fire, a thrill like electricity shot through my whole body, making me wild and reckless. How it would have operated had I stopped longer, I cannot say. I should be careless of my life to try it again. The wind is blowing a hundred miles an hour—the sleet cuts like a knife—and my skin smarts wherever it was struck.

Blows like great guns this P. M. Rain comes down a perfect shower. Runs in streams about our window. We have got pails, buckets, kettles, &c., to catch it and keep from being drowned out. This is worse than the storm of Jan. 2; but we are better prepared to meet it.

8 P. M.—No abatement in the storm yet. Blow! blow! I like it. It is like a roar of thunder all the time.

10:30 P. M.—Still continues. Wind howls now like ten thousand fiends let loose from the infernal regions.

19.—Well, the storm has spent its fury at last. The wild deafning roar has died away, but occasional gusts sweep along, sighing with a low moan, the last dying throes of the wild, terrifying hurricane. It began to abate last midnight. Would like to have the clouds lift a few minutes to see how it served people down on earth. H. has gone down and when he comes back he will report.

It takes a blow from S. E. to get up a storm and keep it agoing.

It also takes a blow from the N. W., up in this altitude, a mile above the ocean, to clear it off. It is cold to-day.

This P. M. we got frost clouds, "clouds made up of minute particles of ice, said to bring death to any one caught in them." That story is a myth. We found them as harmless as a summer vapor.

20.—Ther. 14 degrees below. Clear and pleasant. *Looked away to the south-east and saw the ocean.* Walked down to the ravine. Got a fall and slid down a hundred feet—brought up in a snow bank; was frightened, but not hurt a bit. Hackmatacks are buried in snow. Wind has changed to south-east again. Another storm is on the stocks.

2 P. M.—It is blowing again. It roars again—it howls again. I thought the wind had blown as hard as it could, but it is now worse than ever before. I shall not wet myself to the skin again to hold up that anemometer. I know it blows at the rate of more than a hundred miles an hour. How it roars. But "roar" don't express the noise. Bellow is too tame by half. In a thunder storm the lightning flashes, blinding the sight. Then comes a sharp report which immediately gives way to deep, reverberatory rumbling that shakes and makes everything vibrate with its power, then rolls away and is lost. Now just imagine, if you can, a continual roll of the first reverberations, after the sharp report is over, and you will have some faint idea of what we have this day,—a continual thunder, making everything shake, for hours together.

Have storms like this swept over these mountains for thousands of years, perhaps millions of years, or is this a special storm for the benefit of us two poor mortals who have invaded this bleak and lofty region? Can't tell!

21.—Snows, and there is a drift fifteen feet high on the south side of our house. Had to shovel out our window to let in daylight. 1 P. M.—I am writing by lamplight; the house is completely snowed up.

22.—Ther. 17 degrees below. House still snowed up—time drags!

K*

23.—Have worked with the Theodolite this day. The following are some of the principal points which we have sighted:—

POINTS FROM MOOSEHILLOCK MOUNTAIN.

Mt. Washington	North 70 degrees	East.
Mt. Carrigan	" 88 "	"
Mt. Pigwacket	South 86 "	"
The Ocean seen	" 28 "	"
Lake Winnepisseogee	" 26 "	"
Mt. Belknap	" 14 "	"
Manchester, N. H.	" 4 "	"
Mt. Kearsarge	" 14 "	West.
Mount Carr	" 16 "	"
Mt. Monadnock	" 19 "	"
Mt. Ascutney	" 51 "	"
Mt. Cube	" 54 "	"
Mt. Graylock	" 59 "	"
Killington Peaks	" 61 "	"
Mt. Marcy, N. Y.	North 71 "	"
Camels Hump	" 60 "	"
Lake Champlain	" 52 "	"
Mt. Mansfield	" 42 "	"
Jay Peak	" 11 "	"
Percy or Stark Peaks	" 17 "	East.
Mt. Lafayette	" 58 "	"

24.—Cold. Packed up and have taken part of our things down below the Cold spring. The snow is very deep there, yet the spring runs musical, the same as ever. Cross-bills and other winter birds are very plenty. Coming back, saw where a wolf had crossed the mountain last night. He made a track as large as a dog. Prof. H. froze his feet getting up to the Prospect House yesterday, and thawed them out in snow.

25.—Here it is noon, and I am writing by lamplight, for we have not courage enough to go out and shovel the snow away from our window. Ther. 15 degrees below. Wind blows hard and we cannot get off this mountain to-day. Just went out in the other room and saw a stoat, or ermine, or weasel. He is about eight inches long, small head, full eyes, body pure white, tail five inches long tipped with black. He jumped out of the window where there is a broken light of glass, then turned round and looked back. I made a noise like a mouse, and he went to looking for that animal. They are courageous, very spry and active, and will kill rabbits and hens ten times their weight. No hens up here!

26.—It is stormful, and clouds rush wildly along over the mountain. We have packed up. Our sleds are loaded. We are going to leave the Prospect House,—leave Moosehillock — are going down on earth. What an experience for nearly two

APPENDIX. 579

months we have had up here. Storms, hail, rain, sleet, snow; house rocking, dizzying; wind roaring, yelling, howling, screeching, screaming, moaning, whining, crying; then thundering, one continuous roll so loud that the most powerful voice could not be heard three feet away. And then what sunshine! How grand the thousand snowy mountain peaks around us! The rivers and the lakes, glaring ice, flashing in a flood of glorious sunlight! The ocean! how sublime and how distinctly seen, ninety miles away! No mortals since the world began ever had such an experience on North American mountain top as we have had.

CHRONOLOGY.

Indians in Warren from time immemorial—year	1
Wonalancet in Warren	1675
Waternomee ascends Moosilauke—Acteon's statement—about	1685
Kancamagus in Warren	1690
Captives carried through Warren	1695
Expeditions up towards Warren after Indians	1703
Caleb Lyman kills Pemigewassetts	1704
Lieut. Thos. Baker marches through Warren	1712
Waternomee killed	1712
Capt. John Lovewell kills Indians near Warren	1724
Capt. Sam'l Willard, Jabez Fairbanks, and Col. Tyng, m'ch toward Warren	1724
Capt. John Goffe marches toward Warren	1746
Court's Committee pass through Warren	1752
Acteon Captures John Stark	1752
John Tolford comes to Warren	1753
Capt. Peter Powers marches through Warren	1754
Indians with their captives camp by Wachipauka pond	1756
Capt. John Goffe boating on the Asquamchumauke	1756
Maj. Robert Rogers and his rangers camp by Wachipauka pond	1756
Rogers' Rangers, some of them, pass through Warren	1759
Hunters in Warren	1760
Warren mapped and named	1761
Warren granted to John Page and others, July 14	1763
Warren surveyed	1765
Warren settled	1767
Road cleared	1767
First religious meeting—Congregational—about	1775
Revolution	1775
First mill	1776
Warren incorporated	1779
First town meeting	1779
First training	1780
First public school	1783
Boundary lines settled	1784
The Era of Requisites, about	1795
Methodism first in Warren	1799
Turnpike built	1808
Second war with England	1812
First Permanent Stage	1814
Spotted Fever	1815
First Meeting-house built	1818
Daniel Welch perished on Moosehillock	1825
Mine discovered	1830
Berry brook road opened	1836
Great lawsuit	1842
Railroad built	1851
Warren Common cleared	1859
Prospect House built and road cut on to Moosehillock	1860
Centennial Celebration, July 14	1863

SUBSCRIBERS
FOR THE
HISTORY OF WARREN.

ALBANY, N. Y.
J. Munsell . . 3

ANDOVER.
John M. Shirley . 1

ANTRIM.
W. R. Cochrane . 1

AUBURN.
Benj. Chase . . 1

BENTON.
Chase Whitcher . 1
Ira Whitcher . . 1

BOSTON, MASS.
Guy A. Clifford . 1
John F. Colby . 1
Mrs. H. E. Bryer . 1
Samuel G. Drake . 1
Mrs. Susan Frost . 1
Benj. K. Little . 1
Omar Little . . 1
William Little . 1
Public Library . 1
John E. Lyon . 1
Wm. Parsons Lunt 5
G. H. Tucker . 1

BRIDGEPORT, CT.
W. C. Batchelder . 1

BROOKLYNN, N. Y.
Mrs. Kate Lee . 1

CANAAN.
Caleb N. Homan . 1

CLAREMONT.
H. W. Parker . 1

CONCORD.
Nathaniel Bouton . 1
Sam'l C. Eastman . 1
Asa Fowler . . 1

John H. George . 1
H. H. Kimball . 1
Thos. B. Little . 1
A. S. Marshall . 1
S. B. Page . . 2

DOVER.
S. M. Wheeler . 1

EXETER.
Chas. H. Bell . 2
John J. Bell . 1

FRANKLIN.
Daniel Barnard . 1
Austin F. Pike . 1

GREENLAND.
C. W. Pickering 1

HANOVER.
E. D. Sanborn . 1

HARTFORD, CT.
Geo. E. Merrill . 2

HAVERHILL, MASS.
J. H. Patch . 1
William Patch . 1

HILLSBOROUGH.
J. F. Briggs . 1

HUNTINGTON, MASS.
Ezekiel Dow . 1

LACONIA.
E. A. Hibbard . 1
Mrs. E. M. Jewett 1
T. J. Whipple . 1

LANCASTER.
H. O. Kent . 1

LANDAFF.
Mrs. Mary Clark 1

John Poor . . 1
Daniel Whitcher 1

LAWRENCE, MASS.
D. M. Boynton . 1
W. E. Boynton . 1
Alonzo Jewell . 1
M. P. Merrill . 1

LEBANON.
S. N. Homan . 1

LISBON.
Mrs. S. Kimball 1
Kimball Little . 1
A. B. Woodworth 1

LITTLETON.
J. G. Sinclair . 1

LONDONDERRY.
R. C. Mack . 1

LOWELL, MASS.
Mrs. L. Carleton 1
E. A. Clement . 1
R. T. Clifford . 1

MANCHESTER.
A. W. Bartlett . 1
C. H. Bartlett . 1
Sam'l N. Bell . 2
H. E. Burnham . 1
Andrew Bunton 1
G. B. Chandler . 1
J. S. Cheney . 1
B. P. Cilley . 1
Jos. B. Clark . 1
L. W. Clark . 1
C. W. Clough . 1
L. B. Clough . 1
W. W. Colburn . 1
Geo. W. Colby . 1
Thos. Corcoran . 1
David Cross . 1

APPENDIX. 581

Moody Currier	1
Jesse Eastman	1
Jos. G. Edgerly	1
M. V. B. Edgerly	1
J. E Everett	1
A. G. Fairbanks	1
Jos. W. Fellows	1
John Ferguson	1
J. C. French	1
Sacalexis Glossian	1
Charles Goold	1
E. W. Harrington	1
John Harrington	1
E. D. Hadley	1
Stephen Homan	1
Jacob F. Jewell	1
Abbie A. Johnson	1
J. B. Jones	1
Joseph Kidder	1
E. W. Libbey	1
Nancy J. Libbey	1
H. D. Lord	1
Mary M. Melendy	1
Anson Merrill	1
John T. Moore	1
Chas. R. Morrison	1
Geo. W. Morrison	1
Rodnia Nutt	1
A. C. Osgood	1
Wm. R. Patten	1
David L. Perkins	1
H. A. Prescott	1
D. W. Reynolds	1
Isaac W. Smith	1
Moses E. Smith	1
Frederick Smyth	1
Justin Spear	1
C. W. Stanley	1
Horace Stetson	1
Dan'l L. Stevens	1
E. H. Stowe	1
E. A. Straw	1
Cyrus A. Sulloway	1
William J. Tucker	1
Samuel Upton	1
James A. Weston	1
Darius Wilson	1
Frank L. Wilson	1

MARLBOROUGH, MASS.
Albe C. Weeks	1

MERRIMACK.
L. W. Parker	1

MILFORD.
B. Wadleigh, one for self and one for R. B. Hatch, per order clerk of the court	2

NASHUA.
H. B. Atherton	1
William Barrett	1
W. W. Bailey	1
H. C. Batchelder	1
Joseph M. Copp	1
Dr. F. L. Gerald	1
G. A. Ramsdell	1
Sawyer Junior	1
Gilman Scripture	1

NEW BOSTON.
C. B. Cochrane	1

NEW DURHAM.
C. H. Boody	1

NEWTON, MASS.
I. H. Silsby	1

NEW YORK CITY.
C. A. Fiske	1
Mercantile Lib'ry	1
N. Y. Hist. Soc.	1
Geo. H. Moore	1

ONEIDA, ILL.
E. D. Aiken	1
C. E. Clement	1

PETERBOROUGH.
Charles Scott	1

PLYMOUTH.
H. W. Blair	1
J. A. Dodge	1
J. W. Whiteman	1

PORT HURON, MICH.
J. F. Merrill	1

PORTLAND, ME.
H. C. Peabody	1

PROVIDENCE, R. I.
M. H. Bixby	5

RINDGE.
E. S. Stearns	1

RUTLAND, VT.
G. A. Merrill	1
C. K. Williams	1

SALEM, MASS.
Henry Bixby	1

SPRINGFIELD, MASS.
W. Clogston	1
Columbus Clough	1
M. H. G. Gilmore	1
Curtis B. Newell	1
James Parker	1

TILTON.
J. H. Goodale	1

VERSHIRE, VT.
A. J. Clough	1

WILTON.
C. H. Burns	1

WOBURN, MASS.
A. A. Clement	1
A. E. Clement	1
Mrs. J. B. Flagg	1
Mrs. J. Wendell	1

WORCESTER, MASS.
C. W. Hamilton	1
W. Hamilton	1
A. E. Noyes	1
R. Woodward	1

WARREN.
A. M. Barber	1
J. W. Batchelder	1
R. Batchelder	1
D. E. Bixby	1
Rev. D. C. Bixby	1
James M. Bixby	1
Sam'l B. Bixby	1
Luther Blake	1
J. S. Blodgett	1
C. F. Bracey	1
John L. Clark	1
S. K. Clark	1

HISTORY OF WARREN.

Amos Clement	1	T. Haines	1	James F. Merrill	1
Benjamin Clement	1	Mrs. J. Harriman	1	James S. Merrill	1
Benj. Clement, Jr.	1	N. Harris	1	Jesse Merrill	1
D. Q. Clement	1	Mrs. S. M. Heath	1	N. Merrill 2d.	1
Geo. B. Clement	1	John Hoit	1	Russell Merrill	1
James Clement	1	H. C. Howland	1	Sarah C. Merrill	1
Jas. A. Clement	1	A. M. Jackson	1	George B. Noyes	1
John Clement	1	G. W. Jackson	1	J. H. Noyes	1
Joseph Clement	1	Levi F. Jewell	1	S. M. Noyes	1
R. K. Clement	2	J. S. Jewett	1	Amos T. Page	1
W. Clement	1	Ezra W. Keyes	1	Reuben Page	1
Geo. C. Clifford	1	M. P. Kimball	1	A. M. Pillsbury	1
Z. L. Clifford	1	Mercy J. Knapp	1	E. Pillsbury	1
A. F. Clough	1	C. K. Leonard	1	M. W. Pillsbury	1
C. W. Clough	1	G. E. Leonard	1	Geo. F. Putnam	1
Olcott Colby	1	E. B. Libbey	1	Nath. Richardson	1
D. B. Cotton	1	Geo. Libbey	1	M. J. Sanborn	1
C. W. Cummings	1	Hazen Libbey	1	Jos. Sherburne	1
F. C. Cummings	1	Ira Libbey	1	Darius O. Swain	1
J. T. Cummings	1	John Libbey	1	F. J. Swain	1
Gilman C. Davis	1	Nancy J. Libbey	1	Geo. E. Swain	1
John E. Davis	1	Nath. Libbey	1	S. E. Swain	1
W. S. Doggett	1	Walter Libbey	1	Franklin Towle	1
Jonathan Dow	1	G. A. Little	1	S. Truscott	1
Stevens M. Dow	1	Jonathan Little	1	Jas. O. Tuttle	1
Benj. F. Eastman	1	J. M. Little	1	Russell Upton	1
D. Y. Eastman	1	Susan C. Little	1	E. R. Weeks	1
J. B. Eastman	1	H. B. Low	1	H. W. Weeks	3
Jesse Eastman	1	G. W. Lund	1	Ira M. Weeks	1
Ezra B. Eaton	1	James P. Lund	1	Wm. H. Weeks	1
H. A. Eaton	1	J. D. Marston	1	James Welton	1
James Edgar	1	D. G. Marsh	1	H. A. Whiteman	1
C. O. French	1	Asa Merrill	1	J. M. Whiteman	1
D. A. French	1	G. W. Merrill	1	N. Whiteman	1
Osco H. French	1	Enoch Merrill	1	Levi C. Whitcher	1
A. J. Foote	1	H. N. Merrill	1	Sam. Whitcher	1
A. F. Gale	1	Ira Merrill	1	J. M. Whiton	1
O. S. Gleason	1				

William Little

A Biographical Sketch

Warren Historical Society

William Little

Edward Whitcher

[A close friend of Ira Morse, who married William Little's daughter Lillian in 1898, Edward Whitcher provides a rare profile of Warren's first Historian.]

William Little was born in the town of Warren, on the 20th day of March 1833. The scenery, grand, picturesque and charming in the extreme, amidst which his infancy and boyhood were spent, made a deep and lasting impression upon his youthful mind, and inspired him with a love of the grand and beautiful in nature, "which grew with his growth and strengthened with his strength," and ever remained one of the strong and ruling passions of his soul.

His father Jesse was a physician of high standing and large practice, and the son early developed a tendency and aspiration for professional life, but his youthful ardor and ambition saw wider fields and brighter opportunities at the bar, than in the calling his ancestor had chosen for his life work; and so he directed his educational training with a view to his practice of the law. In this he did not err, and subsequent events proved that he chose wisely and well.

He graduated from Dartmouth College in 1859, and entered upon the study of law in the office of Hon. Thomas J. Smith at Wentworth, and afterwards attended the law school at Albany, New York, from which he graduated, and was admitted to the bar in 1861. It was while at Dartmouth he wrote the first history of Warren 1854. He at once moved to Manchester, N.H. and opened an office, which henceforth was to be the scene of his professional labor. Business came to him at once, and business and political friends swarmed about him. Bold, radical, aggressive, he quailed before none, but accepted encounter from all comers.

He was five times honored by being chosen Manchester representative. Having largely defrayed his expenses while fitting for and attending college, by teaching, he became deeply interested in school work, and for eleven years was a most useful and influential member of the Manchester school board, and was most instrumental and active in securing for the public schools of that city, their highly distinguished exhibit at the Centennial exhibition at Philadelphia in 1876.

He was passionately fond of literature, and, even when intended only for the delectation of intimate personal friends, he delighted in authorship of his rich manuscript, the result of many hours of literary diversion. His most ambitious venture in this direction was his History of Warren, which has been widely read and is universally regarded as one of the best town histories ever published in this state. Its composition was the great literary delight of his life. He was proud of his achievement and had a right to be. No man could have done better, and few as well.

The fame this production brought him, caused him to be employed to write the History of Weare, a work most creditably performed, but in this case the material was furnished for his ready pen, while the History of Warren was all Mr. Little's own work, and he personally gathered both warp and woof, while he explored every known depository of historical data that could add to the completeness of his charming narrative.

He was a great lover of birds, and he often strolled through fields and forest, observing their habits, studying their peculiarities and characteristics.

In 1888, Mr. Little visited Europe and traveled extensively through the British Isles, and in France, Italy, Switzerland and Germany.

Born within the shadows of a great mountain, Moosilauke, his spirits seemed to take on something of the rugged, sterling independence it typified, though this sometimes went against the prevailing beliefs by which he was surrounded. His own beliefs were deeply rooted, tenaciously held as fearlessly as his love of Moosilauke, the roaring tempest, or coming storm.

These characteristics may have not been conducive to universal personal popularity, as the world accepts the term, but they revealed the outlines of the bold, fearless and honest man.

Such a man was William Little.

— From an unpublished manuscript by Edward Whitcher (1914-1974), provided by Mrs. Edward (Esther) Whitcher of Warren.

Additional Biographical Notes, or "How *little* we know about Little."

Robert W. Averill

William Little (1833-1893) was known throughout his life as The Historian of Warren, quite possibly even before his 1870 history was completed, "a work commenced at the age of sixteen and persistently followed" for the next 20 years.[1] There are surprisingly few personal glimpses of its author within its pages, barring the brief Preface. He is absent from the index; the Appendix tersely notes that he was the "son of Jesse and Susan Copp (Merrill) Little, born March 20, 1833; graduated at Dartmouth, 1859; studied law and practiced at Manchester, N.H."; that he was Town Moderator from 1858 to 1860 and also made up the School Committee in 1860.

Luckily, a few brief details are found in a genealogy compiled by George Thomas Little, written in 1882,[2] which provides the following sketch:

> **WILLIAM**[8] [Jesse[7] Amos[6] James[5] Samuel[4] Tristam[3] Moses[2] George[1] (A tailor by trade from Unicorn street, London, England)] born 20 March, 1833, at Warren, N.H.; married 22 Feb., 1870, Annie, daughter of Thomas Dency, who was born 11 Aug., 1845, and died 23 March, 1878. Mr. Little attended the district school, worked on a farm, on a stone quarry, and at peddling till twenty years of age, then fitted for college at Kimball Union Academy, Meriden, and graduated at Dartmouth in 1859. After studying law with Hon. Thomas J. Smith of Wentworth, N.H., and at the Albany Law University, he was admitted to practice, and in 1861 opened a law office in Manchester, N.H. Mr. Little was chosen to the city council for several years, was a member of the legislature five sessions and the candidate of his party

---

[1] Clement, F. C., 1913, The Settlement of Warren, The Granite Monthly, Vol. 15, pp. 233-235.

[2] New Hampshire Historical Society collection.

for the speakership, and has served on the Manchester board of education ten years. He has published a "History of Warren," one of the most readable town histories ever written; a centennial address; a history of the schools of Manchester; and has delivered a few lectures and some political addresses. He has been quite successful in his practice, is in comfortable circumstances, and still resides at Manchester.
    Children: I. Lillian — born 7 Jan., 1871. II. Thomas Dency, born 8 June, 1874. III. Annie Susie, born 27 Dec., 1877; died 13 April, 1878.

[pp. 482-3]

The <u>General Catalogue of Kimball Union Academy (1813-1930)</u>, published in 1880, reveals that William Little attended this local secondary school in 1854-5. His first History of Warren was also completed in 1854. Notes in <u>Dartmouth Necrology</u> by J. M. Comstock (1893-4) state that this interval at K.U.A. was followed by: "... some time at Tufts Coll. [unconfirmed] whence he came to Dart[mouth]. Read Law with T. J. Smith {D.C. 1852} of Wentworth, N.H., with Morrison, Stanley & Clark of Manchester, N.H., and at Albany Law Sch.; pract. Manchester, May 1861 till decease. Memb. Manchester school board 11 years; memb. Leg., 1863, '4, '5, '8.
...D. Manchester, N.H., Dec. 19, 1893, of pneumonia."

II. The History (1870)

As noted above, Little had compiled his first history (170 pages) in 1854, at age 21. In July 1863 he gave a 13,500 word address for the Warren Centennial. He continued to develop his collection of stories, added genealogies, countless footnotes, and a Natural History to complete the 592 page 1870 history. His near absence from his own history may be partially due to his limited years in Warren before his relocation to Manchester, but he also seemed to prefer to work behind the scenes. This is not to say that his presence is not felt. In fact there are rare occasions in this history that his flair for the dramatic is not evident.
    His object, clearly stated in his very first paragraph, was to preserve traditions, tales, memories, legends, anecdotes and events of "our mountain hamlet." But he intended to do this without making his book "dry as a chip." And if this meant altering or inventing a few details then so be it. (Modern historians be warned.) Little sought a "unity of thought, unity of time," or more simply put, a coherent story. He blended local

oral tradition with accounts borrowed by "literary larceny" (to use his own phrase) from both historical and popular literature.

While many of the stories were intended to entertain, Little also recognized the corrective effects of humor. The difficult farming life of the first settlers perhaps made such outlets all the more valuable. But the inevitable competition for land, wealth, and other social emblems also made good targets for Little's stories. In poking fun at his fellow townsfolk, his satire was generally kind. He was careful to avoid taking sides. He notes, "We have even taken pains to make some of our friends show off in good style (p. 520)."

His accounts also demonstrated a typical 19th century optimism, based on the simple idea of Progress (with a capital P). In this period of his life (1833-1870), it was easy to see daily life's physical improvements as technology brought even these northern farm communities into a closer system of exchange with urban areas to the south. In his 1863 Centennial Address reviewing the first hundred years of his hometown, he begins:

> I have no power to describe a century.
> It cannot be comprehended in its details. Compared with all time, it is but an infinitesimal point. Compared with an hour, or a day, it assumes gigantic proportions. To us the past hundred years are replete with interest. They are full of great events — greater than any hundred years which have preceded. Not so great, perhaps, in wars and mighty commanders, as were the centuries of Greece and Rome, but greater in inventions, the steamship, rail car and telegraph; greater in geographical discoveries and the developments of science, but greater yet in the general diffusion of knowledge and the advance of civilization.[2]

Despite this claim of social evolution, there was inevitably an element of 19th Century ethnocentrism in parts of the history. Much of this was ingrained in the source works on Indian society used by Little, but it is likely that he, too, shared the biases of his society. It is unnecessary to note that this was likewise a male-oriented world. In comparison to other writers of the times, Little's mistakes seem limited.

---

[2] Little, W. Address at Centennial Celebration of Warren, N.H. (July 14, 1863). Charles F. Livingston, Manchester, N.H.

The sense of progress is also echoed in his 1870 History:

> Progress in manufacturing has made mighty changes in Warren during its first century, as well as everywhere else. No more do we have the rude camp and log cabin, except in the French settlements... No longer do we have a dearth of books and pictures, with a life of story telling around the hearth, little intercourse with the outer world, roads almost impassable, and hunting and carousing for the chief pleasures and amusements. ... We sit in the midst of our woods and groves in the quietness of the country, a hundred miles from the capital, and are as well acquainted with the movements and incidents of society as though we were almost omnipresent. So much for the advancement of one century. Will the next show as much?
> (pp. 506-7)

But this "advance" had its negative side as well. With rapid industrialization, simple subsistence was no longer an acceptable goal. Other means of personal improvement would be sought, often outside Warren. After reaching its peak population of 1152 in 1860, Warren's most significant "progression" was in the inexorable exodus of its citizens, some to better farmlands in the opening West, others to industrial centers to the south.[3] William Little's own emigration to Manchester is a single example, but there were countless others.

It is ironic to note that Little's history was in part made possible by the educational and professional success of those townspeople who had moved away. This would include Little himself, but also many others. In order to finance his history, Little sought "subscribers," who in turn could be "immortalized in our subscription list (p. 520)." It should be noted that 298 subscribers signed up for 316 books, mostly by single copies. Only 124 subscribers were listed as living in Warren.

He wryly notes that "this pleasant pastime, writing a town history, is a costly one; that we have not, cannot, and shall not make a cent out of it; that, to use an expression of the vulgar world, 'We are a good deal out of pocket by the operation. (p. iv)' " This is confirmed by the Inventory of Wm. Little's estate in 1894. This notes 16 bound volumes of the Warren

---

[3] Joseph Bixby Hoyt, <u>Baker River Towns</u>, 1990, Chapter 6.

History ($8.00) and 200 unbound volumes ($20.00) remaining.[4] These numbers plus those sold by subscription (316) would suggest a first edition run of at least 532.

Despite its decreasing farming population, Warren was able to develop in other ways because of its special location. First, Warren is midway along a natural corridor that connects the two major river valleys of western New Hampshire: the Merrimack and the Connecticut. General McDuffee's survey and plans for a canal through Warren in the 1820's proved untenable, but the construction of the railroad along much the same route a generation later certainly was not. With its completion to Wells River in 1853, the new "Boston, Concord and Montreal" would open new markets to Warren, as well as a major new growth industry: the summer visitor (Hoyt, Chapter 9). The railroad would allow Little and countless others to travel easily both for business and pleasure. In fact, Little was particularly interested in making "pleasure" a business for his home town. Second, there were many natural attractions in the Warren area, not the least of which was Mt. Moosilauke. This upland area would become a special attraction for a growing non-rural populace fleeing stifling summer heat and varied epidemics of swamp fevers and allergic disease.

Little became involved heavily in this last new venture, encouraging summer visitors to spend much of their summer at the fledgling summer lodgings around Warren. These began in 1860 with the construction of the large, one-story stone house on the very top of Mt. Moosilauke. Although much of the mountain, including its summit, is in Benton, the Prospect House was built by a crew of about 18 Warrenites, headed by James Clement and Darius Swain. The first "landlord" of the newly erected Prospect House was William Little, himself. Warren became (and remains) the most frequent approach to the mountain.

Other citizens soon "commenced to keep summer boarders (p. 493)," including Nathaniel Merrill 2d at the base of the Carriage Road — "Merrill's Mountain Home" at Breezy Point; D. G. Marsh at the Moosilauke House near the train station in Warren; and The Moosilauke (Inn) built at Breezy Point in 1886.

Little's particular interest in summer visitors was clearly due to his own special attachment to Mt. Moosilauke. Many of his best tales are those related to wide-ranging accounts of doings on and about the mountain. He had in many ways grown up on the

---

[4] Little's Will and Estate list was provided by Robert Morse, the great grandson of William Little.

mountain. The first "trail" up Moosilauke was cut around 1840 by his uncle (Benjamin) who ran an inn at Warren Summit (Glencliff). He undoubtedly climbed the mountain from many directions. It is likely that the "Bill" of Jobildunk (Joe-Bill-Dunk) Ravine is for Bill Little.

Little provided key support for the first high mountain overwinter expedition in 1870 on the summit of Moosilauke. This was made up of Prof. J. H. Huntington of Dartmouth College and Amos F. Clough, an independent-minded son of Warren and pioneer winter photographer. In November 1870, Little obtained Clough's expedition diary, which was entitled "Journal of Events Whilst on the Mountain." He made substantial alterations to this and added his excerpted version to the Appendix of his 1870 History. Little apparently wanted to smooth over some of Clough's rougher grammar and ideas, as well as enhance the "dramatic" moment. (Both the original and a transcription are in the Dartmouth College Special Collections).

To briefly digress, Amos F. Clough would also provide one of the best features in the 1870 History — its clear photographs. These were originally stereoscopic views, most of which are now lost. Oddly enough an 1871 reviewer felt that the use of photographs was "unwise." He concluded: "The life or durability of a photograph has not been determined, but there are reasons for believing that its life is short as compared with that of an engraving, or of any impressions in ink."[5] These fifteen photographs have, to the contrary, done quite well over the intervening 120-odd years.

For the rest of his life Little would continue this promotional bent, not for any personal financial interest, but to expand this local "industry" for the good of the North Country and for the enjoyment of those unfamiliar with its wonders. He provided many stories for the newspapermen who frequently covered the summer activities around Moosilauke.[6] One newspaper account (c. 1883) noted that Little had "spent some time every summer since youth upon the summit and in exploring the surrounding mountain fastnesses and forest depths, and is familiar with many charming retreats and wild and picturesque scenes which few others have ever witnessed." Another stated: "Judge William

---

[5] The New England Historical & Genealogical Register and Antiquarian Journal, 1871, Vol. XX, p. 304.

[6] These newspaper accounts are contained in the "Tip Top News," a transcription of the clippings kept at the Moosilauke Summit House from 1879 to 1916 (unpublished). — Wm. S. Morse Collection, Dartmouth College Archives.

Little of Manchester, the historian of Warren, N.H., recently made a journey up the Woodstock path, this making his 102nd pedestrian trip to the summit." (Not surprisingly, he was an early member of the Appalachians — the Appalachian Mountain Club, founded in 1876.) He would write half a dozen historical pieces for The Granite Monthly, listed in his Bibliography.

Little was well aware of the large number of summer visitors that passed through the Franconia valley on the other side of Moosilauke from Warren. After the Pemigewasset Valley Railroad reached North Woodstock from Plymouth in 1882, he and others pushed for a passable road between North Woodstock and Warren. In 1882-3 he scouted and helped build a woods path from the Agassiz basin area to Moosilauke's summit, later known as Little's Path. (This would disappear during turn-of-the century lumbering.)

III. CONCLUSION

There are undoubtedly additional details concerning William Little's activities outside of Warren, which may eventually come to light. He also remained strongly interested in education, serving many years on the Manchester School Board, writing a history of the Manchester schools, and after his death making a bequest to the town of Warren for support of its public schools.

He may have returned to Warren in his last years, though it is unclear if this was year round.[7] The family home in Warren along the old Coos Turnpike is pictured below. This house, demolished in the 1970's is only a few yards from the Morse Museum.[8]

To close, I can do no better than to let William Little have the last word — he has reached the end of his 1863 Address to his town and now addresses us, a hundred years (or more) in the future:

---

[7] Roland M. Bixby, History of Warren, 1986, p. 340.

[8] The Morse Museum (July 4, 1928-August 13, 1992) was built within a few yards of this site, and would be associated for much of its long life with Ira H. Morse, Little's son-in-law, and Philip Morse, the grandson of William Little.

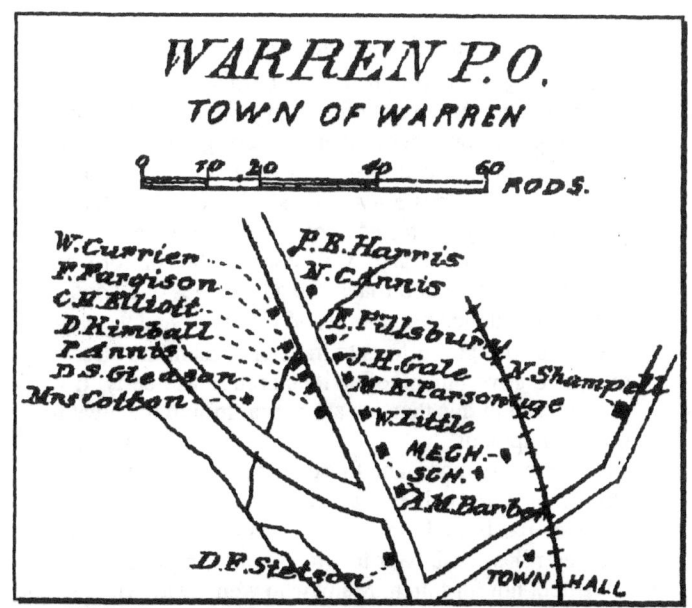

1892 Warren, N.H. — C. H. Hurd & Co. Boston, Mass.

William Little House, Warren, N.H.
Will and Lillian Gordon, Joe Little (Wm. Little's brother)
(Photo given to Edward Whitcher by Philip Morse in 1964.)

The men of the first generation have nearly all passed away. The gray hairs and wrinkled brows of the second show that they are rapidly following. We of to-day can never repay to our ancestors the debt of gratitude which we owe. We can only discharge it by emulating our fathers in handing down to posterity all those blessings which have been so lavishly conferred upon us. We would give to them a territory well cultivated, well stocked, the comforts of good houses and good roads, the advantages of a good education, intellectual, moral and religious, and we should make the strongest efforts to transfer to them the blessings of a good government, of civil and religious liberty. If we do not succeed in this then we are not faithful to the great trust imposed upon us.

A few hours more, and this day shall be lost in the past. No person here shall ever see a similar one return. This occasion has brought many of us strangers together. Many a wanderer has come back to witness once more scenes long unvisited, not forgotten. Many who went away with us shall never more return. Many who have gone and whom we expected to see are not here. Many whom we left behind have gone to their long home, never to come back to us on earth, and we miss their happy faces this day. Let us forget their faults, and imitate their virtues.

We are glad to be here, to greet our friends and recount the scenes of the past.

As we part thoughts of the future fill the mind. Who shall stand in our places on the fourteenth day of July, 1963? May they be our own posterity? May no plundering army desolate this fair valley, no horrid butchery ever stain these hills, no pestilence, no famine, no fierce flood or wild conflagration of nature sweep our descendants away.

Then we can say to our sons and daughters who shall be here in 1963, we have the highest regard, the deepest love for you. May you, our children of the twentieth century, excel in religion, be high advanced in moral power and strong in intellect. May physical strength and the blessings of good health be yours. May you have good farm-houses tastefully adorned, rich gardens smiling with flowers, fertile meadows, green slopes upon the hillside, and pastures alive with flocks and herds. May no "deserted village" ever be yours! Rather may you have busy stores, mills ever musical with the hum of industry, beautiful cottages and comfortable residences embowered with forest trees, wide streets and good sidewalks, large churches ever well filled, excellent school-houses always in good repair, and may your village green, on which the grass grows smooth and even, shaded with wide-spreading maples and waving elms, ever be a place of happy resort!

If to you looking back darkness and barbarity seems to prevail in this age we will not be offended, for we know that not yet have we attained true christian perfection. We will rejoice at your high advancement, at your mastery of the sciences, that you, with your fellow-countrymen, have wrought out so many useful inventions, have explored the depths of the ocean, fully comprehended the earth's crust, the air we breathe, and have sounded with your telescopes the hitherto unknown depths of space.

True the same sky will be over you, the same blue forest-clad hills around you, and the same streams will run musically by you. You will love the light blue of that sky, the deep blue of these mountains, the fresh green grass of summer, the white mantling snow of winter, the bright spring foliage upon the trees, and the deep autumn hues and rich tints cast by the frost upon the forest like a mantle of gorgeous rainbows. To you the crisp frost work, white and clear as heaven's purity, that clings some winter's morning biting cold upon the hacmetacs and lichens of Mount Carr, will be as beautiful as to us. By you the wild grandeur of Moosehillock, the mountain king of the lesser hills, who alone listens to the scream of the eagle, the song of the winds sung in the mosses of the cold gray rocks, and the dirge of the tempest chanted amid the drapery of thick clouds, will be admired as well as by us.

You will love to read the Psalms of David, the sermon of Christ on the mount, the epics of Homer, of Virgil, of Milton, the plays of Shakespeare. We delight in them as well. You will feel indignant at the sight of wrong, of tyranny, ingratitude and revenge. You will sympathize with suffering, and love charity. You have patriotism; domestic affection is yours. We too feel all these emotions, and you cannot be more kind, more true than ourselves. We are filled with warm gratitude for what our ancestors have done for us. We pray that we may bestow upon you the same blessings that we enjoy. Then may you welcomed by us to all the joys of life, be able to transmit the same to your children, and gladly celebrate that day, a hundred years distant, Warren's second Centennial.

Bibliography of Wm. Little

1854 — History of the Town of Warren, New Hampshire from Its Earliest Settlement to the Year 1854, Including a Sketch of the Pemigewasset Indians, Concord, N.H., McFarland & Jenks.

1863 — Address at Centennial Celebration of Warren, N.H. (July 14, 1863). Charles F. Livingston, Manchester, N.H.

1870 — The History of Warren; A Mountain Hamlet Located Among the White Hills of New Hampshire, Manchester, N.H. William E. Moore.

1877 — Chohass. The Granite Monthly, I, 212-215.

1877 — A Brief History of the Schools of Manchester, N.H., Formerly Derryfield, 24 pp., Manchester, N.H.

1877 — Moosilauke - Little's History of Warren. The Granite Monthly, I, 141-144.

1887 — About the Names of Moosilauke, and of Some Other Places. The Granite Monthly, X, 357-365.

1888 — History of Weare, New Hampshire.

1892 — Capt. John White's Scout Journal. The Granite Monthly, XIV, 205-211.

1893 — The Warren-Woodstock Road. The Granite Monthly, XV, 48-55.

1893 — Capt. Eleazar Tyng's Scout Journal. The Granite Monthly, XV, 183-186.

INDEX.

The table of proprietors, page 170, is not indexed, neither are the lists of voters, town officers, subscribers, or tables of names in the Appendix. Indian names are in SMALL CAPITALS.

A.

Abbott, John   259, 288, 321 n, 393 n, 564
     Moses 456
ACTEON, 33 n, 35, 43, 51, 61, 69, 71, 103, 142
Adirondacks 253
Aiken brook 246
     James . 216–218, 232, 243–246
Albert, Henry 508
ALGONQUIN Indians 23
AMARISCOGGIN Indians   25 n, 64, 68, 74
Ambuscade 96, 127
AMOSKEAG Indians . . . 24 n, 50
Animals   158, 219, 229, 237, 248, 251, 318
                 370–377, 526
Annexation 447
Apple trees 210
Arling, Abigail 314–316
AROSAGUNTICOOKS . 93–99, 111–113, 132
Arrows . . . . . . n. 35
ASQUAMCHUMAUKE river . 18–20, 33
              85, 104, 105, 122 n, 190, 345
Atkinson, Theodore, Jr. 163–164, 167, 168
                 173, 176, 178, 199
Auctions 283
Autumn . . 151, 250, 251, 418–420

B.

Badger, David 321
     John 341
Baker, Capt. Thomas . 81–86, 190
     Ponds 109, 122
     River. (See Asquamchumauke.)
Balch, John . . 265–267, 343, 398
Bald hill 19
Balls 309–312
Barber, Albert M. 451
Barker, John 128, 129
     Sarah 362, 433
     Stillman 433
Barn, the first one 240
Barr, Capt. Samuel 95
Barter 386

Bayley Fry 189
Bean porridge 218
Bears   228, 232, 237, 238, 251 n, 325, 371, 372
Beavers 210, 251
     meadow pond . . . 229
     meadows . . 186, 210, 219
Bedell, Capt. Timothy . . 270, 271
Bedsteads 215
Beech hill 20, 325
     District 320
Beef cattle sold to British . . 269, 270
Bell 486
Berry brook 19, 20
     brook road . . . 454–460
Bills paid in produce . . . 356
Birds 377, 527
Bishop, Enos 127–129
Bixby, Benj. 404, 416
     Dudley C. . . . 511, 545
     George . . 372, 404, n. 439, 503
     James M. 532
     Joseph 455
     Moses H. . . 490, 541, 543
     Samuel B. . 455, 480–482, 503
Black brook, (see Mikaseota.)
     hill 254
     mt. 18, 19, 563
Blacksmiths 504
Blanchard, Col. Joseph 93, 130, 137, 138
Blazed paths 111
Blind man's buff 301, 309
Blodgett, Jared S. . . . 486, 492
Blue Ridge 239, 385
Block Houses 100
Blowing a horn 368
Boating on the Asquamchumauke . 101
Bobbins 502
Boody, Rev. Joseph . . 364, 365, 422
Books 400
     Law 350, 352
     Town 350
Boundary lines . . . . n. 337
     feuds . n. 222, 335, 339, 511–513

Bartlett, Chas. H. 481
  Dr. Ezra   354 n, 355-356, 389
                       405, 460, 537
  Dr. Josiah 167 n, 171, 178, 196
                            277, 354
BASHABA . . . . 43, 46 n, 51
Baskets 506
Batchelder brook 19
            Cotton . . . , 394
            Capt. Daniel . . . 508
            Isaiah 229, 260, 277, 292, 337
                              338, 419
            John S. 382
            Reuben . 288, 320, 342, 358
            Stephen 321
            Ward C. 509
Battles 230, 231, 332
  Bennington 269
  Bunker hill 263
  for office 329, 334
  Indian . 44, 62, 66, 67, 83, 91
  Knight with a bear . . 344
  by Rogers' rangers . . 139
  of St. Francis . . . 145
Bounties for falling trees . . 222
  for grist-mill . . . 241
  for killing Indians . . 75
  for killing wild animals . 371
  for saw-mill . . 237, 240
  for settlers . . 196, 197, 225
  for soldiers . . 269, 285, 287
Bowen, Peter. 115, 117
Bowles, Charles . 285, 286, 307, 413, 441
  Lot 286
Bows, Indian . . . . n. 35
Boynton, Joseph . . . 367, 426
  Thomas 358
  Dr. Worcester E. . 546, 554
Bradstreet, Col. Dudley . . 70
Bracey, Chas. F. . . 506, 511
Brainard, Daniel . . . n. 211
Brick 504
Bridges 345-348
Bridle paths . . . 189, 245
Broad arrow mark . . 184, 238
Broadhead, Rev. John . 363, 368
Brock, Billy 420
Brooks 250, 381, 417
Brown, Frederick . . . 407
  Jesse 552
Burnham, Josiah . 321, 339, 413
Burning a piece · . . . 218
Burning of James Aiken's house . 245
Burns, Dr. Robert 321, 355, n. 405, 538
Burnside, Thomas . . . 190
Burials . . . . . . n. 40
Burying cloth 353
  ground . . 27, 295, 359, 487
Burton, Amos . . . 402, 445
Butler, Capt. Wm. 234, 240, 241, 277, 279
  295, 302, 331, 338, n. 341, 352, 363, 385, 387
Button or play 309

C.

Call, Phillip 127
Camp-meeting . . . 366-369
Canal 349, 445-447
Canoes . . . . . n. 36
Captains . . . 297, 391, 547
Captives 67, 88-98, 105, 108, 118, 127, 133
  treatment of by Indians . 45

Cardigan Mountain . . . 318
Carding mill . . . 349, 501
  wool . . . n. 233, 360
Caribou 375-376
Carr Mt. 18-20, 182, 247-251, 254-256, 375, 563
Cascades on Berry brook. . . 324
  on Ore hill brook . . 388
Casualties 559
Catamount 208, 370
Cemeteries . . . 295, 359, 487
Census . . . . . n. 265, 534
Centennial 167, 519
Centre district 320
Certificate money . . n. 333, 356
Chairs 215, 505
Charter 168, 196, 199, 200
Charleston Convention . . 292-293
           district 320
Choristers, ... 260, 542
CHRISTO 107
Chronology 579
Churches . . . 362-365, 481-489
Cider mill 419
Clapboard and shingle mill . . 501
Clark Amos 348
  Daniel . . . . . n. 277
  Stephen K. . . . 500-502
  Thomas 228, 277, 279, 285, 292, 337
                              n. 338
Clearing, first one . . . 210
  first road . . . 188, 220
Clement Amos 506
  Col. Benjamin . 420, 425, 503
  Daniel Q. . . n. 493, 502, 563
  Ephraim 470
  Hill 19
  James . 33, 451-453, 493-498, 516
  Dea. Jona. . 245, 251, 365, 366
  Jonathan 225, 259, 284, 349, 387
  Joseph . . 33, 499, 504, 559
  Moses H. 237, 341, n. 349, 395
  -397, 405, n. 427, 446, 455-458, 501
  Obadiah 33, 222, 238, 267, 279
  n. 284, 293, 297-303, 329, 334, 345
            -348, 398, 441-446, 565
  party . . . 278, 334, 349
  Reuben . 225, 264, 279, 293
  Russell K. 321, n. 380, 429, 483
  William 480-482
Clerk, proprietors . . . 178
  Town 278, 532
Clifford, Absalom . . . 382
  Dorathy . . . 351-353
  Isaac 279, 280
  Hon. Nathan . . . n. 280
  Reuben 423, 424
  Ruel Bela 500
  Russell F. 321
  Timothy . . n. 320, 554
  William 509
  Mrs. Zachariah . . . 434
Climate 20
Clough, Amos 554
  Amos F. 210, 486, 506, 514, 562, 569
  Columbus, ... 486
  Capt. Jeremiah . . . 92
  District 320
  Jonathan . . . 210, 406
  Nathaniel 355, n. 387, 419, n. 428
                  436, 464, 475, n. 499
  School-house 210
  William 465

INDEX. 585

Coal 506
Coasting 316, 317
Cold brook 317, 417
  Spring 492, 563
  Winter 284, 442
Collectors of taxes . 179, 281, 282–284
College graduates 539
Colonels 395, 547
Committee of Safety 266–269, 275, 284–287
  to explore Coos . . 109
  to run lines . . 179, 337
  to build bridges . 345–348
  to build a meeting house 358
    359, 423-428
  to clear roads . 188, 196
  to lay out lots . 189, 220
  to take care of pauper . 352
  to agree with settlers 196, 220
    n. 222
Common 485, 487
Conditions of Charter 169, 174, 187, 200
Constables 279, 281
Constitution 358
Continental Money 282
Converts 368
Convention 292
Cook, Timothy 127
Cooking . . . 306, 307, 399
Coopers 502
Coosuck Indians . . n. 24. 25, 99
Coos Turnpike . . . 384–389
Copp, George W. . n. 321, 426, 441
  John 394
  Joshua 218, n. 265, 267, 285, 292, 331
    352, 358, 499
  Joshua, Jr. . . . 218, 294
  Moses 218, 241, 287, 293, 352, 353
  Sarah 310–312
Copper mine 449
Corporation dinner . . 177, 178
Cotton, Dudley B. 534
  Solomon . . . 455-457
Courts 279
Coventry 212
Craige, Alexander . . . n. 211
  David S. 386
Cross, Daniel 212
  Iron mine 389
  Uriah 343
CULHEAG TRAP . . 37, 208, 376
Cummings survey 339
Currency 356
Cushman, Ebenezer . 500–504, 513
  Francis A. . 500–506, 513
  Mt. . . . 18, 371, 563

D.

Dances 44, 309–312, 420
Dark day 284
Davis brook 353
  Enoch 353
Day, Daniel 416
Death by casualty 559
  by fright 461
  in Warren 552
Dedication 426
Deer . . . 183, 229, 230, 237, 376
Deer Keepers . . . 281, n. 351
Devil's Doings 363
Diana's bowl . . . 192, 562

Diary, Amos F. Clough's . . . 569
  of weather . . . n. 408
Dishes 218
Distances on Moosilauke road . 563
Dodge, Joseph A. 473
Dogs . . . . n. 374
Doggett, W. S. 511
Dow, Ezekiel 321, 543
  James 317, 320, 365, 366, 429, 439, 525
  Jonathan 582
  Col. Stevens M. 261, 321, n. 493, 547
Drafts 285, 391–393
Drawing of lots . . . 192, 548
Dreams 327
Dresses of olden times 208, 231, 233, 260
    310, 311
Drinks . . 261, 278, 302, 311, 413, 443
Drills 351
Drovers 269
Ducked . . . . . . n. 504
Dudley, Gov. J. 73–75, 85
Dustin, Gardner . . . 277, 282
  Mrs. Hannah . 67, 68, n. 428
Dutch wagon . . . 361, 398
  oven 210
Dying 234, 501

E.

Eagles 253, 459, 494
Eames, Capt. Jeremiah . . 267, 270
Early settlers 207–235
East Branch 19
Eastman, Addison W. . 382, 516, 545
  Damon Y. 506
  Jesse 362
  Jesse 394
East-parte district . . 320, 342, 567
  regions 325
  song 568
Eating 307, 412
  human flesh . . . 148, 151
Eaton, Ezra B. . . . 500, 511
Ecclesiastical 257–262, 361–369, 422–430
    541–544
Edgar, James 450, 451
Education 313–321
Egg-nogg 444
Elliott the apostle 55
Elections . . 178, 278, 329–334
Eleven mile tree . . . 192, 339
Ellsworth 247
  Moses . . 394, 433, 462, n. 470
Emerson, Samuel 277
Equinoctial storm 184
Eva 566
Evens, Rev. Edward . . 426–428
  Sergt. David . . 149–151
Exhibitions 516
Expeditions against Indians 75–79, 80–86
    88–91, 93, 96, 118
  to Warren 101, 110, 121–125
    138, 182–186
Express business 398

F.

Fairbanks, Capt. Jabez . . . 89
Fairs 173
Fairies 152, 250
Falling trees 222, 294
Family Record, (see Genealogy.)

Famine	408
among Indians	n. 49
among Rangers	147–156
Farm work	412, 420
Fashions in olden times	233, 260, 310
Federal Constitution	358
Currency	356
Feasts	38, 177, 256, 307
Fellows, Jonathan	269, 293, 341, n. 422
Joseph	321
Perkins	n. 392, 394
Samuel	n. 341, 441
Fifield, Isaac	372
Fire-place	309
Fires	245, 467–471
First land in the world	31
Fishes	528
Fishing	36, 235, 379–383, 417
Fiske, Chas. A.	506, 562
Fisk, Wm. H.	381
Flanders, Samuel	343, 425, 558
Capt. Stephen	342, 373–375, 422
Flax	234
Flip	443
Floats	373
Floodwood company	299, 393
Flowers	242, 318–324
Foote, Cotton	513
Foote, Elias	370
Levi B.	321, 435
Forks district	210, 320
Forts at Coos	100, 113, 118
Wentworth	138
Foster, Jona.	n. 285
Fowling	36, 378, n. 379
Foxglove meadow	235, 516
Foxes	251, 370, 376
Freewill Baptists	364, 483–489
French, Dr. Alphonzo G.	382, 481, 539
David A.	538, 581
Dr. David C.	321, 403, 481, 504, 512
	538, 545
John	321, 545
Joseph	288, 405, 407
Mrs. Dick	324
Osco H.	509
Reuben B.	321, 565
War	126–156
Freshets	347, n. 391
Frogs	249, n. 307, 319, 528
Frost	408
Clouds	577
Feathers	573
Funeral	n. 426
first one	294
Sermon	365
Furniture	215

G.

Game	36, 209, 251, 370
Games	301, 309
Gardening	414
Gardner, John	342
Geese	378
GENEALOGIES:—	
Abbott	553
Barker	553
Bartlett	354
Batchelder	553
Bixby	404
Boynton	554
GENEALOGIES;—	
Bowles	286
Butler	234
Clark	554
Clement	222, 224, 344
Clifford	554
Clough	387, 554
Copp	218
Dow	554
French	554
Homan	312
Jewell	555
Knight	342
Libbey	555
Little	341, 463, 555
Merrill	231, 233, 341, 555, 556
Patch	211, 357
Pillsbury	556
Richardson	556
Welch	341
Whitcher	221, 230
Whiteman	394
Ghosts	388, n. 439
Gilman, Daniel	265
GITCHE MANITO	39, 71, 171, 185
Glen ponds	19, 182, 235, 248, 254, 455, 514
Gods, Heathen	185, 366
Goffe, Capt. John	92, 94, 130, 136
Golden tradition	153
Gookin, Maj.	61
Gospel	174
Gould, John	372
Gove, Capt. John	426
Graduates	539–541
Grantees of Warren	170
Grave-yards	487–489
Greeley, Col. Jona.	166–200, 220, 223, 291
his Inn	n. 168, 176, 291
Grist-mill	240–242, 349, 500
Guns	265, 267

H.

Hackett, Capt. Wm.	n. 225, n. 339
Handsleds	238, 241, 255
Harboard, Jona.	311
Harnesses	506
Harriman, Mrs. James	500
Harty, Capt. John D.	394
Haying	219, 258, 416
Hawkins, Onley	354
Hazen, Capt. John	167, 179
Head, Gen. Natt.	510
Hearse	n. 518
Heath, Dr. Horatio	321, 434
William	230, 264, 287, 293
Heights of mountains	563
Hermits	235, 478
Hidden, Ebenezer	341
John	341
High Street	362
Height-o'-land	20, 325, 386
Height-o'-landers	388
Height-o'land district	320
Highways, (see Roads.)	
Highway surveyors	279, 281
Hilton, Col. Winthrop	76, 80
Hinchson, John	235, 252–256, 259, n. 264
	293
Hobart, Col. David	280, 286
Hogreeves, or Hog constables	281
Hogs	386

INDEX. 587

Holman, Rev. Sullivan . . . 484
H.lmes, Barnabas 287
H.iman, Caleb . . 342, 365, *n*. 414
   Mrs. Caleb . . . 344, 425
Horses 357
Hotels . . . 204, *n*. 206, 348, 387
House burnt by rebel . . . 271
Houses 240
Howard, Col. Joshua . . . 190
   Rice 425
Hunters . . 153, 158, 235, 250–256
Hunters' camp 159, 236
  on Moosehillock . . 229, 253
Hunting by Indians . . . *n*. 37
   party . . . 103, 203, 255
Hunting 250–256
Hurricane 409, 571, 576
  [brook 250, 562
  falls 562
Husking bees 419
Hutchins, Gordon 287

I.

INDIANS 24
  Burials . . . . . *n*. 40
  Camp 128
  Captives 133
  Captured 62
  Fights 92, 95–98, 118, 127–128, 145–148
  Friendly 81–84
  Gods 39
  Killed 116
  Laws . . . . . . *n*. 52
  League 42, 51
  Legends 29
  Marriages 40
  Massacres 92
  Names 25
  Oratory . . . 54–56, 74, 112
  Religion 39
  Revels 44
  Rock . . . 26, 71, 242, 294, 562
  Trail . 20, 149, 183, 189–191, 340
  Tribes 42
  War 46, 59, 75
  in Warren . . 26, 27, 33, 224, 562
Indictments 333, 343
Infantry . . . 297–303, 390–397
Inns, (see Taverns.)
Insects 417, 529
Interregnum 331
Introductory 17
Inventories 282, 551
Iron mine 389

J.

Jackson, Dr. Chas. T. . . . 349
  Geo. W. 470, 505
Jail broken 117
Jewell, Samuel 413, 555
  Levi F. . . . 372, 500, 502
Jewelry 506
Jewett, J. S. 511
Jobildunc ravine 497
Johnson, James 133, 525
Jones, Joseph 354
Josselyn, John, Gent. . . 36, 158
Judges 279–281, 560
Jugglery 53, 54, 517
Jumper 226
Jurors, Grand 329

K.

KANCAMAGUS 64, 110
Kelley pond . . . 19, 326, 499
  William 427, 500
Keyes, Ezra W. . . . *n*. 405, 486
Keyes Ledge, or Mt.Helen, 20, 27, 317–320
Keezer, Lemuel 337, 348, *n*. 368, *n*. 387
  n. 400, n. 414, *n*. 427, *n*. 433, *n*. 504
  Lemuel, Jr. 406, 444
Kimball, Cyrus C. 381
  Heber 490, 543
  Joseph 277, 337
KINEO, Mt. 18, 254, 563
King George's war . . . 91–98
  Phillip's war . . . 60–62
  William's war 88
King's Woods 171, 183
Knapp, Arthur 511
Knight, Betsey 426
  Hannah B. . 259, 363, *n*. 556
  Hill 19
  Nathaniel 316, 352
  Samuel . . 249, 288, *n*. 342, 439
  Mrs. Samuel . . 344, *n*. 363
  Stevens . . . . . , 420

L.

Ladd, Capt. Daniel 96
  Trueworthy 166
Land given to settlers 211, 220, 222, 225
  given to Col. Greeley . . 199
  given to Phillips White . 199
  given to Schools . . . 313
Lane, Col. Chas. 473, 500
Law book 350, 352
Lawsuits . 243, 279, 338, 461–464, 482
Lawyers . . . 462, 481, 535, 542
Lead mine 449, 452
Leathers, Vowell . . . 376, 469
Leavitt, Benj. . . . 182, 189, 192
Leonard, Charles . . . 487, 520
  George E. . . 410, 481, 520
Libbey, Ezra Walton . . 510, 557
  Dr. Ezra B. 413, 505
  George 343, 373, 392, 406, 505, 555
  Hazen 481, 490
  John 343, 458, 555
  Luke . . . 288, 407, 555
  Nathaniel . 307, 310, 392, 409
  Obadiah 413
  Walter 505
Library 559
Lifting at stiff heels 302
Linen wheel 234, 245
Lines settled 337, 511
Little, Amos 341, 385, 404, 410, 423, 427, 443
  Benj. 214, 217, 457
  Benj. K. 379, 514
  George . . . . *n*. 463, 555
  George A. . . . 463, *n*. 541
  Dr. Jesse *n*. 231, 321, 403, *n*. 463
       511, 538, 545
  Jonathan . . . 321, n. 476
  Joseph M. 506
  Thos. B. . . . *n*. 463, 509
Lock 428
Log forts 138
Log houses . . 210, 215–224, 236
Loggerhead 278
Longevity 552

Loons	227
Lost	558
Lots drawn	192, 222, 548, 550
lost	337
for ministers	257
run	192
for settlers	196
for schools	n. 170, 313
Lovewell, Capt. John	88-91, 98
fight	89
Low, Asa	288, n. 396
Jacob	288, n. 396
John	343
Lower school-house	n. 320
Lufkin, Levi	359
Lug-pole	n. 245
Lumber trade	476-477
Lund, Ephraim	n. 211, 227, 264, 288, 293
Ephraim	277, 392
Hosea	416, 505
Joseph	227, 260, 277, 293
Stephen	416
Stephen	418
Stevens Merrill	511
Lyman Caleb	76, 79
Lyon, John E.	n. 472, 563

M.

Mahurin, Capt. Ephraim H.	392
Mail	265, 398-403
Mann, John	212
Manufactures	499-507
MANITOU, (see Gitche Manito.)	
Map of Warren	16, 171, 336, 355, 448
Maple sugar	186, 410
Markets	173
March of Rogers' Rangers	142-156
Marriage, the first	279
Marsh, David G.	n. 493, 569
Marston Hill	20-28
John	255, 279, 293
John D.	470
Joseph E.	350
Sarah	221
Martin brook	183, 451
May, Col. Silas	398-401
May trainings	297
McCarter, Antony	478-479, 503
McDeuffe, Gen. John	384, 445-447, 454
Meader, Paul	342, n. 500, 560
Meader Pond, (see Wachipauka pond.)	
Meeting-house	260, 358, 422-430, 484-489
Meeting at Plymouth	336
of Proprietors	176, 335
religious	258
town	277-279, 351
Merrill, Abel	n. 341, 374, 423, 442
Amos L.	372, 379
Anson	321, 366, 386, 426, 445, n. 462
	503
Benjamin	[390, 426, 435, 444, n.445
	500
brook	19, n. 417
Deaf Caleb	437
Capt. Daniel	368, n. 387, n. 400
	427, 483. 500
David	287, 293
Ira	321, 486, 500
Col. Isaac	321, 470, 481, 487, 502,
	512, 516
Isaac	363, n. 414
Merrill, Jonathan	232, 238, 269, 279, 284
	329-334, 390, 393, 405, 422-428, 500
Joseph	231, 344, 348, 385-390, 400
	406, 436, 437, 500, 555
Capt. Joseph	363, 419
Rev. Joseph	321, 539
Joshua	n. 233, 252-256, 284, n. 386
Lemuel	321, n. 439, 541
Gen. Michael P.	321, n. 385, n. 429
	546
Rev. Nathaniel	n. 321, 364, 386
Nathaniel, 2d	28, 321, 491, n. 493
party	278, 334, 349
Robert E.	n. 363
Russel	n. 471, n. 493
Samuel	213, 327, 342, 379, 386
Samuel	n. 363, 406
Samuel L.	435, 445, n. 461, 481, 486
Stevens	231, 233, 237, 240-246, 252
	-264, 267, 269, 283, 296, 315, 346
	364, 437-439
Stevens, 2d	232, 456, 537
True	449-453
William	394, 445
Meteors	404
Methodists	362-368, 483-489, 541
Mica	n. 316, 453
Middle cascades	562
MIKASEOTA brook	19, 20, 239, 258
Military company	297-303
officers	546-547
Mills	193, 220-222, 237-240, 349, 506
Mills, Anna	310-312
James	n. 501
John	215, 245, 252-256, 259, 263, 287
	294-296
John, Jr.	215, 241, 259, 269, 293, 294
	-296
Widow	353
Millers	501
Minerals	20, 241, 249, 449-453, 530
Mines	449-453
Ministers, Free-will Baptist	286, 364, 365
	542
Methodist	362, 363, 367, 368, 408
	489, 541
Universalist	483, 542
Miracles	78, n. 363
Mist Mt.	18, 563
Moat	n. 317
Moderators	278, 282, 533
MOHAWK Indians	42, 65, 76-79
Money	356
MONTAWAMPATEE	57, 525
Montgomery, Gen. John	390, 392
Morey, Col. Israel	297
Morse, Robert	400, 401
Moose	111, 122, 212, 224, 227, 253-256, 372
	-375, n. 417
Moose yard	253-255
Moosehide breeches	221, n. 265
Moosehillock district	320, 342
falls	344
Mt.	18, 71, 151, 229, 253, 457
	-460, 490-498, 563, 569
Mt. road	563
Moosemeat	272
Moosilauke house	466, 475, n. 493
Morrill, Abraham	189
John	221, 231, 279
Mosely, Capt.	61
Mother Cluck	564

Moulton brook 235, 515
Mount Carr, (see Carr mountain.)
Mountains 495–498, 563
Mt. Helen, (see Keyes Ledge.)
Music 300, 395, 401
Muster day 395–397
Mythology 366, 367

N.

Name of Warren 171
Naming buildings . . . n. 425
NASHUA Indians, . . . n. 24, 25
Necessaries brought from Plymouth 224
Negroes, stealing 108
New emission of money . . . 356
New Hampshire Grants 159–161, 164, 289
NEWICHANNOCK Indians . . . n. 24
Night 312
Niles, Jesse 354
Nathaniel 277
NIPMUCK Indians 24, 26, 28, 42, n. 70, 87
–92, 99, 113
Northern Indians 61
Lights 202, 374
Noyes' Bridge . . . . n. 433
Enoch 414
Joseph 514
Number Four 112, 155

O.

Oak falls . . . 82, 191, 326, 500
Ocean 498, 575
Officers B. C. & M. R. R. . . n. 472
military 296
Proprietors 177
Town 278, 530
U. S., State and County . 560
Oils and essences 504
Old fashioned fire-place . . . 309
Old well 296
Old White Face 371, 372
Oliverian brook 18, 20, 82, 129, 149, n. 190
n. 229
Notch 20, 124
Omens . . . , . . . 431
Oratory 54, 112
Ore hill 449, 453
Ore hill brook 27 388
Origin of the Pemigewassetts . . 29
Orn, Joseph 354
Osgood, Capt. James . . n. 267
OSSIPEE Indians . . . n. 25
Owl's Head Mt. 18. 563
Ox Teams 305, 308

P.

Paddles . . . . . n. 35
Page, Enoch . 196, 220, 225, 338
Gov. John 392
John . . . 166–185, 203, 237
John, Jr. . . . 166–171, 188
Joseph . 178, 196, 220, 233, 338
Samuel B. 462, 533, 534, 535, 541, 563
Pall 353
Palmer, Rev. John E. 483
Panics 289
Panthers 208, 370, 529
Parade 350
Paring bees 464–466

Parker, Rev. L. W. 545
Parties 278, 329–334
Partridges . . . 220, 251, 378, 379
PASCATAQUAUKES . . . n. 24, 42
PASSACONAWAY . . . 51–57, 110
Patch brook 19, 477
bridge 347, 348
Patchbreuckland . . 320, 325, 465
Patch, Daniel . . 356, 392, 446, 455
David . . . . . n. 393
hill 19, 342
Jacob 207, 209, 210, 245, 253, 321, 372
–375
Joseph 207–213, 225, 231, 240, 250–256
263, 271, 284, 351, 372, n. 376, 556
Joseph, Jr. 213, n. 385, 393, 423
n. 461
Mrs. Joseph . . . 272, 288
party . . . 278, 334, 349
PAUGUS 89–91
Paupers 351–353
PAWTUCKET Indians . . . 25
Pearlash 503
Peddlers 395–397
Peg factory 502
Peeling 212, 337, 339
PEER 103
PEHAUNGUN . . . . . n. 70
PEMIGEWASSETT Indians 23–29, 49, 58, 99
land . . 28, 61
Penhallow's Indian Wars . 80, 89
PENNACOOK Indians . . . 24, 60
Pensions 287
People bewitched 435
PEQUAWKEE Indians . n. 25, 89–91
Perusing the law 352
Pestilence 49
Peters, Absalom . 289, 331, 354, n. 384
Peters, Dr. Joseph . . 354, 536
Philip, King 60
Phillips, Lt. William . . . n. 149
Photographers 506
Physicians 354, 536–539
Picked hill 19
Picnics 319
Pierce, Franklin 462
Pine hill 20
District 320
Pillsbury, Moses W. . . 501, 505, 561
Richard 416
Richard . . 345, 416, 556
Thomas . . 385, 416, 436
Pitching quoits 302
Pitch-pipe 367
Pizen 301
Plague 47–50, 404
Plan of the town . . . 339, 355
of Forts at Coos . . 100
Plantation 173
Plants 318, 529
PLAUSAWA 114–116
Plays 301, 309, 465
Pod teams 386
Poets of Warren 564
Politics 357
Pomeroy, Robert . . 151, 525
William 502
Ponds 19, 499
Population 535
Postmasters 403, 542
Post-office 402, 403
Potash 503

Potter, Ephraim	366, 416
Hon. C. E.	n. 55
Pound	350
Poultry	306
Powder and ball	265, n. 290
Powers, Rev. Grant	120, 190, 340
Capt. Peter	120-125, 190, 401
Rev. Peter	258, 260-262, 328, 422
Pow-wow	90
Preachers	n. 427, 541
Preaching	258, 363
pay for	n. 427
Prescott, George W.	403, 414, 445
Presented	333
Prime	289
Proclamations	160
money	174
Produce	308, 386
Proprietors	21, 170, 338
Camp	183, 189
Meetings	168, 178, 180, 185, 188
	192
Records	177, 194
Taxes	179, 188, 193
Prospect House	493-498
Pulling teeth	n. 400
Punch	167, 443
Pungs	386
Puter platters	284
Putnam, Geo. F.	536, 541

Q.

Queen Anne's War	73-79
Quilting bees	462
Quincy, Hon. Josiah	469, n. 481
Quit rents	165
QUOCHECO	66-68

R.

Rabbits	171
Races	343
Raft on the Connecticut	154
Railroad	472-477
Raising bees	424
Ramsey, Mrs. Betsey	365, 425
Daniel	320, 372
Ransom money	106
Rattlesnake Mt.	122, 401
Rebels	264
Red-oak hill	18, 436-438
Regiments, old 13th	392, 395
12th	297
Religion	174
of the Indians	39
Religious meetings	257-262
Report of Surveyor Leavitt	185
Representatives	280, 293, 533
Reptiles	528
Requisites	340-359
Reservation	165, 174, 197, 512
Retreat of Rogers' rangers	147-156
Revolution	200, 263-293
Richardson, Nathaniel	392, 413
Capt. Stephen	260, 409, 433
Ride and tie	436
Riding post	265
Rindge, Isaac	200
Roads	20, 109, 188, 191, 222, 333, 340
	345
Rocks	530
Rocky falls	252

Rogers' Rangers	137-156
Maj. Robert	110, 136-156, 190
Romney	211, n. 469
Roots, Crooks, and Daleys	212
Root, Dr. Levi	354, 537
Rum	265, 346, 388
Runaway pond	186, 219
Running the gauntlet	105
Running town lines	182, 220

S.

SABBATIS	107, 114-116
Sabin, Rev. Elijah R.	362, 422
Sable	209, 370
Salamanders	298, 528
Sale of property to pay taxes	283
Salmon	209, 241, 559
Sanborn, Morrill J.	473, n. 506
SAWHEGANET falls	122
Sawtelle district	320
Saw-mills	193, 220, 237, 499
Scalping David Stinson	105
Scalps	95, 105
Schools	175, 313-321, 517
books	316
committee	534
districts	320
houses	316-321
teachers	314, 321
Scouts	77
Seal of Warren	351
Selectmen	279, 281, 330, 390, 530
Sentimental Acrostic	565
Sentinel Mt.	18, 338, 563
Settlements	207
Settlers	212
Set of drills	351
Set of measures	350
Seven Cascades	152, 202, 497
Seven years war	126-156
Sham-fight	76, 396
Shaw, Henry	293
Sheep marks	414
Sheldon, Lieut. Charles	510
Henry H.	561
Shingle-mill	501, 503
Shoemakers	505
Shooting match	306
Silver mine	449
rill	344
Singing	260, n. 362
Signs	348, n. 389
Smith, David	251, 321, 416, 511, 534
Capt. John	41, 47
Simeon	226, 267, 282, 337
Snakes	528
Society, School-house	n. 341
Soldiers from Warren	264, 285, 293, 390
	509
Solitude	99, 145, 203
Sorcery	53
SOUHEGAN Indians	n. 24
Spaulding, Daniel	190
Spelling schools	517
Spiders	528
Spinning flax and wool	360
Spotted fever	404-407
Spring	101, 298, 409, 410
SQUAMSCOTT Indians	n. 24

INDEX. 591

Stage . . . . 398–400, n. 401
   drivers 400, 402
   horses 400
Starch factories 502
Stark, Gen. John . 103, 109, 139, 264
Stars 312, 374
Stevens Capt. . . . 76, 112, 130, 142
   Maj. True . 365, 425, 458, n. 501
St. Francis Indians, see Arosagunticooks.
Stinson, David 103–105
Stint 558
Stock of provision 290
Stocks 280
Stone, Col. 396
Stores 441–448, 501
Storm 185, 391, 570
Straggler 288
Strangers, well dressed . . . 268
Streamy Valley district . . . 320
String bean company . . . 299, 393
Sugaring 410
Suicide 558
Summer 258, 322
Summit 323, 476
   District 320
Superintending School Committee . 534
Surplus Revenue 456
Surveyors . . . 179, 189, 339, 384
   of highways . . . 279
Swain, Darius 493
   Darius O. 510
Swallows 343
Swingling flax 274, 315

T.

Table 215, 218
Tailors 233, 505
Tanning 502
Tarleton Lake . . . 18, 262, 389
TARRENTINE Indians . . . 42–52
Taverns . . . 168, 223, 348, 387
   keepers 223, 348
Tax collectors 281–284
Taxes 356, 551
   of proprietors . . . 179, 188
   paid in produce . . . 356
Teams to market 343, 386
Teamsters 343, 349, 386
Telegraph 511
Temperance 513
Tempest . . . 184, 391, 571, 576
The serpent 567
Thesbian Lyric 566
Thurston, Asa . . . 403, 445, 502
TITAGAW, Francis 103
Todd, Capt. Andrew 96
Toddy 443
Tolford, Capt. John 109
Toll-gate 385
Tolling the bell 486
Tomahawks 34
Tories 264, 268
Tornado 409
Torture 44, 45
Town books 330, 350
   Clerks 278, 532
   House 486
   lines 168, 337
   lots 192, 548
   map . . . 16, 171, 336, 448
   meetings . . . 277, 282, 557
   officers . . 278, 281, 530–534

Townships laid out 164
Tradeers 441–448, 561
Training day, first one . . 297–303
   held 359
Trapping 159, 208
Treasurer, county 560
   proprietors 179
   town 281
Trecothick 212
Trees 529
Trout 317, 381
True, Eph. 219, 297
Truscott, Samuel 450
Tunnel brook 253
Turkey shoot 306
Turnpike, Coos 384–389
   Coventry 384
Turtles 528
Two Brothers monument . . . 74
Tythingman . 281, n. 365, 366, 429
Tyng, Capt. 80, 89

U.

Uniforms 299
Universalists . . . 483–489, 542
Utensils of Indians 34
Upper school-house . . . n. 320

V.

Varnum, John 366
Vendue 283
Village school 320
Volunteers for the army . 264, 392, 394
Voters . . . 277, 285, 333, 341, 354

W.

WACHIPAUKA pond 18, 128, 138, 239, 382
Wagon, first in town . . . 361, 398
Waldron, Richard . ' . 62, 64–68
Wars 201, 508, 511
   Mexican 508
   of 1812 391–394
   of Revolution . . . 263–293
Warning out of town . . . 353
Warren Admiral . . . 17, 172
Warren . . . 102, 158, 168, 171, 276
WATERNOMEE 69–72, 75, 83, 110, 190, 493
. . . . 508
   falls . . . 202, 375, 562
   Mt. . . 18, 197, 512, 563
Water shed 386, 476
Weare, Meshech 277
Wearing a hat 310
Weaving 346
Webster, Jeremy . . . 177, 185
   Slide Mt. . . 18, 372, 563
Weeks district 320
   Enoch R. . . 420, 446, 463
   Enoch R., Jr. 560
   Henry W. . 471, n. 486, 500, 561
   Ira M. 321, 511
   Mrs. Sarah . . 434, 462
Weights and measures . . . 350
Welch, Aaron 341
   Daniel 558
Wentworth, Gov. B. 91, 129, 162, 167, 194
   Gov. John . 194, 197, 200
WETAMOO 57, 525
Wheelwrights 506

Whipping the cat	505
Whipping post and stocks	280
Whipple, Dr. A. A.	481, 538, 545
Dr. Thos.	400, 405, 537
Col. Thos. J.	462, 516, 538
Walter	502
Whitcher, Chase	229, 266, 362
John	221, 285
Joseph	264, 293
Levi C.	486, 500
Reuben	260, 277, 284
Sarah	322–328
White, Phillips	196–200, 265
Whiteman, C. William	342, 412
Stephen	n. 394, 456, 504
William	n. 394
Whiton, John M.	486, 500, 502
WIGWAMS	34, n. 35
Wild-cat	343, 526
Wild hound	465
Willey Nathan	433
Window shades	502
Winter	202, 305, 442
Witches	225, 431–440
WINNECOWETT Indians	n. 25
WINNEPISSAUKEE Indians	n. 24
Wolf's head falls	192, 562
Wolves	212, 216, 237, 370, 458
WONALANCET	56, n. 60–63, 65
Wrestling	302, 557
Wyatt hill	20
Hobart	479–482, 501, n. 504
Vanness	478–482, n. 504

Y.

Yards	254–256
Young Caleb	285, 293

Z.

Zinc mine	449

THE END.

www.ingramcontent.com/pod-product-compliance
Lightning Source LLC
Chambersburg PA
CBHW071131300426
44113CB00009B/943